Charles Seale-Hayne Library
University of Plymouth
(01752) 588 588
LibraryandITenquiries@plymouth.ac.uk

The Labour Governments
1964–1970

The 1964–1970 Labour Governments presided over an extremely eventful and exciting period of British history. This was the period during which comprehensive schools were being extended and universities expanded, British troops were sent to Northern Ireland, the United States was waging the Vietnam War, the 'permissive revolution' was taking place, immigration became a major political issue, and 'modernisation' became a dominant political theme. In such a tumultuous era, the Labour Government elected in 1964 increasingly struggled to maintain control over unfolding events and unforeseen crises.

This volume of essays provides a comprehensive, yet in-depth, analysis of the policies and intra-party debates of the 1964–1970 Labour Governments, and the problems which Ministers faced in the context of both external events and increasing discontent amongst Labour backbenchers. The book includes chapters on Harold Wilson's political economy, the attempts at reforming Parliament and the civil service, the failed legislation to curb trade union power, the reform and expansion of education, Scottish and Welsh devolution, Labour's response to the breakdown of civil order in Northern Ireland, the application to join the European Economic Community, the scaling down of Britain's role as a global power in international affairs, the dual strategy of promoting good race relations while curbing immigration, the abolition of the death penalty, and the legalisation of homosexual acts by consenting adults.

The Labour Governments 1964–1970 provides a unique account of the period, for not only does it examine a wide rage of policies and issues, it also makes extensive and unprecedented use of primary sources, including previously unpublished Cabinet papers, ministerial correspondence, Ministers' private papers, and interviews with former Ministers. As such, this is the most comprehensive, in-depth and original book on the 1964–1970 Labour Governments ever published.

Peter Dorey is Senior Lecturer in Politics at Cardiff University, UK. He has published numerous books and articles on aspects of British government, the Labour Party, British Conservatism and public policy.

British politics and society
Series Editor: Peter Catterall
ISSN: 1467-1441

Social change impacts not just upon voting behaviour and party identity but also upon the formulation of policy. But how do social changes and political developments interact? Which shapes which? Reflecting a belief that social and political structures cannot be understood in isolation either from each other or from the historical processes which form them, this series will examine the forces that have shaped British society. Cross-disciplinary approaches will be encouraged. In the process, the series will aim to make a contribution to existing fields, such as politics, sociology and media studies, as well as opening out new and hitherto-neglected fields.

The Making of Channel 4
Edited by Peter Catterall

Managing Domestic Dissent in First World War Britain
Brock Millman

Reforming the Constitution
Debates in twenty-first century Britain
Edited by Peter Catterall, Wolfram Kaiser and Ulrike Walton-Jordan

Pessimism and British War Policy, 1916–1918
Brock Millman

Amateurs and Professionals in Post-war British Sport
Edited by Adrian Smith and Dilwyn Porter

A Life of Sir John Eldon Gorst
Disraeli's awkward disciple
Archie Hunter

Conservative Party Attitudes to Jews, 1900–1950
Harry Defries

Strangers, Aliens and Asians
Hugenots, Jews and Bangladeshis in Spitalfields 1666–2000
Anne J. Kershen

Conscription in Britain 1939–1963
The militarization of a generation
Roger Broad

An Enemy Embrace
German migration to post-war Britain
Inge Weber-Newth and Johannes-Dieter Steinert

The Labour Governments 1964–1970
Edited by Peter Dorey

The Labour
Governments 1964–1970

Edited by Peter Dorey

Routledge
Taylor & Francis Group

LONDON AND NEW YORK

First published 2006
by Routledge
2 Park Square, Milton Park, Abingdon, Oxon, OX14 4RN

Simultaneously published in the USA and Canada
by Routledge
270 Madison Ave, New York NY 10016

Routledge is an imprint of the Taylor & Francis Group, an informa business

Transferred to Digital Printing 2008

Typeset in Garamond by Wearset Ltd, Boldon, Tyne and Wear

British Library Cataloguing in Publication Data
A catalogue record for this book is available from the British Library

Library of Congress Cataloging in Publication Data
A catalog record for this book has been requested

ISBN10: 0-714-65619-4 (hbk)
ISBN10: 0-203-32722-5 (ebk)

ISBN13: 978-0-714-65619-9 (hbk)
ISBN13: 978-0-203-32722-7 (ebk)

Contents

Illustrations

Figures

Tables

Contributors

Peter Dorey is Senior Lecturer in Politics at Cardiff University. His books include *British Politics since 1945* (1995), *The Conservative Party and the Trade Unions* (1995), *The Major Premiership: Politics and Policies under John Major* (editor, 1999), *Wage Politics in Britain: The Rise and Fall of Incomes Policies since 1945* (2001), *Policy-Making in Britain, An Introduction* (2005), *Developments in British Public Policy* (editor, 2005) and *The Labour Party and Constitutional Reform* (forthcoming). He is currently writing two monographs, *British Conservatism: The Philosophy and Politics of Inequality* and *The Child Support Agency: A British Policy Disaster?*

James Hampshire is Lecturer in Politics at the University of Sussex. He has recently published *Citizenship and Belonging: Immigration and the Politics of Democratic Governance* (2005).

Kevin Jefferys is Professor of Contemporary History at the University of Plymouth. His books include *The Attlee Governments 1945–1951* (1992), *The Labour Party since 1945* (1993), *Retreat from New Jerusalem: British Politics 1951–64* (1997), *Anthony Crosland: A New Biography* (1999), *Leading Labour: From Keir Hardie to Tony Blair* (editor, 1999), *Labour Forces: From Ernest Bevin to Gordon Brown* (editor, 2002) and *Finest and Darkest Hours: The Decisive Events in British Politics from Churchill to Blair* (2002).

Janet Mather is Senior Lecturer in Politics at Manchester Metropolitan University. She is author of *The European Union and British Democracy: Towards Convergence* (2000), and has written widely on both regionalism, and aspects of European Union politics.

James Mitchell is Professor of Politics at the University of Strathclyde. He has published *Conservatives and the Union* (1990), *Politics and Public Policy in Scotland* (co-authored with Arthur Midwinter and Michael Keating, 1996), *How Scotland Votes: Scottish Parties and Elections* (co-authored with Lynn Bennie and Jack Brand, 1997), *Scotland Decides: The Devolution Issue and the 1997 Referendum* (co-authored with David Denver, Charles Pattie and Hugh Bochel, 2000) and *Governing Scotland: The Invention of Administrative Devolution* (2003).

Helen Parr is Lecturer in Politics at the University of Keele. Her books include *Harold Wilson and Britain's World Role: British Policy towards the European Community, 1964–1967* (2005) and *The Labour Governments 1964–70 Reconsidered* (co-editor, 2005).

Melissa Pine is Lecturer in European History at the University of Plymouth. Her most recent publications include 'Perseverance in the Face of Rejection: Towards British Membership of the European Communities, November 1967–June 1970', in Franz Knipping and Matthias Schönwald (eds) *Aufbruch zum Europa der zweiten Generation: Die europäische Einigung 1969–1984* (2004) and 'Private Diplomacy and Public Policy: The Soames Affair of 1969', *Journal of European Integration History* (January 2005).

Eric Shaw is Senior Lecturer in Politics at the University of Stirling. His books include *Discipline and Discord in the Labour Party* (1988), *The Labour Party since 1979: Crisis and Transformation* (1994) and *The Labour Party since 1945* (1996).

Donald Shell is Senior Lecturer in Politics at the University of Bristol. His books include *The House of Lords* (1988; 2nd edition 1992), *The House of Lords at Work* (editor, 1993), *From Churchill to Major: The British Prime Ministership since 1945* (co-editor, 1995) and *Second Chambers* (editor, 2001).

Kevin Theakston is Professor of British Government at the University of Leeds, and a Fellow of the Royal Historical Society. His books include *Junior Ministers in British Government* (1987), *The Labour Party and Whitehall* (1992), *The Civil Service since 1945* (1995), *Leadership in Whitehall* (1999), *Foreign Secretaries since 1974* (editor, 2003) and *Winston Churchill and the British Constitution* (2004).

Noel Thompson is Professor of History at the University of Swansea and a Fellow of the Royal Historical Society. His most recent books include *Political Economy and the Labour Party: The Economics of Democratic Socialism, 1884–1995* (1996) and *Left in the Wilderness: The Political Economy of British Democratic Socialism since 1979* (2002).

Stephen Thornton is Lecturer in Politics in the School of European Studies at Cardiff University. He has published several articles and chapters on pensions policy in Britain, and is currently completing a monograph entitled *British Pensions Policy since 1945*.

Neville Twitchell is currently completing his PhD at London Metropolitan University, his thesis being on the campaign to abolish capital punishment.

Rhiannon Vickers is Lecturer in International Politics at the University of Sheffield. She is the author of *Manipulating Hegemony: State Power, Labour and the Marshall Plan in Britain* (2000) and *Labour and the World: The Evolution of the Labour Party's Foreign Policy since 1900*, Volume 1 (2004) and Volume 2 (forthcoming).

Introduction

Peter Dorey

There are three discrete justifications for another book on the Labour Governments of 1964–1970, thereby adding to those by Ponting (1989, 1990) and Coopey, Fielding and Tiratsoo (1993). First, the latter half of the 1960s was a singularly eventful one in British politics, for this period encompassed a plethora of economic, political and social developments and difficulties which either necessitated or partly arose from governmental activity. Not only are the issues and problems of this particular period of intrinsic importance and interest to students of post-war British politics, but they also serve to reveal many of the conundrums and constraints which confront contemporary British governments in attempting to devise appropriate policies to address them. In this regard, the 1964–1970 Labour Governments were often either inhibited from pursuing particular policies, or, alternatively, obliged to respond in specific ways, owing to a combination of exogenous crises, domestic circumstances, pressure from organised interests, intra-party dissent over specific measures, and tensions within the Cabinet. It was a fascinating period in recent British political history.

Certainly, some of the disagreements and disputes which variously occurred both at Cabinet level and within the Parliamentary Labour Party transcended traditional ideological tensions between the left and the right of the Labour Party, with socio-educational background becoming a more important variable in shaping attitudes towards particular policies, whilst on a couple of specific issues, links with the trade unions also strongly shaped reactions and responses. In short, after thirteen years in opposition, the social composition of the Parliamentary Labour Party was rather different from that of the Attlee era (and before). As we will note in Chapter 2, an increasing number of Labour MPs seemed to personify the process of *embourgeoisement*, whereby Britain was apparently becoming more middle class as a consequence of increasing prosperity, full employment, expanding educational opportunities and attainment, and an expansion of white-collar occupations. Many Labour MPs emanating from this seemingly more meritocratic socio-economic background had, in some respects, a somewhat different outlook or set of attitudes vis-à-vis certain issues in comparison to older or more working-class Labour parliamentarians. Indeed, this socio-economic and generational distinction occasionally manifested itself not only with regard to particular policies, but also in relation to perceptions about the role of a Labour backbencher: loyal, but largely passive, supporters of the Party leadership, or proactive parliamentarians who sought greater influence and input over governmental policies, and who therefore were not willing to be mere 'lobby fodder' herded hither and thither by the party's whips.

The second justification for a new book on the 1964–1970 Labour Governments is that whilst the two texts referred to at the beginning of this Introduction provide in-depth coverage of particular aspects of those Governments, they do so at the expense of other important aspects. For example, Ponting's *Breach of Promise* (1989, 1990) provides comprehensive coverage (and rightly so, given their intrinsic importance and major impact) of both foreign affairs and the economic problems which beset the Labour Governments, but this means that various other aspects and policies are either glossed over, given only cursory consideration, or accorded merely a passing reference or two. For example, the application to join the (then) European Economic Community is condensed into an eleven-page chapter, whilst the separate issues of immigration (and race relations) and Northern Ireland are subsumed into a single chapter of just twelve pages. Elsewhere, House of Lords reform is examined, but not the experiments concerning reform of the House of Commons, whilst the issue of civil service reform is despatched in barely three pages. Meanwhile, the 1964–1970 Labour Governments' 'social liberalism' – as symbolised by the abolition of the death penalty, and homosexual law reform – is given the briefest of discussion. Moreover, the Labour Governments' initiatives in the sphere of education are also dealt with rather briefly, whilst the growing demands for Scottish and Welsh devolution – and the Cabinet's rather sanguine response – have been omitted altogether.

Similarly, the collection of essays garnered by Coopey, Fielding and Tiratsoo (1993) focus on a relatively narrow range of themes and issues, to the neglect of many others. For example, whilst the Labour Governments' economic record and industrial policy, along with foreign affairs and Harold Wilson's much-vaunted 'scientific revolution', are intelligently and comprehensively addressed, policies pertaining to parliamentary reform, 'the troubles' (and ensuing military intervention) in Northern Ireland, Scottish and Welsh demands for devolution, the expansion of education, legislation concerning immigration and race relations, and the aborted attempt at trade union reform are either conspicuous by their absence or mentioned fleetingly in passing, although space is provided at the end of the book for a substantive chapter on the Conservatives in opposition during this period.

Third, this is the first book on the 1964–1970 Labour Governments to make comprehensive and systematic use of Cabinet papers and ministerial correspondence. Although the 2005 implementation of the Freedom of Information Act (actually passed in 2000, but with its full enactment deferred for five years) has superseded 'the thirty-year rule' – whereby government papers could not be made publicly available for thirty years – during the period when the chapters for this book were being researched and written, the relevant official papers and records had only recently become available in the public domain; they were certainly unavailable to the earlier authors mentioned. The contributors to this volume were therefore encouraged to make extensive use of these Cabinet and ministerial papers, in order to imbue this work with maximum originality and scholarly research, and I am delighted with the amenable and conscientious manner in which they have faithfully fulfilled this particular editorial entreaty.

Even though several of the issues and problems which confronted the 1964–1970 Labour Governments have variously faced British governments since this time, many of them emerged, or were tackled, for the first time in the 1960s. It is sincerely hoped, therefore, that this volume will enrich our understanding of the 1964–1970 Labour Governments, and provide new or deeper insights into the events and developments which confronted Ministers during this period. The repercussions of many of them are still with us today, in one guise or another.

1 Labour in opposition, 1951–1964

Kevin Jefferys

Introduction

Must Labour Lose? was the title of a book published after the Labour Party had suffered a third successive general election defeat in 1959. Answers to the question were not optimistic. Basing their work on a survey of 500 voters, the authors found that Labour was widely seen as an outdated force, representing mainly the poor at a time when 'many workers, regardless of their politics, no longer see themselves as working class' (Abrams and Rose, 1960: 23). It was widely agreed that after the heady days of the Attlee government, the Labour Party had consigned itself to opposition – perhaps permanently – as a result of factional in-fighting. Labour's reaction to the loss of power in 1951 had been to enter into protracted internal disputes between Bevanite 'fundamentalists' advocating an extension of public ownership, and Gaitskellite 'revisionists' seeking to play down nationalisation in favour of social justice.

Apportioning responsibility for this sorry state of affairs tended, in the first instance, to be a continuation of the internal power struggle by other means. Left-wing writers attributed Labour's difficulties to the growing ascendancy of moderate ideas. According to Ralph Miliband (1961), by abandoning a consciously socialist perspective in the early 1950s, the Labour Party betrayed its ideals and alienated its natural supporters. Conversely, revisionists believed Labour was not adapting itself quickly enough to post-Second World War social change. In particular, it was argued that as Conservative governments provided wider home ownership and steady economic growth – thereby allowing greater access to consumer goods such as cars and domestic appliances – so the 'affluent worker' was increasingly aspiring to middle-class habits (Crosland, 1960a). This perspective, of course, reflected the concept of *embourgeoisement*, which became popular amongst some social scientists during the late 1950s and early 1960s, and which implied a continued diminution in support for the Labour Party.

Subsequent research has exposed the inadequacy of these claims, which not only exaggerate the 'socialist' content of 1940s Labourism and the speed of change in post-war society, but also underplay the residual strength of the

Labour vote. In spite of Churchill's return to power, Labour polled over 200,000 more votes than the Tories at the 1951 election – the product of huge majorities building up in urban strongholds. Indeed, Labour's total of nearly 14 million votes was the largest hitherto recorded, and remains, to this day, the largest in the party's history, exceeding 'New Labour's' 13.5 million votes in 1997. Much of what became known as 'consensus politics' in the 1950s resulted from the Conservative belief that the nation remained 'left inclined', firmly attached to the welfare state and mixed economy bequeathed by Attlee's administration (Jefferys, 1997).

Without doubt, the Labour Party struggled during the 1950s to find ways of appealing to those groups at the heart of social change, such as younger voters, but then so too did the Conservatives, as became clear after 1959. Labour's core vote nevertheless remained strong, and the party's weakness in the 1950s should therefore be accounted for in rather more prosaic terms. In a period of sustained economic growth, with living standards rising, there was no compelling incentive for the electorate to change the government of the day, especially as the Labour Opposition seemed happy to trade the unity of the Attlee years for 'civil war' between rival factions. The party's electoral slide, in other words, had as much to do with political as with social determinants, which implied that the possibility of renewal remained strong. The authors of *Must Labour Lose?* concluded that it was wrong to present the party as being in terminal decline; the question they posed could not be answered with certainty in 1960 because 'politics is continually in a state of flux' (Abrams and Rose, 1960: 97–8). It was this 'state of flux' that was to enable Labour to return to power in 1964.

Attlee's final years as leader, 1951–1955

The early 1950s constituted, in the words of Andrew Thorpe, 'one of the most dismal periods' in Labour's history (2001: 126). It certainly looked during these years as if the party 'must lose'. Contrary to expectations immediately after the 1951 election – when Labour stalwarts believed the Conservatives would prove 'unfit to govern' – Churchill's administration grew in stature, gaining popularity as the harsh years of 1940s rationing and austerity finally came to an end. Attlee, by this stage in his late sixties, proved ineffective as leader of the Opposition, and instead of developing a clear and coherent new programme, Labour resorted to bitter intra-party squabbling. For example, in March 1952 a group of 57 MPs defied the party whip by refusing to back an official amendment to the defence estimates, an event which marked the first major act of public defiance by the Bevanites, a faction within the Parliamentary Labour Party (PLP) that developed out of the ranks of the Keep Left group of the late 1940s.

What made this challenge more significant was that, for the first time in a generation, the left had a leader who could attract support throughout the broader Labour movement. Nye Bevan was credited with both successful ministerial experience – as the architect of the NHS – and outstanding skills as an orator, and in 1952 he attempted to build on this by publishing his own political creed. *In Place of Fear* argued that in order to challenge the power structures of British society, democratic socialism needed to become something more than merely a middle way between capitalism and communism. Bevan's work was much criticised for failing to take into account changes since the war, and for proposing remedies that seemed more appropriate to the economic circumstances of the 1930s. Nevertheless, there were signs that the tide was running in his direction. The Bevanite journal *Tribune* was successfully relaunched with an increasing circulation, whilst constituency parties vied with each other to hold 'Brains Trusts' question sessions featuring Bevanite speakers such as Richard Crossman and Barbara Castle. Meanwhile, at Westminster, Bevan's supporters organised weekly meetings to discuss policy papers and were often found socialising together, constituting not so much 'a party within a party', as critics alleged, but rather 'the Smoking Room within the Smoking Room' (Campbell, 1987: 273).

The increasingly high profile of the Bevanites caused considerable consternation on Labour's centre-right. Attlee's private view – that Bevan had the qualities for future leadership – was not widely shared by his senior colleagues, many of whom regarded Bevan as an egocentric demagogue. Those prepared to speak out against Bevanite activity, such as Herbert Morrison and the former Chancellor, Hugh Gaitskell, began to enlist the support of concerned elements within the PLP and the trade union hierarchy. The outcome of a protracted inquest into the revolt over the defence estimates was the reintroduction of Standing Orders, suspended since 1945; henceforth, MPs could only receive the whip if they agreed to abide by majority decisions of the PLP. The revival of Standing Orders marked the eclipse of the unity that characterised the immediate post-war years. Attlee himself, while regretting these developments, believed he had gone as far as possible in disciplining the rebels without causing an open rupture in party ranks; only if unity was maintained, he believed, did Labour have any realistic chance of removing Churchill from power. Yet intra-party tensions increased further still, in spite of Attlee's efforts to adopt a conciliatory line. Nowhere was this more evident than at the party's annual conference in the autumn of 1952.

'The Morecambe Conference', recalled Attlee loyalist Douglas Jay, 'was memorable as one of the most unpleasant experiences I ever suffered in the Labour Party. The town was ugly, the hotels forbidding, the weather bad, and the Conference, at its worst, hideous' (1980: 223). Normal courtesies were cast aside as speakers from Labour's right found themselves booed and jeered from the gallery. Meanwhile, the advance of Bevanite ideas within the party was reflected in the passing of motions backing the principle of a free health service and demanding further nationalisation of 'key and major industries'. The most bitter feelings, though, were reserved for the elections to the constituency section of the National Executive Committee (NEC), where two of Labour's old guard, Morrison and Hugh Dalton, were defeated by two leading Bevanites, Harold Wilson and Richard Crossman. The Bevanites, who could now claim six out of seven constituency places on the NEC, were not afraid to exult in their triumph. News of Morrison's defeat in particular was greeted with howls of delight on the conference floor. Nor was any early improvement likely. To many on the right of the Labour Party, Morecambe demonstrated that if Bevanites in the Commons were an irritation, then Bevanism in the country threatened the whole future of the labour movement. In a hard-hitting speech in Stalybridge the week after the conference, Hugh Gaitskell provoked his opponents by alleging that one-sixth of conference delegates were 'Communist or Communist-inspired'. Hugh Dalton noted in his diary that 'nothing is getting better. More hatred, and more love of hatred, in our Party than I ever remember' (Pimlott, 1986: 601, entry for 24–28 October 1952).

What, then, was at stake in this feuding? In part, the conflict was a battle for the party leadership. With Attlee likely to retire in the not too distant future, right-wingers were determined that he should be replaced by Morrison or, after the Stalybridge speech, by Gaitskell. Equally, Bevan had his own leadership ambitions. The main protagonists clearly saw the dispute as ideological; they believed, in Bevan's words, there was a 'basic conflict over party purpose', between fundamentalists and revisionists. But some important qualifications must be added. In the first place, party disputes in the early 1950s were much less concerned with domestic than with foreign affairs. The principal topics of concern were German rearmament, national service and nuclear weapons. For example, whereas over twenty backbench revolts occurred on foreign policy and defence issues, only one was over nationalisation. Second, neither side had any coherently formulated ideas to apply to domestic politics. Bevanism focused almost exclusively on demands for more nationalisation, whilst the right had not as yet produced any distinctly revisionist agenda. Furthermore, those younger, middle-class Labour MPs who were floating new ideas tended to be viewed with suspicion by old-style trade unionists.

There were, moreover, many shared assumptions between Labour's left and right, notably over the achievements of the Attlee years. Contributors to a 1952 collection entitled *New Fabian Essays*, drawn from all sections of the party, were agreed that – in contrast to what happened in 1930s Britain – the power of capitalism could be subordinated to, and shaped by, the political decisions of a democratic state. This collection also indicated, moreover, that there was a sizeable 'centre' element within the party, many of whom believed that internal feuding was a futile distraction. This suggested that much of the bitterness in the Labour Party during the early 1950s derived from differences of political style and emphasis, compounded by a rapid hardening of individual loyalties (Jefferys, 1999: 44–7).

In the aftermath of the Morecambe conference, Attlee decided the time had come to attempt a firm stand. At the first meeting of MPs in the new parliamentary session, he secured agreement, by 188 votes to 51, for a resolution banning all unofficial groups within the party. Under protest, the Bevanites had no option but to comply. Thereafter, instead of there being a group of 40 Bevanite MPs, Bevanism in the PLP was restricted to a smaller, private discussion group comprising only Bevan's closest followers, such as Richard Crossman, Harold Wilson and Michael Foot. Bevan himself agreed the time had come to mend fences, and in the belief that the Morecambe conference had endorsed many of the policy positions favoured by the left, he put himself forward for Shadow Cabinet elections, signalling that he was prepared to re-enter the Party's mainstream. The result was that throughout 1953 and early 1954 an 'armed truce' was in place. Old antagonisms remained beneath the surface and still occasionally flickered into life, but on both sides there was a recognition that Churchill's government, enjoying the political dividends of economic advance, could only be challenged if the Labour Party displayed unity. Hence, the disruptive scenes in Morecambe were not repeated at the Margate conference in 1953. Instead, delegates approved almost unanimously a compromise policy document entitled *Challenge to Britain*, which combined limited promises of nationalisation with a pledge to remove all National Health Service charges.

In the spring of 1954, however, the armed truce was replaced by a return to more open warfare. Bevan found it ever more difficult to tolerate being in a minority of one in the Shadow Cabinet, especially as Conservative popularity made it increasingly unlikely that his self-discipline would be rewarded by a return to high office. In a debate on foreign policy, Bevan's frustrations got the better of him when he launched a scathing attack that appeared to contradict most of what Attlee had argued on behalf of the Labour Party. After receiving a stern rebuke for what many MPs regarded as megalomania, Bevan announced his resignation from the Shadow Cabinet. Aside from leading to a formal ruling that in future frontbench speakers should stick to defined subjects, this incident had serious implications for the balance of power within the party. In the first place, the disintegration of the Bevanites was confirmed when the runner-up in Shadow Cabinet elections, Harold Wilson, decided to take his mentor's place, provoking allegations of 'Mac-Donaldism' from those on the left.

More importantly, in the short term Bevan had jeopardised any prospect he might have had of succeeding Attlee as Labour Party leader. Not only did Bevan alienate mainstream party opinion, but he also disappointed his friends, who recognised that outside the Shadow Cabinet he had much less authority to promote his ideas. This was confirmed later in the year when he was easily defeated by Hugh Gaitskell for the post of party treasurer. 'Bevan', noted Hugh Dalton in December 1954, 'has been committing slow suicide', and this, combined with the 'melancholy mediocrity of Morrison', made it increasingly likely that Attlee would be succeeded by Gaitskell (Pimlott, 1986: 641, Dalton's diary entry for Christmas 1954). 'The trouble with Nye', one of his supporters later concluded, 'was that he wasn't a team player' (Mikardo, 1988: 151). Bevan, it was felt, could neither work closely with senior colleagues nor, owing to his conviction that socialism was about instinct rather than strategy, provide consistent forward planning. As if to underline the point, he launched a further attack on Attlee in a defence debate in March 1955. This led, despite the imminence of a general election, to another bout of wrangling in which Bevan only narrowly escaped expulsion from the party (Shaw, 1988: 35–50).

The price of Labour's internecine warfare was about to become apparent. After Churchill's retirement, his successor, Sir Anthony Eden, could not resist calling an early election in May 1955. The electoral omens had not looked good for Labour for some time, for in forty-five contested by-elections held since 1951, the Conservatives had not suffered a single defeat; unusually in mid-term, several of these by-elections had actually witnessed a swing towards the Government. In such circumstances, Labour found it difficult to make any distinctive appeal to the electorate. The party's 1955 manifesto was essentially a reworking of *Challenge to Britain*, which Bevan had described privately as 'cold porridge stirred through a blanket'. Neither appeals to the memory of the 1945 government nor promises of a few further measures of nationalisation did much to stir voters. Nor did Labour attacks on high prices make much impact on the steady Conservative lead in the opinion polls, whilst Attlee's request that Eden repudiate his 'dirty' electioneering claim that Labour would bring back rationing failed to instil life into a low-key campaign. Meanwhile, in the constituencies Labour's campaign was hampered by the serious decline in its number of full-time agents since 1951.

When the results were announced, it was no surprise that the Conservatives became the first peacetime government for nearly a century to be returned to power with an increased majority. Press commentators were agreed about the causes of this outcome: in addition to Labour's internal feuding, 'a great many working people are "doing nicely, thank you" – and they don't bother to ask why' (Butler, 1955: 82–94, 160). Yet it would be wrong to exaggerate the longer-term significance of the 1955 result. Both parties recorded lower total votes than in 1951 owing to a fall in turnout, and the Conservatives gained only 11 seats on a small average swing of 1.8 per cent. With membership of trade unions continuing to expand slowly and Labour still commanding 46.4 per cent of the popular vote, there was no indication that the 1955 defeat was irreversible. Internal Conservative inquests noted that Labour abstentions were a crucial factor, and that affluence had not yet gone far enough to dent the 'prejudice against voting Conservative' of millions of working-class voters. In such circumstances, there was actually some concern amongst Conservative strategists that Labour had not been beaten out of sight (Jefferys, 1997: 38–40).

Hugh Gaitskell and the rise of revisionism, 1955–1959

In the aftermath of election defeat, there was a recognition within Labour ranks of the need for change. Party organisation was compared by Harold Wilson in a special report to a 'rusty penny-farthing', and a series of research projects were soon launched in order to reconsider Labour's policies. The major preoccupation of Labour activists, though, as they confronted the prospect of a lengthy Eden administration, was with the party leadership. It was obvious that Attlee, after twenty years at the helm, would soon retire, and the question of his successor occasioned intense speculation. Instead of retiring immediately after the election, Attlee stayed on for a further six months. Critics claim that he did so in order to spite his long-standing rival, Morrison (Hunter, 1959: 222). On the other hand, Attlee believed his early departure was likely to deepen intra-party divisions between the supporters of Morrison and those of Bevan. Whatever his motives, the practical effect was to enhance the prospects of the third contender for the leadership, Hugh Gaitskell. Aside from a forceful conference performance, revealing a passion for social justice hitherto hidden from many party members, Gaitskell's standing was further reinforced by 'Operation Avalanche' – the effort of his old ally Hugh Dalton to dislodge ageing members of the Shadow Cabinet, nine of whom were over 65. By encouraging others to follow his lead in making way for younger candidates, Dalton helped to encourage the view that Morrison's age made him an unsuitable leader. In the ballot amongst MPs that followed Attlee's eventual resignation in December 1955, Gaitskell comfortably defeated Bevan, leaving Morrison in a poor third place.

The new leader was not universally welcomed in the labour movement. To many Bevanites, it was not easy to forgive Gaitskell's close ties with the Party's right wing since 1951, especially his links with the three trade union leaders who controlled about 40 per cent of votes at the party conference: Deakin of the TGWU, Lawther of the Mineworkers and Williamson of the GMWU. The claim that Gaitskell was insufficiently radical to head the Labour Party was one that was to resurface for years to come. So too were the accusations that he relied too heavily on a narrow clique of friends known as the 'Hampstead set', who, like Gaitskell himself, tended to be middle class and Oxford educated. In these circumstances, it was to his credit that Gaitskell was able rapidly to establish himself as party leader. He first managed to exploit the mood for a fresh start by offering past antagonists such as Bevan and Wilson important positions in the new Shadow Cabinet. Within a year, Gaitskell also demonstrated his potential as a national leader during the Suez crisis. For by speaking out powerfully against the Anglo-French attack on the Egyptians and emphasising the theme of 'law not war', he both carried with him the support of the whole Labour movement and played a part in helping to bring down Sir Anthony Eden after the suspension of the Suez operation (Williams, 1979: 279–92).

Gaitskell's leadership also meant fresh thinking about the party's domestic agenda. After the 1955 defeat, the NEC identified several areas of investigation, with the aim of revising policy in order to take account of recent social change. Under Gaitskell's guidance, this process eventually resulted in a series of policy documents that shaped Labour pronouncements until well into the 1960s (Donnelly, 1995: 92–125). In place of the old-style corporate socialism that characterised the Attlee generation, the party was gradually moving towards an ideology that stressed the need to achieve greater social equality. Revisionism did not find expression only in policy committees: in terms of the intellectual argument, Gaitskell's case was greatly strengthened by the publication in 1956 of Anthony Crosland's work *The Future of Socialism*. Crosland, an Oxford-trained economist and a close friend of Gaitskell, argued that one of the main inspirations of British socialism – antagonism towards the evils created by capitalism – was becoming outdated. Now that post-war economic management was capable of delivering much wider prosperity than before, attention should be focused more on the ethical tradition in socialist thinking, especially the principle of equality. In order to progress towards equality, Crosland argued, Labour had to draw up a list of new priorities: these included comprehensive schools for all children, the redistribution of wealth via the taxation system, and the utilisation of public expenditure to remedy social injustices in areas such as housing and health. The Labour left was outraged by Crosland's claim that nationalisation should henceforth play only a minor role in socialist advance, but for many on the centre-right the brilliance of *The Future of Socialism* was to make it a rallying point for a generation to come (Jefferys, 1999: 56–63).

The Bevanite left, by contrast, seemed devoid of new thinking. Bevan was scornful of the 'fresh thinkers' who claimed that socialism needed to be reassessed, yet in spite of differences over public ownership, there were in reality many similarities between the socialism of Bevan and that of Crosland. Where Bevan really parted company was his belief that the revisionists were surrendering to a tide of 1950s affluence and acquisitive individualism that was threatening to destroy communal values. But Bevan had never been able to make this concern the basis of a convincing alternative programme, and the retreat of Bevanism within the PLP meant there was only a negligible intellectual challenge to the revisionist case. A small group of backbenchers sought to revive a defunct group known as 'Victory for Socialism', but the few policy pamphlets it produced served mostly to highlight the weakness of the Labour left.

Indeed, many of the most innovative ideas about socialism in the second half of the 1950s came from outside the party mainstream, from the so-called New Left. This broad movement developed initially amongst Communists disillusioned with Stalinism after the invasion of Hungary in 1956; it was soon joined by those, including academics such as E. P. Thompson and Raymond Williams, who stressed cultural concerns and the need for a more radical conception of politics than now existed within Labour ranks. In the meantime, the champion of the 'old Left' was making his peace with the party leader. Bevan recognised, albeit reluctantly, that Gaitskell's victory in the leadership contest decisively ended the power struggle within the party. After years of frustration on party committees that inevitably reflected the organisational strength of the right, Bevan came to the view that he must henceforth play the role of loyal lieutenant, especially after he was asked to act as Shadow Foreign Secretary. The party's future prospects were a further consideration. Eden's failings as Prime Minister, even before the Suez fiasco, persuaded Bevan, like others, that Labour had a real chance of returning to power. Whilst factional differences might smoulder beneath the surface, it was now accepted that there must be no return to the open warfare of the early 1950s.

The new marriage of convenience between Gaitskell and Bevan certainly allowed the party to develop a more coherent programme. This was seen most dramatically in the case of defence policy. In a famous speech at the annual conference in 1957, Bevan alienated many of his closest followers by declaring that Britain should not unilaterally abandon nuclear weapons. For several years, Bevan had spoken with great passion about the horrors of atomic warfare, but, as John Campbell (1987: 331) notes, he had never opposed the Attlee government's decision to manufacture the bomb, and in many respects he shared the multilateralist orthodoxy of the party leadership. After much agonising, Bevan decided to speak at the Brighton conference in favour of an NEC motion which committed a future Labour government to oppose testing, but to halt production of nuclear weapons only if other powers agreed likewise. To endorse the unilateralist alternative, he claimed after being heckled from the floor of the conference, would be to send a British Foreign Secretary 'naked into the conference chamber', which represented not statesmanship but an 'emotional spasm'.

Bevan's robust language ensured the defeat of the unilateralist resolution by an overwhelming majority, though it cost him dear in terms of personal friendships; the spectacle of witnessing 'Bevan into Bevin', as the *Daily Telegraph* put it, was something close allies such as Michael Foot could never forgive (Foot, 1973: 569–71). The speech highlighted the extent to which Bevan had tied himself to Gaitskell's leadership, and confirmed that Bevanism as a serious force within the parliamentary party was a thing of the past. It was no coincidence that the forces built up by Bevan in the constituencies and the trade unions began, from this point onwards, to channel their energies in new, extra-parliamentary directions, most notably into the newly formed Campaign for Nuclear Disarmament (CND). At the annual conference in 1958, the party's commitment to NATO and to multilateralism was again endorsed, though there was increasing concern about growing support for a more militant position.

Although overshadowed by the drama of the defence debate, the Brighton conference of 1957 also underlined the eclipse of the left on domestic policy. With sullen acquiescence from Bevan, the policy sub-committee on public ownership set up by Gaitskell produced a document entitled *Industry and Society*, which committed a future Labour administration to little more than the renationalisation of steel and road haulage (which had been denationalised by Churchill's 1951–1955 administration). Beyond this, there were only vague references to reviewing the position of industries alleged to be 'failing the nation', and to the possibility of the state controlling investment in private companies by buying a percentage of shares short of ownership (Haseler, 1969: 99–111). In spite of the fulminations of *Tribune*, this position was overwhelmingly backed by delegates in Brighton, and Gaitskell was credited with a triumph which avoided the need to make any potentially damaging commitments in the run-up to a general election. Bevan's behaviour at Brighton was conditioned, at least in part, by the widespread belief that the Labour Party was once again a serious contender for power. In the aftermath of Suez, Labour maintained a clear lead in the opinion polls throughout 1957, and, unlike in the early 1950s, the party could also take comfort from a series of promising by-election results, culminating in the capture of Rochdale and Glasgow Kelvingrove from the Conservatives early in 1958.

However, belief in certain victory was gradually eroded, for Eden's successor as Prime Minister, Harold Macmillan, was soon making political capital out of his claim that the nation had 'never had it so good', and within months the Government's popularity was restored. By-elections in the first half of 1959 showed virtually no swing towards Labour, and opinion polls in the run-up to the election in October 1959 suggested a clear, if modest, Conservative lead (Cook and Ramsden, 1975: 195–6).

The Labour Party entered the election in much better shape than in 1955, for by this time there was little evidence of past policy differences. Whatever their reservations in private, the former Bevanites gave full public backing to a manifesto that focused on social justice and played down nationalisation. More so than in 1955, the Labour Party also had a leader capable, at least at the outset, of forcing the pace. Ironically, it was Gaitskell himself who made a serious blunder by claiming that Labour's improved social provision would not require increases in income tax. Whilst the effect on voters of a single pledge can easily be exaggerated, this incident did appear to mark a turning point. Thereafter, Conservative ministers relentlessly made the claim that Labour was cynically bidding for votes with a series of unattainable promises.

The outcome was a third successive Conservative victory. On an average swing towards the government of 1.1 per cent, the number of Labour voters fell again and Macmillan was able to increase his overall majority to 100 parliamentary seats. The regional pattern of results indicated that wider prosperity was a key determinant in voting behaviour. Most of Labour's losses were concentrated in London and the West Midlands, areas that had prospered during the 1950s, whereas two regions that experienced rising unemployment – Scotland and Lancashire – went against the national trend by recording a small swing to Labour. In many ways, this was a more crushing defeat for Labour than 1955, because it was no longer possible to blame factional in-fighting, and hence commentators were quick to draw the conclusion that the Labour Party looked obsolete in the face of rising living standards.

There was, however, some reason to remain sceptical about the notion of a disappearing Labour vote. The party may not have fared particularly well with younger voters – those unable to remember 'the hungry thirties' – but its appeal in industrialised communities still enabled it to retain nearly 44 per cent of the total vote (Butler and Rose, 1960: 189–201). In reality, any Opposition would have found it difficult to dent the popularity of a government that delivered stable prices and steady growth; Gaitskell defended himself by pointing out that on balance fewer than three voters in every 200 had switched sides. The real question for Labour was to decide in which direction to move: should more full-blooded socialism be given its chance, or was 'the party's weakness that it had not been revisionist enough?' (Howell, 1976: 219).

From Gaitskell to Wilson, 1959–1963

Inquests into the causes of the 1959 defeat reached widely differing conclusions. Douglas Jay, reflecting views he encountered on the doorstep during the election, immediately published a controversial article suggesting that if the Labour Party were to avoid the charge of exclusive association with a shrinking working class, it might have to consider a change of name (1980: 272–5). To the left, it seemed outrageous that the Gaitskellites, having dictated party policy for several years, should claim that defeat demonstrated the need to move further still to the right. Bevan gave vent to his frustration by publicly claiming that Labour had paid the price for fighting not on a socialist programme, but on 'pre-1914 Liberalism brought up to date'. This set the scene for a period of renewed bloodletting which appeared to confirm the worst fears about Labour's future. Gaitskell himself opened up a fresh area of controversy at the annual conference in November 1959. His own explanation for defeat emphasised long-term social change, but also argued that votes had been lost because of the Party's image – especially its association in the public mind with wholesale nationalisation. In common with many of the leading revisionist intellectuals, Gaitskell had long believed that public ownership was only one of several means by which to achieve socialist ends. As a result, he took the famously high-risk strategy of proposing that the Labour Party should amend Clause 4 of its 1918 constitution; this was the clause, reprinted on party membership cards, that stipulated the need to aim for the 'common ownership of the means of production, distribution and exchange'.

For some conference delegates, the leader's suggestion was broadly acceptable, for if Labour were ever to recover electorally, then modernisation was unavoidable. However, this response was far from typical: many Labour activists, including trade union leaders hitherto loyal to Gaitskell, regarded

Clause 4 as the cornerstone of their political outlook. In the words of Henry Drucker, Clause 4 encapsulated the 'ethos' rather than the 'doctrine' of the party. It convinced party members that, come what may, their socialist commitment was fundamentally sound (Drucker, 1979: 8–10). Gaitskell's proposal was not designed to rule out any further measures of nationalisation by a future government, but he found that simply to challenge such a vital symbol was rather like trying to take 'Genesis out of the Bible' (Jones, 1997: 1–21). After several months of heated exchanges, the party leader was forced to back down. By focusing on a symbolic issue – which many moderates thought would not be understood by the general public – Gaitskell unwittingly served to deepen intra-party divisions without furthering the process of policy revision. His own advisers had in fact warned him that he would 'start a battle in the Party that will cause far more trouble than the thing is worth' (Crosland, 1982: 93).

As a result, Gaitskell has been much criticised for his poor tactical sense, and for fighting the wrong battle at the wrong time (Jones, 2000: 306). At the outset, however, he cannot have known that his former union allies would desert him, and Gaitskell himself was convinced that it was not the wrong battle to be fighting. If, as he believed, Labour's real problem was to do not with policy but with image, then it was only by openly demonstrating its willingness to modify this that the party would attract sufficient new voters to secure electoral victory (Marquand, 1991: 133–4). Nevertheless, the very fact of having to back down over Clause 4 had serious implications. Henceforth, Gaitskell had to acknowledge that attachment to his brand of revisionism was not as widespread in the party as he had hoped, and in the short term, criticism was such that the leader even faced an open challenge to his own position.

Unease about the leadership in 1960 crystallised in particular around the defence issue. With its well-publicised annual marches from Aldermaston to London, CND was attracting increasing support for the unilateralist cause, not least amongst a minority of Labour MPs. The main challenge to the party's official multilateral policy, however, came from the trade unions. Unlike Attlee, Gaitskell could no longer rely on the backing of the old pro-right triumvirate of transport workers, miners and municipal workers. In particular, Deakin's successor as leader of the Transport Workers' Union, Frank Cousins, was sympathetic to a range of left-wing policy positions, including unilateralism. By aligning supportive elements at the 1960 conference in Scarborough, Cousins was able to use union block votes to ensure the passage of two unilateralist resolutions and the defeat of the leadership's official statement on defence.

Gaitskell immediately let it be known that he would not accept the view of conference, in theory the supreme policy-making authority. He argued that a unilateralist position was intellectually disreputable and electorally disastrous, and he pledged to 'fight and fight and fight again' against the decision. Within a matter of weeks, though, the party leader was fighting for his own position. Ever since the 1959 election defeat, there had been an undercurrent of concern about his leadership, particularly a belief that Gaitskell spent too much of his time imposing his wishes on reluctant followers and not enough seeking to match Macmillan on the national stage. This view was held particularly by the left, and after the death of Nye Bevan in 1960, many former Bevanites were prepared to back Harold Wilson in a leadership challenge. Wilson stood not on the basis of support for unilateralism, but rather as a 'unity' candidate, opposed to what was said to be Gaitskell's confrontational style of right-wing leadership. In the event, Gaitskell secured a comfortable, if not overwhelming, victory in the PLP ballot, although at the same time Wilson put down a useful marker for the future (Pimlott, 1992: 224–51).

In retrospect, the leadership contest was the start of an impressive fight-back by Gaitskell. During the next year, he was able not only to re-establish his personal authority, but also to put the Labour Party in a position where it was able to benefit from a turnaround in electoral fortunes. 'The crucial task for the next year', advised one of Gaitskell's supporters, 'is to isolate the extreme left and win back or consolidate the left-centre' (cited in Crosland, 1982: 104). This task was greatly assisted by the emergence in 1960 of the Campaign for Democratic Socialism (CDS), a pressure group within the party that sought to disseminate revisionist ideas and to promote revisionists to key positions of power. Transport House turned a blind eye to CDS, showing a leniency it had never extended to Victory for Socialism (Shaw, 1988: 53–5). The new grouping was dominated by 'Hampstead-set' Gaitskellites, though it came to have support from about 45 MPs. It also established a youth section and sought to influence local parties and trade unions, though with varying degrees of success on different issues.

The most potent symbol of Gaitskell's fightback in 1961, the reversal of conference approval for unilateralism, was only marginally influenced by CDS pressure. Rather, some of the major unions, such as those representing the railwaymen and the engineers, decided to endorse a multilateral defence policy in the interests of party unity. The same desire for pulling together could be seen in the support given to a new domestic programme, drawing inspiration from a policy document entitled *Signposts for the Sixties*. This aimed at reconciling different opinions within the party by calling for both social egalitarianism and economic planning to secure a higher rate of growth. By securing support for both his foreign and his domestic policies at Labour's 1961 conference, Gaitskell could be satisfied that his authority had been reaffirmed (Brivati, 1996: 376–403).

These debates over Labour policies took place in tandem with the debate about the political inclinations of the burgeoning middle class, and the extent to which they could be electorally attracted to the Party. Participants in these intra-party debates – one of which was instigated by the NEC's home policy sub-committee – drew markedly different conclusions about the implications for Labour's future electoral support. One perspective was that technological advances would increasingly blur the distinction between the working and the middle classes, whilst yielding new occupational divisions which would actually prove politically beneficial to the Labour Party. In particular, it was suggested that during the 1960s, 'the really dangerous rift in society is likely to lie along the frontier dividing the administrators from the administered, the powerful from the powerless, the machine controllers from the machine minders', such that there was no reason to assume that the interests of white-collar workers would be in conflict with those of manual workers. Indeed, 'since their interests are essentially the same, there will not be a divergence, but a gathering together' (Labour Party Archives, RD.194/January 1962).

Implicit also in this perspective was the view that whilst technological advances and automation heralded a diminution of the traditional working class based in manufacturing and extraction industries, the corresponding expansion of the middle class was less clear-cut, for some non-manual workers were at least partly deskilled, and had lost some of their autonomy, and quite possibly at least some of their status and prestige, as a consequence of technological advances in the workplace, and the ensuing impact on the labour process. This implied that the apparent process of *embourgeoisement* developed dialectically with that of 'proletarianisation' and deskilling in some workplaces (see Braverman, 1974).

Against the cautiously optimistic view that the growing number of non-manual workers would increasingly find Labour an attractive political option were two other, less sanguine perspectives about the electoral implications of the changing occupational structure for the party. One of these was essentially agnostic, noting that the expanding strata of non-manual workers generally evinced an 'essentially empirical approach to life', and whilst many of them were (or were becoming) trade union members, they 'had a strictly utilitarian and non-ideological attitude towards' trade unionism, which entailed deep scepticism about explicitly political activity and campaigns. Consequently, the Labour Party had to acknowledge that 'it is not the slightest use making an ideological or overtly idealistic approach, or relying on past achievements, and far-off fights on matters of principle'. Instead, the party's 'only hope is to enlist the support of the individual [non-manual] worker by direct personal conviction'.

One example of how this might be achieved concerned the Conservative Government's reversion to an incomes policy during the early 1960s, and the stipulation that pay increases should be linked to higher productivity. This, it was pointed out, would serve to exacerbate the erosion of pay differentials between manual and non-manual workers, as manual workers were often more readily able to increase their output – or, at least, do so in an empirically verifiable manner – than many non-manual workers, particularly those in public services, such as nursing and teaching. This afforded the Labour Party an opportunity to secure support amongst some non-manual workers by developing a national pay policy which demonstrated that it 'does not believe that his [a white-collar employee's] wage and salary should be determined by a free-for-all in a market economy' (Jarvis, 1962).

However, this would involve a Labour Government 'interfering' in pay determination in a manner which might actually serve to alienate the very non-manual workers it was seeking to attract, particularly as the Conservative Government's own pay policy was deemed to be harming the material interests of sections of the middle class in particular, owing to their aforementioned difficulty in increasing productivity. More significantly, though, in seeking to appeal to non-manual workers on specific, instrumental, policy issues such as wages and salaries, Labour would be confronted with an acute dilemma, namely reconciling the Party's egalitarian principles with the concern of the burgeoning middle class to maintain, or even restore, their pay differentials vis-à-vis manual workers.

Such conundrums partly underpinned a third, more pessimistic prognosis about the Labour Party's ability to appeal to the growing number of white-collar workers, at least in the short to medium term. Douglas Houghton (a Labour MP since 1949, who subsequently served both as a Cabinet Minister and then as chair of the PLP during the 1964–1970 Labour Governments), for example, suggested that there were several reasons why white-collar workers tended to be suspicious of the Labour Party, most notably because they believed it to be:

- bedevilled by factions and disunity, exacerbated by elements within the party who repeatedly seemed determined to undermine the leadership;
- a predominantly working-class party with little concern for pay differentials and upholding the prestige of non-manual employees;
- dominated by the trade union bosses with their undemocratic card votes at annual conference;
- wedded to out-of-date dogma and to be excessively doctrinaire, a view reaffirmed by the retention of Clause 4. The very word 'nationalisation' aroused strong opposition: they 'want no more of it';
- no longer motivated by a passion for liberty, as exemplified by its apparent toleration of trade union tyrannies and malpractices.

Ultimately, Houghton explained, 'it is the traditional nature, composition and behaviour of the Labour Party that repels, and little we can say will help', particularly when Labour's image, amongst many white-collar workers, is 'fashioned by what happens at the TUC and Labour Party conferences'. As long as Labour was widely viewed as 'the Party of the industrial trade unions', its own claims to be 'the Party of the whole people ... clearly does not carry conviction'.

These observations led Houghton (1962) ineluctably to the conclusion that it was 'going to be extremely difficult in Opposition' to win the political trust, and thus the electoral support, of the expanding middle class, to the extent that 'only in a period of Office can the Labour Party show the white-collared workers that they can give Labour their confidence'. A similar conclusion was arrived at by W. R. Williams, MP (1962), who concurred that

> the conversion of the white-collared – non-manuals – is a long-term policy. I doubt whether we can do very much before the next general election. In the meantime, we must work like the devil to keep the old faithful, the manuals, etc.

This analysis clearly posed a potential electoral paradox for the party, for it implied that only by securing electoral victory, and thus gaining political office, could Labour enact policies which assuaged the anxieties of white-collar workers, yet without attracting the support of white-collar workers in the first place, in an increasingly middle-class society, then Labour might be unable to win the next general election. In that case, of course, the Labour Party's negative image amongst white-collar workers would be perpetuated almost indefinitely.

Yet in spite of such pessimistic political analyses, the beginning of 1962 heralded a growing belief in some quarters of the Labour Party that Hugh Gaitskell could well become the next Prime Minister. After the optimism that preceded the Conservative election victory in 1959 – and the corresponding pessimism which this induced amongst some Labour MPs and supporters, as we have just noted – Macmillan's government was soon beset by chronic economic difficulties. In particular, the need to impose a 'pay pause' on public-sector employees was sufficient to push Labour ahead in opinion polls during 1961. By-election results also indicated a government quickly forced onto the defensive. Although the Liberals made the headlines with a famous by-election victory at Orpington in 1962, Labour was also making significant electoral advances, its success in the Middlesbrough West by-election providing the party's first gain since the general election.

Nor was Labour much damaged in the eyes of the electorate by differences of opinion over the major question of foreign policy in the early 1960s – that of whether Britain should join the Common Market. Many on the revisionist wing of the party shared the Macmillan Government's view that British economic interests could only be secured in the long term by closer integration with continental Europe. Yet this view was far from universal in Labour ranks. The left tended to view the Common Market as a suspect capitalist enterprise, whilst many others disputed the likely economic benefits of membership and/or were worried about the possible undermining of national sovereignty. Gaitskell's attitude was influenced by his belief that British membership would irrevocably undermine traditional ties with the Commonwealth and North America. As a result, he made an impassioned speech at the 1962 conference, citing 'a thousand years of history' as a basis for standing aside from Europe. By siding for the first time with mainstream party opinion against his own more natural supporters, Gaitskell managed to avoid any fresh division that might jeopardise Labour's electoral prospects. He was not, however, to be the beneficiary of the party's improving fortunes. After a brief illness, Gaitskell – at the age of only 56 – died suddenly from a rare disease in January 1963.

Wilson and the Labour victory of 1964

Gaitskell's death left the party momentarily in turmoil. His close friends were shattered, convinced that with his passing had gone any real prospect of revisionism ever being put into practice. Douglas Jay later said that had he lived, Gaitskell would have pursued his aims with a 'sureness of purpose' that had not been seen since the 1940s (Jay, 1980: 287–8). This was a veiled reference to the alleged shortcomings of the Gaitskell's successor, Harold Wilson, who had long been regarded by the Gaitskellites as lacking consistency and 'sureness of purpose'. In a hastily convened and entirely unexpected leadership contest, Wilson won sufficient support from the centre-left of the parliamentary party to defeat two candidates of the right, George Brown and James Callaghan.

In spite of his background as a Bevanite who had resigned over health service charges in 1951, Wilson essentially belonged to the moderate centre of the PLP and presented himself as the candidate of reconciliation. He believed, like Attlee, that Labour was best led by maintaining unity between the different wings of the party; in other words, that he should not follow Gaitskell's more abrasive style (Morgan, 1987: 249–51). As he settled into his new post, Wilson made a point of including several Gaitskellites in his first Shadow Cabinet, notably persuading a reluctant George Brown to continue as deputy leader. Yet inevitably it was those on the left, denied influence under Gaitskell, who most appreciated the change of leadership. Richard Crossman wrote in his diary of a 'psychological revolution in the Parliamentary Party and in the Party in the country', so much so that he was 'irresistibly drawn to clichés of the New Frontier and of comparisons of Harold with Kennedy' (quoted in Morgan, 1981: 983–6, diary entry for 5 March 1963).

In policy terms, Wilson tended to play down both the revisionist emphasis on achieving social equality and the left-wing case for extending public ownership. Instead, he brought to the fore a theme implicit in *Signposts for the Sixties* – namely, that socialism was about science. His central argument was that in order to avoid the 'stop–go' economics of the Conservative Government, Labour should champion a new managerial revolution. As the party of professional managers, scientists, technicians and skilled workers, Wilson believed, Labour would stand for modernisation, in stark contrast to the Conservatives under Macmillan's successor (in the autumn of 1963), the Scottish aristocrat Sir Alec Douglas-Home. 'With Wilson', notes Kenneth Morgan:

> a folksy northerner full of reminiscences of Herbert Chapman's Huddersfield Town in the 1920s, ranged against the aristocratic languour of

Douglas-Home, the contrast between a down-to-earth modernizing Labour Party and grouse-moor Tory Party of the old school was set out in personal terms.

(1990: 231)

Nowhere was this more apparent than at the annual conference in October 1963. The willingness of Gaitskellites to – in the words of Douglas Jay – refrain from behaving as Bevanites had done at previous conferences meant that, compared with the last time the party met in Scarborough, this was a 'positive love-feast' (Jay, 1980: 295; Howard and West, 1965: 38). Wilson used the occasion to enthuse delegates, and the wider public audience, about the idea of harnessing the 'white heat' of the technological revolution. Although there were clearly potential difficulties inherent in this approach, not least of these being what would happen if technical change did not deliver a high-growth economy, for the time being Wilson, with his familiar pipe and Gannex macintosh, carried all before him. The Labour Party had found both a fresh, confident leader and an agreed political rallying cry, and when Douglas-Home finally called an election in October 1964, there was a confident belief in the party that Labour would at last be returned to power.

In the event, the 1964 election proved to be a close-run affair. Labour's manifesto built on the policy-making process of recent years by emphasising the need for growth, innovation and efficiency, and in a series of well-publicised speeches Wilson reaffirmed his commitment to 'a just society, to a dynamic, expanding, confident, and, above all, purposive new Britain' (Butler and King, 1965: 110–16). Labour was generally credited with the better campaign. Whereas Douglas-Home appeared ill at ease on television, Wilson exuded confidence. Nevertheless, when the results were announced, it became clear that Douglas-Home had regained some of the support lost by the Conservatives in the economic downturn of 1961–1962. On an average swing of 2.9 per cent, Labour managed to win an overall majority of just four parliamentary seats, making ground particularly in the North-West and in Scotland.

Clearly, there was just cause for celebration – this was the first outright victory for a 'party of the left' in peacetime since 1906 – but there were also good reasons for not reading too much into the result. In the first place, Labour's share of the total vote had barely risen from 1959; 44.1 per cent was the lowest share of any majority government for forty years. What ultimately explained the Labour victory was a rise in Liberal support and a steep fall in the Conservative vote. In addition, certain regions of the country – for example, the West Midlands, where Labour suffered from accusations of being 'soft' on immigration – had remained strikingly loyal to the Conservative cause. If Labour were to safeguard its tentative hold on office, Wilson still needed to appeal to many more voters. An NEC inquest into the election concluded that 'while we have succeeded in eroding many voters' faith in Conservative policies, much remains to be done to convince the majority of the electorate of the ability of the Labour Party to govern' (quoted in Jefferys, 1997: 195).

Nevertheless, the party's election victory in 1964 was difficult to square with the concerns of only a few years earlier that Labour 'must lose'. The idea that the aspiring 'affluent worker' would inevitably turn to the Conservatives as material conditions improved had taken a hard knock. Indeed, detailed research into the relationship between social class and voting behaviour, carried out in the early 1960s, found little to support the so-called *embourgeoisement* thesis. Manual workers still overwhelmingly saw themselves as working class, and they seldom mixed with white-collar employees, who more openly aspired to middle-class status. Admittedly, in political terms, support for the Labour Party was becoming less instinctive and more conditional or instrumental, dependent on whether the party might deliver on its stated promises, but most manual workers still saw Labour as 'our party'; the share of the working-class vote going to Labour had fallen only marginally since 1951 (Goldthorpe *et al.*, 1968). A further challenge to the so-called *embourgeoisement* thesis during this period, though, emanated from the 'rediscovery of poverty' amongst those termed 'the forgotten Englishmen' (Abel-Smith and Townsend, 1965; Coates and Silburn, 1970).

At the same time, however, interest in politics generally was diminishing in a more leisure-orientated society; individual membership of the Labour Party fell from its peak of just over one million in 1952 to 830,000 in 1964. Yet all the sound and fury of internal divisions in the 1950s had not undermined confidence about the future throughout the movement. With electoral support, and secure in the knowledge that the alliance between the PLP, constituency activists and trade unionists remained firm, Harold Wilson had every reason to hope that the next Labour administration would prove as successful as the last.

With hindsight, it was to become clear that not everything in the garden was rosy. In spite of outward appearances, the long civil war of the 1950s had not been satisfactorily resolved in the minds of many Labour activists. Bevanites and revisionists were willing to sink their differences in the interests of winning power, but in the longer term, both wings of the party hoped to see their tradition prevail. By linking socialism with science, Wilson claimed to have modernised the party in a matter of months, where Gaitskell had struggled over several years. 'Scientific socialism' was a useful means of rallying all shades of party opinion in the short term, yet in many respects Labour seemed ill-equipped to deliver a high-growth, diversified economy, having thought little, for example, about the reaction of trade unionists to the rapidly changing working patterns that inevitably accompanied technological change. Similarly, there were dangers in making bold promises of a 'New Britain'. At the same time as maintaining Britain's global commitments, Wilson pledged that his government would reverse the stagnation of the Tory years by using 'socialist planning' to produce a dynamic, classless society – a society in which the elimination of poverty and the creation of genuine equality of opportunity would become the 'immediate targets of political action'. Seasoned political observers doubted whether the steely commitment to national regeneration shown by Attlee's generation could be emulated by Wilson, who unsettled colleagues during the 1964 campaign by insisting that strategy was best decided on a day-to-day basis. The wisdom of raising hopes that there could be some sort of re-run of 1945 would soon be put to the test. But in October 1964, none of this mattered. The party was back in power. The 'forward march of social-ism', it was hoped, was about to resume.

2 The social background of Labour MPs elected in 1964 and 1966

Peter Dorey

Introduction

By the early 1960s, a clear connection was being established at senior levels within the Labour Party between the changes in British society, noted in the previous chapter, and the consequent need to revitalise and rejuvenate Labour's membership. In this context, 'modernisation' was not solely about updating or revising Labour's policies – vital though this was, as well as sometimes divisive within the party – but also about modernising the party's image vis-à-vis the electorate. Following the 1959 defeat, it was widely acknowledged by Labour strategists that the party needed to adopt a more diverse range of parliamentary candidates, so that these more closely reflected an apparently more middle-class, professional society. With a steady diminution in the number of manual workers employed in heavy industry, and a concomitant increase in the number of administrators, technicians, scientists and sundry other white-collar workers, it was emphasised that 'if we are truly to remain a national movement of all "workers by hand and brain", the new modes of work and social feeling must be reflected in the composition of our membership'. Failure to ensure this would not only mean that Labour's membership and candidates might not prove electorally appealing to the burgeoning white-collar socio-occupational strata, but also that 'their special viewpoints will be muffled for lack of advocates within the Labour Party' (Labour Party Archives, RD.194/January 1962). This perspective echoed the findings of a survey conducted for the party, following the 1959 defeat, by Mark Abrams, and published (with Richard Rose) in *Must Labour Lose?* (Abrams and Rose, 1960). One of the key findings was that

> Labour Party supporters see the Conservatives as exercising a much greater attraction for ambitious people, middle class people, young people, office workers, and scientists. . . . The image of the Labour Party, held by both its supporters and its non-supporters, is one which is increasingly obsolete in terms of contemporary Britain.
> (Abrams and Rose, 1960, quoted in Butler and King, 1965: 66)

The message was clear: the Labour Party needed to modernise not only its policies, but its personnel too.

The 1964 intake of Labour MPs

The 1964 general election saw no fewer than 82 Labour MPs elected for the first time, representing almost 26 per cent of the Parliamentary Labour Party (PLP), and adding to the 22 Labour MPs who had previously first been elected in by-elections since the 1959 general election. In other words, 104 Labour MPs, constituting almost one-third of the PLP, had not been Labour MPs at the time of the 1959 general election. This clearly represented a major influx of 'new blood' into the PLP, and this, coupled with their social backgrounds, was to have a discernible impact on the Labour Party's attitudes and activities during the next six years, but more particularly after the 1966 election, for reasons which will become apparent.

With regard to educational background, for example, Table 2.1 shows that one of the most notable features of the Labour Party's parliamentary intake in 1964 was the decline in the proportion of Labour MPs who had received only an elementary education, and then left school at 14 or 15. In 1945, 43 per cent of Labour MPs had been educated thus, whereas by 1964 this figure had fallen to just under 30 per cent. During the same period, the proportion of university graduates on Labour's benches in the House of Commons increased from 34.2 per cent to 43.9 per cent, with the proportion of Labour MPs having graduated from Oxbridge increasing from 14.5 per cent to 17.7 per cent during the same period.

One important reason for the changing composition of the PLP in terms of educational background was the influx of new Labour MPs elected in 1964, whose education was on average markedly different from that of their counterparts at the previous election. As Table 2.2 illustrates, whereas in 1959 over 45 per cent of Labour MPs first elected in 1959 had received an elementary education only, this proportion had declined to 25.5 per cent in 1964. Meanwhile, whereas 31 per cent of Labour MPs first elected in 1959 had attended university, 45.3 per cent of 1964's new intake had done so.

Table 2.1 Educational background of Labour MPs elected in 1964, compared to 1945 (as a percentage of the Parliamentary Labour Party)

Education	All Labour MPs	
	1945	*1964*
Elementary	43.0%	29.7%
University (any)	34.2%	43.9%
Oxbridge	14.5%	17.7%

Source: Mellors (1978: 50–1).

Table 2.2   Educational background of new Labour MPs in 1959 and 1964

Education	New Labour MPs	
	1959	1964
Elementary	45.3%	25.5%
University (any)	31.0%	45.3%
Oxbridge	4.8%	17.9%

Source: Mellors (1978: 50).

Even more stark is the increase in Oxbridge graduates amongst new Labour MPs during this period, rising from less than 5 per cent in 1959 to nearly 18 per cent in 1964 (Mellors, 1978: 50).

Although these changes can partly be attributed to general socio-economic changes in British society itself from the late 1950s onwards, and a concomitant increase in the number of people attending university, the main expansion of higher education did not occur until the 1960s themselves. Hence, the changing educational background of new Labour MPs between 1959 and 1964 owed much to a conscious decision by the Labour Party to adopt more university-educated candidates after 1959, for, as one commentator pointed out, 'With all the education there is about these days, Labour must show that its candidates are as well qualified as the Tories' (Barker, 1968: 25–6). This sentiment was borne out by Mellors's observation that 'especially in the sixties, there has been a concern to raise the ability of Labour recruits. Labour's leadership ... has been especially vocal in pursuit of this end', for one increasingly important way of persuading the electorate that the Party was 'fit to govern' was to change the characteristics and calibre of Labour candidates and MPs, which therefore 'places a premium on educational qualifications and fluency of speech and ideas' (Mellors, 1978: 50).

Not surprisingly, the increasingly educated character of the PLP was reflected in the changing occupational background of Labour MPs during this period, as illustrated in Table 2.3. Moreover, within this overall decline in the proportion of manual workers elected as Labour MPs between 1945 and 1964, there was a marked reduction in the number emanating from specific working-class occupations. For example, in 1945, 39 Labour MPs had been miners and 27 were ex-railwaymen, constituting 9.9 per cent and 6.9 per cent of the PLP respectively. Following the 1964 election, however, the number of miners on Labour's benches in the House of Commons had fallen to 22, whilst the number of railwaymen had fallen to 10, now constituting 6.9 per cent and 3.2 per cent of the PLP respectively. Again the decline was particularly stark amongst new Labour MPs, for whereas 10 of Labour MPs elected for the first time in 1945 had been miners and 18 had been railwaymen, the new intake of Labour MPs in 1964 included just 4 miners and 4 railwaymen.

Table 2.3 Occupational background of Labour MPs elected in 1964, compared to 1945, based on key occupational categories (as a percentage of the Parliamentary Labour Party)

Occupational background	All Labour MPs	
	1945	1964
Law[a]	11.7%	12.9%
Education[b]	11.9%	16.4%
Other professions	10.4%	11.4%
Non-manual[c]	29.3%	30.9%
Manual workers	27.2%	18.3%

Source: Butler and King (1965: 235); Mellors (1978: 62–4).

Notes
a Barristers and solicitors.
b Teachers and college/university lecturers.
c Political workers, trade union officials, journalists, authors, public relations, etc.

Table 2.4 Occupational background of new Labour MPs, 1959 and 1964

Occupational background	New Labour MPs	
	1959	1964
Law[a]	7.1%	10.4%
Education[b]	9.5%	18.9%
Other professions	11.9%	12.3%
Non-manual[c]	35.7%	25.5%
Manual workers	23.8%	18.9%

Source: Mellors (1978: 69).

Notes
a Barristers and solicitors.
b Teachers and college/university lecturers.
c Political workers, trade union officials, journalists, authors, public relations, etc.

As Table 2.4 illustrates, some of the most marked changes in the occupational background of new Labour MPs actually occurred between 1959 and 1964. For example, in 1959 almost 24 per cent of new Labour MPs had been manual workers, but in the 1964 election the proportion declined to just under 19 per cent. Conversely, the number of new Labour MPs in 1964 who had been teachers or lecturers virtually doubled compared to 1959, whilst the proportion of lawyers amongst new Labour MPs increased from 7.1 per cent to 10.4 per cent between 1959 and 1964.

One other noteworthy characteristic of Labour's new MPs in 1964 was their relative youth compared to those in previous elections during the

1950s. For example, whereas just 10 (23.8 per cent) of Labour's 42 new MPs in 1959 had been in the 21–39 age group, 37 (35.2 per cent) of Labour's 105 new MPs in 1964 were aged under 40, thereby representing a significant infusion of 'new blood' into the PLP.

In short, the Labour MPs elected in 1964 were generally younger and more educated (in terms of formal and higher education), and emanated from more professional occupational backgrounds than their predecessors.

Labour's 1966 intake

The trends discernible in the 1964 general election were further evident in the 1966 election. For example, as Table 2.5 indicates, of the 72 new Labour MPs elected in 1966, no less than 64 per cent had received a university education, with the Oxbridge component constituting just under 24 per cent of all new Labour MPs. Conversely, those new Labour MPs who had only received an elementary education declined further, from 25.5 per cent in 1964 to 13.9 per cent in 1966.

With regard to occupational background, meanwhile, as Table 2.6 illustrates, the proportion of manual workers declined further, with only 12.5 of new Labour MPs in 1966 emanating from working-class occupations compared to 18.9 per cent two years previously. Furthermore, in 1966 none of the manual workers amongst Labour's new MPs were railwaymen, and only 3 were miners. By contrast, the proportion of new Labour MPs who were lawyers rose from 10.4 per cent in 1959 to 18.1 per cent in 1966, whilst the same period witnessed a remarkable increase from 18.9 per cent to 34.7 per cent in the proportion of new Labour MPs who had previously been teachers or lecturers.

The cumulative effect of all of these changes was that in the wake of the 1966 election, more than 48 per cent of all Labour MPs had previously attended university (compared to 33 per cent back in 1945), whilst in terms of occupational background, the 1964 and 1966 intakes meant that almost 44 per cent of *all* Labour MPs came from professional backgrounds, with education and law constituting the two largest occupations in this category. By contrast, less than 17 per cent of Labour MPs could be classified as

Table 2.5   Educational background of new Labour MPs in 1966, compared to 1964

Education	New Labour MPs	
	1964	1966
Elementary	25.5%	13.9%
University (any)	45.3%	63.9%
Oxbridge	17.9%	23.6%

Source: Mellors (1978: 50).

Table 2.6   Occupational background of new Labour MPs in 1966, compared to 1964

Occupational background	New Labour MPs	
	1964	*1966*
Law[a]	10.4%	18.1%
Education[b]	18.9%	34.7%
Other professions	12.3%	4.2%
Non-manual[c]	25.5%	20.8%
Manual workers	18.9%	12.5%

Source: Mellors (1978: 69).

Notes
a   Barristers and solicitors.
b   Teachers and college/university lecturers.
c   Political workers, trade union officials, journalists, authors, public relations, etc.

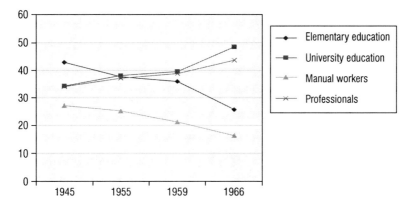

Figure 2.1   Educational background of Labour MPs, 1945–1966.

manual workers (a decline of almost 10 per cent since 1945, and one which was to accelerate after 1966). The PLP of the 1960s, in tandem with British society itself, it seemed, was undergoing a process of *embourgeoisement* (Rose, 1981: 34–8).

The overall impact of the changes delineated above is illustrated in Figure 2.1, which clearly illustrates the increasingly educated and middle-class/ professional Parliamentary Labour Party which was becoming established during the mid-1960s.

Meanwhile, with regard to the rejuvenation of the PLP, 1966 witnessed a continuation of 1964's trend towards the election of younger new Labour MPs, for, as Table 2.7 shows, 41 of Labour's 72 new MPs in 1966 were under 40, thus constituting almost 57 per cent of the new intake.

Table 2.7   Number of new Labour MPs by age cohort in 1966, compared to 1964

Age cohort	New Labour MPs	
	1964	*1966*
21–29	1 (0.9)	7 (9.7)
30–39	36 (34.3)	34 (47.2)
40–49	48 (45.7)	23 (31.9)
50–59	19 (18.1)	5 (6.9)
60–69	1 (0.9)	3 (4.2)
70+	0 (0)	0 (0)

Source: Mellors (1978: 32).

Note
Figures in parentheses represent percentages of the new Labour MPs.

Trade union-sponsored Labour MPs, 1964 and 1966

One other factor characterising the intake of Labour MPs in both 1964 and 1966 was the extension of trade union sponsorship, and their candidature in more 'promising' seats. The number of trade union-sponsored candidates rose from 129 in 1959 to 138 in 1964, and whilst this increase might not appear particularly notable, the actual number elected increased from 93 to 120 (Butler and King, 1965: 235–6), comprising almost 38 per cent of the PLP. Eighteen months later, whilst the number of trade union-sponsored Labour candidates remained the same, the actual number elected increased to 132, a success rate of almost 96 per cent (Butler and King, 1966: 209), although because of the increase in the number of Labour MPs elected overall, the proportion of trade union-sponsored Labour MPs actually declined fractionally to just over 36 per cent. Yet their greater absolute number was to pose various problems for the Labour leadership vis-à-vis certain policy issues from 1966 to 1970, most notably incomes policies, and the introduction of legislation to curb trade union activities. With regard to both of these policies, the strongest opposition generally emanated from Labour's trade union-sponsored MPs (and the Labour left), as will be illustrated in Chapters 5 and 6.

There is one apparent paradox here, namely that the number of trade union-sponsored Labour MPs was increasing (in absolute terms) at a time when the number of working-class Labour MPs was declining. The explanation lies in the changing character of trade union sponsorship during the 1960s: a number of trade unions extended their sponsorship to middle-class Labour candidates. With the number of working-class Labour candidates and MPs declining, a number of trade unions responded by sponsoring middle-class Labour candidates and MPs. Although a few trade unions, such as the National Union of Mineworkers and the National Union of Railwaymen, sought to retain their proletarian image and linkages through their sponsorship of working-class Labour candidates and MPs, others, such as the Transport and General Workers' Union and the National Union of General and Municipal Workers, increasingly sponsored 'predominantly young, graduate, professional candidates' (Mellors, 1978: 105; see also Butler and King, 1965: 236–7; Ellis and Johnson, 1974: 4–14).

Implications for the role and behaviour of backbench Labour MPs

The relative youthfulness and *embourgeoisement* of the PLP in the mid-1960s was itself to have significant implications for party discipline and unity during the latter half of the decade, for 'social and attitudinal cleavages have tended to reinforce each other. . . . The general effect of social changes in the Labour Party over these three decades [1940s, 1950s, 1960s] does coincide with distinct changes in policy preferences' (Mellors, 1978: 121).

In very general terms, Labour's younger, more educated and more professional (in terms of occupational background) MPs tended to seek a more active parliamentary role, and expected to exercise somewhat greater influence over public policy. Furthermore, some of the policy preferences or social attitudes of such Labour MPs were rather at variance with those of Labour's older or more proletarian MPs.

In this respect, some of the new Labour MPs elected in the mid-1960s seemed to reflect the aspect of post-materialism subsequently noted by Inglehart, whereby the apparent satisfaction of basic material needs by the late 1950s and early 1960s facilitated greater concern about ethical, social, environmental or 'lifestyle' issues (Inglehart, 1977). Or as one of Labour's new 1964 entrants observed, 'the articulate young Labour graduate . . . changed the Party's image and ousted the fundamentalist phrases appropriate to the days of mass unemployment and slump', presaging instead 'the liberalism of the new intellectual first-generation middle class'. Furthermore, some of these new Labour MPs emanated from a working class 'from which in many ways they were alienated and whose prejudices they did not share'. They were 'from the working class [but] not *of* it' (Rose, 1981: 34, 39).

Consequently, the socio-educational and occupational backgrounds of such Labour MPs were probably as much of an influence on their parliamentary behaviour and attitudes towards the Party leadership as their ideological disposition in orthodox left–right terms. Or as the editor of Richard Crossman's famous *Diaries of a Cabinet Minister* observed in her introduction, 'Not only were their political attitudes more questioning and intransigent . . . they had high expectations of Parliament's duties and rewards' (Morgan, 1976: 14).

However, Shaw has identified another way in which the changing socio-educational (or class) composition of the PLP from the mid-1960s onwards served to weaken cohesion and discipline. He suggests that prior to this time, when the PLP was generally rather more proletarian in its composition, discipline and loyalty to the leadership derived from a 'social democratic centralism', based on 'a syndrome of norms – loyalty to class and to the union, respect for majority decisions'. However, during the 1960s, as the PLP became steadily less working class in composition, so this mode of class solidarity similarly weakened. Or to put it another way, as the PLP became more heterogeneous, so too did the range of opinions and policy stances within it; compositional changes begat attitudinal changes.

At the same time, Shaw notes, the loyalty to the Labour leadership which had traditionally been provided by the trade unions – who had often constituted what has variously been described a 'praetorian guard' protecting the party leadership against the left – was itself eroded, as Ministers found themselves, in response to economic circumstances and pressures, pursuing policies inimical to the material interests of the unions and their members (Shaw, 1988: 163–4).

Initially, though, during the first Labour Government's eighteen months in office the new influx of Labour MPs posed few serious problems for the leadership and the whips, partly because the Cabinet's measures, introduced with another imminent election in mind, were intended to be popular with voters and the PLP alike. Furthermore, Labour's wafer-thin majority fostered restraint amongst Labour Ministers and backbenchers; Ministers sought to avoid controversial measures, owing to recognition of the problems which might be engendered in securing the necessary parliamentary approval – 'the Government was compelled to act with caution' (Shinwell, 1981: 160) – whilst Labour backbenchers themselves had little desire to pose problems for their leaders after thirteen 'wasted years' in opposition. Labour Ministers and MPs had a common interest in persuading the electorate to return the party with a significantly increased majority at the next election, which everyone knew would be held sooner rather than later.

Hence, it was not until after Labour had been re-elected, in the March 1966 election with a parliamentary majority of 97, that various Labour MPs began displaying greater assertiveness and defiance vis-à-vis the leadership. This was partly due to the controversial nature of some of the policies which the second Labour Government pursued, often in response to stringent economic circumstances and exogenous factors, but also because a sizeable parliamentary majority de facto granted 'backbench rebels' greater licence to oppose their leaders, without a corresponding likelihood of precipitating the downfall of the Government itself. The Government's Chief Whip during Labour's first term was acutely aware of the implications of such a situation, and thus arranged a meeting with Harold Wilson

> about the Party problem which would now confront us. We knew it would be a very different one from that of the past eighteen months. In the 1964–66 Parliament, Party management was the strenuous and

often vexatious, but relatively uncomplicated, physical and arithmetical task of parliamentary survival; now, with an overall majority of ninety-seven, survival was assured. Our difficulties would be political. . . . The tug-of-war [between Labour's left and right] was containable and often provided a creative tension between the two wings when the parliamentary majority was small. In these circumstances, the ultimate sanction of a General Election muted the struggle. . . . But our huge majority removed this sanction, and both left and right could pursue their causes to the point of defying the Government with impunity.

(Short, 1989: 244–5)

Wilson himself had also ruminated on this almost inevitable problem in the immediate aftermath of Labour's 1966 election victory, and resolved that one way to 'keep his troops usefully occupied and out of mischief' was to establish a number of departmental committees (as discussed in Chapter 10) (Short, 1989: 245).

Yet precisely because this was just 'one way', there remained other opportunities and occasions for Labour MPs to articulate their increasing dissatisfaction and disagreement with aspects of policy during the Labour Government's second term of office, with 'cross-voting' (and abstentions) in the House of Commons division lobbies providing the most visible means of dissent. Less publicly overt dissatisfaction with various Government policies was articulated via the weekly meetings of the PLP – with the Wilson Governments' economic policies and the conduct of foreign affairs both eliciting regular criticism from backbenchers, although these were by no means the only policy issues which strained the relationship between Labour's Ministers and backbenchers during the latter half of the 1960s.

Consequently, the combined effect of the changing social background and concomitant attitudes of many Labour MPs elected in 1964 and 1966, coupled with the nature of some of the policies adopted by the Cabinet (more especially after 1966), meant that party management assumed a particular significance for the Labour leadership.

3 The problem of party management

Eric Shaw

Introduction

This chapter explores the internal politics of the Labour Party between 1964 and 1970, focusing on the problem of party management. Party management – sustaining the unity or cohesion of a party and the willingness of its members, at all levels, to work together to promote shared goals – is a vital function within political parties. Cohesion, the co-ordination of collective effort, is the rationale behind party formation; parties seek to harness the energies of their members in the effort to realise shared goals. But equally, conflict – over policy, ideology, strategy and the distribution of power – is inevitable in any mass political organisation. Members will often interpret somewhat differently the precise aims and values of the party, and disagree about the particular policy instruments which best give effect to them. They will have different conceptions of the interests which the party should serve, and how. They will have differing views as to how power should be apportioned within the party, and with what justification. They will also disagree about how best their party can extend its popular appeal. Not least, personalities and ambitions will inevitably come into conflict. It is evident, therefore, that dissension is an inexorable feature of political and intra-party life.

Disagreement, then, cannot be abolished (except by fiat), and it would not be healthy for a party to seek to abolish it, for 'A party without conflict is a dead party. Such parties are monolithic and usually unable to gain support or raise expectations.' Yet, equally, 'a party of total internal conflict will also soon expire – at least in electoral terms. This is the dilemma for all parties' (Heidar, 1994: 96). Balancing the two is what party management is ultimately about. Sustaining unity, regulating internal conflicts, retaining the allegiance and commitment of members, reconciling diverse interests, values and aspirations, welding together disparate units with their own institutional interests and differing political complexions – all these constitute the functions of party managers.

The real question is not *why* conflict occurs in political parties, but how it can be regulated and parties held together – that is, the character of the managerial regime. Management implies authority, since cohesion (or co-ordinated action) can only be effectively secured by a central body endowed with appropriate powers and duties. The way in which the managerial function is performed varies most significantly according to the degree of leadership regulation or constraint, and reflects 'the extent to which activities in a social unit are subject to directives, rather than being left to the free discretion of members' (Eckstein and Gurr, 1975: 53).

In this respect, one can identify two dimensions: organisational structuring and discipline. Organisational structuring refers to the institutional apportionment of managerial powers and duties. To what extent are managerial powers concentrated in the hands of a single body or diffused amongst a range of bodies? If the latter, what is the relationship amongst these bodies: are they bound together by a cohesive leadership elite – an oligarchy, in Robert Michels's terminology? (Michels, 1964). Or are they more pluralistically ordered, reflecting differing views and institutional interests?

The other dimension, discipline, refers to the 'extent to which superiors attempt to influence the behaviour of members of a social unit by means of directives' backed by the threat or use of sanctions (Eckstein and Gurr, 1975: 53). Discipline is partly a function of the capacity of the leadership's capacity to exert discipline, of course, but also a function of its proclivity to do so, or its managerial philosophy.

The main theme of this chapter is a straightforward one: the shift in the Labour Party's managerial regime after 1964 from one characterised by tight organisational structuring and firm discipline to one defined by organisational loosening (or decoupling) and a more liberal disciplinary system. Although these processes occurred in tandem, they were not produced by the same causes. The first, as will become clear, was the outcome of a shifting ideological balance within Labour's ranks, and increasing organisational strains engendered by a clash in policies and priorities, especially between the industrial and political wings of the party. In short, it was not the result of deliberate action. The shift towards a more permissive managerial regime, in contrast, was reflected in the intentions of a new, more liberal type of party manager, politicians who had at one time or another been prominently associated with the left, or dissident, wing of the party, notably the Prime Minister himself, Harold Wilson, and his senior lieutenant and close political ally Richard Crossman.

The chapter is organised in the following way. First, it discusses the peculiar and distinctive pattern of organisational structuring in the Labour Party and its implications for party management. It then turns to the general question of relations between party and government, focusing on the increasing strains between Labour's parliamentary and extra-parliamentary organisations, and its industrial and political wings. The chapter then analyses the management of the Parliamentary Labour Party (PLP), exploring the new liberal philosophy expounded in particular by Richard Crossman, and its application during the so-called Crossman–Silkin regime. The chapter concludes with some brief reflections about the dilemmas of party management within the Labour Party.

The structure of managerial control within the Labour Party

According to Panebianco, 'Every organization bears the mark of its formation, of the crucial political-administrative decisions made by its founders, the decisions which "molded" the organization' (1988: 50). We can apply this hypothesis to the Labour Party, which, unlike most of its Continental sister parties, emerged as a coalition of pre-existing organisations, of which (at least in terms of organisational weight) the trade unions were by far the most important. Hence, it soon became customary to refer to the party's 'industrial' and 'political' wings. Furthermore – again in contrast to the established social democratic model – it first took form as a *parliamentary* body, reflecting its initial modest purpose as a parliamentary vehicle for the articulation of working-class interests. This gave rise to a lasting tension between Labour's *parliamentary focus* and the traditions of internal representative democracy it inherited from the trade unions, and embodied in the doctrine of the sovereignty of conference. Thus, Michael Foot reflected – in the wake of his own traumatic experience of leading the party – on what he dubbed an 'extraordinary feature' of Labour's constitution: the recognition of two sovereign authorities.

> The National Executive, answerable to the party conference, has not the power to dictate to the Parliamentary Labour Party, but nor has the Shadow Cabinet, answerable to the Parliamentary Party, the power to dictate to the National Executive, less still the party conference.
>
> (Foot, 1984: 160)

In the managerial sphere, this 'dual authority' was reflected in the fact that responsibility for managing the PLP was assigned to the leader and his senior colleagues, whilst that for the wider party was vested in the NEC, which was entrusted with enforcing the constitution and rules of the party. For example, it had the power to ratify or refuse parliamentary candidatures, and to suspend or expel members from the party.[1]

These structural features of the Labour Party pushed to the fore two key managerial tasks which only the leadership could discharge. First, the leader must, as Peter Shore explained, 'so manage the Party in the country, in the affiliated trade Unions and in the predominantly socialist constituency parties and their representatives on the National Executive Committee, that damaging public disputes are avoided' (1992: 15–16). Second, and more specifically, according to Richard Crossman (1960b), the party leader had 'to hold together divided and disparate powers', in order to ensure that (when Labour was in office) party and government work together harmoniously, on the basis of an agreed division of functions.

Management of the wider party

During the Attlee administrations, these two managerial tasks had been accomplished in a remarkably trouble-free way. This was due to a pattern of concurrent majorities in which like-minded right-of-centre figures controlled all key institutions. The critical axis in this coalition was the alliance between the Labour Party leadership and the trade unions, for the latter not only disposed of the bulk of conference votes but controlled the election of the majority of NEC members. The existence of this alliance – solidly rooted in a shared ideology, broadly overlapping interests and goals and a measure of social affinity between the leadership groups (Minkin, 1991: 8) – enabled the parliamentary leadership to weld together the various constituents of the party and to preserve a firm managerial regime. On the great majority of issues, the leader and the front bench could rely on guaranteed and firm majorities both in the National Executive and at conference. Elite consensus, and the pattern of concurrent majorities, in turn, facilitated the development of institutional interlock, the welding together of the key institutional hierarchies, and a consensus-sustaining division of functions buttressed by congruent role conceptions. The NEC defined its role as providing general political and organisational support for the Government – as its gatekeeper.

During the Attlee premiership, for example, the NEC 'behaved with a devoted loyalty, publicly mute and privately circumspect in its criticisms' (Minkin, 1978: 298). A key role here was played by the Executive's trade union members (both within the trade union section itself and within the women's section): 'Traditionally overwhelmingly moderate and Right-wing in outlook, they had an instinctive loyalty to the Party's leaders and an often obsessive suspicion of the Left' (Minkin, 1978: 298). In effect, the NEC operated as a managerial arm of the Government (Morgan, 1984: 71–3).

In the early years of the 1964–1970 Labour Governments, this pattern appeared to be replicated, for 'Conscious of the need to sustain the Labour Government', the NEC 'desired to do nothing which would undermine or embarrass it' (Minkin, 1978: 293). Yet not all ran smoothly. Even in the first months of the Wilson Government, Richard Crossman, both a Minister and a member of NEC, was lamenting the lack of co-ordination between the Cabinet and Transport House (the party's head office) (1975: 223). This also bothered Wilson, who felt that Attlee's Government had lost contact with the party, and hence he wanted Crossman 'to do the job of organizing and making sure that the rank and file feel themselves linked with the leadership' (Crossman, 1975: 608, diary entry for 10 August 1966).

Accordingly, as newly appointed Leader of the House and Lord President of the Council, Crossman was charged with 'bridging the gulf which separates the Cabinet from Transport House and the rank and file' (1976: 183, diary entry for 1 January 1967). A variety of mechanisms were henceforth established for this purpose. In 1966, for example, a joint annual meeting was instituted between the NEC and the Government, to provide a forum for the airing and resolution of differences. The same year also heralded the new practice of inviting Ministers to attend NEC policy sub-committees, whereupon they could expound the Government's position when and where it diverged from the party's. Finally, in November 1968 it was agreed to establish a policy co-ordinating committee comprising five Ministers and seven members chosen by the NEC, whose monthly meetings were intended to harmonise Government and party thinking on future policy (Minkin, 1978: 299).

However, far from relations improving between the two wings of the Labour Party, they deteriorated further. As early as New Year's Day 1967, Crossman was reflecting that his task of bridging 'the gulf which separates the Cabinet from Transport House and the rank and file' had 'turned out to be a complete flop' (1976: 183, diary entry for 1 January 1967). Links between the Labour Party in office and the party on the ground remained 'weak and relatively ineffective', and instead of operating as a vehicle for fashioning future policy, the policy co-ordinating committee was used mainly as a forum in which 'the Party raised grievances and Ministers defended their positions' (Minkin, 1978: 293, 299). Indeed, far from party and government working in harmony, relations continued to deteriorate, and divisions began to deepen. Two main sets of factors, political and institutional, account for this divergence.

Rising political tensions

Institutional interlock, or the fusing of the institutions of parliamentary and extra-parliamentary governance in the Labour Party, was rooted ultimately in elite consensus, the common centre-right orientation of both the front bench and the National Executive Committee. However, this was increasingly challenged from the mid-1960s onwards, for three reasons. First, the NEC's seven-person constituency section was increasingly composed of vocal left-wing critics of the Wilson Governments. Second, and more importantly, a new breed of tough, left-wing leaders (most prominently Jack Jones of the Transport Workers and Hugh Scanlon of the Engineering Workers) assumed key leadership positions. Pledged to free collective bargaining and to a left-wing stance on most political issues, they felt little of that instinctive sympathy with the predominantly right-wing Labour leadership that had characterised earlier generations of union leaders. By the end of the decade, 'the old Rightwing "block vote" had disintegrated as the dominant entity on the floor of the Party Conference and the Trades Union Congress.... The pattern of Party Leadership dominance over the Conference was shattered' (Minkin, 1991: 115). Given the fact that such a large proportion of NEC members owed their seats to the trade unions, its compositional balance began to alter, albeit slowly (owing to the many conventions governing the way in which the unions cast their votes). As a result, gradually and haltingly the NEC began to exhibit greater responsiveness to grassroots feeling as manifested in critical resolutions at conference: 'It was prepared now, for the first time in Party history, to be publicly identified with critics and criticism of Labour Government policy' (Minkin, 1978: 300).

It was at this juncture that a third factor began to operate: the widening rift between Labour's industrial and political wings. A key norm governing that relationship was what Minkin has called 'freedom', or 'mutual respect for the independence and institutional integrity of both industrial (TUC) and political wing'. On the one hand, the political side – the PLP – would not seek to encroach, by legislative means, on matters that impinged on the trade unions' core material interests (most notably, wage bargaining and their internal organisational affairs) without their consent. On the other, the industrial side – the trade unions – would exercise 'a conscious self-restraint in the use of potential levers of power' (Minkin, 1991: 28, 30). However the instigation by the 1966–1970 Labour Government of a statutory incomes policy (see Chapter 5) imposed great strains on this norm. These stresses reached crisis point when, in response to a rash of unofficial strikes, the Government published the White Paper *In Place of Strife*, which would have imposed legislative curbs on the ways that the trade unions operated (see Chapter 6). This represented 'a huge break with Party tradition – as clear a breach of the "rules" of the union–Party relationship as had ever been proposed by any Labour Government' (Minkin, 1991: 114).

Trade union leaders from both the right and the left were now prepared to use the NEC as a lever with which to exert pressure on the Government (as indeed were dissenting Ministers, notably the Home Secretary, Jim Callaghan). The clash over *In Place of Strife* highlighted the breakdown of the traditional nexus between the political and industrial wings of the labour movement, and 'severely diminished the confidence of many union leaders – not all on the Left – in the judgement and reliability of the Parliamentary Leadership'. Equally, there were those on the right of the PLP whose dismay at the Government's subsequent retreat resulted in their becoming 'more ambivalent about the value of the union attachment and increasingly worried about protecting the rights of the Parliamentary Party' (Minkin, 1978: 116). The seeds for a future crisis were being sown – though not to be reaped until the fall of the next Labour Government in 1979.

Increasing institutional tensions

These growing political tensions were exacerbated by increasing institutional ones. Earlier, we noted how the pattern of concurrent majorities, an agreed division of functions and congruent role conceptions all helped to cement party–Government relations. However, norms and ground rules are always open to contention and conflicting interpretations, imparting a dynamic element to the way in which political organisations operate. The distinctive organisational structuring of the Labour Party meant that there was always a potential for jurisdictional and personal conflicts between those

NEC members not serving in ministerial posts, but who wished to maintain its traditional high-profile role in policy on the one hand, and Cabinet Ministers keen to uphold the primacy that the conventions of British government accorded them on the other. The problem never really arose during Attlee's premiership, because his Governments could rely upon the solid and unswerving support of the Executive. However, during Harold Wilson's premiership, as the paths of the parliamentary and extra-parliamentary party began to diverge – with the Government consequently suffering an unprecedented range of rebuffs at the hands of conference – there were increasing calls for the NEC to assert more forcefully the policy-making rights of the wider party.

The Government was unresponsive, as Ministers were reluctant to concede to the party any significant role in the formulation of Government policy, and Wilson was determined to demonstrate that Labour could replace the Conservatives as 'the natural party of government'. Ministers were keen to prove that they were responsible administrators, which meant taking whatever policy decisions they believed were appropriate or necessary according to circumstances, irrespective of manifesto commitments, Conference decisions or 'socialist ideology'. Furthermore, 'a public display of independence of the Labour Party in the country' was seen as politically useful (Minkin, 1978: 292).

The result was growing disagreement over the respective rights and competencies of party and Government. If – as Wilson regularly emphasised – it was the Government's responsibility to govern, what precisely was the role of the NEC? As the Minister entrusted with improving relations between the Government and the wider Labour Party, Richard Crossman's thoughts on the matter carried weight. How could the respective jurisdictions of the party in government and the Labour Party beyond be clearly and conclusively determined in circumstances where policy responsibilities overlapped, and personal, political and institutional ambitions conflicted? Crossman's point of departure was that when Labour obtained governmental office, 'the relationship between the Party and its chosen leaders undergoes a change. . . . From that moment they must be seen to govern without dictation from outside'. The first duty of the party was 'to sustain the Government in power at Westminster' (to use the customary phrase). The problem, then (as defined by Crossman's close political ally Barbara Castle), was to prevent the Government and the NEC 'getting too much at loggerheads without sacrificing the basic independence of the Government', for (she continued, expressing a thought shared by the Cabinet as a whole) 'if I am honest, I must admit I wouldn't like as a minister not to be free to modify Party policy in the light of my own greater administrative insight and experience' (Castle, 1984: 516, diary entry for 18 September 1968).

Crossman's resolution of this conundrum was to point to a second, equally substantial, role for the Labour Party: 'the formation of *future* policy . . . the planning of the manifesto[2] for the next General Election, and of the strategy for the second five years'. The NEC should operate as 'the battering-ram of change' – avoiding the fate which, Crossman believed, had befallen the Attlee Governments, of exhausting their radical impetus by running out of ideas (Minkin, 1978: 294). The logic of this functional distinction was that, whilst the Government retained full responsibility for current policy, the National Executive – in full consultation with the Cabinet – should be the prime mover in the planning of the next election manifesto.

The advantage of Crossman's formulation for the Government was that it supplied a (party) constitutional justification for its right to override party opinion (in the form of conference resolutions) where it conflicted with its own policy. The advantage to the party was that it conferred a clear and major role upon the NEC (and, ultimately, conference) in that it had the right to shape Labour's future policy trajectory. However, it presupposed that the Prime Minister, along with his closest colleagues, would be willing to concede to the NEC and to annual conference the power to decide the programme for the next Labour Government. This they were not prepared to do. Nor was this surprising, since the efficacy of the arrangement depended upon precisely the problem it was designed to remedy – political and ideo-logical divergence between party and government – not actually existing (at least in any serious form). Dividing responsibilities between current and future policy made sense only if there were a broad consensus over the direc-tion of the party – as there had been during the Attlee Government. Any significant turn in direction was bound to appear (and be exploited by the critical media) as a rebuke to the Government or a repudiation of its pol-icies. The Cabinet was certainly not going to allow its critics to set future priorities.

The outcome was that whilst in theory the Labour manifesto was sup-posed to be decided by a joint meeting of the NEC and Ministers, in prac-tice the latter made the crucial decisions (Minkin, 1978: 293). This was not surprising. The 1979 manifesto was framed 'under circumstances where the pressures to accommodate were strong (as they normally are in a pre-election period), the assertiveness of the NEC was muted, the prestige of the parliamentary leadership was high and the authority of the Conference was low' (Minkin, 1978: 327–8). Rather than 'a battering ram of change', a means by which a fresh radical drive be imparted to government, 'a bland, cautious and noncommittal document was approved' (Minkin, 1978: 313–14).

This illustrates that whilst there were powerful forces driving Ministers and the wider party apart, there still remained strong ones holding them together, for both understood the vital importance of maintaining a working relationship. The NEC was not insensitive to the difficulties of government, whilst Ministers (or such of them as took an interest) were keen to improve the organisational effectiveness of the party on the ground. Further, though weakened, the pro-leadership right still retained a majority. Above all, there was a common overriding interest in success at the polls. In short, 'both recognised that the party could not survive without a minimal degree of mutual co-operation' (Minkin, 1978: 300).

Yet there were disturbing harbingers for the future. Institutional inter-lock was being displaced by sharpening institutional differentiation. The NEC might have little capacity to influence Labour Governments' policies, but, in turn, Ministers had a diminishing capacity to shape the party's own policy output. The NEC, as the custodian of conference, could safely be mar-ginalised in the construction of policy whilst Labour was in office, but what would happen in opposition? The bald fact was that the NEC possessed the lion's share of managerial powers in the conduct of the affairs of the wider party:

> Whatever independence Ministers might assert and however self-reliant they might feel, there remained the fact that it was the NEC which pre-pared the Party's programme and the NEC which was the government of the Party; the NEC which could ratify or refuse candidatures, and the NEC which could expel from the Party.
>
> (Minkin, 1978: 298)

What would happen if the left gained an outright majority when the Labour Party was in opposition and then insisted on exercising to the full the Exec-utive's prerogatives?

The management of the PLP

When the Labour Party entered office in 1964, responsibility for enforcing PLP discipline was shared between the Chief Whip and the PLP liaison committee. The latter consisted of the Chief Whip, the Leader of the House and three elected members: the chair of the PLP and his two deputies. The Chief Whip was responsible for recommending disciplinary action, subject to the approval of the liaison committee. Any recommendation was dis-cussed by the PLP, with which the final decision rested. Between October 1964 and July 1966, the key managerial posts – Chief Whip, Leader of the House and chair of the PLP – were occupied by traditionalist disciplinarians: Ted Short, Herbert Bowden and Emmanuel (Manny) Shinwell. In any case, Labour's extremely narrow parliamentary majority, and the recognition that another election would have to be held sooner rather than later, as well as the novelty of being back in office after thirteen years, all fostered very con-siderable self-discipline.

In April 1966, the Labour Party was re-elected with a majority of 97 seats. In a Cabinet reshuffle three months later, Richard Crossman was appointed Leader of the House and John Silkin Chief Whip. Wilson intended these appointments to presage a new style of party management, for both Crossman and Silkin were convinced that a 'liberal philosophy' was 'the only way to run a modern Left-wing party' (Crossman, 1976: 95, diary entry for 26 October 1966). They were joined in spring 1967 by the like-minded Douglas Houghton, who replaced Shinwell as PLP chair. All their predecessors had been men of the right, whereas both Crossman and Silkin identified themselves with the centre-left. Whilst former party managers were traditional disciplinarians, both Crossman and Silkin were men of a more liberal stamp and critical of the established managerial philosophy. What I have elsewhere labelled 'social democratic centralism' (Shaw, 1988) comprised three key elements.

First, there was a strong accent on discipline as a means of sustaining party cohesion. Attlee once commented:

> The fact is, in political, as in other forms of warfare, the leader must be able to rely on his troops when he is fighting his opponents. The more the discipline is self-imposed the better, but discipline there must be unless one is prepared to lose the battle.
>
> (1957: 16)

The rationale for this perspective derived from the second element of 'social democratic centralism', namely the doctrine of majority rule. Free and frank discussions should be followed – in the words of Hugh Dalton, a senior Labour Party figure for many years – by 'majority decisions loyally accepted by all. Without some measure of healthy discipline and the submission of the individual to the collective will, there can be no democracy, but only egotism and anarchy' (Labour Party, 1939: 231). This precept was, in turn, underpinned by the third element, the collective theory of representation. This decreed that Labour MPs were elected as representatives of the party, and that the voters who supported them at the polls did so because of their general allegiance to the party and its principles, and not because of their individual qualities. According to advocates of this perspective, such as Clement Attlee, Labour voters had the right to expect that their elected representative would stand by those principles and by the government which sought to give effect to them (cited in Jackson, 1968: 30). Consequently, members of the PLP were required to abide by its standing orders, which stipulated that all must accept collective decisions. Under the so-called conscience clause, MPs were allowed some latitude on grounds of 'deeply held personal conscientious conviction'. But this clause was restrictively defined, and on most political issues Labour MPs were instructed to comply with the majority stance.

The outcome was a tough managerial regime. Some examples will illustrate this. In 1961, Michael Foot (and four other MPs) were expelled from the PLP for defying a three-line whip. The previous year, both Barbara Castle and Richard Crossman had been ousted from frontbench posts for challenging the party line over defence policy. Within the wider party, Bertrand (Lord) Russell – then Britain's most renowned living philosopher – only narrowly escaped expulsion for sponsoring a conference convened by an organisation proscribed by Labour,[3] and then Russell was reprieved only on the grounds that his transgression was an isolated case (Shaw, 1988: 55–6, 62–3).

In its heyday of the 1950s and early 1960s, Crossman had developed a trenchant critical analysis of 'social democratic centralism'. He had been a prominent member of dissident left-wing groups, most notably 'Keep Left' during Attlee's premiership, and the Bevanites in the 1950s, and was, by nature, an incorrigible (and idiosyncratic) nonconformist – one of A. J. P. Taylor's 'troublemakers' (Taylor, 1957). Crossman argued that whilst there was, within modern political parties, a natural tendency for power to accumulate in the hands of senior parliamentarians and professional machine politicians, this tendency was intensified within Labour's ranks by the 'canon of solidarity' which lay at the heart of 'the spirit of trade unionism' (1963: 41–2). The outcome was 'to concentrate power in a few hands and change party democracy into party oligarchy'.

Crossman identified three mechanisms underpinning such oligarchy, the first of which was the elevation of loyalty into 'the prime political virtue required of an MP', whose test was a 'willingness to support the official leadership when he knows it is wrong' (1963: 43). Second was the use of 'the powerful machinery of the whip's office to muster support for the line of the Shadow Cabinet, yet forbidding those who want the Party to modify that line any form of group activity or organisation'. Third was 'exploiting to the full the trade union sentiment that it is in all circumstances disloyal for the minority to oppose a majority decision once it has been taken'. He dismissed 'the system of "democracy" enforced by the PLP's Standing Orders' as 'little less ruthless than the Democratic Centralism of Leninist theory' (Crossman, 1955).

The requirements of party discipline had consequently driven the struggle for power underground, transmuted into 'a conspiratorial matter of cliques and cabals' (Crossman, 1963: 45), and the effect was to damage both the fabric of party democracy and the system of representative government. Of the contest between rival ideas and political currents within a party, the voter 'can only hear the garbled versions leaked to the press by interested parties' and can never know for certain why 'a policy defended for years' was suddenly dropped. To the public mind, politics is 'personified and simplified' into a 'battle between two super-leaders' (Crossman, 1963: 45).

Crossman argued for a more pluralist conception of party democracy, one which placed less emphasis upon the will of the majority, and more upon the ability of minorities to question and challenge – party government by consensus rather than by majority fiat. This would entail a milder and more benign approach to managing the PLP, thereby allowing dissenters the right to organise and publicise their views with minimum hindrance (Crossman, 1955; see also Crossman, 1952). With the sudden death of Hugh Gaitskell in 1962 and his replacement by Crossman's friend Harold Wilson, the erstwhile rebel found himself swiftly transformed from poacher to gamekeeper. At the heart of what became the new managerial philosophy was the belief that – in the words of the liberal-minded PLP chair, Douglas Houghton – 'experience proves that disciplinary action is no remedy for serious discontent, still less for disunity' (1969: 455). Simply trying to suppress dissent by relying on bans, dismissals and expulsion – as had occurred during most of the thirteen years in opposition – had neither crushed such dissent, nor fostered a more cohesive spirit within the party. 'Old fashioned, rigid regimentation', as Crossman put it, was 'unsuitable to a modern party' (1976: 96, diary entry for 26 October 1966).

Furthermore, the general elections of 1964 and 1966 had replenished the PLP with a new breed of 'overwhelmingly middle class' MPs – lawyers, scientists, teachers in technical colleges, etc. (see the Introduction to this volume) – who, Crossman realised, would be less amenable than trade unionists: 'A party of this kind', he concluded, 'can't be led into battle under the old-fashioned, military discipline.' MPs had to be consulted and persuaded, and this required 'an entirely different style of party'. From 1964 to 1966, party managers could plausibly invoke a tiny minority to justify the retention of old methods, but with the rather more emphatic electoral victory in 1966, Labour backbenchers had effectively been 'liberated from the constraints of a tiny majority' and would not buckle under so easily. Crossman fully anticipated that 'those Labour MPs who gritted their teeth and just voted with their feet, and weren't allowed to speak or influence anything, will be seething with life and vitality and energy, and a desire to take an active part in policymaking' (1975: 492–3, diary entry for 3 April 1966). Patterns of party management would henceforth have to adjust to the new temper of the PLP.

The more liberal Crossman–Silkin regime was composed of three main elements:

- a relaxation of the control regime by extending the right to dissent;
- a more informal approach to managing relations with backbenchers;
- the promotion of a more consultative relationship between Ministers and backbenchers.

Widening the 'conscience clause'

The first step was to widen the PLP's 'conscience clause'. This raised two issues: first, the definition of 'conscience' – that is, 'the delimitation of the issues upon which the clause may be legitimately invoked'; and second, the manner in which MPs could demonstrate conscientious conviction (Alderman, 1966: 224). Previously, 'personal conscientious conviction' had been narrowly construed, but Crossman postulated, as a basic tenet of the 'liberal philosophy' of party management, the 'assumption that every member of the Party may well on occasion have to abstain conscientiously; conscientious abstention won't in future be limited to pacifists and teetotallers, but will be recognised as the right of every member' (1976: 95, diary entry for 26 October 1966). As Silkin advised the PLP, it would make much greater political sense if the conscience clause encompassed all political matters, rather than its being assumed that it operated only in the fields of religion, temperance and pacifism (Crossman, 1976: 105–6, diary entry for 3 November 1966). The shifting power currents within the Labour Party – the growing strength of the left in the wider party – also betokened a more relaxed approach to dissent. 'We have to realise', Crossman averred, 'that when a Government suddenly does things which are not in the Party manifesto, and which are profoundly controversial, then members have the right to challenge that Government, and in the last resort to abstain conscientiously' (1976: 95, diary entry for 26 October 1966). In February 1968, the word 'conscientious' was dropped from the provision, which henceforth granted members the right to abstain on 'matters of deeply held personal conviction', finally eradicating the distinction between conviction arising from 'conscience' and from beliefs. However, Labour MPs were still formally debarred from voting contrary to the decision of a party meeting, or abstaining on a vote of confidence in a Labour Government.

A more informal model of party management

Second, Crossman and Silkin consciously sought to copy the (then) more relaxed Conservative model of party management, which entailed relying more heavily on informal methods of control – pressure from colleagues, from constituency parties – and on the lure of ambition. According to Silkin, party management was a 'soft art', whereas relying upon mechanical majorities to force dissidents to comply was counter-productive: it sharpened lines of cleavage and encouraged the adoption of intransigent positions (Shaw, 1988: 161). More attention would henceforth be given to feeling the pulse of the PLP, acting as a conduit between Labour backbenchers and the Government, conveying their concerns as well as transmitting orders from on high. As Crossman wrote in his diary, 'I've got to be in the House of Commons every working day . . . with the boys . . . spending a large amount of time in personal contact . . . talking to people individually and so getting a grasp of the Party's reactions' (1976: 17, diary entry for 6 February 1966). Backbench speeches which departed from the official Government position should not immediately be dismissed as destructive, but treated as 'the natural expression of differing views within the party' (Crossman, 1976: 120, diary entry for 10 November 1966).

Improving communication and consultation within the PLP

Third, the 'liberalisers' improved lines of communication between the Labour Government and its backbenchers. Party unity was bound to be threatened when the Government felt impelled to adopt policies which disturbed large sections of party opinion. This danger could best be averted by 'closer liaison, a coming together if not in joint responsibility, at least in mutual understanding' (Houghton, 1969: 458). It was the responsibility of Ministers to expend more effort in explaining and promoting their policy rather than expecting backbench Labour MPs simply to fall into line. To this end, a range of institutional innovations were introduced, such as more frequent party meetings, which Ministers were invited to attend and speak to, and respond to questions. Also encouraged were specialist subject groups, which sought to foster greater dialogue between Ministers and interested backbenchers over particular issues and policies. In turn, the chairmen of these groups held monthly meetings with the PM. Finally, weekly meetings took place between the Prime Minister and Douglas Houghton, the PLP chair, with the remit of exploring anything 'relevant to the unity and morale of the Parliamentary Party' (Houghton, 1969: 458–60). Indeed, some of these initiatives were part of a more general process of parliamentary reform initiated during the latter half of the 1960s, which itself partly reflected a desire by the party leadership to seek ways of keeping the new breed of better-educated, more professional Labour backbenchers usefully occupied in this particular era of less stringent intra-party discipline (see Chapter 10).

The liberal managerial regime would never have been instigated, nor would it have survived (more or less) intact, without Wilson's approval. Wilson by disposition (he was a tolerant man who disliked confrontation) favoured the liberal approach. He believed that cracking down on dissent by disciplinary means inflamed rather than abated passions. As he later told Barbara Castle in an 'impassioned outburst', 'All along I have believed my duty was to be the custodian of party unity . . . I am determined to avoid the splits of 1959' (quoted in Perkins, 2003: 359).

Tolerance was, however, underpinned by political calculation. Unlike Gaitskell, Wilson lacked a solid power base in the Labour Party. He had acquired a (somewhat misleading) reputation as a left-winger by resigning (in 1951) as President of the Board of Trade, alongside the left's champion, Aneurin Bevan, in protest against the Attlee Government's decision to embark on a massive and (as Wilson convincingly argued at the time) unsustainable armaments programme. Though for a while a senior figure within the Bevanites, Wilson was quick to seize the opportunity of a rapprochement with Labour's right-wing leadership during the 1950s, and for most of the decade before Labour's return to power in 1964 he occupied senior positions in the Shadow Cabinet. Indeed (unlike other Bevanites, such as Richard Crossman, Michael Foot and Barbara Castle), Wilson was by nature a conformist, an insider and a pragmatist, although during these years he still incurred the deep and lasting mistrust of the party's right. The outcome was a paradox: although during his years as Prime Minister his views on policy issues corresponded closely with those of Labour's right majority, he did not enjoy their political support. Indeed, he was constantly (obsessively) on guard against 'right-wing plots' and 'conspiracies' – some of them more than a figment of his imagination – to replace him by either James Callaghan or Roy Jenkins.

To shore himself up, Wilson relied heavily upon a loose grouping of centre-left Ministers, such as Crossman, Tony Benn (at that time close to the Prime Minister), Barbara Castle and Peter Shore. Indeed, throughout his 1964–1970 premiership, Wilson contrived the unusual feat of adopting policies identified with the right whilst relying upon the left to protect him from right-wing efforts to remove him. One Labour MP and Tribune Group member, Ben Whitaker, recalled Wilson talking to left-wing MPs and 'managing to give us the impression that he was on our side, and that but for the bankers, he would be saying the same things as us' (quoted in Pimlott, 1992: 520). In similar vein, the journalist David Wood confessed to being 'constantly astonished by the number of left-wing parliamentary critics who claim they have just had a heart-to-heart private exchange with Mr. Wilson', who also displayed 'a sensitive understanding of their point of view' and (Wood added) a readiness to start left-wingers on 'the ladder of ministerial promotion' (*The Times*, 9 October 1967).

Of course, the new (liberal) managerial regime was by no means without its critics. Right-wing Cabinet heavyweights Denis Healey, Tony Crosland and Roy Jenkins all, at one time or another, complained about disciplinary laxity – using their parliamentary private secretaries (PPSs) (Crossman claimed) 'to stir up dissatisfaction against the Prime Minister and Silkin' (Crossman, 1976: 614, 665, diary entries for 20 December 1967 and 6 February 1968). As Crossman acknowledged, the trio were reflecting the opinion of many 'loyalists' within the PLP, which held that the primary duty of the Labour backbencher was to 'sustain the Government': it was for this, and not their personal views, that they had been elected. The well-publicised spectacle of intra-party 'wrangling', it was claimed, weakened the morale of the PLP, impeded the passage of legislation, diminished the authority of the Government and alienated voters. Not only – so the complaint rang – did such behaviour, licensed by the Crossman–Silkin regime, go unpunished, but disloyalty was actually rewarded as dissidents were hailed in the constituencies as people of courage and integrity whilst the loyalists – whose votes actually kept the Government going – were mocked as time-servers.[4] Why should the majority bear the brunt of rank-and-file obloquy when Silkin's recipe for quelling rebellion appeared to be (as the *Guardian* journalist Peter Jenkins put it) 'a bottle of wine with Stan Orme' (Jenkins, 1970: 67).[5]

Indeed, the liberal regime appeared to do little to stem the rising tide of dissent. For instance, in the twenty months from Labour's triumph at the polls in 1966 to the close of 1967 there were six major revolts: over Vietnam in July 1966; over prices and incomes legislation in August and then again in October 1966; over defence in March 1967; over the European Economic Community (EEC) in May 1967; and finally over prices and incomes once more in June 1967. At one point, Wilson himself appeared to lose patience with the new regime. In March 1967, 62 MPs abstained on the Government's Defence White Paper in protest against the failure to transfer resources from military to social programmes. Wilson reacted furiously, warning that whilst every dog was allowed 'one bite', if he continually bit 'not because of the dictates of conscience but because he is considered vicious', he might not get his licence renewed (*The Times*, 3 March 1967). Crossman, who had not been consulted, was 'livid' (Castle, 1984: 232, diary entry for 3 March 1967). Already engaged in a bitter row with the PLP's hardline chairman, Manny Shinwell, over intra-party discipline, he threatened to resign unless the Prime Minister unambiguously came down in favour of the liberal regime – which he finally did. Shortly afterwards, Shinwell was replaced by the more liberal-minded Douglas Houghton as PLP chair.

Wilson's outburst was – as Barbara Castle recorded in her diary – 'entirely out of character' (Castle, 1984: 232, diary entry for 3 March 1967). He himself claimed (in his memoirs) that his comment was a 'throw away remark' wildly exaggerated by the press (Wilson, 1971: 378).[6] However, he did begin to harbour doubts about the value of the liberal regime, for the situation deteriorated further in the latter half of the Government's term of office, with serious backbench rebellions over reform of the House of Lords, taxation, incomes policy and Vietnam, culminating in the threatened massed revolt over proposals for trade union reform enshrined in *In Place of Strife*.

The attempt to copy the informal Conservative methods seemed to have run into the ground. Though Silkin was deft in handling human relations, Crossman confessed that this was not his 'personal style', and he soon abandoned his plans to spend more time with the troops (Crossman, 1976: 240, diary entry for 15 February 1967). Silkin himself was finally deposed for his apparent failure – with the wave of parliamentary dissent over *In Place of Strife* – to master the party, and replaced by the hearty, convivial but tough-minded right-winger Bob Mellish on the understanding that he would institute much stronger discipline. If this were indeed Wilson's intention (and this is unclear[7]), it was to prove unavailing, for two main reasons. The first was the limits to the Prime Minister's managerial powers. Under the Parliamentary Labour Party's Code of Conduct, an errant MP could be suspended or even expelled from the PLP, but the ultimate, and thus most fearsome, punishment against Parliamentary dissidents – the right to expel them from the party, and hence to prevent their readoption as a Labour parliamentary candidate – was vested in the NEC, not the parliamentary wing of the party. This posed no problem for the post-war Labour administration (nor, indeed, has it done so for Tony Blair's), but with the NEC increasingly sympathetic to the dissidents' positions on key issues (notably industrial relations legislation), there were mounting doubts about its willingness to continue operating as the Government's disciplinary arm.

Second, the Labour Government's ability to assert what we might call normative control – the appeal to loyalty, to allegiance to the party and its leadership – was flagging. Normative control derived much of its disciplinary edge from its roots in a solidaristic attachment to 'the movement', the transposition of the collective norms and experience of trade unionism to party life. In the past (during the social democratic centralist era), it had been the trade union leader and the trade union-sponsored MP who were most insistent upon maintaining intra-party unity, enforced, if necessary, by discipline, and thus least sympathetic to the call of conscience and the rights of dissenting minorities in the PLP.[8] But what if loyalty to one's trade union, to one's class – to 'the movement' – came into conflict with loyalty to the Labour Government itself? This is precisely what happened. Feelings of loyalty and solidarity were being sapped as the discord between the Labour Government and the trade unions intensified. The traditional functional differentiation between the political and industrial arms, which had welded together the various party institutions, disintegrated in the late 1960s as the Government encroached upon the unions' reserved domain of collective bargaining through successive measures of statutory incomes policies. Ironically, it was Manny Shinwell – manoeuvred from his chairmanship of the PLP because of his hostility towards the liberal regime (on his belief in the need for strong intra-party discipline, see Shinwell, 1981) – who told his parliamentary colleagues that if confronted with the choice of loyalty to the Government or loyalty to the movement as a whole, he would unhesitatingly opt for the latter (*The Times*, 9 May 1968). Then came the proposed trade union legislation presaged in the White Paper *In Place of Strife*. The trade union group of Labour MPs – the bedrock of right-wing loyalism – found themselves cross-pressured between loyalty to the leadership and loyalty to the unions. 'Protecting "the Movement" became a major consideration for many MPs who would normally have given the Government loyal support' (Minkin, 1978: 307). Far from reinstalling an astringent disciplinary regime, Mellish advised Wilson that the bill would not pass and he would have to relent. The relaxed managerial regime appeared to have survived its greatest challenge.

Conclusion

Over the past generation, Labour has oscillated between strict and lenient disciplinary regimes – each provoked by disaffection with the other. In response to the strict regime of the Attlee–Gaitskell era, Harold Wilson's premiership entailed a more relaxed approach. The 'Crossman–Silkin regime' – as he rightly pointed out in his memoir – moved 'towards a degree of liberality in party management seldom risked with a Government party; indeed, going far beyond anything the Labour Party had conceived possible in our Opposition years throughout the fifties and early sixties' (Wilson, 1971: 317). But in so far as the intention of this more emollient style was to avoid chronic discord, it failed. The 1964–1970 Labour Governments were racked by dissension within Parliament and beset by sharpening fractures in the party beyond Westminster. Three decades later, the Blair leadership – determined to avoid the strife which, it felt, had so bruised earlier Labour

Governments – imposed a tight managerial regime. On a whole range of issues, such as the selection of parliamentary candidates, the election of party leaders for the new devolved authorities and discipline in the House of Commons, party authorities acquired and sought to exercise a degree of central control unparalleled in the Labour Party's history. However, this so-called control-freakery itself fell into disrepute when Blair's attempts to install favoured candidates as Welsh First Minister and London Mayor foundered, and the Prime Minister, embarrassingly, found himself applauding two men – Rhodri Morgan and Ken Livingstone – whom he (or his spin doctors) had dismissed as unfit for high public office (Shaw, 2004). Equally, the taut disciplinary regime in Parliament – imposed on an apparently compliant PLP – could not in due course avert (in 2003 and 2004) the two largest backbench rebellions in Labour's history.[9]

In fact, criticising the liberal managerial regime for failing to prevent conflict is to invoke the wrong yardstick. The Labour leadership's 'eternal problem', Crossman wrote with his usual perspicacity, was that 'one can't put one's views strongly without being accused of factional strife' (1975: 250, diary entry for June 13 1965). Subsequently, it has become entrenched conventional wisdom to disparage disagreement within political parties as 'squabbles, splits and bickering'. Yet cohesion is not necessarily the absence of contention or conflict, but the outcome of finding the means – effective institutional channels – to regulate and contain it. Without disagreement – open debate over a range of issues – political parties become inert, monolithic bodies manipulated by their leaders. Michael Foot neatly encapsulated the dilemma: 'how to encourage freedom without which political parties will become moribund, whilst not destroying the cohesion without which they will cease to be effective instruments of government?' (1959: 21). No Labour government has been able to resolve the dilemma – perhaps because there is no resolution. Ultimately, it may be a question of a disciplined but sluggish and leaden party, or a quarrelsome and combative but lively one.

Notes

1 The 29-member NEC was elected in a variety of ways. Roughly a quarter were elected by the constituency Labour parties (CLPs), 18 were either solely or largely elected by the unions, and the Leader and Deputy Leader of the Party (elected by the PLP) were ex-officio members.

2 As stipulated by Labour Party rules, the framing of the manifesto is a shared enterprise. The source material for the manifesto is the party's programme, which consists of resolutions and NEC statements adopted by Conference by a two-thirds majority on a card vote. A joint meeting of the Parliamentary Committee (i.e. Cabinet or Shadow Cabinet) and the NEC – the so-called Clause 5 meeting named after the relevant section of the constitution – decides which items of the programme will be included in the manifesto.

3 The proscribed list was a compilation of organisations membership of which was deemed to be incompatible with that of the Labour Party.

4 As Wilson put it, 'the member for "Coketown West" was a hero in his

constituency, and no doubt equally in "Coketown East", simply because he could count on his neighbour to support the Government in the lobbies. This was not political courage: it was the opposite' (Wilson, 1971: 377).

5 Stan Orme was the left-wing MP for Salford West and a Minister in the 1974–1979 Labour Government.

6 He added that his real strictures were aimed at 'some hard-line members of the right wing' who had abstained frivolously as a protest against lax party discipline (Wilson, 1971: 377–8).

7 Though it is what Barbara Castle feared. She wrote to Wilson, '[I]f the strategy is to railroad my Bill [i.e. *In Place of Strife*] through Parliament on a Healey-type regime of reactionary discipline, I will have no part of it' (quoted in Perkins, 2003: 299).

8 'I personally am sick and tired of individuals who get cheap applause by hawking their consciences around', the trade union MP and future Chief Whip Bob Mellish exclaimed at one party conference. 'You have to have honest and clear discipline . . . we must abide by majority decisions' (Labour Party, 1955: 206).

9 These were over Government policy towards Iraq and the proposed introduction of variable top-up fees for university students.

4 The Fabian political economy of Harold Wilson

Noel Thompson

Introduction

Assessments of the political sensibilities, convictions and ideology of Harold Wilson have tended to emphasise their pragmatic nature. Wilson has been viewed as a tactician, not a strategist; as someone noted more for his deft political footwork than for being an ideologically driven politician. Support for Bevan over the budget of 1951, the subsequent gravitation to the left, the challenge to Gaitskell for the leadership in 1960, the embrace and then de facto abandonment of planning in the 1960s, the determination to defend the international value of sterling whatever the deflationary cost and the eventual acceptance of devaluation – these have all been interpreted as driven by considerations of political expediency, rather than by any desire to realise or defend a particular vision of the political economy of socialism. Viewed kindly, all this could be seen in terms of the malleability necessary for political survival in the fraught economic circumstances of the 1960s; viewed more brutally, it furnishes evidence of a devious politician intent on retaining power at whatever cost to the labour movement or the Labour Party's natural constituency.

This chapter does not aim to challenge directly either the favourable or the less favourable judgements of Wilson's political actions. What it will argue, however, is that there was such a thing as a distinctively Wilsonian political economy that underpinned a particular vision of what Britain might become; that it was a coherent vision embodying both a persuasive analysis of Britain's relative economic decline (persuasive, if not altogether sound, but a discussion of the weaknesses of this analysis would require a separate chapter) and a strategy to address it; and that this political economy was fundamental to the relative unity, and the considerable political success, that Labour enjoyed for most of the 1960s. It will also argue that its failings were intrinsic to any late twentieth-century social democratic political economy sculpted with an eye to unifying the party, broadening its social constituency and winning elections, rather than a consequence of the self-seeking, devious behaviour, or lack of political resolve, principle or courage, of the politician who gave it expression.

Fabian political economy

The key to understanding the nature, prescriptive thrust and patois of Wilsonian political economy is to appreciate that he must be located in the long and ideologically powerful tradition of Fabian political economy – something that has been recognised by writers such as Pimlott and Ziegler, but whose implications have not been fully developed (Pimlott, 1992; Ziegler, 1993). This was a tradition that, for good or ill, had furnished the political economy that informed the Labour Party's critical analysis of capitalism and consequent economic strategy for the greater part of its history. Yet whilst it had been challenged, in the 1930s, by new ideas on how to manage a social democratic economy – whose provenance was primarily Keynes's 1930 *Treatise on Money* and 1936 *General Theory* – a cursory reading of the Labour Party's 1945 election manifesto *Let Us Face the Future* is sufficient to show what a powerful influence Fabian economic thinking still exerted within the Labour Party of the early post-war years.

The distinctive characteristics of this political economy were these. It saw in capitalism a system distinguished by waste, inefficiency and economic anarchy, which precluded the sustained economic growth necessary for that high standard of material well-being, for the working population, which industrialisation had made possible. It saw the amalgamation and merger of industrial and other enterprises, which characterised late nineteenth- and early twentieth-century capitalism, as laying the basis for the extension of social ownership and thence a transformation of economic performance. It considered the replacement of entrepreneurs by professional managers as creating a class of functionless drones and, simultaneously, a *nouvelle couche sociale* possessed of the technical skill and professional competence required to manage efficiently economic affairs at either a micro- or a macroeconomic level.

Consistent with this, Fabian political economy lauded the expert and condemned the amateur, celebrated the application of science and scientific management to industry, and sought to apply the methods of (social) scientific investigation both to analyse the nation's economic ills and to furnish a solution to them. And, as regards the latter, the Fabians saw the extension of public ownership as providing the basis for the conscious and purposive planning of economic activity. In this regard, and others, they were the heirs to the optimistic rationalism and associated hubris of the Enlightenment. As Middlemas (1990: 124) observed with regard to the National Plan, it assumed a rationality and simple perception of the national interest which was never likely to fit with institutions' and members' known patterns of behaviour.

Wilsonian political economy

To identify these salient characteristics of Fabianism is to list most, if not quite all, of the distinguishing characteristics of the Wilsonian political economy of the 1960s. To begin with, much of what Harold Wilson and the Labour Party offered in this period was infused with, and invigorated by, an optimistic rationalism: a positivistic faith in the scientific method, a belief that clear and 'new thinking' could 'end the chaos and sterility' that had characterised the economic and social life of Britain in the 1950s (Wilson, 1964a: 229; see also Wilson, 1964b: 14–28), a conviction that 'brains' and 'genius' rightly deployed must necessarily make for economic and social progress, and an associated Fabian belief that forces unleashed by economic self-interest would, independently of a governing will, produce chaos and stagnation. Indeed, one of the reasons for Wilson's opposition to devaluation was that its proponents too often viewed it as a quick, market fix for problems whose solution required reasoned analysis and rational, strategic decision-making. Yet in Wilson's view 'There was no more dangerous illusion than that laissez-faire and a cold east wind [would] do the trick' as regards Britain's economic performance (House of Commons Debates, 5th series, vol. 645, col. 1656).

Moreover, as regards his optimistic rationalism, some of Wilson's most powerful expressions of frustration were reserved for the speculative excesses that undermined the position of sterling, threw the government's strategy into disarray and yet had no intelligible or rational basis in the underlying economic realities. The crisis of the summer of 1966, which forced upon the government another set of deflationary measures to maintain the international value of sterling, at a time when the balance of payments looked strong, was referred to by Wilson as 'one of the nastiest and most *inexplicable* crises sterling had to face'. More generally, speculators were seen as prone to '*neurotic* moods' and herd instincts that precluded the exercise of rational judgement (Wilson, 1971: 251, 272; emphasis added). In this context, Wilson deemed it

> [i]nteresting to ask why, in a summer [1964] when we had a deficit running at a rate of £800 million, there were few selling sterling short, while in a summer [1966] when we were running at a deficit only a fraction of that figure, anti-sterling speculation ran riot. Whatever explanation is given must *transcend economic considerations*. It was *a morbid psychology* with which we had to deal.
>
> (1971: 250; emphasis added)

Rationalism, science and socialism

This faith in rationality, and Wilson's disparagement of its opposite, were rooted in a characteristically Fabian faith in science and a methodological positivism. In Wilsonian political economy, and that of the 1960s Labour Party, science and socialism were seen as interdependent and at times almost synonymous. Socialism 'must [be] harness[ed] to science and science to Socialism'; socialism must 'harness new technologies and the powerful economic forces of our time to human ends'; must 'harness the forces released by science in the service of the community' (Labour Party, 1970a: 4; 1961: 7). Moreover, for Wilson himself the advance of science and the advance of socialism had engendered a pressing contemporary need for the latter to be restated in terms of the former, a point he emphasised in his speech opening the debate on science at Labour's 1963 annual conference (see Wilson, 1964b: 27). It was not just, as a *New Statesman* editorial put it, that Wilson took 'socialism into a world of radio physics and cybernetics', it was also that he saw that world as inherently socialist, with the prospect of 'scientific efficiency' 'both produc[ing] and be[ing] produced by social equity' (*New Statesman*, 4 October 1963: 429). Wilson himself recalled that when, in an interview during this period, he had been 'asked what, above all, I associated with socialism in the modern age: I answered if there is one word I would use to identify modern socialism it was "science"' (quoted in Foot, 1968: 331).

And as with the Fabians, so with Wilson, the creators of this brave new world and the champions of this new scientific rationalism were to be the technician, the scientist, the engineer, the technocrat – in short, the professional expert. 'Skill, talent and brain power [were] . . . the most important national resources'. Labour's 1964 manifesto promised that 'a New Britain' would harness such resources utilising 'our national wealth in brains, our genius for scientific investigation and medical discovery' (Craig, 1975: 260). It was such human capital that would reverse the relative economic decline that had afflicted Britain under the Conservatives, and it was this *nouvelle couche sociale*, the rapidly growing salariat of the 1960s, that would provide the necessary expertise and leadership to translate the scientific and technological revolutions of the post-war period into a material abundance that laid the basis of socialist advance. Tony Crosland in particular attached considerable importance to the point that in the 1951–1959 period, the salariat had increased from 30 per cent to 34 per cent of the population (1960a: 10).

The need for a cadre of professionals and experts

This was an age when the fundamental problems that had dogged Britain could be solved, given the requisite technical skill, scientific knowledge, trained personnel or professional competencies. And, as one commentator was subsequently to observe, 'The advent of the Wilson governments saw . . . the rapid recruitment of professional economists to all ministries and agencies' (Thirlwall, 1987: 230). In effect, it was considered that these problems would be solved independently of social conflict, class struggle or any fundamental assault on the bastions of capitalist power – even if the social apotheosis of those who solved them would ultimately precipitate a kind of social revolution. In this context, Anthony Howard (1963: 294) saw Wilson as 'identify[ing] the Labour Party with the next great social breakthrough in Britain'.

Those who would construct the New Britain were defined not by their class but by their expertise. And when in power, Wilson did move quickly to place in positions of authority 'an impressive array of scientists and industrialists' (Coopey, 1993: 108). Furthermore, the enemy was now defined less by class than by its incompetence or its functionless character. A new socialist demonology was constructed that encompassed the 'dead wood' in 'Britain's board rooms', 'far too many of whom owe their place not to fitness for their job but to family, social and school connexions'; 'the old boy network' with its 'social prejudices and anti-scientific bias'; the 'amiable coelocanths no longer suited to the waters which lap the shores of the world in which we are living'; and the 'gentlemen' who sought their living 'in a World of Players'. These were the social elements whose 'amateurism', 'grouse-moor conception of ... leadership' and 'Edwardian notions' were a luxury that could no longer be afforded in the modern world. What was worse, in alliance with them were 'the spiv, the speculator, the take-over bidder, the land-grabber' – in short, the functionless wealthy whose primary objective was to reap where they had not sown (Labour Party, 1961: 10; 1964a: 234; Wilson, 1964a: 14; 1964b: 87; 1964a: 126). Whilst these 'social parasites' might boast professionalism, it was the professionalism of greed, and if their activities had an economic rationality, it was the rationality involved in the pursuit of their material self-interest. For Harold Wilson and the Labour Party of the 1960s, neither amateurism nor spivvery could have any place in the Fabian and technocratic New Britain which they aimed to build.

The centrality of economic planning

The new rationalism in the conduct of economic affairs that would characterise a technocratic Britain was to be expressed in the conscious, purposive planning of economic activity (for the Conservative origins of the planning and modernisation agenda in Britain, see Tomlinson, 1997). Planning signalled the triumph of rational forethought over amateurism and ad hocery. It gave scope for the *nouvelle couche sociale* to display its professional qualities and exercise its powers. It epitomised the new dirigisme that was fundamental to economic success in the modern world, as evidenced by the performance of France, Japan and the countries of the Soviet bloc. The example of France proved particularly persuasive, with French influence coming, in the early 1960s, through informal meetings, exchanges and a conference in London, in the spring of 1961, involving the NIESR and the Institut de Science Économique Appliquée (Meadows, 1978: 404; see also Leruez, 1975: 87–8). As to the Soviet Union, Richard Crossman was clear that, whatever its political and social diseconomies, Soviet planning was allowing it to outstrip the performance of the Western economies and particularly that of Britain (Crossman, 1960a: 9).

According to post-Keynesians such as Kaldor, Balogh and Robinson, planning was necessary to secure dynamic equilibrium in a market economy (see, for example, Kaldor, 1964; King, 2002: *passim*; Targetti, 1992: 11; Thirlwall, 1987: *passim*). It was also seen as vital to correct regional imbalances (see Chapter 13 in this volume; see also *New Statesman*, 7 December 1962: 809), and it would ensure the advance of the scientific and technological revolutions in a manner that served national ends. Thus, Wilson informed delegates at Labour's 1963 conference that 'with planning, we can harness the new technologies' (quoted in Wilson, 1964b: 18), a claim subsequently echoed in the party's pledge to establish '[a] New Britain – mobilizing the resources of technology under a national plan' (Craig, 1975: 260).

Planning was confidently considered a corrective to the systemic ignorance of investment intentions inherent in atomised decision-making in a free market economy and, as such, it reduced the risk and uncertainty attendant upon expansion (for more on this perspective, see Balogh, 1963). It was also seen as an antidote to the irresponsible exercise of oligopoly and monopoly power that was becoming an increasingly characteristic feature of Western industrial capitalism and that had prevented the market acting as 'a determinate signalling system which will result in optimal decisions' (Balogh, 1963: 12). Such views on the merits of planning were articulated in particular in the work of Labour's economic advisers, such as Thomas Balogh and Nicholas Kaldor, but they clearly resonated with Wilson's own thinking and his direct experience of the success of planning during the immediate post-war period.

The nature of the planning proposed was indicative, but Wilson and Labour Party literature were unequivocal that 'by planning we don't mean the publication of academic statistics and blueprints, but plans and priorities – planning with teeth' (Wilson, 1964b: 47). And certainly, in the approach to the 1964 election there was no shortage of suggestions as to what teeth could be given to plan and planners. Labour's 1961 policy document *Signposts for the Sixties* expressed the need for 'the full resources of government' to be used 'to make sure that it was carried out, industry by industry' (Labour Party, 1961: 13). Fiscal and monetary policy should be subordinated to planning goals: 'Financial policies must be directed to ensure that the investment plan is fulfilled'. Meanwhile, 'tax policies' would 'encourag[e] new investment and the speedier writing off of capital expenditure', whilst guaranteed government orders would be used to stimulate growth where it was thought appropriate. Furthermore, the possibility of 'new publicly-owned undertakings was mooted' (Labour Party, 1961: 15; see also Wilson, 1964a: 23), whereby 'competitive public enterprises' would advance the public sector 'where it [was] most needed', at 'the growing points of the British economy and in the new industries based on science', thereby engendering growth and stimulating private enterprise to do likewise. In addition, it was envisaged that there would be joint private–public ventures, the growth of public enterprise to tackle the regional problem and, as with steel, the nationalisation of whole industries where the existence of monopoly power might require it (Wilson, 1964a: 55; Labour Party, 1961: 18).

> All these kinds of social ownership have their part to play in meeting the dangers of monopoly, in achieving a fair distribution of the national dividend – and, most importantly of all, in helping to fulfil our national plan for economic growth.
>
> (Labour Party, 1961: 18)

Whatever may have happened subsequently, and whatever may have been Wilson's true intentions or real attitude to public ownership, it was clear that Wilsonian political economy, like that of Webbian Fabianism, placed emphasis on its extension. Paul Foot quotes a remark made by Wilson to John Junor, editor of the *Sunday Express*, that Macmillan was 'holding up the banner of Suez for the Party to follow, and he's leading the Party away from Suez. That's what I'd like to do with the Labour Party over nationalization' (quoted in Foot, 1968: 127). The fact remains, though, that he also stated that 'by our nationalization policy, and only by that policy, can we carry out a plan essential for Britain's future' (Wilson, 1961: 468).

Moreover, close to the centre of Labour policy-making, and the ear of the Labour leader, was Thomas Balogh, who, as one commentator saw it, considered

> public ownership ... crucial ... both to a restoration of social balance between public and private expenditure and to the securing of a more equitable distribution of income ... which the purely fiscal revolutionists can achieve only at the risk of failing at the polls or reducing the economy to a state of debility.
>
> (Artis, 1963: 111)

As Balogh himself put it,

> far from [its] being true that progressive taxation can of itself bring about social change, we must recognise that effective taxation demands such powers on the part of the state as can hardly be secured in an economy where the commanding heights of economic power still remain in the hands of a tiny minority.
>
> (Balogh, 1962: 922; see also Balogh, 1963: 7–8)

There is throughout all this a powerful resonance with Webbian Fabianism.

Fabian asceticism, commercialism and consumerism

Finally, as regards the Fabian character of the Wilsonian political economy of the 1960s, there are the powerful parallels between the views of Wilson and those of the Webbs on the business of consumption. Put briefly, the Webbs were suspicious of the business of the private consumer and private consumption. Consumers were manipulated and misled by 'the mendacious advertisement of rival products' and frequently behaved with 'anarchic irresponsibility' (Webb and Webb, 1920a: 324–5; 1920b: 674). In turn, the Webbs advocated, and lived, a self-denying socialism that emphasised public, not private, consumption and looked to institutions such as the cooperative movement to rationalise and guide the latter. Wilson's thinking moved on similar lines. There were the same ascetic leanings that saw in much contemporary private consumption a waste of resources and a perversion of aspirations. What Britain produced should be related 'to the needs of a largely hungry world whose wants are not for consumer luxuries but for the primary basis of life itself – basic, elemental goods and the means of producing them'. In this context, too, Wilson frequently made the distinction between what he termed the 'hard-centre sector of our economy, the metal-using industries' and 'the soft-centre of the consumer sector'. As he saw it, the latter serviced the whims of private consumers 'titillate[d] with striped toothpaste, or all the other lunacies of an Americanised society', while the former focused on 'the needs of the Commonwealth, Latin American and other markets' (Wilson, 1962: 578; 1964b: 49). On these matters, Wilson clearly took a moral stand, and one consistent with a strategy where a fiscal policy aimed at growth would treat 'consumer demand – and not as hitherto, exports and investments – as the residual legatee' (Wilson, 1961: 466). The irony was, of course, that the consumer goods, durable and otherwise, produced by the soft centre of the economy, were those for which export markets were expanding most rapidly in the 1950s and 1960s.

Wilson's conception of the apparently ill-informed and easily duped consumer was also remarkably similar to that of the Fabians. Striped toothpaste aside, post-war industrial capitalism was more generally distinguished by 'the delirium of advertising and the ceaseless drive to produce new and different variants of existing consumer goods and services', with the consuming population in danger of 'sinking back into the syrupy, demoralising persuasion which pours into our homes night after night via the commercial channel'. And it would only be 'when this country loses its soft centre, its candy-floss philosophy, and is allowed to aspire to more astringent policies' that it could 'succeed' (Wilson, 1964b: 26, 60). Here, Wilson became a part of that rationalist tradition that stretches back through the Fabians and Benthamite utilitarians to those onslaughts upon the societal and personal corruption induced by luxury that form an important strand in eighteenth-century civic republicanism.

For someone who sought to win over the salariat, it is perhaps surprising that Wilson's condemnation of some of the material possibilities offered by affluence should have been so fierce. As noted above, such a condemnation did have an economic rationale, but the language is fiercely moral and connects with a Fabian perception of the ideal of service, in contrast to self-indulgence, as central to the civic virtue that would characterise socialism and enable it to function effectively. Thus, it was because of the service they would render that the members of the new technocracy were to be located in the positions of power and decision-making that their abilities merited. Further, the sense of national purpose, the Dunkirk spirit, the national resolve, that was required to deliver the objectives of a National Plan and rejuvenate Britain could not be engendered, and could certainly not be sustained, 'by appeals to materialism, or selfish acquisitiveness, or competitive social emulation' or by 'a self-regarding affluent society' where 'the verb "to have" means so much more than the verb "to be"' (Wilson, 1964b: 56). Rather, they must be informed and inspired by a spirit of service or they would not emerge at all.

The coherence of Wilson's Fabian political economy

It is perhaps due to the fact that, from the 1964 election victory onwards, economic forces outside the control of the Wilson governments blew them hither and thither across the political landscape, that there has been a tendency to regard Wilsonian political economy as an essentially incoherent ragbag of expedients, and a concomitant failure to acknowledge its coherence – a coherence given it by its essential Fabianism. That said, there were some contemporaries, even contemporary critics, who recognised just what had been achieved. Perry Anderson, writing in the *New Left Review*, opined that

> perhaps for the first time in its history, the Labour Party now possesses a coherent analysis of British society ... a long-term assessment of its failure, and an aggressive political strategy based on both. The contrast with Gaitskellism is arresting.
>
> (1964: 4)

Similarly, an editorial in the *New Statesman*, written shortly after Wilson's Scarborough speech at the Labour Party's annual conference of 1963, stated that 'its virtue ... is its relation to a plan in which economic growth, the role of technology, education, the compassionate services, the class revolution and an age of leisure are *all lucidly exhibited as integral elements of one another*' (*New Statesman*, 4 October 1963: 429; emphasis added).

Furthermore, the critical analysis and politico-economic prescriptions of this integrated strategy addressed not only pressing contemporary problems and social concerns, but also those difficulties confronting the Labour Party, and those tensions within its ranks, that had helped to keep it out of power for thirteen years and threatened to keep it from government for another decade. As to the former, Wilsonian political economy provided a compelling analysis of Britain's relative economic decline, which was explained in terms of persistent underinvestment, along with the concomitant failure to exploit the potentialities of the contemporary scientific revolution, and thence an inability to establish a competitive edge in global export markets. These failures were, in turn, rooted in a social structure, and ossified social attitudes, that obstructed the advance in industry, finance and commerce of those whose dynamism, intellectual qualities and professional training merited the possession of decision-making power. Moreover, the absence of a sense of national and social purpose inherent in an economic regime of self-interested laissez-faire prevented a concerted, planned attack upon Britain's failings. In this respect, the macroeconomic ring-holding which was the essence of Keynesian demand management was no longer sufficient. Recourse had to be had to the economic planning that, in the immediate post-war period, had delivered both an export miracle and the construction of a welfare state.

As to Labour's political difficulties and the tensions within the party, there was, during the 1950s and 1960s – and as noted in the previous chapter – a recognition that structural changes in the British economy were effecting an apparent decline in the importance of Labour's traditional social constituency, relative to the rapid growth of a middle-class salariat. Crosland, Gaitskell, Jay and others had taken note of these developments and suggested a change in the character, prescriptive thrust and even the name of the party. For Crosland, 'new social forces [were] . . . at work, gradually breaking down the old barriers between the working and middle classes and slowly giving birth to new and more fluid social gatherings', and so the party needed 'to adapt itself . . . and to present itself to the electorate in mid-twentieth-century guise' (1960a: 13; 1960b: 5). This required, amongst other things, a fundamental revision of its position on Clause 4. Also, given the existence of a cross-party political consensus on Keynesian macroeconomic management and a mixed economy, Crosland (1956: 128–9) believed that party differentiation necessitated the prioritisation of social, as distinct from economic, means of achieving social democratic objectives.

The 1959 Labour Party annual conference clearly showed just how divisive such a perspective could be. Moreover, Britain's relative economic decline, stop–go and the increasing intensity of balance of payments crises were calling into question the whole theoretical basis of the Keynesianism that Crosland, and others, saw as underpinning the existing political consensus on economic policy-making. Besides, even in so far as contra-cyclical demand management did work – and there was a growing body of opinion that began to question its practical efficacy – it was increasingly recognised that it merely ensured that all labour resources were fully utilised, not that they were utilised efficiently. And in the context of a growing appreciation of Britain's relative economic decline, this was viewed as something meriting serious consideration.

What Wilsonian political economy furnished was a strategy that seemed to reconcile the short-run objectives of macroeconomic management with the long-run aims of constructing an efficient and competitive socialist economy, resting on the foundations of substantial social ownership and purposive economic planning, and thence melding right-wing Keynesian revisionism with left-wing Clause 4 fundamentalism. Party literature and Wilsonian speeches told the left what it wanted to hear, but party policy served to reassure the right. Further, while the idea and rhetoric of planning had a strong resonance with the left, the type of planning proposed – indicative planning, with its corporatist, information-disseminating character, and means of implementation that stopped well short of wholesale nationalisation – was something that could be accommodated by the social democratic right (Anderson, 1964: 16). So, for a time, Labour's left and right could unite and fight under the banner of a distinctive Wilsonian political economy, even if the reconciliation was to prove fundamentally unstable.

The political and electoral potential of Wilsonian political economy

In addition, as noted above, planning plus technological advance could provide both framework and opportunities to accommodate the social, career and pecuniary aspirations of the salariat, and certainly, upon becoming Prime Minister, Wilson acquired and appointed 'an impressive array of scientists and industrialists sympathetic to the Labour Party' (Coopey, 1993: 108). As with the Fabians, so with Wilsonian political economy: an emphasis on planning and technological innovation provided an important potential means of broadening the party's social appeal and breaking open the closed establishment and 'closed society' seemingly favoured by the Conservatives (Wilson, 1964a: 9). It also served to highlight the deficiencies and the costs of leaving the functionless drones, the amiable coelacanths and the tweed-suited 'condescending Edwardian masters' in positions of decision-making authority. Although the substance of the Wilsonian critique of Britain in the 1960s, as an 'anti-technological and backward country', has been called into question (see, for example, Edgerton, 1996: 54), the political purchase of the demonology which it allowed Wilson to construct was nonetheless considerable.

Wilson might have wanted, as Paul Foot (1968: 328–9) put it, to replace 'effete aristocratic cabals ... with meritocratic cabals', but in terms of widening the appeal of the Labour Party, the important point is that the latter were both numerically more important and certainly more recruitable than the former. Though critical of Wilsonism, Perry Anderson, writing in 1964, clearly recognised the political opportunities it had created: 'Neocapitalism everywhere demands indicative planning by the state. This planning must necessarily be executed by highly skilled technocrats working within a powerful state apparatus. In England, the whole cumulative tradition of the governing class disables it from this role' (1964: 51).

In 1961, David Marquand had emphasised the need to impress upon 'that growing section of the working class which feels itself to be middle class' that Labour was 'no longer the party of the manual working class alone, that it stands for the ambitious and successful as well as for the poor and unfortunate' (1961: 5). Wilsonian political economy offered the means of doing just that without alienating traditionalists, either by changing the party's name, or by formally abandoning a commitment to the substantial extension of social ownership or, for that matter, the construction of a socialist society.

Furthermore, this apotheosis of the technically able professional middle classes allowed Wilson and the party to talk a language of social revolution that was familiar and congenial to the left, but whose substance was unlikely to alienate the revisionist right. A *New Statesman* editorial (4 October 1963: 429), for example, bought into the view expressed by Wilson at Scarborough that 'a transformation of our attitude to science and technology will more than any other single factor transform our attitude to class', whilst Anthony Howard, even before that speech was made, wrote that 'Mr. Wilson's grand design' had

> identif[ied] the Labour Party with the next great social breakthrough in Britain, the moment when the employed executives, the white-coat brigade, even the drawing-board planners, decide that if they do the work, they might just as well have the power and control as well.
>
> (1963: 294)

This was social revolution of a Fabian kind, the rhetoric of which resonated with the left without the reality alienating the right.

In the late 1950s and early 1960s, there were those on the left who had argued that in pursuit of electoral success, and in order to broaden its social basis of support, Labour must perform the well-nigh impossible task of 'simultaneously attract[ing] a mass of "prosperity-corrupted" electors by giving [the Party] a new and essentially unsocialist face', while 'retain[ing] the support of many who still call themselves socialists' (Hansen, 1961: 11). In fact, by focusing on the middle class in their role as producers, rather than their role as consumers, Wilson did, at least in the short run, manage to square this particular circle, broadening the party's social appeal while retaining the support – indeed, the enthusiastic support – of the left.

In blending his critique of amateurism and incompetence with an attack on the parasitism of functionless property owners and speculators, Wilson also struck other chords whose reverberations transcended the left–right divisions within the party. Such critical rhetoric had been the stuff of Labour's political economy since the party's birth; it had been at the very heart of the critical political economy of both Fabianism and ethical socialism, and it could be developed in the language of moral opprobrium and exhortation as well as that of economic expediency. Also, implicit in the Wilsonian critique of the functionless and unproductive was a contrasting evocation of the ideal of service, the work ethic and socially responsible activity, whose appeal transcended class but lay at the very heart of traditional support for the Labour Party.

Wilson's was also a political economy that not only united the Labour Party but had purchase on the latent fissures in the social constituency of the Conservatives. Thus, for Foot, 'Wilson's bitterness towards the Tories in the 1950s and early 1960s was no more than a meritocrat's irritation with an incompetent and amateurish aristocracy' (1968: 327). Yet this was a bitterness that could be spun in many political ways, some of which might be used to split the bourgeoisie and persuade elements that their interests could best be represented by Labour. The speculative and parasitical could be separated from those productively engaged in useful work. More generally, and perhaps more crudely, the productivism and emphasis on white-heat technological innovation in industry, together with the putative subordination of fiscal and monetary policy to planning in industry, pointed to possible divisions of interest between finance and manufacturing activity – the City and the Federation of British Industries (FBI).

In these respects, therefore, Wilsonian political economy served not only to unite the Labour Party (at least in the short term) and broaden the social basis of its support, but also to sow the dragon's teeth of dissension amongst the Conservatives' traditional supporters. Here it is interesting to note that even as severe a critic as Paul Foot could admit that 'by the time Wilson became Prime Minister in October 1964, he had contrived to unite the Labour Party and its affiliates as it had never been united since 1945' (1968: 304). Moreover, whilst 'in normal circumstances' the 'unanimous approval and praise' he received 'from the Left' could have been expected to 'provoke an opposite reaction from the Right ... during the same period the Right was equally uncritical' (Foot, 1968: 304). Yet it was not that circumstances were abnormal, nor was it, as Foot suggests, that 'the magical transformation in party policy which accompanied the election of Harold Wilson to the leadership' only took place 'in the minds of the Labour Left' (1968: 305). The fact was that Wilsonian political economy, even if it failed the test in the refining fires of practical politics, did indeed offer just those elements and strike just those chords that were most likely to bring together the two wings of the party. Failure to recognise this is seriously to underestimate, and certainly to misunderstand, the nature of Wilson's achievement.

The very language of science and technology also served the twin roles of broadening support and unifying the Labour Party. To begin with, just as planning addressed contemporary concerns about the failure of macroeconomic management to halt Britain's relative economic decline, so, as one commentator has put it, the language of science with its 'appeal to modernity came at a time when technological change had assumed a very high degree of visibility' and when it was unproblematically associated with progress and economic success (Coopey, 1993: 112). Moreover, this implied emphasis on progress and efficiency suggested a political economy to which Croslandite revisionists and fundamentalists could adhere (a point made by numerous writers; see, for example, Coates, 1975). There could be little dispute on political grounds about the need for both, and little disagreement that science and technology were salient to their realisation. But more than that, the language of cybernetics and radio physics implied solutions to pressing problems that transcended political ideology and these ideological divides.

According to Wilson, 'Socialism, as I understand it, means applying a sense of purpose to our national life: economic purpose, social purpose, moral purpose. *Purpose means technical skill*' (1964a: 14; emphasis added). For those who bought into such a restatement of 'socialism in terms of the scientific revolution', the political debates that had riven the party had effectively ended. For national purpose would now be informed and determined by those with the requisite professional or technical knowledge. The positivism of science meant that henceforward decisions would be made not on the basis of priorities determined by an ideologically inspired agenda, but on the more certain basis of what the scientific analysis of problems furnished for policy-makers. Moral imperatives would be replaced by those of a scientific or technical nature. The scope for divisive debate would thus be more narrowly circumscribed, and within the Labour Party that proved for a time to be the case. As one *New Statesman* contributor put it at the time, 'politically the divide between those in the Labour Party who want to seem more socialist ... and those who want to seem less so is thus conveniently bridged: we are all scientific planners now'. As to the 'voters', they 'were offered not a crusade but a better computer' (*New Statesman*, 11 July 1964: 127).

The subsequent failure of Wilson's political economy

Yet if Wilsonian's political economy was Fabian in the ways outlined, it lacked a key Fabian characteristic, a lacuna that contributed to its subsequent failure and that highlights at the same time the necessary impotence of social democratic political economy in the latter part of the twentieth century. What Wilsonian political economy lacked was a sense of the powers necessary to implement its strategy and the determination to acquire them. Webbian Fabianism, the product of another capitalist age, was not lacking in this respect, for the early Fabians were convinced that the state could and should assume the powers required to construct a socialist economy, and they outlined clearly both what those powers were, and how they were to be acquired. A radically redistributive fiscal policy would furnish the wherewithal for a substantial increase in social expenditure, in tandem with a significant extension of public ownership to encompass the greater part, and certainly the most important locations, of economic power. This was the strategy that was embraced by the Labour Party after the debacle of 1931 and, even if somewhat diluted by the late 1930s, it still served to underpin much of what the Labour Governments did in the period 1945–1951.

The explanations for the policy failures of the Wilson Governments are legion and diverse, but most are agreed on this: they were unable to acquire the powers, or use the limited power they did have, to pursue with any success the purposive planned growth that was the *sine qua non* of Wilsonian political economy and the Labour Party's economic strategy. This powerlessness manifested itself in an inability to pursue the desired course of action, or, at any rate, to act only within certain narrowly circumscribed limits, something that was most obvious in relation to the conduct of macroeconomic policy. Wilson himself commented upon the impotence of his Governments in the face of speculative attacks on the pound, even when support was forthcoming from the United States and the IMF, and even when there was no objective basis for the sale of sterling.

As a consequence, the Labour Governments were compelled to pursue deflationary policies, particularly in the summers of 1965 and 1966, thereby leaving their strategy for growth in tatters. Indeed, so swift was the demise of the National Plan that its obituary was contained in its preamble, for whilst stating that the policies set out in it were designed to remedy 'the underlying weakness of the economy' in the long run, the plan also admitted 'the need to protect the balance of payments and the position of sterling in the intervening period'. This was something which inevitably entailed deflationary policies that would 'involve some slowing down in the rate of expansion in the next year or so' (Department of Economic Affairs, 1965: 13).

The Labour Governments might, of course, have abandoned the sterling area and/or devalued earlier, in October 1964, July 1965 or July 1966, and commentators have made out a case for each of these dates. In this regard, Labour's impotence might be seen as self-inflicted. However, as the period following devaluation showed, earlier devaluation would not have prevented deflation and was therefore unlikely to have saved the National Plan (see, for example, Middlemas, 1990: 115). Further, while devaluation and deflation might have given a temporary freedom of manoeuvre, the prescriptive space they opened up was always likely to be narrowly circumscribed. The Labour Governments of the 1960s, whichever strategy they pursued, could not engender either international or domestic confidence, leading one commentator in *The Economist* to observe – in an editorial entitled 'Labour Men, Tory Measures' – after the first markedly deflationary episode in June/July 1965, that

> all that these nine months of Labour government have proved financially, is that when orthodox policies are pursued by a left-wing government they do not attract the same return in financial confidence as exactly the same policies pursued by the Tories.
>
> (*The Economist*, 31 July 1965: 127)

Also, from the time that the Labour Governments contracted substantial loans from the IMF and the United States to defend the international value of sterling, they were, in any case, under considerable pressure from these quarters to eschew devaluation. Powerlessness was, therefore, not just a function of the inaction of the Governments or the actions of speculators, but also a consequence of the external constraints imposed by the agenda of international agencies and the world's premier economic power. As Wilson himself had put it with respect to the Conservatives, when speaking at an election rally in Edinburgh in 1964, 'you cannot go cap in hand to the central bankers as they have been forced to do, and maintain your freedom of action' (quoted in Foot, 1968: 154). Of course Labour might have resisted such pressures but the consequences would have been much the same: devaluation and deflation. All roads led to hell, some by a straight and others by a more circuitous route.

External agencies also served to place limits on the conduct of commercial policy. Even an avowedly temporary measure such as the import surcharges imposed by the Labour Government soon after taking office provoked the ire of the European Free Trade Association (EFTA), and its eventual abandonment. Besides, the possibility of EEC membership precluded any significant progress down the protectionist road, even had the political will been there.

Of course, with regard to the National Plan, most commentators have argued that it was those who formulated it who were responsible for its toothless character. In this regard, unfavourable comparison has frequently been made with French planners, who were able to offer a range of fiscal and monetary carrots and sticks. As Postan put it, 'the French plans were ... comprehensive ... concerned with concrete problems of investment, technology and management, and ... discriminating between individual sectors, industries and firms' (1967: 32; see also Shonfield, 1969: 121–50), whilst the French planners could operate through a substantial public sector, including the principal financial institutions (in marked contrast to Britain; see Pryke, 1966: 5), possessed powers over the direction of investment, and had available to them a range of fiscal incentives and disincentives that they did not hesitate to use in a discriminatory fashion. Moreover, they had the support of a significant section of the business community. As one historian has noted, 'so readily did officials and business leaders agree on main principles, that at least one recent commentator was able to describe the French plans as acts of voluntary collusion between senior Civil Servants and senior managers of business' (Postan, 1967: 35).

Yet the fact was that the Commissariat du Plan had been invested with such powers at a particular historical conjuncture, when defeat in the Second World War was seen as necessitating a substantial redistribution of economic power, and a radical departure from traditional economic thinking and policy-making to rectify the manifest failings of the French economy and deficiencies of French society that had laid the basis for the humiliation of 1940. In addition, there was the strong tradition of dirigisme in France that made planning acceptable across the political and social spectrum. Such circumstances could clearly not be replicated in Britain.

That said, even if the Department of Economic Affairs (DEA) had been vested with the same powers as those deployed by the Commissariat du

Plan, there was still both an absence of the kind of detailed information necessary for effective planning and, crucially, the absence of 'a cadre of officials, actual or potential, with the drive and capacity to execute a technical revolution from the centre' of the kind that the National Plan envisaged (Marris, 1967: 71). The Industrial Inquiry which furnished the greater part of the information that informed the National Plan rectified this to some extent, but it proved a one-off exercise. As a *New Statesman* editorial of September 1966 – entitled 'From H. G. Wells to J. H. Wilson' – observed,

> [T]he truth is that the government, with the best intentions in the world is working in the dark. It lacks the detailed industry-by-industry information on which to base selective decisions, and even if it had the information, it lacks the legislative and administrative machinery to enforce them. It is trying to operate socialist policies with a free market Civil Service structure, and with a statistical machine that Gladstone himself would have found inadequate.
>
> (*New Statesman*, 23 September 1966: 417)

If knowledge was power, then this was redolent of impotence, and, as regards the Civil Service, the eventual triumph of the Treasury over the DEA represented a profound failure to transfer power into the hands of those who sought a radical departure from the traditional Treasury-determined goals of economic policy. This, in turn, meant the supersession of a transformative, long-run economic strategy by the short-run objectives of a fiscal and monetary management.

To have rectified all this would have required a profound revolution not just in the structures but also in the whole ethos of the civil service. Again, the contrast is with France, where the French *étatiste* tradition – the training of the higher echelons of the French bureaucracy and the career mobility between state administration and the private sector – facilitated the effective formulation and pursuit of planning goals. However, leaving aside the immediate political and administrative diseconomies involved in embarking upon such a bureaucratic revolution, even its successful completion would have involved a period of time extending well beyond that envisaged for the National Plan itself. Admittedly, in more propitious economic circumstances the DEA might have gradually eroded the authority of the Treasury, but to assume such circumstances is to assume a solution to the problems that the DEA was created to solve. Or as Middlemas notes, 'As a department planning the economy the DEA could only have had a clear run in a good year like 1962–63; in any other the Chancellor could always argue a higher *raison d'être*' (1990: 121).

Nor was the power of the business community itself challenged – a power that was burgeoning in line with the rapid growth of transnational corporations – because 'This mode of planning did not involve a significant transgression of the market order or business autonomy but sought to enhance the competitive position of British industry' (Shaw, 1996: 74). Of course, the Labour Governments sought to strengthen the Monopolies and Mergers Commission, but its track record was not one to strike fear into the heart of enterprises wielding significant monopoly power. In any case, there existed an ambivalence in Labour's strategy, epitomised by the creation of the Industrial Reorganisation Commission, which sought mergers and amalgamations on the principle that if big was not necessarily beautiful, it was at least more efficient. It was left, therefore, to a later generation of socialists, through their Alternative Economic Strategy, to try to mount a significant challenge to the growing power of transnational companies that, along with other developments, were serving to limit the economic policy autonomy of medium-sized economies like Britain's (for an account of the AES, and its limitations, see Thompson, 2002: 29–69).

Also, in relation to the impotence of Labour in the 1960s, there was the power wielded by the trade union movement. In part this was a consequence of a conjuncture of economic circumstances that favoured greater militancy with respect to pay bargaining. Trade unions operated in a tight labour market for most of the decade, with unemployment often below 2 per cent of the insured working population. Trade union density rose, and the unions increasingly represented a labour force whose expectations and aspirations were conditioned less and less by the experience of inter-war unemployment and more and more by those of an affluent society – a labour force too whose material aspirations were cultivated and ignited by mass advertising. It has also been suggested that in Britain, with 'relatively low productivity growth' and a correspondingly low growth of incomes, 'an aspirations gap started to emerge', efforts to close which again resulted in upward pressure on wage levels (Woodward, 1993: 97). Finally, the demonstration effect of wage explosions on the Continent may have had an impact on the attitudes of British trade unionists (Woodward, 1993: 96). In all these respects the times were not favourable to the implementation of an incomes policy which sought to curb free collective bargaining and transfer substantial power over the determination of wages and salaries to the state. That such a transfer of power was crucial to the delivery of the National Plan in particular, and economic growth in general, there can be little doubt, but except *in extremis*, and in the short run, the trade union movement was unlikely to accede to it.

Furthermore, the structure and, in the late 1960s, the changing leadership of the British trade union movement also militated against the acceptance of an incomes policy as an integral element of planning, as the following chapter will illustrate. Many of the major trade unions witnessed a leftward shift in their leadership, whilst the fragmented structure of the trade union movement as a whole also made difficult the rigorous enforcement of an incomes policy. As to trade union structure, as the contemporary phenomenon of wage drift showed, the capacity of trade unions to control wage increases at a national level was, to say the least, problematic. These problems were compounded by the fact that the TUC was able to exert only limited authority over its constituent trade unions, thereby rendering it unable to play anything more than a short-term role in helping the state control the rate of growth of incomes. In any case, a visceral attachment to the traditional ideal of free collective bargaining meant that the trade union movement tended, for the most part, to regard an incomes policy as an emergency expedient, rather than as something central to the purposive planning of a socialist economy (for the problems of implementing or sustaining incomes policies in post-war Britain, see Dorey, 2001: ch. 9).

As long as the trade union movement retained the power it possessed in the 1960s, the economic strategy pursued by Labour was necessarily circumscribed. And as the 1969 fate of *In Place of Strife* (discussed in Chapter 6 of this volume) made clear, the trade union movement at this juncture had the capacity to prevent its legislative erosion. As soon as it lost this power, was denuded of its militancy and bargained 'freely' and collectively in circumstances that militated strongly against success, as in the 1980s, then the potency of government and its freedom of policy manoeuvre were considerably enhanced. Of course that power was then used not to put in place the planning of incomes as an integral element of a more general economic strategy but to unleash a wholesale attack on the post-war advances that social democracy had made. A powerful trade union movement prevented the implementation of the Fabian economic strategy of Wilsonian political economy; the erosion of its authority put in jeopardy the social democratic legacy.

Conclusion

The 1964–1970 Labour Governments therefore lacked the powers necessary to implement a radical social democratic strategy, and it was a recognition of this that, in large measure, fuelled that ferment of ideas out of which the Alternative Economic Strategy (AES) emerged in the 1970s. For, if it was about anything, the AES was about the rectification of prescriptive impotence. The problem was that the cure proved almost as terminal for Labour as the disease, with the AES playing a significant part in splitting the party, narrowing the basis of its support and projecting it into the political wilderness for almost two decades.

By then, social democracy was clearly impaled upon the horns of a dilemma from which it could not extricate itself. To utilise the exchange controls, import restrictions, changes in the international value of sterling, substantial extension of public ownership and discriminatory use of fiscal and credit policy, which the AES and the left saw as necessary to achieve social democratic objectives, guaranteed the alienation both of the Keynesian social democratic wing of the Labour Party and of that middle-class technocracy which, as consumers and producers, had an interest in a relatively untrammelled capitalism. But not to use them was tantamount to accepting policy impotence.

Further, any serious attempt to acquire the powers necessary to secure control over the rate of growth of incomes threatened the support of an increasingly militant and powerful trade union movement. Not to do so was to risk a growth strategy degenerating into an inflationary spiral. Admittedly, the AES did offer a sweetener to wage-claim continence in the form of increased trade union participation in decision-making at both a macroeconomic and an enterprise level. But by eroding management prerogatives, this also threatened to jeopardise the interests of at least part of the middle-class salariat, and also exacerbate left–right tensions within the Labour Party.

Moreover, even if such powers had been acquired and deployed without the political diseconomies mentioned, and leaving aside the matter of their likely efficacy, there is still the question as to whether they would have proved sufficient to give a British Labour government the freedom of manoeuvre it required in an increasingly interdependent global economy – one characterised by the growing volume and speed of short-term capital movements, increasing exchange rate volatility, and a marked and rapid build-up of inflationary pressures, courtesy of a United States payments deficit that was treated with what could only be termed benign neglect.

Though not deemed so at the time, and while not subsequently acknowledged, it would therefore seem that Wilsonian Fabianism was the last desperate throw of the dice to furnish the Labour Party with a political economy that was manifestly social democratic, that united left and right within the party, that broadened its social constituency and that was in harmony with the neophilia of an age of rapid change and increasing affluence. In that regard, its demise signalled the effective end of the social democratic project. The Wilson and Callaghan Governments of the 1970s advanced (or, as some would have it, retreated) on the basis of an improbable fusion of Keynesian social democracy, an intermittent predilection for monetarism and an increasingly potent Alternative Economic Strategy leftism – a volatile concoction always likely to blow apart both itself and the party. After 1981, the putative unity on the AES terrain of *The New Hope for Britain* proved to be the unity of the 1983 graveyard, and the consequent attempt to revamp Keynesian social democracy under Kinnock convinced neither the party nor, more importantly, the electorate either in 1987 or in 1992. It was, then, only with the abandonment of the social democratic project and the unqualified embrace of neo-liberalism that the party secured the measure of unity and the extension of electoral support which returned it to power in 1997.

Historians will therefore come to view the years 1961–1966 as almost the last occasion, at least in Britain, when the social democratic project found expression in terms of a viable electoral politics, a practical economic strategy and a discourse which struck a chord with contemporary aspirations. What followed with the AES was sound and fury signifying nothing, before the project finally imploded, in the 1990s, not with a bang but with a post-Thatcherite whimper.

5 From a 'policy for incomes' to incomes policies

Peter Dorey

Introduction

For several years after its 1951 election defeat, the Labour Party gave little thought to the issue of incomes policy. This largely reflected the chastening experience of pursuing a wage freeze from 1948 to 1950, and the consequent realisation of just how strongly the trade unions were committed to free collective bargaining, and their concomitant antipathy to State intervention in wage determination (see, for example, Labour Party, 1952: 136). Consequently, only a few on the left were willing to point out that free collective bargaining was likely to prove inflationary in a period of full employment, as well as inimical to Labour's professed egalitarianism, owing to the manner in which workers with stronger bargaining power could secure wage increases which maintained, or even increased, socio-economic inequalities (Bevan, 1961: 138–9; Wootton, 1954: 175).

Only towards the end of the 1950s could one discern a few other senior Labour politicians beginning to consider how the party would address the issue of incomes when next in office. In 1957, Labour's Shadow Chancellor (and future leader), Harold Wilson, argued that as 'wages are at the centre of the cost-push spiral', the Labour Party needed to contemplate 'the conditions in which wage restraint could once again become a reality', for 'the battle against inflation would depend upon its [a Labour Government's] ability to secure an understanding with the unions which would make wage restraint possible' (Wilson, 1957: 66). Sensitive to the trade unions' antipathy to incomes policy, however, the following year heard the Labour Party insist that 'whilst some measure of restraint on demands for higher incomes will be needed . . . no kind of wage freeze is envisaged' (Labour Party, 1958: 37).

Instead, up until the 1964 election, Labour pronouncements on the issue of wages were couched in terms of a 'planned growth of incomes', so that the objective of any incomes policy was *not* 'to keep increases down to a minimum, but [to allow increases] up to the maximum possible', which would ensure that 'incomes policy is not wage restraint. It should allow *real* wages to rise' (Labour Party Archives, RD.433/March 1963). Of course, as far as many trade unions were concerned, the best way to ensure that wages could rise to 'the maximum possible' was to eschew incomes policy entirely, and robustly defend free collective bargaining.

During the first half of the 1960s, therefore, the Labour Party sought to square this particular circle by persuading the trade unions that a 'policy for incomes' was explicitly linked to the objective of economic expansion, rather than being an instrument of deflation. This would ensure that a 'planned growth of wages' was inextricably linked to the maintenance of full employment, continued economic expansion, greater prosperity, and the eradication of remaining pockets of poverty (Balogh, 1963: 14–15). By 1962, the Labour leader, Hugh Gaitskell, was envisaging an incomes policy which would enshrine five main principles: it should contribute to economic expansion; facilitate increased productivity; apply to all forms of income, not just wages; be applied fairly to all sections of British society; and be secured on the basis of voluntary agreement between the 'two sides' of industry (House of Commons Debates, 5th series, vol. 663, col. 1742).

These objectives were also enunciated by James Callaghan – who had replaced Wilson as Shadow Chancellor in 1961 – to Labour's 1962 annual conference, when he explained that 'what we have to do – and this is a gigantic essay in persuasion and co-operation – is to secure the assent of the whole nation to the idea of an incomes policy', albeit one which 'is fair and ... will be equally applied' (Labour Party, 1962: 219). In fact, Callaghan's appointment inadvertently served to underpin the Labour Party's shift back towards an incomes policy – or 'planned growth of incomes', as many diplomatically referred to it, in order to avoid antagonising the trade unions. By his own admission, Callaghan was no economist – his appointment having been due largely to his political stature (Morgan, 1997: 169) – so he immediately began appointing a number of economic advisers. Amongst the team he assembled were a number of Oxbridge academics who had also previously worked in either the Treasury or the economic section of the Cabinet Office.

Having been duly appointed to offer economic advice to Callaghan, one of the first issues to which they turned their attention, during the spring of 1962, was that of incomes policy, often closely linked to Labour's heightened emphasis on economic planning. One of them, Thomas Balogh (who later became Harold Wilson's chief economic adviser), was particularly enthusiastic about developing 'a policy for incomes', believing that some 'general co-ordination of collective bargaining is indispensable if unemployment ... is to be eliminated and expansion accelerated'. Although Balogh acknowledged that 'it would be hopeless for a Central Board or Court to try to fix wages', he did contemplate the creation of a Council of Economic Advisers, which could comment on the extent to which any particular pay award was 'compatible with continued stability of prices and/or the balance of payments' (1963: 14–15).

Meanwhile, at Labour's 1963 annual conference a motion on economic planning presented by the General and Municipal Workers Union, urging the party leadership to devise, in partnership with the trade unions, an incomes policy 'to include salaries, wages, dividends and profits' in order 'to promote sustained economic growth', was endorsed by 6,090,000 votes to 40,000, and supported by all trade unions affiliated to the Labour Party. A few months later, Harold Wilson himself referred to this endorsement twice in one week, in speeches which reiterated Labour's commitment to 'a policy of planned growth of incomes', whereby '*all* incomes, not just wages', along with prices too, would be linked to increases in production. Wilson insisted that whereas the Conservatives invoked incomes policies as part of a deflationary economic package, for the Labour Party 'an incomes policy is the condition of sustained growth, and because a pledge of sustained growth is a condition of that policy'. Furthermore, Wilson (1964a) emphasised that a Labour incomes policy would also be inextricably linked to the party's historic pursuit of social justice.

When Labour won the 1964 election, it appeared to have devised not only an incomes policy which the party itself was satisfied with, but, crucially, one which the trade unions were amenable to, linked as it was to economic expansion, rather than deflation. Indeed, as one 'insider' noted,

> there is no doubt that there was a tacit agreement, or appeared to be one, between certain sections of the Trade Union movement and Labour leaders about the need for certain action – if not an incomes policy, then certainly a declaration of intent which would be meaningful in real terms.
>
> (Williams, 1972: 359)

The Labour Party's 1964 manifesto proclaimed the objective of securing 'a planned growth of incomes broadly related to the annual rate of production' which would be applicable 'in an expanding economy to all incomes: to profits, dividends and rents as well as wages and salaries', but which would 'not be unfairly directed at lower paid workers and public employees' (Craig, 1975: 282).

A joint statement of intent

Within weeks of its October 1964 election victory, though, the Labour Government was actually seeking trade union agreement to a period of wage restraint, owing to the economic situation which Ministers encountered upon entering office. Indeed, at the Cabinet's very first meeting, George Brown (having been appointed First Secretary at the newly created Department of Economic Affairs) explained that 'the economic situation was serious. It appeared to have been deteriorating for some time, and there was a prospect of a large and continuing deficit on the balance of payments' (PRO CAB 128/39, 1st Conclusions, 19 October 1964). Certainly, upon entering office, Ministers had faced considerable pressure from 'the City' to take firm action against an overheating economy and a deteriorating balance of payments position (more particularly with regard to visible earnings), and in this context there was a widespread expectation that the newly elected Labour Government would opt for devaluation.

This was certainly the option being recommended to the Chancellor of the Exchequer, James Callaghan, by two of his economic advisers, Nicholas Kaldor and Robert Neild, but Callaghan and most of his Cabinet colleagues were averse to such a course of action at this stage, partly because of concern that Labour would acquire a reputation amongst the financial community as *the* party of devaluation (owing to the fact that Attlee's Labour Government had devalued in 1949), but also because of concern that by making imports more expensive, devaluation would almost inevitably prompt a drive by trade unions for compensatory wage increases. A further factor militating against the devolution option was an agreement secretly entered into by senior Labour politicians prior to the election, whereby the New York Federal Reserve Bank would provide US support for sterling if economic circumstances were serious enough, thereby obviating the need for devaluation. In fact, this agreement was so secret that most of the new Labour Cabinet were not aware of it (Short, 1989: 37).

Instead, therefore, a *Joint Statement of Intent on Productivity, Prices and Incomes* (hereafter *Joint Statement of Intent*) was published in December 1964, which emphasised the importance of ensuring that 'increases in wages, salaries and other forms of incomes' were in accordance with increases in efficiency and productivity. To this end, the *Joint Statement of Intent* – which was the product of an agreement between Labour Ministers, senior trade union officials, and representatives of Britain's then largest employers' organisations, namely the Federation of British Industries, the British Employers' Federation and the National Association of British Manufacturers (all three of which amalgamated the following year to form the Confederation of British Industry) – heralded institutional machinery 'to keep under review the general movement of prices and of money of all kinds' and 'to examine particular cases in order to advise whether or not the behaviour of prices or of wages, salaries or other money incomes is in the national interest as defined by the Government after consultation with management and unions' (Department of Economic Affairs, 1964).

The body charged with responsibility for undertaking these reviews and examinations was the National Board of Prices and Incomes (NBPI), which was launched in April 1965, although it lacked statutory powers to enforce its reports and recommendations, and was therefore dependent on the voluntary acquiescence and goodwill of management and trade unions. Nor was it empowered to follow up its recommendations to see whether they had been adhered to. Not surprisingly, perhaps, the NBPI had very little impact on the rate at which prices and incomes increased during this period (Fels, 1972: 38–9).

Another institutional innovation invoked by the first Wilson Government was the aforementioned Department of Economic Affairs (DEA), which Wilson established immediately upon entering office in 1964. Harold Wilson envisaged that the DEA would complement the work of the Treasury, and be 'at least as powerful', for whilst the Treasury would retain responsibility for macroeconomic policy and public expenditure, the DEA was to be responsible for economic and industrial planning, boosting British exports, 'increasing productivity, and our competitiveness in domestic and export markets' (Wilson, 1971: 3). However, upon being appointed First Secretary at the DEA, George Brown immediately added prices and incomes to the new department's remit.

A voluntary incomes policy

Although the Labour Government had been elected with a commitment for a 'planned growth of wages', followed by the *Joint Declaration of Intent*, much of early 1965 entailed Brown seeking to persuade the trade unions of the need for voluntary pay restraint, whereby wages and salaries would not increase by more than 3–3.5 per cent per year. The TUC's General Council consented to this proposal, as did delegates attending a specially convened TUC conference in April 1965 (where the TUC's General Secretary, George Woodcock, warned that without such an agreement, the Labour Government would either have to impose a statutory incomes policy or abandon the commitment to full employment) by a vote of 4.8 million votes to 1.8 million, but only in return for a corresponding agreement by Brown that the 3–3.5 per cent 'norm' could be exceeded in certain instances, most notably when there were significant increases in productivity, or in cases of especially low pay. It was also noteworthy that most of the votes cast against this voluntary incomes policy emanated from the Transport and General Workers' Union (TGWU), which had been led by Frank Cousins until his election as a Labour MP in 1964, whereupon he was immediately appointed Secretary of State for Technology. Cousins himself was vehemently opposed to incomes policies based on wage restraint, which ensured that his period as a Cabinet Minister was an increasingly unhappy one, to the extent that he resigned within two years.

Besides that of the TGWU, the other opposition to this voluntary incomes policy came largely from those trade unions whose members were in craft trades or were skilled workers, these being the kinds of employees whose market position enabled them to benefit most from free collective bargaining. This 'labour aristocracy' therefore proved particularly resentful towards incomes policies intended to secure pay restraint, especially when these also entailed an erosion of their 'differentials' vis-à-vis lower-paid workers. Clearly, there were limits to the comradeship and solidarity of the British proletariat in such circumstances.

So why did other trade unions acquiesce in the request for voluntary pay restraint in 1965? Partly, this was due to the exceptions and exemptions which would be permitted for 'increased productivity' – perhaps offering

plenty of scope for creative use of statistics by seasoned trade union negotiators – but it also derived from the trade unions' belief that the Labour
Government really would achieve faster economic growth, and thus a real
increase in wages and salaries, once it had overcome the current economic
difficulties. Neither for the first time nor the last, the trade unions were persuaded that the introduction of a voluntary incomes policy was to be a temporary measure only, and that once the immediate economic problems had
been resolved, there would be a return to free collective bargaining. On this
understanding, most of them acquiesced.

However, this acquiescence also partly reflected the trade unions' relief at
having a Labour Government in office again after thirteen unbroken years of
Conservative rule, which meant that Ministers were, initially at least, able to
draw upon a stock of political goodwill. Moreover, the trade unions fully
recognised that the narrowness of Labour's parliamentary majority in
October 1964 made it inevitable that another general election would be
called sooner rather than later, and this further informed their willingness to
acquiesce in the Government's call for voluntary pay restraint: a more militant and conflictual stance would almost certainly have increased the likelihood of the Conservatives being swiftly returned to power within a year or
two.

It was to become apparent during the next five years, however, that
whilst the linking of pay increases to productivity imbued incomes policies
with greater flexibility, as well as linking them to the Government's own
determination to improve productivity levels in Britain, it also meant that
claims of 'increased productivity' became a common trade union means of
securing pay increases in excess of specified 'norms', irrespective of whether
productivity had really increased to the extent claimed.

Even by the summer of 1965, Ministers were becoming increasingly concerned about the viability of the recently agreed 3–3.5 per cent pay norm,
reflecting growing doubts about the compatibility between free collective
bargaining and voluntary wage restraint. Faced with low economic growth,
and continued balance of payments deficits (£272 million in 1965, for
example), and under increasing pressure from 'the City' and overseas holders
of sterling, July 1965 heard the Chancellor announce cuts in public expenditure, and a postponements of various planned increases in the 'social wage'.
Yet these measures alone did little to allay the anxieties of the business
community, either at home or abroad. Indeed, having previously agreed to
lend its support to sterling, the United States Federal Reserve was also
expressing growing concern about Britain's economic problems and the
Labour Government's apparently inadequate response to them. Such was this
concern that the American Secretary of the Treasury, Henry Fowler,

> doubted whether the voluntary prices and incomes policy which George
> Brown had negotiated would be able to withstand the pressure for wage
> increases to which we were subject. While he did not attempt in any

way to make terms or give us orders, he was apprehensive that if further central bank aid were required, it would be difficult to mount if we had no better safeguard against inflation than the voluntary system. It was in these circumstances that we began first to think in terms of statutory powers.

(Wilson, 1971: 131–2; see also Callaghan, 1987: 189)

At the end of August, Harold Wilson and George Brown cut short their respective holidays and returned to London to meet James Callaghan in order to formulate a stronger policy on prices and incomes. By this time, Wilson himself had concluded that 'the voluntary procedures, resting on the *Joint Declaration of Intent*, were proving inadequate' (Wilson, 1971: 132). Callaghan too was becoming convinced of the need for a stronger incomes policy, for having visited his US counterpart, Joe Fowler, during the summer and been asked 'about the prospects for our voluntary policies', Callaghan 'found [it] increasingly difficult to answer' (Callaghan, 1987: 189). The urgency was not merely due to the economic situation and the anxieties of Callaghan's US counterpart (vitally important though these factors were), but also because the TUC's annual conference was being held at the beginning of September, and Ministers wanted to present any revised policy to the TUC to secure formal trade union endorsement.

A meeting of the full Cabinet on 1 September – attendance at which necessitated various other Ministers terminating their summer holidays – secured ministerial approval for an 'early warning system' whereby trade unions would be required to notify the DEA of imminent pay claims (whilst employers would be obliged to notify the DEA of proposed price increases). The DEA could then, if it wished, refer the proposed increase to the NBPI. The NBPI would henceforth be imbued with statutory powers enabling it to obtain further information from trade unions or employers in connection with proposed pay or price increases, whilst the Secretary of State for Economic Affairs would, in turn, be empowered to enforce any recommendations enshrined in the NBPI's report. Whilst the NBPI was investigating a proposed pay claim, the trade union(s) concerned would not be permitted to pursue industrial action in connection with it.

Although most Ministers endorsed this new policy – Callaghan had actually wanted a temporary wage freeze, but this was strongly opposed by George Brown, so that the 'early warning system' represented something of a compromise – there was hostility from Frank Cousins, who 'exploded with indignation at the proposal to turn a voluntary incomes policy, which he had always distrusted and disapproved of, into a legally controlled policy, which he utterly rejected' (Goodman, 1979: 465). Brown, though, was emphatic that this revised policy was being introduced 'on the strict understanding that this is *not* the first step to statutory wage control', an assertion fully endorsed by Wilson himself (Castle, 1990: 32, diary entry for 1 September 1965). Certainly many Ministers acknowledged that 'there could be no question of seeking to impose a statutory control on wages, since it would be unacceptable in principle and unenforceable in practice' (PRO CAB 128/39, 46th Conclusions, 1 September 1965).

It then took Brown several meetings spanning twelve hours (the final one not ending until after midnight, just hours before the start of the TUC's annual conference) to persuade the General Council of the TUC to accept the 'early warning system' policy, although to do so he was obliged to offer the concession that the proposed statutory powers 'could only be activated by a specific Order in Council requiring the consent of both Houses [of Parliament]' (Wilson, 1971: 133). In return, the TUC's General Council would establish its own vetting procedure via an 'incomes policy committee', to which affiliated trade unions would be expected to submit proposed pay claims. This committee would then consider the veracity of these pay claims, although it would not be empowered to impose any decisions on the trade union(s) concerned. These proposals were then endorsed by delegates at the annual conference – by 5.2 million votes to 3.3 million – after George Woodcock again warned trade unionists that the alternatives would be either 'a movement towards greater direction of the unions . . . or the state says the whole thing is unworkable and gives up the job of maintaining full employment' (TUC, 1965: 472).

The TUC's incomes policy committee was to prove ineffective, though, to the extent that it was subsequently described as a 'complete failure', for although it considered more than 600 pay claims during its first nine months, 'it questioned only a handful, and had no real effect on any of them'. This was, perhaps, unsurprising, given that it met on a monthly basis and thus sometimes dealt with up to fifty claims in one hour (Dorfman, 1973: 138; see also Lovell and Roberts, 1968: 172–3).

Meanwhile, this particular incomes policy, with statutory powers now held in reserve, placed Frank Cousins in a singularly uncomfortable situation, for having been a clear and consistent opponent of incomes policies during his time as leader of the TGWU, he was now obliged, by virtue of the doctrine of collective (ministerial) responsibility, publicly to support it – or at least avoid criticising it in public. Indeed, Cousins was to complain that 'I myself disagree with it so utterly that I can no longer make a political speech. I can only speak on technological problems . . . I think it's time I resigned' (Crossman, 1975: 321, diary entry for 12 September 1965). On this occasion, he did not tender his resignation, but it was to be only a matter of time before he finally did so – a case not of whether, but of when.

Countering criticism of this incomes policy, George Brown offered a three-pronged defence of the Government's approach when he spoke at the TUC's 1965 annual conference. First, he argued that the incomes policy was entirely consistent with the Government's general approach to a planned economy, as enshrined in the National Plan. Second, Brown sought to link incomes policy to socialism, on the grounds that the alternative to such a policy was recourse to free collective bargaining, a method of pay determination which 'puts a premium on those ... with great bargaining power'. In condemning this, he claimed that 'We have been operating the law of the jungle ourselves while condemning it for every other purpose.' Brown's third defence of the Government's reversion to incomes policy was to insist that 'We have no intention of supplanting the voluntary system by government action if the former works' (TUC, 1965: 134).

It was this caveat, 'if the present system works', which put some trade unions on their guard against the Labour Government's recourse to incomes policy, for the clear implication was that if it did not prove successful, more stringent, statutory pay controls were likely to follow. To those trade unions most committed to free collective bargaining, this was provocative indeed. Indeed, Brown's peroration was lent added piquancy by the fact that Frank Cousins was sitting alongside the TGWU's delegation 'seething and burning like a volcano about to erupt ... unsmiling, staring into the middle distance with [a] look of stony resolution'. At the same time, George Brown 'glowered down at his Cabinet colleagues and the entire delegation of the country's largest union: Brown's own union' (Goodman, 1979: 468).

The 1966 wage freeze

Within weeks of being re-elected with a substantially increased parliamentary majority in March 1966, the Labour Government was faced with a national strike called by the National Union of Seamen (NUS). The strike was called in support of a pay claim which significantly exceeded the Government's 'norm', not merely by virtue of the cash increase sought, but also because the NUS was seeking a reduction in the normal working week from fifty-six hours to forty, which effectively meant that whilst on ship, seamen would automatically become eligible for sixteen hours' overtime pay per week. Wilson and his ministerial colleagues considered it vital to resist the NUS's claim, not merely because it far exceeded the 'pay norm', but also because the Cabinet needed to assuage the anxieties of industrialists and financiers, many of whom were even more apprehensive now that Labour's increased parliamentary majority meant that it was likely to govern for a full term, and might also be emboldened to pursue more radical or socialist policies. Wilson therefore alleged that the strike was being fomented by 'a tightly knit group of politically motivated men' in furtherance of 'what is at present the main political and industrial objective of the Communist Party – the destruction of the Government's prices and incomes policy' (House of Commons Debates, 5th series, vol. 730, cols 1612–17).

Even though the seamen's strike was called off within twenty-four hours of Wilson's speech, sterling remained under considerable pressure in the currency markets, and there was a growing expectation in international circles that devaluation was imminent. In an attempt at avoiding devaluation (even though a number of Ministers were now in favour of it, or fatalistically resigned to it), Wilson and Callaghan (backed by the recently appointed Governor of the Bank of England, the IMF and the OECD) secured sufficient Cabinet support for a further tranche of deflationary measures, including more cuts in public expenditure, stricter controls on hire purchase, and higher indirect taxes and postal charges.

There was also to be an immediate six-month 'freeze' on all incomes (but not profits), this to be followed by a further six months of 'severe restraint' entailing a 'zero norm', whereby pay increases would be justified only in cases of improved – and proven – productivity, or in particular cases of low pay. These proposals inevitably incurred the wrath of trade unions and left-wing Labour MPs, but what made them even more controversial was the fact that the 'pay freeze' was to be statutory, enforced by legislation. Indeed, the Labour Government's attempts at securing wage restraint through increasingly stringent incomes policies (the 'planned growth of incomes' by now a distant memory) had already precipitated the ministerial resignation of Frank Cousins, who returned to his previous post as leader of the TGWU (not only Britain's largest trade union at the time, but also a consistent opponent of incomes policies designed to secure 'wage restraint') whilst also remaining a Labour MP, opposing the latest incomes policy from the back benches. When, upon resigning from the Cabinet, Cousins had his final audience with the Queen, and was asked the real reason for his resignation, he replied, 'Because the Government no longer believes in the policies for which they were elected, Ma'am' (quoted in Goodman, 1979: 500).

Having thus returned to the back benches, Cousins immediately tabled a Commons motion, signed by six other TGWU-sponsored Labour MPs, denouncing the recourse to a statutory incomes policy and calling instead for the Government to exercise stricter controls over prices and imports, as well as over the movement of capital, whilst also extending public ownership (House of Commons Debates, 5th series, vol. 731, col. 1792). Meanwhile, Jack Jones, who had been the TGWU's Acting General Secretary during Cousins's time in the Cabinet, complained that the imposition of a statutory incomes policy would 'further tilt the balance in favour of . . . employers and further worsen industrial relations'. Jones alleged that those responsible for the legislation 'are out of touch with day-to-day industrial life and are unfitted to solve its problems' (1986: 178). The TGWU was by no means alone in opposing the imposition of a wage freeze backed by legislation, for at the TUC's 1966 annual conference in September, the Government's new incomes policy was offered 'reluctant acquiescence' by a very narrow margin of 4,567,000 votes to 4,223,000, a result described by Cousins's biographer as 'a moral defeat for the Government' (Goodman, 1979: 518).

Beyond the 'wage freeze' and 'severe restraint'

By this time, the Cabinet itself was becoming increasingly divided over the future of incomes policies, with marked differences of opinion emerging over what should succeed the period of 'severe restraint' when it ended on 30

June 1967. Some Ministers believed that any subsequent incomes policy would need to be backed or enforced by statutory means, for trade unions had already proved unable or unwilling to adhere to a voluntary wages policy which relied upon their own self-restraint. Indeed, Michael Stewart, who was George Brown's successor at the DEA, favoured a permanent incomes policy backed by statutory powers which would be subject to annual renewal by Parliament. Stewart further suggested that future pay increases should be dependent on certain criteria being met, such as increased productivity, labour shortages or low pay, although he did acknowledge that 'an incomes policy should be part of a more general plan to make the distribution of wealth more just'. Nonetheless, by recommending that pay increases should only be permitted on the basis of specified criteria, Stewart was effectively challenging the notion of a routine pay increase for working people every twelve months, for the 'underlying principle should be that no-one was entitled automatically to an annual increase of money incomes' (Stewart, 1980: 194). Also believing that the Government needed to hold 'reserve powers . . . in order to deter selfish minorities who otherwise would use their more than average bargaining position to snatch sectional advantages against a patriotic majority' was Wilson's economic adviser, Thomas Balogh, who was adamant that 'full employment without an incomes policy is impossible' (PRO PREM 13/1875, Balogh to Wilson, 28 February 1967).

Richard Crossman suggested that those Labour Ministers most inclined towards a statutory incomes policy tended to be the Party's 'middle class intellectuals' such as Barbara Castle, Tony Crosland, Crossman himself, and Patrick Gordon Walker. By contrast, he observed that the Ministers most opposed to statutory incomes policies were those with working-class, trade union backgrounds or links (Crossman, 1976: 230, diary entry for 9 February 1967). Amongst this latter category were George Brown, Ray Gunter – described by Crossman as 'a traitor within the walls . . . a kind of TUC agent' (1976: 252, diary entry for 23 February 1967) – Richard Marsh and Fred Peart. It was these Ministers who were most mindful of the voluntarist tradition in British industrial relations, and of the trade unions' commitment to free collective bargaining.

Also opposed to the continuation of statutory incomes policy, but not having working-class origins or notably close trade union links, was Tony Benn (then known as Anthony Wedgwood Benn), who argued that no legislative form of wage control 'could possibly be practicable or effective', and suggested instead that the Cabinet ought to concentrate instead on measures to regulate prices. According to Benn, 'if a firm can give wage increases that don't involve any price increases, there is no reason why the Government should interest itself in that settlement' (PRO PREM 13/1473, Benn to Wilson, 3 February 1967).

Whilst these debates were being conducted, during early 1967, senior Ministers were also holding meetings with the TUC's economic committee in an attempt at securing trade union agreement for an incomes policy to follow the period of 'severe restraint'. Not surprisingly, senior TUC representatives, such as Frank Cousins and George Woodcock, made clear their opposition to any further wage restraint entailing statutory measures, with Woodcock in particular insisting that any subsequent incomes policy would only be effective if the TUC itself was permitted to administer it (PRO PREM 13/1875, 'Meetings between TUC Economic Committee and Ministers', 28 February and 15 March 1967).

Both 'sides' in the ministerial debate over incomes policy sought to justify their perspective on the grounds of a realistic understanding of the character of British industrial relations and contemporary trade unionism. Proponents of a voluntary incomes policy argued that statutory intervention in wage determination was incompatible with the *voluntarist* tradition of trade unions, and their commitment to free collective bargaining. Hence, only an incomes policy based on voluntary agreement between trade union leaders and Ministers would have any reasonable chance of success in the battle against inflation.

By contrast, ministerial advocates of a statutory incomes policy were adamant that it was the voluntarist tradition of British trade unions which rendered a voluntary incomes policy inadequate, for the trade unions would not adhere to it: any incomes policy which was not enforceable via legislation would be ignored or undermined by the trade unions. This meant that a statutory incomes policy was essential – however regrettable – because anything less would invariably prove ineffective, as illustrated by the experience of previous voluntary incomes policies.

Not surprisingly, perhaps, Harold Wilson was sometimes deeply frustrated by the trade unions' stance, to the point of suggesting, on one occasion, that if they would not accept an incomes policy backed by statutory powers, then the Government should respond by reducing public expenditure ('If they take too much in real wages, we shall have to cut their schools, their hospitals, and housing'), whilst a week later an exasperated Wilson half-heartedly mooted the idea of a 'divorce' between the Labour Party and the trade unions (Crossman, 1976: 280, 287, diary entries for 16 March and 22 March 1967).

When, in the spring of 1967, the Government did announce its incomes policy to succeed the period of 'severe restraint', it became clear that a 'zero norm' was to be retained, with Ministers declining to specify any other percentage figure for the maximum permissible pay increases. This reluctance was partly because of the seriousness of the economic situation, but also because they realised that the trade unions would inevitably view any such figure as an automatic entitlement or target. Instead, any pay increases would have to be justified in accordance with specified criteria, similar to those invoked in 1965, most notably increased productivity and the eradicating of low pay (although, perhaps unsurprisingly, no definition was offered as to what constituted low pay, and which groups of workers would thus be entitled to claim pay increases in accordance with this criteria). Furthermore, the Government would reserve the right to delay a pay increase for up to one month, during which time Ministers could consider its merits and implications. If they remained unconvinced that the pay claim was warranted, Ministers could then refer it to the NBPI, which might entail a further delay, this time of three months. Finally, the NBPI could itself impose a further three-month delay if it too remained unpersuaded of the veracity or viability of the pay claim. In other words, workers were not to assume that they would automatically be entitled to an annual pay increase, whilst pay claims adjudged to be excessive or unwarranted could be delayed for up to seven months altogether (Department of Economic Affairs, 1967).

Devaluation and the perpetuation of incomes policy

Having pursued deflation and incomes policies in order to stave off devaluation for three years, the Labour Government was finally forced to relent in November 1967, when sterling was devalued by 14.3 per cent, thereby reducing its value against the dollar from $2.80 to $2.40. However, Ministers were quick to warn the trade unions that devaluation would not presage any relaxation in their determination to secure wage restraint, in spite of the fact that devaluation was likely to yield price increases of up to 3 per cent. On the contrary, if the economic benefits of devaluation were to be realised, primarily in the form of cheaper imports and an improved balance of payments position, then it was deemed even more important to prevent 'excessive' pay increases and restrain domestic demand, for these would almost inevitably lead to further imports, and thus a further series of poor trade figures. Thus was wage restraint transformed from a means of avoiding devaluation to a means of buttressing devaluation.

Consequently, the March 1968 Budget announced a 3.5 per cent pay limit, this to last until the end of 1969, with any increases to be justified only in accordance with the four criteria originally delineated in the 1965 White Paper (i.e. significantly improved productivity; labour mobility and re-allocation; eradicating low pay; and erosion of comparability vis-à-vis workers performing similar tasks). Furthermore, this new incomes policy was to entail the Government increasing from seven to twelve months the maximum period of deferral for a pay (or price) increase deemed excessive or unwarranted.

The legislation giving effect to this latest incomes policy again attracted considerable opposition from particular sections of the Labour Party, most notably from the left, and also from Labour MPs sponsored by trade unions (see, for example, PRO PREM 13/2289, letter to Harold Wilson, 26 March 1968, signed by 23 Labour MPs, including Frank Allaun, Norman Atkinson, Michael Foot, Eric Heffer, Hugh Jenkins, Ian Mikardo and Stan Orme). Such MPs were irked that working people were being blamed – and thus compelled to make economic sacrifices – by a Labour Government for the problems of British capitalism, particularly as there was no corresponding attempt at controlling the wider economy. Instead, workers were effectively being told that it was their wages which were causing the country's economic problems, and that they and their families should therefore endure further hardship in order to restore employers' profitability and Britain's competitiveness (see, for example, Ian Mikardo, House of Commons Debates, 5th series, vol. 765, col. 377; vol. 767, cols 544–5; Mikardo, 1988: 176; Stan Orme, House of Commons Debates, 5th series, vol. 765, cols 354–63). Moreover, Mikardo argued, the Government's prices and incomes policy

> wasn't in fact a policy for prices and incomes – it was merely a policy for restricting increases in wages at the lower end of the scale. It was completely out of balance. . . . Unearned incomes, even the largest, were untouched by any semblance of restriction, and in earned incomes, there was no restriction on professional earnings or managerial salaries: it was only the workers on the shop-floor and in the offices, that is those in the lowest wage brackets, who were to suffer limitations on increases in their pay packets.
>
> (Mikardo, 1988: 176)

Consequently, the 1968 Prices and Incomes Bill (giving statutory effect to this latest incomes policy) prompted several 'rebellions' by Labour backbenchers, who either voted against the bill as a whole (on grounds of opposition to the policy in principle) or against specific clauses, or tabled 'hostile' amendments of their own which they knew Ministers themselves would oppose. On one occasion, for example, the Government's majority fell to 18, when Trevor Park, a TGWU-sponsored Labour MP, tabled an amendment to delete the Government's penal powers over pay (but not price) increases, for this was supported by 23 Labour MPs, whilst at least 20 abstained (*The Times*, 26 June 1968; *Financial Times*, 27 June 1968). Of these 23 Labour MPs, 'almost all . . . were Tribune Group members' (Panitch, 1976: 158), thereby providing an indication of the extent to which hostility to the Labour Government's statutory incomes policies was strongest on the left of the party.

In many respects, though, Ministers should not have been too surprised at the scale of hostility on the back benches, for a meeting of the Parliamentary Labour Party on 8 May 1968 had heard widespread criticisms of the Cabinet's reliance on statutory incomes policies. At the meeting, Roy Hughes explained how trade union-sponsored Labour MPs were experiencing divided loyalties, and this was having a deeply damaging effect not only on morale, but on relations between the Labour Party and the trade unions as a whole. Following on from this, Norman Atkinson expressed concern that through its determination to secure wage restraint via statutory incomes policies, the Labour Government appeared to be 'siding' with employers rather than workers. Manny Shinwell, meanwhile, declared that if he were forced to choose between saving the Labour Government *or* the Labour Party, he would choose the latter. Similar complaints and criticisms were articulated when the Parliamentary Labour Party (PLP) met again the following week, and on this occasion, 42 Labour MPs voted *against* a motion declaring support for the Government's statutory prices and incomes legislation (Labour Party Archives, Meetings of the PLP, 8 and 15 May 1968).

Prior to the introduction of this latest incomes policy, there had been a marked disagreement within the Cabinet committee on incomes policy concerning a proposal from Roy Jenkins and Peter Shore that pay increases ought to be monitored at local level, for this was where the problem of 'wage drift' emanated. Jenkins especially was adamant that such micro-monitoring was vital in order to assuage the anxieties of the international financial community and holders of sterling, and thus to prevent the possible need for further devaluation before the summer. Many other senior Ministers, though, most notably Barbara Castle, George Brown, James Callaghan and Richard Crossman, were aghast at the idea, convinced that it would be neither practicable, nor acceptable to the trade unions. Indeed, when discussion continued in the full Cabinet at the beginning of March 1968, Peter Shore apparently 'collapsed' in the face of rigorous questioning by ministerial opponents of the proposal (Crossman, 1976: 695, diary entry for 7 March 1968), with Barbara Castle observing that 'Peter just doesn't seem to have taken in the impossibility for the Government itself, through a mass of civil servants, to vet thousands of wage increases at plant [factory or workplace] level' (Castle, 1990: 195, diary entry for 7 March 1968).

Peter Shore also found himself at odds with his ministerial colleagues over the duration of the Government's next incomes policy, when he suggested that it ought to operate until October 1970. Wilson pointed out that this might well be about the time of the next general election, in which case Ministers either would find themselves attempting to devise a new incomes policy at a politically sensitive time, or might be abandoning incomes policy altogether. If the second, the Conservatives would accuse the Government of cowardice, opportunism, or appeasement of the trade unions. Wilson therefore secured Cabinet support for an eighteen-month period, this being announced shortly afterwards in the Budget, which would mean that the 3.5 per cent incomes policy would be operational until the autumn of 1969.

Ministers recognised, however, that whilst the latest incomes policy continued to stipulate low pay as a criteria for a pay increase (thereby enabling the Labour Government to proclaim its unyielding commitment to tackling poverty), other workers might seek to exploit such a loophole merely in order to maintain their differentials vis-à-vis low(er)-paid employees. To obviate this problem, therefore, Peter Shore suggested, this time to widespread Cabinet approval, that the 3.5 per cent limit be accompanied by improvements to the social wage, especially family allowances.

Ministers also agreed to consider the introduction of a national minimum wage, although such was the potential political sensitivity of such an innovation that the Cabinet acknowledged 'that there should be no public reference to it', nor any discussion of it with the trade unions (PRO CAB 128/43, 22nd Conclusions, 18 March 1968; 23rd Conclusions, 21 March 1968; see also Labour Party Archives, Re.418/February 1969). In fact, a national minimum wage had already been considered elsewhere in the Labour Party the previous year, before being abandoned owing to the host of problems which it was thought likely to engender, such as the actual figure at which it should be set; the annual rate of increase thereafter; the likely inflationary impact; and the negative response of workers whose pay was just above the minimum wage, and who were thus likely to seek significant pay increases themselves in order to restore differentials (Labour Party Archives, Re.123/April 1967).

Meanwhile, the perseverance with incomes policies was placing the Labour Government's relationship with the trade unions under increasing strain, for what had originally started out as a 'policy for incomes' had then become a voluntary incomes policy, followed by both a statutory incomes policy and a 'zero norm'. What was supposed to have been a temporary period of wage restraint had seemingly become a permanent tool of economic management, and was causing increasing resentment amongst skilled workers and the low-paid alike. Indeed, repeated incomes policies were also causing tension between trade union leaders and their rank-and-file members, thereby undermining the authority and credibility of the former in the eyes of their members.

This, in turn, enabled local-level officials and shop stewards to enter the growing gulf between the national-level trade union leadership and their members at local or factory level. This resulted in both growing concern over unofficial strikes (not sanctioned by the official or national union leadership), and the phenomenon of 'wage drift', whereby local or workplace pay deals were agreed which were invariably somewhat higher than those formally agreed between trade union leaders or the TUC and Ministers at Downing Street or Chequers.

Clearly, the Labour Government's repeated recourse to incomes policy – with no sign of a return to free collective bargaining in the offing – placed many trade union leaders in an invidious position and tested their loyalties to the limit, torn as they were between wanting to support a Labour Government on the one hand, but opposing continuous wage restraint on the other, particularly as the latter was alienating their own members. Not surprisingly, therefore, the TUC's 1968 annual conference heard widespread condemnation of the latest incomes policy, with Frank Cousins insisting that regardless of 'what political background the government has, it cannot get involved in the detail of industrial negotiation', whereupon he urged Ministers 'to keep out before they destroy not only themselves, but us' (TUC, 1968: 555–6). In similar vein, the recently elected leader of the Amalgamated Union of Engineering Workers (AUEW, the engineers' main trade union), Hugh Scanlon, alleged that the Labour Government's approach to securing wage restraint was merely 'a policy on traditional Tory lines' (TUC, 1968: 611), whereupon delegates voted by 7,746,000 votes to 1,022,000 against all statutory curbs on collective bargaining.

The Government's incomes policy suffered a further defeat at Labour's own conference a few weeks later, when delegates voted against it by 5,098,000 votes to 1,124,000. This was in spite of a robust defence of incomes policy by Barbara Castle, who had just been appointed Secretary of State at the new Department of Employment and Productivity (which replaced the old Ministry of Labour). Castle explained that she and her ministerial colleagues had been searching for 'something better than crude industrial power politics, whether practised by industrial tycoons or trade unions'. In so doing, she warned delegates that if the labour movement destroyed the Government's incomes policy without 'being clear [about] what you put in its place, then you will share a very heavy responsibility' (Labour Party, 1968: 152).

It was partly the trade unions' increasing antipathy to incomes policy, and the increasing incidence of unofficial strikes, which persuaded Castle and Wilson of the need for industrial relations legislation, as foreshadowed in January 1969's White Paper *In Place of Strife*. However, as we note in the next chapter, this policy was also undermined by the combined opposition of numerous Labour backbenchers, disagreements within the Cabinet, and the predictable hostility of the trade unions themselves, to the extent that it was eventually abandoned. Indeed, the Labour MPs and trade unions who successfully obliged Wilson and Castle to abandon *In Place of Strife* were often the same MPs and unions who had become increasingly hostile to the Government's incomes policies, particularly those which had a statutory basis. Yet this left the Labour Government bereft of both trade union legislation and an effective incomes policy as the next general election began to loom.

Ministerial despondency increases, 1969–1970

With opposition to further incomes policies increasing throughout the labour movement, and the Government having just been forced to abandon its proposals for legislative reform of industrial relations, many Cabinet Ministers were understandably weary and battle-scarred by 1969, and began to have doubts themselves about the efficacy of continuing to pursue incomes policies. Such doubts would have been fuelled by the 1968 publication of an NBPI report which suggested that since 1965, the Labour Governments' incomes policies had made a difference of about 1 per cent to the overall increase in earnings (National Board for Prices and Incomes, 1968), a revelation which finally convinced some Ministers that 'it wasn't worth all the effort and disputes that it generated' (Ponting, 1990: 377).

Indeed, long before the latest ('zero-norm') incomes policy expired at the end of 1969, the Cabinet had decided that the statutory component would not be renewed or reactivated. Instead, in December 1969 the Government announced that there would be a 'pay norm' in the 2.5–4.5 per cent range, although even this could be exceeded in 'exceptional circumstances', such as in industries with a large number of low-paid workers, or where there were significant increases in productivity. It was also proposed that 'comparability criteria' could be invoked in order to ensure that public-sector workers did not continually fall (too far) behind their private-sector counterparts. This proposed 2.5–4.5 per cent 'pay norm' not only was much more generous than the incomes policies which had immediately preceded it – leading cynics to suggest that a general election was imminent – but also represented a compromise in the Cabinet, for the then Chancellor, Roy Jenkins, had wanted the limit set at 3.5 per cent, but Barbara Castle deemed this 'utterly unrealistic' and, with the backing of Richard Crossman and Peter Shore, suggested 'a realistic range of 2.5–5 per cent'. However, Jenkins was aghast at setting an upper pay limit of 5 per cent (especially as the trade unions were likely to regard this as the 'norm', or 'going rate', rather than an absolute maximum), whereupon the 2.5–4.5 per cent range was agreed for pay deals negotiated during 1970 (Castle, 1990: 366–7, diary entries for 17 and 20 November 1969).

Yet by the autumn of 1969, a growing number of Ministers seemed tacitly to accept that 'the prices and incomes policy is, in fact, in ruins' (Crossman, 1977: 654, diary entry for 24 September 1969), and was having a detrimental impact on the strength and unity of the Labour Party itself (Labour Party Archives, Re.418/February 1969). As Figure 5.1 illustrates, in spite of the various incomes policies devised by the 1964–1970 Labour Governments, the annual average increase in earnings was considerably higher than the increases in the retail price index. Of course, Ministers might have responded that without their incomes policies, the increases in both prices and earnings might have been even greater. However, one commentator has

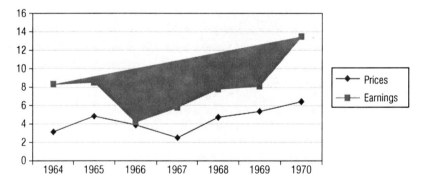

Figure 5.1   Increases in prices and incomes, 1964–1970 (per cent) (source: The Treasury (Annual Economic Trends, 1964–1970)).

suggested that the increase in earnings during 1968 and 1969 was broadly similar to what it would probably have been in the absence of incomes policy (Fels, 1972: 34–8).

Conclusion

Given the upward movement of earnings during the latter half of the 1960s, very few commentators have viewed the Labour Governments' incomes policies as a notable success. One writer has observed that with regard to incomes policy, 'The Wilson years . . . ended in failure as wage-push inflation began to threaten the economic gains achieved by the 1967 devaluation' and 'demands for wage restraint in the wider interest of resolving the underlying crisis of the British economy had come into conflict with the fragmented character of so much of the country's wage bargaining system' (Taylor, 1993: 172; see also Taylor, 1982: 201; Jones, 1987: 81–2). Meanwhile, Towers argues that the 1964–1970 Labour Governments' incomes policies were 'always trying to operate "against the tide" and alongside repeated packages of deflationary measures', whilst at the same time, the 'key problem of wage drift and shop floor control of earnings . . . was not effectively tackled: too much emphasis was placed on aggregate norms'. Nonetheless, Towers does concede that 'in spite of everything, the policy may have contributed towards a dampening of the course of pay and price inflation' (1978: 13–14).

Certainly the 1964–1970 Labour Governments' attempts at pursuing incomes policies (to secure wage restraint, rather than the originally promised 'planned growth of wages') brought Ministers into increasingly bitter conflict with a trade union movement which has always believed, almost as an article of faith, in free collective bargaining – 'free', that is, from political restriction or State interference. Indeed, as we note in the next chapter, the Governments' eventual response to the apparent failures of their incomes policies – apart from imbuing them with statutory rigour – was to pursue industrial relations legislation to curb 'irresponsible' trade union behaviour. Needless to say, this served to strain further, virtually to breaking point, the relationship between the Labour Government and the trade unions, whilst also causing serious divisions within both the Cabinet and the PLP, as we will observe in the next chapter.

6 Industrial relations imbroglio

Peter Dorey

Introduction

During the early 1960s, concern increased amongst political elites and commentators with regard to the relative decline of the British economy, which, it became apparent, was being outperformed by many of Britain's competitors. A range of economic variables, particularly those pertaining to industrial productivity and rates of economic growth, indicated that countries such as France, Italy, Japan, the United States and West Germany were outperforming Britain. What also became apparent was the decline of the British economy in historical (as well as international) context, so that Britain's share of world manufactured exports, for example, had declined from 33 per cent in 1900 to 16.5 per cent by 1960. The former 'workshop of the world' had seen its share of world exports exactly halved in sixty years. In turn, Britain's declining share of world manufacturing exports fuelled a series of balance of payments deficits during the 1960s.

This relative economic decline served to draw attention to Britain's industrial relations, and the apparent role of the trade unions in debilitating the British economy, for, as Taylor has noted, the unions became 'scapegoats of economic decline' (1993: 1–15). Their growing number of critics variously accused the trade unions of impeding increased efficiency, productivity and industrial modernisation through restrictive practices and over-manning, challenging managerial authority, fuelling inflation and undermining profitability through 'excessive' pay demands, and deterring new investment, as well as disrupting output, through strike activity. Certainly, unofficial strikes became a particular source of concern to Britain's political elites, partly because their very unpredictability and ad hoc character rendered them generally more damaging and disruptive, but also because it became apparent, in 1961 (owing to a change in the way that the Ministry of Labour compiled and published strike statistics), that unofficial stoppages accounted for at least 90 per cent of strikes in Britain. What also drew increasing political attention to unofficial strikes during the 1960s was the growing interdependence of British industry, for, as Barbara Castle would explain to her Cabinet colleagues in 1969, 'comparatively small groups of men could abuse their power and throw many thousands out of work, and cause inconvenience or hardship to the public and substantial damage to the economy' (PRO CAB 128/44 Part 1, CC(69) 1st Conclusions, 3 January 1969).

During the early 1960s, the Conservative Governments of Harold Macmillan and then, briefly, Sir Alec Douglas-Home were desperately seeking to uphold the voluntarist (i.e. non-interventionist) industrial relations strategy which had been sustained throughout the 1950s. The voluntarist strategy was partly derived from the Conservative Party's determination to win the trust of the trade unions (thereby banishing the bitter legacy of the 1920s and 1930s), but also owed much to the 'human relations' philosophy which many senior Conservatives espoused, which held that much industrial conflict arose as a result of lack of communication between employers and employees, and a corresponding feeling amongst workers that they were not really appreciated or valued. This meant that minor grievances often flared up into forms of industrial disruption, with factory floor discontent exploited and exacerbated by left-wing militants for their own political purposes. This being deemed the underlying cause of many industrial stoppages by Conservative advocates of the 'human relations' perspective, industrial relations legislation was rejected as likely to make matters worse, by increasing animosity and enmity between management and labour, and playing into the hands of the left (Dorey, 2002).

In spite of increasing calls for trade union legislation by various backbenchers and constituency delegates at the party's annual conference, therefore, the Conservative leadership right up until 1964 insisted that the law could not compel employers and employees to work more harmoniously together; only greater trust, derived from improved communication, consultation and co-operation, could eradicate outdated 'them and us' attitudes in the workplace. Nonetheless, by the early 1960s even Conservative advocates of voluntarism and the 'human relations' approach were becoming exasperated by the apparent unwillingness of trade unions to 'put their house in order' and develop more 'positive' attitudes and practices, and so there was a pledge that if the Conservatives won the 1964 election, some form of official inquiry or royal commission into industrial relations and trade unionism would be launched (Dorey, 1995: 56–62).

The Donovan Commission

A royal commission was established following the 1964 election, but by a Labour Government rather than the Conservatives. As was noted in the previous chapter, by the end of 1964, the Labour Government was already seeking trade union support for an incomes policy, such was the seriousness of the economic situation facing Ministers, and the pressure that the Cabinet was under from the City and overseas holders of sterling. Although the Government had secured the acquiescence of the TUC, it was still concerned that a nationally agreed policy of wage restraint might well be undermined by 'wage drift' as local-level pay deals, often secured in the wake of unofficial industrial action orchestrated by shop stewards at factory level, yielded pay increases higher than the official or national 'norm' formally agreed by the trade unions' official leaders. For that reason, March 1965 witnessed the establishment of the Royal Commission on Trade Unions and Employers' Associations, chaired by Lord Donovan. The Donovan Commission's remit was

> to consider relations between managements and employees, and the role of trade unions and employers' associations in promoting the interests of their members, and in accelerating the social and economic advances of the nation, with particular reference to the law affecting the activities of these bodies.

In spite of the formal even-handedness of both its title and its brief, it was clear that as far as many Ministers were concerned, it was the trade unions that most needed to be 'investigated'.

When the Donovan Commission published its report in 1968, it confirmed what many had already suspected, namely that

> Britain now has two systems of industrial relations. The one is the formal system embodied in the official institutions. The other is the informal system created by the actual behaviour of trade unions and employers' associations, of managers, shop stewards and workers.
>
> (Royal Commission on Trade Unions and Employers' Associations, 1968: 12)

The 'informal system' invariably undermined wage settlements negotiated at the formal, national level, and thus underpinned the phenomenon of 'wage drift', whereby actual official, nationally agreed pay increases and earnings were overtaken, and thus undermined, by local-level, unofficial wage bargaining and settlements, involving shop stewards. Ironically, this gulf between the national and the local in industry was compounded by the recent recourse to incomes policies, for as trade union leaders were increasingly seen to be 'colluding' with Ministers to restrain wage increases, so union members at factory level increasingly looked to shop stewards – who were more visible and 'in touch' owing to their proximity – to represent their material interests more effectively. Consequently, the Donovan Report emphasised:

> Incomes policy must continue to be a lame and faltering exercise so long as it consists in the planning of industry-wide agreements, most of which exercise an inadequate control over pay. So long as work-place bargaining remains informal, autonomous and fragmented, the drift of earnings away from rates of pay cannot be brought under control.
>
> (Royal Commission on Trade Unions and Employers' Associations, 1968: 53)

However, the report emphatically cautioned against the introduction of statutory measures to impose greater order and stability into industrial relations, and to tackle the 'informal system' deemed to be undermining national-level pay deals and incomes policies. Crucially, it insisted that 'the law could not, in any circumstances, assist in the reduction of unofficial strikes.... To take steps in that direction today would not only be useless but harmful' (Royal Commission on Trade Unions and Employers' Associations, 1968: 52, 53).

Labour's political opponents might have expected Ministers to have been secretly relieved by Donovan's defence of voluntarism, providing as it did a case for *not* introducing industrial relations legislation and trade union reform. Yet Harold Wilson and Barbara Castle were actually deeply disappointed by the timidity of the Donovan Report, long as it was on analysis but short on bold recommendations. They had apparently hoped that the Donovan Report would suggest radical reforms, which would then enable the Government to pacify predictable trade union outrage by proposing more modest measures instead as a compromise (Ponting, 1990: 352). Wilson was emphatic that 'the confessed failure of the [Donovan] Commission to find any short-term remedy for unofficial strikes could not be accepted' (Wilson, 1971: 591), particularly as the Conservative Opposition was itself developing a legalistic industrial relations policy to tackle unofficial strikes (a policy which constituted the basis of the ill-fated 1971 Industrial Relations Act), and so, with Wilson's full support, Barbara Castle readily drafted proposals for the reform of industrial relations, with a view to restoring order and stability to British industry whilst *inter alia* providing a fillip for the Government's incomes policies. Indeed, back in May 1968, even before the formal publication of the Donovan Report, Castle had informed ministerial colleagues that whilst there was likely to be much in the report with which they could concur, there was likely to be a need to prepare legislation, if only a short bill, for the next [1968–1969] Parliamentary Session (PRO CAB 134/2936, 'Memorandum by the First Secretary of State', 27 May 1968).

Castle was able to reject the arguments in defence of voluntarism and laissez-faire not merely on the grounds that the existing system was no longer functioning effectively, but also by reminding the trade unions that the previous one hundred years had yielded various Acts of Parliament to grant them legal privileges and protect the rights of their members against employers. Her January 1969 White Paper, *In Place of Strife* – subsequently deemed 'a provocation to strife' by its left-wing opponents (Mikardo, 1988: 176) – contained several measures intended to foster greater stability and order in industrial relations, most notably those:

- to grant employees a statutory right to belong to a trade union;
- to establish a commission on industrial relations which would be able to recommend the formal recognition of a trade union for bargaining purposes;

- to provide compensation or reinstatement in cases of unfair dismissal;
- to empower the Secretary of State to order a twenty-eight-day 'cooling-off' period in the case of unofficial industrial action;
- to empower the Secretary of State for Employment to order a ballot prior to a strike which was judged likely to inflict serious damage on the economy or to the national interest.

Inter-union disputes were to be referred to the TUC to resolve, and if this failed, to the commission on industrial relations. Ultimately, the Secretary of State would be entitled to enforce a commission recommendation by imposing a fine on a recalcitrant trade union or its members. In the latter case, failure to pay the fine could result in an attachment-of-earnings order being invoked.

Castle and Wilson doubtless expected instant and instinctive denunciations of *In Place of Strife* from the trade unions, whose leaders believed that *free* (from State intervention) collective bargaining was sacrosanct – the *raison d'être* of trade unionism, even – but what they had probably not fully anticipated was the degree of hostility which many of the legislative proposals aroused from sections of the Parliamentary Labour Party (PLP) and around the Cabinet table. Indeed, throughout much of 1969 Castle found herself struggling to overcome the opposition of trade unions, many Labour MPs and some of her ministerial colleagues to various legislative proposals intended to curb 'irresponsible' trade union behaviour.

For example, less than a fortnight *before* the publication of *In Place of Strife*, Castle was informing Wilson that James Callaghan 'had made it clear that he was going to oppose her proposals and argue the straight Donovan line' (PRO PREM 13/2724, 'Note for the Record', 3 January 1969), which was a major reason why the Home Secretary was not appointed to the Cabinet committee on industrial relations reform. Callaghan actually harboured three substantive objections to *In Place of Strife*. First, he maintained that the proposed legal sanctions would not prevent unofficial stoppages, thereby proving ineffective. Second, Callaghan suspected that the envisaged legislation would not be approved by Parliament, because of inevitable opposition by sections of the PLP. Third, he was concerned that the proposals would cause a serious rift between the Labour Government and the trade unions, particularly at a time when relations between the industrial and political wings of the labour movement were already strained as a result of the repeated imposition of incomes policies and other deflationary measures. 'From the moment I set eyes on it,' Callaghan recalls, 'I knew such a proposal, which ran counter to the whole history of the trade union movement . . . could not succeed. Barbara galloped ahead with all the reckless gallantry of the Light Brigade at Balaclava' (1987: 274).

By the spring of 1969, Callaghan's outspoken opposition to trade union legislation was such that the Chief Whip felt obliged to send Wilson a telegram (whilst the Prime Minister was visiting Addis Ababa and Lagos) informing him of 'considerable anti-Callaghan feeling in the PLP, probably reinforced by visits to their constituents who appear to be in angry mood', and observing that 'This feeling is shared even by those who are against Barbara's White Paper' and who 'violently resent senior Ministers being allowed to get away with it' [publicly criticising aspects of official government policy with which they disagree]. The Chief Whip urged that 'action must be taken on this point very soon if we are to stop total disintegration' (PRO PREM 13/2785, Mellish to Wilson, undated but *c.*28–30 March 1969). A similar message was sent by Fred Peart (Leader of the House of Commons), who reported 'general resentment at Callaghan's attitude' and cited Cledwyn Hughes's view that 'Jim's actions [are] deplorable' (PRO PREM 13/2785, Peart to Wilson, 31 March 1969; see also Wills to Wilson, 31 March 1969; Wilson Papers, MS Wilson, C. 936, 'Note for the record on industrial relations legislation', 10 May 1969).

Some commentators have drawn attention to Callaghan's own instinctive attachment and loyalty to the trade unions, which, it has been suggested, were 'reinforced by his personal links to the key unions' following his October 1967 election as Labour Party Treasurer (Morgan, 1997: 333), as well as his own background as a former official with the Inland Revenue Staff Association. For figures such as Callaghan, would-be industrial relations reformers like Castle and Wilson possessed an inadequate grasp of internal trade union politics, and thus a naïve faith in the ability of legislation to effect positive change.

Meanwhile, in the Cabinet's first 1969 discussion of the imminent White Paper, it was argued by opponents of *In Place of Strife* that Britain's record of industrial disputes actually compared favourably with that of most other countries, to the extent that this too 'largely undermined the case for legislation'. This argument, in tandem with that pertaining to the likely impracticability or ineffectiveness of legislation in reducing unofficial strike activity, meant that it was not worth 'risking the difficulty and the loss of goodwill within the unions and the Labour Party which [legislation] would entail (PRO CAB 128/44 Part 1, CC(69) 1st Conclusions, 3 January 1969).

Just a few days later, a poll in *The Times* indicated considerable differences of opinion amongst trade union-sponsored Labour MPs, for whilst 60 per cent claimed to approve of secret strike ballots compared to the 25 per cent who were opposed, there was a somewhat narrower margin – 45 per cent to 33 per cent – in favour of a government-imposed 'cooling off' period. Meanwhile, the proposal to make collective agreements between employers and employees legally binding was opposed by 39 per cent of trade union-sponsored Labour MPs, compared to the 37 per cent who supported such an initiative. Overall, the poll found that 37 per cent of such MPs approved of the plan to give legislative effect to these measures, whilst 23 per cent were opposed, but, crucially, 32 per cent were undecided, with a further 13 per cent declining to offer an opinion. One trade union-sponsored Labour MP, and chair of the TGWU group of MPs, Roy Hughes, claimed that Ministers were 'bending as a result of Tory pressure', and warned that 'If the Government went ahead with these proposals, it would be highly detrimental, and Labour would lose the next election' (*The Times*, 8 January 1969).

Some unease was also felt within parts of Whitehall, where there was uncertainty about whether *In Place of Strife* was intended to be an adjunct or an alternative to incomes policies and the search for wage restraint. The day before *In Place of Strife* was published, one senior official wrote to the Prime Minister's Principal Private Secretary urging the Government to make clear that 'while a policy to improve industrial relations may be complementary to an incomes policy, it *cannot* be a *substitute* for it ... to push ahead with it [industrial relations legislation] *at the expense of* incomes policy would ... spell disaster'. Yet it was also recognised that the Government might find it very difficult to persuade the trade unions to accept both a continued incomes policy *and* industrial relations legislation together, unless it could offer the unions more in return by way of positive measures alongside the penal elements proposed in *In Place of Strife* (PRO PREM 13/2724, Graham to Halls, 14 January 1969; emphasis in original).

Also on the eve of the publication of *In Place of Strife*, Wilson was informed that whilst 23 members of the TUC's General Council were opposed to the White Paper, with 16 willing to accept it, 'there is no belly for a fight, except perhaps on the part of Frank Cousins'. However, it was also reported that according to Vic Feather (Acting General Secretary of the TUC), the trade unions were likely to oppose *In Place of Strife* by a majority of three to one, with the 'hard-liners' being the Transport and General Workers' Union (TGWU) (led by Frank Cousins) and the Amalgamated Engineering Union (AEU) (PRO PREM 13/2724, Kaufman to Wilson, 14 January 1969). By this time, Castle herself had been informed by George Woodcock 'that he personally was happy with the package', and felt that if it came to a vote, the TUC's Finance and General Purposes Committee would probably endorse it, although he was not so sure about the General Council (PRO PREM 13/2724, Castle to Wilson, 3 January 1969). Such reports from senior TUC officials may well have led Castle (and Wilson) into underestimating the degree of trade union opposition which would imminently be unleashed by *In Place of Strife*, whilst simultaneously creating the impression that many sceptics and opponents within the trade unions would be open to persuasion once they had made their ritual public denunciations of industrial relations legislation.

Meanwhile, within the Cabinet, alongside the outright opponents of *In Place of Strife* like Callaghan, there were two other discernible strands of opinion. Some Ministers, such as Tony Crosland, recognised the 'need to go beyond Donovan in bringing industrial relations within the framework of the law and public accountability', but were doubtful whether strike ballots would prove effective, whilst the imposition of a 'peace pause' was likely to prove 'not only provocative but (more importantly) ineffective', in which case it was likely 'to make the Government look ridiculous because either it would not be used or it would fail'. If this proved to be the case, 'the Government would appear ineffective, the public would be disillusioned, and the field would be left open for more violent Tory proposals'. An alternative strategy, it was suggested, would be to grant the proposed commission on industrial relations 'more strength, more independence, and additional statutory or judicial powers' (PRO PREM 13/2724, Crosland to Wilson, 6 January 1969), although it was not clear how or why this would be any more acceptable to the trade unions. Also doubtful about the likely efficacy or practicability of empowering the Secretary of State to impose a 'cooling off' period was Richard Crossman, who hoped that its inclusion in the White Paper would prompt the TUC to offer 'an acceptable voluntary alternative', whereupon the measure would be withdrawn by the Government and not included in subsequent industrial relations legislation. Castle, however, was adamant that such a stance would merely indicate to the TUC 'weakness and indecision on the part of the Government' (PRO CAB 128/44 Part 1, CC(69) 3rd Conclusions, 14 January 1969).

The other strand of opinion within the Cabinet was wholly supportive of *In Place of Strife*, accepting that 'it is essential that we bring more order into industrial relations ... we must go beyond Donovan ... the reform of our industrial negotiating machinery is urgent', and thus fully endorsing Castle's proposals for pre-strike ballots and empowering the Secretary of State to impose a 'conciliation pause' when an unofficial strike 'would cause widespread damage to the national interest and to other workers'. Even when it was acknowledged that there might be 'difficulties about enforcement, I do not think, however, we should not make too much of these ... we shall not be forgiven if we fail to grasp this nettle' (PRO PREM 13/2724, Peart to Wilson, 7 January 1969). Furthermore, it was suggested that 'psychologically the existence of the power might make men more careful' (PRO CAB 128/44 Part 1, CC(69) 1st Conclusions, 3 January 1969).

Such differences of opinion meant that four Cabinet meetings in a week (instead of the normal one or two) had to be held, at the beginning of January 1969, before Castle and Wilson could elicit sufficient ministerial support to publish *In Place of Strife* as a formal statement – in the form of a White Paper – of the Labour Government's policy on industrial relations. Yet with a sizeable minority of Ministers remaining implacably opposed, the PLP divided and the trade unions inevitably hostile, it was clear that Castle and Wilson would face the utmost difficulty in translating *In Place of Strife* into an Act of Parliament. Indeed, once formal Cabinet approval had been obtained, a new difference of opinion manifested itself, this time amongst supporters of *In Place of Strife*, concerning the timing of legislation.

Castle envisaged that the White Paper would provide the basis for discussions which would pave the way for legislation in the autumn of 1969, thereby providing her with considerable time in which to persuade hostile

Labour MPs and trade union opponents to support an industrial relations bill, although she also recognised that she was 'taking a terrible gamble, and there is absolutely no certainty that it will pay off', in which case *In Place of Strife* might prove to be 'the political end of me with our own people'. She nonetheless consoled herself with the recognition that 'I am proposing something I believe in' (Castle, 1990: 296, diary entry for 7 January; see also PRO PREM 13/2724, Castle to Wilson, 7 January 1969).

Yet whilst insisting on her determination to introduce industrial relations legislation during 1969, she and Harold Wilson also suggested, right from the outset, that if the TUC advanced satisfactory and credible counter-proposals for dealing itself with inter-union disputes and unofficial strikes, then the Government would be willing to reconsider its own legislative proposals, to the extent of possibly withdrawing what became known as the 'penal clauses' (PRO CAB 128/44 Part 1, CC(69) 2nd Conclusions, 8 and 9 January 1969). This ambivalence over the Government's true objectives – to enact industrial relations irrespective of labour movement hostility, or to invoke the threat of a bill in order to spur the TUC into tackling inter-union disputes and unofficial stoppages – partly reflected the no-win situation potentially facing the Cabinet. Emphasising a tough stance with regard to the need for industrial relations legislation would probably be matched by implacable opposition from the trade unions, possibly embroiling the Government in a lengthy battle which might well damage its popularity and authority. Yet in alluding to their willingness to drop the 'penal pauses' in return for satisfactory initiatives from the TUC, Castle and Wilson were conveying their desire to seek a compromise with the trade unions, in order to avoid controversial legislation. Now whilst this might have been expected to galvanise the TUC into appropriate action, the Government's hints that it was willing to avoid punitive legislation actually encouraged many trade unions to believe that if they stood firm and denounced proposed legislation vociferously enough, the Government desire for a compromise would become even greater. Certainly, by June, as we will note shortly, Castle and Wilson were becoming increasingly desparate in their efforts at avoiding the need to introduce a punitive industrial relations bill, thereby placing the TUC in a stronger bargaining position.

Partly because they were alert to this danger, some of Castle's Cabinet colleagues, most notably Richard Crossman and Roy Jenkins, believed that, whilst *In Place of Strife* was right both in principle and as a basis for legislation, Castle was wrong in deferring a bill until the autumn. Far from providing her with the time in which to win over sceptics and opponents, the eight- to nine-month interregnum was likely to enable hostile Labour MPs and trade unions to mobilise a campaign against Castle's proposed legislation. Such a prognosis led Crossman and Jenkins to urge Castle to introduce a 'a short interim Bill … at once' (Castle, 1990: 295, diary entry for 3 January 1969; Crossman, 1977: 306–7, diary entry for 3 January; PRO CAB 128/44 Part 1, CC(69) 3rd Conclusions, 14 January 1969).

Initially, Castle was 'not prepared to put forward a shorter Bill in which all the emphasis will be on the penal bits. I could not imagine anything more detrimental to my whole philosophy' (1990: 295, diary entry for 3 January 1969), but by April she had changed her mind. Although the reason for this change is unclear, it may well have owed something to the scale of antipathy which was evident on the Labour back benches during a Commons debate on *In Place of Strife*, for in the ensuing division, 50 Labour MPs voted against the White Paper, whilst a further 40 abstained. The scale of such dissent was, Castle reflected, 'more than we had anticipated' (1990: 310, diary entry for 3 March 1969). Three weeks later, Labour's National Executive Committee voted 16 to 5 against legislation based on *all* the proposals enshrined in *In Place of Strife*.

These instances probably served to persuade Castle to accept Crossman's and Jenkins's critique, namely that the longer she left it before introducing legislation, the greater and stronger would be the opposition which would have been mobilised within the labour movement. Certainly, neither Castle nor Wilson was sufficiently impressed by the arguments advanced against legislation by the TUC representatives whom they met at 10 Downing Street on 11 April 1969. The TUC insisted that 'the unions were anxious to pursue the reform of industrial relations on a voluntary basis', an assertion which Castle and Wilson felt belied a conservatism and tardiness on the part of too many trade unions, as indicated by the apparent lack of progress since 1965, when the Donovan Commission had been established. Hence, Castle and Wilson made clear their determination to persevere with limited legislation in lieu of a more comprehensive industrial relations bill, probably in the next parliamentary session, although it was hoped that consultations between the Government and the trade unions would continue in the meantime (PRO PREM 13/2726, 'Note of a Meeting with Representatives of the Trades Union Congress', 11 April 1969).

What doubtless reinforced Castle's and Wilson's determination to introduce a short industrial bill was the Cabinet's difficulties concerning its incomes policies, which in turn increased the need to assuage the anxieties of the City and overseas holders of sterling about the Labour Government's stewardship of the British economy. This particular interpretation is certainly lent credence by the fact that the imminent introduction of a short Industrial Relations Bill – in lieu of a more comprehensive bill in the autumn – was announced not by Castle or Wilson, but by the Chancellor, Roy Jenkins, during his Budget speech on 15 April 1969. Possibly to mollify the trade unions, though, he also announced that the Government would not be renewing its statutory power to delay pay settlements when the existing incomes policy expired at the end of 1969.

The short bill contained just five substantive measures:

- a statutory right to join a trade union;
- the Government, via the Employment Secretary, to be able to order a recalcitrant employer to 'recognise' a trade union, if this were recommended by the Commission on Industrial Relations (CIR);

- workers laid off due to an industrial stoppage in which they were not involved to be entitled to claim unemployment benefit pending their return to work;
- the Government, via the Employment Secretary, empowered to impose a settlement in cases where neither the TUC nor the CIR was able to secure a voluntary resolution to an inter-union dispute;
- the Government, via the Employment Secretary, empowered to impose a twenty-eight-day 'conciliation pause'.

Castle had wanted to include a further clause to impose pre-strike ballots, but was dissuaded by a number of Cabinet colleagues, with Callaghan once again proving a prominent opponent. Wilson staked the authority of the Government on the short Industrial Relations Bill, declaring it to be

> [a]n essential component in ensuring the economic success of the Government . . . essential to our economic recovery, essential to the balance of payments, essential to full employment . . . the passage of this Bill is essential to the continuance of this Government in Office. There can be no going back on that.
>
> (Wilson, 1971: 643)

Not surprisingly, perhaps, the last two of the five clauses were bitterly resented by the trade unions, particularly as continued defiance of either clause would ultimately result in the imposition of financial penalties on the individuals involved, possibly via an attachment-of-earnings order. Nor were the trade unions enamoured with Castle's avowed intention to introduce a more comprehensive industrial relations bill in the autumn. Meanwhile, at a meeting of the PLP on 7 May, its chair, Douglas Houghton, was reported to have claimed that 'The unity of the Party is more important to the nation than the damage to the nation from unconstitutional strikes.' Such strikes were for management and trade unions to resolve: 'The Government should not shoulder the responsibility for unconstitutional strikes' (PRO PREM 13/2726, Report of PLP Meeting to Wilson, 7 May 1969).

When Houghton's claims were reported to the Cabinet the following morning, Wilson pointed out that if such warnings were heeded, Ministers would be 'acquiescing in a dangerous precedent' whereby they would henceforth only be able to govern 'on sufferance, and in the knowledge that there were certain policies which they must not pursue, however necessary in the country's interests they might consider them to be', because of 'the dictation of the PLP'. Callaghan then responded by reiterating his opposition to the Industrial Relations Bill, maintaining not only that it was a response to 'an issue . . . of such little significance' but that its alleged benefits did not warrant 'the destruction of the Labour Party' (thereby effectively echoing Houghton's warning). In so doing, Callaghan called upon his Cabinet colleagues to 'withdraw from the brink of disaster' by accepting that they would be unable to enact the bill in its present form.

Other Ministers effectively echoed Callaghan and Houghton by reiterating their opposition to the short Industrial Relations Bill, pointing out that the Cabinet had underestimated the degree of opposition in the Parliamentary Labour Party. Indeed, in view of the degree of opposition engendered by the bill, it was deemed entirely right and proper that members of the PLP should warn the parliamentary leadership of the consequences of persevering with such a measure, particularly if they believed that the survival of the Labour Party was being jeopardised. Even Ministers who were less strongly opposed to the short Industrial Relations Bill accepted that it would be unwise to issue a public rebuke to Houghton. What was needed, they suggested, was 'to allow time for a calmer approach to the Industrial Relations Bill to develop', something which would certainly not be achieved by further antagonising critics on the Government's back benches (PRO CAB 128/46, CC(69) 22nd Conclusions, 8 May 1969).

The TUC held a special one-day conference in Croydon on 5 June, at which a *Programme for Action* was endorsed by 7,908,000 votes to 846,000. In rejecting 'statutory penalties on working people or trade unions in connection either with industrial disputes or with the compulsory registration by trade unions of their rules' (TUC, 1969: 67), *Programme for Action* proposed instead that the TUC would strengthen its own procedures for dealing with inter-union disputes and official strikes. This would entail the TUC's General Council itself insisting that affiliated trade unions did not authorise strike action without first consulting the TUC, whilst in the case of an unofficial stoppage, the relevant trade union would be obliged vigorously to seek a return to work by those involved.

Neither Castle nor Wilson considered these counter-proposals by the TUC to be sufficient to warrant abandoning the Industrial Relations Bill, for they were not convinced that the TUC's General Council would really be able – or willing – to ensure the compliance of an affiliated trade union which refused to abide by the *Programme for Action*. The ultimate penalty of expulsion from the TUC was not deemed a realistic sanction in Castle's and Wilson's view, not least because the TUC itself was hardly likely to want to take action which would reduce its own membership. Besides, there remained the problem of whether a trade union itself should be held liable, and thus punished, for the 'unconstitutional' actions of individual members. Put another way, even if they had been satisfied that the TUC were able and willing to ensure the compliance of affiliated trade unions, there remained the problem of imposing sanctions on recalcitrant individuals who defied both the TUC and their union by engaging in unofficial industrial action.

However, Wilson and Castle were still hopeful that some kind of agreement with the TUC could be secured, to the extent of indicating that the penal clauses enshrined in the short Industrial Relations Bill could be repealed or amended when the second, more comprehensive, industrial relations bill was introduced in the next parliamentary session. Yet some Ministers believed that the TUC had by this time proved sufficiently receptive, particularly at the Croydon conference, to warrant Wilson and Castle considering the abandonment of the 'penal clauses', at least for the time being. If they did so, they would be able publicly to justify such a move by claiming that it was the Government's proposed legislation which had prompted the TUC to 'put its own house in order' at last (PRO CAB 128/44 Part 1, CC(69) 26th Conclusions, 9 June 1969).

By this time, though, it was quite clear that the opposition of Labour backbenchers against the short Industrial Relations Bill was increasing, particularly with regard to the penal clauses. Indeed, following the TUC's Croydon conference endorsing *A Programme for Action*, a meeting of Labour's Liaison Committee decided that such was the depth of feeling amongst the party's MPs that 'the Government could not count upon enough support within the Parliamentary Party to get this Bill through the House', and warned of 'the inevitable devastating consequences to the Party inside and outside Parliament' of persevering in the face of such opposition. It was therefore deemed vital that Ministers reach an agreement with the TUC 'if a grave split in the Parliamentary Party is to be averted', and to this end it was suggested that the Cabinet should 'take the TUC at their word for the present, put them to the test of experience, and defer any question of legislation until the next Sesssion' (PRO PREM 13/2728, Houghton to Wilson, 16 June 1969). Meanwhile, the Chief Whip was expressing concern about the diminishing amount of parliamentary time remaining before the summer recess, with eight days pencilled in for the committee stage of the Industrial Relations Bill as it currently stood, although 'the position would be much eased if the Industrial Relations Bill proves non-penal' (PRO LAB 43/536, Mellish to Wilson, 6 June 1969).

When a group of senior Cabinet Ministers and the Chief Whip held a pre-Cabinet meeting to discuss how to proceed, Castle lamented that the stance of the PLP in general, and Houghton in particular, 'had greatly weakened the Government's negotiating position', with Wilson alleging that 'Houghton seemed to be working hand and glove with a Member of the Cabinet' (PRO PREM 13/2728, 'Note of a Meeting of the Management Committee', 17 June 1969).

Nonetheless, Castle and Wilson were still inclined to proceed with the short Industrial Relations Bill, believing that whilst the TUC had offered acceptable proposals to deal with inter-union disputes, it had still not provided sufficiently robust proposals to tackle unofficial strikes. If the Government were now to abandon its legislation, therefore, it 'would lose all credibility both at home and abroad ... their authority would disappear'. Again, however, a number of Ministers believed that Castle and Wilson ought to moderate their stance, for 'the gap between the respective positions of the Government and the TUC was now very narrow', to the extent that it was deemed desirable that they should conduct further negotiations with

TUC representatives before deciding definitely to proceed with the short Industrial Relations Bill, particularly in view of the scale of opposition to the bill which by now existed in the PLP (PRO CAB 128/44 Part 1, CC(69) 28th Conclusions, 17 June 1969).

Thus it was that the following morning, Wilson, Castle and their senior officials met members of the TUC's General Council at 10 Downing Street, although this meeting was then adjourned whilst Wilson and Castle held a smaller meeting with just seven members of the General Council. It was from this smaller meeting that a compromise solution was finally agreed upon, entailing a 'solemn and binding undertaking' by the TUC's General Council to strengthen its own procedures for dealing with unofficial industrial disputes, in accordance with the *Programme for Action*. This was unanimously approved by the General Council when the full meeting was resumed following the adjournment (and subsequently by the full Cabinet when it met later the same day). In return for this undertaking, and subject to its subsequent endorsement at the TUC's annual conference in September, the Government would not proceed with the short Industrial Relations Bill, nor would the 'penal clauses' be included in industrial relations legislation planned for the next parliamentary session, or, indeed, for the lifetime of the current Parliament. If the TUC failed to deliver on this agreement, though, then the Government would consider reintroducing the 'penal clauses' in new industrial relations legislation which would entail sanctions (probably in the form of financial penalties), either against individual strikers, or against the relevant trade unions themselves (PRO PREM 13/2728, 'Note of a Meeting with Representatives of the Trades Union Congress', 18 June 1969).

In spite of this climbdown – or, perhaps, precisely because of it – Castle remained determined to introduce a comprehensive industrial relations bill in the next (1969–1970) parliamentary session, although she fully realised that the trade unions 'remain deeply suspicious of any interference in the running of union affairs or any hint of sanctions against unions'. Through the remainder of 1969 and into early 1970, Castle therefore again sought to devise an industrial relations bill which would strike a balance between enhancing certain rights for trade unions and employees on the one hand, but which would reduce both unofficial strikes and the scope for secondary or sympathy action on the other (see, for example, PRO CAB 134/2738, Minutes of Meetings of Ministerial Committee on Industrial Relations, various dates). Some prescriptive content was deemed necessary alongside permissive clauses because, as Harold Wilson ruefully reflected, 'Strikes did not diminish in number, scale or duration after 18 June 1969' (1971: 662).

Such a bill was indeed published at the end of April 1970, although how much opposition the bill would again have elicited from Labour MPs and trade unions was never put to the test, for before it received its second reading Wilson announced that a general election would be held on 18 June 1970. Yet even before this announcement, the Chief Whip was warning

Castle of the practical and timetabling difficulties which the bill would encounter (PRO PREM 13/3275, Mellish [Chief Whip] to Castle, 6 May 1970), given that major items of Government legislation are usually given their first reading before Christmas in order to ensure sufficient parliamentary time for their subsequent stages. Yet Castle had envisaged a swift industrial relations bill 'to demonstrate that the Government was seriously intent on enacting this legislation' (PRO PREM 13/3275, Castle to Wilson, 1 May 1970).

The Labour Party's manifesto for this election intriguingly placed the issue of industrial relations under the heading of 'Industrial Democracy', pledging to give legislative effect to a 'charter of good industrial relations'. This would entail safeguards against unfair dismissal, provide trade unions with the right to statutory recognition by employers, and oblige employers to disclose more information to workers' representatives. However, these measures, clearly intended to prove attractive to trade unions, would be accompanied by an (unspecified) overhaul of negotiation and disputes procedures, rationalisation of trade union structures, and provision for legally binding agreements between trade unions and employers (Craig, 1975: 361).

Conclusion

In many respects, Harold Wilson and Barbara Castle felt compelled to pursue industrial relations reform as a result of the difficulties encountered by the Labour Government's incomes policies. Certainly the search for wage restraint from 1965 onwards (as examined in the previous chapter) served to highlight the veracity of the Donovan Report's observation concerning the 'two systems' of industrial relations which operated in Britain: the formal, national-level system and the unofficial, local-level system, with the latter frequently undermining the former and thereby fuelling 'wage drift'. It was largely to tackle the latter that Wilson and Castle resolved to introduce industrial relations legislation which would curb unofficial strikes, thereby restoring the authority of the official, national-level trade union leadership, with whom Ministers sought to secure agreement over incomes policies.

However, whilst Wilson and Castle might have expected the opposition of the trade unions themselves to the penal measures which *In Place of Strife* proposed, they did not anticipate the degree of opposition which emanated from the Parliamentary Labour Party. This opposition manifested itself amongst two particular 'groups' of Labour MPs and Ministers, and in many respects neatly corresponded to the opposition to the Government's incomes policies. First, there was the hostility of Labour's left (notwithstanding that Barbara Castle herself was otherwise widely viewed as a left-winger), particularly those MPs associated with *Tribune*, who instinctively viewed any statutory curbs on the trade unions as an attack on the right and ability of ordinary working people collectively to undertake industrial action in order to defend or promote their material interests. Moreover, such MPs were inclined to point out that whenever Britain's (capitalist) economy experienced difficulties or crises, it was ordinary working people who were expected to make sacrifices and/or see their representative institutions – namely, the trade unions – subjected to legal curbs; no such blame or restrictions were directed at capital or employers.

The second 'group' of Labour MPs and Ministers who were implacably opposed to *In Place of Strife* were those who were either sponsored by the trade unions or had strong trade union backgrounds. On this particular issue, it was apparent that the loyalty of many of these Labour politicians lay first and foremost with the trade unions, rather than the Labour Government. For them, it was the Cabinet which ought to refrain from placing legislative curbs on the trade unions, rather than the trade unions which ought to accept such curbs. We noted, for example, how within the Cabinet the most implacable opponent of *In Place of Strife* was James Callaghan, a former official with the Inland Revenue Staff Association. However, some of Callaghan's ministerial colleagues apparently suspected that his opposition to *In Place of Strife* was really part of a careful calculation that if he ingratiated himself with the trade unions, he might be able to replace Wilson as Labour leader and Prime Minister (Ponting, 1990: 360, 370–1). It was a supreme irony, therefore, that after Callaghan had replaced Wilson seven years later, in 1976 – albeit through an orderly succession rather than through a Machiavellian plot – his own premiership was effectively destroyed by a major confrontation with the trade unions, namely the 'winter of discontent'.

7 Policy towards the European Economic Community

Helen Parr and Melissa Pine

Introduction

Harold Wilson commented regularly on the subject of Europe before he became leader of the Labour Party. When discussions on the free trade area were under way in the late 1950s, he asked, 'Can we afford to stay out?' The answer was 'I am sure the answer is that we cannot', but he followed it later with 'There is no suggestion that Britain should join the Common Market.' These comments suggest that Wilson was not doctrinaire, but weighed up the costs and benefits and made his decisions accordingly. This pattern would continue over the following years. In the House of Commons debate on the European Free Trade Area (EFTA) in 1959, he noted the distinction between the 'original dreamers and idealists' who had thought up the Community and the 'highly realistic ideas' that they had produced to implement the dreams. Whilst he still resisted entry into the Community, he acknowledged that there was 'a strong desire for a really effective and intimate basis of association between Great Britain and Scandinavian countries on the other hand, and the community of Common Market countries on the other'. He was also worried that Western Europe would attract investment and that Britain would become a scientific backwater. The technological potential of European integration interested Wilson for years as a rationale for membership and as a tool to assist entry.

Thus, Wilson's attitude towards the European Community was never entirely consistent. During the Conservative negotiations for membership in 1961–1963, Wilson displayed a more anti-European attitude, declaring memorably that Britain was 'not entitled to sell our friends and kinsmen down the river for a problematical and marginal advantage in selling washing machines in Düsseldorf'. Realisation that Britain could not get desired terms for the Commonwealth, coupled with the temptation to put pressure on the Conservative negotiators, led the incumbent Labour leader, Hugh Gaitskell, as well as Wilson, to criticise the Conservative bid. The failure of the Brussels negotiations in January 1963 allowed Wilson to elude serious discussion on the Labour Party's future attitude towards Community accession. When Wilson became party leader after Gaitskell's death, he formulated an alternative vision for Labour, centred on regeneration of the Commonwealth abroad and science and technology and economic planning at home. The EEC was not a priority for the incoming Labour Government, although membership of the 'right sort' of Europe was a constant feature of Wilson's rhetoric.

This chapter traces the evolving attitudes of British Cabinet Ministers towards the European Economic Community within the context of the development of Harold Wilson's policy towards membership of the Community. It argues that the primary case in favour of membership of the European Community was political, particularly as the economic arguments for and against joining the EEC were extremely finely balanced because of the weakness of sterling. Wilson compelled Ministers to accept the application in April 1967. Following de Gaulle's veto in November 1967, Wilson continued to direct European policy, restricting discussion of policy and keeping close watch on Ministers' speeches. Thus, ministerial acceptance of the initiative was somewhat 'resigned' or fatalistic, and certainly did not represent a wholehearted endorsement of Britain's future in Europe. Despite this reluctance, it is clear that Wilson had a strategic objective of attaining membership of the EEC. Since the French veto was lifted during his leadership, his initiative must be regarded as something of a success.

Policy towards the EEC, October 1964–March 1966

Between October 1964 and March 1966, the two Ministers most closely associated with a possible move towards the European Economic Community (EEC) were the First Secretary of State and Secretary of State for Economic Affairs, George Brown, and the Foreign Secretary, Michael Stewart. Both agreed that the primary reason to seek British membership of the EEC was the clear-cut political argument: '[U]nless we can evolve a more effective relationship with the European Community, Britain will cease to be a world power' (PRO FO 371/184288/W6/12, Palliser to Nicholls, 9 February 1965; PRO PREM 13/306, Stewart to Wilson, 3 March 1965). Brown and Stewart adopted different approaches to attaining membership. Brown and the Department of Economic Affairs (DEA) favoured the pursuit of a British partnership with the French, an Anglo-French condominium that would lead Europe. An Anglo-French-led Europe would, it was envisaged, simultaneously diminish the Community's adherence to supranationality, whilst strengthening Europe in relation to the two world superpowers, the United States and the Soviet Union. For Brown and the DEA, aligning with the French was also a way of extending Britain's experiment in economic (indicative) planning. The rationale behind indicative economic planning was partly based on the French experience, and some of the Government's economic policy advisers, such as Bill Nield and Stuart Holland, had close links with French economic policy-makers (PRO EW24/53, Nield to Burgh, 24 March 1965; *The Times*, 3 April 1965; Badel, 1999: 237–41;

Leruez, 2002: 177–8). Moreover, the DEA supported technological expansion and, alongside Roy Jenkins's Ministry of Aviation, saw partnership with France as the cornerstone of a genuine European co-operative effort (PRO CAB 134/2134, JRD(65).2, Work of the Committee, Minister for Aviation, 28 May 1965). Only through collaboration could the European economies, which did not have the natural US advantage of a vast domestic consumer market, hope to support the research and development necessary to sustain the most modern technological developments (PRO EW 24/53, Nield to Burgh, 24 March 1965). Britain and France could together be the pioneers of European development in aircraft, space, computers, telecommunications and civil atomic energy.

The approach of Stewart and the Foreign Office towards Community membership was rather different. Far from seeing the French as Britain's primary partners in the EEC, the Foreign Office regarded France as a threat to Britain's position on the Continent. French dominance in the EEC meant that the Community was developing into a 'closed shop' (PRO PREM 13/306, Stewart to Wilson, PM/65/38, 3 March 1965). Economically, the protectionism of the Common Agricultural Policy (CAP) denied access to third country producers, and there was a risk that the French could thwart the Kennedy Round of trade negotiations in the General Agreement on Tariffs and Trade (GATT). French policies towards third countries were also making it difficult for Nigeria to associate with the Community on acceptable terms. The British feared that Nigeria would be forced to choose the EEC over Britain, whereupon other African Commonwealth nations would be encouraged to follow suit: 'France will inherit our place in Africa' (PRO PREM 13/306, Stewart to Wilson, 3 March 1965; PRO PREM 13/306, O'Neill to Stewart, 3 May 1965; Alexander, 2002: 195–7). Moreover, the Foreign Office feared the connection between French political dominance in the EEC and French policy towards NATO. If the French persuaded the Germans to team up with them in a defence partnership, the whole basis of the European and Atlantic alliance could unravel. Thus, the Foreign Office advocated a more vigorous policy towards attainment of eventual membership of the European Community. Expectation that Britain was likely to accede in the future would serve to stiffen the resolve of the Five against acquiescence to French terms and thus help to curb French hegemony in Europe (PRO FO 371/184288/W6/8, Barnes to Hood, 4 February 1965; also PRO PREM 13/306, Stewart to Wilson, PM/65/26, 12 February 1965).

Neither Stewart nor Brown pressed Wilson to make a second attempt to secure British membership of the EEC in 1965. Instead, both argued in favour of 'functional collaboration', which Brown viewed as part of a wider economic approach to the French, whereas Stewart favoured it as a non-controversial means to illustrate Britain's ultimate interest in the Community (PRO CAB 130/227, MISC48, 1st Conclusions, 25 March 1965). Wilson's adoption of the policy of bridge-building in May 1965, seeking an accommodation between the EEC and EFTA, was a response to the pressure from both government departments, although his own attitude suggests a lack of interest in the principle of EEC membership when Labour took office in 1964. Pressed by Brown and Stewart in 1965, though, Wilson appears to have recognised the political force of the argument that Britain needed to augment its influence, both on the Continent and internationally, through a closer relationship with the EEC. Wilson did raise the possibility of eventual membership of some kind of European Community 'based on the Treaty of Rome' when discussing the bridge-building initiative with the Cabinet in May 1965 (PRO CAB 128/39, CC(65) 30th Conclusions, 13 May 1965), but he showed no signs of reconciliation to the type of economic changes which would be engendered by British membership of the EEC. He replied to Stewart's prompting:

> [B]ut what is the right sort of Europe? Unless it was genuinely outward looking and not autarkic it must be inimical to Atlantic and Common-wealth links. The real test is agricultural policy, which in its present form is autarkic and would deal a death-blow to Commonwealth trade.
>
> (PRO PREM 13/306, Wilson comments on Stewart to Wilson, 3 March 1965)

To the Cabinet, he stressed that whilst Britain might have to enter some kind of Community, the EEC would have to 'develop policies acceptable to us' (PRO CAB 128/39, CC(65) 30th Conclusions, 3 May 1965).

Preoccupation with the Commonwealth formed the main argument against Britain's membership of the EEC at this early stage. Douglas Jay, President of the Board of Trade, drafted a paper in June 1965 which argued that entry into the EEC would place a threefold burden onto Britain's balance of payments. The cost of Britain's food imports would rise, as Britain would tend to import more from the EEC than from the Common-wealth. An increase in import costs would, in turn, raise the cost of living, and fuel compensatory wage claims, and thereby make Britain's exports less competitive. Commonwealth exports would encounter reverse preferences in Britain's market, losing the Commonwealth preference and facing the common external tariff (PRO PREM 13/904, EEC membership, President of the Board of Trade, 15 June 1965).

Behind Jay's analysis was a commitment to Commonwealth trade, to the principle of cheap food and to the idea of British constitutionalism and British leadership of a diverse, multiracial grouping (Jay, 1980: 347–408). While Jay's thinking was regarded by officials as 'partisan and emotionally directed', Wilson actually agreed with much of Jay's prioritising of the Commonwealth. Throughout 1965, Wilson genuinely sought to regenerate Commonwealth connections, investigating projects such as linking the planned aspects of the British economy to the needs of the Commonwealth (PRO CAB 130/229, MISC56, 1st Conclusions, 13 May 1965). However, by late 1965 a combination of the Commonwealth's lack of interest, and a conflict with Britain's own multilateral trading policies, rendered Wilson's Commonwealth regeneration programme economically unworkable (CAB 134/1746, ED(ER) (65).32, Meeting with Commonwealth Trade Officials, President of the Board of Trade, 29 November 1965; Tomlinson, 2003: 216–17). Furthermore, the idea of British political leadership of the Commonwealth was challenged by the unilateral declaration of independence in Rhodesia. The anger of the black African nations led the Nigerians to call a special conference in January 1966. On his return from this conference, Wilson endorsed secret studies of the implications of Community membership (PRO PREM 13/905, Stewart to Wilson, PM/66/3, 21 January 1966, reporting meeting of Wilson on 19 January 1966). The demise of the Commonwealth alternative was important in weakening Wilson's resistance to a more accommodating stance towards eventual British membership of the EEC.

A decision to probe: March–November 1966

Between March and July 1966, George Brown became the most vigorous advocate of a move to get into the European Community whilst de Gaulle was still in power. Stewart's Foreign Office was cautious about the implications of an attempt, in the short term, to secure Britain's membership of the EEC. The latter's hesitancy resulted partly from recognition of de Gaulle's likely obstruction; but the main reason for Foreign Office wariness stemmed from the crisis in NATO during this period. Whereas de Gaulle's withdrawal from the command structures of the alliance in March 1966 strengthened the long-term case for accession, in the short term the Foreign Office was concerned that de Gaulle could demand concessions in NATO in return for admitting Britain into the EEC (PRO CAB 148/69, OPD(66).9, The International Consequences of General de Gaulle's Foreign Policy, Foreign Office, 25 March 1966). The Foreign Office, backed by the US State Department, sought a declaration of intent that Britain would enter the EEC eventually, flanked by an invigoration of Britain's informal Continental probes ongoing since March 1966 (PRO FO 371/188347/M10810/458, How to Get into the Common Market, EEOD, 18 August 1966).

Brown, by contrast, maintained that Britain could accede to the Community in the short term. His initial proposal was for a British defence initiative whereby Britain could enter a defence arrangement with the Germans, supported by the Americans, which would prove so popular to European opinion that de Gaulle would be forced to admit Britain to the Community (PRO PREM 13/906, Brown to Wilson, 23 June 1966). Wilson resisted this idea on the grounds that Johnson would not be interested; moreover, US support would only be forthcoming if Britain conceded nuclear equality with the Germans (PRO PREM 13/906, Wilson comments on Brown to Wilson, 23 June 1966). Thereafter, Brown's belief in a short-term route into the Community blended with his interests in the economy. He maintained that Britain should devalue the pound and cut free from the country's inhibiting global role, which would not only signal Britain's commitment to Europe but also facilitate a more dynamic domestic economic policy (PRO PREM 13/907, Brown to Wilson, 29 June 1966). Devaluation could provide a way into the EEC via the support of the French: '[T]hat's what Pompidou said to us. Devalue as we did and you're in' (Castle, 1990: 75, diary entry for 18 July 1966). However, for others in the Labour Government, the July visit of Maurice Couve de Murville and Georges Pompidou, the French Minister of Foreign Affairs and Prime Minister, seemed to rule out French support for British membership, precisely because of Pompidou's suggestion that Britain might have to devalue the pound (PRO FO 371/189127/RF1053/38, Wilson, Brown and Stewart to Pompidou and Couve de Murville, 8 July 1966; PRO FO 371/189127/RF1053/36, Campbell comments on Reilly despatch, 13 July 1966; Roll, 1985: 173; Cairncross, 1997: 146).

Wilson called Ministers together for a meeting at Chequers on 22 October 1966 in order to discuss the question of Britain's policy towards the EEC. Wilson had already decided to seek British membership of the EEC in the short term, and in pursuit of this objective he proposed to undertake – with the new Foreign Secretary, George Brown – 'a tour round Europe . . . to visit the chief capitals and try to clarify the doubtful issues' (Crossman, 1976: 84, diary entry for 22 October 1966). Stewart, now Secretary of State for Economic Affairs, and Brown advanced the primary arguments in favour of a move towards the EEC, their joint paper arguing that, politically, Britain had to seek accession in order to remain a world power. The Commonwealth and EFTA would continue to diversify, and thus diverge away from Britain. Meanwhile, business and industry would become disillusioned should Britain fail to advance towards membership of the EEC, whereupon investment (and jobs) might well be relocated elsewhere. Britain would be unable to muster the influence to enforce its global economic policies: 'we would be left increasingly alone, swimming against contrary economic tides' (PRO CAB 134/2705, E(66).11, Britain and Europe, First Secretary and Foreign Secretary, 18 October 1966).

Not all Ministers supported the political case in favour of entry, with Crossman noting that some – in particular, Tony Benn (new to the Cabinet); Barbara Castle and Richard (Dick) Marsh – fully shared his scepticism about the argument that Britain should 'go into the EEC in order to remain great'. Indeed, Crossman himself advocated the option of a 'socialist offshore island': Britain should expedite the withdrawal of its global defence role, devalue the pound and draw down the reserve role of sterling, and pursue the Swedish route of social democracy, consolidating growth and welfare at home as a priority. Tony Benn, meanwhile, wondered whether Britain should value its outward-looking ties with the United States over and above links with the protectionist European bloc (Crossman, 1976: 84, diary entry for 22 October 1966). Wilson therefore agreed to prepare studies of both the alternative options: 'going it alone' (GITA), and the North Atlantic Free Trade Area (NAFTA), despite awareness that the Americans would be unlikely to support NAFTA.

It was primarily economic concerns which dominated the Chequers meeting, although Wilson suggested that the 'conditions' of EEC member-ship caused much less anxiety than hitherto. With regard to Britain's freedom to pursue an independent economic and foreign policy, Wilson argued that British economic policy was in any case constrained outside the Community, and that de Gaulle hardly found his foreign policy restricted because of Community membership. As for Labour's pledge to protect EFTA and the Commonwealth, EFTA countries were seeking accommoda-tion with the EEC anyway, whilst the Commonwealth countries were tending to diversify their trade away from Britain. Nevertheless, Wilson was careful to emphasise that in seeking EEC membership, the Government would make demands for the preservation of (unspecified) Commonwealth trading arrangements, and that Britain would need to seek amendments to the CAP. The overwhelming concern at Chequers was the weakness of ster-ling, with the officials in attendance – including William Armstrong, joint Permanent Under-Secretary at the Treasury – arguing that the fragility of sterling meant that expectation of membership could precipitate devalu-ation, as speculators sold sterling in anticipation. It could take Britain's economy five years to be ready to withstand the rigours of entry (PRO CAB 130/298, MISC126(66) 1st Conclusions, 22 October 1966).

For some Ministers, such as Crossman, Benn and Castle, who had sup-ported devaluation as a policy option in July, the prospect of a forced devaluation was welcome, although the pro-devaluation pro-Europeans were in a minority: Brown, Home Secretary Roy Jenkins and (to some extent) Education Secretary Tony Crosland. For most Ministers, the potential con-nection between devaluation and EEC membership was a considerable cause for concern, and after the Chequers meeting Chancellor James Callaghan wrote to Wilson to stress his fears that announcement of the tour could lead to sales of sterling, as speculators would anticipate an outflow of capital if Britain did enter the EEC (PRO PREM 13/909, Callaghan to Wilson, 31 October 1966). Yet by the time of the November Cabinet meetings at which the probe was endorsed, Callaghan had changed his mind, arguing that hope of membership would strengthen the short-term prospects for the economy by encouraging investment and illustrating to business and indus-try the framework within which the Labour Government would attain future growth. Callaghan's switch was essential in convincing Ministers to back the probe in these meetings, especially as Callaghan warned that he could not guarantee the strength of sterling – now under further threat because of sanctions in Rhodesia – unless Britain moved towards the Community (PRO CAB 128/41, CC(66) 55th Conclusions, 9 November 1966; Crossman, 1976: 117, diary entry for 9 November 1966). In other words, without the approach to the EEC, the British would not be able to discharge responsibilities to the Commonwealth. Barbara Castle indicated her support for the tour on the basis of this argument alone (Castle, 1990: 93, diary entry for 9 November 1966).

The conditional nature of the tour was important in securing the acquiescence of most Ministers to the policy. The probe implied no prior commitment to the principle of membership and would thereby forestall any adverse speculation against sterling. Wilson promised the Cabinet he would tell the Six that the CAP would distort British agricultural production and lead to a rise in prices and living costs. Acceptance of existing agricultural financing arrangements would pose an intolerable burden on Britain's balance of payments, and would therefore need review. Liberalisation of capital movements would also require safeguards, and Britain's ability to carry out regional policies that prioritised the development areas would have to be ensured. Certain Commonwealth countries would have to seek association, and arrangements would be required in particular for New Zealand trade, as New Zealand was particularly dependent on the British market for its agricultural exports (PRO CAB 129/127, CC(66).149, Europe, Foreign Secretary, 7 November 1966). Agreement for the Commonwealth should be no worse than that reached during the Brussels negotiations in 1961–1963 (PRO CAB 129/127, CC(66).150, Commonwealth Consultations, Commonwealth Secretary, 7 November 1966). Wilson expressly stated that only after exploratory discussions would the Cabinet have to choose whether terms that might reasonably be obtained in negotiations were adequate to justify joining the Community (PRO CAB 128/41, CC(66) 55th Conclusions, 9 November 1966).

Accepting the application, April 1967

A transformation in Wilson's stance became apparent during the Cabinet meetings in April 1967. The Prime Minister's position towards the EEC developed during the tour, as Wilson was confronted with the uneasy truth that any application for EEC membership would have to be unconditional in order to be convincing. Anything less than an unequivocal statement in favour of British accession would prove too simple for de Gaulle to rebuff (PRO PREM 13/1477, Wilson to Zijlastra and delegations, 27 February 1967). Wilson therefore decided, in the closing stages of the tour, to submit an unconditional application to the Six, covered by a statement to the House of Commons outlining minimal areas for negotiation (PRO FCO 30/82, Wilson to Trend, undated, early March 1967 (probably before the Luxembourg visit on 8 March)). His room for manoeuvre constrained by the need to deliver an initiative which was difficult for de Gaulle to reject, Wilson resolved to force through the Cabinet this virtually unconditional initiative. This shift was a radical breach in former British tactics towards the European Community and had an enormous impact on the Labour Cabinet's stance towards eventual entry.

On the eve of discussion as to Labour's next step towards the European Community, Cabinet opinion was divided. In favour of the principle of British entry into the EEC were Brown, Jenkins, Stewart, Lords Gardiner and Longford, and Minister of Labour Ray Gunter. Opposed on principle were Jay, Minister of Agriculture Fred Peart, Transport Secretary Barbara Castle, Minister of Power Richard Marsh, and Scottish Secretary Willie Ross. Undecided were Lord President Richard Crossman, Minister for Technology Tony Benn, Minister without Portfolio Patrick Gordon Walker, Crosland, Callaghan, Commonwealth Secretary Bert Bowden, Minister of Housing Anthony Greenwood, Healey and Cledwyn Hughes (Crossman, 1976: 336, diary entry for 1 May 1967; Pearce, 1991: 312; Castle, 1990: 126, diary entry for 1 May 1967).

The balance of opinion was therefore fine, and the views of undecided Ministers thus assumed great significance. Of importance to Wilson was the fact that Callaghan supported the initiative. In a restricted meeting just before the application was announced, Callaghan effectively staked his career on the retention of the parity of sterling. Neither the April budget nor the July deflation had ended speculation that Britain needed to devalue, and some felt that a turn to the EEC made devaluation more likely (Bank of England, OV44/136 (FU(67)1, 'Contingency Planning: Entry into Europe', June 1967). Callaghan silenced the doubters, suggesting that if sterling went, he would go too. Such a statement had the effect of bringing Ministers to rally behind Callaghan, supporting the line that the advance towards the EEC would strengthen the economy by encouraging expectation of growth and investment (PRO CAB 128/46, CC(67).25th Conclusions, 30 April 1967). Wary of the tenuous prospects for economic success, the Government was faced with a dilemma. To admit that the economy could face devaluation would only make that eventuality more certain. Callaghan had no choice but to argue that European entry would strengthen the economy, in the hope that this would become a self-fulfilling prophecy. Unwilling to jeopardise the Government's prospects, Ministers huddled into line.

It was also significant that of the Ministers listed as undecided, many were uncertain less of the principle of advancing towards the Community than of the timing of the proposed move. Herbert Bowden, Commonwealth Secretary, was a case in point. Outlining the dangers for New Zealand's trade, Bowden argued that Britain had to turn to the EEC in order to sustain current relations with the Commonwealth. Bowden admitted that Britain did have strong emotional ties to the Commonwealth:

> [W]e speak the same language and we understand each other – all the more so because we have largely common systems in administration, the law, the armed forces, education, British merchanting and banking traditions and interests. Oxbridge, Sandhurst, Shakespeare, the authorised version of the Bible are all genuine links.
> (PRO CAB 129/129, C(67).59, Commonwealth Secretary, 'The Value of the Commonwealth', 24 April 1967)

Nevertheless, protecting the developing Commonwealth had become an awkward stance to adopt in recent international meetings: 'in a special sense, Commonwealth Prime Ministers' meetings in recent years have contained examples of Britain clutching vipers to her bosom – and paying for it' (PRO CAB 129/129, C(67).59, 'The Value of the Commonwealth', Common-wealth Secretary, 24 April 1967). Diversification of Commonwealth inter-ests and Britain's need to multilateralise trade on a global basis also meant that the Commonwealth could not remain the tenet of Britain's world role.

Ministers uncertain as to the timing of Wilson's initiative rallied around Denis Healey, whose argument has been summarised in the phrase 'there's no point playing for a rebuff' (Castle, 1990: 123–4, diary entry for 20 April 1967). Healey's stance has been interpreted as principled opposition (Evans, 1975: 67), yet at the Ministry of Defence, Healey had shown strong support for European initiatives, such as pioneering the Euro-group defence proposal to strengthen the European arm of Britain's overseas defence (see, for example, PRO CAB 128/42, CC(67).69th Conclusions, 30 November 1967; Rees, 1999: 64–70). As the application process drew to a close in November and December 1967, Healey argued for a decisive veto in order to clear Britain's tactical grounds to concentrate on more fruitful proposals such as the Euro-group (PRO CAB 128/42, CC(67).69th Conclusions, 30 November 1967). Thus, Healey seemed to support the principle that Britain should move towards Europe, but he queried whether Britain should apply at that time. Why court a failure that could only make the British seem once again the odd man out in Europe? Bowden shared Healey's reservations, for although Bowden agreed that Britain had little choice but to secure membership of the Community, he nonetheless felt it was too early to make the application (Pearce, 1991: 312; Crossman, 1976: 336, diary entry for 30 April 1967).

Healey's position led Wilson to a radical transformation in tactics, as the Cabinet Secretary, Burke Trend, advised Wilson tactically to separate the 'nevers' from the 'not yets'. To do so, Wilson should address directly the political case for joining the EEC (PRO PREM 13/1479, Trend to Wilson, 19 April 1967). Despite the Cabinet's resistance to Trend's argument that even if de Gaulle vetoed, Britain should 'stand on the threshold in a stance of eager expectation', Wilson argued, '[I]f rebuffed, we should not rule out the possibility of joining Europe later' (PRO CAB 128/42, CC(67).22nd, 20 April 1967; Crossman, 1976: 321, diary entry for 20 April 1967). Politic-ally, studies of 'going it alone' (GITA) and the North Atlantic Free Trade Area (NAFTA) revealed that there was absolutely no alternative to member-ship of the Community. NAFTA was not viable because the Americans did not want it, and besides, such a partnership would subordinate Britain to the superior strength of the United States. GITA was plausible but unwel-come, forcing Britain into specialisation of its economy and condemning Britain to a permanently less competitive position vis-àvis its European neighbours. The Commonwealth could not constitute the basis of Britain's long-term future, for the reasons outlined by Bowden; moreover, it was only through entry into the European Community that Britain could hope to preserve its existing Commonwealth ties (PRO CAB 129/129, C(67).52, Cabinet Secretary, 'Alternatives to Membership of the EEC', 14 April 1967). Therefore, in order to retain political independence in the world, Britain had to join the EEC. Wilson argued explicitly that failure to do so would mean Britain would have to follow the United States into Vietnam (PRO CAB 128/42, CC(67).26th Conclusions, 30 April 1967). Europe offered the only basis for the building of Britain's future political independence. Even if the application failed in the short term, the British had no choice but to secure entry in the longer term.

Such a stark rendition of the political case represented a clear departure from Britain's former stance. Wilson's argument had an immediate effect. Healey, the prime target of the tactics, was angered, but recognised the corner into which the Cabinet had been backed (Castle, 1990: 123–4, diary entry for 20 April 1967). It was this political argument that had the greatest effect in securing the Cabinet's rather reluctant support for the initiative. With options foreclosed in this manner, there was literally nowhere else for Ministers to go. For the left, the lack of choice was a consequence of the failure of the government's alternative economic policies. Crossman wrote that the alternative of a 'socialist offshore island' could have been attainable prior to the July 1966 deflation, but now everyone recognised the improbability of such a goal (1976: 320–1, diary entry for 20 April 1967). Tony Benn was in favour of entry, partly because he wished to expand technological links with the Commuity, although he had always been dubious about the ease with which Britain could do this (PRO PREM 13/1850, Benn to Wilson, 24 November 1966). Nevertheless, Benn also felt that the Cabinet's agreement was the result of Britain's economic difficulties: 'those of us who favoured the application were not too worried about the conditions because we were a defeated Cabinet' (1987: 496, diary entry for 20 April 1967). Such views were hardly an emphatic or enthusiastic endorsement of Britain's future membership of the European Community.

The Cabinet's reluctant acceptance that there was no alternative to seeking British membership of the EEC had a further important consequence. Crossman summed this up when he argued that if the application had to be made, then the Cabinet might as well do it as effectively as possible (1976: 320–1, diary entry for 20 April 1967). Acquiescence to the principle meant that the Cabinet then put up very little opposition to the terms under which Britain should accede. All were aware of the likelihood of de Gaulle's veto and knew that too stringent adherence to the terms of entry in advance would hand de Gaulle an easy victory. During the Cabinet meetings, Wilson argued that Britain would seek in advance arrangements for New Zealand's trade and for Commonwealth sugar. Although Ministers acknowledged the unwelcome cost of accepting the Community's system of payment into the agricultural fund, Wilson simply stated that such a system would prove 'inequitable'. He did not promise to make alterations before securing membership (House of Commons Debates, 5th series, vol. 746, col. 312).

The Cabinet's muddying of the entry terms was further in evidence as Brown prepared to deliver Britain's negotiating stance to the countries of the Six in July 1967. Brown expressly told the Cabinet that there was little need to quibble over the details of Britain's negotiating posture. It was more important, Brown argued, to overcome de Gaulle's opposition: 'the immediate purpose must be to assure that negotiation actually began' (PRO CAB 128/42, CC(67).44th Conclusions, 3 July 1967). Britain's priority was to appear to accept all the terms of entry, in the hope of applying diplomatic pressure to de Gaulle. In particular, Brown did not invite thorough discussion concerning the agricultural financing arrangements, arguing instead that Britain should seek to enter the Community before the Six's scheduled agricultural review in 1969. Once a member of the Community, Britain would be better placed to seek changes (PRO CAB 128/42, CC(67).44th Conclusions, 3 July 1967). Yet the Cabinet Office felt it was unrealistic to expect full membership in advance of the 1969 review. Indeed, this point had been made to Ministers during the April discussions, but in the atmosphere of resigned acceptance of the initiative, no Minister opted to challenge the Foreign Secretary.

The application and veto, May–December 1967: Wilson's position

Instead, de Gaulle challenged the British application, vetoing the opening of negotiations on 27 November 1967. The rest of this chapter will show that, if anything, Wilson's commitment to the British application only increased after the French veto. As he told Parliament, 'I do not agree that we are knocking on the door and being humiliated. We have slammed down our application on the table. There it is, and there it remains' (House of Commons Debates, 5th series, vol. 755, col. 239). All the factors that had compelled him to make the application remained – and were even strengthened with the decisions to devalue sterling and to accelerate the withdrawal of British forces from east of Suez. NAFTA remained 'an option that simply did not exist', whilst in the veto period Wilson only mentioned GITA in the sense that Britain was strong enough to stand on its own feet if the application were rejected, or if it failed to secure acceptable terms of entry (PRO PREM 13/2413, Palliser to Day, 30 September 1968). For the remainder of the Government's term of office, Wilson remained intimately involved in both the strategy and the tactics of European policy.

George Brown's pro-European sentiments have already been discussed, but from March 1968 Wilson enjoyed the support of Michael Stewart, who returned to the Foreign Office when Brown finally resigned (Pimlott, 1992: 483–503). There were concerns, both in the United Kingdom and on the Continent, that the replacement of such a well-known pro-European with a less passionate person would be interpreted as indicating a change in British policy (PRO FCO 30/117, Hancock to Morland etc., 18 March 1968; PRO FCO 30/194, Roberts to Maitland, 19 March 1968). However, the change actually proved beneficial to the 'approach to Europe': Stewart got on well with Wilson, and shared ideas about policy and strategy with him – indeed, Wilson made him his 'No. 1 Deputy in grave emergency' (The Papers of Lord Stewart of Fulham (henceforth 'Stewart Papers' or 'Stewart diaries'), STWT8/1/5, diaries, 23 April 1968). His less abrasive style allowed for easier relations with Foreign Ministers abroad, and, according to Castle (1990: 604), his boring and verbose reports allowed him to sneak difficult information past Cabinet. For the first time in the veto period, Britain had a Foreign Secretary who was not only determined to move the application forward, but was also sensitive to the needs and anxieties of friends on the Continent in a way that Brown had not been. Stewart was supported in the Foreign Office by his Minister of State, Lord (Alun) Chalfont, and, following the October 1969 reshuffle, by George Thomson in his new capacity as Chancellor of the Duchy of Lancaster. Together with Wilson, these Ministers made up a formidable team that was entirely united behind the goal of negotiating British membership of the EEC at an acceptable cost.

Contingency planning

As it became clear that de Gaulle might indeed veto the British effort, contingency planning began in the Foreign Office. Wilson insisted that they should be ready for a French '*non*', wondered if they should submit another application immediately, and declared that the Government should 'keep the ball before every meeting' (PRO FCO 30/107, Wilson, handwritten note on Palliser to Day, 25 September 1967). Sir Con O'Neill felt that a French veto would 'be *par excellence* the moment for ñot taking no for an answer". He acknowledged, though, the importance of having the friendly Five on side:

> [T]he Five must *not* acquiesce in the kind of position they adopted in January 1963: namely a reluctant acquiescence in the fact that the French attitude effectively terminated, or interrupted, the possibility of further negotiations with us. Thus, if the French say no, the Five must continue loudly and determinedly, in season and out, going on saying yes.
>
> (PRO FCO 30/107, O'Neill to Statham, 28 July 1967)

O'Neill's path was ultimately followed, whereupon the Foreign Office drafted a paper emphasising that the British application should be 'debated and approved' in all the national parliaments, the international assemblies, and 'in as many bodies and organisations as we can drum up'. While it was recognised that these tactics would not be enough to force de Gaulle's hand, it was equally acknowledged that the point was not to alienate France completely, since 'our major objective is to become part of a European Community which includes France'. The possibility of working with the Five in areas outside the Rome Treaties was raised, as was the notion of the Five holding up progress within the Communities (PRO FCO 30/107, Draft Paper, 'Britain and the European Communities', 16 August 1967). Officials suggested both a 'solemn declaration' by Britain and the Five, and a high-level meeting. The final draft of the paper highlighted the irony of the situation: the Government would need to act quickly after the expected veto, but must not give any hint of the action being considered in the meantime (PRO FCO 30/107, EURO(67).117, 'Action to Be Taken in the Light of an Early French Veto', 6 October 1967).

The secrecy that would become a feature of the Labour Government's European policy was already clearly discernible. Wilson, Brown and Callaghan agreed that contingency planning would be discussed interdepartmentally, but with officials attending in their personal capacity. The papers were therefore not circulated to the different departments. The group of officials from the Treasury, Board of Trade, Department of Economic Affairs and Foreign Office, after consulting the Commonwealth Office and the Ministry of Agriculture, agreed that there was 'no alternative to maintaining the objective of joining the Community and ... this would require the strongest possible reaffirmation of purpose by the Government buttressed by supporting statements in some form by the Governments of the Five' (PRO FCO 30/107, Jackling to Brown's private secretary, 20 October 1967). Months before the veto, therefore, both British policy in case of rejection, and its management, were already determined – without Cabinet discussion.

The 'Opinion', devaluation and the November veto

The publication of the European Commission's 'Opinion' on enlargement in September strengthened British policy. It was ruthless in dealing with the British economic situation, but concluded that negotiations should be opened at once (*Keesings Contemporary Archive* (henceforth KCA), 23169–23170, 1–8 February 1969). Whilst the Five welcomed the Commission's contribution and agreed that negotiations should commence, the French focused on the comments about Britain's economy, and succeeded in persuading the others that they should concentrate on defining the conditions of membership, rather than moving immediately to entry negotiations (KCA 23170, 1–8 February 1969). While the Six were conducting this internal debate, however, the British finally accepted that the parity of sterling would have to be modified.

Many hoped that devaluation would help British European policy by indicating that the Government was prepared to address the country's persistent economic weakness, in preparation for taking on the economic burdens of membership. The Treasury brief stated that devaluation 'will not lessen the Government's determination to join the European Economic

Community', but, rather, would 'put beyond doubt this country's ability to accept the obligations of membership' (PRO PREM 13/2058, Treasury brief, 20 November 1967). Members of the Six were reassuring, with the Belgian Prime Minister, amongst others, writing to Wilson to welcome the economic measures taken by the British government: '[e]lles renforcent le désir du Gouvernement belge de voir rapidement les négociations entamées entre le Royaume Uni et les Six pays membres, dans le perspective d'une adhésion prochaine' (PRO PREM 13/2058, van den Boeynants to Wilson, 21 November 1967; see also de Jong to Wilson, 23 November 1967; Werner to Wilson, 23 November 1967, Kiesinger to Wilson, 4 December 1967). Wilson himself took a somewhat contradictory position, simultaneously believing that the devaluation 'clearly ... ought to help', yet doubting 'whether it will in any way affect the General's long-term strategy' (PRO PREM 13/2058, Wilson to Brown, 24 November 1967). In the event, he was correct on both counts: the Six welcomed the courageous British decision to devalue, but the French Finance Minister, Michel Debré, noted that it would 'not fundamentally change the French view on the British candidature for membership of the Common Market' (KCA 22373, 25 November–2 December 1967). The Belgian and Dutch Foreign Ministers formally recorded their disappointment at the French attitude, but that did not stop it from being confirmed in de Gaulle's press conference, held just nine days after the devaluation announcement (KCA 23170–23171, 1–8 February 1969). So why did the Labour Government persevere? As Kitzinger noted, Wilson could hardly have coined the phrase 'not taking no for an answer' if the answer had looked like being yes (Kitzinger, 1968: 14). Deighton suggests that so much had been invested in the policy that backing off would have been politically unacceptable: 'having got so far, the Labour government clearly could not yet take France's third *Non* as a final no' (2003: 48). Lieber takes a slightly different approach, arguing that once the decision was made, 'Wilson was absolutely determined in his course' (1970: 272). Neither concern for political appearances nor plain stubbornness, however, takes account of the long-term importance of the second British application. De Gaulle's reasons for opposing British entry to the Communities – economic weakness, the 'special relationship', links with the Commonwealth – were the very issues with which British governments were trying to come to terms during the 1960s.

The Cabinet

For the remaining thirty months or so of the 1966–1970 Labour Government, the dynamics within the Cabinet remained virtually unchanged. On a few occasions, Ministers pressed half-heartedly for a reopening of the question of entry in principle, with the most determined of these efforts coming, as might be expected, immediately after the veto. Peter Shore, Secretary of State for Economic Affairs, wrote to Wilson that while I appreciate your wish not to react petulantly to de Gaulle and to await the December meeting of the Council of Ministers, I do feel strongly that, with soft answers, we are in danger of losing a unique opportunity of rallying opinion, of asserting our self reliance, and of identifying ourselves with the national cause. . . . People in Britain, as you have so often observed, are tired of being pushed around. The General's veto compounds the feeling of national humiliation which followed last week's devaluation. . . . Surely this is the moment, in a measured and serious way, to be 'Gaullist' in the British sense and to rally the nation . . . in the task of making ourselves both strong and independent.

(PRO PREM 13/2646, Shore to Wilson, 28 November 1967)

One Minister ruefully suggested as a text for Anglo-European relations an old Confederate song: 'I can't take up my musket / To fight 'em now no more / But I ain't going to love 'em / And that is sartin sure' (PRO PREM 13/1488 (possibly Gordon Walker) to Wilson, 20 December 1967). Later, there were several ministerial calls for a general review of foreign policy, and two such reviews were indeed undertaken, one in January 1968 and the other in July 1969. The second of these entailed Wilson and Stewart seeking a renewed remit, prompted by a perception that the chances of negotiations were increasing (PRO CAB 128/43/CC(68).9, 18 January 1968; PRO CAB 128/44, CC(69).35, 22 July 1969; PRO PREM 13/2629, Graham to Youde, 18 July 1969). Ministers sometimes tried to turn attention towards other options, such as NAFTA, GITA or developing either the Commonwealth or EFTA (PRO CAB 128/42, CC(67).69, 30 November 1967; PRO CAB 128/43, CC(68).9, 18 January 1968 and CC(68).42, 17 October 1968). Finally, there were occasional outbursts against the continuation of a policy that some felt to be at worst humiliating and at best pointless. In February 1968, in what she described as 'one of [her] usual diatribes', Castle told Ministers that they 'all ought to be uttering paeans of praise and thankfulness for the fact that our application to join had been turned down' (1990: 382–3, diary entry for 27 February 1968).

Apart from these somewhat desultory efforts, the Cabinet witnessed a similar apathy to that noted for 1966–1967. This does beg the question of why supposedly 'Euro-sceptic' Ministers like Shore, Castle and Crossman did not protest more forcefully. One of the main reasons seems to concern the doctrine of collective responsibility, for the Cabinet *had* agreed, in 1967, to apply, unconditionally, for entry to the EEC, a decision which had then been reinforced by the then largest peacetime majority achieved in the House of Commons. Certainly when Peter Shore subsequently stepped out of line in March 1970, publicly suggesting that the Government's stance had changed, the rest of the Cabinet were horrified. Shore defended himself vigorously, but was reminded in discussion that all had agreed that whatever differences of opinion of emphasis there existed among individual Ministers, the Government would speak with one voice in public in endorsement of the policy. It was essential, he was told, in what Castle described as 'the biggest trouncing in Cabinet I can remember for a long time', to avoid any appearance of disunity or allow the impression to be created that the Government was prepared to treat a major issue of national policy as the subject of mere party political controversy in the period before the general election. The Government's policy should therefore be reaffirmed in the terms already approved collectively by the Cabinet, and Shore should seek an early public opportunity to put his speech in better perspective, making it clear that it remained the Government's declared purpose to join the Community if acceptable terms could be obtained (PRO CAB 128/45, CC(70).14, 26 March 1970; Castle, 1990: 782, diary entry for 26 March 1970).

A further reason, though (as previously noted), was that the decision had been taken by 'a defeated Cabinet' (Benn, 1987: 496, diary entry for 30 April 1967). By the time of de Gaulle's veto, devaluation had compounded the defeat initially inflicted by the various sterling crises, and the failure of the national plan. Ministerial acquiescence thereafter suggests that Ministers still did not see any realistic alternative to the continued pursuit of British membership of the EEC. Crossman suggested that some Ministers almost abdicated responsibility for European policy, noting that 'We are all too tired, too absorbed in our own interests to feel any great collective responsibility' (1977: 586, diary entry for 22 July 1969; Castle, 1990: 604, diary entry for 22 July 1969). Both Crossman and Castle suggested that they were bored with the whole approach to Europe, using this reason to explain their lack of attention as the 'Soames affair'[1] broke (Crossman, 1977: 373, diary entry for 20 February 1969).

Moreover, some Ministers continued to believe that, given de Gaulle's opposition to British entry, Wilson's approach could never succeed. There was no need to take a stand when the General would do the Euro-sceptics' job for them (Marsh, 1978: 96). Crossman once tried to use this stance to make Wilson rethink, asking, 'For Heaven's sake, why do we assume that negotiations should be resumed as soon as possible, why assume that we want another snub when there is really no chance of our getting in?' (Crossman, 1977: 653, diary entry for 24 September 1969). Finally, in a Cabinet that saw battles over issues like the Rhodesian settlement, selling arms to South Africa and the reform of industrial relations, European policy was simply not deemed important enough a subject over which to resign (Castle, 1990: 548, diary entry for 13 November 1968). The combined effect of these factors provided an opportunity space in which Wilson, Brown and Stewart were able to pursue British accession to the EEC.

Wilson's tactics

Even the somewhat lacklustre protests had to be dealt with, however, and hence Wilson restricted decision-making on European policy to a tight circle – one which excluded most Ministers. Wherever possible, smaller groups or official groups were used instead of Cabinet – at Wilson's express command. So, for example, in reply to a request from Anthony Crosland, President of the Board of Trade, that senior Ministers should meet to discuss events since the veto, the Prime Minister minuted Palliser, '[b]etter be EUR(O). and then the Ministerial committee under George' (PRO PREM 13/2110, note on B. W. Meynall to Maitland, 12 January 1968). Crosland received the same reply in May: Wilson directed him to Stewart and thence to the official and ministerial Europe committees, not to Cabinet (PRO PREM 13/2111, note on Crosland to Stewart, 6 May 1968; Palliser to Maitland, 7 May 1968). Again, when the ministerial committee decided, in April 1968, to cut British participation in European collaboration on space exploration, Wilson instructed Stewart to set up a new committee. This body, under Lord Chalfont, was to explore what space projects Britain could participate in, in order to mitigate the adverse effects in Europe of the above decisions. There was 'no need to inform Cabinet of the names of the committee members' (PRO PREM 13/2364, Palliser to Wilson, 6 April 1968; Stewart to Wilson, 9 April 1968; Palliser to Maitland, 10 April 1968). In October of the same year, Wilson and Stewart agreed that 'since the next stage was to be concerned with how to maintain the momentum in Europe in matters other than those relating to EEC and our application for membership of it', it should be discussed in an ad hoc committee, not the ministerial committee on Europe, with membership of the new group to be suggested by the Foreign Secretary (PRO PREM 13/2627, Palliser to Day, 7 October 1968). Despite Stewart drafting a paper for the purpose, he and Wilson decided, in January 1969, that there was no need to discuss European policy in the overseas policy and defence committee (OPD) or Cabinet before Stewart attended a ministerial meeting of the Western European Union (WEU) and Wilson met with Kiesinger – two events likely to be crucial to the policy (PRO PREM 13/2627, draft untitled Cabinet paper, Hancock to Palliser, 7 January 1969; Palliser to Maitland, 24 January 1969).

Once preparations got under way, in anticipation of the opening of the next round of negotiations Wilson sought even greater secrecy. In studies of the CAP, 'Any figures should be kept very close and . . . there should be no briefing suggesting that the study was well advanced; otherwise there would be strong pressure to reveal its contents publicly' (PRO PREM 13/2629, 'Record of a meeting between the Prime Minister, the Foreign and Commonwealth Secretary and Mr Soames at 2.45 p.m. on Wednesday June 25, 1969 at No. 10 Downing Street'). Again, in July 1969 Wilson told Stewart that 'he did not wish the attempt to establish a total figure for the balance of payments cost of our acceptance of the Common Agricultural Policy to go forward. The difficulty that the speculation on such a figure would cause had been made apparent by recent press reports', and in any case the figure would be meaningless since the Six were about to renegotiate the CAP (PRO PREM 13/2629, Youde to Graham, 14 July 1969). This position was adopted against Stewart's advice, and was augmented by an instruction that individual departments were not to do their own calculations either (PRO PREM 13/2629, Youde to Wilson, 18 July 1969).

An earlier agreement that they should seek a renewed remit for the policy in Cabinet was tempered by the earmarking of this meeting as an opportunity for the Prime Minister to make 'his statement on the need for Departments to maintain discipline' (PRO PREM 13/2629, Graham to Youde, 18 July 1969). During the drafting of the White Paper on the costs of British entry to the EEC, in the winter of 1969–1970, the need for secrecy was held to be absolute, and very few Ministers were involved. In January 1970, an 'inner group' of Ministers was chosen to consider the paper before it went to Cabinet (Jenkins, Castle, Benn, Thompson, Mason and Hughes), and even the knowledge that those Ministers were meeting was confined to the Ministers themselves and the officials directly involved in briefing them (PRO PREM 13/3199, Lloyd-Jones to private secretaries of the Ministers concerned, 7 January 1970).

In addition to minimising the number of people involved in the decision-making process, Wilson directly participated in the drafting of policy papers. As in April 1967, when a joint Wilson–Brown paper was presented to Cabinet as the effort of Brown alone, Stewart presented a paper with considerable input from the Prime Minister to the two Europe committees in May 1968 (PRO PREM 13/2108, Wilson to Brown (in Washington, DC), 20 April 1967, telegram no. 3790; EUR(M).(68).6). Wilson amended both the content and the tone of this paper in an attempt to pre-empt and counter anticipated criticism in Cabinet – its planned final destination. Once again, circulation was initially limited, the paper going first to the Chancellor, the Secretary of Defence and the President of the Board of Trade, then to the ministerial committee on Europe, and only being intended for consideration by the Cabinet after it had cleared these hurdles (PRO PREM 13/2112, Maitland to Palliser, 10 May 1968; Palliser to Wilson, 10 May 1968; Palliser to Maitland, 13 May 1968). Wilson had also contributed to the drafting of a Cabinet paper in February of that year: this paper was intended not to lead to decision but to 'stimulate some thought from our seminarists' (PRO PREM 13/2636, handwritten note on Youde to Wilson, 22 February 1968). Whilst he originally 'did not want the attempt to establish a total figure for the balance of payments cost of our acceptance of the Common Agricultural Policy to go forward' because of the difficulties it would cause in the Cabinet and country, Wilson later ordered that studies should produce a broad range of possible totals, taking into account many different variables, even suggesting those that should be considered (PRO PREM 13/2480, Youde to Graham, 14 July 1969; PRO PREM 13/2629, Wilson to Stewart, 13 September 1969).

Wilson later played a key role in the drafting of the White Paper on the costs of entry, published in February 1970, contributing to several drafts. He not only commented on the tone that he wanted the paper to take – strictly factual, without arguments for or against joining – but also gave instructions on the form of the paper. In so doing, Wilson rejected Foreign Office suggestions that the information could be presented as a Green Paper, 'which would give the impression that the Government policy had changed since 1967 and that the policy was open to debate' (PRO PREM 13/3222, to Brandt, 'Note for the Record', undated: filed in November 1969). Instead, Wilson insisted that it should be a White Paper, containing official Government policy, so that the original question of deciding to apply to join the EEC could not be reopened. He also was minutely involved in the detail of the paper, to the point of checking the arithmetic involved in calculating the costs of entry in his trademark green ink (PRO PREM 13/3198 and 13/3199, Wilson's comments on drafts of White Paper). Wilson further insisted that the White Paper should indicate that 'if negotiations did not produce acceptable conditions we should decline' (PRO PREM 13/3199, note on Nield to Andrew Halls, 14 January 1970).

The Prime Minister tried to encourage Ministers actively to support his European policy – without too much success. In September 1969, Wilson accepted Stewart's advice that 'senior Ministers should be pressed to make committal speeches during the autumn' and that Wilson should speak to junior Ministers about the 'general principles of ministerial conduct' – that is, supporting official Government policy (PRO PREM 13/2629, Wilson to Stewart, 13 September 1969). The result was a minute to all Ministers and junior Ministers in which Wilson wrote:

> I should like to underscore ... the importance of all Ministers taking advantage of opportunities – in speeches, press interviews and other public appearances – to support the Government's European policy; i.e. that we are ready to open negotiations with the Community as soon as possible and join it if the right terms are available. If we are to carry through successful negotiations, on which everything will depend, it is important that the whole Government should present a determined and united front both to our future partners in Europe and to those who are trying to undermine the Government's policies at home. . . . There is no need to be obsessed by safeguards and the negative aspects of our application, though the Government has these fully in mind. There are plenty of positive points to put across about the opportunities that membership would offer for our influence abroad and economic well-being at home.
> (PRO PREM 13/3197, Prime Minister's Personal Minute no. M/62/69,
> 30 October 1969)

This minute demonstrates Wilson's resolve that the European policy should be presented as agreed and undisputed official policy – and perhaps also his acknowledgement that it was neither agreed nor undisputed by all Ministers. Indeed, after the speech by Peter Shore mentioned above, Wilson gave a further instruction to Cabinet Ministers that any speech on the Common Market should be cleared both with the Chancellor of the Duchy of Lancaster and with Sir William Nield, who would in turn consider whether any other Department, in addition to the Foreign and Commonwealth Office, needed to be brought in.

(PRO PREM 13/3197, Moon to Wilson, 13 April 1970)

Ministers were evidently not to be trusted to make the right kind of speeches on their own. Wilson did not, though, force Ministers and Labour MPs to join those institutions that did represent and support official policy, such as the Labour Committee for Europe, anticipating that some would rebel and that there would be a 'sheep and goats story in the Press if some Ministers joined and some did not' (PRO PREM 13/3343, note on minute, Moon to Wilson, 27 February 1970 and 3 March 1969).

The ultimate form of control available to Wilson, however, was the Cabinet reshuffle, for by appointing pro-Europeans to key ministries he could ensure that his own policies would be implemented. He wrote to Stewart in confirmation of a conversation they had in September 1969, saying:

I indicated to you that the forthcoming Ministerial changes could be used to emphasise our commitment to Europe. This however would depend on the decisions you yourself made about the allocation of duties among your new team. This I will leave entirely to you.

(PRO PREM 13/2629, Wilson to Stewart, 13 September 1969)

This conversation reveals both the determination of Wilson to ensure that his Cabinet supported the European policy, and the extent of the trust and harmony of views on Europe between Wilson and Stewart. Together, they worked effectively towards British membership of the EEC.

Conclusion

This chapter indicates first that Harold Wilson's decision to apply for membership of the European Economic Community was a political one (see also Parr, 2006). Wilson viewed EEC membership as a means of dealing with Britain's future world role in the context of, and in response to, Britain's declining links with the Commonwealth, the British retreat from a global defence role east of Suez, and Britain's diminishing influence vis-àvis the United States. Even after the failure of the initiative in 1967, Wilson intended to take Britain into the EEC. Indeed, his backing for a European future appeared to increase after 1967.

Second, Wilson's tactics in dealing with the Cabinet were a departure from previous tactics for securing EEC membership. Rather than balancing domestic doubts about the terms of entry with the diplomatic need to get Britain into the Community, Wilson elected to force through Cabinet an unconditional application, accompanied by a statement to the House of Commons. Wilson adopted the political argument in 1967 that even if Britain did not secure EEC membership in the short term, there was no choice but to accede in the longer term. Such an argument neutralised Cabinet opposition to the timing of the move: it was a question of principle, and Ministers resignedly accepted Wilson's judgement that there was no choice. Because Ministers had endorsed the initiative in principle in 1967, there were no acceptable outlets for ministerial opposition to the continuation of Britain's approach between 1968 and 1970.

Third, European policy under Wilson was an elite diplomatic strategy. Wilson oversaw a tight management of European policy, particularly after the veto, whereby discussion was restricted to small groups, with the Prime Minister overseeing it personally wherever possible. Although ministerial opposition in 1967 to the principle of membership was not as extensive as is sometimes depicted, Wilson's tactics had the effect of muting opposition, which might well have served to store resentment for the future.

Nevertheless, Wilson's approach to the EEC must be regarded as a success. Wilson adopted the strategic goal of Community membership and did all he could to bring that goal closer, despite the unlikely prospect of short-term accession. Wilson's management of the Cabinet created the vital appearance of unity, helping to show that the British really did mean business. Without Wilson's application, the subsequent Conservative Government could not have opened negotiations for membership only twelve days after the 1970 general election (see also Pine, 2003).

Note

1 The 'Soames Affair' was a diplomatic spat between Britain and France that followed proposals on European policy made by de Gaulle to the British ambassador in Paris, Christopher Soames. See Pine (2004).

8 Foreign policy beyond Europe

Rhiannon Vickers

Introduction

Whilst the Labour Party had high expectations of a new, radical political dawn upon winning the general election on 15 October 1964, it faced two major hazards. First, it only had a majority of 4 seats, and this small majority constrained Wilson in both party political and policy issues. Conversely, this situation also provided him with an excuse for not undertaking radical initiatives. Despite being from the centre-left of the party, he appointed many colleagues from the right to his Cabinet. Patrick Gordon Walker, a 'quiet, acquiescent' man (Short, 1989: 21), became Foreign Secretary, shortly to be followed by another right-winger, Michael Stewart. Denis Healey became Defence Secretary, a position that he held throughout the two Labour Governments. However, Harold Wilson also established a new Ministry, that of Overseas Development, the first appointment to which was a left-winger, Barbara Castle.

Second, Labour had regained power at a time of considerable change, when questions were being asked about the role that Britain could, or should, play in the world. Britain still had a vast military commitment across the globe, with troops across Europe, the Middle East and Far East, including Germany, the Mediterranean, Aden, the Persian Gulf and Malaysia. However, it was becoming increasingly apparent that Britain's relative economic decline – relative, that is, to other industrialised countries – meant that it could no longer project itself as a major force in the world in the way that it had during the first half of the twentieth century. It was also clear that Britain had become increasingly dependent upon the United States in terms of security policy. Indeed, Britain's bid to join the European Community had been rather humiliatingly vetoed by General de Gaulle in January 1963, partly because of its close ties with the United States (but also, more generally, because he suspected that Britain was motivated primarily by economic self-interest, rather than genuine partnership and long-term integration with other European states).

Wilson described on how his first day in office he found himself facing a 'stormy welcome':

The Chinese had, the previous day, exploded their first nuclear weapon. . . . There was a telegram appraising the situation in the Soviet Union following the overthrow, less than twenty-four hours earlier, of Mr Khrushchev. . . . There was a telephone call from President Johnson [of the United States]. . . . And, grimmest of all, there was the economic news.

(1971: 2–3)

The economic news was that there was an £800 million balance of payments deficit, knowledge of which the Conservatives had not made public. Wilson's solution to this was to shore up sterling by turning to the United States for financial support, whilst introducing a series of severe financial restraints domestically. Both these measures alienated the Wilson Government from the wider Labour Party. This chapter will argue that the economic problems were greatly to influence, but not determine, Wilson's foreign policy – and it was Wilson's foreign policy, rather than that of any of his rather short-lived Foreign Secretaries. I will focus specifically on three major issues that dominated Britain's foreign policy during the 1964–1970 Labour Governments: relations with the United States, and in particular the escalation of the Vietnam War and the tensions engendered within the Labour Party by Wilson's formal support for America; defence policy, in particular the recognition that, largely for economic reasons, Britain needed to reduce its overseas military commitments, hence the start of a withdrawal from 'east of Suez' from 1967 onwards; and Southern Rhodesia, where the unilateral declaration of independence (UDI) by Ian Smith's white minority government in November 1965 demonstrated Britain's weakness in dealing with the Commonwealth. Subsequent attempts by Wilson to broker a settlement in Rhodesia received a hostile response from sections of the left in the Labour Party, and merely demonstrated Britain's impotence to act alone.

Anglo-American relations

Wilson had undertaken two trips to the United States before the 1964 general election, the first to meet President Kennedy, the second to meet his successor, President Lyndon Johnson. As a result of these trips, and of the favourable news coverage that accompanied them, Wilson felt that he had a special rapport with the Americans in general, and a special relationship with Johnson in particular. However, during 1963 and 1964 the US administration had undertaken a reassessment of Anglo-American relations. Britain's continued economic weakness, combined with the failure of its bid to enter the European Economic Community at a time when the United States was hoping for an increased European role for Britain, resulted in a decline in its importance to the United States. The stormy debates over foreign and defence policy within the Labour Party during the late 1950s, with the left of the party supporting unilateral nuclear disarmament, also meant that a Labour victory was viewed with some trepidation in a US administration more used to dealing with a Conservative government.

Less than two months after becoming Prime Minister, Wilson visited Washington with Denis Healey and Patrick Gordon Walker. A great deal of advance work was undertaken before the visit, with Wilson being warned that he 'should not bank on everything going his way when he got face to face with the President'. It was even pointed out that the President was not looking forward to the talks with anything approaching the same eagerness as the Prime Minister, as he had many other problems on his mind and saw the visit 'as more of a chore than a major act of policy' (PRO PREM 13/103, Mitchell to Harlech, 30 November 1964, with note of conversation with Richard Neustadt on 29 November). Yet despite such warnings, the visit proved fairly successful. The main topics of discussion were, first, the issue of nuclear weapons within NATO and the idea of a multilateral force (MLF), which the United States had proposed under Kennedy but which Britain was largely opposed to, and second, the situation in Vietnam.

The US Congress had authorised Johnson to undertake direct military action in Vietnam in August 1964, following the Gulf of Tonkin incident, and hostilities, and the US commitment to Vietnam, were set to escalate rapidly. During the talks, Dean Rusk, the US Secretary of State, asked for a British commitment regarding Vietnam, stressing that 'it was important to have a significant number of people in the country in order to create the necessary international effect, both in Saigon and Hanoi, and on public opinion in the United States'. Gordon Walker replied that the United Kingdom already had troops in Malaysia comparable to the US presence in Vietnam: 'But he was emphatic that the United Kingdom could not have troops on the ground in Vietnam.' However, the United Kingdom would be prepared to help in other ways which could be made public and which would amount to an increased commitment. These were by training more men in jungle warfare; by having more policy advisers in Saigon; and by co-operating more in the medical field (PRO PREM 13/104, 'The Prime Minister's Visit to the United States and Canada', 6–10 December 1964, p. 31). Wilson sent a message to his colleagues at home to reassure them that 'We have not accepted any new commitment as regards South Viet Nam' (PRO PREM 13/104, telegram from Prime Minister to First Secretary of State, No. 4046, 9 December 1964).

Wilson made much of his personal relationship with Lyndon Johnson, in particular to his Cabinet colleagues. Following his next visit to Washington in December 1965, which had been described in the press as his most suc-cessful to date, he could not help telling them that Johnson had asked him to help turn the Christmas tree lights on in the White House, the first time a British Prime Minister had been given this honour since Churchill in 1943. Barbara Castle noted that 'Obviously the two get on like a house on fire' (1984: 78, diary entry for 21 December 1965). Whilst Johnson did appear to find his first few meetings with Wilson something of a 'chore', he also made an effort to demonstrate the strength of the Anglo-American relationship, for it was felt that the United States' problems would be 'increased by the political or economic demise of the only other Western country which exercises genuine worldwide responsibility' (PRO PREM 13/1262, letter from Sir Patrick Dean, British ambassador in Washington, to C. M. MacLehose, Foreign Office, 6 August 1966).

Indeed, the US administration did need Britain's support. An American review of Anglo-American policy relations noted that 'The simple, hardly debatable answer' to questions of the future of the special relationship 'is that we need the support and sympathy of the British. If they are unable to go it alone, in their relative weakness, neither can we everywhere. We touch one another at too many points and are still affected by what the other does in too many situations to be able to dispense with mutual support of some kind' (US National Archives II, RG59 1964–66, POL 1 UK-US, Box 2786, airgram A-2843 from US embassy in London to State Department, Washington, 'A View of US–UK Policy Relations', 23 May 1966). There were four particular issues. First, the United States still needed Britain's influence within Europe. Second, in economic terms the US administration needed Britain to keep sterling at $2.80, and not to devalue, in order to protect the dollar at a time when the United States was suffering its own balance of payments problems. It was feared in the United States that it might be forced to devalue if the pound devalued, which would cause instability in the international financial system.

Third, with regard to defence, the United States wanted Britain to continue to provide military support both in Germany and across the globe, and in particular to retain its bases in the Persian Gulf, Aden, and Singapore and the Indian Ocean. It was feared that if Britain reduced its defence commitments east of Suez, then the region might fall prey to Soviet influence or control, at a time when the United States was devoting increasing defence resources to Vietnam. Fourth, the US administration wanted British support over Vietnam, preferably by providing troops, but if not troops, then at least strong public diplomatic backing, in order for the United States to present its actions in Vietnam as multilateral rather than unilateral. In particular, '[I]t is extremely important from the point of view of American standing with world opinion that the leading socialist-governed country in the world should support their objectives in South East Asia.' This was true for domestic public opinion as well as international, 'since American public opinion still has a latent sense of guilt which it is much easier to allay when the Administration can point to the moral and physical support of other countries for what the U.S. is trying to do in Vietnam' (PRO PREM 13/1262, letter from Sir Patrick Dean to C. M. MacLehose, Foreign Office, 6 August 1966). To a considerable extent, Wilson agreed with the first three of these four US objectives. It is not necessary to go into detail about Britain's economic and balance of payments problems here, as they have already been discussed in Chapters 5 and 6. Suffice it to say that Wilson and most members of his Cabinet were also opposed to devaluation as a solution to Britain's huge balance of payments deficit, as it would mean revealing the full extent of Britain's economic problems. It would also mean playing into the hands of Labour's opponents who argued that Labour governments were disastrous for the British economy, and that a devaluation took place whenever a Labour government was elected.

The Chancellor of the Exchequer, James Callaghan, had been concerned before the election that a Labour victory would be followed by an attack on sterling. When a sterling crisis followed the budget of 11 November 1964, he was able to turn to the Americans for help, whereupon the Labour Government received large-scale support for sterling from the US Federal Reserve Bank. Then, in the summer of 1965, when the pound came under increasing pressure at a time of dwindling exchange reserves, Wilson agreed to a rescue package from the United States to support sterling and prevent devaluation. This, according to Ponting, came at a price: in return for the rescue package, Wilson had to agree to maintain British worldwide defence commitments, and impose a statutory prices and incomes policy (Ponting, 1989: 52–3). Those involved in making this controversial deal were Wilson, Callaghan and George Brown, but the details of the deal were not made known to their Cabinet colleagues, let alone the public.

Yet debate has raged over whether such an agreement was actually reached, and, if it was, the degree to which the United States was able to use its financial aid as leverage over Wilson (see Bartlett, 1992: 110–11; Dobson, 1988: 213–14; 1990: 250–1; Ponting, 1989: 53–4). To a large extent, Wilson's goals coincided with those of the Americans, namely to avoid devaluation at any price, to maintain defence commitments east of Suez, and to prevent wage and price increases. Wilson, whilst aware of the need to cut defence expenditure, did not want a dramatic decline in Britain's defence commitments internationally. Whilst paying lip service to the need to rationalise Britain's commitments to reflect its loss of its imperial role, Wilson simultaneously emphasised Britain's continuing world role. Roy Jenkins (a Cabinet Minister from December 1965 onwards, and in favour of devaluation) argued that 'if they [Wilson and Callaghan] could get American support for what they wanted to do anyway this could be regarded as serving a British interest and, from the point of view of the 1966 election, even a Labour Party interest' (Jenkins, 1989). What Wilson had managed to do with this agreement was to avoid any commitment to Vietnam.

However, despite this, Wilson 'repeated time after time that the Americans had never made any connection between the financial support they gave us and our support for them in Vietnam', although he also urged Cabinet colleagues to remember that the United States'

> financial support is not unrelated to the way we behave in the Far East; any direct announcement of our withdrawal, for example, could not fail

to have a profound effect on my personal relations with LBJ and the way the Americans treat us.

(Crossman, 1975: 456, diary entry for 14 February 1966)

This could, of course, have been Wilson's way of forestalling criticism from within his Cabinet, for he was, like many successful politicians, an opportunist, and US financial support provided Wilson with the opportunity to rein in recalcitrant colleagues.

Britain and the Vietnam War

Despite pressure from the US administration, Wilson did not provide what Lyndon Johnson really wanted, namely British troops fighting alongside the US military in Vietnam. Wilson was prepared to give the United States verbal and moral support, thus providing the semblance of international agreement over the United States' decision to intervene in Vietnam, and he frequently discussed the situation in Vietnam with Johnson on the 'hotline' between their two offices, and sometimes offered advice. When the Americans launched a heavy bombing attack on North Vietnam following an attack by the Vietcong on 7 February 1965, it was met with widespread criticism both within and outside the Labour Party. Wilson phoned Lyndon Johnson to express his concern at the escalation of the situation, and to urge caution. Wilson also suggested a visit to Washington to talk to Johnson, whereupon, Wilson recalled: 'To my surprise, he let fly in an outburst of Texan temper.' Johnson had angrily said that there was no point jumping across the Atlantic every time there is a critical situation, and that while the international community was willing to share advice, it was not prepared to share responsibility:

> I won't tell you how to run Malaysia and you don't tell me how to run Vietnam. . . . If you want to help us some in Vietnam send us some men and send us some folks to deal with these guerillas. And announce to the press that you are going to help us. Now if you don't feel like doing that, go on with your Malaysian problem.
>
> (Wilson, 1971: 80)

Apparently Wilson was concerned about public opinion in Britain, and at the prospect of speaking in the House of Commons the next day, when he would be questioned on the situation in Vietnam, and would have to reiterate that his Government's policy was to support the United States' actions in Vietnam. Following this conversation, Wilson's Private Secretary commented to him that

> Your telephone conversation with the President about Vietnam, together with other indications, indicate that the nature of American

Foreign Policy, as pursued by President Johnson, is likely to be very different (and less helpful to British interest) from that pursued by President Kennedy. . . . The fact that we have to deal with is that the man who is at present at the head of the United States is basically not interested in Foreign Affairs. . . . The conduct of American Foreign Policy is, therefore, likely to be left to the professionals of the State Department.

(Wilson, 1971: 80)

This was likely to result in a period of reduction of US commitments to the world in general, of 'neo-isolationism'. He noted that there was a similar withdrawal of commitment by the Soviet Union (PRO PREM 13/316, note for Wilson by J. Oliver Wright on future UK foreign policy, 12 February 1965).

Wilson's policy of giving the United States moral support for its war in Vietnam, whilst resisting the pressure to send British troops, satisfied neither the anti-Vietnam War lobby within Britain, nor the Americans, who wanted a more concrete form of support. However, it was, perhaps, the most realistic policy option at the time, given the conflicting pressures on the Government. Ben Pimlott, in his biography of Wilson, noted that 'Wilson, courageously, persistently and despite the strongest inducements, declined to provide [troops]. Words of support were one thing, British lives another' (1992: 388). Peter Shore, a Minister in the 1966–1970 Labour Government, told Pimlott that 'It is hard to imagine any other Labour leader resisting very strong American pressure so successfully', for 'Enormous efforts were made by the Foreign Office, the Treasury, the Americans to get Britain wholly to identify with the war and express this with a military presence' (quoted in Pimlott, 1992: 388–9). This, though, is overly generous to Wilson, for there really appears to have been little enthusiasm from within the Foreign Office for Britain to get stuck in the Vietnam quagmire; it was concerned about the extent of opposition to the Government's limited policy of moral, but not military, support for the United States (PRO PREM 13/689, letter from M. MacLehose at the Foreign Office to J. Oliver Wright, 8 September 1965).

The Vietnam War was, of course, an extremely emotive issue for the Labour Party, and one which caused vociferous criticism of the Wilson Governments. There were many resolutions sent in to party headquarters from constituency Labour Parties and from trade union branches that criticised Britain's support for the war, and the left wing of the party felt that the Labour Governments were being not only weak by refusing to condemn the United States over Vietnam, but also immoral. Nor was it just Labour's rank and file who were critical of the United States' military intervention in Vietnam; during Wilson's visit to Washington in December 1965, he had read out a telegram from Labour MPs demanding an end to the bombing, and explained that if US aircraft bombed North Vietnamese cities, the British Government would have to remonstrate (PRO PREM 13/1271, note by the Prime Minister of conversation with President Johnson, 17 December 1965; also Wilson, 1971: 244).

This situation occurred six months later, when the conflict intensified and the United States started bombing oil installations in Hanoi and Haiphong in the North. On 29 June 1966, Wilson announced that the Labour Government had decided to 'dissociate itself from the bombing of oil installations in the Hanoi and Haiphong areas', and made a statement in the House of Commons to this effect, following repeated requests from his own back benches on 7 July 1966 (House of Commons Debates, 5th series, vol. 731, col. 682). This was a polite way of criticising the United States.

Wilson, whilst urging Johnson 'to reconsider whether this action, whatever its results in terms of immediate military advantage, is worth the candle', hoped that Johnson would understand that he had been left with no choice but to condemn the bombing as a result of ongoing pressure from his party in the Commons, and reassured him that 'this will not affect my general support of American policy in Vietnam' (US National Archives II, RG59 1964–66, POL 1 UK-US, Box 2786, telegram from Department of State to US embassy in London, 28 May 1966, referring to message from Wilson to Johnson, 24 May 1966). David Bruce, the US ambassador in London, reported back to Washington that 'My estimate is that the Prime Minister will weather the storm in the Commons by reiterating the doubtful distinction between disassociation from Haiphong–Hanoi action, and support for basic US policy in Vietnam' (US National Archives II, RG59 1964–66, POL 1 UK-US, Box 2786, telegram from David Bruce, London, to Acting Secretary of State, Washington, 3 July 1966).

At the 1967 Labour Party annual conference, a resolution was narrowly passed which called upon the Government to 'dissociate itself completely' from US policy in Vietnam and to persuade the United States to end its bombing of North Vietnam 'immediately, permanently and unconditionally', and for a peace settlement based on 'the 1954 Geneva Agreement, which required the withdrawal of all foreign troops from Vietnamese soil, and the reunification of Vietnam under the government chosen by the Vietnamese people' (Labour Party, 1967a: 223). The proposer, from the Cambridge Constituency Labour Party, continued that it was high time that this country 'ceased to give one scrap of more comfort or consolation to President Johnson in supporting his ill-begotten, misdirected and wholly criminal policy'. He pointed out the dilemma the government's policy placed Labour Party members in, having to defend British policy while out campaigning:

> I find myself, in answer to questions about Vietnam, having to hold my tongue, cross my fingers and drag my feet, and I am wondering personally how long I can remain in this uncomfortable posture and at the same time have a hand still willing to hold a Labour Party card.
>
> (Labour Party, 1967a: 224)

It was not just sections of the Labour Party which wanted Wilson and his Government to condemn US actions in Vietnam. In 1967 and 1968, an anti-war movement grew in strength and presence, and Wilson was plagued by vociferous anti-Vietnam War demonstrators when visiting towns around the country (Wilson, 1971: 445). Two large demonstrations took place in London in March and in October 1968, which included people from across the political spectrum. One way that Wilson sought to reassure public opinion, and to deal with the enormous pressure coming from within the Labour Party for the Government to reverse its policy and to publicly condemn the United States, was to act as an intermediary for the United States and the Soviet Union in an attempt to broker a deal on the cessation of hostilities (for an account of one particular initiative, see Young, 1998: 545–62).

If Wilson had been successful in brokering a peace deal, this would have legitimised his stance on Vietnam and pleased the Labour Party, whilst also raising his profile as a world statesman who could succeed where so many others had failed. However, Wilson's efforts were not always welcomed by the United States, and the Soviet Union did not necessarily have the authority to negotiate a deal on behalf of the Vietnamese. Consequently, none of Wilson's diplomatic initiatives secured an agreement, which possibly undermined Wilson's international standing whilst distracting him from other foreign policy issues (quite apart from domestic ones, of course). The Labour Party continued to complain vociferously about Vietnam, and Wilson's refusal to condemn the United States undoubtedly hurt the party in terms of alienating many liberals, as well as those on the left. Wilson was seen by many not only as a pragmatist but also as having sacrificed his socialist principles for the sake of keeping in with the Americans. As soon as Labour lost the 1970 election, the party's stance changed to one of outright condemnation of the United States' intervention in Vietnam, and criticism of the Conservative Government for not doing more to secure a US withdrawal.

Defence and Britain's role in the world

There were a number of security issues facing the incoming Labour Government in 1964, but the two most immediate and far-reaching which needed to be addressed were the future of Britain's independent nuclear deterrent, and Britain's overall defence commitments in the context both of mounting financial problems and of the over-stretch of Britain's conventional forces. In each of these, close defence relations with the United States were maintained, and even strengthened (for instance, over defence procurement). Labour's 1964 manifesto, *Let's Go with Labour: The New Britain* (Labour Party, 1964a), had pledged a review of weapons expenditure and a greater emphasis on conventional forces, and promised to end the 'Tory nuclear pretence' of an independent British deterrent by renegotiating the Nassau agreement to buy Polaris from the United States. Buying the American

Polaris missile system, Labour argued, would mean that the United States would in effect have a veto over Britain's use of its nuclear capability, which undermined the whole point of Britain trying to retain an independent nuclear deterrent. Therefore, it was a waste of money. Labour would either cancel the purchase of Polaris, or the Polaris submarines would be handed over to NATO, as

> We are against the development of national nuclear deterrents ... and will put forward constructive proposals for integrating all Nato's nuclear weapons under effective political control so that all the partners in the Alliance have a proper share in their deployment and control.
>
> (Craig, 1975: 272)

However, once in office, Wilson, Healey and Gordon Walker decided not to cancel the purchase of the Polaris missile system, on the grounds that it was too far advanced to be cancelled except at inordinate cost, and accepted the terms of the Nassau agreement negotiated between Kennedy and Macmillan for the purchase of Polaris (Wilson, 1971: 40). This effectively meant rejection of unilateral disarmament, which the left of the Labour Party had been advocating since the late 1950s. As Dean Rusk noted, whilst other defence commitments were being cut,

> The British nuclear deterrent has so far escaped the economy axe. The reason is simple. The nuclear deterrent is the most important of the great power symbols still in British possession. Although Wilson is committed to give it up, he has so far shown no disposition to do so.
>
> (US National Archives II, RG59 1964–66, POL 7 Box 2779, memo from Dean Rusk to the President, 'Visit of Prime Minister Wilson July 19, 1966', 27 July 1966)

Britain's independent nuclear forces not only gave Britain the appearance of power and diplomatic leverage, but also remained the cornerstone of Britain's deterrence against the perceived threat of Soviet aggression during the period of the Labour Governments.

Wilson remained opposed to the United States' proposal for Britain to incorporate its nuclear capability into a combined West European multilateral force (MLF). Instead, he proposed that Britain should put its four Polaris submarines and its V-bomber force, which could potentially launch short-range nuclear bombs on Soviet territory, into NATO as part of an Atlantic Nuclear Force (ANF), on the basis that the United States would contribute at least an equal number of Polaris submarines to the ANF. As far as Britain was concerned, 'This could be represented as taking the British out of the possession of a national nuclear deterrent and would be a real breakthrough toward non-proliferation' (US National Archives II, RG59 1964–66, POL 7 Box 2779, memo from Dean Rusk to the President, 'Visit of Prime Minister Wilson', 19 December 1965). The nuclear weapons would then be subject to collective NATO authority, but, Wilson explained to the House of Commons, the contributors of the weapons would enjoy a privileged position in the management of the ANF, would have a veto over its use, and dissemination of nuclear technology would be prevented (House of Commons Debates, 5th series, vol. 704, cols 434–8).

Part of the rationale for these plans was concern that West Germany might attempt to develop its own independent nuclear deterrent, which was a prospect that appalled both the British and the US administrations. However, the Americans rejected Wilson's plan, and the plans for neither the MLF nor the ANF were developed. Denis Healey, the Defence Minister, also announced the cancellation of the British TSR2 military aircraft, which could launch short-range nuclear bombs on Soviet territory, but, unlike the V-bomber, could fly under the Russian radar system. Instead, Britain would purchase fifty American F1-11 aircraft, a decision which provoked criticism from the left of the Labour Party about job losses. It also increased Britain's reliance on the United States for defence procurement and its nuclear deterrent.

The other main security issue that the 1964–1970 Labour Governments faced concerned the future of Britain's overall defence commitments, given the twin problems of over-stretch of existing defence resources – in particular, troops – combined with the need to cut defence spending in response to Britain's increasing economic problems. When Labour entered office in 1964, Britain still retained the bulk of its global network of military bases that it had assembled during the heyday of the Empire to protect Britain's colonies, and its trade and supply routes. However, by the mid-1960s Britain's financial problems – especially the massive balance of payments deficit – were such that it was clear that existing defence commitments could not be maintained. Indeed, it was estimated that three-eighths of the 1964 balance of payments deficit was accounted for by defence expenditure (Hanning, 1966: 225). Nor was it clear why certain bases had been retained for so long, given that Britain no longer had to protect the trade routes to India, and that 'the political problems caused by large fixed bases in developing countries would increase as fast as their military utility, in the nuclear age, would diminish' (Howard, 1966: 181).

On 16 December 1964, Wilson informed the House of Commons that he would initiate a comprehensive review of Britain's defence needs and commitments. The 1964 defence estimates were for £2 billion, representing 7.1 per cent of gross national product, and this was expected to increase to £2.4 billion during the next five years. Wilson therefore insisted that

> we have to relate our decisions in the field of defence to the broader objectives of our foreign policy and we have to relate both to the realities of the economic position which Britain faces and has, indeed, been facing for the past few years.

Indeed, 'the plain fact is that we have been trying to do too much. The result has been gravely to weaken our economic strength and independence without producing viable defences' (House of Commons Debates, 5th series, vol. 704, cols 418–21).

Consequently, Labour would develop a new defence policy, based on its comprehensive defence review, which would have a £2 billion budget ceiling. However, Wilson, like all his predecessors, did not want to appear to be downgrading Britain's status as a world power. He therefore continued that 'we cannot afford to relinquish our world role – our role which, for shorthand purposes, is sometimes called our "east of Suez" role'. Britain's world role is 'one which no one in this House or indeed in the country, will wish us to give up or call in question'. In particular, Britain had much to contribute to international peacekeeping, either as part of a UN force or on its own, and what impressed 'our American allies' in terms of Britain's claim to be a world power was not its nuclear weapons, but 'our ability to mount peace-keeping operations that no one else can mount' (House of Commons Debates, 5th series, vol. 704, cols 423–6). Denis Healey also emphasised Britain's need to maintain a military capacity of mobile conventional forces outside Europe in order to undertake peacekeeping operations when needed in Africa, or the Middle East or Asia, and to perform a world role that no other country was capable of (House of Commons Debates, 5th series, vol. 704, col. 612).

Labour's defence review

Denis Healey presented the long-awaited defence review on 22 February 1966, calling it 'essentially an exercise in political and military realism'. He outlined how Labour would cut the previous Conservative Government's planned expenditure by 16 per cent through savings gained by getting better value for money, by reducing substantially the deployment of British forces in the Mediterranean and by cutting the level of forces in the Far East once the confrontation with Indonesia was over. Also, from 1968 Britain would give up its Aden base (House of Commons Debates, 5th series, vol. 725, col. 240). Overall, deployment of troops outside Europe would be cut by 30 per cent, but responsibilities east of Suez would continue 'for many years' (House of Commons Debates, 5th series, vol. 725, cols 1778–9). This plan was condemned by many within the Labour Party who had hoped for a more far-reaching review that abandoned Britain's residual imperial role and withdrew from the Far and Middle East, and which subsequently focused on Britain's defence role within Europe. As Waltz remarked, the Labour Government's new defence policy amounted to 'keeping the roles, reducing the means, and changing the rationalizations' of Britain's defence commitments (1968: 156). Christopher Mayhew, Healey's Minister of State for the Navy, resigned in protest at the approach taken by the defence review, arguing that its premise, that Britain's world role and defence commitments east of Suez would be maintained while expenditure would be kept within the £2 billion budget, was 'mistaken'. Indeed, in his resignation speech he said that 'the proposed cuts in resources are not matched by the proposed cuts in commitments and that the result will be strain on the Armed Forces, or dependence on the United States beyond what this House should accept' (House of Commons Debates, 5th series, vol. 725, col. 255).

Shortly after the defence review, Wilson called a general election for 31 March. The 1966 election manifesto argued that the defence review had achieved its objectives, and under Labour there was a new realism in Britain's defence policy (Craig, 1975: 309). Somewhat ironically, Labour's significantly increased parliamentary majority heralded a deterioration in Wilson's fortunes. People's expectations of what the Government could achieve seem to have increased along with the increased Commons majority, but Wilson's ability successfully to solve the multitude of problems confronting Britain appeared to decrease. His colleagues and the electorate were no longer willing to give him the benefit of the doubt.

The balance of payments crisis continued, and impacted on all areas of policy, including foreign policy and defence, and whilst Wilson had been concerned to maintain Britain's role east of Suez, it rapidly became clear that this was no longer sustainable. The tide of opinion shifted during the economic crisis of 1966, and the issue became not whether Britain should withdraw, but when: 'For all Harold Wilson's romantic conception of Britain's world role and his determination to preserve it, economic and political pressures forced his hand' (Darby, 1973: 283). In addition to Britain's economic constraints, the British army was suffering from over-stretch, with 54,000 men stationed in the Far East and 27,000 in the Middle East (Hanning, 1966: 253). There was also increasing nationalist discontent to deal with, as British bases in Aden, Cyprus and the Suez Canal became targets of nationalist agitation and symbols of continued British imperial repression, and thus increasingly expensive to maintain in return for a diminishing degree of security. On 27 July 1967, Denis Healey outlined the Supplementary White Paper on Defence in the House of Commons, which marked the culmination of the Labour Government's defence review and laid out Britain's defence strategy for a projected ten years ahead. This included major cuts in the armed forces in the Far East and South-East Asia, with the removal of forces from Borneo and a reduction in the forces in Malaysia and Singapore, with the intention of withdrawing British forces altogether from Malaysia and Singapore by the mid-1970s – that is, the withdrawal of troops from east of Suez. The precise timing of the eventual withdrawal, though, would depend on progress made in achieving a new basis for stability in South-East Asia and in resolving other problems in the Far East (House of Commons Debates, 5th series, vol. 751, cols 989–94; Wilson, 1971: 422).

The US administration did not approve of Wilson's plans, and continued strongly to urge Britain to keep its military presence in the Far East, but to no avail. The reasons for the ensuing withdrawal of troops were financial, military and political; financially, Britain could not afford to maintain its defence commitments; militarily, British forces were over-stretched and could not meet their commitments; and politically, Wilson wanted an announcement to appease the left of the Labour Party, which was growing increasingly restless over defence issues. Wilson further annoyed the United States in November 1967 by announcing that sterling would be devalued. In January 1968, it was announced that Britain's withdrawal from east of Suez would be accelerated, and would now take place at the end of 1971. Thus, the three main issues on which the United States had sought British co-operation, and which Wilson had agreed to in the first few years of his premiership – no to devaluation, retention of military commitments east of Suez, and, of course, support in Vietnam – had been rejected by the end of 1967.

There were a range of other defence and security issues that concerned the 1964–1970 Labour Governments and which warrant brief mention. Diplomatic relations with the Soviet Union improved following the confrontation over the Cuban missile crisis, and Cold War tensions eased somewhat with the period of déente. Wilson also prided himself on his good personal relationships with Soviet politicians, having made a number of trips to the Soviet Union both before and after becoming Prime Minister. However, the Soviet invasion of Czechoslovakia on 20 August 1968 caused consternation and shock within the Labour Government, whereupon Wilson issued a statement which called the Soviet intervention 'a flagrant violation of the United Nations Charter and of all accepted standards of international behaviour', and recalled Parliament to discuss the situation (see House of Commons Debates, 5th series, vol. 769, cols 1273–1420). He felt that the invasion of Czechoslovakia highlighted the need for vigilance within the Western alliance, and for greater unity within Europe so that it could respond more strongly to any threat to its freedom (Wilson, 1971: 552–4). The Arab–Israeli Six Day War of June 1967 also caused alarm, not least because about 70 per cent of British oil imports came from Arab sources at that time (Crossman files, Modern Records Centre, MSS 154/3/DH/4/68–99, Joint Intelligence Committee report, 'British Economic Interests in Israel and the Arab World', JIC (B) (69) 33 Final, 30 September 1969).

The other (third) main crisis that the 1964–1970 Labour Governments had to deal with was Southern Rhodesia, where the white minority government announced a unilateral declaration of independence in response to Britain's plans eventually to introduce universal suffrage.

Rhodesia

Southern Rhodesia was a self-governing British dependency which was governed on the basis of apartheid and white minority rule. Britain had been urging Southern Rhodesia to widen the franchise to include the black population, whilst the Rhodesian regime wanted to continue its existing system of white rule. The Rhodesian Front had been elected to power in Southern Rhodesia at the end of 1963, and had asked Britain for independence, which the Conservative government had refused. In April 1964, Ian Smith ousted the existing Prime Minister, Winston Field, and immediately threatened a unilateral declaration of independence (UDI) (Blake, 1978: 26–8). This threatened Britain's credibility both in the Commonwealth and in the wider international arena, as the Rhodesian Front regime was seen as completely unacceptable to the rest of the Commonwealth. Wilson refused to grant independence unless the Smith government promised unimpeded progress to majority rule and progress towards ending racial discrimination.

However, Smith was not prepared to offer any concessions, and embarked on a clampdown of opposition groups. The black Zimbabwe African National Union (ZANU) and Zimbabwe African People's Union (ZAPU) were banned, their leaders imprisoned without trial, and the press tightly controlled. Wilson attempted to negotiate privately with Smith in order to find a solution, meeting with him on the occasion of Winston Churchill's funeral on 30 January 1965. No progress was made, and a visit by Smith in October 1965 also ended in deadlock. If anything, Smith returned to Rhodesia with a heightened determination to declare independence, as he had been told that Britain would not retaliate with the use of force. Smith's adviser was convinced that if Britain had threatened to use force, Smith would have backed down, as Rhodesia did not have the capability to resist attack (Flower, 1987: 51).

However, given Labour's wafer-thin Commons majority, Wilson would have needed support from both Labour and Conservative MPs to invade or attack Rhodesia, which would not have been forthcoming. Furthermore, Britain did not have troops in the region that could be mobilised for such an assault, and the cost of military action 'would play havoc with the carefully pruned priorities of the defence budget' (Hargreaves, 1996: 237). Thus, whilst some of the Commonwealth members proposed that Britain consider taking military action to overthrow the Smith regime, it was never a serious option within British political circles. Instead, Wilson went to Rhodesia in a last-ditch attempt to persuade Smith to compromise, to the consternation of his advisers. As Pimlott puts it, Wilson 'believed – as highly intelligent people sometimes do when confronted by an opponent who is behaving illogically – that Smith could still be talked round'. The visit was a disaster, serving to demonstrate Britain's weakness and inability to control events, as 'the ultra-reactionary Rhodesian Cabinet regarded the British premier with macho scorn, while he treated them with head-masterly distaste' (Pimlott, 1992: 369).

Then, on 11 November 1965, the Rhodesian Prime Minister, Ian Smith, issued a unilateral declaration of independence. Britain refused to acknowledge the legal independence of Rhodesia before satisfactory constitutional arrangements could be established for African majority rule, and so declared the Smith government to be illegal. However, whilst insisting that it was the duty of the people of Rhodesia to refrain from doing anything which would assist the illegal Smith regime in its rebellion against the British Crown, Wilson also maintained that it was the duty of public servants in Rhodesia to carry on with their jobs in order to help to maintain law and order (House of Commons Debates, 5th series, vol. 720, cols 349–62). Ultimately, 'The practical effect was to legitimize"the action of public servants, who decided to continue to function just as they always had before November 11, 1965' (Blake, 1978: 389). Smith also acted in defiance of Britain by proclaiming a new constitution.

Southern Rhodesia was an unwelcome remnant of a colonial era, and the problem of what to do about it was one that the previous Conservative Government had also grappled with. Indeed, the Conservative Party was evenly divided over whether to impose sanctions and an oil embargo in response to UDI. However, given Labour's anti-colonial and anti-racist stance, it had more to lose if it failed to take retaliatory action and force Smith to backtrack. Simply transferring the matter to the United Nations, which was what some in the Labour Party urged, would, at the very least, have made Britain look weak, and would itself have achieved little.

Instead, Wilson's response to the announcement of UDI was to impose sanctions on imports from Rhodesia and an embargo against oil exports to Rhodesia, and to freeze its financial assets in London. Wilson thought sanctions would be enough to force the Smith regime to back down, a calculation which led the Prime Minister to reassure the Commonwealth states, at the Commonwealth Prime Ministers' Conference on Rhodesia in Lagos in January 1966, that the collapse of the Rhodesian economy would occur in 'weeks, not months'. In this, he was clearly mistaken. For Wilson had overestimated the effect of sanctions – which were ignored by Rhodesia's main trading partner, South Africa – and underestimated the amount of time it would take for the Smith regime to fall. Subsequently, 'The survival of the Smith regime became a testament to British impotence, and fallen status' (Pimlott, 1992: 381), although this was not yet fully apparent when Britain went to the polls in March 1966.

The Rhodesia problem continued to haunt the re-elected Labour Government throughout its second term of office. In November 1966, Wilson was still trying to find ways of keeping the dialogue going, believing that his ministerial colleagues were being defeatist for feeling that there was no point in further negotiations. Richard Crossman noted that 'The trouble is that for Harold this is his Dunkirk or his Cuba', and he was determined not to admit that Britain had failed over Rhodesia (1976: 114, diary entry for 8 November 1966). Wilson also wanted to bring to an end the criticism he was facing from within the Labour Party, the Commonwealth and the international community. Talks between Wilson and Smith were held on HMS *Tiger* in December 1966 and on HMS *Fearless* in October 1968, but the

Smith regime refused to accept the formula adopted by Wilson of 'no independence before majority rule' (NIBMAR). The ongoing situation revealed Britain's weakness in dealing with the Commonwealth, and its impotence to act alone. Institutionally, the Commonwealth Relations Office was seen to have failed in its purpose. It was renamed the Department of Commonwealth Affairs in August 1966, when it was merged with the Colonial Office (which was abolished in January 1967), then merged with the Foreign Office on 17 October 1968. As Arthur Bottomley, the Commonwealth Relations Minister, publicly pointed out, 'The way in which the Rhodesian rebellion is brought to an end will determine the future of the modern Commonwealth' (Arthur Bottomley Papers, British Library of Political and Economic Science, Box 10, notes for speech 8 March 1966). The Rhodesian 'rebellion' did not end until the late 1970s.

Conclusion

The foreign policy of the 1964–1970 Labour Governments was marked by ongoing debate about Britain's role in the world. Despite the disappointment over Europe, the withdrawal from east of Suez, the failure to reach an agreement on Rhodesia, and the ongoing realisation that Britain's relative economic decline meant that it could not return to the days when Britain really was a great power, Wilson continued to present himself as a player on the world stage. Indeed, his romantic attachment to Britain's world role and its imperial legacy prevented him from accepting sooner what many in his party argued, namely that Britain should retreat from its old imperial commitments east of Suez, not merely for economic reasons but for ideological ones as well. Indeed, in terms of foreign policy – as in other policy areas – there appeared to be little remaining of Wilson the former left-wing Labour MP. This was most obviously demonstrated by Wilson's attachment to the Anglo-American relationship and his attempts to give the United States as much support as possible over its intervention in Vietnam, short of actually sending troops. It was this issue, more than any other, that drained support for Wilson's foreign policy from Labour Party members and sections of the general public.

9   Whitehall reform

Kevin Theakston

Introduction

As with most issues concerning Britain's constitutional and political arrangements, the Labour Party gave little serious thought to the role and (potential)
power of the civil service whilst in opposition throughout the 1950s. This
partly reflected Labour's general disinclination to think critically or theoretically about the structure and operation of governing institutions in Britain,
but also derived from a significant sense of satisfaction following the success
of the 1945–1951 Attlee Governments in establishing a mixed economy and
welfare state. This success tended to allay the suspicions of many of those on
the left who had previously been suspicious about the politics of the civil
service, and who thus feared that a Labour government would encounter
obstruction and opposition – overt or covert – from an 'establishment' civil
service. Indeed, at the end of the Attlee premiership many Labour Ministers
were expressing their respect for a civil service which had apparently co-
operated so conscientiously and professionally with what was widely viewed
as a radical, reforming government. Herbert Morrison doubtless echoed the
sentiments of many of his Cabinet colleagues when he spoke admiringly of
'the meritorious loyalty which the Civil Service quite properly owes and prac-
tises towards its Ministers', and which ensured that 'the British Civil Service
is loyal to the Government of the day' (1964: 52, 345).

Only during the early 1960s – by which time the party had experienced a
decade out of office – did some Labour politicians and left-inclined academics begin to consider the role of the civil service in British politics. Yet
what prompted such reflection was not concern that the civil service would
prove ideologically or politically hostile to a Labour government, but a
certain anxiety in some quarters that the civil service was not sufficiently
suited to assist in the governance of an advanced industrialised society, one
in which science and technology were becoming increasingly important.
What also underpinned certain concerns about the efficacy of Britain's civil
service in the 1960s was the more general realisation that Britain was experiencing relative economic decline, a phenomenon which, indirectly at least,
further cast the civil service in a somewhat critical light.

It was largely in the context of this relative economic decline that some Labour politicians and left-inclined academics began linking the modernisation of Britain's political and governing institutions with economic renewal and revival. As a core component of the 'machinery of government', the civil service was therefore deemed to be in particular need of reform. However, the Labour Party had few clear proposals for reforming the civil service, and its 1964 manifesto was somewhat opaque on the issue, merely alluding to the 'need to make government itself more efficient', which required that 'the machinery of government must be modernised', for 'New techniques, new kinds of skill and experience are needed if government is to govern effectively' (Craig, 1975: 272). However, the ambiguity of Labour's approach to reforming Whitehall was compounded by Harold Wilson's own reverence for the civil service.

Harold Wilson and Whitehall

Harold Wilson was always very much at home in Whitehall. He had a close and intimate knowledge of the civil service machine and its leading personalities, going back to his successful stint as a high-flying wartime 'temporary' from 1940 to 1945, working as an economist and statistician in the economic section of the Cabinet secretariat as an assistant to William Beveridge, and in the Mines Department of the Board of Trade. In 1945, a permanent post in the Treasury had beckoned, but he opted for a political career instead. Twenty years later, as Prime Minister, a contemporary observer described him as displaying 'a profound reverence for the orders and mysteries of the civil service. . . . He would be most upset if he ever thought he had caused serious offence to a permanent secretary' (Watkins, 1966: 171–2). He was proud of being 'house trained', in the Whitehall phrase (Hunt *et al.*, 1964: 18), and generally worked well with civil servants, holding them in high regard. In turn, officials widely respected him as an efficient, industrious, calm, rational and personally easygoing political master (Pimlott, 1992: 347).

Yet Marcia Williams, Wilson's Personal and Political Secretary and a key figure in his Number 10 'kitchen cabinet', believed that a Prime Minister should 'automatically suspect' the activities and the personnel of the civil service, and was therefore dismayed that Wilson did not share her views:

> It is the fact that he does have such an admiration for and such a working knowledge of 'the System' that he tends to lean over backwards in his relationship towards it. He gives it the benefit of the doubt. He doesn't really want to argue with it. He admires the way it is organised and its methods of working. He admires its efficiency and he is often myopic about its failings and its short-comings and its inefficiencies, and this is a great drawback.
>
> (Williams, 1972: 122–3)

Wilson's left-wing colleagues and friends regretted that he was a constitutional traditionalist and a staunch defender of most British institutions, Whitehall included. He was 'too kind to civil servants', complained Marcia Williams, Thomas Balogh and Richard Crossman in September 1965, who believed that he should have more outside advisers and should force through 'fundamental change' in the civil service – all of which the Prime Minister rejected (Crossman, 1975: 333–4, diary entry for 23 September 1965).

It was revealing that within a week of narrowly winning the 1964 general election – at the same time as Richard Crossman was writing in his diary about how, as a new Minister, he felt baffled and isolated by the bureaucracy in his department, and that it was a struggle not to be 'taken over' by the civil service (Crossman, 1975: 21, diary entry for 22 October 1964) – Wilson was sending to the permanent secretaries a personal minute expressing his 'appreciation of the tremendous job you have done over the last few days'. Recalling 'the great names' of 1940s Whitehall (Edward Bridges, John Henry Woods, and so on), he paid tribute to the way that the new Labour Government had been met with 'the fullest co-operation' by top officials, and praised their 'administrative know-how' and 'imagination' (PRO PREM 13/14, Wilson to Helsby, 21 October 1964).

Probably no one capable of admitting that the Board of Trade was 'the department I love' (Wilson quoted in King, 1969: 99) could be regarded as a serious threat to the mandarins (Wilson had been President of the Board of Trade from 1947 to 1951). However, Wilson was not an uncritical admirer of the Whitehall machine, and as a wartime 'temporary' he had apparently grouched about the civil service's lack of drive and the dominance of the elite Administrative Class over specialists like himself (Kellner and Crowther-Hunt, 1980: 27). He claimed to have acquired at that time 'a solid antipathy to the overwhelming power of the Treasury' (Wilson, 1986: 75), and Wilson the grammar-school boy had also relished wartime criticisms of the 'Old School Tie wallahs' (Ziegler, 1993: 35).

Making administrative modernisation a key part of his political credo in the run-up to the 1964 election, he had argued that more specialists, such as economists, technologists and scientists, should be moved into key jobs, and that more outside expert talent should be brought into the new ministries he planned to set up in Whitehall (Technology, Economic Affairs and Overseas Development) from industry, the universities and elsewhere on secondments and through short-term postings. However, he made it clear that he did not plan to bring in 'outsiders' on a large scale, put them 'on top of existing civil servants', or make civil service appointments on political grounds (Hunt *et al.*, 1964: 11–28).

Whilst expressing scepticism about the idea of ministerial *cabinets* of political advisers, Wilson had also expressed concern about what he felt was 'the amateurism of the central direction of government', and therefore proposed enhancing the resources of the Cabinet Office in order for it to support the Prime Minister more effectively in his role as 'an effective executive chairman'. In practice, Wilson as Prime Minister became increasingly close to Sir Burke Trend, the powerful and discreet Cabinet Secretary and an indispensable and trusted adviser and confidant, and whilst the staff of the Cabinet Office did increase in number after 1964, it remained a relatively small outfit. It was still 'mainly a recording (and not even a follow-up) machine', complained Thomas Balogh in 1968 (PRO PREM 13/2126, Balogh to Wilson, 8 January 1968).

Burke Trend was to admit, at the end of Wilson's tenure in 1970, that Number 10 remained 'a large-scale private office' and was 'not equipped to perform wider roles', whilst the Cabinet Office had a primarily secretarial function at the hub of 'a compromise-making system' (PRO PREM 13/3241, 'Machinery of Government: the Central Departments', 10 June 1970). If the Downing Street 'powerhouse' Wilson had talked of creating failed to materialise, he did at least insist on getting his own way over the choice of who should be his Principal Private Secretary, selecting Michael Halls in 1966 (who had worked in his office at the Board of Trade in the 1940s) – but widely seen as out of his depth and a poor appointment in the crucial Number 10 post – and again overruling the Whitehall recommendation when Halls died suddenly in 1970.

Ministers and civil servants in the 1964–1970 Governments

'The idea of some people that a change of government means sabotage from the civil service is, I think, nonsense,' Wilson had declared before he became Prime Minister (quoted in Hunt *et al.*, 1964: 11). From his experience in Whitehall during the 1940s, he was convinced that however great officials' influence might be, the power to get things done rested with Ministers (Ziegler, 1993: 38). He subscribed to the robust 'Attlee view', arguing that 'if a Minister cannot control his civil servants, he ought to go' (Expenditure Committee, 1977: q. 1924) and insisting, in a 1967 interview, that 'Civil servants do what is required once they get a clear lead' (PRO PREM 13/1973 – transcript of interview: 'Where the Power Lies', 10 January 1967).

However, this sanguine perspective was not shared by some of Wilson's closest political friends and allies. Marcia Williams, for example, attributed the disappointing record of the 1964–1970 Labour Governments largely to their 'defeats' in the 'battle ... against the civil service' (1972: 344). She appeared to hate and mistrust the civil service, which she believed Labour should 'purge', starting in Number 10, and Williams clashed repeatedly with the Downing Street civil service staff (Ziegler, 1993: 179–80). Meanwhile, Thomas Balogh, Wilson's Economic Adviser, had firmly established a reputation as a trenchant critic of the Whitehall system, attacking the 'ignorantly dilettante bureaucracy' and arguing that radical reform of the civil service was 'one of the most essential and fundamental preconditions' for a successful socialist government (quoted in Theakston, 1992: 114–15).

Balogh bombarded the Prime Minister with complaints that he was being stymied by officials (and the Treasury in particular) denying him access to crucial papers. 'A large part of the bureaucracy obviously does not share our views,' Balogh told Wilson, alleging too that ministerial responsibility for policy was largely a 'fiction' because of the way in which the Whitehall machine controlled the information available to Ministers, and developed interdepartmental agreements outside political control (PRO CAB 147/7, 147/9, 147/10, 147/75, 147/78).

Wilson, though, publicly scorned a similar claim made in the Labour Party's evidence to the Fulton Committee, namely that some Ministers were 'tools' of their departments because they were kept in the dark and undermined or pre-empted by the official machine (Fulton Report, 1968, vol. 5(2): 655; King, 1969: 109). Balogh loathed, and was loathed by, the civil service, but if Wilson did not really share his views about the mandarins' alleged power and machinations, Richard Crossman certainly did.

Crossman had criticised the Attlee Governments' 'uncritical reliance on Whitehall' in a 1963 *New Statesman* article, suggesting that a successful left-wing government required 'an influx of experts with special knowledge, new ideas and a sympathy for the government's domestic and foreign policies' (1965: 154–5). Giving evidence to the Fulton Committee in 1967, he described the higher civil service as 'a coherent and cohesive oligarchy' and as an organised 'conspiracy' against Ministers (PRO BA 1/6), themes which are repeated throughout his diaries (Theakston, 2003). In many ways, Crossman was a bull-in-a-china-shop figure who had little idea about how to use the civil service machine properly in order to reach his political goals. Yet he believed that determined Ministers could ultimately triumph over civil service obstruction, and in 1970 concluded that Labour's mistakes and failures could not be blamed on the civil service. The real problem, he said, was that the Government did not have a clear enough strategy or sense of direction, and that its policy planning before taking office had been inadequate (Crossman, 1972b: 77).

The suspicions about the civil service harboured in some quarters of the Labour Party, linked to the fear that official attitudes must have been strongly coloured by thirteen years of Conservative rule, were largely unfounded. The top mandarins' group's self-confidence was still pretty high in this period. Dame Evelyn Sharp (Crossman's formidable permanent secretary at Housing) was never afraid to say, 'You've got it wrong, Minister', and Sir William Armstrong (head of the Treasury and then, after 1968, head of the civil service as a whole) believed that the civil servant's job was to bring politicians face to face with 'ongoing reality' (Theakston, 1999: 179, 257).

Yet there was, in fact, much goodwill in Whitehall towards the incoming Labour Government in 1964, rather than blanket hostility. Initially suspicious on class or ideological grounds, Jim Callaghan soon developed a good working relationship with his Treasury civil servants, for instance (Morgan,

1997: 206–7). Relations were much more difficult and turbulent with the more volatile and unpredictable George Brown at the Department of Economic Affairs (DEA) and later the Foreign Office (Paterson, 1993: 175–6, 206–12). However, notions of a 'continuous battle' and 'real resistance or obstruction' were rejected by Tony Crosland, who insisted that the key issue was about harnessing the bureaucracy's 'large fund of knowledge and expertise' (quoted in Theakston, 1992: 17), whilst Roy Jenkins established a clear ministerial authority over the administrative machine at the Home Office, and then the Treasury. He was consequently contemptuously dismissive of the idea that ministerial life involved continuous battering 'against a brick wall of determined departmental opposition' (quoted in Theakston, 1992: 32).

Denis Healey also had no truck with claims of 'bureaucratic sabotage or political prejudice' on the part of the civil service, arguing perceptively that the real problem was 'Whitehall's obsession with procedure rather than policy', which left it 'poorly equipped to handle change', and the system's 'tendency to produce a soggy compromise' (1980; 1989: 376). Meanwhile, whilst Barbara Castle had found, in 1964, that she 'took to the Minister–permanent secretary relationship quite naturally ... [and] had no doubt I was boss' (Castle, 1984: xi), looking back on her time in office she later talked of 'the loneliness of the short-distance runner' (1973).

The idea that Labour Ministers needed political aides and allies in their departments, both to provide an alternative channel of advice and to strengthen political control of the civil service, had developed a momentum during the 1960s. Proposals for ministerial 'brains trusts', along with the appointment of outside advisers into private offices, or ministerial *cabinets*, supposedly based on the French model, were the fashionable prescription (Theakston, 1992: 50–4). However, Wilson was predictably dismissive – 'if I had thought we ought to have a *cabinet* system, I would have done it by now,' he sniffed in 1967 – and other senior Ministers (such as Crossman and Healey) – once they experienced the services provided by an efficient civil service private office in helping to run a Ministry – lost interest in the idea (PRO BA 1/3, 1/6). At the Ministry of Defence, Healey experimented for a couple of years with a small 'programme evaluation group' as a personal think-tank-cum-consultancy-unit, asking awkward questions and generating new ideas – an outfit which proved unpopular with the armed services and the MoD hierarchy. Elsewhere, Labour's so-called irregulars attracted some attention – particularly economists like Robert Neild and Nicholas Kaldor at the Treasury, Christopher Foster at Transport, the social policy expert Brian Abel-Smith at the Department of Health and Social Security (DHSS), and Roy Jenkins's 'fixer' and press adviser, John Harris – but these were not appointed on the scale of the 'special advisers' and 'spin doctors' found in rather more recent governments.

Machinery of government reform

'The biggest single revolution in the structure of Government ever carried out', was Wilson's over-hyped claim about the flurry of machinery of government changes made in October 1964, when he created five new Whitehall departments: the Department of Economic Affairs (DEA), Overseas Development, the Ministry of Technology (MinTech), a Welsh Office and a Ministry of Land and Natural Resources (PRO PREM 13/1971, note for the record, 23 July 1968). The claim that the DEA was dreamed up in the back of a taxi is a myth, because the idea for this new ministry actually emerged from Labour's economic policy discussions in opposition (Clifford, 1997). For example, in the spring of 1963 Thomas Balogh had prepared for Wilson a plan to split the Treasury in order to strike at its 'monolithic supremacy'. According to Balogh, 'Treasury coordination is biased financial coordination', and therefore needed to be counter-balanced by 'an organisation dedicated to expansion' (PRO CAB 147/9, Balogh to Wilson, 25 February 1965; PREM 13/2126, Balogh to Wilson, 8 January 1968). There was a political motivation, too, with Wilson seeking to divide and rule between James Callaghan (at the Treasury) and George Brown (DEA). However, the ill-fated DEA failed to overcome the Treasury's predominance over economic policy, handicapped as it was by an ill-thought-out division of functions between the two Departments, and by a lack of direct executive powers on key issues. The decision to give priority to the defence of the exchange rate ensured that the Treasury would inevitably emerge victorious in the interdepartmental struggles (the DEA was finally abolished in 1969).

Personalities, circumstances and presentational factors always loomed large in Wilson's 'MG' decision-making. William Armstrong, Burke Trend and Sir Laurence Helsby (Head of the Civil Service from 1963 to 1968) strongly opposed the creation of the Department of Health and Social Security in 1968, for example, but Wilson needed to create a big job to occupy Richard Crossman (PRO PREM 13/2690, Crossman to Wilson, 23 July 1968). The DHSS merger was 'hollow' and had 'nothing to commend it in administrative terms' (the two sides of the new ministry having very disparate functions), Armstrong believed, trying to interest Wilson instead in the idea of a 'Department of Social Care' to merge social services and Home Office functions (to tackle the so-called Seebohm agenda). Earlier, Helsby had noted the case for the creation of a hived-off board dealing with health, welfare and social security (akin to the Benefits Agency set up twenty years later). Wilson later admitted that the DHSS merger had been a mistake (Expenditure Committee, 1977: q. 1927), but while in office he refused to 'de-merge' Crossman's empire (PRO PREM 13/2680, Halls to Armstrong, 6 August 1969).

Elsewhere in Whitehall, sensitivity to trade union concerns was a factor behind keeping the Ministry of Power as a separate department, with Wilson believing that a changed 'feeling among the miners' would allow him to let an enlarged MinTech swallow it up in 1969 (PRO PREM 13/2680, Halls to Armstrong, 8 September 1969). The major reorganisation of October 1969 – in which MinTech emerged as a giant and powerful industry/production conglomerate – had the advantage, Wilson envisaged, of outflanking Heath and stealing the Conservatives' industrial policy 'thunder' (*The Times*, 28 July 1969).

The Fulton Committee's (discussed below) terms of reference excluded consideration of the machinery of government, and both Wilson and his senior civil service advisers on these issues were opposed to the idea of an outside inquiry, though there was talk among commentators of the need for a 'new Haldane' to review the organisation and tasks of government. William Armstrong believed that 'you have to see these things from the inside' (Theakston, 1999: 186) – the recommendations of an outside body might prove an 'embarrassment', be 'over-schematic' or 'ignore practical political and administrative factors' (PRO PREM 13/1971, memorandum on Machinery of Government, 18 June 1968). He also advised strongly against the idea of issuing a White Paper on the machinery of government because it could compromise the Prime Minister's personal prerogatives and freedom of manoeuvre (PRO PREM 13/2681, Armstrong to Halls, 30 September 1969). All the same, Armstrong believed that, whilst political considerations could never be disregarded, machinery of government problems were accessible to rational analysis and, as head of the civil service after 1968, was optimistic about the scope for institutional rationalisation and the advantages of 'giant' departments, though he and other permanent secretaries were concerned that the many piecemeal changes of the Wilson years had a cost in terms of a 'disturbance factor' and short-term losses of efficiency.

The Fulton exercise 'put the cart before the horse', Armstrong later argued, in the sense that an inquiry into the organisation and machinery of government should have preceded one into the sort of civil service and civil servants needed in the modern state (Expenditure Committee, 1977: q. 1501). He had ideas of his own, and in his evidence to Fulton, Armstrong advocated a radical transformation of the structure of government, with a division between small policy-making departments and large attached executive agencies with management boards (anticipating the Next Steps reforms of twenty years later) (PRO BA 1/3). In the summer of 1969, he dissuaded Wilson from merging the Ministries of Transport and Power, making the case instead for bringing together Housing and Local Government with Transport. In October of that year, Tony Crosland was appointed to an 'overlord' position as Secretary of State for Local Government and Regional Planning, and by the time of the 1970 election plans had been developed to create an integrated department (see PRO PREM 13/2680, 13/3241).

In the run-up to that election, Armstrong and Burke Trend prepared for Wilson substantial papers about machinery of government reform and the trend to large 'functional' departments, the structure of the Cabinet and the role of the central departments (including arguments for a 'central analytic capability' or planning staff – akin to what became the CPRS 'think tank') (see PRO PREM 13/3241). The Conservatives were receptive to these ideas, for they themselves had been thinking along broadly similar lines, rapid progress subsequently ensuing with Heath's reorganisation of Whitehall in the aftermath of the 1970 election (Theakston, 1996). Had Labour been re-elected, Wilson would have announced the creation of what became (under Heath) the Department of the Environment, though he said that he would not have merged MinTech and the Board of Trade to form the Department of Trade and Industry (Expenditure Committee, 1977: q. 1946).

The Fulton Committee and reform of the civil service

The Fulton Committee reporting on the civil service (1966–1968) was the product of Wilson's 'white heat' phase of technological modernisation and reform (Theakston, 1992, ch. 4; Fry, 1993). Into it flowed long-standing left-wing and Fabian ideas about civil service reform (dating back to the 1930s), the questioning and critical 1960s attitude towards established institutions that were held to be obstacles to economic and social modernisation, and fashionable contemporary ideas about planning, expertise, business methods and management efficiency. Wilson's political need to maintain his image as a reformer also dovetailed with an important reform impulse inside Whitehall itself (there was a recognition in some parts of the civil service that changes were needed).

In opposition, Labour Party opinion about the need for civil service reform had been shaped by Thomas Balogh's blistering attacks both on the Treasury and on civil service amateurism, and by the publication in 1964 of an influential Fabian group report, *The Administrators*, which called for a more professional, specialised and expert civil service (Theakston, 1992: 114–19). *The Administrators* reiterated claims – common on the left – that the civil service was 'plainly out of touch with the times' and 'unfitted to more positive government', based as it was on an amateurish and generalist approach to governance, and characterised by elitism in terms of membership and recruitment. It was thus emphasised that significant reform of the civil service 'may be a pre-requisite to enabling a Labour Government – or any other government – to carry through the modernisation of the country' (Fabian Society, 1964: 3), thereby echoing Balogh's claim, two years earlier, that whilst 'Civil Service reform alone will not restore parliamentary democracy, or Cabinet responsibility in Britain', and could not 'by itself create the basis for a successful Socialist Government', it was nonetheless 'one of the most essential and fundamental pre-conditions of both', and it was 'a challenge to Labour to achieve this and it dare not fail' (1962: 115). Although Labour's 1964 manifesto did not refer explicitly to reform of the civil service per se, it did allude to the 'need to make government itself more efficient', which required that 'the machinery of government must be modernised' via a 'probing review [of] the practices of its own Departments of State' (Craig, 1975: 272).

Great (perhaps excessive) hopes were pinned on the potential effects of changed methods of civil service recruitment and training, and whilst Labour's advisers pressed for certain immediate steps to be taken (such as recruiting more economists), it was felt that a more formal inquiry would be needed to secure full-scale reform.

The critics' talk of the need for something approaching revolutionary change, and a new Northcote–Trevelyan report (a reference to the famous report of 1854), meant a downplaying of the extent to which Whitehall was in fact changing before 1964. Under the Conservatives, there had been major departmental reorganisations (of the Treasury, Education and Science, and the Ministry of Defence), important public expenditure planning reforms, and a new emphasis on management (with the 1961 Plowden Committee); and the setting up of the Centre for Administrative Studies (in 1963) marked a new approach to the training of administrators. Had Sir Alec Douglas-Home won re-election in 1964, he would have appointed Enoch Powell to take charge of the reorganisation of the civil service and Whitehall (Hennessy, 1989: 174).

There was no immediate shake-up of the civil service when Labour took office in 1964, but in August 1965 the House of Commons Estimates Committee produced a critical report on recruitment to the civil service, questioned the role of the administrative class and stepped up the pressure for an inquiry. Playing for time, the chiefs of the civil service advised delay and a cautious approach, saying that Whitehall needed time to settle down after the flurry of machinery of government changes of late 1964 (Theakston, 1992: 121–2). Wilson, however, had come to the view that a committee of inquiry or a royal commission was needed. He endorsed the establishment of a civil service staff college, believing, according to Balogh, that 'the Mendès-France reforms have made all the difference to the knowledge and morale of the French civil service and enabled them to dominate the scene in the Common Market and beyond'. A specialist Economist Class had been set up in 1965 and more economists recruited into Whitehall (numbers growing from 19 in 1963 to 106 by 1967), but Balogh pressed Wilson that more needed to be done to bring them into decision-making (PRO PREM 13/1357, Balogh to Wilson, 6 July 1965). When presented with data showing the continued Oxbridge and public-school predominance in higher civil service recruitment, Wilson pointedly commented that it still seemed to be 'heavily weighted against L.E.A. types' and that 'like tends to perpetuate like' (PRO PREM 13/1357, Mitchell to Anson, 14 September 1965).

On 1 November 1965, Jim Callaghan (the Treasury then being the department in charge of the civil service) formally minuted the Prime Minister with a proposal for 'a wide ranging inquiry' into the civil service, covering the structure, recruitment and management of the service (Wilson later insisted on training being explicitly added to the remit). The Estimates

Committee had envisaged a two-stage process: first a committee of officials aided by outsiders, with the government then reporting on the action it proposed, and if necessary going on to appoint a royal commission. Callaghan, however, argued the need to avoid a prolonged operation and to have just one inquiry that would not take too long. 'Some of the criticism [of the civil service] may be misguided, and if so it needs to be answered with authority,' he wrote, but 'Where it is justified, remedies should be sought – and some of the remedies may have to be pretty radical' (PRO PREM 13/1357). Wilson announced to Parliament the setting up of the Fulton Committee on 8 February 1966.

Lord Fulton (who had worked alongside Wilson during the Second World War, when they had apparently discovered they had similar views on the defects of the traditional mandarin class) had not been the first choice for the chairmanship of the inquiry; the names of Sir Ronald Edwards (chair of the Electricity Council), Sir Eric Ashby (a scientist), Lord Simey and W. J. M. Mackenzie (both academics) had earlier cropped up (PRO PREM 13/1357, Bancroft note of 3 November 1965; Balogh to Mitchell, 5 November 1965; Callaghan to Wilson, 25 November 1965). Lord Fulton was not, in the event, a success, being a poor chairman with little grip on the committee and a limited grasp of its subject matter (PRO PREM 13/1970, Halls to Wilson, 9 March 1968).[1] Indeed, according to Robert Neild, who had actually served on the Fulton Committee, Fulton was 'the most ineffective chairman I have ever known . . . charming but useless', having 'provided no direction' (quoted in Stone, 1997: 54).

By appointing two permanent secretaries and a senior government scientist to the Fulton Committee, Wilson aimed to make the changes it subsequently proposed more acceptable to, and within, Whitehall. Yet, in effect, Fulton was a 'Labour' committee: key members were Labour supporters, advisers and/or friends of the Prime Minister (such as Norman Hunt and Robert Neild, two influential figures on the committee), and its reformist conclusions could be almost predicted in advance.

Two areas of crucial constitutional and administrative importance were corralled off from the Fulton inquiry: relations between Ministers and officials, and the machinery of government. Wilson insisted that Labour did not intend to change the fundamental constitutional arrangement by which civil servants were the confidential advisers of Ministers, who alone were responsible to Parliament for policy (House of Commons debates, 8 February 1966, vol. 724, cols 209–10). Critics later argued that this factor meant that Fulton could not properly address issues of civil service power and its political control, as opposed to efficiency and management issues, and that its report neglected the constraints imposed by the political and parliamentary environment on the organisation and working of the civil service (Theakston, 1992: 130–1). Norman Hunt claimed that these exclusions were a civil service-imposed gag, which the mandarins could later use to undermine the committee's recommendations by arguing that they neglected the wider picture (Kellner and Crowther-Hunt, 1980: 27–8). Yet as we have seen, the idea of an 'outside' review of the machinery of government was anathema both to Wilson himself and to Whitehall. By talking of a 'fundamental and wide-ranging inquiry' in the tradition of the great Victorian reforms of Northcote-Trevelyan, Wilson was perhaps guilty of exaggerating what he hoped would emerge from what was, in fact, a relatively restricted and circumscribed review.

The files show that Wilson was kept in touch with and consulted about the progress of the Fulton Committee's work primarily through his Principal Private Secretary, Michael Halls, but also through meetings from time to time with Lord Fulton and Norman Hunt. Early on, the Prime Minister made suggestions about who the committee should seek evidence from, expressing a concern about giving 'undue weight to ex-Treasury Ministers' (PRO PREM 13/764, Halls to Allen, 9 August 1966). He made clear his support for the establishment of a civil service 'staff college' and the importance of training in economics and business management at an early stage of an official's career (PRO PREM 13/1977, Halls to Nairne, 29 July 1967; Halls to Bailey, 29 July 1967). Sir Laurence Helsby told Wilson that Fulton wanted to keep his committee off the subject of transferring civil service management from the Treasury to a new separate department 'until he has talked to you' (PRO PREM 13/1970, Helsby to Wilson, 16 May 1967). Wilson was also briefed about the drafting of the main recommendations of the report, and informed about internal divisions and arguments in the committee (e.g. over 'the classless service') (PRO PREM 13/1970, Halls to Wilson, 17 and 25 February and 9 March 1968).

Halls was clearly a crucial figure with strong views of his own about the need to reform the civil service. Wilson saw him as 'the epitome of the new management type envisaged by the Fulton committee' (Ziegler, 1993: 315), and later, in 1969, he was pencilled in to take up an appointment implementing the Fulton Report, though in the event the post went to someone else (Haines, 2003: 56). Halls was scathing about 'the failure of Permanent Secretaries . . . either to give a lead or to take an interest in organisation', arguing that the civil service 'establishment' should spend 'more time on efficient management and a little less in their intrigues' (PRO PREM 13/2527, Halls to Wilson, 16 January 1969). When he told the Prime Minister that many middle-rank officials agreed with the criticisms contained in Fulton, that the permanent secretaries were 'so determined to maintain the concept of the Mandarin' that they had 'swept under the carpet' every effort to get them to accept that the management of departments was as important as the policy advice function, and criticised 'the dominance of the civil service by Treasury personnel', Wilson responded, 'I agree with your comments' (PRO PREM 13/1970, Halls to Wilson, 11 May 1968). Halls was a strong champion of the idea of a 'classless civil service', arguing that it was essential to establish 'opportunities for all (eliminating the defects of what is in fact, at present, 'class snobbery') and a new found professionalism'. 'My own personal view is that it is just the kind of radical reform that is essential,' he told Wilson – 'and mine', scribbled the PM in the margin of his memo (PRO PREM 13/1970, Halls to Wilson, 25 February 1968).

The controversial Chapter 1 of the Fulton Report (published on 26 June 1968) – with its condemnation of Whitehall 'amateurism' and calls for 'fundamental change' – was not critical enough for Halls (PRO PREM 13/1970, Halls to Wilson, 8 June 1968). However, Ministers at the Cabinet meeting of 20 June 1968 felt that Fulton's criticisms 'though not without foundation were over-simplified and lacking in balance' (PRO CAB 128/43, CC(68) 31st Conclusions). There was, in fact, a Cabinet battle over the report (Crossman, 1977: 98, 103, 107, diary entries for 17 and 20 June 1968 and 25 June 1968 respectively; Castle, 1984: 464, 468, diary entries for 20 and 24 June 1968; Benn, 1988: 83, 85, 86, diary entries for 19, 20 and 25 June 1968). Members of the Fulton Committee had conducted considerable high-level lobbying of Ministers, senior officials and civil service unions, in order to 'sell' their recommendations (Kellner and Crowther-Hunt, 1980: 56–8).

Wilson wanted a quick response to, and immediate acceptance of, the three central proposals: to set up a new Civil Service Department (CSD) to take over management of the civil service from the Treasury; the creation of a civil service college; and the abolition of classes. However, he was opposed by Roy Jenkins and Denis Healey. Jenkins, the Chancellor, was furious at not having been consulted by Wilson over the removal of management of the service from his bailiwick and for being pointedly excluded from the committee's pre-publication lobbying, and argued for delay and a cautious response. Only Tony Benn and Peter Shore supported Wilson at the first Cabinet meeting on the report (20 June 1968), so that Wilson was thwarted by a combination of apathy, counter-lobbying from the civil service, personal and political rivalries and antipathies, and ministerial log-rolling on quite different items of business. William Armstrong warned the Prime Minister that the Government would 'be in danger of looking ridiculous' if it kicked the Fulton Report into the long grass (PRO PREM 13/1971, Armstrong to Halls, 21 June 1968). It required a second meeting (PRO CAB 128/43, CC(68) 32, item 3, 25 June 1968) before Wilson could successfully manage the Cabinet to secure the decision he wanted, so that he could, as Crossman (1977: 103, diary entry for 20 June 1968) put it, 'improve his image as a great modernizer'.

There was little further top-level political attention then given to Fulton, and in effect the Whitehall machine was given the task of implementing the report (with its total of 158 recommendations), subject to only limited and episodic ministerial involvement (Lord Shackleton was appointed Minister in day-to-day charge of the CSD and was also Leader of the House of Lords). Civil service closing of ranks and opposition to new ideas hindered the Fulton reforms, according to John Garrett, but, more importantly, they were thwarted by the lack of political interest in fundamental change and ministerial neglect of what seemed boring, nuts-and-bolts questions (Garrett, 1980: 191). According to Donald MacDougall, the head of the Government Economic Service in 1969,

> The Report contained some good ideas, but a lot of it was . . . rather general and even woolly; and I was obliged to read, and sit through discussions of long papers by the CSD which I thought were sometimes like sermons. First there was the text – a paragraph from Fulton; then ten pages discussing what it might mean; then another ten considering what might be done about it; and a final section quite often saying why nothing was possible or, worse still, with no conclusion at all.
>
> (MacDougall, 1987: 159)

Wilson himself maintained a close interest for a year or so, and expressed satisfaction with the initial progress made (PRO PREM 13/3098, Wilson to Halls, 15 February 1969), but his attention was diverted elsewhere as other issues crowded in during 1969. The eventual outcome was probably inevitable: a process of piecemeal adaptation and of reforms implemented in a way which entailed less radical change than outside critics of the civil service had hoped.

Fulton's champions blame the Whitehall mandarins for smothering or sabotaging the 'lost reforms' (Kellner and Crowther-Hunt, 1980), but the report did not actually constitute a coherent programme for 'reform'. Indeed, several writers have since noted that the Fulton Report was hardly a radical document (see, for example, Fry, 1981: 156; Jones and Keating, 1985: 147; Ponting, 1990: 261; Theakston, 1992: 129–31). There were plenty of shortcomings, weaknesses and ambiguities in its analysis and recommendations; some ideas were not properly thought through; and many of the detailed proposals turned out to be far from radical or original and simply to endorse developments already under way (e.g. on training). William Armstrong, appointed head of the civil service in 1968, was, within limits, a reformer. He saw the Fulton Report as a catalyst, 'breaking the ice' and providing an opportunity to enable reform ideas and change to come through – but insisted that there could be no 'rash commitment to accept recommendations unexamined', and that the changes needed and made could not be confined to Fulton's agenda in a literal or straightforward way (it was not the public administration equivalent of the Bible, he later said) (Theakston, 1999: 186–7; PRO PREM 13/1971, Armstrong to Halls, 21 June 1968; BBC2 television programme *Man Alive*, 9 May 1978). Burke Trend was another influence for caution, arguing that the Fulton Report should be approached 'pragmatically, with due regard for what is feasible' (PRO PREM 13/3135, Trend to Wilson, 11 November 1969).

Although he remarked that 'the classics boys [had] always been against him' (Castle, 1984: 468, diary entry for 24 June 1968), it was in fact the Prime Minister, Wilson, not 'obstructive' bureaucrats, who vetoed Fulton's proposal for 'preference for relevance' in administrative recruitment (PRO PREM 13/1970, Halls to Armstrong, 23 May 1968). There was weighty permanent secretary opposition to parts of Fulton – with arguments even over the departmental title of the CSD, and a scrap with the Ministry of Defence to secure its location in the Old Admiralty Building (PRO PREM 13/2692).

The vested and sectional interests of the main civil service unions were also an important constraint and could be asserted in the National Whitley Council machinery (the civil service's system of joint consultation) that was used to discuss and oversee the implementation of changes (1968–1973). Union views and interests were taken into account, and this process gave an opportunity for the two largest unions, the Society of Civil Servants and the Civil and Public Servants' Association (representing rank-and-file executive and clerical staff), to work with the mandarins of the traditional administrative class to keep out the specialists and maintain the so-called vertical barriers between classes that protected their members' jobs.

The baroque civil service personnel and grading structure – with over 1,400 different classes and groupings – had been an easy target for the Fulton Committee. William Armstrong accepted the need to simplify the system and reduce the rigidities, but he felt that Fulton's proposal for a 'classless' unified grading structure went too far and was unrealistic and unworkable (PRO PREM 13/1970, Armstrong to Halls, 9 May 1968). Class with a capital 'C' was involved. Fulton went along with the standard 1960s criticisms of the mandarin class for being too isolated and exclusive: the Labour Cabinet might be dominated by the Oxbridge educated, but it was undemocratic and unfair if the higher civil service was too. Wilson wanted what he called 'an open road to the top'. Officials were concerned about the cost implications, pay scales and other technical administrative details, arguing (rightly) that any change would be a complex and lengthy process, but he was more interested in radical-sounding talk about 'abolishing' classes and apparently bold reforms that would overturn the social class stereotypes in Whitehall (Kellner and Crowther-Hunt, 1980: 63–4). The CSD worked on plans to introduce an 'open structure' for the 700–800 officials in the top three grades, to amalgamate the old Administrative, Executive and Clerical classes, and put in place new groupings for scientists and professional and technical staff (these reorganisations eventually taking place under Heath in 1971–1972). Michael Halls and Norman Hunt (who kept in touch with Number 10) complained during 1969–1970 that Armstrong and the CSD were watering down Fulton's proposals and that little would change as a result, but there is no sign that Wilson paid much attention (see PRO PREM 13/3099, 13/3100). An inquiry into recruitment methods rejected (in its 1969 report) claims of bias, but the pre-Fulton elitism in terms of the social and educational backgrounds of 'high-flyer' recruits broadly continued into the 1970s (Theakston, 1992: 154–5; 1995: 101). Wilson failed to break the mould in this sense in Whitehall (though there have been changes over the longer term).

The Fulton Report was largely based on collectivist assumptions about 'big government' and a belief in a large civil service (Theakston, 1995: 90). Labour Ministers were more concerned about extending public services than limiting the size of the public-sector payroll. The 'non-industrial' (white-collar) civil service expanded by almost 20 per cent between October 1964 and April 1970 (up from 412,000 to 493,000), and with the 'industrial' civil service seeing a 13 per cent cut, the overall size of the civil service rose from 652,000 to 701,000 over that period (a net increase of 7.4 per cent, compared to 1.3 per cent from 1959 to 1964) (PRO PREM 13/3092, memo by F. Cooper, 5 June 1970). Conservative Party and press criticisms kept the government on the defensive on this issue and anxious to 'bury the bad news', as one Number 10 aide put it, by slipping out information about increased civil service manpower figures on Budget day in 1970 (PRO PREM 13/3092, Gregson to PM, 6 February 1970). A 'standstill' had been announced as part of the post-devaluation crisis measures in January 1968, but the government found it difficult to keep the lid down on departmental pressures for increased staff numbers. Roy Jenkins, the Chancellor, was convinced that there was 'a lot of over-staffing in the Civil Service' (PRO PREM 13/1969, Jenkins to Armstrong, 23 July 1968), and Wilson hit upon the idea of appointing a panel of businessmen and industrialists to review staffing, and undertake a programme of inquiries into particular areas of work, seeking staff savings and improved efficiency.

However, the Bellinger Panel (starting work in late 1968) met with predictable opposition from the 'staff-side' unions, and scepticism from permanent secretaries. Thirteen investigations had been carried out by the time of the 1970 election, but the direct results were extremely modest (eliminating a couple of hundred posts) (see PRO PREM 13/3092). Michael Halls was disappointed at the progress made by Bellinger, telling Wilson firmly that there was scope for staff cuts and greater efficiency in the big blocks of executive and clerical work, and complaining that senior staff needed to take the issue more seriously (PRO PREM 13/2527, Halls to Wilson, 16 January and 1 August 1969). However, serious axe swinging, large-scale staff cuts and a determined programme of 'efficiency scrutinies' were to come only after 1979, with Mrs Thatcher; unlike her, Wilson did not aim to 'take on' the civil service and attack 'bureaucracy'.

Another area where there was very little post-Fulton progress during the remainder of the Labour Government's term of office was in terms of 'hiving off' government functions to agencies or bodies separate from the main Whitehall departments. Wilson announced a review of possible areas for 'hiving off' in November 1968, later prodding the machine with the claim that this was 'a high priority in modernisation' and asking for 'some of the major and more spectacular cases' to be brought forward (PRO PREM 13/3097, Wilson to Halls, 15 February 1969). A CSD steering group considered various cases, but officials strongly emphasised the possible pitfalls and problems (see PRO PREM 13/3242). By 1970, William Armstrong was warning about the barriers 'against the really large scale diffusion of power by hiving-off within the public sector' and the dangers of surrendering control whilst retaining responsibility (PRO PREM 13/3241, 'Machinery of Government 1970 – Organisation of Government functions', 11 June 1970). Wilson was quick to veto the proposal to sell or hive off the state management districts (government-owned pubs and breweries, mainly in Carlisle) (PREM 13/3242, Halls to Armstrong, 26 March 1970)!

Government secrecy

Previous Labour Governments had left the traditions of 'closed government' and Cabinet secrecy undisturbed, but official secrecy started to become a significant issue on the political agenda in the 1960s. Fabian reformers argued that it was an obstacle to good policy-making: 'it prevents the tapping of a sufficiently wide range of expert advice and ... it narrows public discussion of policy issues' (Fabian Society, 1964: 22), whilst the Fulton Committee was concerned that the administrative process was shrouded in too much secrecy, and hence, urged the Wilson Government to establish an inquiry, with the intention of 'getting rid of unnecessary secrecy in this country' (Fulton Report, 1968: paras 277–80).

Harold Wilson – who 'combined in a bizarre fashion an opener's temperament with a paranoia about leaks' (Hennessy, 2003: 29) – deserves credit for pushing through the 1967 Public Records Act, which reduced from fifty to thirty years the time limit placed on the opening of government records (PRO PREM 13/742, 13/1957). When Wilson consulted the other party leaders, Jo Grimond indicated that the Liberals favoured releasing records after twenty or twenty-five years, but Heath and the Conservatives initially drew the line at forty years, concerned that a shorter period would result in the public disclosure of files about appeasement in the 1930s. The Labour Cabinet decided on a thirty-year rule in August 1965, but there was unhappiness and foot-dragging in Whitehall (and by some Ministers).

At one stage, Wilson toyed with the idea of the general release of documents after forty years but with a mechanism for access within that period, whereupon a 'partially open' period would place the onus on departments to justify the continued withholding of information after twenty-five years. Sir Burke Trend and the permanent secretaries had disliked this option, worried that it would be the thin end of a wedge. Prime ministerial pressure had to be maintained to prevent departments like the Foreign Office and the Lord Chancellor's Department subverting the new legislation's objective by reclassifying and holding back even more material (PRO PREM 11/1077, Wilson to Crossman, 22 December 1966; Crossman, 1976: 328, diary entry for 25 April 1967).

Wilson did 'see some merit in an enquiry [into official secrecy] of the kind suggested by the Fulton Committee, involving outsiders' (PRO PREM 13/1972, Shackleton to Wilson, 27 September 1968), but again senior officials (and, it turned out, other Ministers) were opposed. William Armstrong thought it 'by no means clear that an enquiry by a body of outsiders – the bulk of whom would probably be naturally biased against secrecy – would advance matters' (PRO PREM 13/1970, 'The secrecy of official information', draft memo of 16 May 1968). He acknowledged that the Official Secrets Act was 'restrictive', albeit 'extremely difficult to enforce', and was brought into 'disrepute' by ministerial leaks, although it was not in itself a barrier to the adoption of a more liberal policy towards the ('authorised') release of government information (PRO PREM 13/1972, Armstrong to Halls, 17 June 1968). In November 1968, Wilson was reported as being 'not in any particular hurry to reach conclusions' about these issues (ibid., Halls to Walker, 26 November 1968), but he was stirred into action in January 1969 when Heath called for a review of government secrecy. Not wanting to be outmanoeuvred, Wilson announced that 'the whole question of the release of official information, including the Official Secrets Act, should now be under consideration' (PRO PREM 13/2528).

Various names were mooted for the chairmanship of an inquiry committee, although when Wilson suggested Lord Aylestone (a former Minister, Bert Bowden), Michael Halls warned him that he 'might well come out with a far too liberally minded report – almost Swedish' (PRO PREM 13/2528, Halls to Wilson, 21 February 1969). Whitehall's anticipation of the problems and dangers lurking down the 'open government' road is clearly indicated in an official brief prepared for the Prime Minister (PRO PREM 13/2528, 'The Release of Official Information', 5 March 1969). Doubts were expressed about 'how far there is a real public demand' for the release of more background 'factual and statistical information', which would in any case be costly in terms of civil service staff numbers required to implement it. Through 'the Green Paper approach' – the first of which appeared in 1967 – the Labour Government had already started to make more information available and extend public consultation, it was claimed. However, it was judged that greater openness about the processes of decision-taking and policy-making would not be 'practicable or expedient', because it would open up to the public gaze the role of 'subjective judgments' and 'the reactions of various interests at home and abroad'.

Consequently, the terms of reference of an outside inquiry, if there had to be one, should be framed in such a way as to 'minimise ... the risk of embarrassment'. With regard to Fulton's proposal for progressively relaxing the convention of civil service anonymity – an idea which Wilson had favoured in the early days of the government but had apparently become 'much more cautious' about (PRO PREM 13/1970, Halls to Armstrong, 22 May 1968) – the catch here was that senior officials could become identified as personally responsible for the advice given on particular issues, and the corollary of that would be that 'they should be free to disclose in what respects their advice had not been accepted by Ministers'.

Labour Ministers needed little persuading, and Jim Callaghan later summed up their executive mentality with his comment that 'we are not going to tell you anything more than we can about what is going to discredit us' (Theakston, 1992: 159). In March 1969, the 'inner Cabinet' (the parliamentary committee) finally rejected an outside inquiry as likely to push the Government further than it wanted to go (PRO PREM 13/2528, Trend to Wilson, 24 March 1969). Instead, a rather limited and bland White Paper, *Information and the Public Interest*, was issued in June 1969 (Cmnd 4089, 1969), putting a positive gloss on the Government's record in making more information available. Irrespective of whether this modest move was sufficient to pacify those in the Labour Party calling for 'the provision of much more background information and a much greater knowledge of the machinery through which advice is turned into a draft Bill, or conflicts of advice resolved or reconciled' (Labour Party Archives, Re.440/April 1969), a ministerial briefing paper about the White Paper mocked the 'fashionable current myth that the quality of public business would be improved if it were carried out in a kind of goldfish bowl' (PRO PREM 13/3096, 'Information and the Public Interest: Background Notes for Ministers', 19 June 1969). Certainly many Ministers were, by this time, convinced that the Government had gone as far as it could, or should, in disclosing information – 'our record on improvements both in the collection of intelligence and in the supply of information is quite unusually good' – to the extent that instigating further mechanisms for disclosure would

> cause us a good deal of unnecessary embarrassment by exposing to the public eye sensitive areas in which we have good reason for not being completely forthcoming ... [by] releasing more information with regard to those areas when the discretion we are at present using is wholly justified.
>
> (PRO PREM 13/2528, Crossman to Wilson, 20 March 1969)

The White Paper's tone of self-congratulatory benevolence was in sharp contrast to the actions of Labour's Attorney-General, who in March 1970 initiated the *Sunday Telegraph* secrets trial (concerning leaked information about Biafra embarrassing to the government). This backfired, though, thereby giving the open government cause a fillip a year later (when Labour was in opposition) when the defendants were acquitted and the judge declared that section 2 of the Official Secrets Act should be 'pensioned off'. In April 1970, the Foreign Office and the MoD were still stridently opposed to weakening the secrecy laws and wanted to resist a review 'for as long as possible', officials describing a 'public interest defence' in secrets cases as 'clearly unacceptable', but Wilson recognised that this line was increasingly difficult to hold and was prepared to signal publicly that 'there is a case for considering the operation of the Official Secrets Act' (PRO PREM 13/3473). The outside review that Ministers and Whitehall had wanted to avoid finally materialised in the shape of the Franks Committee, but appointed by

Heath's Conservative Government (elected in June 1970) and reporting in 1972 – although legislation to reform the much-criticised 1911 Official Secrets Act was only finally passed in 1989 (the 1974–1979 Labour Government defaulting on its freedom of information manifesto pledge).

Conclusion

It is a fair criticism that Harold Wilson's political style and his basic institutional conservatism reinforced each other between 1964 and 1970. Absorbed into the Whitehall ethos, he arguably came to regard the smooth process of business through the official machine as the equivalent of successfully dealing with real problems. Most other Labour Ministers too, as Ponting argues (1990: 174), 'settled down into the routines and rituals of Whitehall life, content to be in office'. As with their counterparts in the 1945–1951 Labour Governments, most Labour Ministers in the 1964–1970 administrations came to rely on and admire their officials for their bureaucratic professionalism, policy advice and neutral competence. However, on the left of the Labour Party the experience of office rekindled the traditional suspicions of the civil service, with the Treasury especially suspected of obstructing or sabotaging radical socialist reform. Such suspicions fuelled calls after 1970 (and still more so during and after the 1974–1979 Labour term of office) for major reform of Whitehall, in order to check bureaucratic, and strengthen ministerial, power, to appoint more politically committed advisers, and to increase government accountability (Theakston, 1992: *passim*).

In this context, it is worth pointing out that Tony Benn, in his diaries for the 1960s, certainly complains about 'the Civil Service network' and about problems with his civil servants, but that he only really developed a full-blown critical analysis of bureaucratic power after he moved sharply to the left in the 1970s. Indeed, his technocratic thinking in the 1960s led him to criticise the civil service for its lack of dynamism, ideas and initiative, and to endorse the Fulton Report, without apparently appreciating that a more professional and expert bureaucracy might also be a more powerful one (Benn, 1987: 182, 220, 226–7, 307, 354–5; diary entries for 10 November 1964, 17 and 25 February 1965, 6 August 1965 and 23 November 1965).

Both Wilson (1964–1970) and then Heath (1970–1974) were fascinated by the machinery of government, although Wilson's ad hoc and very political approach to the issues showed little evidence of strategic purpose or design (in contrast to Heath's). Whatever their differences in character and personal style, both – as successive Labour and Conservative Prime Ministers – tended to exaggerate what could be achieved by rejigging official machinery and reshaping the pattern of Whitehall departments. Embracing the then fashionable 'bigger is better' business management ideas, there was an element of wishful thinking in their belief that institutional tinkering and relabelling could solve deep-seated economic and policy problems

(Campbell, 1993: 222). Later, by the mid-1970s, politicians and senior Whitehall officials became much more sceptical about the likely benefits of structural redesign in central government.

Much of the debate about the civil service in this period is dominated by the Fulton Report and its fate. In many ways, Fulton was opportunistic – 'in telling politicians what they wanted to hear and in seizing upon existing trends and dressing them up as something new' (Drewry and Butcher, 1991: 54). The report's derogatory tone raised hackles but the actual proposals were, on the whole, far from radical or original. The Fulton exercise may have largely served to assist, encourage and accelerate developments which were already under way in Whitehall or in the pipeline. The Fulton reform programme was just starting to take shape and gather momentum when Labour left office in 1970, but it ran out of steam a few years later under Heath. There were real improvements in training, organisation and management, but it is true to say that by the late 1970s Whitehall had changed in more evolutionary, piecemeal and modest ways than outside critics had wanted (Garrett, 1980: 3, 191). In some respects, the Fulton Report laid the foundations for or foreshadowed the radical Whitehall reorganisations and reforms of the 1980s and 1990s (executive agencies, financial management reforms, etc.), but it cannot be claimed that either Fulton or Wilson's Labour Government directly generated them; the real political clout was provided by Margaret Thatcher, who had her own agenda and motives (Theakston, 1995: 107).

Note

1 Twenty years later, Margaret Thatcher did not bother with the likes of Fulton, pushing through major civil service (and other reforms) without the cloak of an outside 'non-political' inquiry by the 'great and the good' or deference to established interests.

10 Parliamentary reform

Donald Shell

Introduction

With regard to the reform and modernisation of Parliament, the 1964–1970 Labour Governments are probably best remembered for the abortive attempt to reform the House of Lords. That a major bill to remove hereditary peers, and to reconstitute the basis of membership for the upper House, should have received all-party endorsement, been introduced as a Government bill, received a comfortable majority at second reading, then been abandoned in committee, was remarkable. The repercussions of the loss of this bill, the Parliament (No. 2) Bill, were still being felt thirty years later when the Blair Government made the next serious attempt to reform the Lords. Yet when the Labour Party narrowly won the 1964 election, it was not House of Lords reform that was uppermost in its mind, but reform of the House of Commons, and whilst progress in this sphere may have seemed modest at the time, there were some changes whose significance have only become apparent or appreciated in the years since.

Parliament appeared particularly ripe for reform in 1964, for at the time both the House of Commons and the House of Lords seemed to be a mumbo-jumbo land (see, for example, Hughes, 1966), performing strange rituals based on archaic traditions which had no relevance to a country about to undergo, in Wilson's phrase, 'the white heat of technological revolution'. Yet the Conservative Party hardly appeared equal to the task of bringing Parliament up to date, in spite of having introduced the 1958 Life Peerages Act. Many of their leading figures appeared pompous, out of touch and ineffective, and what few ideas they did put forward for reforming Parliament seemed modest indeed.

Elsewhere, though, there were more propitious prospects and prognoses for parliamentary reform. In 1964, a group of academics and professional officers in both Houses had come together to found the Study of Parliament Group, and whilst this body had no programme for reform per se, it certainly helped to encourage discussion about reform, and put some proposals firmly on the agenda. Its members produced ideas, gave evidence to parliamentary committees and published scholarly work advancing the case for changes in the way Parliament did its work in order to improve its effectiveness.

In the same year, Bernard Crick, one of the founder members of the Study of Parliament Group, wrote a vigorously argued book, *The Reform of Parliament*, which attracted considerable attention. His main thesis was that the procedures of the House of Commons were still geared to the idea that it exercised real power – over every piece of legislation and even every expenditure estimate. But party government meant that this was no longer so. The theory that best fitted the facts, according to Crick, was that 'Parliament influences the electorate which has the real power to control the Government', and hence 'Control means influence, not direct power; advice, not command; criticism, not obstruction; scrutiny, not initiation; and publicity, not secrecy' (1964: 28, 80–1). Crick's remedy was thus for reforms which would enable Parliament to become a body better able to provide scrutiny of government, its legislation, its policies, and the efficiency and effectiveness of governmental activities. High on the list of desirable reforms were specialist or select committees, which could investigate areas of government activity, take evidence and report their conclusions.

A similar diagnosis was offered in the Penguin book *What's Wrong with Parliament* (the title deliberately lacked a question mark, because it was intended to be an exposition, not a question), also published in 1964, and written pseudonymously by two House of Commons clerks known as Andrew Hill and Anthony Whichelow. It was the need to reform Parliament so that its activities were better able to ensure the accountability of an expanded and strengthened government, that pre-occupied these authors; 'there should be,' they wrote, 'beneath Parliament's grand function of debating Government policies, a considerable stratum of Parliamentary activity designed to establish the facts and question the thoroughness with which those policies have been thought out' (Hill and Whichelow, 1964: 45). This again pointed to the desirability of greater committee activity within Parliament, and for Hill and Whichelow it was parliamentary committees – as opposed to party committees – which were most likely to provide for enhanced parliamentary scrutiny and effectiveness. They also recommended, though, that Parliament should be better publicised, especially through television, and that MPs should be better paid and resourced.

The Labour Party cautiously endorses parliamentary reform

Immediately upon becoming leader of the Labour Party in 1963, Harold Wilson was including Parliament within the ambit of his reform agenda, not only proposing the creation of an 'Ombudsman', but also talking of the need to shift the balance between the executive and the legislature, and of enabling MPs to make a greater contribution to policy-making and legislation. Citing his own experience of studying the role of select committees in formulating nineteenth-century railway legislation (!), he outlined his ideas on establishing select committees consisting of MPs under the chairmanship of a Minister, taking evidence and then producing reports with draft bills (cited in Crick, 1965: 339). Thus, when Labour won the 1964 general election, the whole issue of parliamentary reform was firmly on the agenda, although it was not generally perceived as a high priority. Shortly after leading Labour to electoral victory, Wilson ruminated further on the potential for such committees, suggesting that such an initiative would serve to show that the Government 'far from being arrogant in its relations with Parliament is desirous of giving more work and authority to the House as a whole', whilst also providing 'useful and constructive employment' for Labour backbenchers (PRO PREM 13/1053, Wilson to Bowden, 21 November 1964).

Bowden, having been appointed Leader of the House (of Commons) following Labour's election victory, was rather less enthusiastic about granting Labour MPs a pre-legislative role, wary that this might actually slow down, rather than expedite, the Government's legislative programme in the Commons, but he did acknowledge that some form of specialist or subject committees 'would be useful in giving backbenchers varied and interesting work and the feeling that they were contributing to policy', and suggested that such committees might be developed to carry out investigations into specific topics and policies, whereby they could 'call for papers, interview Ministers, officials and other Members, *but would not be expected to come up with legislation*' (PRO PREM 13/1053, Bowden to Wilson, 3 December 1964; emphasis added).

Yet such initiatives had not been evident in Labour's election manifesto, which despite its overall length – 7,000 words – referred only to the need to subject 'Parliament itself [to] continuing and probing review' along with the 'Departments of State, the administration of justice, and the Social Services' (Craig, 1975: 272). Furthermore, the parliamentary situation that confronted the Labour Government after the 1964 election veered very much in the direction of management and containment, rather than boldness and reform, for with such a narrow majority the Government's priority was clearly to present itself as competent and united, in order to secure a rather more comfortable majority when it went to the polls in the not too distant future.

Nonetheless, parliamentary reform was not entirely abandoned in the short 1964–1966 Parliament, for whilst Ministers were naturally not inclined to implement contentious proposals, especially those that might make life more difficult for themselves, a few initiatives were introduced during this period. Probably the most important and innovative of these concerned proposals for a Parliamentary Commissioner for Administration, more commonly known as an 'Ombudsman' (discussed later in the chapter), which Wilson had first publicly mooted in a speech in Stowmarket, Suffolk, in July 1964 (for a full account of the development and establishment of the Ombudsman, see Stacey, 1971).

Improving MPs' resources and facilities

With regard to the salaries and facilities available to MPs, there were at least three discrete issues to be addressed. First of these was the question of whether or not being an MP was really a full-time occupation. For most Conservatives it was not (many of them happily combining attendance at Parliament with their careers in 'the City' or at the Bar), but for most Labour MPs it was, and this partisan difference imbued the argument about salaries with a partisan edge. Second was the question of expenses, and how these should be reimbursed. Prior to 1964, this had been done through allowing MPs to claim £750 of their £1,750 annual salary as expenses set against tax. Third was the more general question of the facilities available to MPs to help them with their Parliamentary work. Ultimately, these were matters that the House of Commons itself had to decide, a somewhat invidious task because it involved Members deciding their own salaries and resources. The previous Conservative Government had set up a committee of non-parliamentarians to make recommendations, but this committee, known as the Lawrence Committee after its chair, Sir Geoffrey Lawrence, had simply recommended a straight salary increase to £3,250, while dodging the issue of expenses and facilities by claiming that these lay outside its terms of reference. The newly elected Labour Government immediately implemented the salary increase, thereby ensuring that MPs now received remuneration of modest decency. A pension scheme was also launched, albeit one which was remarkably ungenerous, providing a former MP with fifteen years' service with a pension of £900 at age sixty-five.

The whole question of what was really expected of MPs, and what resources were needed to enable them to fulfil their roles and responsibilities in an appropriate and effective manner, was in effect side-stepped. Later, reimbursement for travel and for the use of telephones was gradually improved, but to an extent that now looks remarkable for its sheer parsimony. And looking ahead for a moment, in 1969, a secretarial allowance of £500 per annum was introduced, enough perhaps to offer half-time employment to a fairly junior secretary. Of course the constituency demands upon MPs were vastly less than they were later to become in subsequent decades. Denis Healey recalls how, until 1964, he personally produced handwritten replies to all constituency letters, doing this whilst sitting in the Commons library (1989: 144–5). No personal offices were available for MPs, and only a minority had personal desks, either in multiply occupied rooms or in corridors. The House of Commons Library was still a pale shadow of what it was later to become. The attitude of younger MPs was exemplified by Richard Marsh (later to be Wilson's youngest sacked Cabinet Minister) when he commented during a debate in 1963, 'Any Member of Parliament who finds the Library adequate cannot be doing a proper job', whilst in 1966 a select committee rather proudly reported that 'the Library now has nine graduates including three specialised in economic matters'. By 1969, the number of graduates had apparently reached twenty.

To many backbench Labour MPs, it was the facilities of the House and proper recompense for what they felt were the legitimate expenses of doing their job that mattered far more than the salary level. And certainly these were matters that had an impact on the effectiveness of Parliament. Pressure to improve conditions for MPs was therefore linked with procedural reform. A Labour backbench reform group was established during the first Labour Government, chaired by David Kerr, whereupon a working group of the Parliamentary Labour Party (PLP) was also created, although the latter seemed simply to sit on the subject and muffle it, as it was probably designed to do. However, the Select Committee on Procedure was reconstituted, and produced a number of reports which gently ventilated the case for reform in a positive manner. Indeed, this revived Select Committee on Procedure gave a very respectful hearing to three professors of politics – all founding members of the Study of Parliament Group – invited to give oral evidence.

The case for more specialised and investigatory select committees gradually gained greater credence, although the idea that Ministers might appear before such bodies was described as a 'drastic constitutional change' by the then head of the civil service, Laurence (later Lord) Helsby (quoted in Wiseman, 1970: 199), whilst Herbert Bowden, Leader of the Commons, thought that neither Ministers nor civil servants should appear (PRO PREM 13/1053, Bowden to Wilson, 19 April 1966). In spite of such scepticism and conservatism, the Labour Party's 1966 manifesto suggested somewhat greater boldness, with a section entitled 'Modernising Parliament' declaring that

> Improvement and modernisation of the work of Parliament is essential to reinforce the democratic element in modern Government. Changes must improve procedure and the work of committees, and reform facilities for research and information. Consideration is being given to the broadcasting of Commons proceedings, in order to bring Parliament closer to the people it represents, and to increase the sense of public participation in policy making. Legislation will be introduced to safeguard measures approved by the House of Commons from frustration by delay or defeat in the House of Lords.
>
> (Craig, 1975: 307)

Labour's re-election with a comfortable parliamentary majority clearly presented the Government with new opportunities and new challenges. The caution and hesitancy with which it characterised its agenda of parliamentary reform during its first term of office could now, it seemed, be jettisoned in favour of more innovative and imaginative measures. Certainly, as was noted in Chapter 2, many of the new Labour MPs in the House of Commons after the 1966 election were drawn from professional occupations, and they were eager to make the Commons their workplace and to ensure its (and *inter alia* their) effectiveness. Simply being Members of the House, privileged to be close observers of those who wielded power, was not enough. They wanted scrutiny to be effective. They wanted to bring into the public domain more of the information upon which Ministers and civil servants based their decisions. If backbenchers remained frustrated in their attempts to bring this about, their discontent was likely to make them fractious, awkward, even rebellious, thereby greatly exacerbating the problems of party management discussed earlier in Chapter 3.

Of course, from the Government's perspective a cohort of more active or assertive Labour MPs was potentially problematic, for it raised the spectre of Ministers being subject to much greater scrutiny from their own backbenchers, in addition to that naturally emanating from the opposition parties. It was this realisation which probably accounted, in large part, for the appointment of Richard Crossman as the new Leader of the House. Though in retrospect his interest in parliamentary reform makes his appointment as Leader seem obvious, at the time this was far from the case. Tam Dalyell, Crossman's Parliamentary Private Secretary (and subsequent biographer), was later to write:

> In twenty-seven years in Westminster, I do not recollect anything to parallel the amused incredulity among the older and more senior denizens of the palace – elected members and clerks of the House of Commons alike – with which the appointment of Crossman as Lord President of the Council and Leader of the House of Commons was received.
>
> (Dalyell, 1989: 149)

Previous Leaders of the House of Commons had traditionally been men who knew the place well through long years of diligent participation, and who could both gauge the mood of the House and guard its traditions, politicians who could carefully soothe its ego at times of tension, and steer the House into calm waters when turbulence threatened. Yet not only had Crossman taken very little interest in the House hitherto, he had hardly even been there. Reflecting in his diary on his appointment, a few days after it was announced, he wrote:

> For days now I've been sitting at my desk, reading the documents and mugging up on the organisation and history of Parliament. It's difficult because I know as little about it as I did about housing twenty months ago. Although I've been a backbencher for nearly twenty years I've really done very little in Parliament. I've taken no interest in procedure and not very much part in debates because I thought Parliament a profoundly unimportant and boring place. But at least in writing about its ineffectiveness, I've consistently advocated reform. Now, ironically, I've

got to see if I can get the case for reform across. After looking at the papers I've a feeling I've got some luck on my side since a package of reforms has been prepared.

(Crossman, 1976: 17, diary entry for 29 August 1966)

Crossman had an intellectual curiosity about the constitution, and the manner in which it had changed. Indeed, in 1963 he had written an introduction to the Fontana edition of Walter Bagehot's *The English Constitution*, in which he relegated the Cabinet and, by implication, the House of Commons to being merely 'dignified' – rather than efficient – parts of the constitution (Crossman, 1963: 54). Speaking in a Commons adjournment debate the day after his appointment, Crossman referred to his 'strong prejudice in favour of Parliamentary reform', because 'Parliament has declined, is declining, and should not decline any further' (House of Commons Debates, 5th series, 24 August 1966). Crossman was convinced that 'the modern House . . . had lost its main function of controlling the Executive' and therefore needed to 'reshape itself and redefine its functions if it ever wanted to be anything again' (1976: 165, diary entry for 14 December 1966). Bernard Crick thus deemed Crossman to be 'the first reforming Leader of the House in modern times' (1964: xi).

The 'package of reforms' to which Crossman alluded included specialist select committees, the introduction of the Ombudsman, the possible televising of Parliament, transference of the committee stage of the Finance Bill from the floor of the House to a standing committee, and the alteration of Commons hours of business, in particular through the introduction of morning sittings. None of this seemed very exciting to Crossman, for much of it constituted detailed procedural initiatives, hardly matching the grand ideas he had espoused and highly unlikely to meet the sweeping criticisms of the British system of government that he was ready to make. Yet they did represent a start, and however limited their intellectual attraction to the new Leader of the House, there were good political reasons for pushing forward with such reforms; Labour's new backbenchers, if not given some real and sensible work to do, would almost certainly grow restless and troublesome. The devil would make work for idle hands – a point not lost on Crossman's Cabinet colleagues.

However, the PLP was in two minds with regard to the reform of Parliament. There were plenty of older members who regarded the whole idea of reform as a dangerous red herring, believing that Government backbenchers were there to keep the executive strong, to ensure it could push its laws and policies through Parliament, and to discredit the Opposition as much as possible. Giving backbenchers tools to make scrutiny of the executive more effective would only make the work of government harder. It was a distraction from the great political battle between the two rival political machines. This attitude was illustrated in the argument Crossman records as having taken place in Cabinet when he presented his reform proposals in mid-

November. According to Crossman, a 'ghastly discussion' took place lasting nearly two hours, with Ministers emphasising the extra work such reforms would create, and applauding Michael Stewart, still at the Department of Economic Affairs, when he declared that Labour backbenchers should be thankful that as a 'socialist government we want to keep the Executive strong, not to strengthen Parliamentary control'. Crossman reflected on how Ministers who had individually been committed to parliamentary reform had become 'Whitehall figures who've lost contact with Parliament' (1976: 130, diary entry for 17 November 1966).

Far from being deterred by the conservatism and complacency – 'pure nonsense' – of some of his ministerial colleagues, though, Crossman's belief in the need for parliamentary reform was strengthened further, not least because he envisaged that Ministers and their departments would be compelled to sharpen up by a little more pressure from Parliament. Besides, granting Labour backbenchers a more active or extensive role in the parliamentary policy process not only would (it was hoped) pacify the aspirations of a cohort of more educated and professional MPs who were not prepared to be treated as mere 'lobby fodder', and thereby forestall growing unrest on the Labour back benches, but also fitted neatly with the Parliamentary Labour Party's more liberal managerial regime of this period, as was discussed in Chapter 3.

The Parliamentary Commissioner for Administration

A very positive note was struck immediately after Labour's 1966 election victory, with the establishment of a Parliamentary Commissioner for Administration (PCA), more commonly known as the Ombudsman – an innovation which commanded widespread support within the PLP, although some MPs had initially been anxious that their own roles and responsibilities might be undermined.

As indicated above, the preparations for establishing an Ombudsman had actually begun after Labour's 1964 election victory, whereupon a Cabinet committee endeavoured to develop proposals for an Ombudsman which would not undermine the role of MPs, and which would allay the concerns of some senior officials in Whitehall, who were anxious about the potentially detrimental impact on the work of their departments.

The most significant modification to the original idea of an Ombudsman was that citizens would not have direct access to the Ombudsman themselves, but would be required to make representations through MPs. In other words, unlike Ombudsmen elsewhere, the British version would be a Parliamentary Commissioner – even the word 'Ombudsman' was at the last minute deleted from the bill – accessible not directly by members of the public, but only through MPs, and unable to enforce remedies, but reporting to a specially created select committee of the House, which could follow up reports as it saw fit. Crucially, therefore, the Parliamentary

Commissioner for Administration was to provide a means of giving expression to parliamentary control rather than detracting from it, an instrument increasing the weaponry available to MPs, rather than the creation of a rival champion. This meant that the Commissioner could only examine matters for which Ministers had direct responsibility to Parliament, thereby excluding areas that many considered the most frequent source of citizen grievances, including local government, the nationalised industries and the National Health Service. Nonetheless, this did not prevent the Labour MP Sydney Silverman from describing the creation of the Parliamentary Commissioner for Administration as 'the greatest constitutional amendment that this House of Commons has ever approached since the days when universal suffrage became applicable to our electoral system'. It would contribute greatly, he claimed, to making 'the individual House of Commons backbench Member's defence of his constituents against the Executive more effective than it has ever been' (House of Commons Debates, 5th series, vol. 734, col. 124).

Yet in spite of Silverman's eulogy, there was considerable uncertainty as to how the office of Parliamentary Commissioner would develop. The word 'maladministration' was left deliberately undefined, though it was made clear that the exercise of discretion in the taking of decisions was not included. Crossman, during the second reading of the bill, offered a catalogue of possible qualities that might result in maladministration: 'bias, neglect, inattention, delay, incompetence, inaptitude, perversity, turpitude, arbitrariness and so on', although it would be for the Commissioner to work out in detail what this meant.

The first Parliamentary Commissioner for Administration, whose appointment was announced even before the bill had gained its second reading, was the former Comptroller and Auditor General Sir Edmund Compton, someone familiar with the role of being a servant of the Commons, but also someone well versed in the ways of Whitehall. Indeed, perhaps because of his familiarity with its ways, there was some nervousness in Whitehall over Sir Edmund's appointment, exacerbated by the story that Sir Edmund, when asked whether he preferred being Ombudsman to a permanent secretary at the Treasury, had replied by quoting Pope Leo X: 'Now that God has given us the papacy, let us enjoy it.'

The first report made by the Commissioner was very low-key, greeted by a *Times* leader headed 'Ombudsman or Ombudsmouse?', but by the end of 1967 the Parliamentary Commissioner for Administration had risen to prominence over a report on Sachsenhausen. This found that the Foreign Office had indeed been guilty of maladministration in the manner that it had handled claims for compensation from some of those incarcerated in this concentration camp during the Second World War. The Foreign Secretary, George Brown, was intransigent in defence of the Foreign Office, but parliamentary debate, and a further report from the select committee, secured a new decision favourable to the claimants. The significance of this case for Parliament was that this new parliamentary officer had succeeded on a matter upon which several senior MPs had campaigned for years to no avail. The Ombudsman had won his spurs, and thereafter there was never any question of this newly created office being removed. On the contrary, the Ombudsman concept was extended to other areas during the 1970s, most notably local government and the health service.

Expanding parliamentary select committees

The expansion of Parliament's system of select committees was more fraught, and met with less obvious immediate success. Nonetheless, a considerable expansion did occur, and in subsequent Parliaments this too was extended, rather than reversed. The argument for such committees had slowly and cautiously been developed during Macmillan's Conservative administrations in the late 1950s and early 1960s. The existing Estimates Committee and the Select Committee on Nationalised Industries offered some guidance as to the roles further select committees might fulfil, envisaging cross-party backbench investigatory committees, which would probe the work of the executive through inquiry and evidence-taking. They would not deal directly with draft legislation, though, because it was accepted that no government would want this for its own bills, but they would examine the making of policy as well as the quality of administration.

Also proposing the extension of such parliamentary committees was the Study of Parliament Group, whose evidence to an inquiry – during the first year of Wilson's premiership – by the House of Commons Procedure Committee emphasised that

> to enable the House to arrive at a correct judgement on the workings of administration and on the Government's conduct of affairs, some process of enquiry is needed. Specialist committees are needed to scrutinise the actions of government in their own fields. The main weakness in Parliament's present methods ... is the limited ability to obtain the background facts and understanding essential for detailed criticism of administration or any informed discussion of policy. Specialist committees ... could go a long way to remedy this.
>
> (Fourth Report of the Procedure Committee, 1964–1965, HC 303: 134, 137)

Crossman secured Cabinet approval to establish two experimental committees, one to cover a subject, namely science and technology, and the other to examine a Whitehall department, the Ministry of Agriculture. In the 'ghastly' Cabinet discussion referred to earlier, Crossman had few supporters, but crucially the Prime Minister 'helped a great deal', and Wedgwood Benn and Barbara Castle were also helpful (Crossman, 1976: 131, diary entry for 17 November 1966). Certainly Wilson believed that such committees would 'not only provide useful work [for the increased number of Labour MPs accruing from the 1966 election victory] but would give a very forward looking image to Parliamentary reform' (PRO PREM 13/1053, Wilson to Crossman, 6 April 1966).

When Crossman introduced the Commons motion to appoint these two committees on 14 December 1966, he began his speech by speaking grandly about the decline of Parliament and the growing power of the state, and the consequent need for reform to restore the balance. The House still behaved as though it was a sovereign body, but along with the House of Lords it had in fact surrendered most of its effective powers and had become the passive forum in which the struggle for power was fought out between the parties. Parliament urgently needed reform if it were again to fulfil its historic roles. Crossman believed that Wilson, who was sitting alongside him on the front bench, was shocked by the tone of this part of his speech. However, there then came what Crossman planned as a deliberate anticlimax, what he described in his diary as his 'mousy little proposals' (Crossman, 1976: 165, diary entry for 14 December 1966), the most important of which were the specialist select committees. A comfortable majority supported the proposals.

The terms of reference of the new committees were those of the traditional select committees: 'to send for persons, papers and records', but, clearly, much would depend on how this was interpreted, and how ready the executive would be to co-operate. There was something of an assumption within government that the new committees would be kept on a tight leash, with the whips controlling their membership in order to keep potential troublemakers off. These committees would also, most Ministers assumed, be steered into investigating innocuous topics, possibly matters where Ministers might actually welcome some parliamentary probing, but certainly not areas of real political controversy. To a considerable extent, Crossman himself shared this perspective, for he certainly did not want them to become sharply confrontational. Hence, he became very angry with the Agriculture Committee when it became 'silly' and 'made an ass of itself' (Crossman, 1976: 392, 660, diary entries for 21 June 1967 and 5 February 1968).

There was also initial resistance within the Cabinet to the notion that Ministers could be required to appear before a select committee and 'cross-examined'. Indeed, Crossman discovered that 'the majority were really against Ministers appearing at all', with Michael Stewart and James Callaghan again amongst the most passionate critics. Stewart 'couldn't understand how any socialist could propose to limit the powers of the Government by creating Specialist Committees to poach on their preserves', whilst Callaghan deemed the proposal 'an outrage'. Their hostility was shared by George Brown, Ray Gunter, Richard Marsh and William Ross (Crossman, 1976: 308, diary entry for 11 April 1967).

Soon after the establishment of the committees, Crossman met the Labour backbench reform group and heard David Kerr complain that the committees 'were packed by the Whips and have no genuine independence'. Crossman tried to explain why giving them the kind of autonomy these backbenchers wanted was 'impractical in a British Parliament'. But at the same time, he reflected:

> I am beginning to realise that the complete control which the Chief Whip keeps on the selection of members and the assumption that he and each Minister has that they will in future be able to control the business and forbid the committee to do anything of which they disapprove is really unconstitutional.
>
> (Crossman, 1976: 235, diary entry for 13 February 1967)

Some ten weeks later, at a subsequent meeting of the same group, Crossman was apparently accompanied by the Chief Whip, whereupon Members argued that it was intolerable for the Chief Whip to be able to remove MPs from a committee if they offended him. Silkin patiently but persistently explained the important 'constitutional principle' that Whips had to keep control of patronage with the Prime Minister, and this meant imposing discipline by 'giving people jobs and by taking them away'. Crossman reflected that he wanted a core of members to 'grow old and hoary' on committees, but although 'I sympathised with my young Parliamentary reformers, I couldn't support them' (1976: 327, diary entry for 24 April 1967).

The committees were sessional, which meant that both they and their individual members were, in effect, on probation. The Agriculture Committee in particular quickly encountered Whitehall hostility. In part, this was because of the topics it chose to investigate, which were precisely those that it was given to understand the Minister, Fred Peart, wanted it to avoid, namely the machinery of the annual farm price review and the effects on agriculture of Britain's proposed entry to the European Common Market. The latter topic also led to the committee insisting on a visit to Brussels in order to collect evidence. This resulted in an angry stand-off with the Foreign Office, which clearly felt that meddling by inexperienced MPs in matters they did not really understand would only make life more difficult for the experienced diplomats who had ongoing responsibility in these delicate matters. (The Science and Technology Committee met similar opposition when it wished to send sub-committees to America and Europe) (PRO PREM 13/1983, Peart to Crossman, 30 January 1968). Certainly the chosen topic of investigation by the Agriculture Select Committee on this occasion prompted concern in Whitehall that select committees might 'become a law unto themselves' (PRO PREM 13/1983, Trend to Wilson, 31 January 1968).

At the commencement of the new parliamentary session in November 1967, Crossman announced that the Agriculture Committee would be established for just one more session, and its membership increased from

16 to 25, seemingly in order to add party loyalists and make the committee more cumbersome. Eventually the committee was disbanded in February 1969, with its final report providing something of a swansong, claiming that it had 'no evidence that the Government did consider the opinions of the Committee'. Nor did the Government reply to any of its reports.

However, the Science and Technology Committee did gain credibility and secure its position. It investigated the civil nuclear power industry, a move welcomed by Anthony Wedgwood Benn (soon more commonly known simply as Tony Benn), the Minister responsible for this area, who subsequently said how helpful he found its work. Meanwhile, other specialist committees were created, one to cover the Department of Education and Science in 1968, another to cover Scottish affairs in 1969, and one to examine the Department of Overseas Aid and Development also in 1969. Two further select committees were established by legislation, one (already referred to) to oversee the work of the Parliamentary Commissioner for Administration and the other to monitor race relations, an area of growing tension where the Labour and Conservative front benches generally wished to maintain bipartisanship (hence Edward Heath's sacking of Enoch Powell from the Shadow Cabinet in April 1968, immediately following Powell's notorious anti-immigration 'rivers of blood' speech in Wolverhampton).

Meanwhile, the terms of reference of the Nationalised Industries Committee were extended, as were those of the Select Committee on Statutory Instruments. Despite a reduction in the membership of the Estimates Committee (because the pool of members able and willing to serve on select committees was limited), there was much more investigation going on through select committees in 1970 than there had been in 1966. Furthermore, small adjustments were gradually made in the nature of select committee activity. Meetings to hear evidence took place in public for the first time in 1966. Expert assistance, which had been refused to the Estimates Committee in 1965, was given to that committee in 1966, and then in 1967 to the Nationalised Industries Committee, before becoming a normal feature of select committee life by 1968. Initially the costs of any overseas travel had to be negotiated separately for each trip with the Treasury, but by the 1968–1969 session a modest budget for such travel had been fixed for allocation by select committee chairmen collectively. Sub-committees were initially not allowed, but both the specialist select committees won the right to appoint sub-committees.

The development of select committees during this period was therefore untidy, and along with advances came periodic setbacks. By the spring of 1969, the Labour Party's Home Policy sub-committee was expressing its regret that 'the Government appears to have hardened its heart against new select committees', even though – or maybe because – such committees were 'the best means available' of 'maintaining effective oversight of the administration' (Labour Party Archives, RE.440/April 1969). Crossman's successor as Lord President of the Council, Fred Peart, displayed little enthusiasm for

•

the select committee 'experiment', observing that those which had been established had proved rather more independent than originally envisaged, and somewhat less responsive to Ministers' own suggestions concerning topics for investigation. He thus suggested that the experiment should cease at the end of the current Parliament and then be reviewed (PRO CAB 134/3032 P(69) 1st Meeting, 27 January 1969). Yet in spite of these disappointments and disavowals, the Labour Government's experiment with select committees can be viewed as having provided a precursor for the far more comprehensive select committee system that was subsequently established a decade later.

Improving scrutiny and the use of time

Much of the effort of successive procedure committees had gone into devising ways to save time on the floor of the House, especially if this could allow for more topical debates and more backbench participation. Small changes were made, including the introduction of standing committees for the second reading of non-controversial bills. But the most useful change to the Government was one that took the Finance Bill off the floor of the House. This happened by stages, and was not without considerable inter-party acrimony. Ancient rights and privileges were involved in abolishing the Committee of Ways and Means (a whole House committee, allowing any member in theory to take part in debates on increases in taxation). The first Finance Bill to be taken in standing committee was in 1968, although according to Crossman, the Chancellor, Roy Jenkins, reported adversely on this to the parliamentary committee of the Cabinet, because it meant so much more work for both Ministers and Government backbenchers. Crossman records that he asked, 'Do you mean the Bill is much more thoroughly handled in Committee upstairs than on the Floor of the House?', to which Jenkins replied that this was undoubtedly the case, because 'on the Floor we can get away with murder in the course of the night because nobody's there, but in a Committee of fifty they attend'. Crossman was left reflecting how this encapsulated the dilemma of parliamentary reform. Increasing parliamentary control was not what Ministers wanted, for it was in their interests to keep control weak. But the Finance Bill has ever since been divided, with most of it being dealt with in a standing committee. This was a change the executive definitely wanted, and one for which Ministers were prepared to pay a price. Part of that price was to allow specialist select committees to be established.

Modernising the House of Commons

Crossman drew a distinction between modernisation and reform, explaining that the former meant things like a more efficient voting system, improved facilities for members, perhaps televising the House. The latter, however, involved altering procedures, for example to enable the House to 'provide a continuous and detailed check on the work of the Executive'. Crossman was in favour of both modernisation and reform, but it was clearly the latter about which he had come to feel passionate, and which he saw as most difficult. Nevertheless, some attempts were also made at modernistaion.

One of these involved the media and Parliament. When D. N. Chester prepared a paper on the British Parliament during the period 1939–1966, he began with a list of thirty-four events which had occurred. The last of these was: 'On Friday 19 November 1965, for the first time a notice was posted outside the St. Stephen's entrance to the House of Commons informing the public of the business to be taken in the following week.' This captures the reluctance of Parliament to adapt itself in order to accommodate the legitimate interest of the electorate in its affairs. The major issue was whether Parliament should be televised. In April 1966, the state opening was televised for the first time. A select committee to investigate the matter was established in August that year. It recommended an experiment whereby a continuous feed of all the proceedings of the House could be made available for broadcasters to use, on either radio or television. But the Commons rejected the proposed experiment by a single vote (131 to 130) in a thin House on 24 November 1967. Crossman was the only Cabinet Minister who voted, and he recorded how angry he felt at being left isolated by so many of his ministerial colleagues. Later, the House of Lords did hold an experiment with closed-circuit television, and the Commons one with radio. But there was little enthusiasm for publicly broadcasting Parliament, and it was another decade before live radio transmission from the Commons began, and over two decades before television carried proceedings.

The theme of modernisation also involves the hours during which the House sits. As much more recent debate has illustrated, this has always been a far from straightforward matter. On the one hand, MPs with outside jobs tend to oppose morning sittings, so the argument is sometimes cast in terms of full-time versus part-time politicians. But those who work full-time may well prefer to keep mornings free for committee work or other political activity – and this group can include Ministers who prefer to keep mornings free for work in their Whitehall departments. Furthermore, many MPs are not averse to evening sittings, especially when their family home is too far away for a daily commute. All might agree that very late sittings ought to be avoided, partly because such can make the House look ridiculous, but morning sittings are not necessarily a remedy for late or all-night sittings, as Crossman was to discover.

The 1965 Procedure Committee had recommended an experiment with morning sittings, and Crossman supported this, at least in principle. However, he was uneasy about the precise proposals for morning sittings which he inherited upon becoming Leader of the House, recognising that they constituted 'a most half-hearted proposal' which would 'merely consist of a collection of bits and pieces of business', and, as such, would be 'a miserable solution'. However, as it had already been approved by the Procedure Committee, Crossman felt obliged to persevere with the proposal (Crossman, 1976: 24, diary entry for 6 September 1966), whilst making it clear to a meeting of the PLP, on 23 November 1966, that morning sittings should be regarded as an 'interim solution' pending more coherent and consistent parliamentary reforms (Labour Party Archives, minutes of PLP meetings).

Commencing in February 1967, the 'experiment' involved 10.00 a.m. sittings on Mondays and Wednesdays (Tuesdays and Thursday mornings already occupied with standing committees), although to avoid antagonising MPs with jobs elsewhere, it was intended that no parliamentary business of real importance would be conducted during these morning sittings. The experiment was thus a compromise, and therein lay the seeds of its failure, for if important parliamentary business had been arranged for a morning sitting, the appropriate Ministers would often be unable – or unwilling – to attend, owing to their required attendance elsewhere (such as meetings of the Cabinet or one of its many committees, for example, or working in their departments). Certainly George Brown, as Secretary of State for Economic Affairs, believed that it 'would be impossible' to run his department effectively if he were obliged to attend morning sittings, an objection shared by Denis Healey at the Ministry of Defence (PRO PREM 13/1678, Brown to Strauss, 28 September 1965; Healey to Strauss, 14 October 1965; see also Anderson, 1968: 147). Yet if morning sittings were only allocated unimportant business, then, clearly, few MPs would deem it worthwhile attending, whereupon morning sittings would be adjudged a failure. This was indeed the case, and so there was little surprise that the experiment was not continued into the 1967–1968 parliamentary session.

Certainly Labour MPs were divided in their opinion as to the merits of morning sittings, as Crossman had discovered when he first presented his proposals concerning the future of the 'experiment' to the Parliamentary Labour Party in June 1967. Indeed, such were the various views expressed when these proposals were presented to Labour backbenchers on 7 June 1967 that discussion had to be adjourned, and resumed at another PLP meeting the following week. On both occasions, it became apparent that morning sittings did not enjoy widespread support amongst Labour's backbenchers, many of whom were engaged in committee work at this time of the day. This, in turn, led to a relatively low rate of attendance at most morning sittings, which further meant that genuinely important governmental business could not be considered at such times. Furthermore, the changing composition of the Labour Party, entailing MPs and Ministers who themselves emanated from professional backgrounds, meant that they too – like many of their Conservative counterparts – variously needed to be elsewhere during mornings, a point made by some of the backbenchers at the PLP meeting on 14 June 1967 (Labour Party Archives, minutes of PLP meetings).

It is clear that 1966–1968 was an especially productive period in relation to reform of the Commons. Labour's comfortable election victory brought into the House many Members who wanted reform. The mood in the country also favoured reform. Crossman possessed seniority and the self-confidence to argue the case for reform, and the political skill to prosecute that cause. Looking back, one may be struck by the timidity of the reforms, but at the time some of them certainly appeared radical, and it is significant that many of them have subsequently been built upon. The trend towards membership of the Commons being regarded as a full-time occupation has continued, as has the development of facilities and the enhancement of salaries. The select committee system was further developed in the 1970s with the advent of the Expenditure Committee, then from 1979 onwards with a comprehensive system of select committees covering every Whitehall department. Experiments that failed in the 1960s now look more like proposals that were simply ahead of their time, such as broadcasting or televising Parliament, or the adjustment of sitting hours. Yet the question remains as to how well directed this change really was, a point we will return to after considering the attempts to reform the House of Lords.

Reform of the House of Lords

When the 1964 and 1966 Labour manifestos referred to the House of Lords, they simply alluded to the need to constrain the power[1] to delay legislation retained by the upper chamber. Undoubtedly, old Labour hands had in mind the struggles that had taken place in the past over power of the Lords, for whilst the House had generally been co-operative vis-àvis the 1945–1951 Attlee Governments, there remained a sharp awareness of the problems that a more 'obstructive' House of Lords could pose for a Labour government. The manifesto pledges were effectively a warning to the House of Lords (and *inter alia* the Conservatives, whose peers constituted the largest party bloc in the Upper House) that if it started to become unduly obstructive, then the Labour Government was armed with a manifesto pledge to deal, in whatever way it chose, with the remaining power of delay that the House possessed.

   Yet, of course, when Labour entered office in 1964, the House of Lords was already undergoing very considerable change, for the effects of the 1958 Life Peerage Act (and to a lesser extent the 1963 Peerages Act) were becoming increasingly apparent. Largely as a result of the 1958 Act, the membership of the House of Lords was changing – not suddenly but slowly, not dramatically but inexorably – as life peers arrived in steadily increasing numbers. The Labour Party in the Lords was growing in strength, as were the cross-benches, and the old conservatism of the House was being supplanted by a new liberalism. In 1965, for example, peers gave a 100-vote majority to the proposal to abolish the death penalty, a matter on which, nine years earlier, they had dug their heels in by insisting on retention (see Chapter 18). Surprisingly, too, the initiative for changing the law in a liberal direction on homosexuality (see Chapter 19) and abortion originated from the Lords.

The Conservative Party in the House of Lords was initially quite prepared to behave with restraint, for it had no wish to provoke Labour into rashly reducing the powers of the House further still, or even removing them altogether. There was a tacit recognition that the Government must be allowed to have its way, so when the House defeated the Government, there was generally a readiness to concede at the second time of asking. Gradually, however, the political situation changed, and as the Labour Government lost support in the country, especially in 1968, the Opposition began to feel less restrained, and Conservative peers became more awkward (from the Government's point of view). This change of mood was to have serious consequences for Labour's attempt to reform the House of Lords, of which more in a moment.

For many Ministers in the 1964–1970 Labour Governments, it was the House of Lords' power which remained the crucial issue. When attention first seriously turned to reform of the Lords early in 1967, it was the need to curb the power of the Lords that drove consideration, whilst later, when the Government ran into serious embarrassment over the Lords, some Ministers, including the Prime Minister, instinctively turned back to the question of power. A short bill, dealing only with power was an attractive option, apparently so much simpler than tackling the more complex issue of composition. If the power of the House of Lords were reduced, or even removed altogether, then the composition of the second chamber might almost cease to matter. Maybe the House would gradually just fade away as people lost interest in being members? Maybe it would remain as a kind of decorative feature of the constitution, possibly still useful as a retirement home for politicians, but without the capacity to trouble the Commons?

However, as Labour's intra-party discussions on Lords reform proceeded, those most closely involved soon realised that to consider the power of the House of Lords in isolation presented substantial difficulties. For a start, any bill which merely curtailed the power of the Lords would certainly be delayed by the House of Lords itself. Moreover, if peers were so minded, it would not just be the one bill dealing with power that would suffer; the Government's whole legislative programme could be severely mauled by an upper House that felt itself under sentence. Certainly, if the Labour Government's standing in opinion polls was weak, the Conservative Opposition would have a particular incentive or justification for proving obstructive. Furthermore, even if a bill curtailing the power of the Lords were successfully passed, a failure simultaneously to change the House's composition might still result in peers proving rather obstructive with regard to government legislation. After all, the House of Lords undertook a considerable degree of legislative work on behalf of the Government, such as improving bills which were still in a rather raw state when they completed their Commons stages, and thereby ensured that the House of Commons and its MPs did not become completely overwhelmed. Moreover, many non-controversial or 'technical' bills commenced in the House of Lords, prior to being debated in the Commons. In normal circumstances, the House was diligent and co-operative in these respects, but if unduly provoked, it could easily turn uncooperative and awkward, in which case, Ministers and MPs would have to reckon with the consequences.

The possibility of pursuing a more comprehensive programme of Lords reform actually received encouragement from the Conservative Opposition. Just as a ministerial committee was beginning its deliberations on Lords reform, in April 1967, a debate took place in the Lords initiated by a Labour backbench peer, Lord Mitchison. The Conservative deputy leader, Lord Harlech, made clear that if Labour found the present composition of the Lords frustrating, so did the Conservatives, because having a built-in majority for one party was not really a rational basis on which to run a second chamber. He suggested that hereditary peers should be limited in number to between 50 and 75, chosen not by election but according to the frequency of their attendance. However, the Cabinet committee appointed to consider the subject had terms of reference which excluded composition. Even so, Crossman and the Chief Whips in both Houses had conferred two days before its first meeting, and devised a strategy for getting composition on the agenda without going back formally to the Cabinet, lest their ministerial colleagues nipped 'talk of radical reform in the bud' (Crossman, 1976: 313, diary entry for 14 April 1967).

Discussion continued throughout the rest of the spring and summer of 1967, culminating in a two-day meeting of Ministers at Chequers in September. Gradually the main lines of the eventual proposals were settled. Should the Government have an overall majority in the reformed House? Government Ministers in the House of Commons said 'yes', but Lords Ministers argued for a majority over the Opposition parties, but with cross-benchers holding the balance. What about the possibility of having a two-tier membership, with some members of the reformed House having a right to speak but not to vote? The attractiveness of this option increased amongst those most closely involved in the discussions, particularly when it was also recognised that 'voting membership' could thereby be restricted to regular attendees, whilst allowing others to contribute to debates and generally to the work of the House. Such a scheme could also be helpful initially in allowing peers by succession who had already inherited their seats to continue in the House (as non-voting members) rather than face sudden removal. This would not only soften the blow for them, and make the reform more palatable to the Conservative Opposition, but it would also facilitate continuity with regard to the work of the House of Lords.

By October 1967, the Cabinet had been persuaded of the case for reforming the House of Lords' composition and power simultaneously, whereupon the Queen's Speech on 31 October stated:

> Legislation will be introduced to reduce the present power of the House of Lords and to eliminate its present hereditary basis, thereby enabling

it to develop within the framework of a modern Parliamentary system. My Government are prepared to enter into consultations appropriate to a constitutional change of such importance.

Janet Morgan explains that the second sentence of this quotation had been inserted after this draft paragraph of the speech had been shown to Lord Carrington (Morgan, 1976: 174–5). The two front benches in the Lords were, by this time, regularly exchanging ideas about reform of the House of Lords, and Crossman had intended that the two-writ proposal would again emerge after all-party talks got under way, as a kind of concession made by Labour. But Lord Longford had already explained the proposal and the rationale for it to the Conservative leadership. (Under the two-writ proposal, some peers would receive a writ giving them full rights of membership, including the right to vote, but others would receive a non-voting writ allowing them to attend the House and to take part in proceedings, but not vote. Those in the latter category could include existing hereditary peers, perhaps those beyond a specified retiring age and maybe those who attended below a certain frequency level.)

When the all-party talks commenced (for a detailed discussion of these, see Morgan, 1975), the key players on each side, particularly Crossman and Carrington, convinced each other that they really wanted to reach an agreement. Naturally there were difficulties, but gradually these were resolved through negotiation, and compromises accepted. For example, in return for accepting the two-writ scheme, the Conservatives sought a longer period of delay than the six months from third reading in the Commons that Labour was offering. Consequently, a compromise of six months from the date of disagreement between the two Houses was reached.

A further disagreement concerned the timetable for the implementation of the proposed changes. The Conservatives wanted them delayed until the start of a new Parliament (i.e. after the next general election), but Labour wanted to bring them in as soon as the bill was passed. Compromise here had almost been reached, but an increasingly partisan atmosphere undermined final agreement. For, during these all-party talks, the authority of the Labour Government was being weakened by both by-election defeats and losses suffered in local elections, resulting in many Labour local councillors losing office. With the Labour Government experiencing a loss of support in the country, Lord Carrington found it increasingly difficult to restrain his colleagues in the House of Lords, and with other important items in the Government's legislative programme reaching their Lords stages during the late spring and summer of 1968, he told Crossman that 'We've missed the quiet time' (Crossman, 1977: 87, diary entry for 28 May 1968).

Yet it was not just Conservative peers who were proving problematic, for some of Crossman's own ministerial colleagues seemed uninterested in House of Lords reform. Crossman recalled that at 'one enormously important meeting' of the Cabinet committee on Lords reform,

> Fred Peart, the Leader of the House, turned up without having read the draft, and Jim Callaghan ... wasn't even bothering to attend, though his Department [the Home Office] is responsible for the Bill. From their point of view, Lords reform is a lost cause. They won't knife it, kill it; they'll let it go until it dies or collapses ignominiously.
>
> (Crossman, 1977: 72, diary entry for 22 May 1968)

Indeed, Callaghan had made clear his lack of interest in Lords reform several months earlier, suggesting that 'this was a kind of bread-and-circuses stunt – or at least would be regarded as such', a view apparently shared by George Brown, who warned that reform of the House of Lords 'would be regarded as trying to distract attention away from the real issue of unemployment' (Crossman, 1976: 481, diary entry for 18 September 1967; see also Castle, 1990: 284, diary entry for 5 December 1967; see also PRO PREM 13/1686, Notes of meeting between Wilson and senior Ministers on Lords reform, 18 September 1967). Many Labour MPs also believed that too much time and energy were being expended on House of Lords reform, rather than on more important or urgent economic issues (for a general overview of Labour politicians' ambivalence over, or antipathy towards, reform of the House of Lords in the twentieth century, see Dorey, 2000). Several Labour MPs also pointed out that there was little public demand for Lords reform (Labour Party Archives, Meetings of the PLP, 19 June and 3 July 1968: PRO PREM 13/3403, Notes of meeting with Douglas Houghton, Charles Pannell, Emmanuel Shinwell, Dingle Foot and George Strauss, 25 March 1969).

The growing antipathy of Conservative peers by the spring of 1968, in the context of the Labour Government's own loss of popularity in the country at large, and lack of enthusiasm for Lords reform amongst Labour Ministers and backbenchers alike, provided the context for the infamous vote on the Rhodesia Sanctions Order in late June, when peers defeated the Government by 193 to 184, the first time the House had ever carried a vote against a piece of delegated legislation upon which the House still had (and still has) an absolute veto (although no objection was made when a new order was presented shortly afterwards).

Wilson wanted to bring in a 'short, sharp' bill dealing with the power of the House of Lords immediately (Wilson, 1971: 608), but during a lengthy discussion – 'a slogging match' – Crossman reiterated his argument that this could not be viewed as satisfactory, telling the Prime Minister, 'Their composition is their power', and warning Wilson that attempting to reduce or remove the Lords' power in isolation from reforming their composition would almost certainly result in the Lords wreaking havoc on the Government's legislative programme (Crossman, 1977: 101, diary entry for 19 June 1968: PRO PREM, 13/1686, Crossman to Wilson, 19 June 1968).

However, Wilson was emphatic that the all-party talks were over and that the Government reserved its right to bring in 'comprehensive and radical legislation'. Meanwhile, even when Crossman was no longer Leader of the Commons – having been appointed Secretary of State for Social Security in November 1968 – he retained overall responsibility for Lords reform. Whilst the key players were pessimistic about the prospects of comprehensive reform, the proposals that had emerged from the all-party talks were revived later in the year, and it was these which formed the basis of the White Paper published in October. However, the relative lack of ministerial interest in House of Lords reform was ominous, and the Cabinet apparently took only eight minutes to approve the paper (Crossman, 1977: 226, diary entry for 17 October 1968). When it was debated in the House of Commons, Crossman led for the Government, but he reckoned only 150 MPs overall heard any of the debate, and the only real support came from frontbench speakers. Backbenchers were either uninterested or hostile. The Government carried the vote, but on a two-line whip, 47 Labour MPs voted against. The Conservatives had a free vote, and only 47 supported the White Paper, whilst 104 voted against. Nevertheless, this produced a respectable Commons majority of 270 to 159. In the Lords, a three-day debate culminated in a 251 to 56 vote in support of the White Paper. The 108 Conservatives who voted in favour heavily outnumbered the 43 Conservatives who opposed the plan. All 72 Labour peers who voted, and overwhelming majorities of both Liberals and cross-bench peers also supported the White Paper. The reason for the strong support in the Lords lay partly with the positive attitude of party leaders to the proposals, and the general feeling that this was the best way forward for the House.

One particular aspect of the White Paper which aroused opposition was the proposal to pay salaries to voting peers, a feature which many MPs – including many on the Labour benches – feared might lead to 'an abuse of [prime ministerial] patronage' (Crossman, 1976: 417, diary entry for 8 July 1967). There was also concern that the payment of salaries to 'voting peers' would render it necessary 'to ensure that a corresponding amount of work is done' (PRO PREM 13/1686, Trend to Wilson, 10 October 1967). As such, when the Parliament (No. 2) Bill was published, just before Christmas 1968, the proposal to include salaries had been dropped. The second reading debate took place on 3 February, with the Prime Minister leading for the Government, and the House voting 285 to 135 in support of the bill. But whilst only 25 Labour MPs defied their whip by voting against, on a free vote Conservatives divided 58 for the bill and 103 against.

Because this was a constitutional bill, it was accepted that the committee stage would take place on the floor of the House. Initially the Government planned five days for this, but although the Opposition front bench were in support of the bill, there was no question of an Opposition whip being applied, and the 'usual channels' simply did not operate on the bill. Hence, the Government had little chance of curtailing debate unless it applied a guillotine, and in this respect its difficulties quickly became apparent, as the bill's opponents – on both sides of the House – were able to talk endlessly on points of order, and table amendments on matters of detail. For example, on the second day of the (standing) committee stage, one Labour back-bencher, Robert Sheldon, spoke for two hours and twenty minutes on an amendment to Clause 1, leading a despondent Crossman to refer, in his diary, to 'another disastrous day on the Parliament Bill' (1977: 370, diary entry for 18 February 1969).

In this context, the Cabinet – never entirely enthusiastic about Lords reform in the first place – began to waver, yet as news of its misgivings leaked out, so the opponents of the bill become further emboldened. Ministers who were not supportive of the reform plans were reluctant to abandon the bill, fearing that the Government's loss of authority would set a damaging precedent, particularly as Labour backbenchers were increasingly making clear their unhappiness about other aspects of the Government's programme at this time, most notably incomes policy and imminent industrial relations reform (PRO CAB 128/44, Part 1, 10th Conclusions, 27 February 1969, and 11th Conclusions, 6 March 1969).

Meanwhile, scenting a tactical victory, the Conservative Opposition firmly rebuffed Crossman's overtures seeking their support for a guillotine or for sending the bill 'upstairs' (to a traditional standing committee). After twelve days in committee and over eighty hours of time on the floor of the House, on 17 April Harold Wilson announced that the bill would be dropped. To make this defeat seem a little less painful, he emphasised that dropping the Parliament (No. 2) Bill was intended to make way for the imminent Industrial Relations Bill (discussed in Chapter 6 of this volume). Meanwhile, Wilson insisted that the Government reserved its right to bring in other measures to reform the Lords.

The ill-fated Parliament (No. 2) Bill was not widely mourned. Regardless of its intellectual appeal to those who had thought seriously about the future of the second chamber, the politics of the bill were wrong on several counts. It was nominally an all-party measure, but the Labour Government had never obtained a firm commitment of support from the (Conservative) Opposition, and so once the all-party talks had broken down, a consensual bipartisan approach became impossible. Crossman noted that the committee stage of the bill showed 'only too well what happens when you try to run the House without the usual channels' (1977: 385, diary entry for 26 February). Yet, crucially, within both the Labour Cabinet and PLP, support for the bill was never more than half-hearted. To many Ministers and backbench MPs alike, the preparations for the bill had steadily led to a scheme of ever greater complexity, with a two-tier membership for the Lords, with attendance levels and retirement ages being specified, and the evidence for the supposed viability of the scheme residing in complex statistical models worked out under Lord Shackleton's supervision. All this simply strengthened the feeling that a much simpler solution to the problem posed by the Lords was possible.

Yet few Ministers had any real understanding of the House, another point frequently bemoaned by Crossman, who felt their simple-minded solutions would raise far more problems than they solved. Many Labour MPs failed to appreciate just how vital the second chamber was to the work of Parliament: if it were not there to consider bills, two further Commons stages would be necessary. For example, Michael Foot declared himself to be 'a fervent abolitionist', and was anxious that any reform (rather than outright abolition) would merely serve to imbue the House of Lords with greater legitimacy and longevity, whilst also rendering it even more obstructive of Labour Governments (House of Commons Debates, 5th series, vol. 777, cols 84–90; see also Robert Sheldon, ibid., cols 110–14). Crossman, though, was convinced that 'it's jolly useful to have a second chamber' (1976: 94, diary entry for 26 October 1966).

One other aspect of the bill which highlighted the dilemma of Lords reform for Labour MPs concerned the proposal to replace hereditary peers by nominated or life peers. This too raised concerns about an extension of prime ministerial patronage, particularly as some commentators during the 1960s were becoming concerned about the rise of prime ministerial government. Indeed, Crossman himself was arguably the first to articulate this concern, in his foreword to a revised edition of Bagehot's *The English Constitution* (Crossman, 1963). Subsequently, when discussions about Lords reform broached the issue of replacing hereditary peers with appointed or life peers (as opposed to elected members), Crossman was amongst those in the Labour Party – and beyond – who were alert to the danger of strengthening prime ministerial patronage (PRO CAB 134/3114, PL(67) 2nd Meeting, 5 June 1967), and thus the vital need 'to avoid the odium of excessive patronage that would be incurred by the establishment of a nominated House of Lords completely under Government control' (PRO PREM 133/1686, Trend to Wilson, 5 September 1967).

Ironically, the legislation for which the Parliament (No. 2) Bill was ostensibly withdrawn for, the Industrial Relations Bill, also failed to reach the statute book because of Labour backbench hostility (as was noted in Chapter 6). It seemed that, having flexed their muscles on one bill, Labour backbenchers were sufficiently emboldened to do so on others, thereby vindicating the warnings of those Ministers who had argued that abandonment of the Parliament (No. 2) Bill would weaken the authority of the Government (Crossman, 1977: 441, diary entry for 16 April 1969). Crossman himself was subsequently to reflect ruefully on 'what fools we were to drop the Parliament Bill in favour of the Industrial Relations Bill, and then to drop the Industrial Relations Bill' (1977: 602, diary entry for 30 July 1969). Indeed, one (unnamed) Minister wryly remarked at the time that the Labour Government was abandoning 'a Bill to limit the power of the peers in favour of a Bill to limit the freedom to strike' (PRO CAB 128/44, Part 1, 18th Conclusions, 16 April 1969).

Conclusion

Many commentators reflected, at the end of the year, how 1969 had become the year of the backbencher. This cast doubt on the veracity of Crick's argument that the job of the Commons was to scrutinise the executive, not pretend that it had the ability to defeat the Government. Ronald Butt had taken issue with Crick when he (Butt) published his seminal study *The Power of Parliament* (Butt, 1966), in which he argued that academics often missed what journalists saw, namely that behind the scenes the Commons was much more influential over government, as it had been through the centuries. It was important to recognise, however, the varying and changing ways in which this influence was expressed. In modern times, it had ceased to be through defeat on the floor of the House; instead, it took place through pressures exerted within parliamentary parties. Crossman recorded an occasion when he had lunch with Ronald Butt and was impressed by his argument about the role of the Commons (1976: 192, diary entry for 9 January 1967). Subsequently, of course – and as Norton has since documented (1975, 1978, 1980) – the way in which Government backbenchers expressed their disagreement with their front bench changed again as defeat on the floor of the House became a feature of the House of Commons, first under the Heath Government, and then of course with considerable regularity under Labour again in the later 1970s. The dissidence of MPs as expressed in the division lobbies of the Commons has been a growing phenomenon ever since.

A final irony, therefore, is to contemplate that the greatest achievement vis-àvis Parliament of the 1964–1970 Labour Governments was to remind MPs of the power they could assert simply by failing to support their Government in the division lobbies. This, it can be argued, was of rather greater significance than concrete reforms involving select committees or other procedural changes. Perhaps the diagnosis as to what was wrong with Parliament was too shallow, and the prescriptions ineffective. Meanwhile, House of Lords reform remains one of the great might-have-beens. If that had been accomplished, the hereditary peers would have been almost totally removed by the gentle process of attrition by the time that (New) Labour came to power in 1997, pledging, once again, to reform the House of Lords, and similarly losing its reforming zeal during the subsequent term of office.

Note

1 The House of Lords' power of delay was limited to a maximum of just over one year, as a result of the Attlee Government's 1949 Parliament Act.

11 Scottish nationalism and demands for devolution

James Mitchell

Introduction

Scottish nationalism was thought to be defunct only a few years before the 1964 general election. Having created problems for the previous Labour Government headed by Clement Attlee, the Scottish home rule movement had receded to the fringe of Scottish politics. Attlee's Government had responded to a public petition – supposedly 2 million Scots had signed the 'Scottish Covenant' in favour of home rule – by reforming Parliamentary procedures, establishing a Scottish Economic Council and undertaking some minor administrative reform. Combining these symbolic actions with aggressive attacks on the movement, particularly those who supported independence, Attlee's Government had seen off the home-rulers. The central message Attlee's Government had hoped to convey was that it was sympathetic to Scottish distinctiveness but that the socialist project necessitated strong government from the centre. No Scottish Labour politi cian articulated this view as powerfully as had Aneurin (Nye) Bevan in Wales, but the message was the same.

The Scottish national movement's relationship with the labour movement had long been ambiguous. At its foundation, the Labour Party supported home rule. Keir Hardie's platform in the 1888 Mid-Lanark by-election, the first election contested by an independent Labour candidate, had included support for home rule, and Hardie had been active in the Scottish Home Rule Association. This tradition was carried through to the inter-war period, with many of the Red Clydesiders arguing for what amounted to Scottish independence. But as Frank Bealey noted long ago, Labour's ideological 'stock pot' (1970: 1) contained many ideas, not all mutually compatible. The experience of the Attlee Government and its subsequent position in Labour folklore as the only unambiguously successful Labour Government, combined with the national movement's attacks on Attlee's centralisation (supported by an opportunistic Conservative Opposition), marked a watershed.

As the Scottish national movement receded in the 1950s, so the Labour Party's unionism hardened. Under Clement Attlee's leadership, Labour remained theoretically committed to home rule, but it was clearly a low priority, especially as experience of government, coupled with perceptions that socialism and equality required central demand management and central imposition of standards and policies, shifted the party's ideological stance towards centralisation. Home-rulers still existed within Labour's ranks, but by the late 1950s the party was turning its back on its historic commitment. In 1957, for example, Labour's Scottish executive came out against a Scottish parliament on 'compelling economic grounds', whilst the following year witnessed the Scottish Labour conference reject a Scottish parliament. The *Glasgow Herald* carried two articles – obituaries to a political movement – in July 1959 (*Glasgow Herald*, 8 and 9 July 1959). Entitled 'Is Nationalism in Decline?', these pieces argued *inter alia* that nationalism's outlook was 'unpromising if it depends on what are variously known as the British, English, and Quisling"political parties' (*Glasgow Herald*, 9 July 1959). Labour, it was maintained, 'though full of ex-Home Rulers, is suspicious or hostile'. Home rule appeared to have been removed from the agenda, although there still remained a handful of home-rulers within the Labour Party in Scotland, and these continued to espouse its cause. One of the most prominent of them, from the 1960s onwards, was John Mackintosh, Professor of Politics at Strathclyde University and sometime Labour MP.

The Scottish National Party (SNP) had stood aloof from the broader home rule movement in the late 1940s, arguing that petitions criticising Labour would not bring about home rule. Only the challenge of electoral politics would force the issue – an analysis that could not be faulted. The problem was that electoral support was not forthcoming. Lipset and Rokkan (1967) had identified four key social cleavages explaining voting behaviour across Europe: Church–State, centre–periphery, urban–rural and social class. As elsewhere, class was the key determinant in electoral politics in Scotland, although religion played its part too. Class and religion were most important, but these social cleavages were mediated by each political party seeking to win support beyond its core. The Scottish Conservatives styled themselves the Scottish Unionist Party between 1912 and 1965 to attract working-class Protestants, thereby highlighting the complexity of voting behaviour. An urban–rural divide was evident too, with Labour being the urban party. The centre–periphery tension existed, but operated in a different way from that suggested by Lipset and Rokkan. In opposition, each party became the party of the periphery, articulating grievances against London government, but in office each became defensive once more. The SNP's efforts to break through as the party of the periphery proved difficult. In part, this reflected the electoral system, which was not generous to minority parties. The 1950s marked the high-water mark of the two-party system. In 1955, Labour and the Conservatives combined to take 96.8 per cent of the vote in Scotland. The Nationalists also struggled to break through in a system in which the other social bases – most notably class – dominated.

During the 1950s, Labour shamelessly attacked the Conservatives for failing to take account of the Scottish dimension, just as the Conservatives had done when Attlee was Prime Minister. Playing the Scottish card came easily to Labour, and the party saw no incompatibility with its growing opposition to home rule. At the 1959 election, Labour started to pull ahead of the Conservatives in Scotland, heralding the long, almost uninterrupted, demise of the Scottish Conservatives. In opposition, Labour in Scotland could not resist the temptation to play the Scottish card. In the 1959–1964 Parliament, Labour in Scotland had it relatively easy, although issues such as nuclear disarmament divided the party in Scotland as elsewhere. Jimmy Maxton had famously remarked that 'If you can't ride on two horses at the same time, you shouldn't be in the bloody circus.' Yet Scotland permitted Labour to do this comfortably, for whilst the London-based Labour Party would form a government at Westminster, and therefore needed to be responsible and moderate, the party in Scotland was Labour's radical conscience, more left-wing but ultimately impotent. The tension would only become significant when Labour entered office.

The rise of nationalism

Whilst its obituary was being written, the Scottish home rule movement was regrouping. Key figures active in the Covenant were reaching the conclusion that electoral pressure alone would provide the pressure for home rule. One senior figure from the 1940s wrote of his conversion to this strategy. James Porteous, secretary of the Scottish Covenant Association, wrote to a friend in 1963 that there was no point pretending that the home rule pressure groups had any real purpose and that the differences between the Association and the SNP had diminished (Mitchell, 1996: 98–9). Porteous, however, differed from the generally held view that the SNP had little hope of electoral success, and was shortly to join the SNP, convinced that it offered the best hope for progress towards the goal of a Scottish parliament.

Early signs of the SNP's potential were evident in various by-elections. In Glasgow Bridgeton in 1961 and West Lothian in 1962, the SNP did creditably. The latter by-election brought Tam Dalyell, an Old Etonian and former chair of Cambridge University Conservatives, up against Billy Wolfe, the rising star of the SNP, in what was to be the first of six electoral contests in which these two confronted each other in the constituency. Dalyell had dispensed with his erstwhile Conservatism for the Labour Party, to represent the constituency of his ancestral family home just outside Edinburgh. The Conservatives lost their deposit in the by-election and Wolfe won 23 per cent of the vote. Dalyell's view that Labour should never compromise with the Scottish Nationalists was established early (even though twice later – before the 1974 elections and again before 1997 – Dalyell included a commitment to devolution in his election address). Yet not all by-elections pointed towards an SNP advance. In Kinross and West Perthshire in late 1963, Sir Alec Douglas-Home romped home as Conservative Prime Minister after renouncing his peerage in the House of Lords in order to become an MP. The SNP won only 7.3 per cent of the vote. At the general election held a year later, the Scottish Nationalists won 2.4 per cent of the vote across Scotland, contesting 15 seats.

So long as Labour was in opposition and the Conservatives remained in power, voters were more likely to turn to Labour than to the SNP to express opposition to the party in power, hence the SNP's prospects would require more than a Labour Government. A successful Labour Government would continue to attract support, and so the SNP's best prospects lay in an unsuccessful Labour Government. At the general election held two years later, the Scottish Nationalists secured 5 per cent of the vote, having contested 23 seats. Labour's problems, and thus the SNP's opportunity, were not long in coming after the 1966 general election. Two events within two months of the election had an impact on the future course of the Labour Government's actions vis-àvis devolution. The first was the seaman's strike in May 1966. The strike itself was symptomatic of a broader problem that afflicted Wilson's Government. His Government's relations with the trade unions both reflected and reinforced the general sense that something was wrong in the governance of the United Kingdom, and thereby undermined Wilson's determination that Labour should henceforth replace the Conservatives as the 'natural party of government'. Industrial relations problems and economic crises during the 1960s did little to create an image that the United Kingdom was a successful political entity. Wilson's modernisation rhetoric had played a significant part in encouraging a view that the State could deliver for its citizens – and that included Scots. The disillusionment that set in soon after the 1966 election was therefore felt in Scotland as much as elsewhere. However, the difference here was that there was a vehicle for voters to express that disillusionment that did not exist in England.

The other significant development which would play its part in determining the Labour Government's response to Scottish nationalism was related to the modernisation agenda. In late May 1966, Wilson announced that a royal commission (chaired by Sir John Maud) would review local government in England and Wales – the 'biggest [review] this century'. It would be followed by a similar announcement of a royal commission on local government in Scotland which would be headed by Lord Wheatley, former Labour MP and, incidentally, father-in-law of Tam Dalyell. Debate on regional and local government reform across Britain inevitably became enmeshed in debates on devolution.

The first dramatic signs that nationalism was on the march actually came from Wales, where Gwynfor Evans, leader of Plaid Cymru, the Welsh nationalists, won Carmarthen in a by-election in July 1966, overturning a Labour majority of over 9,000 votes. The SNP had long had close relations with Plaid, and were understandably buoyed up by the result in Wales. The following March, a by-election in Glasgow Pollok presented Labour with a challenge. The sitting Labour Member had died, whereupon Esmond Wright, one of the new breed of media dons, an historian who had a high profile on local television, won the seat for the Conservatives. In his short time as MP before he was defeated at the 1970 general election, he would articulate a view, which was developed by Ted Heath as Conservative leader, that the Scottish Conservatives needed to modernise and that this included supporting a measure of home rule. Labour's defeated candidate was Dick Douglas, who would later be elected in Dunfermline and defect to the SNP in the late 1990s. Wright's victory owed much to the strong SNP performance, because the SNP's 28 per cent share of the vote was largely drawn from Labour, and allowed the Conservatives to sneak through and take the seat. It was to be the Conservatives' last by-election victory in Scotland in the twentieth century.

Scottish nationalism had infected the Scottish body politic, although its evident ability to attract Labour voters to a greater extent than Conservative voters did little to persuade many in the Labour Party to support home rule. Labour and SNP would become rivals for the same voters, and this competition for votes did little to move Labour in Scotland to a nationalist position. The Conservatives, on the other hand, had seen their Scottish vote decline from its 1955 high point. Ted Heath had succeeded Sir Alec Douglas-Home in August 1965, the first Conservative leader elected by the party's MPs rather than 'emerging'. Heath's view was that the Conservatives needed a new image north of the Border, particularly as nationalism was the 'biggest single factor in our politics today', as he told Richard Crossman (Crossman, 1976: 550–1, diary entry for 2 November 1967).

Part of the Conservatives' response was to rename the party in Scotland, so that from 1965 it would be styled the Scottish Conservative and Unionist Party, rather than the Scottish Unionist Party. The party's 'grouse moor image', about which the Conservative populist Teddy Taylor would complain, was damaging, and Heath thus called for imaginative and electorally appealing policies. This led Heath to make what became known as the 'Declaration of Perth' at the Conservatives' 1968 Scottish conference, when he advocated a moderate form of devolution, entailing a body which would be partly directly elected and partly indirectly elected, and imbued with powers to initiate and consider legislation, but leaving Westminster with the final veto.

It came as a surprise to most delegates, including those few who supported devolution, but it shook up Scottish politics. A ginger group within the Scottish party – the Thistle Group – emerged, arguing for devolution and thereby indicating that Conservatives were seizing the initiative. Douglas-Home was placed in charge of a committee to look in detail at the idea of Scottish devolution, and produced a report in March 1970. *Scotland's Government* proposed a Scottish convention with limited powers, whose 125 members would be directly elected on the same day as the House of Commons. However, by this time Scottish nationalism had receded, whilst opposition to devolution within the Conservative Party had become more vocal. Nonetheless, for a brief period in the late 1960s the Conservatives took the initiative and set the pace compared to the 1964–1970 Labour Governments.

The SNP manifesto in 1964 urged voters to 'put Scotland first', and this was to be its main slogan for almost a decade. By contrast, Labour came close to forgetting to mention Scotland in its 1964 manifesto. Tony Benn recorded in his diary that Jim Callaghan woke up in the middle of the night realising that there was 'nothing about Scotland or Wales' in the draft manifesto (Benn, 1987: 138, diary entry for 8 September 1964). The SNP campaigned vigorously in local elections, and in 1965 it was given its first party political broadcast. Billy Wolfe, candidate in West Lothian in 1962, argued that Scotland subsidised the rest of Britain. This would be a key theme in its campaigns and one that Labour in government was forced to respond to. At its 1966 annual conference, the SNP claimed a tenfold increase in its membership in four years, from 2,000 to 21,000 by the end of 1965, and estimated to be nearer 30,000 six months later (*Glasgow Herald*, 4 June 1966). Even allowing for hyperbole, the evidence of the record attendance of 600 delegates at the conference suggested that the party was advancing.

At local elections in May 1967, the Scottish Nationalists won 60,000 votes in Glasgow, although they failed to win a seat, but in Stirling Robert McIntyre, former SNP leader, became Provost. The real breakthrough, however, came in Hamilton that November. Hamilton had been a rock-solid Labour seat where Tom Fraser had secured a 16,576 majority over the Conservatives in a two-way contest in 1966. When he then resigned to become chairman of the Hydro Electric Board, Labour chose Alex Wilson, a miner with NUM support, against the wishes of many party supporters. The SNP candidate was Winnie Ewing, who was all that Wilson was not: an articulate, charismatic young lawyer. In the words of one history of the home rule movement, 'Television cameras and photographers' lenses gobbled her up' (Harvie and Jones, 2000: 84).

The backdrop was important, for in November 1966 the Government had announced that it intended to take the United Kingdom into the European Economic Community (EEC), although opinion polls showed opposition to EEC membership. The Scottish Nationalists had argued at their conference five months earlier that all negotiations should recognise Scotland as an independent country. The SNP message again was 'put Scotland first'. It was populist and successful. Economic crises were just around the corner. In July 1966, the Government had imposed a wage freeze. Controversy had surrounded the Government's incomes policy, and trade union dissatisfaction had undermined Wilson's Government. Within weeks of the by-election, sterling was devalued.

Options and Cabinet disagreements

The Labour Government's range of options included ignoring the Scottish nationalist threat for fear that focusing on it would provide it with publicity. This was not amongst the various options that were considered, because the threat was deemed sufficiently serious. It was also historically rooted. A paper presented in 1947 to Attlee's Government by the then Secretary of State for Scotland had accepted that the nationalist movement included elements that had legitimacy (PRO CAB 21/3329, 'Scottish demands for home rule or devolution: Memorandum by the Secretary of State for Scotland', November 1947). Back then, the options considered were to be those considered again by the Labour Government twenty years later: an attack on separatism, especially its economic consequences; parliamentary reform; administrative reform; buying time through some kind of inquiry; and various other means of appeasing Scottish sentiment. Not surprisingly, there existed various views within the Labour Party and Cabinet as to which response should be adopted.

At one end, Richard Crossman argued for radical constitutional change, including Scottish home rule. At the other were those, including the Scottish Secretary, Willie Ross, who were inclined to focus on attacking the SNP. In his biography of Crossman, Tom Dalyell, who had been Crossman's Parliamentary Private Secretary, maintained that the bad relations with Ross 'turned Crossman into a devolutionist' (1989: 223), but this seems implausible. Crossman was certainly critical of the way in which Ross operated as Scottish Secretary, his diaries recording his irritation that Ross and his friends 'accuse the Scot Nats of separatism but what Willie Ross himself actually likes is to keep Scottish business absolutely privy from English business' (1977: 48, diary entry for 6 May 1968).

Cabinet activity around the subject of devolution developed following Hamilton, and the Parliamentary Labour Party (PLP) also urged action. Reflecting on the Hamilton result in a note to the Prime Minister, Crossman concluded that whilst there might be a Poujadist element to nationalist support, Hamilton confirmed what each of them had suspected after the Rhondda, Carmarthen and Glasgow Pollok by-elections, namely that it would be 'unwise to disregard the growing feeling that Wales and Scotland are not getting a fair deal from Whitehall and the growing demand for further devolution including some kind of Scottish and Welsh Parliament' (PRO CAB 164/659, Crossman to Wilson, 13 November 1967). Wilson had suggested the Stormont model (as used for the governance of Northern Ireland until 1972) for Scotland in an earlier conversation, and Crossman could see 'no reason why all the responsibilities of the Secretary for Scotland should not be transferred to a Scottish Government'. He suggested that a small group of Ministers be convened to consider this and offered to submit the first paper. Burke Trend, as Cabinet Secretary, though, was more cautious, urging that care be taken 'since the susceptibilities of other Ministers are involved' (PRO CAB 164/658, Trend to Wilson, 4 December 1967).

Crossman favoured a committee which he would chair, consisting of junior Ministers, and whilst Trend was surprised by this, he accepted that the subject 'might benefit from a fresh and perhaps unconventional approach' (PRO CAB 164/658, memo to Wilson from Trend, 17 January 1968). A committee[1] was established, chaired by Crossman, '[t]o examine the implications of further devolution for Scotland and Wales, and to report their conclusions to the Home Affairs Committee' (PRO T227/2871, Trend to Crossman, 16 February 1968). Crossman's agenda was clear: he wanted to push the case for devolution, and had indicated support for this in a television discussion in February 1968, which provoked reaction. Labour's Glasgow Govan MP put down a question to the Prime Minister asking whether the Lord President's views represented Government policy. The reply was evasive, merely that a transcript of the discussion had been placed in the Commons Library (House of Commons Debates, 5th series, vol. 759, cols 1225–8, 27 February 1968).

The PLP questioned Wilson on the policy in June, whereupon the Prime Minister responded that Crossman should get together with Ross and George Thomas, Welsh Secretary, to produce a paper on devolution. However, the Lord President doubted the value of this course of action, suspecting that 'the result of such tripartite collaboration would be the lowest common denominator and not the highest common factor of consensus' (PRO CAB 164/658, Crossman to Wilson, 25 June 1968). On one thing, though, the three Cabinet Ministers were agreed: the Treasury should be asked to provide economic arguments concerning what Ross described as the 'folly of separation'. Ross also supported some of the less radical responses which Crossman proposed, including the transfer of a 'major part of a Whitehall office' to Scotland – the Civil Aviation Department within the Board of Trade being suggested – and the establishment of a Select Committee on Scottish Affairs, though he foresaw difficulties in having its meetings routinely conducted in Edinburgh (PRO CAB 164/658, Ross to Wilson, 8 July 1968). Ross was, though, adamantly opposed to Crossman's long-term goal of directly elected regional councils in England, Scotland and Wales. Notably, he thought this might work best in England:

> I can just see this working in England, where the central government would be operating at a different geographical level; but I cannot see it operating in Scotland or Wales, except on a basis of virtual fiscal and therefore economic separation, or else in a way that left central government with little power while still having to carry the main financial burden.
>
> (PRO CAB 164/658, Ross to Wilson, 8 July 1968)

Meanwhile, a similar analysis, but reaching quite different conclusions, was being developed by a group of Scottish Conservatives. The Thistle Group, including future Conservative MPs Michael Ancram and Peter Fraser, argued that fiscal independence was 'vital' and that it could see 'no bar to a separate monetary policy for Scotland' (Thistle Group, undated: 11).

Ross's conservatism found sympathy in the upper reaches of the civil service, though, where Sir William Armstrong, head of the home civil service, saw costs in terms of administrative efficiency, and increases in staff numbers following further devolution (PRO CAB 164/658, Memorandum to Wilson's Principal Private Secretary from Armstrong, 8 July 1968). Crossman apart, there was little sympathy amongst Government Ministers and senior officials for devolution, and this lack of enthusiasm was replicated on Labour's back benches.

Territorial finance

Meanwhile, the Treasury was considering the financial status of Scotland. Scotland had traditionally been treated as a separate entity for some public financial matters, but not all, and there had long been a debate as to how to calculate public income from the component parts of the United Kingdom. A parallel debate was also going on – which inevitably became embroiled in the devolution debate – concerning the extent to which the Scottish Office should have flexibility in the control of public spending for which it had responsibility. Judith Hart, Labour MP for Lanark, and Paymaster-General, was keen on allowing for more flexibility in spending priorities determined by the Scottish Office. For her, this was about 'decentralisation at least as much as about expenditure' (PRO T227/2871, Hart to Ross, 21 January 1969). John Mackintosh had described the public expenditure process in his 1968 book, noting that

> The expenditure for the Scottish Office is not voted as a single sum leaving Scottish Ministers free to move money from roads to schools or to industrial development as they feel priorities require. The investment in school building is worked out as part of a national policy on this subject, and the money for hospitals is negotiated between English and Scottish Departments of Health acting together and the Treasury. Thus there are financial, administrative and heavy political pressures brought to bear on St Andrew's House to make it operate in a manner and according to priorities which are as close as possible to those of White-hall. It is scarcely surprising that as a result few can distinguish between Scottish and English patterns of action. . . . The great pride of the civil service is not that it has developed special methods or a different emphasis in Scotland, but rather that no gap can be found between Edinburgh and London methods so that no politically awkward ques-tions can be raised.
>
> (Mackintosh, 1968: 132)

Mackintosh's solution was devolution, whereby a democratically elected body would have the 'positive incentive to be different, to take local needs into consideration rather than to struggle to be the same' (1968: 133). Yet his arguments did not find favour amongst Treasury officials, and a note by one of them, commenting on his book, argued that Mackintosh did not appreciate that the control of public expenditure was important in the management of the economy, and that Mackintosh conceived it only in terms of providing public finance for expenditure. Mackintosh was also criticised for passing 'very lightly over the question how the Treasury should be associated with these processes', and his assumptions on the 'very great degree of freedom for the regional governments to switch expenditure between one service and another' were doubted, given the 'fairly homogeneous' nature of the items involved. Nor had Mackintosh taken into account the dynamic impact of changing priorities over time, it was alleged. It was conceivable that choices would be made which would have an impact on the extent of demand on real resources. The economic impact was felt to be absent from Labour's most ardent home-ruler's analysis. For example, a United Kingdom-wide national incomes policy, that key element of the Wilson Government's economic strategy in the 1960s, was felt to be impossible under Mackintosh's proposals (PRO T227/2871, note to officials by P. R. Baldwin, Treasury, 'Scottish and Welsh Expenditure', 7 February 1969).

The Scottish Office was less keen on having the ability to alter spending priorities than colleagues in the Welsh Office. In a letter to a Treasury colleague, Douglas Haddow, Scottish Office Permanent Secretary, argued that it was rarely possible to depart from the English pattern except, for example, in housing, as Scotland had a larger public sector. The reason given was that the Scottish Secretary found it difficult coping with complaints from those using services, who 'drew unfavourable comparisons between Scottish and English programmes of trends' (PRO CAB 151/45, Haddow to Vinter, 12 December 1968). The phrase that was used frequently in much of the correspondence was that Scotland might wish to 'shade the allocations a little differently from England', but, in essentials, the desire was to follow English spending patterns.

Willie Ross himself had no doubts. In a letter to Judith Hart, he argued that there was no benefit, presentationally or practically, in a system under which Scotland received a total allocation and was left to distribute it as it wished, and opposed a 'major official exercise on this'. He argued that Scottish needs 'should be, and should be seen to be, the basis for Scottish allocations' (PRO CAB 151/45, Ross to Hart, 13 February 1969). Ross cited the allocation for public housing and feared that the alternative system would require the Scottish Office to find 'off-setting reductions in other sectors'. Ross could see no advantage in gaining greater autonomy to prioritise according to Scottish needs when, as he saw it, this was already evident in the generous housing budget, which also provided Scotland with a total spending advantage. Ross was determined to maintain both Scotland's spending advantage and his own control over this, even if for most items he followed English spending patterns.

Emerging strategy

The royal commissions on local government complicated matters. In mid-July 1968, the Prime Minister called a meeting to discuss devolution, at which a two-stage approach was agreed. Plan A involved proposals that could be implemented within the lifetime of the Parliament, and Plan B might be announced in a White Paper after taking account of the recommendations of the royal commissions. The latter was a classic way of buying time. Plan A had three elements: the education of the public; administrative devolution; and parliamentary devolution.

The educative material would be assembled by the Treasury, Scottish and Welsh Offices, and included in ministerial speeches. This propaganda offensive was designed to undermine the SNP, for shortly afterwards Hamilton, a Treasury official, noted that the 'election of Mrs Ewing has galvanised the Scottish MPs into asking a flood of questions' on Scottish public finances (PRO T328/227 14 November 1967). The same day, the *Financial Times* also referred to the 'flood of Parliamentary Questions from Winnie Ewing and others' in its report 'A Balance Sheet for Independence' (*Financial Times*, 14 November 1968). Jack Diamond, Chief Secretary of the Treasury, was brought in to help combat the SNP's claims that Scotland subsidised the rest of the United Kingdom. A letter to Dickson Mabon, Scottish Office Minister of State, from Diamond privately admitted that figures which Billy Wolfe, an accountant by profession, was using on Scotland's financial position were probably about right and that it was Mabon who had got his figures wrong, though, 'Certainly I would not like it to be thought the Treasury accepts the SNP calculations' (PRO T331/438, draft of letter to Mabon from Diamond, 15 January 1969). A number of Scottish Labour MPs approached Treasury Ministers requesting help in challenging nationalist claims. Willie Hamilton, MP for Central Fife, had sent Jim Callaghan, Chancellor of the Exchequer, an SNP leaflet asking for comments in 1967 (PRO T328/227, Hamilton to Callaghan, 15 May 1967). Gregor Mackenzie too sent an SNP leaflet to the Treasury requesting help in April 1967, and in October wrote to Harold Lever, Financial Secretary to the Treasury, to assist with 'economic, financial and particularly taxation policies' during the Hamilton by-election (PRO T328/227 correspondence, October 1967).

Considerable effort was expended by officials and Ministers attempting to undermine SNP claims. Against this, the SNP's resources were meagre but caused considerable difficulty. Two decades earlier, the Attlee Government had set up an inquiry into Scotland's economic and financial position, which reported in 1952 (Catto, 1952), by which time Labour was in opposition. A new report was considered but rejected, not least because its subject would be subsumed within the workings of a Royal Commission on Constitutional Affairs which would be set up in 1969. Additionally, it was doubted whether it would silence the SNP, which would challenge the basis on which the statistics had been collected (PRO T328/227, draft memorandum on 'Scotland and Wales: Public Expenditure and Taxation', 23 November 1967).

Administrative devolution had long been the main method of appeasing Scottish sentiment (see Mitchell, 2003 for its history). This included adding new responsibilities to those already held by the Scottish Office. Crossman proposed that responsibility for ancient and historic buildings, along with tourism, in Scotland should be handed over to the Scottish Office, and that the promotion of tourism overseas should be a shared responsibility with the Board of Trade. In 1969, responsibility for royal parks and gardens, and ancient monuments, was transferred from the Ministry of Public Buildings and Works to the Scottish Office (see MacDonald and Redpath, 1979).

By parliamentary devolution, the Government simply meant reforms in parliamentary procedures at Westminster to accommodate Scottish interests. Crossman explained that

> the objective should be to make visible in Edinburgh and Cardiff, respectively, the elements in the Westminster Parliament which devote themselves specifically to Scottish and Welsh affairs, and to do this in a way which demonstrates that these bodies are taking real decisions on matters of importance to the two countries concerned.
> (PRO CAB 164/658, 'Devolution to Scotland and Wales: Memorandum by the Lord President of the Council', July 1968)

The Scottish Grand Committee might sit in Edinburgh. This idea had a long pedigree, and had been attempted on an experimental basis during the Second World War by Tom Johnston, Scottish Secretary, but he had concluded that 'there was little purpose in a frequent repetition of the experiment – it had no teeth – and that I had better fall back upon the area group meetings in London' (Johnston, 1952: 152). Indeed, this idea came to nothing until John Major's premiership in the 1990s. More successful was the proposal to have a Scottish Affairs Select Committee, and alterations in the power of the Scottish Grand Committee.

Plan A, Crossman maintained, would establish Labour's 'bona fides' and would place it in a credible position to outline its proposals for the next Parliament. Some consideration had been given to supporting either a national assembly for Scotland or a royal commission on Scottish government, and these had found favour amongst some Ministers at a Cabinet meeting in July 1968. For Crossman, a national assembly was a first step towards federalism, and to attract 'men of substance and calibre' it would need to have 'some means of influencing policy'. Yet this was a very vague notion that had little support either inside the Government or amongst senior civil servants. A note to Fred Peart, whilst he was Lord Privy Seal, set out arguments against some of the proposals for parliamentary devolution, even though it noted that the Prime Minister is dead set on seeing some such system come into operation, and . . . we must therefore presumably take it to be our job to find how it can be worked rather than develop arguments in depth about how it cannot.

(PRO CAB 164/658, Ward to Peart, 2 August 1968)

Both Peart and John Silkin, the Chief Whip, were opposed to the idea of grand committees sitting in Edinburgh and Cardiff, and, according to an internal note to Sir Burke Trend, 'were reluctant to consider whether the thing could be done if Ministers collectively took the view that it should not be done'. Both thought it 'unwise to make concessions to the Nationalists'. Economic problems had given rise to support for the SNP, and 'when the economic situation improves most of the Nationalist vote will disappear' (PRO CAB 164/658, 'Note on Devolution', Nunn to Trend, 7 August 1968). This was the classic protest vote theory (see MacLean, 1970 for the best articulation of this). Yet even if the economic situation did not improve, sittings of the Scottish Grand Committee would not substantially affect public opinion. The Redcliffe-Maud Commission had not yet reported and might have implications for devolution. As time passed, Crossman's radicalism was either watered down, pushed down the agenda or simply blocked.

A royal commission was the main idea that emerged over the summer of 1968 inside the Home Affairs Committee, to which Crossman's committee reported. Initially the idea had been for a royal commission on Scottish affairs. A Royal Commission on Scottish Affairs under Lord Balfour had been set up, in 1952, by the Conservatives, as part of their response to the home rule agitation in the late 1940s. When the Balfour Report was published, two years later, it proposed an extension of administrative devolution (Balfour, 1954). Heath had, of course, set up a constitutional committee to look at Scotland's constitutional status, and it was felt necessary to ensure that the Labour Government's inquiry should have a higher status and wider remit.

The idea of a royal commission on the constitution, with a broader remit than just Scotland, emerged. There was a debate as to whether the inquiry should be a Commonwealth constitutional commission or a royal commission, with the Home Secretary preferring the former and the Scottish Secretary the latter. It was agreed that it should take evidence in public to 'ensure that the Scottish and Welsh Nationalist Parties were compelled to submit specific proposals to scrutiny and public discussion' (PRO MISC 215(68), 'Future Policy', 23 October 1968). Judith Hart was unconvinced of the case for a commission, arguing instead for the Government to complete its own study and then propose a package of proposals. This, she claimed, 'would then avoid the danger of stimulating a possibly declining nationalism in Scotland by appearing to shelve the issue until after 1970–71' (PRO MISC 215(68), 28 October 1968). In the event, though not quite as she had feared, this is what happened. The Royal Commission on the Constitution was set up in 1969 and reported in late October 1973, recommending devolution. This report was published just a week before a by-election in Glasgow Govan, and the SNP won the seat from Labour.

Meanwhile, the timing of responses was seen as important by the 1966–1970 Labour Government. Crossman later questioned his own idea that the Government should approach the problem in two stages. Whilst supporting an attack on the nationalists, Crossman feared that there was 'no great enthusiasm' for elements of Plan A, and launching initiatives before the reports of the royal commissions on local government was premature and 'exposes us to the criticism that we are trying to placate nationalist opinion' with short-term expedients rather than working out a 'coherent long-term policy' (PRO CAB MISC 215(68)1, 15 October 1968). He too had doubts about the value of another royal commission and hoped that the local government reports would allow the Government to work out its own solution. In the event, Scottish nationalism receded in importance, thereby allowing the Government to scale down the priority attached to Scotland's constitutional status. The royal commission was still established, although it did not publish its findings until 1973, when its report, favouring devolution, prompted another, stronger wave of Scottish nationalism, which the 1974–1979 Labour Governments were obliged to deal with.

The changing backdrop

As was previously noted, the early years of the 1966–1970 Parliament were marked by suggestions that Scottish nationalism was a growing threat. By the end of the Parliament, though, the Hamilton by-election was viewed more as its high-water mark than as the launch pad of a growing threat. The Conservatives had played the Scottish card forcefully, but Heath had created trouble for himself by attempting to impose a policy of home rule against the wishes of his party. The Liberals consistently argued in favour of home rule, with Jo Grimond, Orkney and Shetland Liberal MP, moving a Commons motion on home rule in February 1966. Another Liberal MP, Russell Johnston, introduced a Scottish self-government bill on St Andrew's Day (30 November) 1966, and David Steel, who had been elected as a Liberal MP in a 1965 by-election, had written a pamphlet in 1968 (Steel, 1968). Books had been produced making the case for home rule or independence (Mackintosh, 1968; Paton, 1968). The General Assembly of the Church of Scotland passed a 'Deliverance' calling for the appointment of a royal commission on self-government for Scotland in 1968, and *The Scotsman* newspaper launched a campaign for a federal system enshrining a strong element of Scottish home rule.

The all-out attack on the SNP and 'separatism' was supported across the Labour Government, and Whitehall civil servants were enlisted in the battle. Indeed, Whitehall, particularly the Treasury, could not fail to be involved, as Ministers were inundated with parliamentary questions following Winnie Ewing's by-election victory in Hamilton. Labour's message in Scotland was clear: Scotland gained a great deal from London, particularly through the activities of the Scottish Office and its Secretary of State, and the SNP was in danger of jeopardising this.

By the end of the Parliament, the Scottish national movement had run out of steam. This was most evident in the South Ayrshire by-election in March 1970, when Jim Sillars easily held the seat for Labour, and the SNP came in a poor third. Sam Purdie, the SNP candidate, had previously been an election agent for Labour in Ayrshire, and Sillars would later describe him as his 'political twin' (1986: 32). Sillars shared the title 'Hammer of the Nats' with fellow Ayrshireman Willie Ross, for both earned a reputation for robust opposition to the SNP. In 1968, Sillars had co-authored a pamphlet entitled *Don't Butcher Scotland's Future*, and gained an early reputation as a hardline Unionist opponent of Scottish nationalism. The pamphlet was classic Sillars: punchy, acerbic, populist. Labour won the day, and three months later, in the general election, regained Hamilton from the SNP. The SNP hype and expectations created by Hamilton meant that the party's otherwise creditable performance in the general election was seen as a failure. The SNP had the resources to fight 65 seats, won 11.4 per cent of the vote, and succeeded in winning the remote Western Isles from Labour.

Conclusion

In the foreword to his book *The Claim of Scotland*, the philosopher H. J. Paton remarked, 'Politicians concerned with Scotland are almost nationalistic when they are out of office: when they form a government they become obstinately and even blindly unionist' (1968: 10). This certainly proved true of Harold Wilson's 1964–1970 Labour Governments. Willie Ross, as Shadow Scottish Secretary, had happily attacked the Conservatives whilst Labour had been in opposition, but proved reluctant to consider devolving power to Scottish institutions once in office. However, Paton's comments do not quite capture politics under the Labour Governments. In his own way, Willie Ross was a nationalist, and irritated ministerial colleagues with his relentless support for Scotland and efforts to maintain control of his fiefdom. However, Ross's nationalism was the antithesis of that espoused by John Mackintosh, who was as opposed to Ross remaining in office as Secretary of State for Scotland as he was keen to hatch plots to undermine and unseat Wilson himself. Mackintosh supported a Scottish parliament, but had few friends for this cause inside Parliament, and especially not in the Government. Dick Crossman, ever the reformer, sought to win approval for plans that would eventually lead to a Scottish parliament. The rise of the SNP made this appear plausible, but the SNP's subsequent demise would remove any such prospect.

The 1964–1970 Labour Governments engaged in symbolic and administrative changes designed to demonstrate that Labour's sympathies lay with

Scotland, just as the 1945–1951 Labour Governments of Clement Attlee had done. The most significant measure was the Royal Commission on the Constitution. However, unlike the Catto Inquiry, which Attlee had set up to look at Scottish financial and trade statistics, but which had little impact when its publication coincided with the retreat of Scottish nationalism, the 1973 report of the Kilbrandon Commission on the Constitution gave sustenance to the Scottish home rule movement, particularly at a time when the SNP, fuelled by the discovery of North Sea oil, was once more advancing.

Under Harold Wilson's first (1964–1966) Government, Labour was still wedded to an approach whereby the United Kingdom required a high degree of central government. Equality and economic planning, it was believed, required centralism, and hence devolution was seen as a threat to both social justice and economic prosperity. Centralist unionism had come to overwhelm Scottish nationalism, which had been one element in the 'peasant's stockpot' of ideas at the Labour Party's foundation, in the period after 1945. The rise of nationalism affected Scottish politics but did not infect Labour to any great extent. Apart from a few MPs, Labour had long abandoned any serious commitment to Scottish home rule, to the extent that this had become instinctive to the party. In 1970, the widely held belief that Labour had 'seen off' the Scottish Nationalists appeared to justify the strategy. When Labour returned to office in 1974, though, such confidence proved premature.

Notes

The author wishes to acknowledge the support of the ESRC (grant no. L219252026).
1 Its composition was Lord President of the Council (chair), Secretary of State for Economic Affairs, Ministers of State at the Scottish Office, Department of Education and Science, Ministry of Housing and Local Government, and the Welsh Office, the Attorney-General, the Financial Secretary to the Treasury, and Joint Parliamentary Under Secretary of State at the Home Office.

12 Welsh nationalism and demands for devolution

Peter Dorey

Introduction

The constitutional conservatism highlighted in the previous three chapters was also evident in the 1964–1970 Labour Governments' stance towards Wales, and the growing demands for devolution which were articulated during the 1960s. Labour had never taken Welsh nationalist sentiments particularly seriously, tending instead to dismiss devolutionary demands as the manifestation of economic grievances. Hence, when such sentiments have been expressed, Labour's instinctive, and *economistic*, response has been to suggest that Welsh grievances will dissipate once a Labour government's 'socialist' economic and industrial policies deliver or restore prosperity and employment. The most that the Labour Party has been willing to contemplate in response to Welsh nationalism has been administrative devolution, not parliamentary and legislative devolution, and this was certainly the case in the 1960s.

Labour and 'the Welsh question' prior to 1964

The Labour Party had never evinced serious concern about Welsh nationalist sentiments, particularly when these were articulated in support of a parliament for Wales. Admittedly, at its annual conference in 1918 (when it formally committed itself to a socialist programme and Clause 4), the Labour Party adopted a resolution which suggested that 'along with the grant of Home Rule to Ireland, there should be constituted separate statutory legislative assemblies for Scotland, Wales and even England, with autonomous administration in matters of local concern', yet the Labour leadership, most notably Ramsay MacDonald, displayed a marked lack of enthusiasm, even though the official commitment to home rule was subsequently reiterated in Labour's 1929 manifesto. Moreover, this early formal endorsement of 'home rule all round' owed much to the electoral dominance of the (pro-home rule) Liberal Party in Wales at the beginning of the twentieth century, the Liberals having won 33 out of Wales's 34 seats in the 1906 election. Thus, the Labour Party's 'original impulse towards devolution was part of the heavy ideological baggage inherited from Liberalism', so that 'the electoral alliance which became the Labour Party at the beginning of the [twentieth] century happily accepted the old Liberal and radical demand of Home Rule all round' (Jones and Jones, 2000: 242), although 'this was a demand which the party could accommodate, given the vague formulation' (Jones and Keating, 1985: 34).

Ultimately, though, the formal commitment to home rule was never seriously promoted or pursued by the Labour Party overall, least of all by the parliamentary leadership. Instead, the Labour Party's stance towards Wales was of a dirigiste character, whereby economic or social problems in Wales were to be ameliorated by the 'correct' policies pursued nationally by a Labour government at Westminster. This dirigisme thus melded economism with *statism*: what Wales was deemed to need was the implementation of apparently socialist policies from the centre (London), rather than greater autonomy or self-government (see, for example, PRO CAB 129/6 (46)21, 'Memorandum by Herbert Morrison', 27 January 1946). Indeed, to the extent that Wales was acknowledged to suffer socio-economic disadvantage or deprivation, the Labour Party tended to insist that this alone rendered greater autonomy impractical, if not impossible: Wales would be too weak economically to be granted self-government. What Wales needed, therefore, was a Labour government at Westminster, not a parliament in Cardiff or Swansea, for many of the industrial and economic problems experienced in south Wales in particular 'were of a character that could not possibly fall within the administrative duties of a Secretary of State for Wales', for they required action 'on a much wider basis' (Labour Party Archives, Research 56/October 1943).

Nor should it be assumed that this anti-devolutionist stance was the preserve of English Labour MPs, arrogantly imposing a centralist perspective on their pro-devolution Welsh comrades. On the contrary, whilst some Labour MPs in Wales did indeed support a 'Welsh dimension' to public policy (particularly in the form of a Secretary of State for Wales), many others seemed to share Aneurin Bevan's view that he did not know the difference between 'a Welsh sheep, a Westmorland sheep and a Scottish sheep', and pointing out that

> My colleagues, all of them members of the Miners' Federation of Great Britain, have no special solution for the Welsh coal industry which is not a solution for the whole of the mining industry of Great Britain. There is no Welsh problem.
> (House of Commons Debates, 5th series, vol. 403, col. 2312)

In a subsequent parliamentary debate, Bevan reiterated his objections to Welsh devolution by insisting that it was 'rather cruel to give the impression to the 50,000 unemployed men and women in Wales that their plight would be relieved and their distress removed by this constitutional change', for it would be 'trying to pretend that deep-seated economic difficulties can be removed by constitutional changes' (House of Commons Debates, 5th series, vol. 428, col. 405). Indeed, in the same parliamentary debate the President of the Board of Trade, Sir Stafford Cripps, dismissed the notion of a Welsh economic plan by insisting that none of the economic problems or developments pertaining to Wales were 'local in character in the sense of being financed or originated from Wales' (House of Commons Debates, 5th series, vol. 428, col. 311). Or as the Neath MP, D. J. Williams, insisted, 'What Wales needs . . . is not separation from Britain but closer integration with the British economy . . . Wales has not had a fair share of British prosperity' (House of Commons Debates, 5th series, vol. 428, col. 363).

The Labour Party's opposition to a Welsh parliament was maintained throughout the 1950s, although in 1954 a new document entitled *Labour's Policy for Wales* did enunciate, instead, the case for administrative devolution, and recommend the provision of more parliamentary time to debate Welsh affairs. *Labour's Policy for Wales* maintained that

> The Labour Party is not unsympathetic to the spirit which animates the proposals for a Welsh Parliament. Looking back to the pre-war days of mass unemployment and economic stagnation, it is easy to understand why Welshmen should seek to control their own affairs. . . . But in our view, it is a serious error in political thinking to trace the cause of past and present Welsh problems to the constitutional arrangements which exist between Wales and the rest of the United Kingdom. The basic cause of pre-war distress was the failure of successive Tory Governments to combat the spread of unemployment. Wales was one of several areas of the United Kingdom . . . which suffered great hardship as a result . . . the prosperity of Wales is bound up with the prosperity of the United Kingdom as a whole. . . . The industrial life of the United Kingdom and Wales which has emerged organically over the centuries, merges and mingles into one economic system.

It was therefore quite clear that in rejecting demands for a Welsh parliament, the Labour Party was continuing to view the problems of Wales from a predominantly economistic perspective and that devolution, particularly legislative devolution, was deemed to be irrelevant to the problems which underpinned devolutionary demands and aspirations in Wales.

However, *Labour's Policy for Wales* did contain one new institutional proposal, namely the establishment of a Minister for Welsh Affairs, who would be allocated a seat in the Cabinet. It was also suggested that the Council for Wales and Monmouthshire should be made 'a more representative and more effective organ of Welsh opinion', although precisely how this was to be achieved was not made explicit. Such opacity owed much to the fact that, as the party subsequently admitted, *Labour's Policy for Wales* 'was mainly concerned with refuting the demands of the Parliament for Wales Campaign' (Labour Party Archives, Re.533/April 1959).

In spite of – or possibly because of – the policy document's rejection of the case for a Welsh parliament, 1955 witnessed the Labour MP for Merthyr Tydfil, Stephen O. Davies, introduce a private member's bill to create a parliament for Wales. This, however, was defeated by 48 votes to 14, with only 5 of Labour's Welsh MPs voting in favour, and subsequently being strongly rebuked by the party's national leadership for so doing (B. Jones, 1983: 22; Jones and Jones, 2000: 253). The following year also witnessed another Welsh Labour MP, Goronwy Roberts, present a petition calling for the establishment of a parliament for Wales. This petition had been signed by 250,000 people (representing about 14 per cent of the Welsh electorate), but as the vote on the previous year's parliament for Wales bill had indicated, there was little support for a Welsh parliament amongst Labour MPs in Wales (Philip, 1975: 257–8).

The Welsh devolutionist case was reiterated by the 1957 publication of the Third Report of the Council for Wales and Monmouthshire, which addressed the issue of government administration in Wales. The report highlighted a number of deficiencies pertaining to Welsh administration, most notably insufficient co-ordination between government Ministries concerning the implementation of policies in Wales, coupled with the low rank of civil servants in Wales, which effectively prevented them from exerting much influence or speaking with much authority, either in Wales itself or in Whitehall. The report also expressed concern at the inadequate position of the Minister for Welsh Affairs, established by the Conservative Government in 1951 but only operating within the remit of the Home Office.

This report prompted a renewed debate within the Labour Party concerning its approach to Wales, although initially this did not yield any discernible shift in its stance. For example, the NEC's home policy sub-committee remained unconvinced of the case for any significant degree of Welsh devolution, even of a purely administrative character, insisting that 'any Government wishing to act on Welsh affairs has perfectly adequate machinery at its disposal for any measures that it proposes to take'. Besides, it was argued, it remained 'extremely difficult to find out what Welsh people *really* want', so that in the 'absence of ... concrete evidence, experimentation surely cannot be justified'. Thus, the Labour Party rejected the case for a Secretary of State for Wales, claiming that 'perfectly adequate machinery ... already exists' for the implementation in Wales of policies agreed at Westminster and Whitehall. Ultimately, the NEC's home policy sub-committee maintained, 'there are very few major problems that have an exclusively Welsh character about them', and thus 'we must regard the case for a Secretaryship of State [for Wales] as not proven' (Labour Party Archives, Re.221/November 1957).

However, a tripartite committee was established at the end of 1958, comprising four representatives each from Labour's MPs in Wales, the party's National Executive Committee, and the Welsh Council of Labour. Significantly, the chairman of this committee was James Griffiths, both a Welsh

MP and Deputy Leader of the Labour Party (since February 1956), and strongly in favour of administrative (but not legislative) devolution for Wales. In the context of wider favourable circumstances at this time, Griffiths was able to convince Gaitskell and the NEC to accept the case for a Secretary of State for Wales (Griffiths, 1969: 164; see also Jones and Jones, 2000: 254). Thus did Labour's 1959 election manifesto declare that 'The time has now come for the special identity of Wales to be recognised by the appointment of a Secretary of State', a pledge which was reiterated in the 1964 manifesto and subsequently implemented with immediate effect.

This shift in the Labour Party's position reflected several developments pertaining to 'the Welsh question' during the latter half of the 1950s. First, far from granting Wales its own Secretary of State, the Conservative Government in January 1957 transferred responsibility for Welsh affairs from the Home Office to the lower-ranking Ministry of Housing and Local Government. Furthermore, when the post was later allocated by Harold Macmillan to a Conservative peer, Lord Brecon, rather than an MP from the House of Commons, *The Economist* was moved to observe that it 'represents one of the most curious political appointments since Caligula made his horse a consul' (21 December 1957: 1034).

Second, October 1958 witnessed the resignation of Huw Edwards as chairman of the Council of Wales, because of his growing frustration with the Conservative Government's apparent disregard for the Council's views and recommendations, including the call for a Secretary of State for Wales.

Third, and finally, as the tripartite committee noted in one of its first reports, the Labour Party's position in a number of Welsh constituencies was potentially susceptible to 'Welsh National propaganda'. It was not that Plaid Cymru was deemed likely to win any Welsh seats at this time, but that the narrowness of Labour's majority over the Conservatives or Liberals in constituencies such as Anglesey, Brecon and Radnor, Carmarthen, East Flint, and Merioneth meant that a relatively small swing from Labour to the Welsh nationalists would be sufficient to allow the election of the Conservative or Liberal candidate (Labour Party Archives, Re.533/April 1959).

The tripartite committee therefore published a report which recommended the establishment of a Minister for Welsh Affairs who would be granted full Cabinet status *and* spared other departmental responsibilities. It was also proposed that a Welsh Grand Committee be established to consider the implications for Wales of imminent legislation and the administrative issues involved. It was envisaged that these proposals would be in lieu of a comprehensive review of the machinery of government and administration, not merely vis-à-vis Wales, but England and Scotland too, whose purpose would be 'the establishment throughout the whole of Britain of a system of central, regional and local government' which would prove 'much more responsive to the needs and desires of ordinary people than is our present system' (Labour Party Archives, Re.534/April 1959).

From the end of the 1950s onwards, therefore, the Labour Party was formally committed to establishing a Welsh Office, which would be represented at Cabinet level by a Secretary of State for Wales, and which would thus entail a more coherent and systematic mode of administrative devolution. However, the twin proposals for a Welsh Office and a Secretary of State for Wales, with a seat in the Cabinet, were not accompanied by any commitment to an elected assembly or legislative body for Wales, although there had, throughout this period, been talk of an elected – as opposed to government-appointed – Council of Wales. Instead, the Labour Party overall seemed to maintain the view that the 'special problems of the Welsh economy', namely the heavy reliance on a small number of geographically concentrated extraction industries such as coal and tinplate, coupled with 'the geographical isolation of much of rural Wales', as problems whose 'origins [were] in natural and political factors' (Labour Party Archives, Re.540/May 1959). Indeed, because 'Wales has for centuries been integrated with the rest of Britain, both politically and economically, it is now undesirable as well as impracticable to separate their economic affairs' (Labour Party Archives, Re.557/May 1959).

Into the 1960s, meanwhile, there remained those in the Labour Party in Wales who were adamant that 'the political, industrial and social history of the Welsh nation has inclined our people naturally and instinctively towards Socialist thinking', thus ensuring that 'the majority of Welshmen find the best means of giving expression to their aspirations within the Labour Party', to the extent that there was 'very little evidence they will demur from their former loyalty' (Labour Party Archives, RD.387/January 1963).

The Labour Party's commitment to establishing both a Welsh Office and a Cabinet-ranking Secretary of State for Wales was thereafter sustained through the early 1960s, although the party also continued to insist on Wales's 'national status within the Parliamentary framework of the United Kingdom', thereby refusing to countenance legislative devolution via a Welsh Assembly (Labour Party Archives, RD.386/January 1963). Even when particular industrial or economic problems were acknowledged to exist in Wales, these were often presented as arguments *against* legislative devolution, with the Labour MP for Cardiff South, James Callaghan, amongst those insisting that 'the prosperity ... of many of the people of Wales is bound up with the prosperity of the United Kingdom as a whole' (Labour Party Archives, RD.407/February 1963).

In similar vein did Cledwyn Hughes prepare a draft position paper for Labour's working party on Welsh policy which emphasised that the party's 'policy of planning for economic growth ... will have a special significance for Wales', whilst proposed dirigiste institutions such as a national industrial planning board would further 'help to fortify and expand Welsh industry', and thereby ensure that 'Wales will thrive side by side with England and Scotland' (Labour Party Archives, RD.385/January 1963). In short, Labour's approach to Wales during this period sought to meld a willingness to countenance limited executive devolution with greater economic centralisation, reflecting a continued top-down approach to politics and policies by the Labour Party.

The 1964–1970 Wilson Governments and Welsh devolution

Labour's 1964 manifesto reiterated the party's commitment to establishing a Secretary of State for Wales, and with Labour electorally successful after thirteen years in opposition, the Government duly established the Welsh Office, whilst also providing the Secretary of State for Wales with a seat in the Cabinet. The new Welsh Office was charged with responsibility for housing and local government, trunk roads and economic planning, although it was also responsible for overseeing the implementation in Wales of the policies of various other Government departments. The modesty of its functions and the paucity of its powers reflected a minimalist approach to Welsh nationalist sentiment by the incoming Labour Government, with Richard Crossman deriding 'the Department for Wales' as 'an idiotic invention ... a completely artificial new office ... all the result of a silly election pledge' (1975: 117, diary entry for 3 January 1965). Almost eighteen months later, Crossman was similarly dismissive of the 'miserable recommendation' of the then Secretary of State for Wales, Cledwyn Hughes, for 'a co-opted Welsh Council, which, as far as I could see, would do nothing but supervise tourism', although Crossman did concede 'that it was no good attacking Cledwyn since he was faced with a very difficult political reality. He had to move forward far enough to hold his position' (1976: 377, diary entry for 12 June 1967).

To the extent that Labour MPs and Ministers considered Welsh nationalist sentiment at this time, the blithe assumption seemed to be that the establishment of the Welsh Office, politically headed by a Minister of Cabinet rank, combined with the pursuit of the correct economic policies (after 'thirteen wasted years' and neglect arising from Conservative rule), would serve to diminish nascent demands in Wales for devolution. However, according to George Thomas, initially Minister of State for Wales and later promoted to Secretary of State as successor to Cledwyn Hughes, 'By setting up the [Welsh] Office, the Labour Government had opened the floodgates for nationalism' (1985: 95), a view apparently vindicated by the electoral advances of Plaid Cymru during the mid-1960s. In this respect, therefore, the Labour Government appeared, at least in the short term, to be in something of a no-win situation in the face of growing Welsh nationalism. Failure to establish the Welsh Office, headed by a Minister of Cabinet rank, would almost certainly have been cited as evidence by Welsh nationalists that the new Labour Government was just as insensitive to Welsh aspirations and distinctiveness as its Conservative predecessor, thereby boosting support for Plaid Cymru. Yet in fulfilling its pledge to establish a

Welsh Office and appoint a Secretary of State for Wales, the newly elected Labour Government was effectively acknowledging that Wales was something of a 'special case' warranting its own government department and Cabinet Minister, and in so doing provided a fillip to Welsh nationalists, who felt that they had been vindicated, and were now emboldened and more confident in pushing for greater autonomy and self-government.

Meanwhile, the view of many Labour MPs and Ministers that economic regeneration and industrial investment would yield a corresponding decline in nationalist sentiment in Wales clearly reflected the aforementioned economism which permeated Labour's stance with regard to regional inequalities and concomitant socio-economic problems in Wales (and other regions of the United Kingdom). Nationalist sentiments and demands continued to be attributed primarily to grievances emanating, ultimately, from economic problems, the remedy for which lay in the pursuit of 'socialist' economic policies, not in constitutional tinkering and political devolution. Thus, it was assumed – or hoped – that once the benefits of Labour's economic policies – particularly those implemented in the guise for a National Plan which enshrined regional planning (see Chapter 13) – the grievances which apparently fuelled Welsh nationalist sentiments and aspirations would be pacified, thereby dissipating the concomitant demands for Welsh political devolution. This was certainly the perspective attributed to Harold Wilson by Richard Crossman, the latter claiming – after several frustrated attempts at convincing his ministerial colleagues to treat devolution more seriously and positively – that

> He doesn't understand either devolution or nationalism because he is basically an economist and a manager who sees things in terms of economic problems, and for whom anything non-economic is either foreign policy, nuclear weapons, etc., but not nationalist movements among people in his country.
>
> (1977: 193, diary entry for 18 September 1968)

Consequently, and as part of the 1964–1966 Labour Government's penchant for economic planning, 1965 saw George Brown's Department of Economic Affairs establish both a Welsh Planning Board and a Welsh Economic Council. Whilst the former was to be primarily administrative in nature, the latter was to be a representative forum with an advisory and consultative capacity. However, this was deemed to undermine the rationale of the Council for Wales and Monmouthshire, which was therefore disbanded in 1966. What Westminster gave Wales with one hand, it took away with the other.

It was, therefore, hardly a coincidence, that 1966 witnessed the remarkable success of Plaid Cymru in a by-election held in Carmarthen on 14 July. The by-election was held just four months after the general election, owing to the death, in May, of the incumbent Labour MP, Lady Megan Lloyd

George. When the by-election was held, the Plaid Cymru candidate, Gwynfor Evans, increased his vote from 7,416 in March to 16,179, whilst Labour's support slumped from 21,221 to 14,743.

Plaid Cymru almost secured another by-election victory the following year, when the Party's candidate in Rhondda West reduced Labour's majority from 16,888 (in the 1966 election) to 2,306, whilst in 1968 a by-election in Caerphilly saw the Labour Party's majority of 21,148 cut to just 1,874 by the Plaid Cymru candidate. Such results, coupled with advances by the SNP in Scotland (as noted in the previous chapter), obliged the Labour Government to treat nationalist aspirations in Wales with at least a little more care and consideration than they had received hitherto. Certainly Crossman was convinced that whilst such by-election results 'may well have strong *poujadist* motives ... we should be unwise to disregard the growing feeling that Wales and Scotland are not getting a fair deal from Whitehall' (PRO PREM 13/2151, Crossman to Wilson, 13 November 1967). Along with the increasing electoral support for Plaid Cymru, this 'growing feeling' was buttressed by opinion polls conducted during this period, which suggested that up to 60 per cent of Welsh voters wanted a Welsh parliament to run Welsh affairs (*Western Mail*, 22 November 1967 and 25 September 1968).

Consequently, there were four main responses by the Cabinet. First, a tranche of legislation was introduced which was directly applicable to Wales, most notably the 1967 Leasehold Reform Act (for the significance of this measure in Wales, see Griffiths, 1969: 181–3; Abse, 1973: 142–4) and the 1967 Welsh Language Act, whilst the 1969 Development of Tourism Act established the Welsh Tourist Board.

Second, a Cabinet committee on devolution was established, this meeting periodically during 1968 before being disbanded in November of that year. George Thomas, who had by this time replaced Cledwyn Hughes as Secretary of State for Wales, drew the committee's attention to the distinction between parliamentary devolution and administrative devolution, and made clear his support for the latter. Not only did he believe that a Welsh parliament would weaken Wales's position vis-àvis Westminster, but he also feared that it would actually encourage the minority who wanted an independent Wales to make further demands to this end.

By contrast, Thomas argued, administrative devolution did not weaken 'the essential unity of the United Kingdom' or the sovereignty of Parliament, and was 'consistent with both the democratic principles and economic strategies of our Party'. He therefore recommended that further responsibilities, most notably those pertaining to agriculture, education and health, be devolved to the Welsh Office in Cardiff. At the same time, he envisaged a strengthening of the newly formed Welsh Council, to be a part-nominated, part-elected body whose role would be similar to that of the Greater London Council. Indeed, he made clear his vision of the Welsh Council as 'a local government rather than parliamentary body', one whose members would have 'plenty of executive and advisory work to keep them busy', and thus would be unlikely 'to transgress on the work of Ministers, of the House of Commons, or of the existing local authorities' (PRO CAB 134/2697, DS(68)11, 19 April 1968).

Thomas's emphasis on the local government – rather than parliamentary – character of the proposed Welsh Council was also intended to assuage the anxieties of those Welsh Labour MPs who feared that such a body would reduce their own role and status. He was adamant that administrative devolution would enable 'details of policy' to be determined in Wales, in a manner appropriate to Welsh circumstances, whilst ensuring that 'the main decisions continue to be decided in London for the [United] Kingdom as a whole' (PRO CAB 134/2697, DS(68)11, 19 April 1968). Furthermore, it reflected Thomas's own attitude: 'Despite a genuine pride in my Welsh heritage, and my eagerness to advance Welsh culture, I have never believed in Welsh nationalism' (1985: 95). Thomas was convinced that administrative devolution via a partly elected Welsh Council, 'with functions taken over from the field of nominated bodies who were now operating in the twilight zone between central and local government', would not 'weaken the essential unity of the United Kingdom. On the contrary, they would bind Wales more surely into this unity' (PRO PREM 13/2151, Thomas to Wilson, 28 June 1968). Moreover, he was emphatic that 'If we reject Parliamentary devolution, it is the more necessary for us to advance in administrative devolution', and to this end he was convinced that 'an elected or partly elected Welsh Council dealing with administrative functions is both practicable and advisable', and 'would provide a dramatic and revolutionary change in administration on an all-Wales basis' with regard to 'activities which at present fall between central and local government'. Thomas did acknowledge, though, that 'The question of finance is obviously not easy to settle' (PRO CAB 165/821, Memorandum by the Secretary of State for Wales – Commission on the Constitution', August [precise date not stated] 1969).

The Cabinet committee on devolution itself concluded that the case for a Welsh parliament was far less convincing than for Scotland, for whereas Scotland already had a long-established separate legal system, which gave credibility to the demand for a Scottish legislature, 'the emotional basis' of the 'separatist movement' in Wales was deemed primarily to be the Welsh language itself, which was only spoken by a minority of the population. Furthermore, it was argued that in spite of recent successes for Plaid Cymru, the electoral situation in Wales was less threatening to the Labour Party than it was in Scotland (PRO CAB 134/2697, DS(68)23, 30 May 1968).

However, the Cabinet committee on devolution rejected Thomas's proposals for a partly elected Council for Wales, explaining that

> The more we studied them, the more disinclined we felt to accept what is bound to be an unsatisfactory compromise between local and central government; in particular, we felt that the analogy with the Greater

London Council is misconceived. In so far as it was effectively an organ of local government, a Council for Wales would be a top tier above a second tier of County and County Boroughs, and a third tier of District Councils. . . . In so far as the Council was still tied to central government, it would be regarded by Nationalist sympathisers as a miserable half-way house to the separate Parliament they really want.

(PRO CAB 134/2697, DS(68) 23, 30 May 1968)

Also rejected by the ministerial committee on devolution, albeit this time in accordance with Thomas's own views, was the notion that the Welsh Grand Committee should conduct its sittings in Cardiff, a decision taken largely on the grounds that, embarrassingly, this 'would increase public awareness of its ineffectiveness', although it was acknowledged that if a parallel proposal for the Scottish Grand Committee to meet in Edinburgh was adopted, 'it would be difficult to resist pressure for the Welsh Grand Commitee to meet in Cardiff' (PRO CAB 134/2697, DS(68)23, 30 May 1968; see also PREM 13/2151, Thomas to Peart, 9 August 1968). Evidently Ministers were rapidly realising that the more they considered the issue of devolution, the greater the number or complexity of constitutional, political and practical problems they raised.

The third response of the 1966–1970 Labour Government to growing Welsh nationalist sentiment and increasing support for Plaid Cymru, was to widen the jurisdiction of the Welsh Office – something which both George Thomas and his ministerial colleagues on the devolution committee had recommended. In April 1969, administrative responsibility for agriculture and health services in Wales was added to its remit. However, the question of whether education should also be devolved to the Welsh Office was left unresolved, to be determined at an unspecified later date, whilst a suggestion that the headquarters of the new Countryside Commission for England and Wales should be located in Wales was opposed by the Minister of Housing and Local Government.

However, these administrative initiatives were to be accompanied by a 'vigorous and sustained campaign of public education . . . emphasising the benefits to be gained . . . from economic and political unity', and explaining how the present 'unitary structure' of government in the United Kingdom was in the best interests of the Welsh people (PRO CAB 134/2697, DS(68)23, 30 May 1968).

Fourth, as was noted in the previous chapter, a Royal Commission on the Constitution was established, although the 1966–1970 Labour Government 'was far from committed to changing the constitution, but wanted an excuse to do nothing in the face of Nationalist success in the by-elections in Scotland and Wales' (Drucker and Brown, 1980: 54), 'doubtless in the hope that the problem would either solve itself or go away' (Jones, 1983: 23).[1] That the Labour Government was stalling was indicated by the fact that although the establishment of the royal commission was announced in the autumn of 1968, its actual members were not appointed until April 1969.

In terms of debates within the Labour Party over nationalist aspirations and advances within Wales during the second half of the 1960s, beyond the premise that devolutionary demands were merely a transient manifestation of short-term economic grievances which would soon dissipate, two contrasting assumptions were drawn about the likely consequences of granting the Welsh people their own elected assembly. Many Labour politicians, including some of the party's Welsh MPs, shared George Thomas's concern that establishing an elected body in Wales was likely to embolden Welsh nationalists and encourage Plaid Cymru to go further in demanding autonomy or independence for Wales.

However, Labour MPs who were sympathetic to the cause of Welsh devolution tended to draw the opposite conclusion, namely that granting the people of Wales their own elected assembly would actually serve to undermine separatist sentiments, on the grounds that establishing democratic institutions in Wales would 'begin to engage people's loyalties and diminish nationalist support till the demand for total separation was lost in a healthy competition ... for control of the Welsh Parliament or Assembly'. Conversely, it was 'the refusal to grant a measure of self-government when it is ardently desired that is most likely to lead to increasing pressure and more extensive demands for autonomy' (Mackintosh, 1968: 150, 164).

Consequently, there was some disagreement within the Labour Party over what evidence it should submit to the Royal Commission, along with divergent views concerning the recommendation of specific proposals. For example, the executive of the Labour Party in Wales prepared a draft submission which recommended the establishment of a seventy-two-seat Welsh senate with a range of legislative powers (Labour Party in Wales, 1970). This was deemed too federalist in orientation not only by the Labour Party leadership in London, but by several Welsh Labour MPs, and also George Thomas (B. Jones, 1983: 23). Indeed, Thomas reiterated the argument that a Welsh parliament 'would inevitably lead to clashes and crises that would precipitate demands for complete separation', whilst a 'division of responsibility for legislation would be both cumbersome and needlessly expensive in resources', although once again he did suggest that 'an elected or a partly elected Welsh Council dealing with administrative functions is both practicable and advisable'. Thomas also suggested that statutory instruments which mainly or solely concerned Wales should be approved or rejected by the Welsh Grand Committee, rather than by the whole House (of Commons) (PRO CAB 165/821, 'Commission on the Constitution: Memorandum by the Secretary of State for Wales', August 1969), although this particular proposal caused some concern in parts of Whitehall, where it was suggested – with the judicious phrasing typical of senior civil servants – that '[t]he implications would need thorough consideration'.

Meanwhile, realisation that the Welsh Council of Labour was preparing to submit rather more pro-devolution recommendations to the Royal Commission on the Constitution than the Scottish Labour Party caused considerable consternation to Labour's NEC, which warned that 'there is some danger of the Party nationally looking rather silly', and therefore suggested that 'it would be much better if all three parties spoke with precisely the same voice' (Labour Party Archives, Re.540/November 1969).

The Welsh Executive was subsequently 'persuaded' to modify its proposals, to the extent that when it did present its submission to the Royal Commission, it actually dismissed the idea of a legislative assembly for Wales on the grounds that 'it would reduce the effectiveness of Welsh MPs and the influence of Wales in the UK, and would jeopardise the unity of the country as a whole' (quoted in B. Jones, 1983: 23). Instead, the emphasis was once again on an elected Welsh council – in spite of the antipathy to such a body by some Ministers on the devolution Cabinet committee – whose role would primarily be to provide advice and administrative oversight concerning the implementation of government policies in Wales, although, by virtue of being elected, it was also intended to ensure a degree of accountability to the Welsh people. Labour's 1970 manifesto, then, referred explicitly to the Welsh Labour Party's support for an elected council, whilst rejecting 'a policy of separatism or a separate Parliament for Wales' on the grounds that either would be 'detrimental to the true interests of the Principality' (Labour Party, 1970a: 17).

One further reason why the Labour Party seemed unable to offer a more coherent and constructive approach with regard to Welsh devolutionary demands during the later half of the 1960s was that the Government was awaiting the outcome of a separate Royal Commission on Local Government in England, chaired by Lord Redcliffe-Maud. This was established in May 1966, and was due to report three years later. Given the extent to which local government reform in England was likely to impact on Wales too – local government reform in England and Wales traditionally being approached or pursued in tandem – Labour's consideration of Welsh devolution was further impeded by uncertainty over the wider reorganisation of local government which was likely to follow publication of the Maud Report. Thus was it deemed necessary for the Cabinet to adopt a 'Plan A, to do what we can now to create a good atmosphere, and Plan B after the Maud Report' (Crossman, 1977: 145, diary entry for 18 July 1968), although, of course, by the time the Maud Report was published, the Royal Commission on the Constitution had commenced its inquiry, so that Labour remained bereft of clear or firm ideas for Welsh devolution. Once again, Labour's lack of 'joined-up thinking' in this sphere was evident in the fact that there were two separate royal commissions during the latter part of the 1960s, one on local government and one on the constitution, although Ministers would doubtless have pointed out that the Maud Commission had already been established before the 'threat' from Welsh nationalists – as evinced by the electoral advances and successes of Plaid Cymru – had become apparent.

Conclusion

Beyond the commitment to establishing a Welsh Office headed by a Secretary of State (who was to be a full member of the Cabinet), the Labour Party entered office in 1964 with no clear policies concerning devolution, even though it had had thirteen years in opposition, during which time it could have given some consideration to such issues. That it had failed to do so was due to a number of factors. First, and most generally, the Labour Party has never seriously considered constitutional issues in a coherent or consistent manner: to use modern parlance, there had been a singular lack of 'joined-up thinking' concerning the political and territorial arrangements and framework of the United Kingdom. Certainly Richard Crossman acknowledged that there existed 'tremendous natural inhibition in the [Labour] Party against home rule, and against constitutional innovation of any kind ... very little support except for purely opportunist reasons' (1977: 69, diary entry for 19 May 1968).

Second, but inextricably linked to this aspect, the Labour Party has largely been characterised by an atheoretical and pragmatic approach to the art of government, and has effectively vied with the Conservatives in its explicit eschewal of 'textbook theories' and abstract political ideas. Instead, the Labour Party's parliamentary leadership in particular has tended to pride itself on its pragmatism and 'realism' in addressing issues and tackling problems, and paraded its disinterest in 'ivory tower ideas' as a virtue, a symbol of its political wisdom and maturity. A key result of this, however, has been a serious lack of serious consideration about the nature either of capitalism or, in this particular context, the constitution and the political framework of the United Kingdom. This has imbued the Labour Party with a marked degree of conservatism on many issues, not least of these being constitutional reform. Or as Anderson observed in the mid-1960s,

> Traditionalism and empiricism henceforward fuse as a single legitimating system: traditionalism sanctions the present by deriving it from the past, empiricism shackles the future by riveting it to the present. A comprehensive, coagulated conservatism is the result, covering the whole of society with a thick pall of simultaneous philistinism (towards ideas) and mystagogy (towards institutions), for which England has justly won an international reputation.
>
> (1966: 32)

Third, and again intimately linked to the above, few Labour politicians have given serious or systematic thought to constitutional matters, with many MPs and Ministers deeming such issues to be of low salience, especially compared to bread-and-butter issues such as education, employment, health and welfare provision. Labour politicians have been inclined to justify their lack of interest in constitutional matters by pointing out that such matters are of little interest to the wider electorate: there have been few votes to be won by promoting constitutional reform. Moreover, the antipathy of many Welsh Labour MPs to devolution (beyond that of an administrative character, as opposed to parliamentary devolution and self-government) has effectively served to legitimise the lack of interest of Labour MPs as a whole in such an issue. The tacit view of many Labour MPs in England has been that if few of their comrades in Wales were overly concerned about securing parliamentary devolution for the Principality, why should they themselves concern themselves with such an issue?

Fourth, and yet again following on from the above, the Labour Party's approach to a range of issues and problems has been imbued with a high degree of economism, whereby solutions – or, at least, the amelioration of particular problems – are deemed to derive from the implementation of the 'correct' economic and industrial policies by a Labour government. Such policies, it has blithely been assumed, will either reduce the scale or scope of particular problems (such as crime, for example, by tackling the socioeconomic deprivation assumed to underpin much crime and antisocial behaviour), or by pacifying the grievances which were apparently fuelled or fostered by a sense of economic disadvantage and injustice.

Certainly there was a widespread view in the Parliamentary Labour Party that the surge in support for Welsh nationalism and Plaid Cymru in the 1960s owed much to a sense of grievance in Wales after 'thirteen wasted years' of neglect by the Conservatives, and that once the Labour Governments began tackling the economic and industrial problems of the Principality, thereby restoring economic growth and prosperity, then support for a Welsh parliament and/or self-government would dissipate. Of course, such policies would take time to come to fruition, thereby obliging the Labour Party hastily to search for measures which would neutralise the threat posed by Plaid Cymru in the meantime. Thus it was that a series of laws were implemented which were directly and solely applicable to Wales, and various proposals discussed, at ministerial level, for administrative devolution to Wales, possibly in the guise of a partly elected Welsh council (although the ensuing discussions revealed a marked lack of support for such an institutional innovation, partly because it might actually serve to strengthen or legitimise the Welsh nationalists' case for a parliament for Wales, and partly because many Welsh Labour MPs and local councillors were concerned that their own roles and status might be undermined by the establishment of a Welsh council which was imbued with administrative and executive authority).

Finally, Harold Wilson announced the establishment of a Royal Commission on the Constitution, a move clearly intended simultaneously to buy time whilst seeking to give the impression that the Government was taking the issue of devolution seriously: such an important matter could not be rushed, but needed serious consideration by 'the great and the good'. Yet once such a body had been established, the Labour Party's internal wrangling over its own submission to the Commission once again revealed the incoherent character of its approach to Welsh devolution. Yet the problems posed for the Labour Government by the issue of Welsh devolution in the late 1960s paled almost into insignificance compared to the problems which the issue posed a decade later: the devolution issue did not go away, as expected, but instead returned to wreak havoc on the 1974–1979 Labour Governments.

Note

1 Far from resolving itself or disappearing, 'the problem' was subsequently to return to haunt, and wreak havoc upon, the Labour Party during the latter half of the 1970s.

13 English regional policy

Janet Mather

Introduction

Elected after thirteen years of Conservative rule, the 1964–1970 Labour Governments entered office pledging radical reforming and modernisation. Harold Wilson and his ministerial colleagues presented themselves as dynamic and innovative, a break with the thirteen wasted years of Conservative rule, hence ideas encapsulated within the metaphorical theme of 'the white heat of the technological change' were plentiful. Labour's regional policy, which was to help deliver the great National Plan, assisted by decentralised economic government, was intended to be a significant component of this avowedly new approach.

However, radicalism is not the only perspective. Actions undertaken by any government are responses, to differing degrees, to underlying ideology, needs and circumstance, tempered by the personalities of those who try to implement proposals. In the case of Labour's regional policy during the 1960s, elements of all these factors can be discerned. Labour's political thought, as I shall show, has always enshrined a decentralist strand, yet it was certainly not the only main political party that was interested in devolving powers during the 1960s. During this time, the need to rejuvenate the regions was becoming increasingly apparent, owing to growing evidence of chronic rather than acute industrial decline – that is, decline that was persistent but not terminal. There was also growing concern about the imbalance in industrial location and population movement between the north and the south of Britain. Circumstances did not *dictate* the 1964–1970 Labour Governments' regional policy, but, whilst the preceding Conservative Governments had not contributed greatly towards the structural reforms needed for regionalisation, some tentative moves had been undertaken upon which a more radically inclined government – as Harold Wilson's purported to be – could build. Finally, there appeared to be suitably able and enthusiastic individuals available to pursue such a project.

An analysis of these factors, which forms the first section of the chapter, helps to explain why some form of regional policy was inevitable. It also accounts for the way in which Labour's regional policies evolved, as discussed in the second section. It does not explain the 'failure' of the policy, which resulted from other factors – mostly deriving from the difference between policy initiation and policy implementation, coupled with what one of Wilson's predecessors, Harold Macmillan, had termed 'events', although personalities and personality clashes were also contributory factors. These factors will be examined in the third section of the chapter.

The origins of Wilsonian regionalism

Philosophical perspectives of the 1960s

Since 1918, the Labour Party has considered itself to be a 'democratic social-ist' party. Whilst the two words are generally linked in a single phrase, its deconstruction demonstrates the dual nature of Labour political thought: 'socialism' necessitates central planning so that economic inequalities may be evened out, whilst 'democracy' requires devolution (of power) so that political inequalities may be reduced by means of empowering non-elites. The Labour Party has thus had some difficulty, albeit unacknowledged for the most part, in reconciling the two aims. The political thought of the Fabians displays the dilemma, for in the context of regionalism and devolu-tion its authoritarian perspective argues that state collectivism may be applied both centrally and locally (Wright, 1986: 11), whilst in its pluralis-tic guise it has consistently advocated decentralised self-government.

Wilson's contemporary experience of Fabianism was of the second school of thought. The economist David Steele, then vice-chair of the Young Fabian Group, published a Young Fabian pamphlet, *More Power to the Regions*, in 1964, which provided a detailed argument and plan for the setting up of powerful regional councils. Steele (1964: 33) suggested a two-tier system: one tier for planning and one with executive power 'which would derive its authority from either central government or enlarged local government'.

Wilson himself, however, was essentially a centralist and corporatist. His concern was the delivery of an 'entirely new concept' (Shrimsley, 1964: 5): a *national* economic plan. Wilson and many of his ministerial colleagues understood that the success of such a plan depended, in part, upon regional involvement, so that the details of the National Plan could be tailored for successful implementation (Clifford, 1997:103; Dunwoody, interview with author, December 2003). Yet Wilson did not believe – there is no evidence that he even considered the issues – that devolution of political power was needed, or that popular participation was desirable. However, as will become apparent, some of his ministerial colleagues held rather different views.

It is difficult to ascertain how deeply Wilson and his Cabinet colleagues were moved by the Young Fabians' advocacy; Labour's policies did not reflect Steele's proposals to any significant extent. However, decentralisation was on the wider political agenda, and Steele's contribution may have added to its momentum. It is clear that the party was aware of it, because in December 1967 Labour's Study Group on Regional Policy (Working Group B, 224/Dec) referred to Steele's pamphlet. Meanwhile, the other two main parties were developing a regional dimension, demonstrating that they shared Labour's ambiguity in thought. The Liberals were proponents of 'power to the regions', using democratic participation as the criterion. For example, Harry Cowie (1964: 18), from the Liberal Party Research Department, argued that people would be unlikely to participate in regional regeneration unless they felt involved in the political processes. The Conservative Party, however, approached the matter from an efficiency perspective, claiming that decentralisation of power was needed in order to make government more effective. For example, A. R. Ilersic (1964: 208) of the Institute of Economic Affairs suggested popular elections for regional authorities, as a counterbalance to the powers of the Whitehall executive, which impeded *efficiency*, rather than democracy. Both parties, however, agreed that regional government was a permanent feature of the United Kingdom's political landscape (Cowey, 1964: 20; Ilersic, 1964: 207).

Needs

There is a clear impression that the notion of regional governance was one whose time had arrived in the 1960s. All three major parties agreed with the principle, and all three had policies for its implementation. It is less clear, however, why this should be so. Lord (William) Rodgers of Quarry Bank, who as a young junior Minister was largely responsible for implementing the policy, thinks that the main motivating factors were perceptions of declining industry and, in particular, of a poor distribution of human resources, rather than political ideology, particularly amongst the intellectual left during the previous decades (Rodgers, interviewed by author, November 2003).

As it turned out later, there was relative economic decline in the 1960s, although this was a familiar experience in the United Kingdom (Woodward 1993: 73). Unemployment was low compared with pre-war rates (although it was rising, because of deflationary policies and a downturn in the trade cycle) (Department of Trade and Industry, 1989). However, a regional response seemed to be required because the spread of unemployment was uneven, reflecting the decline in heavy industries such as shipbuilding and coal (Department of Trade and Industry, 1989), which affected some regions harder than others. Between 1952 and 1962, employment in Scotland, Wales and the northern regions had increased by 3.9 per cent, compared to 12.6 per cent in the other regions (Labour Party, 1969). In May 1964, the Northern region suffered from the highest unemployment rate: 3.3 per cent. The lowest rate, in the Midlands, was only 0.9 per cent (Smith, 1965: 125). The Labour Government was more concerned, however, about the 'drift' from the North to the South, for figures showed that the south-east of England was becoming more heavily populated – by 2.5 per cent between 1951 and 1961 – whilst northern England and Wales saw their populations decline by 2 per cent during this period (Smith, 1965: 126). Since employment opportunities in the surviving traditional industries were concentrated in the North and Midlands, the growing population imbalance had become an issue. Manners *et al.* (1980: 12) note that the government also thought that regional planning would assist in controlling inflation and increasing economic growth by directing resources into the less prosperous North of the country.

However, these were by no means the only issues which inspired the Labour Governments' development of regional policies. There were also political reasons. Local government was regarded as being a problem, partly because the days of municipal socialism had declined and partly because the need for comprehensive wartime planning had encouraged post-war governments to look closely at local government functions. Labour itself had previously played a significant role in depriving locally elected units of political power, particularly with regard to health and education, as well as other statutory undertakings. Concerns about local electoral apathy had begun to surface, along with worries about the outdated and complex structure. Also, the extent of some problems such as urban sprawl, which was sub-national in origin, seemed to require a more methodical system based on larger units of government (Ilersic, 1964: 202). A government that was interested in grand plans, like Wilson's administration, could look upon carefully structured (and limited) regional government as the means of tackling several increasingly salient issues simultaneously.

Circumstances

In addressing these challenges, the Labour Governments of 1964–1970 were not presented with a blank sheet of paper upon which to write. Governments had been attempting to divide the United Kingdom, or at least England, for administrative purposes since the turn of the century. In 1964, though, Labour was faced with a medley of arrangements, including regional boards for public services and for utilities (whose boundaries were not coterminous) dating from the 1940s. In 1946, the Treasury had defined 'Standard Regions' using different boundaries again, and other government departments had been required to accommodate themselves towards them. However, these bodies were based in, rather than centring upon, the regions in which they were located. A paper presented at a Labour party weekend conference on regional planning commented that

> It is clear than many of the organisations established on regional lines are completely divorced from any real regional thinking. A large

number were created in the post-war period when regionalism was almost as topical as it is today, but they have stagnated and become merely units of administration which could have taken any size or shape and still have had as much to do with regional planning as they have now.

(Labour Party, 1966a)

So far as regional economic planning was concerned, actions had been undertaken since 1928, when an Industrial Transference Board was formed with the purpose of assisting workers to move from declining industries to the newer, expanding businesses. 'Special Areas' of economic concern were designated in 1934, whilst the 1945 Distribution of Industry Act redefined and extended the Special Areas, renaming them 'Development Areas' to reflect the contemporary concern about industrial development (rather than unemployment) and putting them under the control of the Board of Trade (BoT). The BoT was empowered to undertake any actions necessary to attract and maintain industry within the Development Areas, whilst restricting the issue of Industrial Development Certificates to discourage development in the South-East (Department of Trade and Industry, 1989).

In 1958, the Conservative Government introduced the Distribution of Industry (Industrial Finance) Act, which added smaller areas, selected on the basis of growing unemployment, to the Development Areas. However, the Government considered that the structure of the Distribution of Industry Acts was too inflexible to deal with regional problems, since additional designation of Development Areas would continue to need parliamentary approval. Therefore, in 1960 it adopted its Local Employment Act, which delegated the power to determine Development Areas, now called 'Development Districts', based on the smaller Local Employment Exchange areas, to the BoT (Department of Trade and Industry, 1989).

Two years later, in 1962, the Conservative Government instituted the National Economic Development Council (NEDC), which, although primarily concerned with increasing the rate of growth in the United Kingdom, focused attention on deficiencies in *regional* planning that were preventing desirable development (McCrone, 1969: 142). The following year, the Government published two White Papers centring upon Central Scotland and North-East England respectively, designating them permanent 'growth areas' which would continue to receive assistance even after their unemployment rates fell (Department of Trade and Industry, 1989). These White Papers have been characterised as 'a first step towards regional planning' (McCrone, 1969: 126).

Local government too had acknowledged the need to tackle industrial decline, as evinced by the formation of ad hoc organisations concerned with industrial development, which by 1963 covered most of England, although excluding the relatively prosperous South-East outside London (Mather, 2000: 14). Sub-national awareness of regional distinctiveness also seemed to be growing. Manners *et al.* refer to a growing disenchantment with central government that fostered 'the emergence of a more articulate regional spirit in provincial England, and increasingly vocal nationalistic movements in Scotland and Wales' (1980: 14). Other parties recommending the establishment of regional government included *The Economist* journal and the Federation of British Industries (one of the forerunners of the Confederation of British Industry). It was in the context of such developments and demands that Labour entered office in October 1964.

Individuals

The composition of the new Labour Cabinet was interesting with regard to the future – and fate – of regional policies. Harold Wilson was, of course, a powerful figure, and, initially at least, seemed to be an enthusiast for regional development, although, as already noted, Wilson viewed it as means to an end. Certainly, according to Gwyneth Dunwoody – who helped define Labour's regional policy during the period from 1966 to 1970 – Wilson's approach to this issue was essentially pragmatic (Dunwoody, interviewed by author, December 2003).

There was also Wilson's First Secretary of State, George Brown – appointed also as the Minister for the newly created giant Department of Economic Affairs (DEA), which was to be responsible for regional policies. It was noted also that in pre-election statements, Brown (cited in Smith, 1965: 20) had hinted that he was considering moving towards future *elected* regional bodies. Brown's agenda was supported by an equally enthusiastic William Rodgers (Lindley, 1982: 173; Rodgers, 2000: 89) a former General Secretary of the Fabian Society, who was appointed Parliamentary Under-Secretary at the DEA from 1964 to 1967.

Brown had two powerful weapons: his position (it was he who deputised for Wilson in the Prime Minister's absence) and his personality – described by a contemporary as 'a sometimes quixotic blend of deep emotion and powerful intellect' (Shrimsley, 1965: 5). Brown *was* an enthusiast for both nationally planned economic growth and what would now be termed 'devolution'. In his memoirs, he confirmed that he wanted his regional councils to be 'embryos of something that could become a new form of regional government' (Brown, 1971: 108). In his memoirs of the Labour Governments of 1964–1970, Wilson recounted how Brown gave life to his 'bare instructions' by 'touring the country, in vigorous formal meetings and turbulent evening sessions', and by strengthening the role of Regional Planning Boards (Wilson, 1971: 97).

However, Wilson and Brown were certainly not the only powerful individuals in the Cabinet during this period. Other prominent figures included James Callaghan, the Chancellor of the Exchequer; Douglas Jay, President of the Board of Trade; and Richard Crossman, Minister for Housing and Local Government. Eventually, as we shall see, the approach of these three, backed by their senior civil servants, at first limited the effectiveness of Brown and the DEA, and eventually triumphed over them.

The story of Wilsonian regionalism

As already noted, the 1964–1970 Labour Governments inherited a confused structure of regional institutions, and ultimately did little to simplify this. Boundaries for services already based on the regions were left untouched. However, Labour's manifesto was focused upon planning as a remedy for relative regional decline. Labour's 1964 manifesto pledged that

> [t]o bring together the different tasks of regional planning, and the different Ministries concerned, Labour will create Regional Planning Boards, equipped with their own expert staffs, under the general guidance of the Ministry of Economic Affairs. These Planning Boards will work closely with representatives of the local authorities, both sides of industry and other interests in the region.
>
> (Craig, 1975: 261)

The idea was for the boards to represent 'mini-Whitehalls' (Wilson, 1971: 97). It turned out that the final sentence meant that the Government would upgrade the existing 'boards for industry' into what became 'regional economic councils', which were composed of representatives from all interested sectors and which were to have an overall responsibility for regional economic planning, covering all issues with a regional dimension.

The Labour Party had been preparing its regional development strategy since January 1964, when its finance and economic policy sub-committee established a working party, under James Callaghan's chairmanship, to 'make proposals for policy for national planning of regional development and for the machinery to carry it out' (Labour Party, 1964b). Even at this stage, the party must have decided upon regional councils, as well as boards, since the working party's reports seem to take them as a given. There is no discussion in the reports about *whether* regional councils should be instituted, only about *how* they should be developed.

This working party met five times during January and February, and produced a draft report at the end of February, with a final report in March 1964. At its first meeting, on 13 January 1964, the working party considered a series of questions relating to regional planning. These included the designation of regional boundaries and whether existing regional institutions should be expected to change theirs; economic development (particularly what should be the role of public enterprise); planning (which powers should be transferred; who should draw up regional plans – local councils or the new regional councils); and involvement of other institutions such as universities and hospitals. Most importantly, it considered the machinery of the new structures.

The answers that came forward were indicative of the current state-centric mode of thought. Whilst regional plans should be drawn up by the new regional bodies, rather than by local authorities, the question of new *powers* was considered settled. It was merely a matter of the extent to which central, rather than regional, government should exploit the powers it already had. The Ministry, the working party commented, already possessed great power, but currently it was only exercised after local authorities had drawn up their plans; it should be used before (Labour Party, 1964b, 27 January).

With regard to the machinery for regional government, decision-making powers were to be in the hands of the centre. The Government would exercise them through relevant Cabinet committees at the national level – at this stage, the designation of the relevant committee was left vague – and through the (more highly integrated) regional offices of the central ministries, supervising the Regional Joint Planning Board, which would be in the hands of regionally based ministry civil servants. However, the National Economic Development Council ('Neddy') through its sectoral divisions ('little Neddies') would have an advisory status at national level, and the new regional development councils would act similarly at the regional level

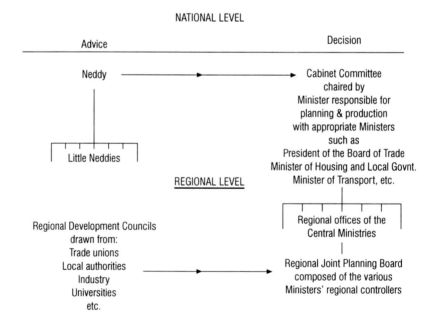

Figure 13.1   Structure of the new regional development machinery, 1964 (source: The Labour Party (1964d)).

(see Figure 13.1). The new councils would have no executive capacity. Public enterprises were to have a high profile (Labour Party, 1964b, 20 January).

The sensitive question of the status of the regional councils was considered, although left unresolved in a rather odd fashion. Two drafts of the working party's report were produced, in February 1964. The first stated that there would be no 'regional parliaments', since these would interfere potentially with national government perspectives and offend devotees of local government:

> The Regional Development Councils will be bodies of great importance and their creation will make it unnecessary to establish 'regional parliaments' at least in the first instance. The arguments against elected bodies of this type are in any case strong. The problems of regional planning will often have to be considered from the national standpoint. Furthermore a regional parliament would not satisfy those who believe in the special virtue of local government.
>
> (Labour Party, 1964c, February)

This statement, however, was omitted from the second draft, published almost immediately afterwards (Labour Party, 1964d), and did not appear in the final report published in March (Labour Party, 1964e). It is difficult to decide whether, in view of the enthusiasm shown by some members of the Labour Government (possibly including some of those on the working party), it was thought to be too controversial to rule out elected bodies at this stage, or whether it was considered wiser not to raise the issue of potentially elected sub-national bodies at all. A member of that committee, Lord Callaghan, in 2003 had no recollection of the decision, although he thought that the working party was probably trying not to offend its Scottish members (letter to author, November 2003). The working party contented itself with determining which groups would be appointed to the councils: representatives from both sides of industry, from local industry and local government, and from universities and hospitals (it was decided that this would be sufficient involvement for these bodies).

By July 1964, George Brown was also involved with the policies. He convened and chaired a Labour Party weekend conference on regional planning (Labour Party, 1964f) composed of specially invited guests. These were drawn from the Shadow Cabinet (for example, Callaghan and Stewart); public enterprise (E. F. Schumacher represented the National Coal Board); industry (Ralph Oppenheimer and David Steele represented the NEDC); trade unions (Foundry Workers, and the Transport and General Workers); local government (T. Dan Smith was a participant); the professions (for example, the Institute of British Architects) and academe (for example, Richard Titmuss from the London School of Economics). The conference considered three papers: on economic policy; on physical planning; and on the machinery for regional planning. The latter argued, like the working group, that regional planning should close the gap between 'physical' and 'industrial' planning – an issue which presaged subsequent disagreements between Brown's DEA and the BoT, as well as between the DEA and the Ministry of Housing and Local Government (MOHLG).

These pre-election activities indicate that when the first of Harold Wilson's Governments was elected in October 1964, its plans for regional development were further advanced than its manifesto implied, and once George Brown was appointed Minister for Economic Affairs events moved very quickly indeed. His DEA included a regional policy division, which involved regional aspects of policies of industry, employment, land use and transport (Clifford, 1997: 192), and therefore Brown was responsible for implementation. Wilson (1971: 97) was impressed with the speed with which Brown and his team acted. By the end of 1964, Brown's Under-Secretary, William Rodgers, had organised a conference on regional planning (albeit accompanied by a degree of bureaucratic obduracy (Rodgers, 1981: 157)).

On 25 February 1965, the eight English regions[1] and Scotland and Wales[2] had provision for both regional economic planning boards and regional economic councils (see Figure 13.2) (Wilson, 1971: 97). Brown wanted them to be called 'Planning Councils' (Brown, 1971: 180), but Crossman objected to this on the grounds that the name implied interfer-

Key:

1. Northern
2. North West
3. Yorkshire and Humberside
4. West Midlands
5. East Midlands
6. East Anglia
7. South West
8. London and South East

Figure 13.2   English planning regions, 1965.

ence with local government's powers over physical planning, so the word 'Economic' was added to the title (Crossman, 1975: 89, diary entry for 7 December 1964). Brown thought that this created 'enough ambiguity ... to go ahead without too much fuss' and hoped that economic and physical planning would eventually become fused (1971: 108), whereas Crossman, presciently, thought that this made the plans 'inadequate and meaningless' (1975: 93, diary entry for 10 December 1964). The councils contained figures representing both sides of industry, local politics and academe, carefully selected by William Rodgers, who recalls (interview with author, November 2003) that he chose them to reflect the younger and less traditional approaches to regional development. They included acquaintances of Rodgers from his Oxford or Fabian days (Rodgers, 2000: 90). The boards consisted entirely of civil servants, and each was chaired by a bureaucrat from the DEA.

The institutions were operational by April 1965, except in the South-East, where indecision about the boundaries delayed progress until April 1966. The role of the bodies was to devise and then monitor a regional plan co-ordinated with the National Plan, which was published in September 1965 after some delays (Wilson, 1971: 185) and which called for 25 per cent growth over a five-year period (Snell-Mendoza, 1996: 139). Initially it was intended that the plans would be drawn up by the boards, in consultation with the councils, which were to be concerned with 'broad strategy' (McCrone, 1969: 230). However, by March 1966 this responsibility had switched to the councils, although, since these had no executive powers, there needed to be no commitment on the part of government to carry out the plans. In the absence of necessary statistics and expertise, regional plans were devised only slowly (McCrone, 1969: 143), to the extent that by 1967 only Scotland had a recognisable plan. Yet by this time, the National Plan itself had effectively collapsed, owing to the 1966–1967 sterling crisis, so was not put into operation. The Labour Party's own analysis, towards the end of the Government's second term, could claim only that the councils had played a valuable part in terms of collecting and disseminating regional statistics, although it argued that the establishment of regional machinery was in itself an important achievement (Labour Party, 1969, 1970b).

It is important to recognise, however, that the development of regional policies under Wilson reflected the somewhat variable structure and approach that he inherited. Whilst the inauguration of boards and councils represented Wilson's 'grand plan' approach to regional development via regional planning, it took place alongside a number of policies, some of which were Labour innovations whilst others owed much to initiatives undertaken by his predecessors. This was particularly the case from 1966 onwards, after Brown left the DEA and was replaced by Michael Stewart. Callaghan's biographer notes that: 'In effect the transition from Brown to Stewart meant that the DEA, heralded with such bravura, was an increasingly enfeebled department' (Morgan, 1997: 247–8). It does seem to have changed the focus of regional policy, for instead of taking a systemic and rational approach, looking towards structural change as a means of delivering the governmental agenda, the recently re-elected Labour Government adopted a more pragmatic and incremental approach. For example, whilst controls on office development had been placed on potential *London* developers in 1964, these were extended throughout the South-East and the Midlands in 1966 (McCrone, 1969: 130). At the same time, the Government persuaded some of its own departments to locate outside central London, and within the Development Areas (Labour Party, 1970a).

In 1966, Labour's Industrial Development Act replaced Development Districts with Development Areas. The intention of this Act was to enable more flexibility for developers by removing the strict employment criteria of the Development Districts, thus enabling developers looking for beneficial terms to select any site within the generously designated Development Areas (McCrone, 1969: 127–8).

From incremental changes to existing (Conservative) policies, the 1966–1970 Labour Government was later forced into a form of crisis management in its regional policy, thereby rendering its policy reactive, rather than developmental. In autumn 1967, the impact of the 1966–1967 economic squeeze led to closures of coal mines, hitting employment prospects in areas already in receipt of assistance under the new Development Areas (McCrone, 1969: 128). In response, the Government designated the affected regions as 'Special Development Areas', giving them access to particularly favourable terms for investment – but not to sufficient public investment or planning to enable them to become growth areas. As McCrone (1969: 128) points out, since the growth potential was not even considered as a criterion for achieving 'Special Development Area' status, this policy development moved even further away from the notion of economic growth, and into the area of managing (and therefore accepting) industrial decline.

Why did Wilsonian regionalism 'fail'?

It would be untrue to state that Labour's policies failed in the sense of not developing a regional approach. A number of useful policies, within the context of a general approach towards regionalisation, were advanced and implemented. Indeed, Woodward (1993: 98) suggests that these count amongst the successes of the Wilson years. However, the policies did fail, in so far as they could be held primarily responsible, to solve the problem of uneven industrial decline and employment distribution. More particularly, in terms of a 'grand design' approach the Wilsonian structural approach falls under the heading of those policies that promise much but deliver little. Regional planning, as McCrone (1969: 142) noted in the late 1960s, 'cannot yet be said to have had a significant effect on the regional problem'.

There are three kinds of explanation for unsatisfactory policy outcomes. First, failure may be explained in terms of factors outside the control of policy-makers. Thus, the Labour Governments' regional policies were unsuccessful because, despite the best efforts of those seeking to implement them, the national economy, and decisions taken about it, ensured that they were foredoomed. Second, policy failure may be said to be due to the shortcomings of those involved, and perhaps due to the greater expertise and experience of those with different priorities. According to this explanation, George Brown was not equal to the task of establishing and defending a newly created ministerial department whose remit subsumed that of several older and more established ministries. Those lower down, from Ministers and national bureaucrats to the regionally based civil servants and chairmen of the regional economic councils, had insufficient time, commitment or ability to be able to deal with the hostility of existing vested interests on the one hand, and with the lack of public interest in their endeavours on the other. A third explanation is structural, ascribing failure to the policy itself, whereby either the policy is poorly conceived or its vision and actions are too limited to achieve success. In this case, it could be argued that Wilsonian regionalism needed to go much further than establishing a new department that would oversee economic regional boards, composed of civil servants who were required only to consult unelected regional councils, and without executive powers, based on arbitrary regions.

Unfortunately for the Labour Governments' regional policy, all three explanations seem to play their part, and the weighting of them seems to be about even in terms of explaining its failure.

It's the economy, stupid![3]

A Marxist determinist would argue, as the above heading suggests, that most policy outcomes reflect the performance of the economy, stressing that this is also outside the control of individual governments, and, by extension, that only a change in the economic system could make much difference. A more pluralist perspective could give similar weight to the impact of economic performance, whilst believing that how the economy performs does depend upon governmental policy decisions. The experiences of the Labour Governments of 1964–1970 actually support both perspectives. On the one hand, it was the sterling crisis of 1966–1967 that ultimately undermined the National Plan, after which the notion of regional planning became irrelevant (Labour Party, 1970b). On the other hand, according to Bill Rodgers (2000: 88), the decision of the Wilson government not to devalue in 1964 condemned the DEA, and with it regional policy, from the start (a view he reiterated in an interview with the author in November 2003):

> [T]here was uncertainty about how [the DEA] would perform. This uncertainty was increased by the decision, reached within twenty-four hours, by Harold Wilson, George Brown and Jim Callaghan in most secret conclave, not to devalue the pound. . . . Although George had

been (and remained) in favour of devaluation, he had not fought for it
with the vigour he brought to other issues. As a result, the Government
embarked upon three wasted years and the DEA had an uphill struggle
from the beginning.

The sterling crisis, amongst other phenomena, led to deflationary cuts, and
restrictions on public and private expenditure worth over £500 million
(Clifford, 1997: 107), which made forward planning and investment problematic. The National Plan's forecasts were nullified, and this meant that
sub-national planning had no solid foundation. At the same time, the
Government's earlier decision not to devalue meant that its ability to
manoeuvre in a crisis was limited, and it was unable to defend its position.

The white heat of technological change may have been insufficient to
withstand the more enduring flame of international capitalism, but this did
not by itself mean that planning itself, at national or regional levels, was
inconceivable. In a different political climate, it could have survived by
taking into account the new realities. In the 1960s, it did not – probably
because other, equally inexorable, forces were at work.

Policy failure, personalities and departments

As has already been noted, the fortunes of Wilsonian regionalism were
closely aligned with the DEA. In keeping with the radical flavour of the
incoming Labour Government in 1964, this was an entirely new department
(other departments were also established at this time, but the DEA was the
most important one). It was designed to liberate the enterprise and fervour
of the new administration, which, it was perceived, were otherwise likely to
be held in check by the Treasury and other more established departments.
The DEA was intended to be an important and influential ministry. As Bill
Rodgers recounts in his memoirs, 'we were to be as pervasive in our influence as the Treasury' (2000: 86).

This ambition ensured that the Treasury would see the DEA as a rival. In
addition, the creation of an entirely new department by definition means
that the responsibilities of existing departments may be challenged, and in
1964 the BoT and the MOHLG, as well as the Treasury, justifiably felt
threatened by the DEA. Their fears, as well as their contempt, were epitomised in the Treasury's nickname for the DEA: the 'Department of Extraordinary Aggression' (Morgan, 1997: 209). The more long-standing
departments, however, had time and experience on their side when it came
to re-establishing their positions.

Callaghan, upon becoming Chancellor, found that Wilson expected the
DEA to assume the more significant role in terms of the economy. Opinions
now differ as to why the DEA was created in the form that it was. There was
certainly an imperative to find a prestigious job for Brown (Wilson's chal-
lenger for leadership of the Labour Party) that would keep him, with his

well-known lack of diplomacy (Morgan, 1997: 247), away from the Foreign Office (although this was to prove only a temporary respite, since Brown achieved his ambitions in August 1966, when he was appointed to the Foreign Office in a Cabinet reshuffle (Morgan, 1997: 247)). On the other hand, Pimlott (cited in Clifford, 1997: 107) suggested that the DEA was created as the embodiment of Labour's belief in long-term indicative planning. There was also a view that the 'dead hand' of the Treasury might be lifted if its responsibilities were lightened. The Treasury's traditional 'economic orthodoxy' (Brown, 1971: 95–6), allied to a not very impressive recent record, could easily be seen as a potential block on an innovative administration unable to realise Wilson's vision of a 'fundamental reconstruction and modernisation of industry' (Wilson, 1971: 24). Callaghan himself thought that the Treasury was in need of reform and revitalisation, although, conveniently, he also agreed with Douglas Jay, who held the possibly self-interested view that 'the right solution was to see that the responsible Department was led, organised and staffed to do its job properly', rather than have it replaced or supplanted (Callaghan, 1987: 164).

Characteristically, Wilson left it to the major players – Brown and Callaghan – to work out the details of the power-share by means of a concordat (Brown, 1971: 99; Callaghan, 1987: 164). After the dust had settled following weeks of talks, the Treasury had lost the responsibility for economic development to the new department. It was still to be mainly responsible for short-term planning, but the DEA would be primarily responsible for long-term planning – although Rodgers (2000: 88) points out that 'primarily' did not mean 'only' or 'exclusively'; Wilson was not too keen on such a distinctive division – as well as prices and incomes policy, regional policy and overseas economic policy (Wilson, 1971: 26). The Treasury was left with powers relating to fiscal and monetary policy in the new government (Shrimsley, 1965: 6). Callaghan, who had followed his Conservative predecessor, Selwyn Lloyd, as the chair of the National Economic Development Council (NEDC), also agreed to cede this position to George Brown (Shrimsley, 1965: 6; Callaghan, 1987: 164).

In his memoirs, Callaghan admits that 'George had the better of the argument' and, with permissible bias, continued: 'but the Concordat represented a verbal truce rather than a true meeting of minds with a genuine and rational division of responsibilities' (1987: 164). Brown, meanwhile, claimed that it was never formally accepted, and that this was the root of future disputes between the two departments (1971: 99). The outcomes reflected the fact that Brown, at least at the start of the 1964–1966 Labour Government, was the more powerful cabinet member (Rodgers, 2000: 88). However, the Treasury was the more powerful department, which, as Brown resignedly noted, 'once the heady first days had gone, and the novelty had worn off', enabled it to reassert itself (1971: 100). The Treasury also had the 'intellectually dominant' Sir William Armstrong, a veteran workaholic, as its Permanent Secretary, whilst the DEA had Sir Eric

Roll, who was apparently both less experienced and less committed (Morgan, 1997: 211). Indeed, Brown (1971: 97) subsequently regretted not having considered inviting Sir William to become his Permanent Secretary at the DEA.

These factors meant that Treasury policies, even without personality clashes between Ministers, were likely to impinge on the success of the DEA's policies. Analyses by the Labour Party during the 1960s confirmed that the Treasury was unhelpful, with Labour's study group on regional planning commenting that it stood in the way of integrating nationalised industries into regional planning (Labour Party, 1967b). For example, because the Treasury demanded a fixed return on capital, it was impossible to implement differential fuel pricing by region, thereby depriving the Government of a powerful regional planning instrument. Besides this, 'crude Treasury thinking' on investment grants denied the Cabinet the opportunity to provide inducements for public enterprises to locate in deprived areas. Rodgers (1966), in a confidential memorandum to the incoming Minister for Economic Affairs, Michael Stewart, stated that the chairmen of the Regional Councils had also met Treasury obstruction: 'Charles Carter (Chairman of the North West Regional Economic Council) has been anxious to set up a planning unit attached to the Council and feels that he has been frustrated, especially by the Treasury.'

The BoT too suffered something of an identity crisis as a result of the formation of the new Ministry. As shown earlier, the BoT had initiated regional policies under the former Conservative Government, but most of these had been annexed by the DEA. Again, however, there was no clear-cut distinction between the responsibilities of the two departments, since the BoT retained distribution of industry policy, which had regional implications. Bill Rodgers, in his memorandum to Michael Stewart, commented that the DEA's policies had a tendency to 'contrast' with the BoT's 'more conventional' approach, although the outcome had been 'an uneasy truce' rather than all-out warfare (Rodgers, 1966). Gwyneth Dunwoody (interview with author, December 2003) thinks that the BoT's approach towards the regions had much more pragmatic success than the ephemeral DEA, which she characterised as being 'dogmatic' in economic terms.

Richard Crossman also had concerns specifically in relation to the regional policies aspect of the DEA's responsibility. The empowerment of a *regional* tier of authority suggested encroachment upon *local* government control. The MOHLG had fought – and won – the battle to keep *physical* planning from the Ministry of Land and Planning (another new ministry) in the early days of the Wilson government (Crossman, 1975: 25, diary entry for 22 October 1964), but the DEA was responsible for *economic* planning. Crossman suspected, with good reason, according to Brown's memoirs (1971: 108), that Brown was keen to take over physical planning as well, and, whilst he was hopeful that a powerful DEA would downgrade the Treasury, he did not want it to be at the expense of his own department (Crossman, 1975: 88, diary entry for 7 December 1964).

Local councillors too were uneasy, for whilst, in theory, they did not stand to lose powers to the new institutions, they nonetheless sensed a threat. As Bill Rodgers (1966) commented, 'Local authorities were bound to be jealous of the new Councils despite their limited advisory role.' There was also a potential for a clash with the Ministry's housing policies, with the MOHLG supporting population dispersal by means of overspill accommodation, and the Development Area policy aiming to concentrate it (Labour Party, 1967c). These potential conflicts thus made for a 'delicate relationship' between the heads of the two ministries (Crossman, 1975: 68, diary entry for 22 November 1964).

These issues need not necessarily have foredoomed Brown's initiatives. However, Brown's personality, which was erratic and volatile, meant that the necessary staying power and the ability to show the 'kind of leadership necessary to face the Treasury on equal terms' was lacking (Crossman, 1975: 161, diary entry for 18 February 1965). Bill Rodgers (interview with author, November 2003) characterised Brown, whom he had backed for the leadership of the Labour Party, as a maverick – a 'man of huge talent – but flawed'. This view accords with other contemporaries' opinion of him. Crossman thought Brown was initially a great success (Crossman, 1975: 116, diary entry for 3 January 1965), but 'fickle' and 'schizophrenic . . . the wear and tear is showing in him after the first four months . . . we shouldn't reckon on our First Secretary being there overlong unless he mends his ways' (Crossman, 1975: 161, diary entry for 18 February 1965). Callaghan also acknowledged that Brown had 'tremendous talents and energy', but similarly found him 'trying' (Callaghan, 1987: 164, 82).

Less significant than Brown's personality in terms of the overall short-term success of the policy, but more significant in terms of the particularised longer-term achievements, were the characteristics and abilities of the sub-national actors. The appointment of staff for the Boards was in the hands of the civil service. Appointees tended to be of inferior quality. In his September 1966 memorandum to Stewart, Rodgers commented that although he had a high opinion of the East Anglia and South-East boards (which were staffed from Whitehall),

> [e]lsewhere, I remain doubtful whether they are universally of a sufficient quality. Two of the Board Chairmen are fully up to their job. Others are competent within limits although they could hardly hope to hold the same rank in Whitehall. The regional representatives of other departments also vary in quality. Some are certainly perfectly good: I know of one who is disastrous.

Besides this, as Mackintosh (1968: 105) noted, there was an inherent problem in determining their relationships with Whitehall and with the regional councils. Since the Boards' staff were appointed by the Ministry, and depended upon it for their progression, it was more likely that they would defer to the Ministry in case of conflict. This weakened their standing with the councils, and simultaneously weakened the councils' effectiveness.

On the other hand, Rodgers was pleased with the people appointed as chairmen and members of the regional councils, and in his memorandum to Stewart, declared that 'We were . . . fortunate in the Chairmen we chose. Dan Smith, in the Northern Region, and Charles Carter, in the North-West, are probably the best two.' Not all were as satisfactory, with Rodgers noting that

> Kenneth Keith and Maurice Hackett, in East Anglia and the South East respectively, have served for much shorter periods. I have never been convinced that Keith had his heart in the job. Hackett is certainly interested; my doubt would be about his capacity for leadership.

The problem was that expertise and enthusiasm on the part of the Councils' members was not met with a commensurate response from the Government. From mid-1966, an internal Labour Party study group on regional planning undertook a survey. As a starting point, it noted that there were 'marked differences between the work of the councils [that were] not wholly due to differences in geography and demography or industry'. It commented that these might be accounted for by the more direct links between central government and Scottish and Welsh regional structures, which was lacking in the relationship that central government had with the English regions. The study group found that councils' effectiveness was inhibited by a lack of information, which it thought resulted from 'a certain amount of jealousy from central and local government departments' (Labour Party, 1966b).

At least the Treasury, the BoT and the MOHLG could not be accused of a lack of concern about regional planning councils, although this concern did not necessarily extend to the members of the councils. For example, the Yorkshire and Humberside council knew nothing about the proposal for a Humberside new town: the MOHLG had not informed them (Labour Party, 1966b; similar examples of the failure to inform and consult may be found in Mackintosh, 1968: 101–9). However, a paper presented to the Labour Party's conference on regional policy in October 1966 offered a rather different perspective, noting that many Ministries, particularly Health and Education, seemed uninterested in them, although Barbara Castle was noted as an exception, for she did develop her department's [Transport] links with the regional councils (Labour Party, 1966a: weekend conference; paper 3). The report of Labour's study group on regional planning policy, a confidential document published in 1970, commented that other departments seemed to be 'unaware of the fact that they have a regional role' (Labour Party, 1970b).

The lack of co-operation and information meant that the enthusiasm of the more able members of the Regional Councils steadily dissipated. Mackintosh (1968: 105) noted that prominent members began to resign or to threaten to resign within a few years of being appointed. Meanwhile, in his aforementioned memorandum to Stewart, Rodgers suggested that it was important to keep the Regional Councils 'busy and interested'. However, with the failure of the National Plan, the shortage of adequate information to enable full economic and social surveys, and the lack of any real executive powers, this would prove to be a tall order.

Structures

Part of the problem with Labour's English regional policy was structural. There were two main aspects concerning the way in which the regional institutions were established that affected the policy outcomes. First, there was the question of power alluded to above, which in turn raised questions about how the policies were to be co-ordinated horizontally – at the centre and within the region itself – and how they were to be co-ordinated vertically – between the centre and the regions. Second, there was the question of the status of the regional institutions and, from this, the relationship they were to have with the wider electorate.

Lacking executive power, the boards and councils had to operate in tandem with a number of governmental agencies, each of which had different regional policies responding to different regional agenda. A Labour Party document entitled *Future Regional Policy* (1967d) recognised that the regional bodies had to operate via the BoT factory programme, and its controls over industrial building and location, office building and investment grants; via a Treasury control over public (including local government) expenditure; via MOHLG's new towns policy; and via the DEA. The policies of these Ministries did not always coincide with individual regional imperatives, nor was it always possible to co-ordinate them amongst government departments. The boards and councils thus found themselves constantly seeking to hit a series of moving targets, thereby making it impossible to develop an internal coherence. The Labour Party (1969) commented that their success depended upon being taken seriously by central government, but implied that this had so far been lacking.

As noted earlier, the question of whether the new regional councils were to be elected bodies with executive powers was considered and effectively discounted at an early stage. If 'regional parliaments' were to move onto the agenda, it would only be when the regional economic councils had proved their worth. However, this placed the councils in a paradoxical situation. Unelected councils do not merit executive powers – a point that was conceded by Labour's Study Group on Regional Planning Policy in its February 1970 report – but councils without executive powers are not worth electing. Similarly, unelected bodies, especially those without executive powers, lack the authority to be effective, so by setting effectiveness as a criterion for achieving electoral status, the government ensured that the regional councils would remain politically impotent.

By the time that Michael Stewart inherited the DEA (in 1966), Bill Rodgers had changed his mind about the benefits of an elected body with executive powers. In his memorandum to Stewart, Rodgers commented that

> There is bound to be pressure in the interim for changes in the machinery designed to give Councils executive power and to introduce an elected element. Reluctantly, I can see no alternative to resisting this, at least until the Royal Commission has reported and the Government has made up its mind.

This comment does not explain his change in attitude, except inasmuch as Rodgers was responding to political realities: it was clear that the re-elected Labour Government was no more enthusiastic about instituting a new range of elected powerful bodies than it had been initially. A Labour Party background paper, *The Future of Regional Planning*, presented to an internal Labour Party conference in October 1966, argued that 'it would be wrong for [Regional Councils] to wield any significant power until they themselves are satisfied with the information and statistics available to them' (Labour Party, 1966a). The question of how they were to achieve such satisfaction without the authority to demand adequate information was not addressed. The same paper noted that the Government's failure to streamline regional boundaries made 'regional government' unfeasible, and that there was no reason to introduce the regional discord that might result where there was no historical demand for it:

> The Government has carefully refrained from giving the impression that the exercise in regional planning is a step towards regional government – and certainly the structure of regional councils and boards amounts to no fundamental steps in that direction. If all government administrative boundaries were made to conform to the planning regions something like regional government would be on its way. No very convincing case has been made out for this so far. Countries as small as Great Britain which have anything like a structure of regional government generally retain it only as an inheritance from the past, when the country was not united.

This observation ignores the point that it was essentially *economic* differences amongst regions that had given rise to the 1964–1970 Labour Governments' policy on developing regional structures in the first place. However, it does pinpoint the problem for regional governance – namely that in England there is only a limited sense of *political* regional distinctiveness.

It was, in part, this lack of identification with regional boundaries that meant that there was no pressure, except from the councils themselves, for the Labour Government to change its stance. Also, as noted above, there is little sign that the new regional infrastructure gained the affection of either local government or the other governmental Ministries. Nor did the councils become household names within their regions. Meetings of the boards and councils were held in private, and their proceedings attracted little publicity (Mather, 2000: 20–1). Again, elections might have fostered greater public interest, but in the circumstances there was no public demand for elections either.

Conclusion

This chapter has argued that there was a balance of factors that meant that the Labour Governments' regional policy was unlikely to make much impact in terms of devolved or economic governance in the United Kingdom. It could, and did, given its inherited infrastructure, make incremental inroads upon regional development, and within these limits it may even be argued that the Labour Governments did rather well. However, what mainly ensured the failure of Labour's regional policy was the domino effect, whereby the sterling crisis led to the downfall of the National Plan, which in turn led to a sidelining of the new regional institutions. Whether this fate was inevitable, though, depended also upon the policies themselves; had the institutions been constructed in such a way as to allow them to find a place in the hearts and minds of those connected with or affected by them, they might have discovered a degree of unassailability. In fact, however, the Labour Governments lacked sufficient ideological clarity to offset the effects of Brown's ministerial shortcomings, coupled with his political opponents' determination to secure their own positions in the interdepartmental warfare arising from the creation of a new, and – of particular importance – apparently or potentially more *powerful* Ministry.

From this perspective, the 1964–1970 Labour Governments present a picture of an administration that tried, but failed, to change the pace and delivery of British governance. Perhaps, as Barberis (1992: 58) suggests, these Governments promised too much, or possibly their supporters expected too much. Regional policy, within this context, epitomises this kind of failure. The 'white heat' of technological revolution was intended to electrify all parts of the United Kingdom's economy by empowering the regions. Instead, its modest decentralisation had, at most, the effect of temporarily illuminating the potential. Subsequently, in the 1970s, the Labour Party did not continue to pursue, with any conviction, the regionalisation of economic governance. National planning, and with it the use of decentralisation as a means of implementation, had fallen from favour. Labour's attempt to politicise devolution by offering elected assemblies to Scotland and Wales during the 1970s was met by enough public apathy to indicate that the public's imagination had not been enthused either (Mather, 2000: 23). Ironically, the Labour Governments' lukewarm regional policies serve to demonstrate the limitations of its centralising agenda, a lesson that subsequent Labour Governments appear to have borne in mind. However, the

Labour Governments of 1964–1970 at least provided an experience of regional policies that would thereafter be available to any government concerned about economic regeneration and devolution, and devolution, rather than national planning, appears to have a long-term shelf-life.

Notes

1 The boundaries chosen bore some resemblance to the Standard Regions, but were amended to enable the London area to be separated from the rest of the South-East and to give the Humberside area a separate regional identity.
2 The Northern Ireland government also adopted a planning approach for 1964–1970 based upon Professor Thomas Wilson's report published in 1965 (McCrone, 1969: 226).
3 This phrase was first advanced as a campaign slogan in 1992 by President Clinton's adviser James Carville, who was emphasising the significance of the economy for political success.

14 From indifference to intervention

Labour and Northern Ireland

Peter Dorey

Introduction

It is widely acknowledged that the 'Irish Question' was generally accorded low saliency by the Labour Party until the emergence of 'the troubles' during the latter half of the 1960s (Morgan, 1984: 200), for although Labour had originally been in favour of 'home rule all round', the issue was certainly not ascribed much importance, given the party's primary goal of securing parliamentary representation in order to advance the material interests of the organised working class. Indeed, as Jones and Keating (1985: 170) noted, the Labour Party's formal, yet unenthusiastic, support for home rule owed much to its concern to remove the Irish Question from the agenda, lest it served to divide the labour movement in England, Scotland and Wales, whilst also hindering Labour's commitment to change through peaceful, constitutional channels.

Ultimately, nationalism was considered a digression from the Labour Party's pursuit of economic and social reform materially to benefit ordinary working people, particularly when the nationalism in question was suffused with a deep and divisive religious dimension. Or as Jones and Keating express it, until the late 1960s, 'Labour ... found it politically expedient to disregard the constitutional and moral issues raised by Northern Ireland', and was 'prepared to ignore a question which only muddied the waters of the socio-economic priorities the party had set itself'. Certainly, after the settlement of 1921, 'Labour's concern for Ireland and Irish problems rapidly and perceptibly declines' (Jones and Keating, 1985: 168, 170), to the extent that 'the Labour Party ... never developed any coherent policy on the Province' (Ponting, 1990: 336).

Labour's stance vis-à-vis Northern Ireland, 1945–1964

By the time that the Labour Party won the 1945 general election, it had accepted the position of Northern Ireland within the United Kingdom and was formally committed to maintaining the constitutional status quo with regard to Ireland. Indeed, the Attlee Government actually strengthened

Northern Ireland's status in the United Kingdom, first by bestowing on the province the right of veto over any change to its border with the Irish Free State, and second, by stating categorically, in May 1949, that 'it is no part of the business of this Government ... to take the initiative to diminish the territory of the United Kingdom' (Herbert Morrison, House of Commons Debates, 4th series, vol. 46, cols 1957–9).

The occasion for this declaration was the passing of the 1949 Ireland Act, of which Section 1 (2) reiterated that 'In no event will Northern Ireland or any part thereof cease to be part of His Majesty's dominions and of the United Kingdom without the consent of the Parliament of Northern Ireland.' Certainly, having been elected in July 1945, the Attlee Government had generally been at pains to avoid alienating or antagonising the Unionist community in Northern Ireland, even though there was significant anxiety at all levels of the Labour Party over the socio-economic deprivation and discrimination endured by the Province's Catholic community (see, for example, PRO CAB 129/2, Memorandum by Addison, 7 September 1945; PRO CAB 21/1838, Pakenham to Attlee, 11 January 1949; PRO PREM 8/1464, Cabinet conclusions, 12 May 1949; House of Commons Debates, 5th series, vol. 438, cols 1467–1530). The Attlee Government's approach, however, was to keep intervention in Northern Irish politics to a minimum.

This partly reflected recognition of the majority viewpoint in Northern Ireland with regard to the Province's status in the United Kingdom, but also derived from acknowledgement of the active support provided by the Province during the Second World War, as compared to the neutral stance adopted by Eire (and the latter's subsequent refusal to join NATO). Indeed, according to Philip Noel-Baker, a Commonwealth Relations Minister, 'without the help of Northern Ireland, Hitler would have won the submarine war and [we] would have been defeated' (quoted in Barton, 1993: 5). In similar vein did Herbert Morrison observe that Northern Ireland's active contribution to the war effort, compared to the formal neutrality of Eire, was 'bound to have a permanently modifying effect on many people's opinions' in Britain (quoted in Donoughue and Jones, 1973: 307–8; PRO CAB 21/13, 12 September 1946).

Although many Labour politicians hoped, and even assumed, that Northern Ireland and Eire would one day be reunited, the Attlee Government's stance was to avoid explicit advocacy of unification, and instead win the trust and co-operation of Northern Ireland's Unionist community. Morrison apparently spoke for many senior Labour politicians when he informed Éamon de Valera, leader of Fianna Fáil and three times Prime Minister of Eire (and, many years later, a President of the Republic of Ireland), in the autumn of 1946, that any raising of the issue of partition would result in 'a storm in Ulster', an 'explosion of no advantage to any of us' (PRO CAB 129/13, Memorandum by Morrison, 16 October 1946).

This remained the formal stance throughout Attlee's premiership, with the Cabinet readily accepting that they 'would be ill-advised to appear to be interesting themselves in this matter, which fell under the jurisdiction of the Northern Ireland government' (PRO CAB 128/14, Cabinet conclusions, 12 May 1949), a point which was reiterated by Herbert Morrison a few months later at Labour's annual conference, when he insisted that

> It would be most unwise for us or anybody else to seek to involve the British Labour Party in internal Irish politics ... we do not want to interfere with the internal politics of Ireland ... it would be inexpedient and unwise for us to be embroiled in all the excitement of internal Irish politics.

Accordingly, the Attlee Government sought to ensure that the 'festering and acknowledged grievance of Northern Ireland remained a relatively minor issue' (Morgan, 1984: 200). This certainly did not mean that Labour politicians were opposed to the principle of Irish (re)unification, but this ultimate desire for a united Ireland was a long-term aspiration, and one which the Party ought not to be seen to be actively pursuing. Instead, there was a vague hope that time would somehow heal the divisions between the North and South, and that an 'inevitability of gradualness' would eventually foster a spirit of co-operation leading to a united Ireland. It was Morrison, again, who articulated what soon became the prevalent, but ambiguous, perspective of the Labour leadership until the 1960s, namely that

> the wisest course on all sides was not to hurry the partition issue. Time was a great healer, and ... it would be a great healer between the three parties concerned, namely Great Britain, Eire, and Northern Ireland, but if the issue was raised in any precipitate manner, first class trouble might ensue ... Northern Ireland would not be a consenting party, at any rate in anything like the early future ... much was to be gained and nothing was to be lost by a policy of developing good co-operative relations ... but not precipitating the issue of partition.
> (PRO CAB 21/13, 12 September 1946)

A week later, Addison, Secretary of State for Dominion Affairs, endorsed Morrison's perspective, claiming that whilst 'it is no doubt right and inevitable that Northern Ireland should enter into some kind of closer relationship, in which event, the Government should not discourage 'the North and South of Ireland in any move that they make with the object of getting together', it was also the case that 'for the present our only safe course is to maintain silence' and 'decline to be drawn on the matter of partition' (PRO CAB 129/13, 18 October 1946). The recommendations of Morrison and Addison were then approved at a Cabinet meeting at the end of October (PRO CAB 128/6, 29 October 1946). Thereafter, the Labour Party hardly considered Northern Ireland for the next twenty years.

During the early 1960s, there was some desultory consideration about the possibility of a future Labour government appointing a Northern Ireland Office in Whitehall, along with a junior Minister for Northern Irish Affairs, thereby providing a conduit for closer co-operation between Westminster and Stormont, particularly with regard to economic and fiscal matters. There was also a suggestion that Northern Ireland might also be allocated an additional three seats at Westminster, but only in return for a reform of electoral law in Northern Ireland to eradicate the gerrymandering deployed to reduce Catholic representation at Stormont (Labour Party Archives, RD.550/November 1963). Overall, though, it was emphasised that the Labour Party had 'always shown the most scrupulous respect for the constitutional position of Northern Ireland' (Labour Party Archives, RD.578/November 1963), and hence when Labour won the 1964 general election there existed a 'blank wall of incomprehension and ignorance about Ulster', to the extent that MPs who 'knew about Saigon [Ho Chi Minh City in Vietnam] or Salisbury [Rhodesia; now Harare in Zimbabwe] seemed to know nothing of Stormont'. Some Labour MPs were also wary of showing any interest in Northern Irish politics because they were 'worried at the delicate balance of religious controversy in their own Constituencies' (Rose, 1981: 179). Certainly Labour's 1964 manifesto had referred to Northern Ireland only under the heading 'plan for the regions', whereby regional planning (under the auspices of the National Plan) was intended to provide Northern Ireland, along with England, Scotland and Wales, with greater 'control over the location of new factories and offices, inducements to firms to move to areas where industry is declining [and] the establishment of new public enterprises', measures which 'will be required ... to build up the declining economies in other parts of the country' (Craig, 1975: 261).

Of course, had the Labour leadership been more cognisant or concerned about the growing grievances of the Catholic community in Northern Ireland, and their allegations about systematic discrimination by the Protestant/Unionist majority, they might have appreciated the risks – in the context of Northern Ireland's unique politics – of pledging greater regional control over economic and industrial affairs; delegating more economic decisions to Northern Ireland might readily have exacerbated extant inequalities and grievances between the two communities in the Province. Yet Labour's manifesto not only casually categorised Northern Ireland as a region akin to Scotland and Wales, but implied that its problems could be ameliorated by regional planning and economic regeneration (albeit in accordance with the National Plan).

Cautiously encouraging social reform in Northern Ireland

However, after the October 1964 election victory (and more particularly after the party's re-election eighteen months later), the Labour Government was obliged rapidly to acquaint itself with the internal politics of Northern

Ireland, as escalating problems in the Province increasingly embroiled an increasingly crisis-stricken Cabinet. Even during the first Labour Government's term of office, there had been a growing awareness, in some quarters of the Labour Party, of systematic discrimination against Catholics by the Protestant/Unionist-dominated regime in Northern Ireland (the Protestants by this time well into their fifth decade of unbroken domination in Stormont, the parliament of the Province), to the extent that Harold Wilson, the Labour Prime Minister, himself began to take a closer interest in Northern Ireland's politics. At the very least, Labour's wafer-thin parliamentary majority in the wake of the 1964 election served to draw attention to the propensity for Northern Ireland's Unionist MPs to vote with the Conservative Opposition in most divisions (Labour Party Archives, Information Paper No. 22, August 1966; Rose, 1981: 179). Meanwhile, Wilson's growing interest in the reported plight of the Catholic community in Northern Ireland was such that in May 1965 he met the Northern Ireland Prime Minister, Captain Terence O'Neill, in London, to discuss O'Neill's progress in pursuing a 'programme of ending discrimination in housing allocations and jobs and generally improving the lot of the [Catholic] minority in Northern Ireland' (Wilson, 1971: 99).

In August of the following year, at a meeting between Wilson, Roy Jenkins – certain aspects of Northern Ireland governance being located within the jurisdiction of the Home Office, but 'filed away under the heading General", with 'no policy briefings, and no boxes whatsoever on how to handle Northern Irish affairs' (Morgan, 1997: 347) – and O'Neill, the latter explained that whilst he had made considerable progress during the previous two or three years (which Wilson readily acknowledged) and fully intended to pursue further reforms in the future, he nonetheless 'gravely underlined the threats to his position and to the reform movement' and was thus convinced that having 'moved so far and so fast by Northern Ireland standards ... there must be a period of consolidation' for at least several months, in order to prevent 'a dangerous and possibly irresistible tide of reaction' by hardline Ulster Unionists who believed that O'Neill was effectively pursuing a policy of appeasement (Wilson, 1971: 270).

O'Neill then resumed his reform programme in Northern Ireland in January 1967, paying particular attention to the laws pertaining to local government elections, and housing, but in so doing he continued to attract increasing hostility from many of his own colleagues at all levels of the Ulster Unionist Party, this reaching unprecedented levels in April when he dismissed one of his fiercest critics, Harry West, the Northern Ireland Agriculture Secretary. Up until this time, Northern Ireland 'rarely, if ever, came before the Cabinet' (Callaghan, 1973: 1–2). Deeply concerned and exasperated by their Government's apparent complicity and complacency concerning Northern Ireland, three Labour MPs undertook a fact-finding visit to Northern Ireland in April 1967 at the invitation of Gerald Fitt (who was subsequently to form the Social Democratic and Labour Party). Their ensuing report cited evidence of routine and widespread discrimination against Catholics in Northern Ireland, and of gerrymandering to enhance Unionist domination in elected political institutions, and therefore called for the appointment of a royal commission to examine the governance of the Province (Rose, 1981: 194–8). This call was ignored by the Cabinet, with Wilson doubtless anxious that establishing such a royal commission would be viewed as provocative by the Unionists in Northern Ireland, whilst making it even more difficult for O'Neill to persevere with his cautious reform programme in the Province.

Ministers face a rapidly deteriorating situation

It was in October 1968, though, that 'the troubles' really erupted, as the (Catholic) Northern Ireland Civil Rights Association (NICRA)[1] defied a ban imposed by the Northern Irish Minister for Home Affairs and persevered with a march through Londonderry. The marchers then found themselves embroiled in a bloody conflict with police, with several of them hospitalised. Unionist apprehension at the emergence of NICRA was compounded by a suspicion, harboured by some senior figures, most notably William Craig (Minister for Home Affairs in the Northern Ireland Government), that the IRA 'played a major part in the civil rights movement' and was fomenting unrest amongst the Catholic community in Northern Ireland (Callaghan, 1973: 11).

The few Labour MPs who had already been developing an interest in Northern Ireland's politics, and in particular the position of the Catholic community in the Province – since the 1964 election, Paul Rose and Stan Orme had 'led a new group of Labour MPs who persistently attempted to prise open Northern Ireland problems' (Callaghan, 1973: 1–2) – now became more vocal in demanding ministerial action. Rose – who had been one of the three Labour MPs who visited the Province in April 1967, and co-authored the report calling for a royal commission – now called upon Wilson to transfer control of the Royal Ulster Constabulary to Westminster (House of Commons Debates, 5th series, vol. 770, col. 1088), a request which the Labour leader firmly rejected.

Instead, the Cabinet's approach was to continue demanding concessions and reforms from the Unionists vis-àvis the Catholic community in Northern Ireland, although Wilson did warn the Unionist leadership that if such reforms were not forthcoming, then the Labour Government might feel obliged 'to apply sanctions such as reconsidering the financial arrangements between the two countries, or even changing their constitutional relationship' (quoted in Callaghan, 1973: 10; see also O'Neill, 1972: 147). Wilson also suggested that 'a fundamental reappraisal of our relations with Northern Ireland' would be necessitated if 'Captain O'Neill were overthrown, or what he was trying to do were overthrown, by extremists' (House of Commons Debates, 5th series, vol. 772, col. 690).

O'Neill did seek to introduce further reforms to ameliorate the discrimination and deprivation endured by Northern Ireland's Catholic community, but these were not enough to pacify an emboldened NICRA. The proposed reforms, were, however, too much for many of O'Neill's own Unionist colleagues, to the extent that in late April 1969 O'Neill was replaced as Unionist leader and Northern Ireland Prime Minister by Major James Chichester-Clark, who had resigned from the Northern Ireland Government's Cabinet a few days earlier, claiming that the time was not yet right for some aspects of O'Neill's reform programme, most notably the introduction of 'one man, one vote' for local government elections in the Province (another opponent of various of O'Neill's reforms, William Craig, had already resigned as Minister for Home Affairs by this time). Not only did hardline Unionists consider O'Neill to have gone too far in appeasing the Catholic minority, but they also resented what they saw as interference in the internal affairs of the Province by Westminster. Or as Arthur and Jeffery express it, a section of the Protestant majority 'objected to what [they] considered to be a policy of appeasement orchestrated by an alien Labour Government and carried out by its O'Neillite puppets' (1988: 8–9).

The resignation of Captain O'Neill was doubly disconcerting for the British Government. First, and most immediately, there was concern that civil unrest might increase, particularly if 'the Paisleyites[2] ... take to the streets in celebration of Captain O'Neill's downfall ... [whereupon] the civil rights elements may counter this'. Second, it was deemed inevitable that O'Neill's successor would be further to the right, which would clearly have serious implications for the Labour Government's attempts at persuading the Unionists to implement reforms intended to ameliorate the condition of the Catholics in Northern Ireland. As Home Secretary, Callaghan suggested that if the British Government continued to intervene as little as possible, and instead encouraged Northern Ireland to solve its own problems, 'this could be a means of influencing the new Government not to veer too sharply to the right' (PRO CAB 130/416, MISC 238(69)3, 'Memorandum by the Home Secretary – Northern Ireland: Resignation of Captain O'Neill', 28 April 1969).

Significantly, in adhering to this largely non-interventionist approach – acknowledged to be merely 'the least unsatisfactory course' (PRO CAB 130/416, MISC 238(69) 2nd meeting, 21 April 1969) – the Labour Government failed to pursue the action alluded to the previous autumn, when Wilson had intimated that the Cabinet would tolerate neither the obstruction of the reform programme nor the ousting of O'Neill as Northern Ireland leader. On both counts, the Unionists successfully called the Labour Government's bluff, and in so doing they also seemed to imply that the toleration which Labour had previously shown towards Unionist domination in the Province, and the Party's unwillingness to challenge partition, counted for nought.

The Cabinet realises how limited are its options

For much of the spring and summer of 1969, it was the restoration of civil order in Northern Ireland which preoccupied the Ministers most closely involved, owing to the seriousness of the clashes and street violence arising from rival marches and demonstrations in the Province. The Northern Ireland Cabinet committee – comprising Harold Wilson, James Callaghan (Home Secretary), Lord Gardiner (Lord Chancellor), Denis Healey (Defence Secretary), Elwyn Jones (Attorney-General), Fred Peart (Lord President of the Council), Roy Jenkins (Chancellor of the Exchequer) and Michael Stewart (Foreign Secretary) – acknowledged that 'it was impossible to evade British responsibility if there was civil war or widespread rioting' in the Province, in which case 'the police . . . or the government can ask for British troops to come', but they naturally hoped that such a scenario could be avoided for as long as possible. However, it was emphasised that if and when British troops were despatched to the Province, they should not be viewed by the Province's Government as a means of helping it to maintain repressive (anti-Catholic) policies (Crossman, 1977: 463, diary entry for 29 April 1969; see also Callaghan, 1973: 15; PRO PREM 13/2842, Healey to Wilson, 14 February 1969; PRO CAB 130/416, MISC 238(69) 4th meeting, 29 April 1969).

Certainly there was a recognition amongst some Ministers that the sending in of British troops – a move which looked increasingly likely by this time – would itself raise two crucial issues for the Government. First, it was clearly recognised – not least by Wilson himself – that the deployment of troops to Northern Ireland to maintain or restore order might be construed by many Catholics as an attempt 'to maintain the Orange faction in power' (PRO CAB 128/44 Part 1, 19th Conclusions, 24 April 1969). Indeed, there was also a recognition that military intervention might well 'exacerbate the situation with which it was designed to deal', in which case, political intervention would itself become 'unavoidable' (PRO PREM 13/2842, MISC 238(69) 1st meeting, 19 February 1969 and MISC 238(69) 2nd meeting, 21 April 1969).

The second issue which would necessarily be raised if troops were despatched to Northern Ireland was whether Westminster would simultaneously need to impose direct rule on the Province. Understandably, many Labour Ministers baulked at such a course of action, particularly when Wilson warned that the 'constitutional consequences might be very grave', and 'once we were involved, it would be difficult to secure our withdrawal' (PRO CAB 128/44 Part 1, CC(69) 19th Conclusions, 24 April 1969), for 'once the English are involved in Ireland, they find it difficult and costly to extricate themselves' (PRO PREM 13/2842, Trend to Wilson, 18 February 1969).

Whilst the Ministers most closely involved in the preparations to send in British troops – namely Wilson himself, James Callaghan, as Home Secretary, and Denis Healey, as Defence Secretary – worked with senior officials to draft a bill which would suspend the Northern Ireland constitution, and thereby impose direct rule from Westminster, they were emphatic that this was merely a contingency measure, one whose activation they clearly hoped to avoid. Yet they were also rapidly becoming aware that other options concerning Northern Ireland were extremely limited. As early as February 1969, for example, a Cabinet committee had ruminated on the possibility that 'independence for Northern Ireland might be a preferable alternative' to military intervention and the imposition of direct rule. Certainly it was acknowledged that 'The threat of declaring Northern Ireland independent might have a profound effect on the population there', and therefore it was suggested that a working party of senior civil servants should consider what forms of independence might be imposed, along with their 'judicial and financial implications' (PRO CAB 130/416, MISC 238(69) 1st meeting, 24 February 1969). However, at this meeting the Home Secretary, James Callaghan, made it clear that this was not a viable option, for quite apart from the constitutional status of Northern Ireland as an integral part of the United Kingdom, independence could hardly be enacted in the context of growing sectarian violence and civil unrest. Independence would not be a viable option 'until peaceful conditions had been firmly established for some time' (in which case, Callaghan might have added, the case for independence would probably have been obviated anyway). Moreover, Callaghan pointed out that an independent Northern Ireland, bereft of economic and financial links with Britain, would not be a viable entity. Furthermore, 'there could be substantial British interests at stake in the fields of defence, agricultural produce, that massive industrial investment that has gone into Ulster, and mineral and other rights in the Irish Sea'. One further argument advanced by Callaghan against contemplating independence for Northern Ireland was that 'the repercussions for Scotland and Wales . . . would be profound' (PRO CAB 130/416, MISC 238(69)1, 'Memorandum by the Home Secretary – Northern Ireland: Political Appreciation', 24 February 1969). Yet given that the Labour Government was ostensibly contemplating forms of devolution for Scotland and Wales during this period, Callaghan's line of reasoning was a source of bemusement to MPs such as Paul Rose, who wryly observed that 'At a time when devolution was being preached from Aberdare to Aberdeen, the opposite was being proposed for the only part of the United Kingdom which has a historical connection and geographical unity with another nation state' (1981: 183).

Callaghan reiterated these arguments against granting independence to Northern Ireland at a Cabinet committee meeting at the end of April, emphasising that independence would be both unacceptable to the main political parties in Northern Ireland, and an abdication of the British Government's constitutional responsibilities and obligations to the Province. Moreover, Callaghan pointed out that if independence were imposed on Northern Ireland, the prospect of civil war would be greatly increased, whereupon 'the Irish public would be likely to intervene' (PRO CAB 130/416, MISC 238(69) 4th meeting, 29 April 1969).

Callaghan had already speculated about applying financial pressures or sanctions on a reactionary or oppressive government at Stormont, and discussed the feasibility of such an option with the Treasury, but readily recognised that, far from facilitating an improvement in Northern Ireland's political situation, it was likely to 'alienate opinion and strengthen resistance'. Furthermore, it was soon recognised that financial sanctions would probably 'hit at the very people we are seeking to help', namely the already economically impoverished and socially disadvantaged Catholic community (PRO PREM 13/2842, Callaghan to Wilson, 17 February 1969).

Also rejected outright was the suggestion from the future SDLP leader, John Hume, that United Nations troops be deployed in Northern Ireland as an alternative to the British army. Hume explained that 'there was now a complete loss of respect for the police force in Londonderry[3] ... indeed, an attitude of hatred towards the police had developed'. Whilst emphasising that he was not an alarmist, Hume warned that 'they were sitting on a time bomb in London, and that if action were not taken soon, it would be too late' (PRO PREM 13/2843, unsigned Memorandum to Wilson, 17 July 1969). However, Ministers deemed any United Nations involvement as highly inappropriate in view of Northern Ireland's constitutional status as part of the United Kingdom, for this meant that the ultimate responsibility for matters of security in the Province lay with the British Government itself.

One other option briefly considered, before being firmly rejected, was that of a Round-Table Conference to be held at Lancaster House, comprising representatives from both the Northern Ireland Government and other groups in the Province, in order to examine the nature of hostilities and grievances in Northern Ireland. Yet it was recognised that determining the membership of such a body would itself be highly problematic: if it were too narrow, then certain viewpoints would inevitably be excluded, raising questions about the representativeness of such a body; yet if its membership were much wider and all-embracing, then the Irish Government in Dublin might claim a right to a seat. This, of course, would be totally unacceptable to the Unionists, to the extent that they might well boycott the Round-Table Conference altogether. Yet not to include Ireland would antagonise Dublin, and 'a hostile Republic is an enemy to progress'. Even beyond the initial question of composition, though, it was acknowledged that 'It is not realistic to suppose that the result [of establishing such an inquiry] would even approach an agreed set of recommendations ... the most that could be hoped for is some lowest common denominators which might point the way towards progress', whereupon 'it would be left to the Northern Ireland Government to take up and give effect to such results as emerged' (PRO CAB 130/416, MISC 238(69) 3rd meeting, 25 April 1969: PRO CAB 130/416, MISC 238(69)3, Memorandum by the Home Secretary – Northern Ireland: Resignation of Captain O'Neill, 28 April 1969).

Meanwhile, in the context of a rapidly deteriorating situation in the Province, Callaghan rejected as 'ill-considered' a suggestion from a deputation of Labour MPs that he should visit Northern Ireland personally, claiming that to do so would embroil him even more deeply in the Province's problems. Also dismissed was the option of banning the forthcoming Apprentice Boys march in Londonderry on 12 August, for whilst the Cabinet was acutely aware of the likelihood of further serious disorder, there was also a recognition that so well established and popular was the event that 'any attempt to ban it would provoke more trouble' (PRO CAB 128/44, CC(69) 39th Conclusions, 30 July 1969).

For their part, Unionist politicians were warning British Ministers that any suspension of the Northern Ireland Parliament would be widely regarded by 'Protestant opinion . . . as a step in the direction of a merger with the Irish Republic'. Chichester-Clark explained that as the present constitutional position was that there would be no change to the Province's status without the approval of the Northern Ireland Parliament, the suspension of Stormont by London would effectively remove this crucial safeguard. (PRO PREM 13/2843, Cubbon to Gregson, 8 August 1969). Chichester-Clark also informed Callaghan directly that 'We were . . . appalled – I do not understate our reaction – to learn that in the event of a deployment of troops, you were proposing . . . to consider a complete, albeit temporary, suspension of the Government of Northern Ireland.' Such a move, Chichester-Clark emphasised, 'would be wholly unacceptable to the great majority of Ulster people . . . I must make it clear to you that the people of Northern Ireland are as determined to have their own Government as the people of the South were from 1919 on', before warning ominously that 'You should consider the history of how Dublin Castle tried to cope with Sinn Fein at that time.' Moreover, Chichester-Clark queried why there should be any constitutional or political need to suspend the Northern Ireland Government as the *quid pro quo* for deploying British troops in the Province to restore civil order. As Northern Ireland itself was an integral part of the United Kingdom, it 'never for a moment occurred to us that its role in relation to Northern Ireland differed in any way from that role in relation to Great Britain', for ultimately, 'the British Army is our Army too'. Accordingly, the Northern Ireland Cabinet was convinced that the despatch of troops to the Province need not be accompanied by a suspension of its constitution and the imposition of direct rule, although clearly matters pertaining to security, and law and order, would ultimately be subject to Westminster accountability, albeit 'in the context of the normal co-operation between the two Governments' (PRO PREM 13/2843, Chichester-Clark to Callaghan, 6 August 1969).

At a meeeting between Callaghan and Chichester-Clark two days later, the latter strongly reiterated that 'moderate Protestant opinion' would view with the deepest concern any significant amendment of the 1920 Government of Ireland Act, especially the suspension of the Northern Ireland

Parliament. Indeed, the Northern Ireland Prime Minister claimed because that Stormont was viewed as a bulwark against Irish reunification, its suspension or abolition would be viewed by Unionists as 'a step in the direction of a merger with the Irish Republic', and 'the Protestant reaction would be widespread, and might be very violent indeed'.

In reply, Callaghan pointed out that whilst suspension of the Northern Ireland constitution was not an objective of the Cabinet, the British people would certainly expect that any deployment of troops, intended to restore order to the Province, would be accompanied by some political control over the role of the army, along with related policies. In such a situation, the Home Secretary argued, intervention from Westminster would become inevitable, with the Northern Ireland Government acting effectively as agents over a very wide field. Chichester-Clark did not demur too much from this characterisation of possible developments, although his apparently sanguine stance may well have reflected Callaghan's own acknowledgement that the British Government was unlikely to seek a suspension of Stormont, owing to 'the likely Protestant reaction' (PRO PREM 13/2843, Cubbon to Gregson, 8 August 1969). Callaghan subsequently recalled that

> It was unthinkable in these circumstances that either the British Government or Parliament would have supported a proposal to hand over British troops to prop up a regime which had lost so much authority, unless reforms were made ... use of British troops would make political intervention inevitable.
>
> (1973: 24, 27)

British troops are despatched to Northern Ireland to restore order

Such was the violence and disorder which subsequently accompanied the Apprentice Boys march that when Callaghan held an emergency meeting with Wilson in Cornwall (the Prime Minister having been on holiday in the Isles of Scilly) on 14 August, the Home Secretary warned that a formal request by the Northern Ireland Government for the deployment of additional[4] British troops in Northern Ireland was now inevitable, and advised Wilson that when the request was received, they should accede to it, albeit emphasising that British troops were being deployed in the Province solely to assist in the restoration of law and order, whereupon they would then be withdrawn 'as soon as possible' (PRO PREM 13/2844, 'Note of a meeting' between Wilson and Callaghan, 14 August 1969). Or, as Barbara Castle recorded a few days later: 'We had agreed to put troops in to *restore* law and order, but not to keep them there indefinitely to *maintain* it', and certainly not 'maintain a reactionary Government' (1984: 699–700, diary entry for 19 August 1969). If – and only if – it proved impossible to effect their quick withdrawal, then the British Government would need – in spite of

Chichester-Clark's clear stance and dire warnings on the matter – to consider the subsequent constitutional and political arrangements between Westminster and Northern Ireland. In this discussion, whilst acknowledging that the deployment of troops was by now inevitable and unavoidable, Wilson insisted on the need to avoid giving any impression that the British army was acting 'in the interests of one section of the community against those of another' (PRO PREM 13/2844, 'Note of a meeting' between Wilson and Callaghan, 14 August 1969). Moreover, Wilson and Callaghan clung to the hope that 'the mere presence of British troops would be enough to restrain both sides without the soldiers having to fire a single shot, and would also be sufficient to end the mob rule that existed in parts of the Province' (Callaghan, 1973: 45).

The expected formal request for British troops to be deployed in Londonderry (and subsequently in Belfast) was tendered in the late afternoon of 14 August, with Callaghan – as previously agreed in his discussion with Wilson – granting this request whilst flying back to London from the Isles of Scilly. As Callaghan subsequently acknowledged, at this stage the Labour Government still lacked an overall strategy for dealing with Northern Ireland, beyond that of crisis management and damage limitation: 'we were living from hand to mouth, and making policy as we needed to' (Callaghan, 1973: 70).

Subsequently, on 19 August 1969, following disorder and violence in Derry and Belfast, the small group of British Ministers dealing with the Northern Ireland situation met – at 10 Downing Street – their counterparts from the Northern Irish Government to evaluate the situation. Chichester-Clark expressed his concern that whilst there had been a significant and swift restoration of law and order, the immediate withdrawal of British troops was likely to be followed by renewed violence in the two cities. He also acknowledged, however, that, due to 'a campaign of vilification', the police forces of the Province had become 'discredited among some sections of the community', thus seriously compounding the problem of restoring order to the streets of Belfast and Londonderry. His solution was to appoint the General Officer Commanding in Northern Ireland, General Sir Ian Freedland, to take charge of the RUC with regard to security matters in the Province. In response, Wilson insisted that this could only be a short-term measure, lest the hostility being directed towards the RUC was then turned against the British army itself, the latter 'at present generally accepted throughout Northern Ireland [as] impartial and . . . in no way involved in sectarian or other disputes', and thus enjoying 'the confidence of all sections of the community'.

The Home Secretary, however, insisted that before taking any decision about control of the RUC, the role of the 'B Specials'[5] had also to be considered, for they were 'the subject of grave concern throughout the remainder of the United Kingdom' (although the Northern Ireland Home Affairs Minister retorted that they had been deployed for many years as a peacekeeping force 'without complaint'). Healey also expressed concern about the alleged activities of the B Specials, claiming that, according to the General Officer Commanding, they had used excessive force, and thereby 'aggravated the problems faced by the British forces in restoring law and order'.

Callaghan and Healey encountered some initial resistance from the Northern Ireland Ministers when they suggested that the B Specials should be disarmed, with Chichester-Clark claiming that obliging them to hand in their weapons might actually yield a further breakdown in law and order in the Province because some sections of the community would feel that their safety had been compromised, whilst others would feel less need to refrain from violence if they knew that the B Specials were unarmed (PRO PREM 13/2844, 'Note of a Meeting' between senior British and Northern Irish Ministers and officials, 19 August 1969).

Meanwhile, just to make absolutely sure that there were no doubts or misapprehensions, Wilson issue his own 'Downing Street Declaration, on 19 August 1969, which asserted that

> The United Kingdom Government reaffirms that nothing which has happened in recent weeks in Northern Ireland derogates from the clear pledges made by successive United Kingdom Governments that Northern Ireland should not cease to be a part of the United Kingdom without the consent of the people of Northern Ireland or from the provision in Section I of the Ireland Act, 1949, that in no event will Northern Ireland or any part thereof cease to be part of the United Kingdom without the consent of the Parliament of Northern Ireland. The border is not an issue.
>
> (Cmnd 4154)

Yet having committed British troops to restore civil order to the streets of Northern Ireland, whilst reaffirming the constitutional status of Northern Ireland, the Cabinet found its policy options severely limited. As we have already noted, many Labour politicians had remained in blissful ignorance of the complexities and sectarian character of Northern Ireland's politics until the emergence of 'the troubles' during the later part of the 1960s. For example, barely three months before the additional troops had been sent to Belfast and Londonderry, Crossman was emphasising, in the Cabinet, 'that we need some political intelligence ... if we have to know about Russia and every other country in the world, we should at least spend some money finding out something about Northern Ireland'. For example, Crossman asked

> whether we had any reliable information on the work of the Royal Ulster Constabulary (RUC). Did we have any objective view as to how far they were oppressive to the Catholics? Of course, I gather they are

oppressive, but we haven't got any reliable picture of the degree of their oppression.

Crossman's stance was endorsed by the Defence Secretary, Denis Healey, who suggested that 'we shall be as blind men leading the blind if we have to go in there knowing nothing about the place' (Crossman, 1977: 478–9, diary entry for 7 May 1969; see also Callaghan, 1973: 22).

With both independence and economic sanctions ruled out (the latter likely to prove particularly damaging to the already economically disadvantaged and socially deprived Catholic community), and Wilson reaffirming – via the Downing Street Declaration – that Northern Ireland's constitutional status as a full part of the United Kingdom would remain unchanged until or unless the people and/or Parliament of the Province expressly stated a wish for change, the Cabinet soon realised that, politically, its only option was to continue seeking to persuade the Protestant majority to end its discrimination against the Catholic minority. Yet this was itself highly problematic, for it was precisely this approach which had initially been pursued by Wilson and O'Neill, and had ultimately led to the latter's replacement by Chichester-Clark, because of resistance from more hardline Unionists. Or as Callaghan clearly recognised:

> We must restore confidence among the Roman Catholic minority without inflaming the Protestants beyond endurance . . . it must be our object to persuade Major Chichester-Clark of the need for overt and urgent measures to secure the confidence of the minority in Northern Ireland.
>
> (PRO PREM 13/2844, 'Memorandum by Home Secretary: Northern Ireland', 19 August 1969)

Yet in the zero-sum politics of the Province, it is difficult to see how any meaningful measures to 'restore confidence among the Roman Catholic minority' could be attained without 'inflaming the Protestants beyond endurance'.

Moreover, the initial expectations of Labour Ministers that the troops would soon be withdrawn were soon confounded, for as Callaghan reported to the Cabinet, a few days after returning from a visit to Northern Ireland at the end of August, 'the prospects were very bleak, and he saw no hope of a solution . . . the only solutions would take years, if they could ever work at all' (Crossman, 1977: 636, diary entry for 11 September 1969).

To compound ministerial despondency, it became increasingly apparent that having initially 'been generally welcomed, in particular by the Catholics', according to Callaghan (PRO CAB 128/46, CC(69) 41st Conclusions, 19 August 1969) – the longer British troops remained in Northern Ireland, the more they were perceived by the Catholic community to be defending Unionist domination in the Province, rather than acting purely as an impartial peacekeeping force. In fact, virtually from the outset Wilson had foreseen the possibility of 'public hostility being diverted from the police to the British troops' after the initial 'honeymoon period' (PREM 13/2844, 'Notes of a meeting at 10 Downing Street, between British and Northern Irish Ministers and officials', 19 August 1969). With equal fore-sight, Crossman had feared 'that once the Catholics and Protestants get used to our presence, they will hate us more than they hate each other' (1977: 620, diary entry for 17 August 1969). Such pessimistic prescience was proven during the spring of 1970, by which time hardline Nationalists, via a resurgent IRA, were attacking the British army itself, claiming that it was, in effect, an occupying force maintaining the subjugation of the Catholic community. This was certainly the perspective promoted by the IRA, which initially claimed that only it – rather than the RUC and the British army – could 'protect' Catholic communities in Northern Ireland. Yet in resorting to its own campaign of bombings and shootings, the IRA served to ensure that the British Government would be unable to withdraw the army (however much it wished to do so), partly because the ensuing bloodshed would probably be even greater if troops were withdrawn in such a context, and partly because to do so would be widely viewed as a shameful surrender to terrorism by Ministers in London.

Yet the Defence Secretary, Denis Healey, in an earlier (mid-September 1969) visit to Northern Ireland, had been warned by Brian Faulkner (Minis-ter of Development in Northern Ireland) that 'unless the troops quickly restored law and order" (meaning the authority of Stormont) in the Catholic strongholds, if necessary by force, there would be a serious backlash from the Protestant majority' (PRO PREM 13.1845, Healey to Wilson, 22 September 1969). The Labour Government was discovering – as any other British Government would have done – that in the complex, conflictual and centrifugal politics of Northern Ireland, what was viewed as 'neutral' or 'impartial' in London was invariably viewed rather differently in the Province.

Conclusion

As Ponting observes, given that the Labour Government 'had never expected to be caught up in the tangled sectarian politics of Ulster', it is 'difficult to see how any government could have acted differently'. Certainly, 'in August 1969 it had little alternative but to use troops, given the scale of disinteg-ration in the Province' (Ponting 1990: 341). Yet having so committed British troops, albeit on what was intended to be a short-term basis, the Labour Party was now obliged to give more consideration to the 'tangled sectarian politics' of Northern Ireland. However, its room for manoeuvre and original thinking was extremely limited, for with Irish unification evidently a distant or long-term goal, and one which would be dependent on the consent of the Province itself, the Labour Government had few alternative options. Those that had been variously proposed – most notably unilaterally withdrawing from Northern Ireland and thereby imposing independence on the Province; imposing financial sanctions; establishing a Round-Table Conference; inviting the United Nations to provide neutral peacekeeping troops, instead of the British army – were all swiftly rejected as inappropriate, impracticable or undesirable. Consequently, the Labour Government was left with the short-term objective of eliminating the violence, whilst simultaneously urging the Unionists to implement further social reform in order to improve the civil rights of the Catholic community.

Yet whilst these aims 'were understandable', they were also, according to Joe Haines (appointed as Harold Wilson's Press Secretary in January 1969), 'incompatible, for it was the burgeoning civil rights movement which provoked the Protestant violence' (1977: 113). Nonetheless, these were precisely the aims which the Wilson Government did pursue from August 1969 until the election in June 1970, when its manifesto reiterated that all citizens in Northern Ireland were 'entitled to the same equality of treatment and freedom from discrimination as obtains in the rest of the United Kingdom, irrespective of political views or religion' (Labour Party, 1970a: 18). The crucial question which confronted the Labour Party (and subsequently the Conservatives too), though, was how this objective could properly realised, given the unique character and history of Northern Irish politics.

Notes

1 The Northern Ireland Civil Rights Association (NICRA) had been formed in 1967 'and had mobilised chiefly around the issues of reforming the restricted local government franchise, gerrymandered local government electoral boundaries, the inequitable allocation of public-sector housing and discrimination in the provision of public sector employment' (Cunningham, 2001: 17; see also Labour Party Archives, home policy committee, 'Northern Ireland', Re.398/January 1969).

2 A reference to the supporters of the Reverend Ian Paisley, who was rapidly establishing himself as a vehement and vocal opponent of O'Neill's reform programme and the 'appeasement' of the Catholic minority. Paisley subsequently, in 1971, left the Unionist Party – believing it had gone too far in offering concessions to the Catholic community – to form (and lead) the Democratic Unionist Party (DUP), which represented a strand of 'diehard' Unionism for which 'virtually any concessions to the civil rights lobby were seen as a recognition of the legitimacy of Catholicism and the resurgence of nationalist irredentism' (Cunningham, 2001: 18). Paisley was still leader of the DUP thirty-four years later, in 2005.

3 Policing in Northern Ireland was undertaken by the Royal Ulster Constabulary (RUC), the overwhelming majority of whose officers were Protestants. For that reason, a growing number of Catholics became convinced that the RUC was either unable or unwilling to defend them from attacks by Protestant extremists. Indeed, it was in the context of such loss of confidence that the IRA re-emerged, initially persuading some Catholics that only it – rather than the official forces of law and order – could be relied upon to provide protection for Catholic communities in Northern Ireland. Yet this, in turn, merely served to strengthen

the suspicions of those Protestants who viewed the Catholics as a politically disloyal and untrustworthy minority, whose aspirations and attitudes were tantamount to treachery and treason against Northern Ireland's constitutional status and political system. Here, as in many other aspects of Northern Ireland's volatile politics, the actions of one section of the community served to confirm the suspicions and thus harden the attitudes of their counterparts, thereby compounding the trend towards political polarisation in the Province.

4 Various battalions of British troops were already routinely present in Northern Ireland prior to, and irrespective of, the emergence of 'the troubles' (just as various parts of England had permanent army bases). In April 1969, however, in the context of increasing sectarian violence, additional British troops were deployed in Northern Ireland, with particular responsibility for protecting 'vital installations', most notably electricity and water supplies.

5 The B Specials were the Ulster Special Constabulary, a body of 8,000 police volunteers: 'In private, its members were farmers and shopkeepers who had volunteered for special constabulary duties ... and were a wholly Protestant force ... seen by the Protestants as their shield against the IRA' (Callaghan, 1973: 18–19).

15 Education, education, education

Peter Dorey

Introduction

There were three particular developments in the sphere of education under the 1964–1970 Labour Governments, namely the promotion of comprehensive schools, the expansion of higher education in general, and the creation of the Open University in particular. However, the first two were policies inherited, rather than initiated, by Harold Wilson's 1964–1970 Labour Governments, so that they were 'building on existing developments and following trends that were already apparent ... very much swimming with the tide' (Ponting, 1990: 130). Another initiative, to raise the school leaving age to 16, was postponed, and was not implemented until 1973. Each of these developments will be discussed below, but first it is important to indicate why education was such an important sphere of policy for Labour Governments. Two main reasons can be identified, the first of which is economic whilst the second is social, although attempts were made to meld them together (as 'New Labour' and the Blair Governments sought to do thirty-five years or so later).

Education provision in Britain has invariably been closely linked with the requirements of the wider economy, a linkage known by many social theorists and educational sociologists as the 'correspondence theory'. This means that education provision has evolved and changed in tandem with the development of industrialisation and the requirements – material and ideological or normative – of the capitalist economy at different historical junctures or social epochs (see, for example, Althusser, 1973; Bernstein, 1977; Bourdieu, 1974; Bourdieu and Passeron, 1977; Bowles and Gintis, 1976; Durkheim, 1947, 1957; Illich, 1973; Miliband, 1973, 1977; Willis, 1978).

By the 1960s, it was becoming more widely recognised that economic trends and associated changes in the character of the labour market were making it increasingly important that British workers acquire new or improved skills and qualifications, in order to ensure the competitiveness of the British economy. As Harold Wilson argued, in a series of keynote speeches in early 1964, 'An industrial economy which is dedicated to rapid change will require flexible and generous arrangements for training adult workers who become redundant through the progress of technology.' At present, Wilson maintained, Britain was 'not training enough skilled workers', although he also emphasised that 'it is just as important to train our great army of technicians, craftsmen', as well as 'our brilliant scientists' (1964a: 35; see also Wilson, 1964b: 14–28).

The trend thus appeared to be towards a much more technocratic and scientific society, although administrative and managerial occupations were also expanding rapidly. It is in this context, perhaps, that Wilson's 1963 peroration about creating a new Britain transformed 'in the white heat of the technological revolution' assumed greatest resonance. If Britain was becoming a more technocratic and science-orientated society, then it was essential for the education system to be modified to provide a suitably qualified workforce. Or as Wilson himself explained to delegates at Labour's 1963 annual conference, 'to train the scientists we are going to need will mean a revolution in our attitude to education, not only higher education, but at every level' (1964b: 136).

Indeed, some commentators suggested that Britain's relative economic decline – which was becoming more apparent and thus more widely acknowledged during the early 1960s – was at least partly attributable to the education system. In a Fabian Society tract, for example, John Vaizey (1962: 15–17) alleged that a significant factor contributing to Britain's economic stagnation was a shortage of skilled labour on the one hand, and the monopoly of elite positions subsequently occupied by those who had received a public school education. The clear implication was that education reform was a prerequisite of economic regeneration.

The second reason why education policy assumed such significance for the 1964–1970 Labour Governments was social, and reflected the critique of continued socio-economic inequalities articulated by Crosland in *The Future of Socialism* (1956). Crosland had argued that many of the structural inequalities endemic in capitalism, and which the Labour Party was formed to ameliorate, had indeed been tempered, if not eradicated altogether, by the policies implemented by Attlee's 1945–1951 Labour Governments (and which were broadly maintained by the 1951–1955 Conservative Government), most notably full employment, parity of power between capital and (organised) labour via collective bargaining and trade unionism, progressive – and redistributive – taxation, and the welfare state, with services such as education and health provided free at the point of delivery irrespective of a person's income or social background.

Crosland was keenly aware that inequalities continued to exist, some of which he accepted were unavoidable or relatively unproblematic. His mode of socialism did not entail the pursuit of complete equality, least of all in terms of wealth: 'I am sure that a definite limit exists to the degree of equality which is desirable. We do not want complete equality of incomes, since extra responsibility and exceptional talent require and deserve a differential reward' (Crosland, 1956: 149). Other forms of inequality, however, Crosland deemed unwarranted and eradicable, most notably those which denied equality of opportunity and social mobility to members of the working class.

Crosland readily acknowledged that such inequalities could not be ameliorated by further expansion of public ownership, or by increasing further the levels of income tax imposed on the better-off. In both of these areas, government had gone about as far as it could: to go further would probably prove counter-productive, such as squeezing out the wealth-creating private sector (which remained dominant overall, in spite of Labour's nationalisation programme in the latter half of the 1940s) and deterring the investment on which so many jobs – and, ultimately, the maintenance of full employment – depended. Consequently, Crosland envisaged that further reducing social inequalities, and facilitating greater equality of opportunity and social mobility, was to be achieved mainly through the education system. For Crosland, 'Education, not nationalisation, was to be the main engine in the creation of a more just society' (1982: 69), but this made it absolutely vital that 'the Labour Party gives education a much higher priority than in the past, and comes to see it as of far greater significance to socialism than the nationalisation of meat-procuring or even chemicals' (1956: 207).

One of the main aspects of Labour's education policy during the 1960s, and one that Crosland himself became indelibly associated with, was that of expanding comprehensive schooling.

Expansion of comprehensive schools

By the early 1960s, commitment to the 'comprehensivisation' of British secondary education was a firm Labour Party commitment, with Wilson insisting, in his speech to Labour's 1963 annual conference, that

> The school system in Britain remains the most divisive, unjust and wasteful of all aspects of social equality. . . . As Socialists, Democrats, we oppose this system of educational apartheid, because we believe in equality of opportunity. But that is not all. We simply cannot as a nation afford to neglect the educational development of a single boy or girl. We cannot afford to cut off three-quarters or more of our children from virtually any chance of higher education.
>
> (Labour Party, 1964b: 19)

Crosland's appointment as Secretary of State for Education and Science, in January 1965, therefore provided him with a direct opportunity to tackle the educational inequalities which both he and Wilson found so offensive. Crosland did not initiate the policy to promote comprehensive schools – comprehensive schools had been slowly expanding under the Conservatives during the 1950s, from thirteen providing for 12,000 pupils in 1954 to 175 attended by a total of 179,000 pupils in 1963, although there still remained nearly 1,300 grammar schools in 1963, which were attended by a total of

722,000 pupils (for an account of the evolution of comprehensive schools during this time, see Fenwick, 1976: Chapters 4 and 5, and p. 148 for statistics) – but he certainly drove the policy forward in the mid-1960s, and, for many observers, he became personally associated with it, given the extent to which such schools seemed to correspond to his political philosophy and critique of social inequality in post-war Britain.

Yet what was perhaps also rather surprising, given his notorious pledge 'to destroy every fucking grammar school in England' (quoted in Crosland, 1982: 148), was Crosland's relative restraint and pragmatism in pursuing the expansion of comprehensive schools. This partly derived from the fact that, just a week prior to Crosland replacing Michael Stewart at the Department of Education and Science,[1] the Cabinet had decided against compulsion in seeking to ensure that local education authorities established comprehensive schools. Michael Stewart had recommended that local education authorities should be 'required' to submit plans for comprehensive reorganisation, fearing that whilst many would submit such plans willingly, others would not. Such a requirement, to be stipulated in the form of a circular issued to local education authorities, would then be enshrined in a bill to be introduced in the next parliamentary session. Stewart argued that legislation was necessary 'both to prevent absolute refusal by some local authorities, and to satisfy all authorities that this is firmly and permanently national policy'. Stewart readily acknowledged, though, that 'there will be controversy about the principle of imposition of a central Government policy on local authorities. This may be a contentious issue' (PRO CAB 129/120, Part 1, C(65)4, 'Comprehensive Secondary Education', 14 January 1965).

It certainly was, to the extent that most Cabinet members were deeply sceptical about the wisdom of the degree of compulsion which Stewart was proposing. Indeed, it was felt that reference to compulsion and legislation should be avoided as far as practicably possible, with the public emphasis being on the Labour Government's confidence that the vast majority of local education authorities would respond positively and constructively, and on a voluntary basis, to a ministerial request to submit their plans for reorganising their secondary schools on comprehensive lines. Given that there was already a 'growing acceptance of the comprehensive principle', the Cabinet was convinced that legislation should only be introduced as a last resort, if and when it became evident that the existing approach was not working (PRO CAB 128/39, Part 1, C(65) 2nd Conclusions, 19 January 1965).

Crosland shared the view of many of his ministerial colleagues that such a programme of educational reform would probably be more successful if achieved on a voluntary basis, rather imposed by government diktat. Indeed, for this reason, and 'strongly influenced by my meetings with the Association of Education Committees' (quoted in Kogan, 1971: 189), Crosland decided to 'request', rather than 'require', local authorities to submit plans for establishing comprehensive schools, this request expressed in 'Circular

10/65', issued in July 1965 (see below). The prevailing ministerial perspect-ive appeared to be that 'if we approach them reasonably, I think we shall get a reasonable answer' (House of Commons Debates, 5th series, 12 November 1964).

Crosland's confidence that a voluntary approach would elicit a more con-structive response than compulsion was underpinned by his recognition that as 'we inherit an elaborate non-comprehensive school structure, which cannot be forcibly dismantled ... the Labour Party could never impose a comprehensive system *rapidly* on the entire country' (1956: 198; emphasis added). Instead, he proposed that 'a Labour Government should explicitly state a preference for the comprehensive principle, and should actively encourage local authorities – and such advice carries great weight – to be more audacious in experimenting with comprehensive schools' (1956: 205). As such, Crosland fully acknowledged that the transition to comprehensive schooling would take 'considerable time', suggesting (in 1965) that 'in five years, such progress could be made that the comprehensive system would be accepted as the normal pattern, towards which all local authorities were working, though necessarily at different speeds' (*The Times*, 8 February 1965). In this respect, he was echoing the perspective of his recent predeces-sor at the Department of Education, for Michael Stewart had acknowledged that it 'would be neither possible nor desirable to impose one method or one time-table on all authorities' (PRO CAB 129/120, Part 1, C(65)4, 'Compre-hensive Secondary Education', 14 January 1965).

This reflected the various sources of opposition which the Labour Govern-ments' policy of comprehensivisation engendered during the latter half of the 1960s, most notably from various (usually Conservative-controlled) local authorities, and sundry groups of parents whose children were attending existing grammar or grant-maintained schools. There was also scepticism, if not outright hostility, from some teachers' unions and associations, although this often derived from resentment over an alleged lack of consultation with them about the reorganisation of secondary education, rather than opposi-tion to comprehensivisation per se (Fenwick, 1976: 131). However, Crosland maintained that, whilst he and the Labour Party were fully com-mitted to pursuit of 'comprehensivisation', he had 'long meetings with all the main bodies', so that 'the consultation was real and genuine ... took months and months.' Indeed, fully cognisant that an Education Secretary 'can't, in this country, railroad through policies regardless of the views of local authorities and teachers', Crosland claimed that he 'was greatly influ-enced by what the National Union of Teachers said in my consultations with them on the draft of *Circular 10/65* about the need for local authorities gen-uinely to consult the teachers' (quoted in Kogan, 1971: 175, 189).

The first Labour Government's desire to pursue comprehensivisation in a relatively flexible and non-confrontational manner – allegations about lack of consultation notwithstanding – was not only reflected in the timescale and multi-speed transition envisaged, but also in the fact that Circular

10/65 provided local authorities with no fewer than six models to choose from in determining how to reorganise the secondary schools within their jurisdiction, although it was made clear that the optimum model would be fully comprehensive schools for pupils from the age of eleven upwards.

Michael Stewart, during his three-month tenure as Secretary of State for Education following Labour's return to office in October 1964, adumbrated six discrete reasons for pursuing the expansion of comprehensive education (PRO CAB 129/120, Part 1, C(65)4, 'Comprehensive Secondary Education', 14 January 1965):

- The 'fallibility of all the methods used in the attempt to assess the potential capacities of children when they are $10\frac{1}{2}$ years old.'
- The 'wide local variations in the standard of attainment' which children of this age needed to achieve in order to secure admission to a grammar school.
- The uneven pace of development of secondary schools, to the extent that some could no longer provide 'the more academic courses of study for which many of their pupils are suited'.
- The existing 'separatist system tends to divide society'.
- In many areas, primary schools 'are tempted to concentrate on getting pupils through the 11-plus tests', to the detriment or partial neglect of apparently less academically gifted pupils.
- The preparation for, or actual implementation of, comprehensive reorganisation by local education authorities in recent years had been patchy or limited (in terms of the actual number or type of schools involved in certain areas), and some of the schemes have been 'ill-advised'. It was therefore 'time to give a national lead, indicating the principles to be observed, and the kind of problems likely to arise in different areas when reorganisation is planned'.

Following the Labour Government's re-election in 1966, there was increasing pressure, at all levels within the party, for legislation to hasten or strengthen the process of comprehensivisation in the face of continued recalcitrance from opponents of comprehensive schools. Various parents' groups pursued legal action through the courts – in some cases, taking their grievances as far as the High Court and the Court of Appeal – usually alleging that either local (education) authorities or the Department of Education had acted *ultra vires*, or were breaching particular aspects of the 1944 Education Act, whose provisions continued to provide the template for the bulk of secondary schooling in Britain. One such case concerned a well-organised campaign by parents in Enfield, bolstered by an appeal fund which raised £4,000, who instructed lawyers to serve a High Court writ on Enfield Borough Council to prevent the reorganisation of local schools on comprehensive lines. When their case was rejected by the High Court, the parents' group took their case to the Court of Appeal, which invoked a temporary injunction on the grounds that Enfield council had not fully complied with certain procedural requirements stipulated in the 1944 Education Act (Fenwick, 1976: 142; Crossman, 1976: 479, n. 2).

By this time, Ministers themselves were coming to the conclusion that legislation would be required to maintain the momentum of comprehensivisation and overcome what appeared to be 'guerrilla tactics' by opponents of comprehensive schools (for an overview of how opponents were seeking to slow down comprehensivisation, see Corbett, 1966). The potential for delay and obstruction was clearly considerable, for as an editorial in *The Times Educational Supplement* (18 March 1966) had suggested,

> the wisest attitude for those who oppose comprehensive policies . . . will be to regard the campaign against them as having to be long drawn out, to be waged for a generation and through the lifetime of several governments. . . . A diplomatic resistance, the skilful use of delaying tactics, a certain haziness in plans presented for the future are weapons which local authorities can use to effect when satisfied that their present provision of secondary education is efficient and just.

Thus it was that during the autumn of 1967, a small group of senior Ministers met to discuss how the Government should proceed in the context of resistance to comprehensivisation by a number of local authorities. Whilst they acknowledged that there was a strong political case for 'a really controversial Bill in which we had public opinion on our side', they also accepted that 'no Bill we could put forward could give the Government last resort powers to compel a recalcitrant local authority by such devices as putting in Commissioners', which meant that 'even after we had passed a Bill, there might well be up to a dozen authorities which effectively prevented the introduction of comprehensive education in their respective areas by putting up bogus schemes'. For these reasons, the initial inclination was to publish a White Paper near the next general election, which would then provide the basis for a major education bill at the beginning of a third term of office. There was, though, agreement in favour of an immediate short bill to address the issues raised by the Enfield case (PRO PREM 13/3168, Crossman to Wilson, 24 October 1967).

Throughout the 1967–1969 period, however, Ministers and civil servants encountered a number of administrative, political and semantic problems in attempting to devise legislation which would provide a statutory underpinning to the Government's comprehensive policy vis-à-vis recalcitrant local education authorities and sundry parents' associations.

Indeed, the semantic problems themselves often served to highlight wider or more fundamental administrative and political difficulties. These semantic problems manifested themselves in two particular ways. First, Patrick Gordon Walker, having been appointed Secretary of State for Education in August 1967, was a little concerned that reference to a 'new school' –

whereby a grammar school was transformed into a comprehensive school – might be vulnerable to a judicial decision decreeing that genuinely 'new schools require new buildings', although Crossman was not unduly concerned about such a likelihood, reasoning that a legal challenge on such grounds would 'build up the case for general legislation' (PRO ED 207/22, Note of discussion between Secretary of State for Education and Lord President of the Council, 25 September 1967).

A more substantive semantic conundrum concerned the form of wording to be employed in order to ensure that grammar schools continued to be replaced by comprehensive schools. Clause 1 of a draft education bill prepared in November 1969 by Edward Short (who had, by this time, replaced Patrick Gordon Walker as Secretary of State for Education) made explicit the intention of abolishing 'selective schools' (grammar schools), in order to give statutory effect to the Government's aim of extending comprehensive education. Furthermore, the clause also stipulated that admission to a secondary school should *not* be on the basis of pupils' ability or aptitude.

However, Harold Wilson was concerned that Clause 1 sounded 'too negative', and urged either that a more positive form of wording be deployed, or that the bill's wording referred to ending the 11-plus (as a criterion of admission to a secondary school) rather than ending grammar schools per se. Wilson was also anxious that the reference to 'ability or aptitude' was 'dynamite', and thus urged the Cabinet's legislation committee to discuss alternative forms of wording (PRO ED 207/19, Gregson [Wilson's Private Secretary] to Tanner [Gordon Walker's Private Secretary], 24 November 1969).

The precise wording of Clause 1 had already been subject to considerable discussion between senior officials in the Department of Education, parliamentary counsel, and the Attorney-General, and it was in this context that wider administrative and political difficulties became apparent. First, it was realised that if Clause 1 were worded in a manner which stated that local education authorities were legally required to provide non-selective secondary schools, then this obligation might result in recalcitrant local education authorities 'establishing two (and only two) comprehensive schools' in their area (but with all remaining schools continuing to be 'selective' with regard to which pupils they admitted), whereupon they would, technically, have fulfilled their statutory obligations under the terms of the proposed legislation. The Government 'cannot take the risk of the Bill being given this interpretation, which would stultify its main objective' (PRO ED 207/19, Gamble to Gregson, 24 November 1969).

Yet alternative forms of wording proved equally problematic, it was discovered. For example, if the clause stipulated that (all) secondary schools maintained by local education authorities had to be non-selective, then this would 'have no application to those local education authorities which maintain a significant element of selectivity by taking up grammar school places in direct grant schools'. Yet to extend the application of Clause 1 to direct grant and independent schools (i.e. those not maintained by a local educa-tion authority) would itself involve the Government 'taking a position about the future of the schools which Ministers are not yet in a position to take (and . . . are not in a position to be likely to take during the lifetime of the present Parliament)', this last point constituting a reference to the Newsom Commission, which the Labour Government, as we shall see, had launched in 1965 to consider the future of public (fee-charging) schools. With regard to Wilson's own suggestion that the bill should legislate against the 11-plus, rather than against grammar schools themselves, it was noted that 'as the 11+ itself has no statutory existence, one cannot legislate to abolish it' (PRO ED 207/19, Gamble to Gregson, 24 November 1969).

This last observation alluded to the fact that the 1944 Education Act (particularly section 8), which had constituted the framework of secondary education up until this time, obliged local education authorities to ensure that sufficient primary and secondary schools were available to meet the needs of children in their area, but did not stipulate the basis of admission to each school. This meant that local education authorities were effectively permitted to provide a variety of secondary schools. Three types prevailed, namely grammar schools (where admission was based on 'ability or aptitude' as evaluated via the 11-plus exam), secondary moderns and technical schools. Consequently, local education authorities had been under no statutory oblig-ation to provide comprehensive schools per se.

These discussions about the precise wording of the proposed education bill were conducted in the context of growing ministerial concern, by the autumn of 1969, that the drive towards establishing comprehensive schools was losing momentum, with at least twenty-five education authorities having either failed or refused to submit the proposals requested four years earlier, or, having had their proposals rejected as unsatisfactory, failing to submit revised proposals. Although some delay had been caused by lack of resources for carrying out the necessary building work to convert schools to comprehensives, much of the ensuing lack of progress was attributed to obstructiveness by various Conservative-controlled local authorities.

Consequently, it was not until February 1970 that a bill – containing just eight clauses – was finally introduced which imposed a statutory obligation on recalcitrant local education authorities to submit plans for the reorganisa-tion of their schools along comprehensive lines. The bill was still in (stand-ing) committee, though, when the general election was called, thereby ensuring that it would not reach the statute book unless the Labour Govern-ment were re-elected and the bill reintroduced in the new Parliament. This was clearly the Labour leadership's intention, for Labour's 1970 manifesto pledged that the Government having 'vigorously pursued' comprehensive reorganisation since 1965, a third term of office would herald legislation 'to require the minority of Tory education authorities who have so far resisted change to abandon eleven plus selection'. This would take the form of 'a new Education Bill to replace the 1944 and subsequent Acts' (Craig, 1975: 352).

The extent to which the 1964–1970 Labour Governments succeeded in expanding comprehensive education is illustrated in Table 15.1. It indicates that by 1970, the number of comprehensive schools had quadrupled as compared with 1965, and now exceeded the number of remaining grammar schools for the first time. Also by 1970, for every two pupils still attending a grammar school, three were attending a comprehensive school. However, closer perusal of Table 15.1 reveals that neither the grammar schools themselves nor the number of pupils attending them declined as rapidly as comprehensive education expanded. This suggests that much of the increase in the number of, and attendance at, comprehensive schools during this period derived from the decline of secondary moderns and technical schools (the other two elements of the tripartite system of secondary education). In other words, grammar schools, and the number of pupils of pupils educated at them, declined relatively slowly during the period of the 1964–1970 Labour Governments, and undoubtedly exasperated those in the party who were most enthusiastic about 'comprehensivisation'. Nonetheless, the trend did continue even when the Conservatives were back in office after June 1970 and Margaret Thatcher became Secretary of State for Education, to the extent that by 1972, 893 grammar schools remained, whilst the number of comprehensives had risen to 1,591.

No action against public schools

One important aspect of the 1964–1970 Labour Governments' reform of secondary education which warrants brief comment concerns the omission of public schools from the ministerial drive to comprehensive schooling. After all, in purporting to imbue the education system with egalitarian principles, and seeking to promote equality of opportunity, the Labour Governments of 1964–1970 might have displayed the same hostility towards the public

Table 15.1   Expansion of comprehensive education, 1964–1970

Year	Type of school		Total number of pupils attending (000s)	
	Comprehensive	Grammar	Comprehensive	Grammar
1964	195	1,298	199	726
1965	262	1,285	240	719
1966	387	1,273	312	713
1967	508	1,236	408	695
1968	748	1,155	606	656
1969	962	1,098	773	632
1970	1,145	1,038	937	605

Source: Fenwick (1976: 148).

schools as they did towards grammar schools and the principle of selection via the 11-plus. Certainly Ministers could argue that grammar schools and public schools alike both reflected and reinforced a form of educational apartheid between middle- and working-class pupils, which in turn perpetuated class divisions and differing occupational opportunities beyond full-time education. Indeed, some Labour politicians deemed the public schools even more socially divisive and elitist than the grammar schools. For example, in a letter to *The Times* in the late 1950s, Manny Shinwell argued that

> We are afraid to tackle the public schools to which so many wealthy people send their sons, but, at the same time, we are ready to throw overboard the grammar schools, which are for many working-class boys the stepping-stones to universities and then a useful career. I would rather abandon Eton, Winchester, Harrow and all the rest of them than sacrifice all the advantages of the grammar school.
>
> (*The Times*, 26 June 1958; see also Shinwell quoted in Doxat, 1984: 41)

Crosland himself had previously made precisely such criticisms during the Labour Party's thirteen years in opposition, alleging, for example, that even if state education were enormously improved,

> we shall still not have equality of opportunity as long as we maintain a system of superior private schools, open to the wealthier classes, but out of reach of poorer children however talented and deserving. This is much the most flagrant inequality of opportunity, as it is the cause of class inequality generally, in our educational system: and I have never been able to understand why socialists have been so obsessed with the grammar schools, and so indifferent to the much more glaring injustice of the independent schools.
>
> (Crosland, 1956: 260–1)

Yet as we have just noted, Crosland himself seemed far more concerned about grammar schools than about public schools during his tenure as Secretary of State for Education. Indeed, in sharp contrast to his notorious utterances concerning grammar schools, there are no reports of Crosland vowing 'to destroy every fucking public school in England'. On the contrary, on one occasion, having become Secretary of State for Education, he declared that 'I'm not frightfully interested in the public schools' (quoted in Crosland, 1982: 149).

However, part of this reluctance to attack the public schools derived from an acceptance – however reluctant or grudging – that principles of liberty were involved, for as Crosland observed,

> A democracy cannot forbid people to found schools and charge for going to them. In any case, outright abolition [would be] unenforceable;

parents and teachers would devise a way to get round the law. Further
waste of resources: many teachers at, say, Eton and Winchester, would
emigrate.

(Crosland, 1982: 149)

This perspective was apparently shared by many of Crosland's colleagues, for
as Wilma Harte, a senior civil servant in the schools branch of the Department of Education and Science during the 1960s, recalled:

[W]e always knew, or perhaps just suspected, that the Labour Government had no real political will to deal with the . . . independent schools.
This was partly because of the old problem of freedom of the individual
. . . but more importantly, because they could never make up their
minds whether these schools are so bloody they ought to be abolished,
or so marvellous they ought to be made available to everyone.

(Crosland Papers, 5/1)

Ultimately, it was the latter approach which the Labour Party tacitly
adopted, so that rather than seeking to abolish or outlaw public schools, the
goal was to improve the standard of education in State (comprehensive)
schools, to the extent that the public schools would eventually cease to be so
attractive or advantageous to the wealthy, although 'if parents want to send
their children to some inferior fee-paying school for purely snobbish reasons,
that's their affair' (Crosland, 1982: 149–50).

Crosland did establish, in 1965, a Public School Commission, chaired by
Sir John Newsom, whose remit was to consider ways in which public schools
might be better integrated with the state system, although he suggested at
the time that 'it will take a couple of years to complete its findings, but
that's OK as there's no money currently available at Education to reform the
public schools' (Crosland, 1982: 149; see also 'Independent Schools',
Crosland Papers, 5/2). The Commission actually took three years before publishing its report, in July 1968, and the 'half-baked' (Pimlott, 1993: 512)
recommendations contained therein, mainly about admitting a wider social
mix of pupils, were 'shelved by the Government as being too costly' (Radice,
2002: 143; see also Perkin, 1989: 450), although Crosland recalled that
'nobody much liked it [the report]' anyway (quoted in Kogan, 1971: 197).
Besides, by the time that the Newsom Commission's report was published,
Crosland was no longer Education Secretary.

Moreover, as was noted earlier, the obligation to provide comprehensive
education applied to those schools which were maintained by local education
authorities, and therefore was not applicable to public schools, which, by
definition, were independent of local education authorities.

Expansion of higher education

The outgoing Conservative Government had been committed to a significant expansion of higher education, but two years prior to winning the 1964 election the Labour Party was contemplating an even greater programme of expansion. Against the 1962 tally of 155,000 people in higher education, Labour suggested that this figure should be increased to 350,000–400,000 by 1970, and further raised to 700,000 by 1980.

As indicated above, Labour viewed such expansion both as an economic necessity and as socially desirable. An NEC study group noted the 'increasing demand for skilled manpower and the growing tendency of the professions for full-time training, e.g. solicitors, actuaries, accountants, etc.' (Labour Party Archives, RD.275/June 1962), and asserted that Britain's standard of living and prosperity could no longer be ensured by natural raw materials or a pool of unskilled labour, for the nation's 'primary asset is the brain-power and skill of its scientists, engineers, research workers and technicians, administrators and professional men and women', and so, 'the economic expansion of the nation requires many more highly skilled and professionally trained people'. Indeed, it was even suggested that 'Britain's economic stagnation is a direct result of its neglect of higher education', so that the expansion of higher education 'is one of the most urgent and important questions before the nation ... a matter of national survival' (Labour Party Archives, RD.368/December 1962), to the extent that the next Labour Government 'will treat Higher Education as a National Emergency' (Labour Party Archives, RD.266/May 1962).

This proposed expansion was also linked explicitly to Labour's professed social egalitarianism and belief in equality of opportunity, for increasing the number of universities (and thus university places) was deemed integral to the goal of facilitating greater social mobility for young people from working-class families. It was emphasised that every boy and girl who achieved the requisite entrance requirements for admission to a university should be guaranteed a place, so that university education became 'a right of democratic citizenship' (Labour Party Archives, RD.275/June 1962), and thus 'no longer ... a privilege, but a right for all able young people, regardless of their families' class, income or position' (Labour Party Archives, RD.368/December 1962). However, although this was a widely supported objective, one Labour MP did draw attention to a

> tendency for young men and women from working class homes, and who have been educated up to university and collegiate levels, mainly through the unceasing effort of educational reformers in the Labour Party ... to break from us when they join professional ranks. They become most conscious of the new status, and are inclined to bite the hand that fed them.
>
> (Williams, 1962)

To achieve this expansion of higher education, Labour Party thinking in opposition envisaged two discrete stages: a short-term 'crash programme' to achieve the 350,000–400,000 intake target by 1970, and then a longer-term strategy to attain the 700,000 target by 1980. It was acknowledged that the 'crash programme' would entail bigger lectures and recruitment of more part-time tutorial staff in universities, as well as an obligation on more students to attend their local university, so that they could live at home whilst studying. This last aspect reflected a recognition that in many smaller towns and cities, particularly those where new universities had been established, there were acute shortages of accommodation (not merely for students, but also for staff employed by the university).

All these measures and problems, it was anticipated, would be directly addressed during the second, long-term phase of university expansion, whereupon it was envisaged that Britain would have a total of seventy universities by 1980, more than double the early 1960s tally. Among the towns and cities provisionally earmarked for a new university during this period were Blackpool, Burnley, Darlington, Doncaster, Carlisle, Halifax, Redruth, Southport and Watford (Labour Party Archives, RD.368/December 1962).

Yet on being elected in October 1964, the new Labour Government swiftly abandoned its own plan to create a large number of new universities, although it did proceed with the creation of ten universities in accordance with the Robbins Report, the establishment of these particular universities already being close to completion by the time that Labour entered office. Beyond this, however, the Labour Government quickly decided that 'it would not be necessary, with one possible exception, to create additional universities or to promote any further institutions to university status in the next ten years', although it readily accepted the target – decreed by the outgoing Conservative Government – of providing 390,000 places in higher education by 1973–1974, of which 218,000 would be in universities (PRO CAB 129/120 Part 1, C(65)11, 'The development of Higher Education – Memorandum by the Secretary of State for Education and Science', 29 January 1965).

Instead, most of this proposed increase in the number of students attending university was to be achieved primarily by increasing the student intake of existing universities, rather than building new ones. In opting to expand extant universities, the Government, and particularly the Cabinet social services committee, chaired by Crosland, appeared to be strongly influenced by the advice proffered by the University Grants Committee (PRO PREM 13/291, Trend to Wilson, 30 January 1965; PRO CAB 128/39 Part 1, CC(65) 6th Conclusions, 1 February 1965).

Moreover, it was polytechnics which the 1964–1970 Labour Governments soon deemed to be the key to widening access to higher education and imparting the (vocational and technical) skills which the British economy increasingly required, and to this end no fewer than thirty polytechnics were established in 1966. The development of polytechnics also reflected Anthony Crosland's view that there should henceforth be 'a move away from our snobbish, caste-ridden, hierarchical obsession with university status', Crosland once confessing that he was 'not frightfully interested in the universities' (Crosland, 1982: 147, 159).

The particular emphasis on polytechnics was maintained, and actually increased somewhat, during the Labour Government's second term of office, to the extent that, in 1969, the NEC's study group on higher and further education was suggesting that any further resources for post-18 education 'should go to the institutions which provide for part-time students, for continuous experimentation with new courses, and for qualifications below degree level', namely the polytechnics. This proposed shift of emphasis and resources was linked to an acknowledgement that the expansion of universities had not hitherto been accompanied by any corresponding increase in the number of working-class students attending them (Labour Party Archives, Re.420/February 1969).

There was, though, a parallel commitment to expanding colleges of education, primarily to provide teacher training, for Crosland was convinced that 'ultimately, both education and economic expansion depended on an increase in the number of teachers in the schools' (CAB 128/39 Part 1, CC(65) 6th Conclusions, 1 February 1965).

Further expansion of higher education was promised in Labour's 1970 manifesto, although it was recognised that this 'will require very careful planning'. Indeed, by this time the party leadership was proposing – via the party's 1970 election manifesto – that a third successive Labour Government would 'undertake an early review of the whole field' of higher education (Craig, 1975: 353).

Creation of the Open University

The establishment of the Open University has variously been deemed one of Harold Wilson's proudest achievements. Indeed, Wilson himself subsequently adjudged it 'one of the greatest achievements' of the 1964–1970 Labour Governments (quoted in Ziegler, 1993: 475), whilst his former Chief Press Secretary, Joe Haines, deemed the Open University to represent 'the single greatest step in the history of higher education', one which was 'truly ... his monument' (Haines, 1998: 2, 3). Similarly, Clive Ponting believed it to represent the 'greatest innovation ... perhaps one of the most revolutionary policies' of the 1964–1970 Labour Governments, and possibly 'the most lasting monument to the work of this Labour Government ... a truly imaginative idea' (Ponting, 1990: 133, 134, 390). One of Wilson's Cabinet colleagues subsequently suggested that the Open University 'was an achievement which can be mentioned in the same breath as the establishment of the National Health Service' (Foot, 1984: 39), whilst one of Wilson's biographers depicted the Open University as 'a brilliantly original and highly ambitious institution which took the ideals of social equality and

equality more seriously than any other part of the British education system'
(Pimlott, 1992: 515).

As with many novel political ideas and initiatives, the precise origins or
parentage of the idea for an Open University have proved difficult to pinpoint accurately. The first *public* allusion to what was then termed a University of the Air was made by Harold Wilson himself during a speech in
Glasgow in September 1963, and the biographer of Jennie Lee (the Minister
whom Wilson subsequently appointed to oversee the establishment of this
university) clearly attributes the idea to Wilson himself (Hollis, 1997: 297).
Yet the initiative had been under consideration by an internal Labour Party
policy committee since March of that year, although Wilson himself subsequently claimed that the idea first occurred to him during his flight back to
Britain from lecturing at the University of Chicago at the beginning of
1963, where an innovative degree system had already been established,
entailing a mixture of postal correspondence, television lectures, telephone
tutorials and face-to-face seminars (Hollis, 1997: 298, 302).

Also central to developing the idea from the outset, it would appear, was
the sociologist Michael Young, who had himself contemplated the notion of
an 'external teaching' college for adult learners during the early 1960s.
Wilson's Glasgow speech about a 'university of the air' indicated to Young
that his idea was shared at the very highest political level, and he was subsequently 'perceived to be the educational inspiration behind the OU [Open
University]', the 'other man who could claim authorship of the OU' (Hollis,
1997: 303; see also Jefferys, 2000: 109).

The development of the Open University was born of the recognition that
whilst a Labour Government would be committed to a major expansion of
university education, there would remain many people who would be unable
to attend a university on a full-time three-year basis, and whose only
opportunities for obtaining post-18 educational qualifications were either to
attend evening classes or enrol on correspondence courses. The former, it was
noted, were not appropriate or accessible for some people, whilst the latter
were 'often of a very poor quality' (Labour Party Archives, RD.776/May
1964). It was also recognised that there were many older adults whose post-
school education had been terminated either by financial hardship, and thus
a necessity to go out to work at the earliest possible opportunity, or, particularly in the case of women, by family responsibilities. In this context, an
open university would provide a major educational means of providing
equality of opportunity to women and the working class, precisely the two
sections of British society traditionally most denied or deprived of a university education.

The problems of citizens unable to attend a traditional university, owing
to family or employment commitments, could therefore be overcome, it was
suggested, by establishing a University of the Air, whereby degrees would
be studied for via a variety of media: television and radio programmes,
postal correspondence, local tutorials, taped (cassette) recordings, and short

residential courses. Because obtaining airtime might be difficult, owing to television and radio's scheduling of other programmes, it was thought that a new, fourth TV channel might be launched, which would be exclusively devoted to programmes for the University of the Air (Labour Party Archives, RD.776/May 1964).

The proposal was not included in Labour's 1964 manifesto, though, partly because it required more careful consideration, but also because Wilson was concerned that it might not attract sufficient support, particularly as Iain Macleod, a senior and highly respected Conservative Minister, denounced the notion of an open university as 'blithering nonsense' (Haines, 1998: 2). However, Wilson's enthusiasm for a University of the Air was sufficient to ensure that he was not deterred by such antipathy, some of which emanated from his own colleagues (see below), and so, following the 1964 election victory, Jennie Lee was appointed Minister of the Arts, but with special responsibility for pursuing the University of the Air, whereupon 'under Wilson's protection, she became the midwife and guardian of the Open University' (Haines, 1998: 2).

Lee established and chaired an advisory group on the proposed University of the Air, whose six meetings during the summer of 1965 considered the basic issues such as the type of degree courses and subjects which would be offered; the envisaged target 'audience'; the format by which teaching was to be conducted; and the funding implications. Perhaps unsure whether the advisory group was supposed to be considering the principle and feasibility of a University of the Air, or developing concrete proposals for actually establishing such an institution, one member asked Lee whether they were meant to be keeping an open mind on the project: 'No', replied Lee, who clearly subscribed to the latter view of the group's role (PRO ED 188/104, Minutes of the University of the Air Advisory Group, 1st meeting, 8 June 1965).

What was subsequently agreed during this and the other five meetings (the last being held on 4 August 1965) was that the University of the Air would be an independent university in its own right – and not an appendage of an existing university or set of universities (as some Ministers and officials had initially envisaged) – which would be vested with full degree-awarding powers. It would mainly be concerned with degree courses, but would also offer various professional and vocational courses. The courses would be taught through a variety of media: television and radio broadcasts; postal correspondence; tutorials in local or regional centres; and short residential or summer schools. Admission was to be open to all, irrespective of previous qualifications, upon payment of an enrolment fee. In view of its primary role in extending educational opportunities and widening access to those unable to attend traditional universities, Lee was not unduly concerned about insisting on a concomitant research requirement: 'I do not regard a research function as an essential condition for the constitution of a university . . . I do not think it necessary . . . that it [the University of the Air] should undertake its own research' (PRO ED 188/104, Lee to Crossman, 28 October 1965).

There were also protracted discussions, both in the advisory group and amongst Ministers themselves, about how the University of the Air should be televised (given that it was not to be confined only to radio broadcasts). In particular, there was debate about whether a separate (fourth) television channel would need to be established, devoted almost entirely and exclusively to educational programmes, or whether the University of the Air should be transmitted via existing channels. The latter option, though, raised further issues, not least whether the university's programmes ought to broadcast at 'peak times', thereby maximising potential audiences and subscribers, or during off-peak hours, when the television channels had more 'vacant slots'.

The former option was not attractive to ITV, concerned as it was about the likely loss of advertising revenues which might result from the broadcast of 'minority interest' programmes at peak times. Yet Ministers themselves were concerned that if the University of the Air were in any way dependent on advertising revenues, then its reputation might be damaged from the outset, and its standards possibly compromised (PRO CAB 129/124, C(66)27, 'University of the Air – Memorandum by the Lord President of the Council [Bert Bowden]', 4 February 1966). On the other hand, Lee was equally concerned that the University of the Air would not attract sufficient viewers and subscribers if its programmes were broadcast only during early-morning or/and late-night 'off-peak' television slots, and hence she was adamant that a fourth television channel was urgently required, insisting that 'unless we are prepared to establish a genuine open university, based on the fourth network, we shall expose ourselves to the charge of gimmickry, and alienate all the most worth-while elements in the academic world' (PRO T 227/2356, Lee to Bowden, 7 February 1966).

Lee's work in developing proposals for the University of the Air was conducted in the context of considerable elitism and scepticism emanating from some of her senior Labour colleagues, and it was a reflection of her own determination, and the full backing received from Harold Wilson, that the project came to fruition. For example, in clear contrast to Lee herself, Richard Crossman was concerned that a university primarily concerned with teaching would not have an adequate research function, something which he deemed 'an essential condition . . . in the eyes both of university dons and of students seeking degrees'. Crossman feared that without such a research role, 'the University of the Air's degree will not be held in high esteem'. Crossman thus wondered whether the proposed University of the Air might be better viewed 'as a kind of extension of a group of universities, say London, Sussex, Colchester for the south; and Liverpool, Manchester, Sheffield for the north; plus a separate one for Scotland' (PRO ED 188/104, Crossman to Lee, 4 November 1965). As we have already noted, Lee emphatically rejected such a perspective.

Also rather sceptical was Anthony Crosland, who was Secretary of State for Education (and thus Lee's departmental superior) from January 1965 to August 1967. Whilst he refrained from actively opposing Lee's work in developing proposals for a University of the Air – 'Tony Crosland was frightened of her and knew that ... she would immediately complain direct to Wilson' if he attempted to hinder her (Ponting, 1990: 133) – Crosland remained unconvinced about the desirability or necessity of such a body, believing that the expansion of higher education, and the widening of access to socially disadvantaged, mature or part-time students – a principle which he fully supported in accordance with his social democratic philosophy – could readily be achieved through the planned development of polytechnics.

Of course, he may also have been partly concerned that a University of the Air would have to be funded out of the Department of Education's existing budget at a time when it was already committed to the expansion of other forms of higher education, the 'comprehensivisation' of secondary schools, and the raising of the school leaving age from 15 to 16 (the latter subsequently postponed for financial reasons). Certainly Crosland was alleged to have claimed that 'he cannot find room for any such expenditure [for the University of the Air] within his allocation', an alleged claim which Treasury officials deemed it 'not possible to accept', not least because it was tantamount 'to saying that he regards the University of the Air as of lower priority than anything else in his programme' (PRO T 227/2355, Rampton to Isaac, 31 January 1966). Of course, Crosland almost certainly *did* view the University of the Air in this way, but was unable to prevent Lee – backed by Wilson – from persevering.

However, there also appears to have been a certain coolness in their professional relationship, with Lee deemed 'something of a lone wolf', and Crosland anxious that 'if he tries to assert the normal authority of a Minister over a Parliamentary Secretary, Miss Lee may take umbrage on the ground that whatever the [constitutional] theory, she reports to you [Wilson]'. On the other hand, it was felt that as Lee 'is not the most systematic of people', it was quite right 'that he [Crosland] should exercise some supervision over Miss Lee'. Wilson himself was therefore asked to 'explain to her gently that ... she ought to take her Secretary of State into her confidence' (PRO CAB 164/564, Mitchell to Wilson, 8 February 1966). Many officials, more generally, were deeply sceptical about the whole project, believing 'that sooner or later, the whole idea of the University of the Air would be dropped like a hot potato', having proved 'to be a "flash in the pan" ... the whole thing would die a natural death in a relatively short time' (Perry, 1976: 13, 14).

Meanwhile, departmentalism also provided a source of opposition to the proposed University of the Air, with some officials in the Department of Education unconvinced about the need for such a body, given that other forms of higher education were already being expanded, and unsure about who precisely a University of the Air was intended to serve or attract. These concerns were quite apart from, or in addition to, those pertaining to funding, with DES officials anxious that expenditure might have to be diverted from other education programmes and reforms, particularly in the context of the serious economic difficulties which beset the Labour Government from 1966 onwards. Officials in the Department of Education were inclined to the view that the University of the Air represented 'a diversion of effort to the wrong ends, an unnecessary frill at a time when resources for badly needed developments over the whole range of education were extremely scarce' (Perry, 1976: 13).

The Treasury, of course, was also concerned about the financial implications of the proposed University of the Air. The Post Office, meanwhile, represented at ministerial level via the Postmaster General, was worried that if a fourth television channel, being mooted at that time, was deemed an educational channel, and thus either partly or wholly commandeered by the University of the Air, then the Post Office would lose the potential revenues which would otherwise accrue from a commercial channel primarily funded via advertising revenues.

Reservations concerning likely costs were still evident when Lee presented firm proposals for the University of the Air to the full Cabinet in February 1966, the same month as these proposals were published in a White Paper. In particular, it was pointed out that unless the Treasury were willing to provide additional funding – which it was disinclined to do – then other educational objectives and policies would need to be re-examined. There was thus a suggestion that the University of the Air be launched as a pilot scheme in order to ascertain the level of public interest, and the operational and broadcasting costs involved, before launching it in full.

Lee was adamant, however, that if the University of the Air was introduced on such an experimental basis, as if by stealth, then its impact on the public would be dissipated and its potential success and popularity undermined from the outset – a view apparently shared by a majority of Ministers serving on the Cabinet committee on broadcasting (which at the time was examining proposals for a fourth television channel, and considering the extent to which this would be responsible for transmitting programmes for the University of the Air). Their view – like Lee's – was that 'an experimental approach would destroy much of the impact of the University on the public'. Nonetheless, it was agreed that the associated White Paper, outlining the educational aspects and advantages of the University of the Air, should omit the issues of cost, and also avoid references to the parallel debate about the extent to which the proposed fourth television channel might be primarily used for educational programmes (PRO CAB 128/41, CC(66) 6th Conclusions, 8 February 1966; PRO CAB 129/124, C(66)27, 'University of the Air – Memorandum by the Lord President of the Council [Bert Bowden]', 4 February 1966).

The proposed University of the Air was also included in the Labour Party's 1966 manifesto (albeit now referred to as the Open University), where it was emphasised that 'It will mean genuine equality of opportunity for millions of people for the first time' (Craig, 1975: 305). Lee had, by this time, renamed it the Open University, mainly to counter the objection that a series of television and radio programmes were hardly sufficient to constitute a university (*The Times Educational Supplement*, 5 February 1965). Certainly it was judged that the appellation 'Open University', rather than University of the Air, 'may be more accurate ... less emotive' (PRO CAB 164/564, Trend to Wilson, 10 October 1966).

Yet having originally faced scepticism, if not outright hostility, deriving from a mode of middle-class, elitist snobbery which doubted that an 'open' university could ever be academically or intellectually comparable to any of the traditional universities, Lee subsequently found the fledgling Open University being criticised from some on the left for not being sufficiently working class in terms of the students it was attracting and enrolling. Certainly there was a discernible misogyny and sexism which looked with disdain at the extent to which the Open University was attracting 'housewives' and 'middle class, middle aged women', or what one LEA Director of Education contemptuously referred to as 'middle class women in hobby education' (Hollis, 1997: 311, 330), rather than working-class men. Yet Lee dismissed such churlish criticism by arguing that 'the most insulting thing that could happen to any working class man or woman was to have a working class university' (Jennie Lee Papers, Lee to Christodoulou [the OU's first Secretary], 12 January 1971).

Following Labour's re-election in March 1966, plans for the Open University gradually became somewhat clearer and firmer, in spite of the serious economic problems which the Government soon encountered. Indeed, just weeks before the election, the vexatious issue about whether programmes would be broadcast by a proposed fourth television channel or via BBC2 was witnessing a shift towards the latter, with Harold Wilson suggesting to the full Cabinet that further consideration ought to be given to both 'the need for peak-hour transmission ... and to the possibility of using spare hours on BBC2 ... thus avoiding the cost of a fourth network'. Given that Lee was emphatic about the need for 'peak-hour' broadcasts, Wilson's stance seems to have been crucial in steering her away from her insistence hitherto on the necessity of a fourth television channel (PRO CAB 128.41, CC(66) 6th Conclusions, 8 February 1966).

However, the Cabinet committee on broadcasting also noted another potential argument against establishing a fourth channel partly or wholly devoted to Open University programmes, namely that these would effectively be ghettoised, whereas if they were broadcast on BBC2 they might attract a wider audience. In support of this line of argument, it was noted that

BBC experience suggests that the comparatively large audiences gained by some of their educative programmes consist to a considerable extent of people who have been watching earlier programmes of a more general

kind. This 'inheritance factor' ... would not apply to programmes confined to a separate educational network.

(PRO T 227/2355, Ministerial Committee on Broadcasting: B.(66)2 –
Interim Official Report on 'University of the Air', undated,
but *c.* February 1966)

It is not clear, though, why attracting a wider audience – beyond those
studying with the Open University – should have been deemed an important consideration if such programmes were *not* broadcast via a commercial
channel (which would naturally want to attract large(r) audiences in order to
secure advertising revenues). One can only assume that either audience size
would provide an indication of whether or not it was justifiable or 'cost-
effective' to use BBC2 programme slots for Open University broadcasts, or
that a larger audience – even if not all were Open University students –
could subsequently be cited as evidence that the BBC was fulfilling the
educative dimension of its Reithian mission to educate, inform and enter-
tain.

Meanwhile, although the Cabinet had not yet formally given its approval
to Lee's plans for the Open University – officially it remained an aspiration,
rather than an agreed and definite commitment – Lee effectively acted and
publicly spoke of it as if it were merely a matter of when – rather than
whether – it would be launched. She 'always ... indicated total conviction
that the new institution would come about' (Perry, 1976: 23). Such confidence was probably derived from both personal commitment and determination by Lee, and the reassuring recognition that she (and the Open
University) had Wilson's full support (MacArthur, 1974: 9). Of course, Lee's
continued preparation for the Open University established a momentum
which effectively ensured that it would indeed become reality – a kind of
self-fulfilling prophecy.

With Wilson backing the proposal, and Lee now willing to accept that
its programmes would be broadcast on BBC2 (rather than on a new fourth
channel partly or wholly devoted to Open University programmes, as she
had originally wanted), the initiative moved nearer to fruition. Determined
to maintain the momentum – and further acting as if the Open University
was a certainty, rather than a possibility – Lee secured Cabinet approval, in
September 1967, to establish a planning committee whose role would be to
finalise plans for the Open University. That the Cabinet granted its approval
for Lee to establish this planning committee was effectively a de facto
endorsement of the Open University itself, suggesting, perhaps, that by this
time Ministers who had hitherto been lukewarm or sceptical about the proposal were resigned to it. According to the Open University's first Vice-
Chancellor, 'It is almost as if Jennie's continued pressure finally wore down
the opposition' (Perry, 1976: 23).

The establishment of the planning committee – representing the second
phase of the Open University's development: 'one of academic, rather than

political, endeavour' (Perry, 1972: 1) – along with the calibre of its membership, seemed to convince many who until then had been sceptical (including some academics themselves) that the Open University would soon become a reality. Chaired by Sir Peter Venables, the Vice-Chancellor of Aston University (and also Vice-Chair of the Committee of Vice Chancellors and Principals (CVCP)), other members of the planning committee included the Vice-Chancellors of Cambridge University, Exeter University, Hull University and Sussex University, and a professor each from Edinburgh University, the London School of Economics and Nottingham University. Furthermore, five of the nineteen-member planning committee had previously served on the advisory committee.

However, Lee had only been able to announce the planning committee because the funding issue had apparently been resolved over the summer of 1967. During July 1967, the Chancellor had apparently been persuaded to grant a special allocation of money for the Open University so that it would not need to be financed at the expense of other Department of Education commitments and projects. This seemed somewhat surprising in the context of the economic difficulties with which the Labour Government was obliged to grapple from the summer of 1966 onwards. However, according to Jennie Lee's biographer, two factors seemed to have proved key in this respect. First, Lord Goodman, chairman of the Arts Council (and subsequently a member of the planning committee responsible for bringing the plans for the Open University to fruition once Cabinet approval had been attained), provided a memorandum detailing projected costs, but 'based on ... wildly inaccurate figures' (Hollis, 1997: 321). Indeed, several years later, Goodman confessed that 'When I see the figure I mentioned ... I ought to blush with shame', and admitted that the Open University 'might not have been established except for my foolish miscalculation' (House of Lords Debates, 23 May 1974). Moreover, according to Ralph Tooney, Lee's Permanent Secretary, officials within the Department of Education also realised that 'these estimates were far too low, but for reasons of expediency, the point was not pressed home' (quoted in Hollis, 1997: 321).

The conservatism of the costs cited seemed to convince the Cabinet that maybe the Open University could be afforded after all. Second, though, and perhaps more importantly, the Treasury was persuaded to finance the Open University on 'the understanding that Wilson would support Callaghan (the Chancellor) in Cabinet on a tough package of [public expenditure] cuts if Callaghan protected the OU' (Hollis, 1997: 321; see also Perry, 1976: 23).

The Open University finally began teaching its first intake of students in January 1971, its academic year running in tandem with the calendar year, which in turn enabled academics in traditional universities to teach short (one- to two-week) intensive 'summer schools' for Open University students in the summer vacations).

As well as being widely viewed, subsequently, as possibly Harold Wilson's greatest legacy (notwithstanding the fact that Jennie Lee was actually the Minister who did most of the work in bringing it to fruition!), the Open University could also be viewed as successfully combining 'Labour's commitment to educational expansion, with a socialist remedying of disadvantage, with a contemporary fascination with technology and the media, and with the nation's economic need to skill its labour force' (Hollis, 1997: 314). In hindsight, it offered an excellent example of 'joined-up government' long before the phrase itself became associated with a later Labour Prime Minister.

Postponement of the raising of the school leaving age

Although raising the school leaving age from fifteen to sixteen had been official Labour Party policy in 1964 and 1966 (it had also been the official policy of the Conservatives), the economic difficulties which afflicted the Labour Government after its re-election in 1966, and the consequent curbs on public expenditure, meant that the plan to raise the school leaving age in 1971 was deferred until 1973. Indeed, in the context of these economic stringencies Cabinet members were to discover that 'comprehensivisation' itself had a negative impact on plans to raise the school leaving age, for it became apparent that 'the building programme for schools up to 1970 will do no more than provide for the extra numbers resulting from the rising birth-rate and the raising of the school leaving age, it is not going to be possible for LEAs to undertake building work to adapt existing schools for comprehensive purposes' (PRO PREM 13/3168, Trend to Wilson, 28 February 1966). Effectively compelled to choose between maintaining the reorganisation of secondary schools on comprehensive lines *or* raising the school leaving age to sixteen, the second Labour Government opted to prioritise the 'comprehensivisation' of secondary education. In deciding, therefore, to defer the raising of the school leaving age, some Ministers had a tacit Micawberish hope that economic circumstances would improve in the ensuing period – with a concomitant beneficial impact on public expenditure – and that the school building programme would have advanced further.

In the meantime, though, it was recognised that deferring the raising of the school leaving age was somewhat inimical to the Labour Government's goal of increasing equality of opportunity in education, and widening access to higher education, for deferral 'means giving a continued advantage to the child whose parents decide that he [*sic*] should stay on voluntarily', and for this reason some Cabinet Ministers, especially those who themselves emanated from working-class backgrounds, such as George Brown, James Callaghan, Ray Gunter and George Thomson, were deeply unhappy about this proposed deferral (Crossman, 1976: 408, diary entry for 4 July 1967, and 636–7, diary entry for 5 January 1968; Ponting, 1990: 305).

Anthony Crosland, though, in spite of being of middle-class origins, was also antipathetic to this cost-cutting proposal, viewing it as being in conflict with his own strongly held views concerning the link between extending education and establishing a more egalitarian society. When asked by Richard Crossman who would be affected by deferral, Crosland replied archly, 'Only 400,000 children. But they're not our children. It's always other people's children. None of us in this room would dream of letting our children leave school at fifteen.' George Brown then turned to Patrick Gordon Walker (Education Secretary at this difficult time) and said, 'I want a straight answer to a straight question: If you had to choose between these 400,000 fifteen-year-olds and university students, which would you help?' When Gordon Walker replied, 'If I had to make such a choice, I suppose I'd help university students', Brown's response was 'May God forgive you' (quoted in Crosland, 1982: 194). Brown subsequently described the decision as 'one of the greatest betrayals a Labour Government, so overwhelmingly composed of University graduates, could make of the less privileged people who, after all, had elected it' (1971: 175).

As these exchanges indicate, the Cabinet meeting which finally agreed to defer the raising of the school leaving age was a fraught affair, for the issue 'raised important issues of principle and social justice, since the different educational opportunities available to the children of the middle class and of manual workers respectively were the main source of class division', thereby rendering it 'wrong for 400,000 children a year to be deprived of educational opportunity which should be available to all'. Against such arguments, though, proponents of deferral (for two years) claimed that 'expenditure on ... comprehensive reorganisation and on teacher training was of greater importance than the leaving age in achieving educational equality'. In summing up the discussion, Wilson acknowledged that, on grounds of social justice, the Cabinet was reluctant to defer the raising of the school leaving age, but that 'for reasons of economic necessity ... there was a balance of view in favour of deferment by two years', albeit on the condition that there would be no further deferral (PRO CAB 128/45, CC(68) 2nd Conclusions, 5 Janaury 1968). This 'balance of view' belied the fact that the Cabinet was evenly divided over deferral, to the extent that Patrick Gordon Walker, as Education Secretary, effectively had a casting vote on this particular issue, which he then used to support the Chancellor in opting for deferral. This rendered him the focus of considerable 'silently displayed' contempt around the Cabinet table (Crosland, 1982: 194). Indeed, George Brown apparently threatened to resign over this issue, but ultimately only Lord Longford actually did so, claiming that 'if I swallowed this, there was nothing I wouldn't swallow' (Crosland, 1982: 195–6), although his resignation (as Lord Privy Seal and Leader of the House of Lords) 'passed largely unnoticed' (Ponting, 1990: 306).

Thus it was that one of Labour's policies expressly intended to ameliorate class inequality in education was compromised by the economic exigencies which afflicted the Labour Government following its re-election in 1966. The Government had committed itself to raising the school leaving age to sixteen, in order to tackle a situation whereby pupils from working-class homes generally left school a year before their middle-class counterparts (thereby ensuring that the latter invariably completed secondary education with more educational qualifications, and thus much more likelihood of proceeding to further and higher education, which, in turn, greatly enhanced their career prospects and future earning potential), but the urgent need to curb public expenditure ensured that, in the sphere of education policy, the proposal to raise the school leaving age was effectively sacrificed – albeit temporarily – in order to protect other aspects of the 1964–1970 Labour Governments' education (expansion) programme.

Conclusion

The expansion and reform of education, at all levels, was a key policy objective of the 1964–1970 Labour Governments, and one which was pursued with considerable success, although various measures which became indelibly associated with these Labour Governments had already been initiated under the previous Conservative administration. With the exception of the raising of the school leaving age, which was postponed, for reasons of financial stringency, for two years, the 1964–1970 Labour Governments maintained and accelerated the expansion of comprehensive schools, and also presided over a steady expansion of higher education, both of which had already been instigated by the Conservatives prior to 1964.

However, when Labour entered office, the party's pre-1964 proposals for expanding higher education through the building of many new universities were swiftly and significantly modified, so that whilst the Labour Government elected in 1964 continued with the ten universities already under construction (in accordance with the recommendations of the Robbins Report), Labour's own plans for a further batch of new universities in towns such as Blackpool, Doncaster, Halifax and Watford were immediately abandoned. Instead, the expansion of higher education was to be achieved by obliging existing universities to increase their student intake (which, in turn, tacitly implied that they had henceforth to be more efficient and cost-effective in the way that they deployed their staff and utilised their lecture theatres and seminar rooms), and also by increasing the number of polytechnics (which would have a special responsibility for the provision of technical and vocational education). For many commentators, though – and for Harold Wilson himself, it seems – the jewel in the crown of the 1964–1970 Labour Governments' educational reforms was the creation of the Open University.

All the educational reforms pursued by the 1964–1970 Labour Governments were intended to achieve two broad objectives, one economic, the other social. Economically, the expansion of education was deemed essential to ensuring that Britain had the well-qualified and highly skilled workforce necessary to compete and progress in a world increasingly shaped by science and technology. In order to improve the competitiveness of Britain's economy, it was deemed vital that the country produce more administrators, engineers, researchers, scientists and technicians, as well as more skilled workers and professionals in general.

Socially, Labour's commitment to the expansion of education was inextricably linked to the party's social egalitarianism, whereby it sought to increase educational opportunities for children from working-class backgrounds. This, in turn, was intended to ensure that more working-class pupils would secure the educational qualifications necessary to attain the better-paid jobs, which would then enable them to escape the 'cycle of deprivation' whereby the children of unskilled manual workers usually grew up to become unskilled manual workers themselves.

For the 1964–1970 Labour Governments, educational expansion was supposed to provide the basis for both economic modernisation and social mobility: a more efficient economy and a fairer society were supposed to be established in tandem. It was envisaged that employment opportunities and life chances would henceforth be based on 'what you know, not who you know', and that with knowledge, not nepotism, constituting the basis of occupational appointment and career advancement, the British economy would become more dynamic and innovative as a result. That, at least, was the assumption and the intention.

Note

1 Michael Stewart became Foreign Secretary in a Cabinet reshuffle necessitated – just three months after Labour's general election victory – by Patrick Gordon Walker's defeat in a by-election in Leyton (although he did win the seat in the 1966 general election). The by-election had been called expressly to secure Gordon Walker's return to the House of Commons (and thus enable him to continue as Foreign Secretary) following his defeat in Smethwick in October 1964.

16 Towards public–private partnership

Labour and pensions policy

Stephen Thornton

Introduction

At first glance, the period from 1964 to 1970 does not appear a particularly significant era in the development of post-war retirement/old age pensions policy in the United Kingdom. In terms of legislation designed for the bulk of National Insurance (NI) retirement pensioners during the first two Wilson Governments, there was little to show other than three increases in the rate of the standard pension, in 1965, 1967 and 1969. Moreover, these upratings, which followed similarly spaced Conservative increases in 1958, 1961 and 1963, were, as Heclo argues, 'fairly mechanical decisions' merely designed to prevent old age pensioners from slipping too far behind general wage and price increases (1974: 258).

First appearances, however, are regularly deceptive. Though the legislative output of the 1964–1970 administrations did indeed lack sparkle, this period did include the Government's presentation of a scheme that marked 'a major improvement to British pension provision' (Blackburn, 2002: 284). In January 1969, a White Paper entitled *National Superannuation and Social Insurance* was introduced, which contained details of a scheme designed to transform the existing predominantly flat-rate state pension regime into one based on the concept of earnings-relation. This plan was developed from an earlier scheme outlined in the policy document *National Superannuation: Labour's Policy for Security in Old Age* (Labour Party, 1957), drawn up during the Labour Party's long period in opposition. However, just weeks before legislation based on the White Paper was due to receive royal assent, it fell, alongside the Wilson Government, in June 1970. Had it succeeded – as a similar scheme had in Sweden – then it is possible that pensions policy in the United Kingdom would have progressed down a track very different from that which it subsequently followed (Pierson, 1994; Glennerster, 1995; Myles and Pierson, 2001).

The purpose of this chapter is not directly to attempt to explain the complete failure of national superannuation to materialise during the 1964–1970 period. This ground is well covered (e.g. Crossman, 1972a; Heclo, 1974; Kincaid, 1975; Shragge, 1984; Baldwin, 1990; Glennerster,

1995; Fawcett, 1996; Bridgen, 1999). Rather, through use of archive material the main aim is to track the development of one aspect of pensions that Crossman singled out as a 'really formidable problem' (1972a: 20).

This problem concerned 'contracting out', the mechanism by which an individual could contribute less to a State scheme – and thus receive less benefit in return – providing that he or she had an adequate alternative provided by the occupational pensions sector. With occupational pensions then providing the vast majority of pensions outside the state system, the stringency of conditions for contracting out greatly influenced the relationship between the public and private sectors. Moreover, changes to the policy on contracting out made during the late 1960s were amongst the most significant attempted, as they explicitly marked the Labour Party's acceptance of a significant role to be played by the private sector in the delivery of pensions.

Though, as we shall see, the problems surrounding contracting out are not fully representative of all the alterations made to Labour's pension scheme during the 1964–1970 period, focusing on these particular problems does allow attention to be drawn to some important aspects of the wider policy process. These aspects include the constraining role of earlier policy decisions (what has subsequently been termed 'inheritance in public policy' (Rose and Davies, 1994)) and the influence of particular pressure groups.

Background

In 1957, the Labour Party published its ground-breaking document *National Superannuation: Labour's Policy for Security in Old Age.* This document was the result of discussions by the Labour Party's study group on security and old age, and was largely the work of academics Richard Titmuss, Brian Abel-Smith and Peter Townsend. Very unusually for a policy document from a party in opposition, *National Superannuation* was a highly detailed piece of research, and – though far from flawless – it did present a well-crafted and nearly intelligible model with which to ameliorate the struggling existing state pension system.

It had been apparent since the early 1950s that the existing Beveridge-inspired flat-rate system was under strain. One problem was that the standard NI pension was proving to be inadequate, leading to increasing numbers of pensioners finding themselves in the position of being able to claim means-tested benefit – not that all did. Another problem was that the inflexibility of the system encouraged many of the more affluent to augment their state benefit through the expanding, and largely unregulated, occupational pensions sector – a sector expensively subsidised through a system of tax allowances.

To provide a solidaristic solution to this growing problem of 'two nations in old age' (Titmuss, 1953: 7), national superannuation was designed to provide a state pension to satisfy nearly all, this to be achieved through a 50 per cent increase in the basic pension, backed by a new level of earning-related pension, which would eventually build up to a third of an individual's lifetime average earnings, to be financed through the establishment of a 'National Pensions Fund' (Labour Party, 1957). If achieved, this scheme had the potential to fulfil Titmuss's goal 'to break the power of private insurance' (Labour Party Archives, study group on security and old age, minutes, 4 July 1956).

Despite the hopes of national superannuation's most prominent political advocate, Richard Crossman, that Labour's proposed pension plan would attract votes, it was certainly not enough to prevent a third successive electoral defeat in the 1959 general election. Nevertheless, despite Labour's defeat, aspects of the scheme did materialise – as part of the Conservative Government's response both to the perceived failings of the existing system and to Labour's own pension scheme. Thus, after much internal debate Harold Macmillan's Government introduced the National Insurance Act 1959. This somewhat muddled piece of legislation created what was termed a 'graduated' pension for some of the more affluent – a pension based loosely on the earnings-relation concept, but designed merely as cost-saving, meagre add-on to the established flat-rate benefit. In addition, and with probably greater significance, this Act gave the opportunity for certain firms to partially contract out themselves and their employees from the state scheme, something that, deliberately, gave a great boost to the occupational pension business.

Meanwhile, the Labour Party expressed continued commitment to national superannuation in policy documents such as *Signposts for the Sixties* (Labour Party, 1961) and *New Frontiers for Social Security* (Labour Party, 1963), and the 1964 election manifesto (Craig, 1975: 265). However, it was also clear, as the early 1960s progressed, that this pension scheme was no longer starring as Labour's most prominent social security proposal. This demotion was partly in response to persistent opinion within the ranks of the labour movement that national superannuation failed to address the primary social security issue of the period. This opinion was articulated by a delegate at the 1960 Party Conference when he claimed that, though the proposed scheme was fine for future provision, 'what we are concerned with now is the immediate position of the old people as they are today' (E. Roberts in Labour Party, 1960: 102). Partially in response, in the 1964 manifesto the top-listed pledge was simply to raise the existing levels of NI benefit. The pledge to introduce a wage-related scheme to cover retirement and, additionally, sickness and unemployment was placed third, coming after mention of a proposed 'incomes guarantee'. This was a scheme designed to secure for widows and the retired extra benefit without their having to resort to traditional means-tested methods, in this case by extending the existing tax system to give as well as take (Craig, 1975: 265).

Following Labour's narrow election victory in October 1964, those expecting the early introduction of at least some aspect of the 1957 scheme, such as the introduction of earnings-related pension contributions, were to be disappointed. Though it was quickly announced that the NI pension was to rise by a considerable 18.5 per cent – to be financed through flat-rate contributions, despite this being regarded by the 1957 scheme's authors as 'a poll tax, which hurts the poorest most' (Labour Party, 1957: 8–9) – all that was said about national superannuation was that it would become one aspect of a major review of social security. As Labour's policy-makers had been working on the scheme for the best part of a decade, there was surprise in some quarters that there was anything left to review.

It was at this stage that the pensions policy process became even more confused than usual. Indeed, at Cabinet level pensions policy became a matter of crisis management, for the pledge to raise pensions – alongside other proposals involving public expenditure – proved a catalyst for an attack on sterling in late 1964 that left Harold Wilson, in particular, very nervous (Wilson, 1971: 31). Admittedly, the generous uprating was salvaged and did go ahead in April 1965, but the difficult economic situation persisted. With the shadow of devaluation looming over the Government, the first significant social security casualty was the pledge to introduce the 'income guarantee', although poor planning, and extreme hostility from the Inland Revenue, also proved to be major factors responsible for this abandonment in July 1965 (PRO T 227/2216, National Insurance Review Committee, 20 November 1964). All that remained was the introduction of the Supplementary Benefits scheme – a rather more cosmetic attempt to lessen the stigma attached to means-tested benefits.

The sense of crisis at ministerial level would not have been helped by certain organisational arrangements. For reasons obscure, Wilson initially appointed Crossman – national superannuation's political champion – to head the Ministry of Housing, and divided political responsibility for pensions between Margaret Herbison, as Minister of Pensions and National Insurance – though significantly without the status of a seat in Cabinet – and Douglas Houghton, as a non-departmental 'overlord' with responsibility for social security matters in Cabinet. This arrangement did not work swimmingly: even Burke Trend, the Secretary to the Cabinet, commented on 'a background of personal difficulty' between the pair responsible for social security (PRO PREM 13/1209, Trend to Wilson, 18 May 1966).

Whilst all hell was breaking loose at the top level, deep down in Whitehall an interdepartmental committee of officials was quietly remodelling Labour's pension scheme. Shortly after the 1964 election, an Official Committee on Social Security Review was established to examine the benefit system. Chaired by Sir Clifford Jarrett, Permanent Secretary at the Ministry of Pensions and National Insurance (MPNI), this committee – a direct successor to a Working Group on Pensions established earlier in 1964 by the Conservatives – did not feel constrained by Labour's past policy proposals. As Jarrett himself remarked,

> while we must certainly take account of proposals put forward in Labour Party documents over the last few years, the subject is one of such

intricacy that a proper examination of alternatives is needed and the answers should not be pre-judged.

(PRO T 227/2216, Official Committee on Social Security Review, 5 February 1965)

By June 1966, this Official Committee on Social Security Review had formulated almost all the basic elements that were to become the basis of the 1969 White Paper (PRO T 227/2217, National Insurance Review Committee, 23 June 1966). This included significant shifts from Labour's pre-election policy, including decisions to change the earnings-relation formula, to reduce the scheme's redistributive element, and to use a pay-as-you-go, rather than a funded, system of financing. Distractions at ministerial level partly explain why civil servants were able to achieve this remodelling. However, it was also a reflection of the fact that Labour's pensions policy-makers in opposition were not, by 1964, able to present a coherent pension scheme (Bridgen, 1999). Officials reviewing Labour's social security plans found many holes in the proposals – not least on costing – and commented that 'National Superannuation''was not then [in 1957 and 1958], and is even less now, an answer to all questions' (PRO PIN 47/141, 'Matters Relating to Labour Party Policy', 13 March 1964).

At ministerial level, some calming was achieved in early 1967 by the appointment of Crossman as chair of the freshly established ministerial sub-committee on earnings-related pensions. This followed Houghton's departure from the Cabinet in January of that year, a significant development because Houghton did not rate the earnings-related pension scheme as his social security priority; his priority was the income guarantee that he himself had largely shaped during Labour's last few years in opposition (see PRO CAB 147/125, 'A Re-appraisal of Social Policy', Houghton to Wilson, 22 December 1965). Crossman's appointment thus lent impetus to the Government's commitment to introduce at least some version of the original 1957 pension scheme.

Though Crossman's appointment did foster a fresh drive to get the scheme implemented, it did not significantly alter the path along which pension proposals had been pushed by the Jarrett Committee. Perhaps the most striking example was the loss of the pledge to create a 'national pensions fund'. Crossman was utterly opposed to dropping the funded option, claiming that maintaining the existing pay-as-you-go system for national superannuation would be tantamount to introducing 'another version of the Tory swindle' (1977: 153–4, diary entry for 23 July 1968). The official committees, however, strongly favoured the pay-as-you-go option (PRO T 227/2216, Working Group on Pensions, 6 October 1964). The civil servants won, leaving Crossman to note ruefully, after a twelve-hour battle with officials, that he was 'fighting both the Ministry [of Social Security, formerly MPNI] and the Treasury in support of a properly funded scheme' (1977: 176, diary entry for 27 August 1968). Moreover, as his editor pointed out in the accompanying footnote, Crossman simply did not possess the actuarial skills to compete in such a contest (Morgan in Crossman, 1977: 176).

This battle was repeated over changes to the earnings-relation formula – whereby the original plan to retain a base level of flat-rate pension was replaced, by officials, with a proposal to introduce just one earnings-related level of benefits for all (PRO PIN 47/147, Working Group on Pensions, 18 August 1964). Crossman was far from convinced about the efficacy of this change, involving, as it did, a complicated banding formula designed to retain a sizeable element of redistribution in the scheme. Indeed, he told officials that he sometimes felt that 'it would be better to scrap this appallingly elaborate scheme' (1977: 53, diary entry for 8 May 1968). It was not scrapped, though, and this mandarin-driven alteration to the original scheme – like that to retain pay-as-you-go – appeared in the 1969 White Paper.

Thus, in some respects it could be argued that the main role of the ministerial sub-committee on earnings-related pensions in the development of the 1957 scheme was simply to accept the recommendations of its corresponding committee of officials. However, over one highly significant issue the Jarrett Committee was unable to set the agenda. This issue was contracting out; and this will be the focus of the next section.

Reluctant accommodation with the private sector

As was suggested earlier, one of the more striking differences between the original 1957 scheme and the 1969 'remake' concerned the terms for the proposed future relationship between the public and private sector in terms of pension delivery. Regarding the 1957 attempt, breaking the power of insurance industry was a clear goal. Moreover, this pension scheme could have achieved such a goal through a combination of providing competition through a generous state scheme, and by applying particularly stringent contracting out conditions – ones that suggested the provision by occupational schemes of some form of protection against inflation (Labour Party, 1957: 41). The potential prospects for providers of private occupational pension schemes were quickly perceived in the City, as, on announcement of the 1957 scheme, 'the shares of the insurance companies fell sharply' (Hannah, 1986: 56). The Prudential Insurance Company lost £2.4 million from the value of its shares within four days of the scheme's publication (Heclo, 1974: 266).

Despite this reaction, there was little sign of Labour's flinty stance on future relations with the private sector softening before the 1964 election – aside from the quiet dropping of a proposal to allow employees to contract in and out on an individual basis (Labour Party Archives, Study Group on Security and Old Age, minutes, 14 July 1959). Indeed, in a draft social security plan from 1962 there remained the prospect of 'very severe conditions for contracting-out of National Superannuation' (Labour Party Archives, Study Group on Security and Old Age, 'A Draft Social Security Plan', RD.216 (Revised), March 1962).

However, by January 1969 this position had changed drastically. Rather than threatening the private pension sector's very existence, the Labour Government was effectively saying, perish the thought: 'there is no question of the State provision replacing occupational schemes. On the contrary, its structure will leave ample scope for their continued development' (Department of Health and Social Security (DHSS), 1969a: 38). This was to be achieved by dint of presenting a State scheme which was less generous than that proposed in 1957, particularly for the more affluent, thus lessening potential competition for the private sector, and – of particular interest here – by the introduction of a unique system of contracting out known as abatement; a system that, crucially, did not require the private pension sector to 'inflation-proof' its wares. Indeed, it was proposed that the State would actually step in, if necessary, to guarantee the standard of contracted out employees' pension (Department of Health and Social Security, 1969b). Crossman could justifiably boast, in January 1970, that '[n]o Government has taken more trouble than we have to protect the pension interests in introducing a new State scheme' (House of Commons Debates, 5th series, vol. 794, col. 61).

As the policy change occurred after the 1964 election, an obvious area for investigation would be the interdepartmental committees of officials led by Jarrett. However, as will be illustrated, on this issue at least, the officials did not take a strong line. Rather, existing explanations have focused on the fact that although Labour's policy on the issue of contracting out remained relatively static during the period between 1957 and 1964, the wider world of private pension provision had not. Sustained by the inadequacies of the Beveridge system, and encouraged by the Conservative reforms, private-sector pension coverage expanded considerably, the numbers with pension scheme membership outside the state sector increasing by over 4 million between 1956 and 1967 (Hannah, 1986: 145). Indeed, by the mid-1960s towards half the national workforce was contributing towards an occupational pension. A little later it was accurately stated that 'Britain has one of the most highly developed systems of occupational pensions to be found anywhere in the world' (National Association of Pension Funds (NAPF), 1968: 4).

This expansion of the occupational pension market is an important aspect of Fawcett's concept of the 'Beveridge's strait-jacket' (1996: 21). She argues that the Beveridge-inspired reforms, *inter alia*, provoked this expansion, and this in turn established a number of 'lock-in''effects' (1996: 21). These 'lock-in effects', it is argued, made it increasingly difficult for policy-makers to veer from the path that British pensions policy was following – a path which, at the time, was paved with an expanding occupational pensions sector. As Fawcett explains, 'efforts the Labour party made to protect those covered by occupational schemes indicates the importance of policy 'lock-in'.' Government action was strongly influenced by the sheer numbers of employees covered by the private sector' (1996: 41). Araki (2000) makes a similar point, arguing that structural obstacles forced Labour policy-makers to accept the private sector, though he puts greater stress on the actions of the Macmillan government hastening private-sector expansion.

Aside from the pressure from sheer numbers involved, another significant element of this private-sector expansion was the growing strength of those various groups committed to maintaining a viable occupational pensions sector. From the perspective of the business community, the insurance industry was able to become 'a powerful interest group' (Fawcett, 1995: 155). In particular, as Heclo argues, '[b]y far the most important, well-organized, and well-staffed interest group concerned with superannuation was the Life Offices Association [LOA]' (1974: 267). This organisation first bared its teeth over state superannuation by leading a quite ferocious barrage of opposition to the 1957 scheme (Hannah, 1986: 56), and its bargaining power only increased with the expansion of occupational schemes.

However, not all the pressure to safeguard occupational schemes came from business groups. As Hannah argues, Crossman was forced to become 'very aware that any new scheme would have to take note of the now clearly established pensioning institutions, if only because the white collar unions within the TUC [Trades Union Congress] would insist on it' (1986: 59). Heclo (1974), like Hannah, is also keen to highlight the role of the trade unions in pressing Labour's policy-makers to support a viable contracting out system. In support of this view, it is clear that the TUC – through the medium of its Social Insurance Committee, which held regular meetings with the Labour Party's Study Group on Security and Old Age – did indeed increasingly moot concern about the future of occupational pension provision (Labour Party Archives, Study Group on Security and Old Age, minutes, 14 January 1958 and *passim*). Moreover, it was particular white-collar unions – those that ran their own schemes – that provoked the TUC's concern. One of these, the National Association of Local Government Officers (NALGO), was particularly vocal, with a shrill plea to Crossman to 'avoid the risk of 'castration''of existing schemes' typical of their viewpoint (NALGO, 1969).

There will be a return to these explanations in the conclusion, but it is worth pointing out at this stage that the growing muscularity of concerned pressure groups was not the issue that caused Crossman the greatest anxiety in the months prior to the 1964 election. Rather, what bothered him most was one particular, slightly esoteric development in the expansion of the private pensions market. In a newspaper article written in December 1963 – one that caught the eye of officials at the Ministry of Pensions and National Insurance (MPNI) – Crossman noted the presence of a 'small but important segment' of the population covered by occupational pension provision that was more generous than the State could hope to offer, particularly during the inevitable transition period following the introduction of a new scheme (PRO PIN 47/141, 'Matters Relating to Labour Party Policy', 13 March 1964). As Crossman explained, 'For at least ten to fifteen years, employers like I.C.I. will pay better pensions than the State can provide, even in a good State graded scheme.' This had severe implications for policy on contracting out, because, as officials noted, 'if a scheme could not see a way to continue to be contracted out, it would have, in most cases, either to be severely cut back or abandoned altogether' (PRO PIN 47/141, 'Matters Relating to Labour Party Policy', 13 March 1964), and this, in turn, had political consequences. As Crossman later commented, 'If ICI workers could be told by their firm, or by the trustees of their pension scheme, that we were requiring their pensions to be cut by 40 per cent, I did not see much chance of winning the election' (1972: 21). As will be illustrated, it was indeed Crossman's – and officials' – realisation that electoral harm was a possible consequence of introducing a pension scheme without a viable system of contracting out that drove the Labour Governments' reluctant accommodation with the private pension sector.

Regarding the attitude of civil servants to the private sector, it is worth noting that most were very wary indeed. Officials – particularly those working at the Treasury – had illustrated their antipathy to the idea of extending the role played by the private sector during the compromised creation of the 1959 National Insurance Act (Bridgen and Lowe, 1998; Bridgen, 2000). This hostility continued into the Wilson era, with the Official Committee on Social Security Review declaring that, as things stood, they did not believe the private sector could provide 'an adequate and almost universal system of pensions'. The Committee even suggested that 'it might be necessary to consider the practicality (in both administrative and political terms) of not merely curbing the growth of occupational schemes but virtually bringing them to an end over a period – if that is the desired objective' (PRO CAB 134/3303, Official Committee on Social Security, 10 March 1967). To give a little more colour to this point, Crossman noted the desire of certain officials to tell representatives from the occupational pensions industry 'to go to hell" (1972a: 21).

For all that, with regard to contracting out, officials found themselves in a similar position to that of Crossman. They supported the idea that if contracting out were to continue, then it should only be with stringent terms attached in order to guarantee that occupational schemes matched equivalent state provision (PRO CAB 134/3303, Official Committee on Social Security Review, 10 March 1967). However, practicalities again got in the way. As one member of the Official Committee on Social Security Review ruefully conceded,

[I]f only pension schemes that were satisfactory in these respects were allowed to exist, some schemes might be wound up or fail to be established either because of the cost of these improvements was so great that the contributions employers were willing to pay and to require their employees to pay would not be sufficient to finance a basic pension that looked like a worthwhile amount, or because of the administrative complications.

Consequently, the politically unpalatable situation would exist where 'there would be several decades before the major part of the improvement in pension provision took effect'. As a result of this dilemma, doing nothing was an option seriously considered (LPA, HART/11/3, Theo Cooper, 'Control of Occupational Pension Schemes', 14 July 1967).

In short, the Official Committee did not fully settle the issue of contracting out and this 'hot potato' was thrust back to its corresponding ministerial sub-committee, which appeared in no hurry to grasp it. As late as March 1968, Crossman, as chair of this body, was still prevaricating. In a letter to the Prime Minister, Crossman admitted that

> [t]he Committee tends to the view that instead of trying to resolve this issue at this stage it might be wise to envisage a presentation in the White Paper next Autumn which sets out the two alternatives [a scheme including contracting out and one without], invites public discussion and reserves the final decision until all the interests concerned have had an opportunity to give their views.

However, in a rhetorical question to complete this letter's final paragraph, Crossman indicated that he realised which direction the wind would blow by embarking on this consultation exercise by asking, 'would this in fact commit us willy-nilly to contracting out?' (PRO PREM 13/2394, Crossman to Wilson, 11 March 1968).

In an ideal world, Crossman would have discontinued contracting out. He was clearly envious of countries, such as Sweden, that had been able to set up an earnings-related pension system without resorting to contracting out (1977: 206, diary entry for 30 September 1968). As he explained to Wilson,

> [I]f we were starting *de novo* we would design a universal State scheme covering every employed worker up to $1\frac{1}{2}$ times the average male earnings; and we should limit private schemes to the useful purpose of providing extra cover beyond the level and on top of benefits of the State scheme for any groups of workers the firm might wish to benefit in this way.
>
> (PRO PREM 13/2394, Crossman to Wilson, 11 March 1968)

However, as Crossman was only too well aware, he could not start '*de novo*'; the existing extent of private pension coverage prevented it. Moreover, Crossman simply could not overcome his original problem that contracting out was developed as an important safeguard designed both to allay the fears of workers (in I.C.I. for example) about the future of their pension schemes and also to reduce the danger of an all out propaganda campaign by the insurance interests which could easily panic the electorate.

(PRO PREM 13/2394, Crossman to Wilson, 11 March 1968)

With a viable system of contracting out reluctantly accepted as inevitable, one task remaining was to decide on what form it would take. It proved to be a difficult job, as determination to create a wholly earnings-related scheme prevented easy adaptation of the existing contracting out system. To explain, the National Insurance Act 1959 had introduced the concept of *partial* contracting out, whereby it was only possible to 'opt out' of one particular portion of a multi-part state pension scheme – the 'graduated' pension in this instance. This maintained an element of universal contribution in the scheme and allowed for the possibility of redistribution (Atkinson, 1977). A similar system – though with considerably less friendly conditions attached – had been proposed in Labour's 1957 pension scheme. However, because of the proposed abolition of the flat-rate standard pension, the model introduced in the 1969 White Paper had no handy 'part' from which partial contracting out could take place.

Discussion on the way forward focused on a new variation on the partial contracting out theme, one termed 'abatement'. The plan here was for contracted out employees, and their employers, to pay a lower percentage of contribution than those who did not contract out. In return, the contracted out employee, when retired, would be awarded a reduced state pension, with the approved occupational pension available to at least make up the shortfall. According to Heclo, this abatement idea had – to borrow John Kingdon's phraseology (1995) – been floating around the 'policy primeval soup' since 1959, when it 'was created by a senior representative of the insurance companies' interests, and through a series of informal talks within the close network of London actuaries, the idea gradually spread among experts'. Civil servants were 'quick to seize on the new approach', though other insurance interest groups were less easily convinced, and it took until the mid to late 1960s before abatement became a key element of pensions policy (Heclo, 1974: 276). Certainly the Official Committee on Social Security Review automatically assumed that a system of contracting out would 'be based on an abatement formula' (PRO CAB 134/3303, Official Committee on Social Security Review, 10 March 1967).

Thus, to summarise, if Labour's pensions policy-makers thought contracting out was inevitable, then, because of 'spill-over' from the proposal to abolish the flat-rate element, the system proposed had to be one based on the abatement concept, as this was the only method yet conceived in which partial contracting out would work in a wholly earnings-related pension scheme. Crossman accepted this argument but was far from happy with it, admitting that these new terms for contracting out were 'feasible, though enormously complicated' (PRO PREM 13/2394, Crossman to Wilson, 11 March 1968). Significantly, Crossman also realised that accepting this scheme ended hopes of forcing the private sector to protect its products from inflation. He remarked that this scheme 'requires the State to bear the full cost of any dynamic element in the pension of those contracted out, since dynamism [inflation-proofing] is the one feature of our State scheme which cannot be reproduced in a private scheme' (PRO PREM 13/2394, Crossman to Wilson, 11 March 1968).

After considerable agonising, on 11 September 1969 Crossman – by this stage Secretary of State at the newly created Department of Health and Social Security (DHSS) – informed the Cabinet of the decision to opt for a pension scheme that included abatement. In so doing, he made it clear that he had not solved the problem he had mentioned in the newspaper article way back in 1963. Having noted the sharp rise in the number of occupational pension schemes, Crossman declared that

> [i]t was undesirable – and would not in any case be politically acceptable – for the Government to compel those in charge of occupational schemes to wind them up when the State scheme was introduced and it would accordingly be necessary to take them into partnership.
> (PRO CAB 128/42, 43rd Conclusions, 11 September 1969)

The battle over the details

Once the decision to include a contracting out option had been made, the only matter left to decide regarded details – though, of course, this is where the devil lurks. The most important of these details concerned the levels to be set for pension abatement and contribution rates for those contracted out. This was significant because, as Heclo highlights, the gap between abatement rate and contribution 'was the economic breathing space that would make private schemes profitable or unprofitable' (1974: 276). Crossman's diaries suggest that negotiations to set the tightness of this breathing space were fraught. They were certainly the battleground for the revival of a long-running departmental division of opinion over contracting out. In this episode of the dispute – which had its roots in the preparations for the 1959 Act – it was explained that

> [t]he Department of Health and Social Security [a successor of the MPNI] was anxious to give generous terms so that the existing private occupational schemes would not campaign against the state scheme but the Treasury wished the terms to be stiff because they had in mind the effect on government revenue.
> (Crossman, 1977: 616, footnote to entry dated 13 August 1969)

When it came to actual figures, the influential figure of the Government Actuary, Sir Herbert Tetley, made calculations that initially led to the suggestion that an occupational scheme would provide its members a pension of 1 per cent of each year's earnings for men in return for a reduction of 1.25 per cent from both employees' and employers' national superannuation contributions (Department of Health and Social Security, 1969b; Crossman, 1977). This became known as the 1:1.25 ratio, and was a figure with which the Treasury was content (Crossman, 1977: 616, diary entry for 13 August 1969). Calculations based on women's relative longevity, earlier pensionable age, and earning patterns led to the Government Actuary's frugal recommendation that 'the pension abatement for women (corresponding to 1 per cent for men) is 0.55 per cent of earnings' (Department of Health and Social Security, 1969b: 16).

Though they accepted the calculations regarding the reduced rate for women (Department of Health and Social Security, 1969b: 7), groups with an interest in maintaining occupational pension profitability were unhappy with the proposed male ratio of 1:1.25. Bodies such as the LOA, the Confederation of British Industry (CBI) and the nationalised industries were angling for a more generous one of 1:1.5 (Crossman, 1977: 663, diary entry dated 2 October 1969). Crossman had already noted that 'the pressures from the occupational pension schemes and the representatives of the T.U.C. are now becoming formidable' (1977: 626, diary entry dated 4 September 1969). He had been particularly unnerved by the TUC conference in September 1969, noting at Cabinet level that it 'had been shown by debates at the recent Trades Union Congress the earnings-related scheme was not popular and there were serious political objections to fixing the ratio at less than 1:1.3' (PRO CAB 128/42, 43rd Conclusions, 11 September 1969).

Thus, Crossman and his departmental officials were keen to come closer to the 1:1.5 mark than the Treasury wanted. Crossman was, in his words, willing 'to pay a little more danegeld to get agreement' (1977: 625, diary entry for 4 September 1969). The 1:1.3 figure was the one agreed at the 11 September Cabinet meeting (PRO CAB 128/42, 43rd Conclusions), Crossman having negotiated with Roy Jenkins, the Chancellor of the Exchequer, a few days earlier (Crossman, 1977: 632, diary entry for 8 September 1969). Ironically, though, Crossman discovered, in the month following this Cabinet meeting, that the TUC as a whole was not all that enthusiastic about generous abatement terms, despite 'certain anxieties from the Firemen and from NALGO' (Crossman, 1977: 682, diary entry dated 13 October 1969).

Anyway, when the National Superannuation and Social Insurance Bill was introduced on 17 December 1969, it did include a viable system of contracting out. This time round, it was based on a unique system of abatement set at a (male) abatement ratio of 1:1.3, and, crucially, it did not require the private pension sector to 'inflation-proof' its wares. Indeed, so unusual was the scheme that Crossman proudly remarked that it 'had not been attempted in any other country', adding for effect, 'I challenge the Opposition to give me any example, even from Venezuela' (House of Commons Debates, 5th series, vol. 794, col. 60).

The reaction of the insurance industry to these terms was in marked contrast to the 'panic in the City' response of 1957. As Crossman ruefully commented following the announcement of the new details,

> The whole idea that our terms would be so unworkable, harsh and damaging to the pensions interests has been quietly dropped. Even the other day at a meeting of the National Association of Pension Funds, Mr. Michael Pilch of Noble Lowndes – and one cannot have a bigger pensions pundit than Mr. Michael Pilch – made an informed guess that the number contracted out would be 7 million, compared with the $5\frac{1}{2}$ million contracted out today.
>
> (House of Commons Debates, 5th series, vol. 794, col. 60,
> 19 January 1970)

Of course, there was never an opportunity to test the validity of Mr Pilch's prediction, as Crossman's scheme never left the debating chamber. However, even though the pension plan fell at the last fence, it is clear that changes made during the 1964–1970 period to Labour's policy towards the private sector – exemplified by the more accommodating terms for contracting out in 1969 compared with those from 1957 – were permanent. This was displayed when Wilson's Labour Party returned to power in 1974 – though without Crossman, who died in April of that year.

In 1975, only two decades after the Labour Party conference had decided that an earnings-related pension scheme was an idea worth exploring, Barbara Castle successfully introduced the State Earnings-Related Pension Scheme (SERPS). Though in this version the abatement system was ditched – being deemed 'both complex and artificial' (Department of Health and Social Security, 1974: 15) – a key aspect that did remain from the 1969 plan was the promised 'partnership with well-founded occupational schemes' (Department of Health and Social Security, 1974: iii). In a reflection of the policy process of the 1960s, Labour's policy-makers in the 1970s found much at fault with the private sector but, like Crossman, were forced to concede that '[a] crucial factor in determining the future pattern of pension provision is the existence in this country of thriving occupational pension arrangements' (Department of Health and Social Security, 1974: 14).

To bring this aspect of Labour policy up to date, the accommodation grudgingly pledged in the 1960s and 1970s has evolved into something more explicit. Following another long period in opposition, the Labour Government of Tony Blair has had to adjust to a near-two-decade period in which the already secure position of the private pensions industry has been heartily bolstered – not least by the drastic weakening of SERPS. This era also witnessed the dominant position of occupational pensions challenged by the government-promoted expansion in personal pensions. In such circumstances, Labour's pension reform proposals for the twenty-first century possess strong echoes of Crossman's acceptance of the virtual inevitable – though whereas in 1969 Labour's proposed partnership with the occupational pension sector was clearly an uncomfortable marriage of convenience, by 2002 this relationship with a now much more diverse private sector has become passionate. As triumphantly announced in a recent Green Paper, the United Kingdom is deemed to be in a good position

> to meet the demographic challenges because of its system of targeted state support coupled with a well-developed, funded private pensions system. . . . The continued success of the UK approach to pension provision relies on the renewal of the partnership between the Government, individuals and employers, underpinned by a competitive and accessible financial services industry.
>
> (Department for Work and Pensions (DWP), 2002: 19)

Conclusion

Though the period from 1964 to 1970 did not witness the passing of any legislation to excite even those few who find pensions policy fascinating, it was nonetheless a hugely significant era. That the long-awaited national superannuation scheme did not materialise was important because, as Glennerster argues, had such a scheme been 'implemented in 1965 [it] might have gathered support from those who were drawing its pensions by the time Mrs Thatcher came to power and the political climate changed' (1995: 114). In such circumstances, it is likely that the pro-market pension reforms of the 1980s would have been much more difficult to push through (Pierson, 1994).

However, as this chapter has illustrated, even if a version of Labour's 1957 pension scheme had been passed during this period, the 1964–1970 Labour Governments' policy-makers had already accepted the requirement to accommodate the private sector. Indeed, in Crossman's case this acceptance had grudgingly occurred prior to the Labour Party gaining power in 1964. Thus, though the future of UK pension development might have been significantly different had the scheme succeeded in the 1960s, it is unlikely that the current position of the British insurance industry – as one providing pensions on a scale much larger than typical for a member of the European Union – would have been greatly changed.

As regards explanations for this development, it is worth highlighting again that though the interdepartmental committees of officials led by Clifford Jarrett did play a significant role in altering various aspects of Labour's pension scheme, contracting out was not one of those aspects. Indeed, according to Crossman (1972a), officials tended to regard representatives of the insurance industry with less warmth than he did himself. Rather, it does appear that aspects of the expansion of the occupational sector during Labour's long period in opposition were key to the change in policy.

To turn first to explanations that highlight the role of pressure groups in the policy process, particularly those within the labour movement, it is clear that groups like the LOA and NALGO were strident in their protests to save generous contracting out conditions. Moreover, Crossman was far from averse from discussing matters with some of these groups; indeed, he expressed pride that 'we have consulted the vested interests, briefed them before legislation, brought them right in – the T.U.C., the C.B.I., above all, the Institute of Actuaries and the Life Association people' (1977: 276, diary entry for 29 November 1968). Furthermore, as illustrated earlier, he was particularly alarmed by noises coming from the unions during negotiations to set the abatement rate. However, it is worth noting that such bodies were largely outside the main policy community during the key early stages (Labour Party Archives, HART/11/3, 'Contracting out under the new pension scheme', 25 July 1967). Furthermore, when a group such as the LOA was allowed in – interestingly, before talks with the TUC and CBI – officials at the Ministry of Social Security made certain that it was for '<u>technical</u> discussions' only, 'not negotiations' (Labour Party Archives, HART/11/3, 'Contracting out under the new pension scheme', 25 July 1967; emphasis in original). Thus, though the role of pressure groups was important, there were other factors at play that prompted Labour's change of heart regarding contracting conditions.

One such factor was probably more significant than direct representations from pressure groups. It is clear that from as early as 1963, Crossman was aware of a massive structural obstacle that blocked attempts to destroy the insurance industry. Fawcett suggests that the 'immovable object' was the vast membership of the occupational sector, and this legacy from a variety of earlier policy-makers does appear to be the key factor that influenced Labour's change of tack. To be a little more specific, the single biggest constraint acting on Crossman was the political problem that by the mid-1960s many thousands of occupational scheme members, working for munificent firms such as ICI, would almost inevitably become worse off during the first years of the planned new state pension scheme if, as seemed likely, those running the occupational schemes felt compelled to close them or make them less generous. Moreover, these thousands of members would, in Crossman's repeatedly expressed view, make the government responsible pay dearly. As he later admitted, '[u]nless we made special arrangements with the private schemes, they would tell their members that the wicked Labour Government was depriving them of their pensions. So this was politically very, very dangerous indeed' (1972a: 20).

Clearly, Crossman was no special friend of the private pension industry, and would – as he mentioned in the aforementioned note to Wilson – have abolished contracting out if granted the opportunity to start '*de novo*'. However, that was not an option available, and Labour's policy-makers were compelled to make a gesture of partnership to the occupational pension industry. Moreover, as illustrated, this was a tremendous compromise from the position back in 1957 when, had its terms been implemented, *National Superannuation* threatened to 'kill the bulk of their [the insurance companies'] expanding business in pensions' (Hannah, 1986: 56). As usual, idealism was beaten by pragmatism.

17 Immigration and race relations

James Hampshire

Introduction

In the course of just six years, the Wilson Governments of 1964–1970 extended and tightened immigration controls, whilst at the same time creating a wholly new legal framework outlawing racial discrimination and incitement. As several commentators have argued, the combination of restrictive immigration laws with progressive race relations legislation marked the beginning of a policy linkage that has continued down to this day. Shamit Saggar has described this linkage as the 'limitation–integration equation', by which restrictive immigration controls are conjoined with integration and anti-discrimination measures as part of a broad policy package (1992: 77; cf. Favell, 2001: 110–22; Hansen, 2000: 128–9). This chapter aims to show how the limitation–integration equation was developed as a political strategy to maintain support from opposed constituencies within the Labour Party, as well as the country as a whole. The intention was to appease anti-immigrant sentiment by restrictive immigration controls, and placate liberal and left-wing progressives with race relations legislation.

Appraisals of immigration and race relations policies have diverged sharply. Political scientists and historians have been highly critical of government approaches to immigration, often arguing that racist attitudes influenced policy-makers (Carter *et al.* 1996; Layton-Henry, 1992: 78; Paul, 1997: 177–80; Spencer, 1997: 136). Although a recent study has challenged the allegations of state racism made by the 'racialization school' (Hansen, 2000: 10–16), the received opinion among academic commentators remains that UK immigration laws developed as 'racialised controls' (Geddes, 2003: 33). Perhaps surprisingly, the literature on race relations policy is smaller and less riven with controversy. Overviews of the politics of race invariably touch upon race relations policy (e.g. Layton-Henry, 1992; Messina, 1989; Saggar, 1992; Solomos, 2003), but there is a dearth of closely researched studies of race relations policy-making. The major exception to this is Erik Bleich's recent study (2003) of race politics in Britain and France, which argues that ideational frames shaped race relations policy-making.

This chapter focuses on both the immigration and the race relations policy-making processes during the time the 1964–1970 Labour Governments were in office, particularly on intra-party debates. It argues that under Wilson the Labour Party adopted a restrictionist and populist approach to immigration. Although this was strongly opposed by many within the party, Labour was driven to tighten immigration controls largely owing to electoral considerations. By way of contrast, in the area of race relations the Government took a principled and anti-populist stand, and notwithstanding its gradualist approach and the compromises it adopted in the process, it pursued progressive policies. There was no electoral advantage to be gained by such a stance, and significant pressure groups opposed race relations legislation.

Labour's approach to immigration

On entering office in October 1964, the Wilson Government inherited an immigration regime defined by two previous pieces of legislation: the British Nationality Act of 1948 and the Commonwealth Immigrants Act of 1962. The Attlee Government had passed the British Nationality Act in response to a decision by the Canadian Government to introduce its own citizenship, as a result of which Canadians would possess British subjecthood only as a consequence of their being Canadian citizens (Hansen, 1999a). In order to shore up the indivisibility of British subjecthood, the British Nationality Act formalised an expansive, imperial conception of citizenship, under which all subjects of the Crown, whether born in the 'mother country' or in one of the colonies, enjoyed the same status (citizenship of the United Kingdom and Colonies) with identical rights to enter and settle in the United Kingdom. The 1948 Act was one of the dying gasps of the British Empire, and its unintended consequences would cause constitutional and political headaches up until 1981, when it was finally superseded by the second British Nationality Act. In 1948 it had not been foreseen that substantial numbers of colonial citizens of the United Kingdom and Colonies (CUKCs) would exercise their right to migrate to the United Kingdom, hence it did not occur to politicians at the time that the British Nationality Act would become an institutional obstacle to immigration controls (Hansen, 2000: 53). Effectively, short of overhauling UK citizenship law, any attempts at control would in future have to discriminate between persons with the same citizenship status – a legally, not to mention politically, difficult situation.

During the 1950s, as CUKCs from the Caribbean and South Asia migrated to Britain, the Conservative Governments considered passing legislation to restrict their entry, but the decision to impose legislative controls was not made until 1961 (various administrative controls were employed prior to this, however; see Spencer, 1997: 46–8). The main reason for the 'open door' policy of the 1950s was a belief, held by many Conservatives, that immigration legislation aimed at colonial immigrants would hasten calls for colonial independence and thus act as a spur to the break-up of Empire and Commonwealth. As Nigel Fisher observed, 'the ties which bind this Commonwealth together are few and tenuous and no-one wants to see them further weakened' (*Guardian*, 28 September 1961). However, as the numbers of immigrants grew and levels of popular discontent increased, and, crucially, as the Government began to perceive its future primarily in European rather than colonial terms, the balance tipped in favour of control. Following the racist violence in Nottingham and Notting Hill, London, in 1958, the Conservatives considered immigration legislation once again, and in 1961 resolved to restrict the right of entry of colonial immigrants (see PRO CAB 128/35, CC(61)55, 10 October 1961).

The Commonwealth Immigrants Bill was presented to Parliament in November 1961. It sought to abolish the right of entry for all Commonwealth citizens except those born in the United Kingdom or those holding a UK passport issued under the authority of the UK Government. A limited employment voucher scheme was created for those no longer automatically entitled to enter the country. From the Opposition benches, Labour vociferously attacked the bill. Hugh Gaitskell described it as 'a plain anti-colour measure' (House of Commons Debates, 5th series, vol. 649, col. 799, 16 November 1961), whilst Patrick Gordon Walker, Shadow Foreign Secretary, berated Rab Butler for advancing a piece of legislation that contained 'barefaced, open race discrimination' (House of Commons Debates, 5th series, vol. 649, col. 706, 16 November 1961). This high moral tone was supported by the use of various procedural mechanisms to try to wreck the legislation, as well as repeated votes against it. None of these was successful, and in February 1962 the bill passed its third reading by 277 votes to 170 (House of Commons Debates, 5th series, vol. 654, col. 1278, 27 February 1962).

Prior to 1964, therefore, the Labour Party had a broadly 'pro-immigrant' record, having opened the door to colonial citizens (albeit unintentionally) in 1948, and then, during 1961–1962, attacking the Conservatives' decision to close the door. It might have been expected that the Labour Party would continue such an approach in government, but once it was back in office matters were very different indeed. In fact, Labour's position on immigration actually began to shift before the election of October 1964. Shortly after the 1962 Commonwealth Immigrants Act reached the statute book, Labour Party statements became more circumspect, and appeared to renege on previous commitments to repeal the Act. By late 1963, the Labour Party, now led by Harold Wilson, had reconciled itself to immigration controls (Foot, 1965: 175–6), and Labour contested the 1964 general election with a manifesto commitment to 'retain immigrant control' because 'Labour accepts that the number of immigrants entering the United Kingdom must be limited' (Dale, 2000: 120). Somewhat awkwardly, however, Wilson maintained that Labour opposed the 1962 Commonwealth Immigrants Act because it had been imposed on the Commonwealth without consultation and was 'inspired by colour prejudice' (MS. Wilson c. 1370, Birmingham immigration speech, 6 October 1964).

Following its narrow election victory in 1964, Labour not only declined to repeal the previous Government's immigration legislation but actually proceeded to enact further restrictions. This was largely a matter of political expedience, for a Government with a parliamentary majority as slim as Wilson's at this time could hardly afford to be cavalier about such a volatile electoral issue. As Shamit Saggar has pointed out, there was a 'rich electoral dividend' to be gained from tough immigration policies, and Labour's volte-face reflected a belated recognition that its earlier liberal stance was out of touch with grassroots sentiment (1993: 255). At the time, Richard Cross-man acknowledged that 'immigration can be the greatest potential vote-loser for the Labour party if we are seen to be permitting a flood of immigrants to come in and blight the central areas in all our cities' (1975: 149–50, diary entry for 5 February 1965). In accordance with this perspect-ive, less than a year after being elected the Labour Government acted to place further limits on the number of colonial immigrants permitted to move to Britain.

The 1965 White Paper

The Labour Government's first major policy initiative in the field of immi-gration was the 1965 White Paper *Immigration from the Commonwealth* (HMSO, 1965). Having renewed the 1962 Commonwealth Immigrants Act shortly after entering office, the Labour Government undertook a review of its operation. The Cabinet dispatched Lord Mountbatten to consult with Commonwealth governments about the possibility of their exercising some control over emigration, in an attempt at fulfilling Wilson's campaign pledge that a Labour Government would seek 'a system of agreed Common-wealth control' with the countries concerned (MS. Wilson c. 1370, Birm-ingham immigration speech, 6 October 1964). Mountbatten's mission was entirely unsuccessful and had little effect on the White Paper. Most Com-monwealth governments were uncooperative, and, besides, the Labour Government had already made up its mind on the core aspects of its policy by the time Mountbatten reported (Hansen, 2000: 148–9). The White Paper revised the immigration voucher system, abolishing Category C (for those without a pre-arranged job or skills in short supply in the economy) and reducing the quotas for Categories A and B, so that the total number of labour vouchers went from 20,800 to 8,500 per year (HMSO, 1965: 13). This tough line on controls was balanced by measures aimed at the integra-tion of already settled immigrants. Building on Wilson's appointment of Maurice Foley as Ministerial Coordinator of Policy on Integration (Saggar, 1993: 260; cf. PRO HO 376/139, Integration of Commonwealth Immi-grants, 1965), the White Paper made provision for various integrationist measures, including the establishment of a National Committee for Commonwealth Immigrants (NCCI).

Despite these attempts to mollify liberal opponents of immigration controls, the White Paper met with a chorus of disapproval from within the Labour Party. A wide range of MPs, constituency party associations and Labour activists attacked the Government's policy. As one letter-writer to the Prime Minister observed, it appeared that 'we . . . have gone back on so many of the firm principles enunciated by Hugh Gaitskell only a few years back' (MS. Wilson c. 891, Fred Moorhouse to Harold Wilson, 10 August 1965). In August 1965, a group from the Research Department wrote to the Prime Minister to express their 'disgust' and 'shame' at the White Paper. Not for the last time, the view that the limitation–integration equation was imbalanced was expressed: the restrictions were 'draconian' whilst the integration measures were 'utterly inadequate' (MS. Wilson c. 891, Judy Bernstein *et al.* to Harold Wilson, 11 August 1965). Wilson replied that the policy was consistent with the Labour Party's manifesto commitments and struck a reasonable balance between 'a number of conflicting factors', which went unspecified (MS. Wilson c. 891, Harold Wilson to John Lyttle, 8 September 1965).

Criticism of the Government's stance intensified during the run-up to the party's 1965 annual conference. In September a group of Labour MPs, including David Ennals, Michael Foot and Shirley Williams, signed an Appeal for a Rational Immigration Policy, which attacked 'the severe and arbitrary nature of the restrictions' contained in the White Paper. They argued that the Government's policy was not founded on 'real study or understanding . . . but appears to be based on too close attention being paid to expressions of fear, prejudice and muddled thinking'. The White Paper should be withdrawn, they claimed, and a thorough review of immigration legislation undertaken, in order to create an 'up-to-date humane, democratic and rational law'. Most revealing of all was their clarion call to resist racism and prejudice: 'We call on all people of liberal and humane opinion, *as well* as on the whole Labour movement . . . to resist the pressures of ignorance and racialism' (MS. Wilson c. 891, Appeal for a Rational Immigration Policy, 21 September 1965; emphasis added). Probably unintentionally, this statement betrayed the fact that there was plenty of illiberal opinion amongst the Labour movement as a whole. As on so many other issues, the Government was caught between its progressive and populist wings, and its immigration policy was being driven by the latter.

At Labour's annual conference, a motion urging withdrawal of the 'reactionary White Paper' was debated, with Alice Bacon, a Home Officer Minister, defending the Government's policy by drawing attention to the provisions on integration and urging delegates to 'go back to their trade unions and their constituencies resolved to do all possible to make at home those immigrants who are with us' (Labour Party, 1965: 220). Similar appeals to the Government's integration measures, as well as its anti-discrimination legislation (to be dealt with later in the chapter), became the main means by which the party leadership rebutted liberal critics of its stance on immigration. In 1965, the strategy appeared to have worked – the resolution was defeated by 4,736,000 votes to 1,581,000 – and over the next few years the Government refused to budge on its restrictionist approach. Indeed, in 1968 it responded to an anti-immigrant panic by passing its most controversial measure of all.

Kenyan Asians and the 1968 Commonwealth Immigrants Act

The Commonwealth Immigrants Act of 1968 was rushed through Parliament in just seven days as a response to the so-called Kenyan Asians crisis. The 1968 Commonwealth Immigrants Act was perceived to be – and was passed as – an emergency measure, and there was no consultation beyond the upper echelons of the Government about the decision. For many, then and now, it represented a capitulation to racist hysteria and a betrayal of Kenyan Asian CUKCs fleeing persecution.

The crisis was created by the 'Africanisation' policy of the newly independent Government of Kenya, under which Kenyans of Asian origin were, among other things, excluded from sectors of the economy and removed from the civil service. Many Kenyan Asians who held CUKC status began to flee Kenya for Britain. These people were not subject to immigration controls because the 1962 Act had excluded from such controls those born in the United Kingdom and those holding a UK passport *issued under the authority of the UK Government*. Most colonial CUKCs held passports issued by colonial governments and were therefore subject to controls. The Kenyan Asians (and many other African Asians) held passports issued by the High Commission under the authority of London and were therefore exempt from the existing legislation. Kenyan Asian CUKCs were able freely to enter the United Kingdom, and did so as life in Kenya became increasingly unpleasant for those who did not accord with Jomo Kenyatta's idea of a true African. British newspapers, radio and television widely reported on these arrivals, and anti-immigrant propagandists warned of the 'flood' to come. Public opinion polls showed that around 70 per cent of Britons wanted further controls to prevent this (Hansen, 1999b: 161 n. 39).

The Government responded precipitately, making the decision to act during two heated Cabinet meetings in early 1968. On 15 February, the Home Secretary, James Callaghan, sought approval from the Cabinet to introduce legislation withdrawing the right of Kenyan CUKCs to enter the United Kingdom. The flow of East African migrants was increasing, and if left unregulated 'might become a flood'. Whilst he was aware of the obligations that the previous Government had undertaken upon the independence of Kenya and other colonial territories, and also cognisant of the international conventions that prohibited the denial of the right of entry to citizens, Callaghan urged the need for action. He claimed that an 'influx' greater than 'we could absorb' would undermine the integration strategy and jeopardise support for the forthcoming Race Relations Bill (PRO CAB 128/43, CC(68)13, 15 February 1968; cf. PRO CAB 129/135, C(68)34, Memorandum by the Home Secretary, 12 February 1968). Cabinet opinion was divided. The Commonwealth Secretary, George Thomson, was unpersuaded by Callaghan's appeal to the limitation–integration equation and claimed that the proposed legislation would be widely condemned as racial discrimination. Furthermore, Thomson alleged that it constituted a breach of faith, was contrary to international principle and would be unworkable in practice. Ultimately, Thomson argued, the Bill 'creates a second-class category of citizens of this country who have no right of entry into any part of it'. It would render the Kenyan Asians effectively stateless (PRO CAB 129/135, C(68)35, Memorandum by the Commonwealth Secretary, 12 February 1968).

In response, the Attorney-General, Sir Elwyn Jones, claimed that the Government's position in relation to international agreements was 'difficult but not impossible'. He argued that in the case of the Universal Declaration of Human Rights, the United Nations Convention on Racial Discrimination and the International Convention on Civil and Political Rights, the action might be justified by the fact 'that the people concerned did not in any real sense belong to this country' (PRO CAB 129/135, C(68)36, Memorandum by the Attorney-General, 14 February 1968).[1] Given the divisions within the Cabinet, a final decision was deferred until the following week.

At the next Cabinet meeting, Callaghan once again insisted that it was 'essential and urgent' to impose restrictions immediately, because Kenyan Asians were now arriving at a rate of 200–300 a day. 'If this rate of entry were to continue,' he warned, 'the pressures on the social services would be such that large additional expenditure would be required, particularly on education and housing, and our race relations policy would be in jeopardy.' It was imperative, he claimed, that 'we . . . legislate so as to deprive citizens of the United Kingdom and Colonies who did not belong to this country . . . of their automatic right to enter this country', adding that 'wide support could be expected in this country for a policy on these lines' (PRO CAB 128/43, CC(68)14, 22 February 1968).

The Commonwealth Secretary remained opposed to the proposal, but the balance of opinion had shifted against him, and that afternoon the Government tabled a bill that removed the right of entry for CUKCs 'with no substantial connection with this country'. Such was the perceived urgency that Commonwealth governments were not consulted about the decision. Wilson's 1964 commitment to 'full and proper consultations with *all* the parties' affected by immigration legislation, which had been one of his main arguments against the 1962 Act, was now abandoned. Ironically, David Ennals, who two years previously had called for a 'rational' approach to immigration policy, was given the task of piloting the legislation through Parliament.

A further irony was that the Labour Government sought to defend its own policy by portraying it as a logical extension of the 1962 Act, despite having attacked that piece of legislation just a few years earlier. In Parliament, Callaghan argued that the 1968 Commonwealth Immigrants Bill simply closed a loophole in the primary legislation. Claiming that Labour was 'fully committed to the development of a multi-racial society in Britain', he also referred to Rab Butler's idea of non-belonging citizens to justify the distinction that was being drawn between different CUKCs (House of Commons Debates, 5th series, vol. 759, col. 1249, 27 February 1968). This failed to pacify fierce opposition to the legislation from prominent Labour and Conservative MPs,[2] many of whom denounced the action as racially discriminatory, but the whips prevailed and the bill was given its third reading on 1 March 1968. When the Speaker announced that the Lords had passed the bill without any amendments and the royal assent had been given, several MPs cried 'shame' (House of Commons Debates, 5th series, vol. 759, col. 1917, 1 March 1968).

The 1968 Commonwealth Immigrants Act (CIA 1968) extended immigration controls to all CUKCs except those who had been born, naturalised or adopted in the United Kingdom, or who had at least one parent or grandparent who had been born, naturalised or adopted in the United Kingdom. In addition, the Act extended the powers of immigration officers in a number of ways, and made it an offence for ships or aircraft to allow an illegal immigrant to land. A quota of entry vouchers for Kenyan Asians was provided (1,500 heads of households a year plus dependants), but this was well short of the total number entering up until February. Within the category of CUKC there were now two distinct statuses, one with right of entry to the United Kingdom, one without. To use Callaghan's own terms, some citizens were 'United Kingdom belongers' while others were 'colonial belongers' (PRO CAB 129/135, C(68)34, Memorandum by the Home Secretary, 12 February 1968), and this was now the basis for two different sets of rights.

In a rather defensive passage in his autobiography, Callaghan claims that in 'an atmosphere of alarm, resentment and panic', and with the 'danger of a serious deterioration in race relations', he could do no other than remove the Kenyan Asians' right of entry to the United Kingdom (Callaghan, 1987: 265). What is certain is that neither he nor any other Minister made a serious attempt to counter the lurid tabloid stories of 'tidal waves' and 'floods', or put the humanitarian case for accepting the fleeing Kenyan Asians. In hindsight, the Labour Government's approach in 1968 compares unfavourably with the response of the Heath Government to the similar plight of Ugandan Asians in 1972.

If the 1968 Commonwealth Immigrants Act was of dubious morality, there was no doubt that it had popular appeal. As Randall Hansen has put it, the 1968 Act 'was loathed by liberal opinion and loved by the public' (1999b: 164–5). Members of the NCCI hinted at collective resignation, and the European Commission of Human Rights ruled that the 1968 Act was in violation of its convention, but British public opinion was firmly behind the law. This might explain why, unlike in 1965, Labour's 1968 conference did not include any motions calling on the Government to repeal the Act. The Home Office reported on its 'balanced policy' of restriction and integration, and a vague motion calling for a national immigration policy 'based not on colour but on the social and economic needs of the country' was carried, but there was no explicit condemnation of the Act (Labour Party, 1968: 283). Labour had completed its volte-face on immigration: the experience of being in government and, above all, electoral considerations had pushed party policy towards outright restrictionism. By 1968, Hugh Gaitskell's denunciation of the Conservatives' immigration proposals must have seemed like a very distant memory.

Labour and race relations

For liberals and progressives, the capitulation to anti-immigrant sentiment in 1968 was a nadir for Wilson's Labour Government. Having criticised the Conservatives whilst in opposition, Labour had itself resorted to a populist policy of restrictive immigration controls once in power. In contrast to this, the Labour Governments' record on race relations gave progressives much to cheer. The development of laws and institutions to tackle racial discrimination and incitement was a genuine and, in the circumstances, far from inevitable achievement. Furthermore, unlike the populist approach to immigration, the process by which race relations was placed on the agenda and legislated for was largely elite driven. Neither pressure group activity nor electoral considerations can explain why the Labour Governments legislated twice – in 1965 and 1968 – to outlaw forms of racism. No significant immigrant lobby groups influenced the legislation, at least in 1965, and, in general, recently arrived immigrants were not in a position to apply pressure to policy-makers. Nor can the drive to legislate against racial discrimination be explained in terms of electoral advantage-seeking, for immigrant communities were not sizeable enough to constitute a significant electoral force themselves, and policies perceived as 'pro-immigrant' were an electoral liability in the anti-immigration climate of the 1960s. It is therefore worth asking why race relations legislation was passed at all.

In his recent study of 'race politics' in Britain and France, Erik Bleich argues that four factors influenced the 1964–1970 Labour Governments to pass legislation outlawing racial discrimination: a desire among the party leadership to prevent social disorder of the sort that was unfolding in the United States; guilt felt by many Labour MPs over the party's approach to immigration, which fed into support for integrationist measures; changing evaluations of the extent of racism in British society; and a perceived need to depoliticise race and remove it from the sphere of electoral competition (Bleich, 2003: 43). Bleich's second factor was particularly important, for along with integrationist measures, anti-discrimination initiatives were part of the Government's strategy to minimise intra-party divisions by mollifying those who opposed its immigration legislation. It should also be noted that the role played by a few key individuals who were committed to anti-racism on principled grounds was important. Overall, the development of race relations legislation was the result of an uneasy combination of pragmatic and principled reasoning. The Government's concern about potential social disorder, as well as disorder on its own back benches, combined with a genuine desire to tackle racial discrimination from key actors, were the key explanatory factors.

Origins of Labour's commitment to race relations

While in opposition during the 1950s, the Labour Party leadership did not see race relations as a priority, as was apparent in 1952 when the NEC shelved an internal report on racism which recommended legislation to outlaw racial discrimination (Lester and Bindman, 1972: 108). The Parliamentary Labour Party, however, included several members with a demonstrable commitment to race relations, with individual MPs, most notably Reginald Sorensen and Fenner Brockway, seeking to introduce anti-racist bills on a number of occasions. Indeed, Brockway tabled no fewer than nine private members' bills whilst Labour was in opposition (Bleich 2003: 41), but, without backing from the Conservative Government, all went the way of most such proposals.

A turning point in the evolution of Labour Party policy on race relations came in the aftermath of the 1958 'race riots' in Nottingham and Notting Hill. In response to the racist violence witnessed that summer, the NEC issued a statement committing the party to legislation outlawing discrimination in public places (Lester and Bindman, 1972: 109). In March 1963, after yet another of Brockway's private members' bills had been rejected by Parliament, the new party leader, Harold Wilson, told an anti-apartheid rally that 'when we have a Labour majority we will enact it as a Government measure' (MS. Wilson c. 891, Commitments on Racial Discrimination and Incitement, undated). In July 1964, this was confirmed when the NEC adopted a draft Race Relations Bill (PRO HO 376/18, Society of Labour Lawyers: Third Report of the Race Relations Committee, November 1966), and a commitment to legislate against racial discrimination and incitement in public places was included in Labour's 1964 election manifesto (Dale, 2000: 120).

Although race and immigration did not figure prominently in the 1964 election overall, one constituency result signalled the potentially explosive impact of 'playing the race card'. In Smethwick, the Shadow Foreign Secretary, Patrick Gordon Walker, lost his seat to his Conservative opponent, Peter Griffiths, who had campaigned on a racist platform, using the slogan 'If you want a nigger for your neighbour, vote Labour.' Against a national swing to Labour of 3.5 per cent, in Smethwick there was a swing to the Conservatives of 7.2 per cent (Foot, 1965: 64). Virtually every observer attributed the result to Griffiths' stance on colonial immigration, and many drew bleak conclusions about the extent of racism in British society, and the potential of race and immigration as electoral issues. The Smethwick incident sent shock waves through the Labour Party and galvanised support for race relations legislation. In the debate on the Queen's Speech, which repeated the Government's commitment to outlaw racial discrimination, the new Prime Minister denounced Griffiths as a 'parliamentary leper' (House of Commons Debates, 5th series, vol. 701, col. 71, 3 November 1964). For his efforts, Wilson was attacked by Conservatives (several walked out of the chamber in protest), a few Labour Party MPs and, for altogether different reasons, the Mission to Lepers (MS. Wilson c. 80, Rev. Davidson to Wilson, 4 November 1964). Wilson's comment was not just parliamentary point-scoring, but a reflection of his personal distaste for racism (Pimlott, 1992: 510). Notwithstanding his personal feelings on the issue, however, Wilson was acutely aware of the political conundrum presented by the Smethwick result, and his attack on Griffiths should be seen in this light (Saggar, 1993: 259–60). In a letter to the Archbishop of Canterbury, he wrote that 'unless this problem is dealt with head on, I am afraid that it will foul our politics not only in the next Election but over a very considerable period of time' (quoted in Ziegler, 1993: 174).

If Smethwick redoubled the leadership's commitment to the limitation–integration equation, it also showed how volatile the whole strategy was. While the immigration side of the equation involved a tightening of pre-existing controls and had populist appeal, the race relations proposals marked a new departure for UK law and, as a 'pro-immigrant' measure, they were politically risky. Accordingly, on race relations the Government proceeded gingerly, adopting a gradualist, problem-solving approach. The first round of legislation yielded a weak law, which was only extended as its limitations became increasingly apparent.

The 1965 Race Relations Act

The Government having committed itself in principle to legislation, it remained to be seen what form the Race Relations Bill would take. Disagreements at the drafting stage focused on whether outlawing racial incitement was practicable. The Home Secretary, Frank Soskice, insisted that it was, but he had to overcome the scepticism of civil servants at the Home Office (PRO HO 376/68, Miscellaneous Correspondence, 1965). There was also concern from some Ministers that the draft was too limited, because of its exclusion of housing and employment, and the decision not to include religious discrimination. In the Cabinet Home Affairs Committee, Soskice acknowledged this and even noted that 'a measure of the limited character now proposed might be criticised by the Government's own supporters'

(PRO CAB 134/1997, H(65)5, 12 February 1965). Nevertheless, a limited draft bill outlawing certain forms of racial discrimination and incitement was presented to the Cabinet for approval in February (PRO CAB 128/39, CC(65)11, 22 February), and then published in April.

The Race Relations Bill reflected most of the backbench proposals that had been suggested in preceding years, particularly with regard to employing the criminal law to punish racial discrimination. However, this proved to be extremely controversial, and a campaign to replace the criminal provisions with a conciliation machinery backed up by the civil law was launched from within the party. A group of Labour lawyers, who were influenced by the North American model of race relations, argued that an administrative machinery with enforcement through the civil courts would be a more effective way of tackling racism (Bleich, 2003: 54–7).[3] Anthony Lester and other members of the Society of Labour Lawyers allied themselves with the recently formed Campaign Against Racial Discrimination (CARD) to lobby Labour MPs to adopt their proposals. CARD was also successful in persuading the Conservatives to support its proposals, largely because it gave the Opposition the tactical ability to oppose the substance of the Government's bill without appearing to be against good race relations per se (Lester and Bindman, 1972: 113).

With the Conservatives opposed and many Labour MPs unsatisfied with its criminal provisions, the Race Relations Bill was heavily criticised during its second reading in the Commons, and when the House divided, it passed by only a narrow margin of 261 to 249 votes (House of Commons Debates, 5th series, vol. 711, col. 1050, 3 May 1965). This convinced the Government that it should accept the substance of the Society of Labour Lawyers/CARD proposals, whereupon it took the unusual step of amending its legislation between the second reading and the committee stage. The bill was redrafted and the criminal provisions replaced with a conciliation mechanism and civil law enforcement. The desire to generate a consensus, both within the Labour Party and across party lines, had led to a significant shift in the Government's position. In standing committee the bill was still criticised by Labour MPs over its exclusions, notably employment and housing, and also over the modest powers of the proposed Race Relations Board (House of Commons Debates, Standing Committee B, Race Relations Bill, 25 May–1 July 1965). However, with Conservative support the Government was able to withstand the proposed changes to its legislation, and the bill received the royal assent on 8 November.

The 1965 Race Relations Act, which established the form of race relations legislation that exists to this day, had two main dimensions: first, it rendered certain types of discrimination unlawful; and second, it established an institutional mechanism to deal with complaints of discrimination. The Act outlawed discrimination on grounds of 'colour, race, or ethnic or national origin' in specified public places, including hotels and restaurants, venues for public entertainment such as cinemas and dance halls, public transport, and public facilities maintained by local authorities. The exclusion of discrimination in the areas of housing and employment was widely commented upon.

A Race Relations Board (RRB) was established to enforce the Act. The RRB, a small organisation consisting only of a chairperson and two members, was charged with overseeing the work of local conciliation committees, which it was required to establish under the terms of the legislation. Not only was the RRB small, it also had limited powers. It could not take the initiative to tackle discrimination unless an individual complainant approached one of the local conciliation committees, and it had no powers to compel the attendance of witnesses or the disclosure of information. Nor was it responsible for the decision to institute legal proceedings against persons or institutions suspected of discrimination. Only if a conciliation committee was unable to achieve a settlement would the Board report the case to the Attorney-General or, in the case of Scotland, to the Lord Advocate, who would then decide whether to bring civil proceedings.

Thus, the decision to prosecute was not in the hands of the institution that had been established to oversee the Act. The Attorney-General's role as a gatekeeper reflected the Government's wish to avoid large numbers of contentious cases reaching the courts: as a member of the Study Group on Commonwealth Immigration put it in 1964, the intention was to prevent 'trivial prosecutions . . . by over-sensitive people' (MS. Wilson c. 1367, Prof. Martin to Greenwood, 7 July 1964). Overall, the various stages through which a complaint had to proceed meant that the whole process was slow and cumbersome.

Given these limitations, it is little wonder that Erik Bleich describes the 1965 Race Relations Act as 'a whimper of a law' (2003: 61). Certainly those on the left of the party, as well as many liberals, were unimpressed, considering the Act to be 'toothless and a sop' (Pimlott, 1992: 510). However, although the Act was limited in power and scope, even to the point of ineffectiveness, it still had a twofold importance. First, it broached the *principle* of anti-discrimination, such that, notwithstanding the Government's public declarations that it hoped further legislation would not be necessary, in future it would become increasingly difficult to justify inaction if evidence of racism in employment or housing were forthcoming. In this sense, the 1965 Race Relations Act's declaratory effect was significant indeed.

Second, the *institutional framework* of the Act was of tremendous long-term importance. The mechanisms adopted – an administrative agency and civil law punishments – have formed the basis for Britain's race relations policy through to the present day. Whilst the scope and powers of the legal and administrative machinery have been extended, its basic structure has not been altered. Indeed, the development of race relations policy after 1965 provides an example of what institutionalists describe as path dependence (see Pierson, 2000). In addition, despite its weaknesses the RRB became an institutional focus for those committed to extending the legislation, as well as a source of information about racism in British society.

Between the Acts

After the 1966 election, there was little reason to think that the Government would turn its attention to race relations again. Anti-discrimination measures were not popular with the electorate, organised labour was hostile to regulation of employment, and segments of the Labour Party were accordingly unenthusiastic (Rose, 1969: 535). Yet within two years, a second Race Relations Act was passed, expanding the areas in which discrimination was illegal and strengthening the RRB. The speed with which new legislation materialised was largely due to three interrelated factors. First, a group of progressives working within and alongside the new immigrant and race relations institutions lobbied for further legislation. Second, from December 1965 these groups had a powerful ally in the Cabinet in the figure of the new Home Secretary, Roy Jenkins, who was personally committed to anti-discrimination legislation, especially in the field of employment. Third, sceptics found it increasingly difficult to oppose the progressive lobby as a body of evidence emerged to show that racial discrimination was widespread, notably in those areas that had been excluded from the 1965 Act.

Those within the Labour Party who were committed to expanding and strengthening the race relations policy came from various quarters. In Parliament, a few MPs and Lords provided the momentum, with Maurice Orbach and Fenner (now Lord) Brockway each tabling private members' bills to extend the 1965 Act in order to include housing, employment, and insurance and credit services. Their bills also proposed an increase in the membership of the RRB, and empowered it to conduct its own investigations and issue enforceable orders against discriminators. Both failed in Parliament, and were in any case largely intended to stimulate debate and generate momentum for Government action. Orbach withdrew his bill after its second reading (House of Commons Debates, 5th series, vol. 738, col. 952, 16 December 1966), whilst Lord Brockway's bill was rejected at second reading in the Lords just three days later (House of Lords Debates, 5th series, vol. 278, col. 1910, 19 December 1966). The striking similarity between their proposals and the legislation introduced in 1968 indicates the extent to which their interventions helped shape the policy agenda.

More influential were the members of the Society of Labour Party Lawyers, particularly its leading campaigner on race relations, Anthony Lester. In November 1966, the Society's Race Relations Committee lent its weight to the calls for new legislation, recommending in its third report that a Government bill should be introduced along similar lines to those advanced by Orbach and Brockway (PRO HO 376/18, Third Report of the Race Relations Committee, November 1966). There was a growing feeling among race progressives that the Government's existing policy was inadequate to deal with the realities of racism in British society. Many of them had always regarded Soskice's 'package deal' (PRO PREM 13/382, Soskice to Wilson, 4 January 1965) as something of a Faustian pact, but during 1966 and 1967 dissatisfaction reached new levels. Following the restrictions created by the 1965 White Paper, and complaints from the RRB that it was unable to tackle racism in a comprehensive way owing to its lack of powers, the limitation–integration equation was increasingly viewed as grossly imbalanced. In a scathing report, which he sent to Maurice Foley at the Home Office, Lester argued that

> the premise on which the Immigration White Paper was based was that a restrictive immigration policy would take the issue out of politics and so enable the Government to have a decent policy on race relations. Immigration has been severely curtailed, and Labour won back Smethwick, but the other side of this dubious bargain has yet to be fulfilled.
> (PRO HO 376/158, 'Labour's White Problem' by Anthony Lester, 9 May 1966)

In a letter to Roy Jenkins, Lester described the 1965 Race Relations Act as a 'shoddy job' and enclosed a 'shopping-list of discontents': the Government should commit itself to extending the race relations legislation to cover all public places, as well as employment, housing, credit and insurance services, and it should strengthen the RRB (PRO HO 376/158, Lester to Jenkins, 29 January 1966).

In response to this lobbying, the Government began to reconsider its race relations policy. A meeting of Ministers was called to discuss the situation in February 1967, at which Jenkins advanced the case for further legislation. He reported that the Government was coming under pressure to strengthen the 1965 Act, not only from Labour backbenchers but also from various Ministers, and progressives such as Lester. The main opposition at the meeting came from the Minister of Labour, Ray Gunter, who warned that the CBI and TUC were both opposed to race relations legislation covering employment. Jenkins acknowledged that it would be 'most unwelcome to the TUC', but the RRB and others had made a compelling case for action and would be 'very disappointed' if nothing was done (PRO HO 376/18, Note of a meeting on possible race relations legislation, 8 February 1967). The assembled Ministers agreed to establish a working party in order to consider legislative proposals, which would then be presented to the Cabinet.

The working party duly reported that the 1965 Race Relations Act had been subject to extensive criticism and that the Government had therefore come under pressure to widen its scope, strengthen the powers of the RRB, and include religion in the definition of discrimination. The report claimed that the Act contained 'obvious deficiencies' and argued that there was a powerful case for widening its provisions to include employment, housing and insurance. It also concurred with progressives on the need to strengthen the RRB. It recommended that the Board should receive some powers of investigation, although the decision to institute civil proceedings should remain with the Attorney-General and Lord Advocate (PRO HO 376/18, Report of the Home Office Working Party on Race Relations, undated 1967).

The Ministry of Labour continued to oppose the proposals, and responded to the report by claiming (on the basis of declining unemployment figures for colonial immigrants) that racial discrimination was probably a diminishing problem. The Ministry further claimed that some of the complaints received by the RRB about discrimination in employment were the result of 'deliberate efforts by immigrant organisations who sent school-leavers to apply for employment which at least in some cases they had no intention of accepting'. Although the existence of some racial discrimination was 'indisputable', the Ministry claimed that there were difficulties in identifying and distinguishing racist motivation for non-hiring from 'other reasons, e.g. poor English or physique or lack of experience of British methods etc.'. If further legislation was passed, there was a risk that 'an employer by engaging a particular race, or too many of them, would lay himself open to strike action on the part of his other employees'. Furthermore, some employers would 'be placed ... in a disadvantageous trading position' if they had to employ 'coloured workers' against public opinion. Although the 'moral force' of legislation would help the employer in these instances, employers would be 'placed in an exposed position and public policy would be enforced at their expense' (PRO HO 376/18, Race Relations: Employment. Paper by the Ministry of Labour, undated February 1967). As an alternative to statutory provision, the Ministry proposed the establishment of a conciliation machinery under its own auspices and with representatives from the CBI and TUC, similar to the Courts of Inquiry that dealt with industrial disputes.

What swung the argument against the Ministry of Labour and in the progressives' favour was the emergence of powerful new evidence that racist discrimination was in fact widespread and profound, and that the existing mechanisms were inadequate to deal with the problem. The annual report of the RRB, published in April 1967, stated that 70 per cent of complaints about racial discrimination fell outside the scope of RRA 1965, primarily in the areas of housing and employment, and it was this kind of racism that 'most seriously affected the day to day existence of coloured people' (Race Relations Board, 1967: 15). The report pointed out the inconsistency of accepting the principle of non-discrimination whilst there was strong evidence of substantial discrimination in areas excluded by the Act: 'the same principle might successfully be applied to other areas where discrimination occurs' (Race Relations Board, 1967: 12). Even more decisive evidence came from Political and Economic Planning (PEP), which, as a widely respected and influential research organisation, could not be accused of bias in the way that the RRB had been by the Ministry of Labour. Based on interviews with immigrants and potential discriminators, and above all, on a series of 'situation tests' in which representatives from three groups – a non-white immigrant, a white immigrant and a white Briton – applied for employment, accommodation and car rental, the PEP report was seen by politicians and experts as a credible and objective assessment. It concluded that there was 'substantial discrimination' in employment, housing and services (PEP, 1967: 8).

The PEP's report served to convince several politicians of the need for further race relations legislation, and newspapers which had previously been sceptical or hostile, including *The Times*, also shifted their stance (Bleich, 2003: 77). The Labour Party Research Department's working party on race relations considered the report to be 'extremely valuable' and, on the basis of its findings, agreed that proposals should be put forward to extend the race relations legislation (LPA, LPRD file, report of Working Party on Race Relations, April 1967).

The PEP and RRB reports were the catalysts for Government action. In July 1967, the decision to present a new bill to Parliament was taken by the Home Affairs Committee, subject to Cabinet approval. Roy Jenkins produced a memorandum proposing that RRA 1965 be extended to cover all public places, housing, credit and insurance services, and, most controversially, employment. He also proposed that the RRB be strengthened in various ways, most notably by giving it the power of independent investigation (PRO CAB 134/2854, H(67)23, 19 July 1967). The memorandum cited evidence from both the PEP and RRB reports in support of his argument.

Once again, though, the Ministry of Labour opposed the proposals on the grounds that both the CBI and TUC were resistant,

> not because they were prepared to tolerate discrimination but because they feared that in a dangerous and delicate situation the wrong kind of legislation would inhibit the efforts which industry was already making, with some success, to contain the problem by means of its own conciliation machinery.

They proposed that 'the problem should be left to industry's own conciliation efforts' or, if Government must be involved, that the existing machinery be supplemented by a process of conciliation and enforcement under the Minister of Labour, but without legal sanctions (PRO CAB 134/2854, H(67)23, 19 July 1967).

The Committee were not persuaded, however, and Jenkins carried the day. Further disagreements over housing, employment and applicability to the Crown and the police force were resolved during the second half of the year, but the details of this lie beyond the scope of the present chapter (see PRO CAB 134/2859, H(68)1, 5 January 1968). Early in 1968, the Cabinet agreed to present a new Race Relations Bill to Parliament.

The 1968 Race Relations Act

Unlike its 1965 predecessor, the 1968 Race Relations Bill was not substantially amended as it passed through the legislature, although this is not to say that its passage was entirely smooth. Progressives tried unsuccessfully to have religious discrimination included, whilst opponents of the bill, including Enoch Powell, tried to wreck it. The Conservatives tabled a reasoned amendment declining to give a second reading, on the grounds that they wanted credit and insurance services, as well as small businesses, excluded from its remit, but then in the committee stage they joined with progressives to ensure that the Crown was made liable for discrimination (Lester and Bindman, 1972: 145–6). Following the Cabinet reshuffle of November 1967, it was left to James Callaghan, as the new Home Secretary, to carry the legislation through Parliament. Given the febrile atmosphere of the first half of 1968 – the Kenyan Asians crisis and CIA 1968 in February, and Enoch Powell's 'rivers of blood' speech, delivered to a Conservative meeting in the Midlands just three days before the bill's second reading – the Government was successful in securing a bipartisan approach. Callaghan, who placed more emphasis on the bill's declaratory effect than on its details, successfully steered a course between progressives and sceptics, often allying with the Conservatives to outvote both progressives (on Labour's back benches) and populists on a number of points (Bleich, 2003: 83). Consequently, the bill drafted under Jenkins in 1967 was substantially unchanged when it was placed on the statute book. The 1968 Race Relations Act extended the breadth of coverage of anti-discrimination measures: employment, housing, and credit and insurance services were now to be covered by the law. The administrative machinery was retained, and the RRB was given the power to investigate discrimination without receiving a prior complaint. The Act also created the Community Relations Commission to promote harmonious community relations and advise the Home Secretary. A further important development was Callaghan's announcement that a select committee on race relations and immigration would be established to give Parliament a more direct role in race relations (House of Commons Debates, 5th series, vol. 763, col. 67, 23 April 1968).

Conclusion

This chapter has explicated the Wilson Governments' mixed record on race relations and immigration policy – liberal on race relations, illiberal on immigration controls – and has argued that the Government pursued a conscious strategy designed to satisfy conflicting constituencies both within and outside the Labour Party. Whilst progressives opposed the 1965 White Paper and viewed CIA 1968 as a shameful episode, it was hoped that they could find something to cheer in the Government's principled stance on race relations. Conversely, anti-immigrant populists who opposed the race relations policy were to be mollified by the application of strict immigration controls – at least, this was the Government's intention. The limitation–integration strategy was typical of Wilsonian pragmatism: an attempt to appear to be all things to all people, as the Prime Minister himself was wont to do (Pimlott, 1992: 218). Whatever its merits as a means of adapting to a racially and culturally diverse society, then, there was certainly a political logic to the Government's approach. Indeed, some commentators have considered it to be a strategic masterstroke (Hansen, 2000: 128–9).

Normative assessments of the Government's record tend to vary according to the relative weight given to each side of the equation. For example, Michael Banton has defended the 'liberal hour' of 1965–1968 by stressing the Government's integrative measures and its recognition of racial harmony as a 'public good' (1985: 46, 126). There is much to be said for this. Given the depth of anti-immigrant sentiment amongst the British electorate, and the Labour Government's wafer-thin majority during 1964–1966, it is difficult to see how Labour could have avoided taking a restrictionist approach to immigration – although this hardly exonerates its response to the plight of Kenyan Asians in 1968. On the other hand, the legislation to outlaw racial discrimination was, as we have seen, driven forward by principled individuals within the party and accepted by the Government despite the fact that such policies promised no electoral reward and were opposed by the trade unions.

However, even a brief consideration of the longer-term implications of the limitation–integration equation raises awkward questions for such a sanguine assessment. This is especially significant given that the policy linkage forged between 1965 and 1968 remains largely intact to this day. Therefore, a full evaluation of the Wilson Governments would have to take account of policy effects after 1970. Two points must suffice to illustrate this here. First, both the immigration and the race relations policies left a considerable degree of unfinished business, and neither went far enough to satisfy either populists or progressives. The incompleteness of these policies was shown by the Heath Government's decision to legislate on immigration in 1971, and by the next Labour Government's decision to extend its anti-discrimination measures once again in 1976. Curiously, Callaghan claims in his autobiography that he knew at the time that RRA 1968 was not strong enough, and was merely an 'interim measure' on the way to more robust legislation (1987: 269).

Second, and more importantly, the limitation–integration equation has had a profound, and not entirely benign, effect on Britain's development into a multiracial society. This is because of the conflicting demands of the equation. The portrayal of immigration as a 'problem' or 'threat' that has often accompanied arguments for limitation sits uneasily with attempts at integration and has undermined the promotion of good race relations. Indeed, it has been argued that the problematisation of immigration (and more recently of asylum) has retarded the development of a re-imagined British identity and encouraged racism (Hansen and King, 2000; Back *et al.*, 2002). Hence, in so far as the race relations paradigm established in the late 1960s requires zero immigration, it is a deeply flawed way of managing diversity. As Andrew Geddes notes,

> the reality of continued flows appears to have produced illiberal responses to new and unwanted immigration, all in the name of good race relations. The relation between an illiberal path to supposedly liberal objectives is at the heart of the British politics of citizenship and immigration.
>
> (2001: 765)

Given that this tension has its origins in the years 1964–1970, the record of the Wilson Governments should be considered in this light.

Finally, even the policy package's short-term political success must be questioned when account is taken of the role of immigration in the 1970 election. Enoch Powell's rise to popularity following his 'rivers of blood' speech on 20 April 1968 showed the extent of support for an anti-immigrant stance amongst the electorate. The Government was certainly rattled by Powell's intervention and the spectre it raised of immigration becoming a new political cleavage. At a May Day rally in Birmingham in 1969, Wilson called on both Government and Opposition 'to take these inflammatory issues out of politics' and insisted that he was not prepared to let 'calculating orators' stoke up racial conflict (MS. Wilson c. 896, Labour Party News Release, 5 May 1969). Heath largely heeded Wilson's call, and most Conservatives avoided explicit anti-immigrant rhetoric, but the attempt to depoliticise the issue and remove it from the election failed: immigration was the fourth most salient issue for voters in 1970. Indeed, it has been argued that despite Powell's removal from the Shadow Cabinet, support for his anti-immigration views won the Conservatives the 1970 election (McLean, 2001: 145–52; cf. Studlar, 1978). If this analysis is correct, it suggests that despite the Wilson Governments' restrictionist immigration policies, Labour was perceived as too 'pro-immigrant' by the electorate in 1970. In this regard, its principled approach to race relations appears more impressive, and its failings as much a comment on British society as on the Government itself.

Notes

1 The Attorney-General noted that the European Convention on Human Rights (ECHR) presented greater difficulties. Article 3 of the Fourth Protocol provided that no person should be deprived of the right to enter the territory of the state of which he or she was a national. However, he pointed out that although the Government had signed this protocol, it had not yet ratified it.

2 Prominent opponents of the bill in the Labour Party included Michael Foot, Anthony Lester and Shirley Williams. Conservative opponents included Iain Macleod, Nigel Fisher and Ian Gilmour.
3 The concern was that the high standards of proof required for criminal prosecutions would mean racism went unpunished.

18 Abolition of the death penalty

Neville Twitchell

Introduction

By 1964, capital punishment and its abolition had become one of the great unresolved questions of British politics. It aroused tumultuous passions on both sides of the argument despite its peripherality to the mainstream of political debate. The issue had surfaced time and again both inside and outside Parliament since the early nineteenth century, and the scope of the death penalty had been steadily narrowed to the point where it was in operation, effectively, only for the offence of murder, and even then only for certain types of murder. The status quo was embodied in the Homicide Act of 1957, which retained hanging as the penalty for five types of murder (capital murder), whilst for other classes of murder the penalty was life imprisonment. In the Act, 'capital murder' was murder: (a) committed in the course or furtherance of theft; (b) committed by shooting or causing an explosion; (c) committed to effect an escape from lawful custody; (d) of a police officer in the execution of his duty; or (e) of a prison officer in the execution of his duty. It was also a capital offence to have been convicted of committing murder on more than one occasion.

As we will note, this Act constituted an uneasy and hard-wrung compromise that satisfied few. No one doubted that matters could not stand there for long, and for dedicated abolitionists this was very much unfinished business. The coming to power of a Labour Government in October 1964 provided the long-awaited opportunity to conclude matters in their favour, for there had long been strong opposition within the Labour Party to the death penalty.

Labour and capital punishment prior to 1964

The 1929–1931 Labour Government had established an all-party select committee to look into capital punishment, which, after much deliberation, recommended total abolition for an experimental five-year period. The Conservative members, however, withdrew from the committee in disagreement with its conclusions, and the Government took no action on the report before it fell in 1931. The Labour Party conference of 1934 committed a future Labour government to abolition (Christoph, 1962: 35), and in 1938 an unsuccessful attempt was made to include abolition in the National Government's Criminal Justice Bill.

In 1945, the election of a Labour Government with a large parliamentary majority fuelled the hopes of the abolitionists, but they were to be disappointed. It was not until the third session of the Parliament that the Government introduced a Criminal Justice Bill, yet this made no mention of hanging. This omission prompted Labour backbenchers, headed by Sydney Silverman,[1] to table an abolitionist clause at report stage, which was carried by a majority of 23 despite the official hostility of the Government. Of the Labour members voting, nearly three-quarters supported it, and more than four-fifths of the backbenchers. Only a Government prohibition on Ministers voting for it prevented the majority being much larger. Of the 72 Government Ministers in the Commons, 44 abstained, many of whom were abolitionists, although a majority of the Cabinet voted against the abolitionist clause. However, five Cabinet Ministers – Aneurin Bevan, Arthur Creech-Jones, Stafford Cripps, Philip Noel-Baker and Harold Wilson – abstained in the vote. Also abstaining were the Government's four law officers, including Solicitor-General and future Home Secretary Frank Soskice (Christoph, 1962: 51). However, the clause was heavily defeated in the House of Lords, and after an attempt to get a compromise clause through the upper house failed, the Government persuaded its backbenchers to drop the issue in order to ensure that the bill reached the statute book.

Further backbench attempts to legislate for abolition in 1953 and again in 1955 foundered, although a number of highly controversial murder cases were by now focusing wider attention on the question, and had begun to shake the hitherto invincible opposition of the general public to abolition. A House of Commons debate on the hanging question in February 1956 revealed a majority for abolition, whereupon a ten-minute rule bill introduced by Silverman the previous November was revived and supported by 292 votes to 246. The bill was then defeated in the Lords, albeit by a smaller majority – 298 to 95 – than in 1948.

The Conservative Government then took matters into its own hands by introducing the bill which became the 1957 Homicide Act, and which, as noted in the introduction to this chapter, included partial abolition of the death penalty. It also enshrined other reforms to the law relating to murder, such as the introduction of the partial defence of diminished responsibility.

Yet the abolitionists were scarcely assuaged, and almost the entire Labour Party opposed it, though the Conservative abolitionists fell into line behind the Government. The bill made scant sense from a legal viewpoint, because the distinction between the two categories of murder bore little or no relevance to the degree of culpability of the offender or the moral heinousness of the offence. A murderer could stab, strangle and decapitate the victim but so long as he (or she) was careful not to run off with the victim's wallet, that murderer was safe from the gallows. The Homicide Act was ridiculed by lawyers and disliked by both abolitionists and retentionists. Both sides continued to lobby, some hard-core retentionists for a return to the position before the Act and the abolitionists for all-out abolition; but both were stonewalled by the Home Secretary, Rab Butler, who insisted that Act 'be given time to work'. It was clear that the position would not change so long as there was a Conservative Government. Meanwhile, the number of executions fell to even smaller numbers than before – down to three or four a year from an average of a dozen between 1900 and 1957. There the position rested until Labour was returned to office in October 1964.

The course of events, 1964–1970

The Prime Minister, Harold Wilson, detested the institution of hanging, as did the Lord Chancellor, Gerald Gardiner, and most of the Cabinet were middling to strong abolitionists who had consistently voted for abolition. No member of the new Cabinet, and scarcely any member of the junior ministerial ranks for that matter, had voted for its retention since the late 1940s. Moreover, an overwhelming majority of the Parliamentary Labour Party (PLP) were in favour of abolition. Yet abolition was not and could scarcely have been Government policy, for it was one of a small group of 'conscience' issues, conventionally never the subject of party manifesto or platform, initiated from the back benches and decided by a free vote in the Commons and Lords. Nonetheless, by 1964 the Labour Party had become so strongly abolitionist that, uniquely, abolition had been included in the Queen's Speech, if only to the extent of a pledge to provide time for a free vote on the issue: 'Facilities will be provided for a free decision by Parliament on the issue of capital punishment' (House of Commons Debates, 5th series, vol. 701, col. 40), although no such pledge had been included in Labour's 1964 manifesto. However, an indication of the extent of the Labour Government's, and particularly Wilson's, commitment to abolition is that the Cabinet agreed that any Minister (of whatever rank) who opposed abolition should 'preferably' abstain rather than vote against, notwithstanding that it was officially a free vote. This message was to be communicated downwards by the Cabinet to junior Ministers and Parliamentary Private Secretaries (PPSs) (PRO CAB 128/39, CC(64) 15th Conclusions, 15 December 1964).

It was in this context that the abolitionists seized their opportunity, with a private member's bill being duly introduced – almost inevitably, by Sydney Silverman – under standing order no. 37. The second reading debate took place in December 1964, with Silverman characteristically passionate in his advocacy. His speech in the House of Commons, which was prefigured in an article in *Tribune*, was scathing about the anomalies created by the Homicide Act and the political machinations which had brought it about (Silverman, 1964). He argued that no one had had a good word to say about the Act, which was a politically motivated compromise (House of Commons

Debates, 5th series, vol. 704, cols 870–90). Following a fierce debate, the House divided 355–170 in favour, a majority of 185. Only one Labour MP voted against, whilst just over a quarter of Conservatives voted for it.

Despite the essentially non-partisan character of the debate, party politics resumed normal service almost immediately as the Conservative Opposition tabled a motion to take the committee stage of the bill on the floor of the House, which would have either left the bill vulnerable to a filibuster or disrupted the Government's legislative timetable if it gave it time. The Government 'whipped' its MPs to defeat the motion by a majority of 18. The Conservatives portrayed this as a betrayal of the Government's pledge to treat the bill as a non-party matter, though it might just as easily have been perceived as an Opposition tactic to disrupt the Government's schedule, given that everyone knew that the Government was heavily, if unofficially, committed to the bill. The bill thus went to a standing committee which included a large abolitionist majority, in line with the second reading vote. It deliberated for five weeks, defeating all attempts to dilute the bill before a Conservative retentionist MP, Forbes Hendry, stood up on a Friday afternoon when the House was thinly attended and proposed that it be brought back to the floor of the House. Hendry's motion passed by 128 votes to 120, with MPs voting on strictly party lines (House of Commons Debates, 5th series, vol. 707, cols 1809–12).

The Government had been ambushed and the bill duly returned to the floor, but the Government retaliated by deciding to sit on certain mornings to debate the bill (against the furious objections of the Conservatives), and the committee stage thus started all over again. Again, with one exception, all retentionist amendments, often designed to reinstate the effect of the Homicide Act, were defeated. The one amendment that succeeded was to require that a confirmatory vote be held within five years (that is to say, by July 1970) in both Houses, in default of which the *status quo ante* would be restored. This amendment was tabled by Henry Brooke, the former Conservative Home Secretary, who had been converted to the abolitionist camp but whose abolitionism was cautious and empirical. The bill received its third reading in July, by 200 votes to 98, this time with no Labour MPs voting against.

The bill then secured substantial majorities in the House of Lords on both its second and its third readings, with Labour peers overwhelmingly in favour. The change in the attitude of the Lords to some extent reflected the liberalisation of the establishment in the intervening years, but there were other factors. There had been a big infusion of Labour peers, mainly as a direct consequence of the 1958 Life Peerages Act, who, together with their Labour colleagues in the Commons, were mainly abolitionist. Also, the mood of the judicial and episcopal benches was very different from what it had been previously. The Archbishop of Canterbury, Michael Ramsay, was a convinced abolitionist (unlike his predecessor, Fisher), as was Lord Chief Justice Parker (very unlike his predecessor, Goddard), and it is probable that they heavily influenced their junior brethren in both cases. In 1948, the Bishop of Truro had wanted to extend the death penalty to offences other than murder!

The Murder (Abolition of Death Penalty) Act thus reached the statute book in November 1965. Although the Act abolished hanging as the penalty for murder, it remained (technically) the penalty for treason, piracy, arson in government dockyards, and mutiny (and other grave offences under the various Armed Forces Acts). However, once the death penalty had been abolished for murder, it became almost inconceivable that it would be invoked for any other offence.[2] The Act abolished hanging in England, Wales and Scotland, but abolition in Northern Ireland was not officially secured until the enactment of the 1973 Northern Ireland (Emergency Powers) Act (passed, ironically, when terrorism in the Province was at its height). Life imprisonment (with a recommendation by the trial judge as to minimum sentence before parole be considered) replaced hanging as the automatic penalty for murder.

However, the passage of the Murder (Abolition of Death Penalty) Act scarcely put an end to the debate, and events soon contrived to reignite the whole abolition controversy. Indeed the retentionists scarcely waited for the ink to dry on the parchment before demanding reintroduction, at least for the murder of police and prison officers. Opponents of abolition were not slow to seize on any rise in the murder rate as evidence of the deterrent effect of the rope, irrespective of statistics demonstrating that the rise was not significantly greater than prior to abolition. Moreover, a number of sensational murder cases hit the headlines. In October 1965, the so-called Moors murders (for which Ian Brady and Myra Hindley were subsequently convicted) came to light, and in August 1966 three police officers were murdered in a confrontation with robbers in Shepherd's Bush, London. The latter, in particular, accelerated demands for the reintroduction of hanging for the murder of police officers, which were resisted by the new Home Secretary, Roy Jenkins. Indeed, Jenkins issued a statement to the effect that major policy could not be determined on the basis of a single event. It did not endear him to the police force, which subsequently barracked him at the next annual meeting of the Metropolitan Police Joint Branch Boards (Jenkins, 1991: 200–1).

It was in this context that Duncan Sandys, in November 1966, tabled a motion to introduce a bill to restore capital punishment for the murder of police or prison officers, although this was defeated by 292 votes to 170 (House of Commons Debates, 5th series, vol. 736, cols 1409–18). What was most surprising about this motion, though, was that 16 Labour MPs voted for it, 6 of whom had voted for the Silverman abolition bill on second reading.

The next few years saw repeated demands for reintroduction in sections of the popular press and in the Commons. These were bolstered by the trend in the opinion polls, which had moved towards abolition in the years leading up to 1965 and now moved back sharply in the other direction, so that by the late 1960s there was a large majority for restoration. Sandys made another attempt in June 1969 to engineer restoration by seeking leave to bring in a bill to cause the Abolition Act to lapse automatically after five years (i.e. by November 1970) and thus to require a new bill to be passed rather than a mere confirmatory vote if the suspension of the death penalty were to continue. This too was heavily defeated.

Against this background, the question arose as to how and when the affirmative resolutions required by the 1965 Act were going to be dealt with. The Cabinet agonised over the timing and tactics to be adopted. The relevant section of the Act was silent on these questions, though clearly the intention behind the provision was that Parliament should have before it a full five years' statistics to consider. The first question was whether the Government should leave matters to the back benches or take the initiative itself. Silverman was no longer on hand, having died in 1968, and the Cabinet resolved to take the latter course, evidently feeling that this was too grave an issue to be left at the mercy of the back benches, given its very limited time allotment for private members' business. There was little enthusiasm for proceeding on the basis of the original bill in 1964–1965, with the Government pulling the strings whilst backbenchers took centre stage. Any shallow pretence of Government neutrality was now firmly cast aside.

With regard to the issue of timing, Harold Wilson was anxious to get the business out of the way well before the next general election (due by March 1971 at the latest, but, of course, actually held in June 1970), so that the question did become a contentious election issue (Wilson, 1971: 924–6). The Cabinet initially resolved to hold the vote in the spillover of the 1968–1969 session, so that in the event of a defeat the situation could be rescued with another vote in the 1969–1970 session, or even further legislation (PRO CAB 128/44, CC(69) 24th Conclusions, 22 May 1969; CAB 129, C(69)48, Cabinet Memorandum Presented by the Home Secretary (Jim Callaghan) and Secretary of State for Scotland (William Ross), 6 May 1969). However, a reassessment of the position led to the Cabinet resolving to postpone the votes until the 1969–1970 session. This seems to have been motivated partly by the realisation on Callaghan's part that the 1968 murder statistics were probably going to be more favourable – from the abolitionist viewpoint – than was first thought, and moreover a Home Office Research Unit was preparing a full set of statistics (see Table 18.1) comparing figures over the entire period since the promulgation of the Homicide Act, which he felt should be in the public domain before any final decision be made.

The table shows the number of persons convicted of 'normal' murder – that is, excluding murders committed by the criminally insane. The division into capital and non-capital is necessarily an estimated one for the years from 1965 onwards when the distinction had been abolished and must be treated with caution, given that the criteria for the distinction were not always

Table 18.1   Murder convictions, England and Wales, 1957–1968

	Capital murders		Non-capital murders		Total murders
	Number	*Percentage of total*	*Number*	*Percentage of total*	*Number*
1957	12	21.1	45	78.9	57
1958	11	23.4	36	76.6	47
1959	9	15.8	48	84.2	57
1960	11	21.6	40	78.4	51
1961	7	13.0	47	87.0	54
1962	4	7.1	52	92.9	56
1963	7	11.9	52	88.1	59
1964	10	13.2	66	86.8	76
1965	17	22.1	60	77.9	77
1966	29	33.0	59	67.0	88
1967	24	26.7	66	73.3	90
1968	26	27.1	70	72.9	96

Source: Home Office Research Unit.

tested in court, being no longer relevant to guilt or sentence. The figures are subject to retrospective adjustment in the light of the outcome of court cases. Many factors must be borne in mind when assessing the significance of the figures, such as the possibly greater willingness of defendants to plead guilty once hanging had been abolished. The table updates a comparable Home Office document of 1961 (PRO CAB 128, CC(69) 45th Conclusions, 25 September 1969; PREM 13/2552; HO 291/1551, 'Capital Punishment – Abolition of Death Penalty – Consideration by Ministerial Committee'; HO 291/1552, 'Capital Punishment – Abolition of Death Penalty – Review of the Murder (Abolition of Death Penalty) Act 1965').

The Labour Government must also have been sensitive to any accusation of bulldozing the Commons or denying it the fullest picture possible, whatever its private feelings were or whatever the tactical constraints acting upon it. It was finally decided, after much collective hand-wringing, to proceed with the resolutions in Commons and Lords in December 1969. The Conservatives nonetheless attacked the Government for holding the vote prematurely and thus limiting the scope of the crime figures that the House could scrutinise before making a decision (see, for example, PREM 13/2552, Callaghan to Wilson, 26 November 1969), but, as usual, all parties allowed a free vote. The debate was duly held in December 1969 and resulted in large majorities for abolition in both Houses.

The voting was 343–185, a majority of 158, and therefore very similar figures to those pertaining to the second reading five years previously. Labour MPs voted by 278 to 2 for the motion (House of Commons Debates, 5th series, vol. 793, cols 1293–8). The two Labour restorationists were Peter

Doig (Dundee West) and Jack Dunnett (Nottingham Central), plus David Ensor (Bury) as teller. (Ensor joined the Liberals in 1972.) The independent ex-Labour MP Desmond Donnelly (Pembroke), who had broken with the party the previous year, also voted for restoration. All four had supported the Silverman bill on second reading in December 1964. Tomney, the solitary Labour retentionist of December 1964, spoke against the motion but did not register a vote. In the Lords, the confirmatory resolution was passed without a vote, an amendment proposed by Viscount Dilhorne (former Conservative Attorney-General and Lord Chancellor) to the effect of extending the experimental period till 1973 being defeated by 220 votes to 174, after what was widely regarded as a consummate speech by Lord Chancellor Gardiner (House of Lords Debates, vol. 306, cols 1317–22).

There the matter has rested despite periodic attempts – most notably in 1973, 1975, 1979, 1983, 1987 (twice), 1988, 1990 and 1994 – by sundry Conservative backbenchers to restore the rope, usually for specific categories of murder. All these attempts have been defeated, with a discernible trend towards ever larger abolitionist majorities, largely irrespective of the party in power and the balance of forces in the House.

Evaluating and explaining Labour Party attitudes vis-à-vis the death penalty

Clearly, the Labour Party was the engine of abolition. Why did support come largely from the left and centre of British politics? As previously mentioned, it had been the second Labour Government of 1929 which had established the select committee charged with looking into the question, and the Labour contingent of which that recommended suspension of the death penalty. The Labour Government of 1945–1951 passed a Criminal Justice Bill containing an abolition clause (albeit over the hostility of the Government itself). The secretary of the umbrella abolitionist organisation (the National Council for the Abolition of the Death Penalty), John Paton, was by 1945 a Labour MP. The future Lord Chancellor Gerald Gardiner QC was from the mid-1950s joint chairman of its successor body, the National Campaign for the Abolition of Capital Punishment, and was groomed for the position as Lord Chancellor in the early 1960s by Harold Wilson partly because of his stance on the issue (Wilson, 1971: 89). Meanwhile, the future Home Secretary Roy Jenkins had strongly advocated abolition, along with a raft of other social reforms, in his *The Labour Case* (1959). Virtually all senior figures in the Labour Party had, by the 1950s, been converted to abolition, including the former Home Secretary Chuter Ede, who had opposed abolition when in office (one of several Home Secretaries who waited for their departure from that office to undergo their conversion). Meanwhile, it was Labour MPs (and Labour peers) who had provided the overwhelming bulk of parliamentary support for abolition each time the matter had arisen, as indicated by Table 18.2.

Table 18.2   Party breakdown of significant divisions on abolition of the death penalty, 1948–1969

Year	Lab Ab	Con Ab	Lib Ab	Total Ab	Lab Ret	Con Ret	Lib Ret	Total Ret
1948	215 (54.3)	16 (7.3)	7 (63.6)	245	74 (18.7)	145 (66.5)	0 (0)	222
1953	189 (64.3)	4 (1.2)	2 (33.3)	195	15 (5.1)	241 (74.8)	0 (0)	256
1955	194 (66.0)	17 (5.3)	3 (50.0)	214	5 (1.7)	239 (74.2)	1 (16.7)	245
1956 (Feb)	240 (86.6)	48 (14.0)	4 (66.7)	292	3 (1.9)	243 (70.6)	0 (0)	246
1956 (March)	235 (84.8)	46 (13.4)	5 (83.3)	286	8 (2.9)	254 (73.8)	0 (0)	262
1964	267 (84.2)	80 (26.3)	8 (88.9)	355	1 (0.3)	168 (55.3)	1 (11.1)	170
1966	255 (70.4)	30 (11.9)	7 (58.3)	292	16 (4.4)	153 (60.7)	1 (8.3)	170
1969	277 (79.6)	52 (19.8)	11 (84.6)	343	2 (0.6)	180 (68.4)	2 (15.4)	185

Notes
Ab = abolitionist; Ret = retentionist. Con. includes National Liberals and Ulster Unionists.
The totals include assorted 'Others'. Figures in parentheses are the percentages of that party's MPs voting for or against abolition.

The figures shown in the table provide a striking illustration of the extent to which voting followed party lines, notwithstanding the supposedly non-partisan character of the issue and the fact that it was almost always decided by a free vote. As early as 1948, a large majority of Labour MPs were abolitionist, and the majority would have been greater had not the Government prevented the payroll vote from supporting it. By the mid-1950s, the retentionist minority had dwindled to single figures and by 1964 to only 1, and despite some slight 'backsliding' in 1966 (when the vote centred on reintroduction for the murder of police officers only) the PLP has remained almost solid for abolition. Was the PLP really this unanimous? It is likely that there was more than one Labour MP opposed to abolition in 1964, but that all save one were unwilling to extend their opposition to the division lobbies. A few of the abstentionists were doubtless pro-hangers. Though it was a free vote, there must have been considerable peer-group pressure, if only tacit, to conform. It had become almost an article of faith on the left to be against hanging, and cognitive dissonance may have played a role.[3]

This begs the question as to *why* the overwhelming majority of Labour parliamentarians were opposed to the death penalty. After all, the Labour Party was, at least theoretically, the party of socialism, the working class and trade unionism. Superficially there is no connection between economic and industrial policy on the one hand, and penal policy on the other. Why, for example, should a belief in nationalisation and redistributive taxation predispose one towards a belief in more lenient sentencing? Much of the answer seems to reside in the fact that Labour had been the party of social, humanitarian and penal reform almost from its inception at the turn of the century, emerging as it did from the plethora of late-Victorian radical movements. It naturally embraced 'progressive' causes. Its origins lay partly in Nonconformism, and though none of the Churches (except for the Quakers) officially opposed hanging, there was slightly more support for abolition amongst Nonconformists than amongst Anglicans and Roman Catholics.

The Labour Party placed far less stress than its Conservative opponents on law and order (particularly with regard to punitive measures and custodial sentences for criminal offences), perhaps because it was less exercised about maintaining the social status quo. Intellectually it tended to take a rather deterministic view of behaviour, and therefore sought solutions to crime and deviancy in the amelioration of the socio-economic conditions which it thought fostered them. There was less ardour for retributive punishment, and more emphasis on corrective measures and rehabilitation. Labour had advocated and brought about the end of corporal punishment and the introduction of probation and suspended sentences, and generally favoured the alleviation of prison conditions. Moreover, it was Labour MPs who provided the bulk of support for many other social reform campaigns that came to fruition in the mid to late 1960s, pre-eminently for law reform on homosexuality (see Chapter 19), divorce and abortion (for a discussion of these measures, see Marsh and Chambers, 1981; Marsh and Read, 1988; Pym, 1974;

Richards, 1970). Finally, the gallows may have been perceived as a tool of an archaic judicial establishment that was loathed by much of the Labour Party, which saw the judiciary as an ally of Conservatism, and thus frequently willing to exert its power against the interests of Labour and the trade union movement.

Moving down the hierarchy of politics, it seems very likely that support for abolition was also strongly favoured by the great majority of Labour Party direct constituency members (though hard data are lacking for this), who were generally slightly to the left of the PLP anyway. There seems to have been no case where a Labour member was in dispute with his local party over his attitude to abolition (whether pro or anti). This is in stark contrast to the Conservative Party, where several abolitionist Tories faced severe criticism from their constituency parties and in some cases intense pressure to alter their stance.

However, if we turn from Labour politicians and Labour Party members to Labour (or potential Labour) voters, a very different picture emerges, as illustrated by Table 18.3. It is almost certain that the majority of those who had voted Labour in October 1964 did not support abolition, and that some may even have viewed it with alarm and dismay. Furthermore, the clamour to restore hanging, as measured by the opinion polls, increased sharply in the months and years that immediately followed, in the wake of the rise in the murder rate and of violent crime generally. People were unpersuaded by the arguments of the abolitionists that this would have happened anyway, and that it was unrelated to abolition.

These polls are a small sample taken from years when the issue was to the fore, and the figures would of course have varied considerably from poll to poll, but they and many others taken at different periods of time demonstrate the striking mismatch between the balance and configuration of opinion in Parliament and amongst the general public respectively. Not only was there a consistently large majority for retention (or restoration), unlike in the Commons, but the breakdown shows that there was always a large majority for retention even amongst Labour voters, though admittedly not quite so large as amongst Conservative voters. Breakdowns by social class consistently showed an equally large majority for hanging amongst working-class voters as for middle-class voters (although middle-class Labour voters, perhaps more ideologically motivated, were probably more 'liberal' in their attitudes to the death penalty – as well as other 'moral' issues – than the average working-class Labour voter, a nuance not revealed by the polls from which these data are extrapolated). Thus, Labour MPs have always been very much out of step – a phenomenon sometimes referred to by political scientists as 'ideological disjuncture' – with the bulk of their supporters in the country on the hanging issue. Significantly also, the majority for hanging seemed to increase in all groups in the years immediately after abolition to a point higher than in 1948, probably reflecting the rise in the number of murders, which was widely perceived as a matter of cause and effect.

Table 18.3   Views on the abolition of capital punishment by party preference, 1948–1969[a]

Date	Lab Ab[a]	Lab Ret[a]	Lab D/K[a]	Con Ab	Con Ret	Con D/K	Lib Ab	Lib Ret	Lib D/K	All Ab	All Ret	All D/K
1948	35	56	9	16	79	5	26	64	10	26	66	8
1956	38	46	16	30	51	19	39	45	16	34	47	19
1964	26	62	12	17	73	10	26	64	10	21	66	13
1966	16	81	3	11	87	2	23	74	3	15	82	3
1969	16	82	2	8	89	3	19	79	2	12	85	3

Source: Opinion poll data: various.

Notes

a   The precise wording of the question varied from poll to poll but not in substance, except that in 1966 and 1969 it would necessarily have referred to restoration rather than retention. Sources: 1948 = BIPO, Survey 167, 10 May 1948, cited in Christoph (1962: 54). The question related to whether the respondent approved of the recent Commons vote to suspend capital punishment for an experimental five-year period. 1956 = Mass Observation, *A Report on Capital Punishment* (1956), cited in Christoph (1962: 120). 1964 = NOP survey December 1964 and 1966 = NOP survey September 1966, both courtesy of Mr Nick Moon of NOP. 1969 = Marplan survey, published in *The Times*, 24 October 1969, reported in Block and Hostettler (1997: 261).

Key: Ab = abolitionist; Ret = retentionist for some or all classes of murder; D/K = don't know/mixed feelings/unclassifiable response; Lab = Labour voter; Con = Conservative voter; Lib = Liberal voter; All = all respondents. Figures are percentages of that party's voters.

Did this weigh with Labour MPs and were any dissuaded from voting for abolition or from voicing abolitionist views by the knowledge that most of their actual or potential supporters did not agree with them? Hard evidence is necessarily difficult to obtain, but the indications are that it did not. Many Labour MPs (and some Conservatives) felt too passionately on the issue to allow themselves to be deflected, and, if challenged, used the occasion for a strident assertion of Burkeian independence (the MP as a representative entitled to exercise their judgement on issues, rather than acting merely as a delegate of those who elected them). It is unlikely that abolition would have been included in election addresses, but on the other hand it must have been a frequent topic at election meetings and during canvassing, particularly in the 1966 general election that immediately followed abolition.

For example, Stan Newens, a newly elected left-winger in 1964 and a co-sponsor of the Silverman Bill (and a member of the standing committee), may well have been typical in thinking that the issue definitely cost him votes, though finding it impossible to quantify. He recalls it being mentioned frequently on the doorstep and as having been approached by local police officers, individually and collectively, who were adamantly opposed to abolition. Feeling had been heightened by the fact that a murderer had recently been run to earth near the constituency (Stan Newens, Labour MP for Epping 1964–1970, interview with author, 1999). This view is reinforced by an article in the *Sunday Times* entitled 'Hanging: The Smethwick of '66?', which highlighted the salience of the hanging issue during the 1966 general election campaign in the North-West region especially (*Sunday Times*, 27 March 1966).

The most fascinating illustration of the disparity of views on hanging between Labour politicians and Labour voters was provided when, in the 1966 general election, Sydney Silverman, the champion abolitionist, was challenged in his Nelson and Colne seat by an independent candidate who fought almost exclusively on a pro-hanging platform. Patrick Downey was the uncle of one of the victims of the Moors murderers, which had occurred near Silverman's Pennine seat (whilst the abolition bill was passing through Parliament), and was passionately opposed to abolition. It was the only instance of a candidate fighting almost exclusively on that issue and consequently became the focus of intense media attention. Intriguingly, he was an erstwhile Labour voter, a declared socialist and a friend of Will Griffiths, left-wing Labour MP for Manchester Exchange. His platform, in so far as it extended at all beyond hanging and a tougher stance on law and order, was for a better deal for old-age pensioners (*Burnley Evening Star*, 1 and 11 March 1966; *Nelson Leader*, 4, 18 and 25 March 1966). Silverman largely ignored the Downey candidacy, treating it with an air of equable indifference, and fought chiefly on the national issues and easily retained his seat with an enhanced majority. His vote had declined by 2,000 but the Conservative vote had dropped even more (Hughes, 1969: 192). Downey, however, gained a very remarkable 5,000 votes, and in so doing he saved his deposit (the only 'Other' candidate to do so in the 1966 election) and achieved the highest poll ever for a genuine independent who was not a former MP in a general election since 1945 (Butler and King, 1966: 291).

Conclusion

As a result of Labour's victory in 1964, the House of Commons had a large and unequivocal abolitionist majority for the first time since 1951, and for the first time there was a Government that was collectively, if unofficially, favourable to abolition and prepared to give an abolition bill time and support. Equally, the Government could not and did not introduce an abolition bill itself, because that would have been to flout the convention that these matters be left to free votes and private members' bills. The bill piloted by the veteran left-winger Sydney Silverman passed the Commons and Lords by sizeable majorities, though not without a few alarums and excursions. This, however, was in the teeth of opposition from several interest groups, notably the police and prison service, and against a background of hostility from a majority of the public. This hostility grew rapidly in the immediate aftermath of abolition with the rise in the murder rate and of violent crime generally. Repeated attempts to reintroduce hanging foundered, and the necessary confirmatory vote went through both Houses easily in 1969, consolidating abolition.

The issue succeeded in uniting almost the whole of the Labour Party, a remarkable feat during years when rebellion against the Government became commonplace (at least after 1966). Indeed, it was one of the few non-divisive issues in a party that was riven with dissension on almost everything else. Even other 'conscience' issues failed to unite the party as comprehensively. It represented the culmination of a twenty-year campaign driven pre-eminently by Labour politicians, and, the 1960s *Zeitgeist* notwithstanding, it is hard to envisage that hanging would have come to an end when it did but for the election of a Labour Government in 1964.

Notes

1 Sydney Silverman, Labour MP for Nelson and Colne from 1935, an obstinate and indefatigable left-winger, became the driving force behind each and every attempt to abolish the rope from then onwards (Hughes, 1969).
2 The last vestiges of capital punishment in Britain were laid to rest with the passage of the Crime and Disorder Act 1998, which formally abolished capital punishment for treason and piracy, and the Human Rights Act of 1998, which abolished it for offences under the Armed Forces Acts. In 1999, the UK Government ratified Protocol 6 of the European Convention on Human Rights and the Second Optional Protocol to the International Convention on Civil and Political Rights, which effectively committed the Government never to reintroduce the death penalty.

3 Cognitive dissonance theory postulates, *inter alia*, that people will seek to eliminate or reduce an apparent logical inconsistency or disharmony between beliefs and actions, either by altering their actions or by rationalisation of their motives for acting discordantly (Secord and Backman, 1974: 70–80). Thus, the anti-syllogism 'Labour MPs overwhelmingly support abolition – I am a Labour MP – I do not support abolition' may have created dissonance.

19 Homosexual law reform

Peter Dorey

Introduction

It was in August 1954 that a committee, chaired by Sir John Wolfenden, was appointed to consider the law and its operation with regard to homosexual offences (and prostitution), and the treatment of those convicted of such activities. The committee's report, published in 1957, included the recommendation that sexual acts between consenting males over the age of twenty-one should be decriminalised, although anal intercourse itself was to remain illegal. In making this recommendation, the Wolfenden Committee – as it became known – explained that

> We do not think it is proper for the law to concern itself with what a man does in private unless it can be shown to be so contrary to the public good that the law ought to intervene in its function as the guardian of the public good.
>
> (Wolfenden Report, 1957: paragraph 52)

The Wolfenden Committee could be said to have been 'in tune with the majority of informed opinion'. Certainly, amongst the forty-six organisations that submitted evidence or written memoranda to the Committee's inquiry, the 'balance of influence and argument favoured change' (Richards, 1970: 70).

However, the Wolfenden Committee was also emphatic that the advocacy of decriminalisation was 'not to be taken as saying that society should condone or approve homosexual behaviour ... the limited modification of the law which we propose should not be interpreted ... as a general licence to adult homosexuals to behave as they please' (Wolfenden Report, 1957: paragraphs 22 and 124). In these (and various other) respects, some writers have viewed the Wolfenden Report as a rather inconsistent and contradictory document (see, for example, Warner, 1983: 83–4).

Attempting to focus Labour's attention on social liberalism

Whilst the Wolfenden Committee was conducting its inquiry (but quite separately and independent of it), Anthony Crosland was ruminating on what sort of issues and objectives the Labour Party ought to focus on in the years ahead, having achieved many of its economic and industrial objectives. Crosland was seeking to steer the Labour Party away from pure economism and Fabian/Webbian asceticism, in order that it could address (what today would be termed) 'quality-of-life' issues:

> We need not only higher exports and old-age pensions, but more open-air cafes, brighter and gayer streets at night, later closing-hours for public houses . . . and so on *ad infinitum*. . . . Total abstinence and a good filing-system are not now the right sign-posts to the socialist Utopia.

Warming to this theme, Crosland then turned

> to the more serious question of socially-imposed restrictions on the individual's private life and liberty. There come to mind at once the divorce laws, licensing laws, prehistoric (and flagrantly unfair) abortion laws, obsolete penalties for sexual abnormality, the illiterate censorship of books and plays, and remaining restrictions on the equal rights of women. Most of these are intolerable, and should be highly offensive to socialists, in whose blood there should always run a trace of the anarchist and the libertarian, and not too much of the prig and the prude. . . . Socialists cannot go on indefinitely professing to be concerned with human happiness and the removal of injustice, and then, when the programmes are decided, permitting the National Executive Committee, out of fear of certain vocal pressure-groups, to become more orthodox than the bench of bishops.
>
> (1956: 355–6)

Crosland returned to these themes six years later, rejecting the claims of some left-wingers that if the Labour Party were not more radical with regard to nationalisation, it would be almost indistinguishable from the Conservatives. Crosland pointed out that there were many 'policies which a radical, progressive, revisionist Labour Party would stand for', amongst which would be '[l]ibertarian reform of existing laws on capital punishment . . . homosexuality . . . and so on' (1962: 131).

Yet there is little evidence that such 'libertarian' views or sentiments were more widely shared in the Labour Party during this time, although they may well have become more extensive after the 1964 and 1966 elections, when, as was noted in Chapter 2, many younger, university-educated Labour MPs were elected for the first time. Certainly, when Labour's 1961 policy document *Signpost for the Sixties* was being drafted, both Hugh Gaitskell and his successor as party leader, Harold Wilson, expressed their unhappiness at the proposed inclusion of a passage which endorsed the recommendations of the Wolfenden Report. Wilson warned that this might well cost the Labour Party 6 million votes, an anxiety shared by Gaitskell, who enquired, 'Can't we be sure this time not to say things which are going to lose us votes?' The passage in question was therefore not included in the published version (Thompson, 1993: 139).

The Wolfenden Report nonetheless provided a basis for parliamentary reformers to pursue a change in the law regarding homosexuality, with a House of Lords debate on the topic held in December 1957 and three debates in the House of Commons, in 1958, 1960 and 1962. The 1960 debate was prompted by a motion, tabled by the Labour MP Kenneth Robinson, calling for early implementation of the Wolfenden Report's recommendations, although it was defeated by 213 votes to 99 in the ensuing Commons division. Most Labour participants in the debate were supportive of reform, with several of them – including Anthony Greenwood, Douglas Jay and Roy Jenkins – subsequently becoming Cabinet Ministers in 1964–1970 Labour Governments. However, the Conservative Government was generally unsympathetic, arguing that public opinion was not yet ready for such a change in the law (see, for example, Home Secretary Rab Butler's speech, House of Commons Debates, 5th series, vol. 596, col. 370). Two years later, another Labour MP, Leo Abse, sought to introduce a private member's bill to give legislative effect to the recommendations of the Wolfenden Committee, but this too was defeated in the House of Commons, albeit by the rather narrower margin of 178 votes to 159, an indication, perhaps, that parliamentary opinion was shifting somewhat (House of Commons Debates, 5th series, vol. 713, cols 611–20).

Labour is obliged to consider its policy on legalising homosexuality

The first occasion on which the 1964–1966 Labour Government was obliged to consider its stance vis-à-vis the recommendations of the Wolfenden Committee was in the spring of 1965, when Lord Arran tabled a motion in the House of Lords, calling for attention to be given to the recommendations of the Wolfenden Committee, with a view to legislating on its recommendations concerning private homosexual acts between consenting adults. Lord Arran subsequently introduced a bill to this effect, which successfully completed its stages in the House of Lords in October 1965.

A fortnight before Lord Arran's motion was tabled, the Cabinet's home affairs committee discussed what the stance of Government Ministers in the House of Lords should be, both during the debate and in any subsequent division. The Home Secretary, Frank Soskice, acknowledged that 'the strongest opinions are at present widely held on both sides', and so the

Government 'would not think it right either to advise against implementation or to come out in support of it'. Yet he was also 'reluctant ... to adopt a wholly neutral attitude', preferring instead to offer 'some guidance to the growing body of opinion now in favour of a change in the law on how ... a change might be brought about'. Consequently, he suggested that this 'guidance' should be for supporters of such a change in the law to introduce a private member's bill, so that 'Parliamentary opinion may express itself' through a free vote in the House of Commons (PRO HO 291/198, H(65)32, 'The Law Relating to Homosexual Offences', 28 April 1965).

This stance was generally endorsed by the home affairs committee, but it was also agreed that, whilst maintaining a stance of formal neutrality, the Government might – subject to Cabinet approval – indicate its willingness to make time available for a subsequent private member's bill. There remained, however, some concern in the committee that even this cautious commitment might be 'unwise' (PRO HO 291/198, H(65) Home Affairs Committee, minutes of meeting held on 30 April 1965).

One particular concern was that if the Government did indicate a willingness to make time available for a private member's bill in the next parliamentary session, then subsequent failure to do so, due to the volume or urgency of the Cabinet's own measures, might expose the Government to continued pressure on the issue from pro-reform MPs (PRO PREM 13/1563, Trend to Wilson, 5 May 1965). In fact, it was a Conservative backbencher, Humphry Berkeley, who subsequently introduced a private member's bill, early in 1966, calling for reform of the law on homosexuality, and although this was actually given its second reading, it proceeded no further, owing to the calling of a general election.[1]

However, the progress of both bills indicated that there existed considerable support in both Houses for a more liberal approach to homosexuality in Britain, whilst Roy Jenkins, having replaced Soskice as Home Secretary in December 1965, suggested to the Cabinet's home affairs committee that opinion polls indicated that 'a majority in the country is now in favour of a change in the law', in which case the Government ought to adopt 'an attitude of benevolent neutrality' towards Berkeley's bill (PRO CAB 134/2852, H(66)6, 18 January 1966). Or as the Cabinet Secretary judiciously expressed it, 'it should be possible ... to indicate sympathetic understanding for the point of view of the promoter of the Bill without suggesting hostility to that of its opponents' (PRO PREM 13/1563, Trend to Wilson, 2 February 1966).

Following the 1966 election, Lord Arran reintroduced his bill in the House of Lords (which again approved it), whilst a Labour backbencher, Leo Abse, introduced a similar measure – the Sexual Offences (No. 2) Bill – under the House of Commons' ten-minute rule bill procedure, which was then supported by 244 votes to 100. However, for it to have a realistic chance of reaching the statute book required – as with most private members' bills – that the Government provide time for it.

Having already met with Richard Crossman, Lord President of the

Council and Labour's Leader of the House, to secure his agreement to make a half-day available for Abse's bill (PRO HO 291/198, 'Note of a meeting with the Lord President of the Council', 6 September 1966), Jenkins then persuaded the Cabinet to grant Abse's bill a half-day to receive its second reading. Jenkins reminded his ministerial colleagues of the support already given by peers to Lord Arran's bill in two successive sessions, and the Commons' endorsement of Berkeley's bill at the beginning of the year, a bill which might well have reached the statute book if the general election had not intervened, and parliamentary time had otherwise been available.

Jenkins also pointed out that if this issue was not resolved, the administration of criminal law with regard to homosexual offences would be made more difficult (PRO PREM 13/1563, Trend to Wilson, 25 October 1966). However, he also suggested that if it did provide time for Abse's bill, the Government ought to maintain a stance of formal neutrality, an acknowledgement that the issue was one which aroused strong feelings, both in the Cabinet itself and in the Parliamentary Labour Party (PLP). In spite of the reservations of some Ministers – Harold Wilson himself had previously expressed doubt about the wisdom of such a course of action via a handwritten annotation on a letter from the Government's Chief Whip (PRO PREM 13/1563, Silkin to Wilson, 21 September 1966) – the Cabinet agreed to provide Abse with a half-day for his bill, although there remained some concern that in so doing, the Government might come under pressure from other MPs seeking time for their own private members' bills. In the meantime, Labour MPs would be permitted a free vote on the bill, it being recognised as a 'conscience issue' (PRO CAB 128, CC(66) 52nd Conclusions, 27 October 1966).

Supporting homosexual law reform, but not condoning homosexuality

What was perhaps most notable about the contributions of Labour MPs to the second reading debate was the attitudes towards homosexuality of those actually proffering support for the Sexual Offences (No. 2) Bill. On a number of occasions, Labour MPs were at pains to emphasise that in seeking to remove private homosexual acts between consenting males from the ambit of criminal law, they were not necessarily expressing approval of homosexuality itself. Most of the support which was proffered for the bill derived from a combination of compassion and tolerance, rather than approval of homosexuality. Indeed, even the sponsor of the bill, Leo Abse, argued that the concern hitherto of criminal law to prohibit and punish homosexuality had diverted attention from

> the real challenge of preventing little boys from growing up to be adult homosexuals ... the question of how we can, if at all possible, reduce the number of faulty males in the community. How we can diminish

the number of those who grow up to have men's bodies but feminine souls?

(House of Commons Debates, 5th series, vol. 738, col. 1078)

However, Abse later acknowledged that his exposition in support of the bill was 'presented in a form which violated my private beliefs ... it was only by insisting that compassion was needed for a totally separate group ... could I allay the anxiety and resistance that otherwise would have been provoked'. Hence, 'in presenting my case ... the arguments were, perforce, highly selective, and to that extent, I acknowledge that my case was fraudulent, but one does one's best' (Abse, 1973: 153, 154). Certainly, when he spoke in support of the bill, Dr David Owen observed that none of the MPs speaking in favour of giving it a second reading 'had condoned homosexual behaviour', adding that 'it would not be my wish that the House [of Commons] should be seen to condone it' (House of Commons Debates, 5th series, vol. 738, cols 1108, 1111). Owen explained that his support for the bill, like that of many other MPs, was not derived from approval of homosexuality, but on grounds of liberty, whereby what consenting adults did in private should not be subject to criminal law. In qualifying their support for the bill in this manner, many of the Labour reformers were effectively echoing the perspective of Lord Longford, Labour's Leader in the House of Lords, who had once declared:

> Never let it be thought for a moment, even by the ignorant and ill-disposed, that if we bring our law into conformity with what is general practice in Europe, we are condoning homosexuality. We are doing no such thing ... we condemn it as utterly wrongful.
>
> (House of Lords Debates, 14 December 1957, col. 743)

One particular anxiety expressed by some MPs who otherwise supported the bill concerned the Merchant Navy, for which they sought exemption. Indeed, Simon Mahon, the Labour MP for Bootle (on Merseyside), tabled a reasoned amendment during the second reading debate,[2] calling for the bill to be opposed on the grounds that it 'fails to afford the exemption and protection to the Merchant Navy, now provided in the Bill to Her Majesty's Royal Navy, Army, and Royal Air Force', and would therefore foster 'circumstances which can lead to the corruption of young seamen, and to conditions which will be prejudicial to the best interests of the Merchant Navy, and to ... discipline and good order at sea' (House of Commons, 5th series, vol. 738, col. 1068).

The National Maritime Board had itself lobbied for such an exemption, with representatives meeting Abse himself on two occasions, whilst also holding informal meetings with both the Home Office and the Board of Trade. Meanwhile, the General Secretary of the National Union of Seamen wrote to the Prime Minister urging exemption for the Merchant Navy from the provisions of the Sexual Offences Bill. He explained that whereas on dry land individuals could readily secure privacy, there was, in practice, no such privacy on board a ship, so what might be an appropriate change in the law for homosexual acts conducted privately in civil society was not appropriate with regard to the close confines of a ship which was at sea for weeks or months at a time, and where men thus unavoidably lived in very close proximity to each other (PRO, HO 291/129, Hogarth to Wilson, 16 November 1966). In this context, Abse indicated that if the sponsors of the reasoned amendment did not push it, he in turn 'would in no way resist' an amendment in (standing) committee stage which met their concerns about the Merchant Navy (House of Commons, 5th series, vol. 738, cols 1075–6).

Abse was true to his word, for the ensuing committee did indeed accept an amendment to the Sexual Offences Bill exempting the Merchant Navy from its provisions, and therefore largely assuaging the objections underpinning the 'reasoned amendment' tabled at the end of the second reading debate. Peter Mahon, however, observed that this exemption merely 'makes a bad Bill slightly more palatable' so that his opposition to the bill remained 'undiminished . . . in the full knowledge that this is not the sort of legislation which the people of our country desire to see' (House of Commons Official Report, Standing Committee F, 19 April 1967, cols 9–10).

One other issue raised by the Sexual Offences Bill concerned the age of consent for private homosexual acts between consenting adults, namely at what age was someone to be legally deemed an adult? The Wolfenden Report had urged that the age of consent be set at 21, on the grounds that 'all things considered, the legal age of contractual responsibility seems . . . to afford the best criterion for the definition of adulthood in this respect' (Wolfenden, 1957: paragraphs 65–71). However, as the Labour Government was known to be considering lowering the 'age of majority' (in accordance with the imminent recommendations of the Latey Committee), the question was raised whether Abse's bill would reflect this anticipated change in the age of adulthood. This, of course, posed something of a dilemma for those Labour MPs and Ministers generally supportive of the Sexual Offences Bill, for if it stipulated the age of 21 when the 'age of majority' was likely to be reduced to 18, this effectively constituted a form of discrimination against homosexuals: a heterosexual couple would be able to have sex at the age of 18, but two men of the same age who did so would still be liable to prosecution.

Roy Jenkins, in reiterating the Government's formal neutrality with regard to the Sexual Offences Bill, maintained that it was for MPs themselves to decide whether to table amendments to the bill during (standing) committee stage, with a view to reducing the age of consent to 18. However, Jenkins also noted that one of the reasons why the Wolfenden Committee had opted for the age of 21 originally was 'the desirability of protecting the young man of 18–21 who leaves home for the first time and who might be particularly vulnerable to attentions and pressures of an undesirable kind' (PRO HO 291/129, Jenkins to Houghton, 20 March 1967), a perspective endorsed by Abse himself when the issue of the age of consent was again raised during the (standing) committee stage of the Sexual Offences Bill (House of Commons Official Report, Standing Committee F, 19 April 1967, cols 30–1). In upholding this stance, Abse

> aroused the anger of the Homosexual Reform Society who considered 21 far too high an age, but I would not accommodate them, both because I was unconvinced they were right, and because of tactical reasons . . . [to] disarm my opponents of the Bill.
>
> (Abse, 1973: 154)

Abse's Sexual Offences (No. 2) Bill was effectively given an unopposed second reading in December 1966, apparently because the leading Conservative opponent 'was too drunk too stand up and object at the right moment' (Ponting, 1990: 265), or too 'sozzled', as Richard Crossman explained to Barbara Castle (Castle, 1990: 100, diary entry for 20 December 1966).

Yet in some respects, the Government unwittingly created a new problem for itself, because having provided parliamentary time for Abse's bill to receive its second reading, the Cabinet was confronted with the question of whether it should henceforth provide time for the remaining parliamentary stages, which would need to be completed in order for the bill to reach the statute book. If it did not do so, then it might be criticised for having 'wasted' time in permitting the second reading (as well as having fuelled the expectations of reform-minded Labour MPs, who would subsequently feel betrayed), yet if it did provide further parliamentary time, it would be difficult to maintain a stance of formal neutrality: a Government which was indifferent to such a bill would hardly provide parliamentary time for it on two occasions. Furthermore, if Ministers did provide further parliamentary time for the remaining stages of Abse's bill, the sponsors of other private members' bills would almost inevitably feel aggrieved that they had not been similarly indulged. On balance, though, the Cabinet Secretary suggested that Wilson might 'think that the Bill's prospects are bright enough to be worth giving it a day' (PRO PREM 13/1563, Trend to Wilson, 10 May 1967).

Discerning tensions between social authoritarianism and social liberalism amongst Labour politicians

Yet although Abse's bill had received its second reading, this did necessarily mean that an enlightened approach to homosexuality was widely shared in the Labour Party; numerous MPs, especially those representing industrial constituencies in northern England and Scotland, were deeply unhappy at the measure. Crossman noted how two senior Government whips, George

Lawson (MP for Motherwell) and Walter Harrison (MP for Wakefield), were amongst those Labour MPs who 'objected fiercely that it [the Sexual Offences (No. 2) Bill] was turning our own working-class support against us' (Crossman, 1976: 171–2, diary entry for 19 December 1966). Meanwhile, at a weekly meeting of the Parliamentary Labour Party, Kevin McNamara alleged that many Labour MPs were opposed to the bill, believing that the Government had already gone too far 'to facilitate legislation that had no bearing on our Socialist programme'. Not only was such a measure likely 'to do us no good in the country', but there were, in any case, far more pressing and worthwhile matters on which Government time and energy ought to be spent (Labour Party Archives, minutes of a meeting of the PLP, 29 June 1967). A similar sentiment was conveyed by a local party activist to Lincoln's Labour MP, Dick Taverne, namely that Parliament 'spent all its time debating Bills for homosexuals when [it] should be discussing unemployment' (Taverne, 1974: 38).

Such sentiments echoed those expressed at a meeting of the PLP just over two years earlier, when – in the context of both proposed homosexual law reform and abolition of the death penalty – it was suggested that the Labour Party was in danger of being perceived as 'the Party that cared more about the "odd people" in society, such as murderers and homosexuals and the like, rather than the ordinary, hard-working members of the community' (Labour Party Archives, minutes of a meeting of the PLP, 12 May 1965).

Emmanuel (Manny) Shinwell, chair of the PLP, apparently shared this deep distaste, to the extent that he 'stalked the [House of Commons] tea rooms whipping in his trade union acolytes to defeat' the decriminalisation of homosexuality, and 'making known, as ever, his contempt for the intellectuals who would bring disastrous opprobrium upon the Labour government' (Abse, 1973: 149).

Also viewing the bill with the utmost displeasure was George Brown, who claimed that 'society ought have higher standards', and warned that 'This is how Rome came down.' If the bill was passed, he anticipated 'a totally disorganised, indecent and unpleasant society', insisting that 'You must have rules! We've gone too damned far on sex already' (quoted in Castle, 1990: 54, diary entry for 11 February 1966).

Richard Crossman himself seemed ambivalent about his own stance, claiming at one stage to 'strongly favour the Bill' (1976: 172, diary entry for 19 December 1966), having already gone to the House of Commons on one particular occasion to sit 'on the Front Bench quite deliberately to give support to Leo Abse, who was moving his Ten Minute [Rule] Bill on homosexual reform in order to prove there is a majority in favour of changing the law' (1975: 561, diary entry for 5 July 1966), but later declaring that

the 'Buggers' Bill' [is] an extremely unpleasant Bill and I myself didn't like it. It may well be twenty years ahead of public opinion; certainly

working-class people in the north jeer at their Members at the weekend and asking them why they're looking after the buggers at Westminster instead of looking after the unemployed at home. It has gone down very badly that the Labour Party should be associated with such a Bill.
(Crossman, 1976: 407, diary entry for 3 July 1967)

Crossman also noted that Harold Wilson, as 'a perfectly sincere Sunday Methodist' with 'a number of moral convictions', was 'against the legal reforms to deal with homosexuality or abortion'. Wilson's willingness to grant parliamentary time to Abse's bill apparently owed less to support for the legislation per se than to the consideration that 'it was clearly better to let the House of Commons debate the matter freely now and to provide time for this than let the subject drag on until nearer the election'. It was with 'this highly tactical argument' that Wilson was 'persuaded . . . to drag the rest of his colleagues along with him' (Crossman, 1976: 159–60, 97, diary entries for 11 December and 27 October 1966).

The most trenchant criticism of the bill by a Labour MP, though, came during the third reading, when Peter Mahon alleged that it was 'by no means unnatural to have absolute revulsion against a Bill of this type', and 'impossible for normal people not to be extremely worried by it, as many of my [Preston South] constituents are'. Mahon then denounced what he considered to be 'a bad Bill now and . . . will be a bad Bill till the end of time . . . because homosexual acts are a perversion of natural function'. Mahon claimed that his attitude towards homosexuality was 'to hate sin and love the sinner', but that in legalising homosexuality the bill was 'inimical to the decency, dignity and moral fibre of the nation', particularly as Britain already had 'a growing number of depraved people who openly flaunt their depravity'. Becoming increasingly indignant, Mahon neared the end of his speech by claiming that the bill 'asks us to bless that sickness [of homosexuality] with lawful approval', when the House really ought to be 'legislating to prevent homosexual practices'. Mahon even claimed that 'When one finds a flaunting of homosexuality, one feels . . . the desire "to land him one in the chops"', before recommending that 'this House should do the same to the Bill' (House of Commons Debates, 5th series, vol. 749, cols 1504–8).

However, only one other Labour MP – Elystan Morgan – joined Mahon in the 'no' lobby to vote against the bill's third reading. The bill was thus given its third reading by 99 votes to 14, although some of those supporting it were Conservative MPs, including Nicholas Ridley (the latter becoming a loyal Thatcherite in the 1980s).

Abse himself subsequently alleged that 'the resistances against homosexual reform arose largely from the imperfectly resolved homosexual drives of some of the Members [of Parliament] themselves', whereupon 'they equated relaxation of the law with the relaxation of the control which they were anxious at all costs to preserve over their own repudiated feelings'. Such people, Abse claimed, 'can react over-determinedly to a plea for a toleration of homosexuality, for they are ever fearful that they may yield to its attractions' (1973: 145, 146, 155).

It seems highly likely, though, that many of those Labour MPs who were unhappy about supporting the legalisation of homosexuality in the latter half of the 1960s were genuinely concerned about the less enlightened and illiberal views of their constituents, particularly those representing more industrial or maritime working-class constituencies. Although the British left has often lauded, and even romanticised, the notion of close-knit working-class communities, with their concomitant connotations of 'proletarian solidarity', this can too readily manifest itself in an insularity and hostility both to 'outsiders' (an 'us' and 'them' mentality which can readily provide one of the bases for racism) and to new ideas or lifestyles. As a Labour philosopher, Richard Wollheim, noted when he reviewed Richard Hoggart's eulogy to working-class life *The Uses of Literacy*, whilst there was indeed much which socialists could admire about working-class communities, there was often, also, 'a lack of curiosity about the unfamiliar and the unknown [and] a residual puritanism in sexual matters', and this aspect of working-class insularity was generally 'unadmirable and ultimately undesirable' (Wollheim, 1961: 12; Thompson, 1993: 138).

Certainly it has variously been noted – and not only in Britain – that people in lower socio-economic groups, or who have received only a limited formal education, tend to be rather more authoritarian on certain social or moral issues than those in higher socio-economic positions in society, and those who have received an education beyond the formal or statutory minimum (see, for example, Lipset, 1969: 97–130). This 'working-class authoritarianism' has therefore posed a problem for the Labour Party in certain policy areas, on which the party's formal principles – most notably internationalism, and opposition to discrimination against 'minority' sections of society – have not been wholeheartedly or consistently reflected in the attitudes and values of some of its working-class supporters. In this respect, therefore, when Labour Governments, such as those led by Harold Wilson in the 1960s, have introduced 'permissive' or anti-discriminatory legislation, they have sometimes done so in spite of the attitudes of much, if not most, of the party's working-class social constituency, which has, in turn, made things uncomfortable for some Labour MPs who otherwise support such legislation but who may then have to face criticism and some opprobrium in their constituencies.

Why Labour's social liberals persevered with homosexual law reform

On the other hand, though, with regard to issues such as removing private homosexual acts from the ambit of criminal law, in addition to their own strong personal commitment to eradicating such discrimination (on grounds of both social equality and individual liberty), Labour's progressive reformers may well have judged that as British society was apparently becoming more middle class (the sociological concept of *embourgeoisement* was in vogue for much of the 1960s), then the more intolerant views and values which we have noted amongst sections of the working class would correspondingly diminish and dissipate. In this regard, Labour's reformers might have envisaged that even if they were ahead of public opinion in the 1960s, socio-economic changes in British society – along with the expansion of education – would result in public opinion moving in their direction and, in time, catching up with their more progressive or liberal stance.

Furthermore, those Labour Ministers and MPs most supportive of such measures as homosexual law reform might also have reasoned that even if some Labour voters disapproved of them, this was unlikely to lose the Party many votes at subsequent general elections, for two reasons. First, the 1960s were part of the era of class and partisan alignment, with the former referring to a close correlation between socio-economic or occupational background and support for a particular political party – in this case, the majority of the working class voted Labour – and the latter referring to the strength and consistency of support for, and identification with, a particular political party. Until about 1970, up to 40 per cent of voters identified 'very strongly' with a political party, and 90 per cent identified with either Labour or the Conservatives. Even when the Conservatives secured their three consecutive general election victories in the 1950s, Labour's share of the vote remained at 43–46 per cent (compared to the 27 per cent it slumped to in 1983). In this context, Labour's liberal reformers might have calculated that the party's working-class supporters would still vote Labour in subsequent general elections, even whilst disapproving of 'permissive' legislation and reforms.

Second, but following on from this last point, Labour's liberal reformers might also have adjudged issues such as homosexual law reform to be of 'low salience' to most voters, compared to so-called bread-and-butter issues such as economic stability, education, full employment, health provision, pensions, etc., which were most important to people politically. In other words, homosexual law reform was unlikely to have much impact on how most people voted in a general election, compared to the state of the economy or whether unemployment was rising, for example. Of course, some Labour MPs opposed to 'permissive' reforms could argue that their low salience to voters constituted a very good reason for not 'wasting time' on such matters; they would gain the Labour Party no additional votes, and might lose a few amongst those voters who did feel particularly strongly about such issues. Against this, of course, Labour's liberal reformers could retort that if an issue such as homosexual law reform was of low salience to the vast majority of voters in terms of how they would vote in a general election, then the party had little to lose by pursuing such reforms, for even voters who did not personally endorse such measures would still vote primarily on the basis of such issues as the economy, employment, pensions, etc. Furthermore, Labour might also attract some votes from the newer, younger generation of professionals who, it was assumed, tended to be more socially liberal in their views, and were perhaps increasingly concerned about quality-of-life issues, or what Inglehart (1977) subsequently identified as 'post-materialism'.

Conclusion

That the 1964–1970 Labour Governments reformed the laws concerning homosexual acts between men aged 21 or over owed much to the commitment of three individuals: Leo Abse, as the sponsor of the relevant private member's bill; Roy Jenkins, as Home Secretary; and Richard Crossman – in spite of the ambiguity over his own views about legalising homosexuality – as Leader of the House. The two last-named were both instrumental in persuading their Cabinet colleagues to provide time for Abse's bill (without which it would almost certainly have failed to reach the statute book).

Certainly the attitude of many Labour MPs and Ministers seemed to be one of unenthusiastic support, a willingness to endorse reform of the law, primarily on the grounds of individual liberty, rather than a strong commitment to such liberalisation. Indeed, the prevalent view amongst Labour parliamentarians was that supporting the legalisation of homosexual acts (between males over the age of 21) was derived from tolerance and/or compassion towards homosexuals, not actual approval of homosexuality per se. Indeed, so prevalent were such views that even Abse himself felt obliged to couch his case, in the parliamentary debates on the Sexual Offences (No. 2) Bill, in terms of the need for homosexuals to be the beneficiaries of compassion and understanding from others whose private lives accorded with what society deemed normal.

Moreover, whilst not more than 2 Labour MPs voted against Abse's bill, it became apparent that a number of Labour MPs representing more 'macho' industrial constituencies in the north of England and Scotland resented being expected to support or publicly defend their Government's tacit support for Abse's bill. Indeed, it seems that, sociologically, support for the liberalisation of the law on homosexuality was strongest – or least antipathetic – amongst the newer, younger, increasingly university-educated, middle-class Labour MPs who had been elected in the 1964 and 1966 general elections, a factor which Abse (1973: 152) himself acknowledged. In other words, without wishing to overstate or oversimplify the case, it does seem as if attitudes towards homosexual law reform in the Labour Party in the latter half of the 1960s – and thus a distinction in social attitudes between authoritarianism and libertarianism – corresponded, to a notable degree, to age cohorts and class background amongst Labour MPs, and even to the region of the country in which an MP's constituency was located (see, for example, Thompson, 1993: 141).

Notes

1 When introducing his bill, Berkeley suggested that public opinion seemed to have shifted in favour of changing the law on homosexuality, in accordance with the Wolfenden Report's recommendations. However, he then lost his Lancaster seat in the March 1966 election, a defeat which he subsequently attributed to his promotion of the bill (Berkeley, 1972: 129).
2 Amendments are not usually tabled at the second reading stage, because this stage is concerned with the principles and purpose of a bill, rather than its technical provisions. However, a 'reasoned amendment' is sometimes tabled – albeit usually by the Opposition – specifying why the bill should not be granted a second reading.

Conclusion

Peter Dorey

Introduction

Many commentators have judged the 1964–1970 Labour Governments to have been a disappointment overall, their failings having outweighed or outnumbered their achievements. Ponting in particular has declared these Labour Governments to have been in 'breach of promise', their record being 'a series of lost opportunities' which meant that, apart from their having carried out some commendable and enduring social reforms, 'In retrospect, it is difficult to see the government as other than a comparative failure' (1990: 400, 408). Jefferys has also characterised the 1964–1970 Labour Governments as a comparative failure, meaning in comparison with the successful reforms and legacies of the 1945–1951 Attlee Governments, against which 'Wilson's record looks especially threadbare.... The comparative failure of the 1964 Wilson Government by contrast with the Attlee Government of 1945–51 is startling', although Jefferys also acknowledges that the 1964–1970 Labour Governments did enact some valuable social reforms which benefited many citizens who had hitherto suffered deprivation, disadvantage or discrimination. Yet in spite of these welcome measures, 'The sense of failure nevertheless persists' (Jefferys, 1993: 60, 77–8). A similarly stark contrast between the dynamism and achievements of the 1945–1951 Attlee Governments and the disappointments and atrophy of the 1964–1970 Labour Governments is provided by Howell (1976: 245), whilst David Marquand (a Labour MP during this period) readily acknowledges that 'few modern British governments have disappointed their supporters more thoroughly than this', and admits that Ponting's charge that the 1964–1970 Labour Governments 'were guilty of "breach of promise" is impossible to fault', for 'the Wilson era ... was an era of lost innocence, of hopes betrayed' (Marquand, 1999: 155, 156, 158).

Meanwhile, three Marxist critiques of the apparent failings and ideological bankruptcy of the 1964–1970 Labour Governments are offered by Foot (1968), Coates (1975: ch. 5), and Miliband, in the postscript to the second edition of his *Parliamentary Socialism* (1972), although as Marxists have invariably characterised the Labour Party as merely a bourgeois reformist party preoccupied with 'humanising' or propping up capitalism, rather than overthrowing it in order to establish 'true socialism', one would hardly expect such writers to offer a more positive verdict!

Moreover, such critics – 'the betrayal school' – are quite reasonably accused by Hennessy of exuding 'an air of puritan unreality about the freedom of scope and manoeuvre available to the Wilson administration' (2001: 350), even though Hennessy himself is by no means uncritical about aspects of Wilson's premiership. Also offering a more sympathetic or 'realistic' appraisal is Walker, who suggests that historical distance and hindsight cast a rather more favourable light on the 1964–1970 Labour Governments, thereby providing scope for 'a more balanced judgement', whereupon 'Harold Wilson's historical reputation will recover' (1987: 186).

Although all governments and premierships are subject to differing, often diametrically opposed, evaluations and judgements (these often reflecting the political perspective of the authors), the 1964–1970 Labour Governments appear to have yielded divergent critiques for two main reasons. First, the overall achievements and record of these Governments are mixed, meaning that commentators can choose to focus either on the apparent failings, most notably in the economic sphere but also, perhaps, in the realm of constitutional reform, or on the social reforms, which are widely viewed as having been much more successful, and thereby earned the 1964–1970 Labour Governments their reputation for having been socially liberal and progressive.

The second reason why the 1964–1970 Labour Governments have been particularly prone to divergent critiques concerns the character of Harold Wilson's leadership itself, with one perspective deeming him to be a leader lacking in clear principle and political vision (even seeking political power for its own sake), and another, much more charitable, account which holds that Wilson did have a discernible strategy and set of goals, but that these were cruelly destroyed by exogenous events and factors beyond Wilson's – and his Governments' – control, and which, moreover, would almost certainly have overwhelmed any government and its leader during this period.

Summarising the 1964–1970 Labour Governments' record

As we have just noted, it is largely their economic record which underpins many of the critical accounts of the 1964–1970 Labour Governments. Not only were those Governments beset by serious economic problems virtually from the moment they entered office, as noted by Thompson in Chapter 4, but these in turn had significant ramifications for various other professed policy objectives. Moreover, the extent to which these Governments were routinely buffeted by economic difficulties (most notably sundry balance of payments deficits, foreign exchange and currency crises, sluggish economic growth, and inflationary pressures in the economy), and thus repeatedly obliged to engage in forms of crisis management and pursue ad hoc, short-term or reactive policy initiatives did much to foster the enduring image of an administration – and, more particularly, a Prime Minister (as will be discussed) – bereft of clear objectives, overall strategy or long-term vision. The 1964–1970 Labour Governments often seemed either to abandon or postpone planned policy initiatives, or hastily to adopt unplanned ones, in desperate response to debilitating economic vicissitudes. Whilst all governments are obliged to respond to exogenous events to varying degrees, the 1964–1970 Labour Governments did seem to suffer more than most in this regard, so that the optimism felt by many on the centre-left in 1964 soon dissipated, to be replaced by disappointment.

The economic situation and its consequences

Croslandite revisionism, as examined by Jefferys in Chapter 1, and Wilson's 'Fabian political economy', as discussed by Noel Thompson in Chapter 4, both, in their respective ways, envisaged that through the application of the correct political and administrative techniques, a Labour government would be able to achieve steady economic growth, promote industrial regeneration and sustain full employment. In achieving these objectives, moreover, Labour would be able to pursue a range of vitally important social goals whose combined and cumulative effect would be to establish a fairer society, with more opportunities and improved life chances for those from working-class backgrounds, but without needing to resort to punitive measures – such as higher income taxes – against the better-off. Moreover, social democratic revisionism and Wilsonian political economy significantly downgraded the importance of nationalisation, the pursuit of which, if it occurred, would be based on pragmatic or strategic grounds, rather than as a matter of ideology or doctrine. Instead, the Labour emphasis in the run-up to the 1964 general election was that (indicative) planning was more important than further nationalisation (and outdated disputes about the formal ownership of the means of production), and that such planning would enable a Labour government to foster a mutually beneficial partnership between private industry and the public sector.

This perspective was also intended to render the Labour Party electorally attractive to the burgeoning salariat. If economic growth could be attained through planning and technocratic rational economic management, then all sections of British society would materially benefit. Social democratic revisionism and Wilsonian political economy would be positive-sum; the rising tide would raise all boats.

Yet immediately upon being elected in October 1964, the (first) Labour Government was confronted with a much more serious economic situation than had been envisaged, and this immediately had serious implications for several of Labour's other policy objectives, for, as we have just noted, many of these had been predicated on achieving steady economic growth.

Certainly a key casualty of the economic problems which increasingly engulfed the 1964–1970 Labour Governments was that of the National Plan (for a brief overview of the purpose and creation of the National Plan, see Opie, 1972: 166–70), and the much-vaunted regional policy through which this grand vision was to be implemented (for an analysis of the link between the National Plan and regional policy, see Hardie, 1972: 218–22). Yet whilst the National Plan, and *inter alia* regional policy, were promoted as key policy tools for revitalising British industry, regenerating the economy and tackling regional inequalities, they also assumed *a priori* that an incoming Labour government would be able to secure steady and sustained economic growth. Indeed, right from the outset the National Plan seemed overly ambitious, to the extent that 'a great deal of wishful thinking [was] involved' (Jones and Keating, 1985: 86), owing to the fact that 'The [National] Plan is designed to achieve a 25% increase in national output between 1964 and 1970', and 'involves achieving a 4% annual growth rate of output well before 1970' (Department of Economic Affairs, 1965: paragraph 6). Instead, the average rate of growth from 1964 to 1970 was a thoroughly disappointing 2.2 per cent, not only much less than that envisaged by the National Plan (on which so much else depended) but also rather less than the rates of growth attained during this period by Britain's economic competitors, most notably France, Italy, Japan, United States and West Germany. Britain's sluggish economic performance was also indicated by a continued diminution in the share of world trade in manufactured exports, for whereas Britain had enjoyed 16.5 per cent of such trade in 1960 (itself down from 33 per cent at the beginning of the twentieth century), by 1970 it had fallen to barely 11 per cent. Thus, when commentators talked about Britain's *relative* economic decline, they were usually making both historical *and* international comparisons: how Britain's economy was performing compared to previous periods of the twentieth century, and how the British economy was now (under)performing compared to other industrialised nations.

Throughout this period, the 1964–1970 Labour Governments found it difficult to exercise mastery over economic events and crises, and spent the first three years pursuing a series of deflationary measures as an alternative to devaluation, although in November 1967 the Cabinet was obliged to resort to devaluation anyway. Yet long before succumbing to the dreaded devaluation, a series of deflationary measures – particularly the deflationary package introduced in response to the July 1966 crisis – effectively meant 'a virtual abandonment of the big idea of growth-through-planning' (Hennessy, 2001: 288; see also Jones and Keating, 1985: 87). Or as another commentator observed, the deflationary package of July 1966, 'to deal with the foreign exchange crisis, destroyed not only economic growth and full employment, but the National Plan as well, and the concept of planning' (Opie, 1972: 177), including, it should be emphasised, regional planning. To the extent that the second Labour Government retained a regional policy, it was one which was essentially reactive, rather than proactive, and, in the absence of sustained economic growth, one which sought to cushion the impact of deflation and industrial contraction. In other words, the remnants of regional policy became less a method of fostering growth in deprived reasons, and more a means of managing continued economic decline and nascent deindustrialisation. The optimism of 1964 and 1965, when economic (and regional) planning had been proudly proclaimed as the bold new innovation which would reverse Britain's relative economic decline and reduce regional inequalities, now seemed a distant, and naïve, memory.

Yet as Janet Mather shows in Chapter 13, it was not just economic circumstances and crises – crucial though these were – which fatally undermined the 1964–1970 Labour Governments' National Plan, and its associated regional policy. Also seriously hindering the effective application of the National Plan from the outset was interdepartmental rivalry and Whitehall turf wars, the rapid development of which provided another indication of Labour's failure or unwillingness to think seriously about 'machinery of government' issues (in spite of the pledge in the 1964 manifesto). Certainly, with the benefit of hindsight the political historian can see that economic planning and regional policy were almost inevitably going to lead to conflicts between departments, the most obvious of which was the inherent tension between the Department of Economic Affairs (DEA) and the Treasury. The DEA was intended to provide a counterweight to the Treasury (although another rationale for its creation was to provide a suitably prestigious ministerial post for George Brown!), which had variously been criticised – as it often still is – for failing to heed the needs of Britain's industrial and manufacturing sectors. It was intended that the new DEA would focus on long-term planning and industrial regeneration whilst the Treasury concentrated on more short-term economic issues, along with macroeconomic strategy in general. However, not only did the Treasury view the DEA as a rival rather than a partner (equal but different), but the economic problems which beset the 1964–1970 Labour Governments from the outset soon enabled the Treasury to assert its dominance, particularly as a series of deflationary packages and short-term crisis measures took precedence over the long-term perspective and expansionary expectations of the DEA. Thus, whereas the DEA and regional policy had aimed to reverse the decline of industry and concomitant loss of jobs in the north of England, Scotland and Wales, the deflationary packages invoked by the Treasury, coupled with its traditional prioritisation of the interests of 'the City' over manufacturing industry (financial capital over industrial capital), ensured that the DEA constantly struggled to achieve its objectives. To the extent that there was any semblance of partnership between the Treasury and the DEA, it was one in which the DEA was very much the junior partner (so much so, that it was abolished in 1969, after barely five years in existence). Nor was it only the Treasury which looked askance at the DEA: the Board of Trade, along with the Ministry of Housing and Local Government, were also concerned that aspects of the DEA's remit and policy initiatives would impinge upon their own jurisdiction and priorities – concerns also shared by many local authorities.

Meanwhile, having entered office promising the trade unions that it was committed to a planned growth of wages (also under the auspices of the National Plan), the 1964–1966 Labour Government immediately found itself seeking to secure trade union acquiescence for a series of incomes policies to secure wage restraint. Initially, the incomes policies were voluntary, and the trade unions were willing to accept them, partly to assist 'their' Labour Government after the party had endured thirteen years in opposition, and partly because the unions were persuaded that such wage restraint was a temporary, short-term measure born of exceptional economic circumstances. However, when these circumstances failed to improve, the Labour Governments found themselves resorting to the imposition of ever more stringent incomes policies, these eventually backed by statutory powers, and variously setting a 'zero norm', which in theory challenged the notion of an automatic annual pay increase. Moreover, whereas the Labour Governments initially envisaged incomes policies to constitute part of the deflationary strategy to avoid devaluation, once devaluation was finally accepted as unavoidable, incomes policies became integral to ensuring that devaluation 'worked', not least by preventing wage increases which would then be spent on more imports and thereby perpetuate Britain's balance of payments difficulties.

Not surprisingly, the trade unions became increasingly resentful at the imposition of successive statutory incomes policies to secure wage restraint, and relations between the industrial and political wings of the organised labour movement became ever more strained. Moreover, incomes policies created conflict not only between trade union leaders and Ministers, but also between those union leaders and their ordinary rank-and-file membership, the latter increasingly wondering whether their national leaders were representing them vis-à-vis the Government or acting as the Government's de facto agents policing ordinary trade unionists. Into the gulf stepped local-level officials and shop stewards, often pursuing local-level pay deals which were in breach of those formally agreed or determined in London, and thereby contributing to the phenomenon of 'wage drift'. Moreover, the gulf between national-level trade union leaders and their rank-and-file members meant that the former found it increasingly difficult to exercise authority over the latter, whereupon unofficial strikes became another source of political concern.

The Labour Governments' response was to propose legislation to place industrial relations and, *inter alia*, the trade unions in a clear legal framework, entailing statutory restrictions on the ability to pursue strike action. Although the Government – or rather the Employment Secretary, Barbara Castle – also offered the trade unions certain statutory rights as part of the proposed package of industrial relations reforms, the 'penal clauses'

enshrined within *In Place of Strife* offended not only the trade unions themselves, but also sections of the Parliamentary Labour Party. In particular,
trade union-sponsored Labour MPs were vehemently opposed, as was most
of the left. There was also strong opposition within the Cabinet from James
Callaghan, the Home Secretary. The combined and cumulative effect of such
opposition, characterised by both breadth and depth, was that *In Place of
Strife* was eventually abandoned, leaving the Labour Government without
either an effective incomes policy or industrial relations legislation as the
next general election loomed on the horizon. Such a situation, of course,
further compounded the image of a Government bereft of a coherent strategy and sense of political purpose.

Constitutional confusion and conservatism

Only marginally less disappointing were the 1964–1970 Labour Governments' attempts at modernising the machinery of government, most notably
through reforms of both the civil service and Parliament. Although Labour
had entered office in 1964 declaring that 'the machinery of government
must be modernised', there was a remarkable lack of specificity or sense of
strategy about how this modernisation was to be achieved, beyond references
to the need for new skills and techniques, coupled with a 'probing review
[of] the practices of its [the Government's] own Departments', whilst with
regard to Parliament there was a Delphic declaration that 'we shall not
permit effective action to be frustrated by the hereditary and non-elective
Conservative majority in the House of Lords' (Craig, 1975: 272). However,
in 1964 nobody knew – least of all Labour MPs – what precisely the newly
elected Labour Government intended to do by way of modernising the
machinery of government or preventing the hereditary peers from obstructing the Government's policies. After all, as Jones and Keating (amongst
others) have noted, the Labour Party has rarely thought seriously or
systematically about Britain's constitutional arrangements and system of
government, so that when it has occasionally promoted the 'modernisation'
of various political or administrative institutions – as in 1964 – it has been
'in a rather piecemeal fashion' characterised by 'the same ambiguities and
tensions which have ... historically marked its approach to the institution
and power of the state' (Jones and Keating, 1985: 140, 141).

This lacuna in the party's approach to 'machinery of government' and
constitutional issues partly derived from Labour's economism, the belief that
social and political problems are primarily to be solved by implementing the
correct economic strategy in order to secure expansion and growth (a point
already noted above), but was also a consequence of a strong strand of atheoretical anti-intellectualism which has tended to permeate much of the
Labour Party leadership, and which has therefore militated against critical
consideration concerning the operation of power in British society and the
State. Moreover, the Labour leadership has generally accepted the premises

of the Westminster model and thus assumed that political power derives from the winning of a majority of seats in the House of Commons, whereupon a politically impartial and neutral civil service loyally serves the Government and its Ministers, and faithfully assists in the implementation of the Cabinet's policies once these have formally received parliamentary approval.

Certainly, with a few exceptions on the party's left, most Labour politicians have not deemed the power of the senior civil service to be a serious problem. Indeed, various Labour leaders have insisted that Ministers who complain about 'domination' by their civil servants are probably weak or ineffective Ministers, and this certainly appeared to be the view of Harold Wilson. Where Wilson and some of his Labour colleagues were critical of the civil service was with regard to its being somewhat old-fashioned and over-reliant on the 'gifted amateur'. In this respect, it soon became apparent that Labour's mid-1960s emphasis on 'modernisation' meant rendering the civil service more professional, dynamic and meritocratic, this to be achieved primarily – in accordance with the recommendations of the Fulton Report – through reforming both its recruitment procedures and its internal structures, whereupon the civil service would be imbued with a much stronger managerial ethos, better suited to the governance of a complex, advanced industrialised society.

However, what Wilson did not seem to appreciate – or did not deem problematic – was that a more 'professional' and 'expert' civil service would almost certainly be (even) more powerful, and might sit uneasily alongside other professed Labour commitments pertaining to 'democratisation' and regionalism. Again, though, it would seem that Wilson's thinking – if that is how it can be described – was that a more dynamic and efficient civil service would itself be more effective in aiding a Labour Government resolving to 'modernise' Britain.

In the event, as Kevin Theakston notes in Chapter 9, the Fulton Committee was given a modest remit, and consequently proffered a correspondingly modest set of proposals which were, in turn, only partly implemented. Or as one of Wilson's biographers wryly notes, 'the Fulton report, in itself only a shadow of what Wilson had once intended, was no more than the shadow of a shadow by the time it had worked its way through to implementation on the ground' (Ziegler, 1993: 315). In instructing the Fulton Committee to inquire into 'the structure, recruitment and management, including training' of the civil service, Wilson was effectively 'precluding examination of the machinery of government as a whole, or the relationship between Ministers and civil servants' (Jones and Keating, 1985: 146), even though modernisation of the machinery of government had been pledged in Labour's 1964 manifesto. This derived not only from Wilson's own lack of intellectual interest in more substantive constitutional questions, but also from his own long-standing respect for the British civil service, a reverence whose origins could be traced back to his own experience working in the

Cabinet Secretariat, followed by a stint in the Board of Trade, during the Second World War.

Also characterised by ambiguity about overall objectives, as well as partly undermined by lack of support from Labour MPs and Ministers themselves, were the 1964–1970 Labour Governments' attempts at reforming Parliament, as examined by Donald Shell in Chapter 10. On the few occasions that Labour Governments have sought to 'modernise' the House of Commons, it has become apparent that what Ministers have really wanted – albeit couched in the rhetoric of making the House more 'efficient' or 'effective' – is to expedite the passage of the Government's legislation (and other measures formally requiring parliamentary approval) more smoothly and swiftly. What Ministers have not wanted is for the House of Commons to be rendered more powerful or 'effective' with regard to subjecting the Government's bills and policies to greater scrutiny and delay. In other words, Labour Governments, as much as Conservative Governments, have not wanted to alter the balance of power between the executive and Parliament from the former to the latter. In accordance with their interpretation (or instinctive, uncritical acceptance) of the Westminster model, Ministers invariably maintain or assume that it is the role and duty of Parliament to 'support' the government of the day, not seek constantly or consistently to obstruct it. As such, Labour Ministers have invariably expected Labour MPs loyally to support their government in the House of Commons, not hinder it by demanding opportunities or institutional innovations which would enable them to play a more active or critical role vis-à-vis public policy. On the other hand, as we have previously noted, the 1964 and 1966 intake of Labour MPs was generally younger and more educated than previous cohorts, and therefore desirous of playing a more active role in the policy process (which posed a problem with regard to party management, as discussed by Eric Shaw in Chapter 3).

One of the Labour Government's experiments in modernising the House of Commons – and one which reflected the leadership's lack of clear or coherent thinking about such matters – was the introduction of morning sittings. Ostensibly intended to reduce the extent of late night sittings, it soon became clear that many MPs preferred to use their mornings to focus on committee work or dealing with constituency problems, whilst various Ministers insisted that they needed to address departmental matters in the morning. In an attempt at pacifying such concerns, it was proposed that morning sittings would not deal with important or controversial matters (these to be left until the afternoon or evening sessions), but this merely reduced the incentive for MPs to attend the morning sittings, because little of value was likely to be discussed or determined. Not surprisingly, the experiment with morning sittings proved short-lived.

Somewhat more successful was the experiment with select committees, and with hindsight it can be seen that these laid the foundation for the departmental select committee system established just over a decade later.

In the latter half of the 1960s, though, only two select committees were initially established (with a few more created in 1968 and 1969), although even these occasioned unease, with some Ministers (and civil servants) concerned about the potential for such bodies to conduct inquiries into politically sensitive or controversial topics, and 'become a law unto themselves' (PRO PREM 13/1983, Trend to Wilson, 31 January 1968).

At the very least, there was some anxiety in the Cabinet and Whitehall that select committees would lead to 'meddling' in the executive's work by inexperienced MPs. There was also a degree of uncertainty about the obligation of Ministers to appear before such committees if summoned, to what extent they would be required to give evidence when so summoned, and whether such appearances would be in addition to their other parliamentary appearances. If Ministers were henceforth to appear before such committees in addition to their other appearances at the despatch box, then there would clearly be issues concerning their workloads, unless there were a corresponding reduction in their other parliamentary appearances, in which case, the Cabinet Secretary pointed out to the Prime Minister, 'the implications of such a shift in the relationship between the Executive and the Legislature are considerable' (PRO PREM 13/1983, Trend to Wilson, 19 April 1966).

Meanwhile, some backbench MPs complained about the role of the whips in determining which MPs were appointed to sit on the committees: there was a suspicion amongst some backbenchers that select committee membership would be used by the whips to 'reward' those Labour MPs who were adjudged to have been sufficiently supportive of the Government. In other words, it was feared that, far from enhancing the role and influence of Labour backbenchers, select committees would effectively become a 'management tool' for the whips, whereby Government 'loyalists' would be appointed to serve on them at the expense of more critical or outspoken backbenchers.

Yet with regard to another parliamentary reform during this period, it was Labour MPs who sought jealously to defend their role against a potential external threat, namely the Parliamentary Commissioner for Administration (the Ombudsman). The initial proposal caused anxiety amongst backbenchers who feared that their role as constituency representatives (seeking 'redress of grievances' for their constituents) would be undermined if aggrieved citizens could contact the Ombudsman directly – hence the significance of creating a *Parliamentary* Commissioner for Administration, whereby citizens could not contact him or her directly, but only via their MP. Moreover, the Ombudsman would be answerable to Parliament via a select committee. The creation of the Ombudsman, once initial anxieties over potential role conflict had been pacified, soon proved to be probably the most successful of the 1964–1970 Labour Governments' parliamentary reforms.

It was certainly rather more successful than the aborted attempt at reforming the House of Lords. As noted earlier, Labour's 1964 manifesto had contained only the vaguest of references to reform of the House of Lords, and the 1966 manifesto confined itself to a pledge that 'legislation will be introduced to safeguard measures approved by the House of Commons from frustration by delay or defeat in the House of Lords' (Craig, 1975: 307). Yet it was not clear exactly how such legislation would be framed, or such 'frustration' would be prevented. Of course, the implication was that action would be taken against the hereditary peers, but once the re-elected Labour Government began considering the options, it became apparent that such action would itself raise a host of constitutional conundrums: would action be taken against the House of Lords only if and when it sought seriously to obstruct the Labour Government, or would the House of Lords be reformed regardless? Would Labour seek to remove the hereditary peers entirely, or only a number of them, sufficient to deprive the Conservatives of their dominance in the House of Lords? Would it flood the House of Lords with Labour peers (under the provisions of the Life Peerages Act) in place of the hereditary peers, or alongside them (and in either case, would not the appointment of more Labour life peers entail a controversial increase in prime ministerial patronage)? Would any reduction in the hereditary peers be accompanied by the election of their replacements, and, if so, how – and by whom – would they be elected? Would a Labour government reduce or remove the House of Lords' (one-year) power of delay? If it reduced the power of delay to, say, six months, the Lords might be inclined to deploy that delay rather more frequently, yet removing the power of delay altogether would effectively enable the House of Commons (and, in effect, the Government) to pass any measure or bill it wanted, however ill-advised or draconian it might be, without being compelled either to think again or to reintroduce it in the following session, having taken stock of the objections raised. Moreover, if the power of delay was reduced or removed, would not the question of composition become less relevant or controversial?

In spite of initially securing the somewhat surprising support of the Conservative front bench for reducing the number of hereditary peers, thereby making a bipartisan approach to House of Lords reform seem possible, the second (1966–1970) Labour Government was unable to reach internal agreement on how to address these questions, and thereby devise a package of reforms which was both coherent and commanded the overall support of the Parliamentary Labour Party (PLP). Not only did different Labour MPs and Ministers favour different measures for reforming the House of Lords, but some, most notably Michael Foot, maintained that nothing short of outright abolition would suffice, whilst some other MPs and Ministers deemed House of Lords reform to be a dilettante digression from the much more important policy issues (economic management, employment, welfare provision, social reform, etc.) which ought always to be the primary focus of a Labour government. That the Blair Governments, thirty years later, grappled, over three successive terms, with the issue of how to reform the second chamber – with many of the above conundrums and conflicts arising again – illustrates just how vexatious the issue of House of Lords reform has been for the Labour Party (Dorey, 2000).

Labour's atheoretical and generally uncritical approach to constitutional issues, along with the party's deep-rooted economism, also had serious implications for the 1964–1970 Labour Governments' response to growing demands for devolution which emanated from Scotland and Wales during the latter half of the 1960s. Many Ministers were inclined to dismiss such demands as the temporary and emotive manifestation of economic griev-ances in Scotland and Wales which would dissipate once the benefits of Labour's economic policies and regional plans facilitated industrial regenera-tion and new employment in the depressed and deprived regions of Britain. Indeed, with regard to Wales in particular, the economic problems which were blithely assumed to fuel demands for devolution were cited as a key reason why Welsh self-government was not economically viable. The eco-nomic problems endured by Wales – and Scotland – could, it was main-tained, only be successfully tackled by a Labour Government at Westminster implementing 'socialist' policies which would reverse indus-trial decline and ameliorate regional inequalities.

At the same time, Labour's constitutional conservatism militated against any serious consideration of the political – and power – relationship between London, Cardiff and Edinburgh: the continued 'union' of England, Scotland and Wales was taken for granted, as was the sovereignty of the (Westmin-ster) Parliament. Ministers did acknowledge, however, that because of a variety of cultural and historical factors, coupled with the existence of its own educational and legal systems, Scotland already enjoyed a limited degree of autonomy (certainly much more so than Wales), but this was generally viewed as an argument against further political devolution. Indeed, as James Mitchell explains in Chapter 11, the stance of most Minis-ters – not least the Scottish Secretary, Willie Ross – was that any form of devolution beyond the transfer of limited administrative functions to Cardiff and Edinburgh would merely fuel nationalist demands and be cited by the Scottish National Party and Plaid Cymru as a vindication of their respective campaigns. Hence, beyond limited administrative devolution, and a sugges-tion (which was not pursued) that the Scottish and Welsh Grand Commit-tees be permitted to sit in Edinburgh and Cardiff respectively, the 1964–1970 Labour Governments' response to the political advances of the SNP and Plaid Cymru was to emphasise how much Scotland and Wales ben-efited, particularly economically, from the existing constitutional and finan-cial arrangements. That the two nations were experiencing various economic and industrial problems during the 1960s was deemed by Ministers to be precisely the reason why Scotland and Wales ought to look to a Labour Government at Westminster (rather than seek self-government) to pursue precisely the type of 'socialist' policies which would generate growth, revi-talise industry, and create new jobs to replace those which had been lost. In the meantime, though, pending economic recovery, a royal commission was established, doubtless in the hope that it would provide the Labour Government with a breathing space, whilst also moving devolution off the political agenda for a while.

No such stalling tactic was available with regard to Northern Ireland, however. The speed with which the Province descended into social unrest and civil disorder during 1968 and 1969 compelled the Labour Cabinet to respond with the utmost urgency. The hitherto cautious approach, entailing various reforms to ameliorate the socio-economic conditions of the Catholic community in Northern Ireland – during a fifth consecutive decade of Protestant/Unionist political dominance in the Province – was ultimately judged too little, too slow, by many Catholics, and too much, too soon, by many Unionists. Yet once 'the troubles' fully emerged in Northern Ireland during 1968–1969, the Labour Government had little time in which to contemplate an alternative strategy and was obliged to resort to crisis management – in the form of military intervention – in order to contain the ensuing violence and restore order to the Province. Having sought to avoid such a drastic course of action for as long as practically possible, the Government found that once it had become directly embroiled in Northern Irish politics, it was almost impossible to extricate itself.

Foreign affairs

The economic difficulties which plagued the 1964–1970 Labour Governments also had a major impact on aspects of foreign policy during this period. Not least of these was a growing realisation amongst Ministers that Britain could no longer afford to maintain a military presence around the globe (particularly as technological advances were rendering military weaponry increasingly expensive), and that instead a more modest international role needed to be adopted. As Rhiannon Vickers explains in Chapter 8, this entailed the post-1967 scaling down of Britain's military presence and bases 'east of Suez', and the tacit recognition that Britain was a medium or middle-ranking world power – even though the Government's public rhetoric often suggested otherwise – unable to match the might of the United States or the Soviet Union. However, as Britain reduced its overseas military commitments, so the 'special relationship' with the United States, coupled with Britain's support for NATO, became even more important (although Wilson's refusal to send any British troops to assist the Americans in Vietnam did cause some tension in the 'special relationship' at the time).

The scaling down of Britain's global commitments, coupled with the country's serious economic difficulties, also had major repercussions for the 1964–1970 Labour Governments' stance towards the European Economic Community (EEC), discussed by Helen Parr and Melissa Pine in Chapter 7. Labour had formally opposed the Conservative Government's application for British membership in 1961 (which was rejected in 1963), and many in the party remained opposed to British membership of the EEC, either because they viewed it as a 'capitalist club' whose commitment to free trade would be inimical to various of Labour's avowed socialist policies, or/and because of continued reverence for the Commonwealth. Harold Wilson himself had initially been somewhat indifferent or uncommitted either way, and one commentator has suggested that

> Wilson was not a natural European. He was a classic representative of that special kind of English insularity which kept his domestic emotions bounded by the Scilly Isles at its extremity (where Wilson had a holiday bungalow) and his global emotions confined to the Commonwealth [and] the 'Old Dominions'.... His tilt towards Europe, like so much else in his first premiership, was the result of economic setback, and the need to find alternative, external sources of dynamism-by-association.
>
> (Hennessy, 2001: 311)

Labour's 1964 manifesto was itself ambiguous with regard to the pursuit of EEC membership, pledging that 'we shall seek to achieve closer links with our European neighbours' (Craig, 1975: 268). However, with Britain's global role being reduced, various Commonwealth countries acquiring independence (even though special trade agreements were often retained), and the EEC outperforming Britain economically, many Ministers – including, crucially, Wilson himself (ever the pragmatist) – in the 1964–1970 Labour Governments adopted a much more positive view of the EEC and became convinced that it was in Britain's interests – diplomatic, economic and political – to seek membership, even though the subsequent application was also rejected.

Social policy and social reform

The 1964–1970 Labour Governments did enjoy rather greater success with regard to various of their social policies and reforms, and it is in these spheres that the image of a liberal administration was forged. Certainly these Governments presided over a significant extension of both comprehensive (secondary) schools and higher education, although both of these trends had been instigated under the previous Conservative administration. The one educational objective which the Labour Governments did fail to achieve was the raising of the school leaving age (from 15 to 16), a commitment which was deferred for two years – to the clear chagrin of many Ministers – owing to economic exigencies.

Nonetheless, the expansion of education was one policy area where the 1964–1970 Labour Governments genuinely seemed to have a clear sense of purpose and strategy, for 'comprehensivisation' and the growth of universities and polytechnics were explicitly intended simultaneously to serve the requirements of the British economy and labour market, whilst also providing the increased educational opportunities deemed necessary to reduce existing socio-economic inequalities. After all, in accordance with Crosland's (1956) critique, the revisionist perspective held that the key to reducing remaining inequalities was through improving or increasing equality of opportunity to those who were traditionally disadvantaged. This, rather than higher taxes on the better off, or more State control of industry via nationalisation, was deemed by Labour's centre-right to be the most desirable and effective means of giving practical effect to the party's egalitarian principles and thereby ameliorating remaining class divisions (by levelling up rather than levelling down). This perspective was particularly evident with regard to the establishment of the Open University, which has widely become viewed as one of the proudest and most enduring achievements of the 1964–1970 Labour Governments, and which provided the opportunity for what has much more recently become known as 'lifelong learning'.

With regard to the economic objectives of Labour's educational policies, the expansion of higher education in particular was viewed as crucial to providing the increased number of administrators, managers, scientists, technicians and sundry other professionals whom the party deemed vital to the modernisation – and thus competitiveness – of the British economy.

One of the measures which did much to earn the 1964–1970 Labour Governments their subsequent reputation for social liberalism was the legalisation of homosexuality (for men aged 21 and over), although many of those who supported this reform made it clear that they were not condoning homosexuality per se, but giving effect to the principle that private acts between consenting adults should not be subject to statutory prohibition or State interference. Moreover, this particular reform did cause unease amongst some Labour MPs who represented more traditional industrial, working-class constituencies, either because these did not share the social liberalism of more middle-class and better-educated Labour MPs and Ministers, or because they felt that such a reform was being given too much time and attention at a time when the Labour Governments were faced with serious economic problems. That the 1964–1970 Labour Governments did preside over the legalisation of homosexuality – albeit via a private member's bill – thus owed much to the indefatigable efforts of a few committed individuals, not least Leo Abse, the backbench sponsor of the bill, Roy Jenkins, the notably liberal Home Secretary, and Richard Crossman, Labour's Leader of the House, who thus ensured that sufficient parliamentary time was made available for the bill (even though the Government maintained a stance of formal neutrality).

Not dissimilarly, as Neville Twitchell explains in Chapter 18, the abolition of the death penalty was another of the 1964–1970 Labour Governments' liberal or 'civilising' measures which was nonetheless at odds with the views of many of the party's own supporters (and much of the wider electorate), whilst also enabling Labour's opponents to depict the party as being 'soft on crime'. Again, too, this reform derived from a private member's bill for which sympathetic Ministers then made time available in the Government's parliamentary schedule, and in so doing helped to 'remove an act of barbarism from the British way of life' (Lapping, 1970: 216).

These reforms, along with similar measures liberalising the laws pertaining to abortion and divorce, and the abolition of theatre censorship, were seen by those who supported them as necessary to provide an affirmative answer to the question: 'Is Britain Civilised?', which had been the title of the last chapter of Roy Jenkins's book *The Labour Case*, published as part of a 'Penguin Special' series in the run-up to the 1959 general election (Jenkins, 1959). However, critics and opponents of these reforms saw them not as 'civilising' measures, but as heralding Britain's degeneration into a 'permissive society', the alleged consequences of which have subsequently become increasingly apparent in terms of civil disorder, moral decay and social breakdown, as well as, ironically, a decline in civility. Yet it is perhaps worth noting, in passing, that those who routinely accuse Labour governments of constant intervention, interference and meddling in people's lives, of imposing a 'nanny state', and of posing a threat to individual liberty, tend to be the very same critics who complain the loudest when those same Labour governments enact measures to grant (greater) freedom to those citizens and minorities whose lives and freedoms have hitherto been diminished by discrimination or constrained by a conservative-minded conformity!

Although the 1964–1970 Labour Governments effectively defied the disapproval of many of their working-class supporters (and much of the British public generally) in pursuing these two liberal reforms, Ministers felt rather more constrained by electoral opinion regarding the twin issues of immigration and race relations, analysed by James Hampshire in Chapter 17, and so pursued a dual strategy (an approach which most British governments have adhered to ever since). Two particular measures – the 1965 White Paper *Immigration from the Commonwealth* (HMSO, 1965) and the 1968 Commonwealth Immigrants Act – were enacted, both of which placed restrictions on the right of Commonwealth citizens to settle in Britain. Whilst many Labour MPs found these restrictions deeply distasteful, the Cabinet was acutely aware of the Government's electoral vulnerability on the issue of immigration, for failure to act would inevitably be exploited by the Conservative Party and much of the tabloid press, both of which would contribute – as they still routinely do today – to a sense of public alarm over 'excessive' immigration, and then claim that they were merely reflecting the anxieties of the British public. Just how susceptible Labour was to racist sentiments amongst sections of the electorate – not least amongst parts of the otherwise Labour-voting white working class – had been dramatically illustrated by the defeat of the incumbent Labour MP, Patrick Gordon Walker, in Smethwick (West Midlands) in the 1964 election, following a racist campaign by the (winning) Conservative candidate. Further evidence of the extent to which racist sentiments could readily be fuelled was subsequently provided by the groundswell of public support offered to Enoch Powell after his 1968 'rivers of blood' speech, when dockers and meat-porters in east London marched in support of Powell. The 1964–1970 Labour Governments thus found themselves torn between upholding the party's formal commitment to anti-racism and internationalism on the one hand, and the electoral imperative to be seen to be curbing 'excessive' immigration on the other, lest they be punished at the polls.

At the same time, however, the Cabinet persevered with a commitment to improving race relations in Britain, with legislation placed on the statute book – also in 1965 and 1968 – outlawing discrimination on racial grounds (in spite of reservations from some Home Office officials about whether this was really practicable). Although some Labour MPs thought it slightly disingenuous that their Government was simultaneously seeking to curb Commonwealth immigration whilst outlawing racial discrimination, Ministers inclined to the view that, far from being a contradictory stance, it was an entirely coherent and consistent approach, for good race relations, and genuine acceptance of immigrants already resident in Britain, depended on the indigenous population being assured that immigration was not 'out of control' (a perspective generally subscribed to by most subsequent governments through to the present day). One account of the 1964–1970 Labour Governments – written by a Labour Party member during this period – deemed its race relations policy to have been '[o]ne of the few areas where the final judgement of history ... seems likely to be strongly favourable' (Lapping, 1970: 109).

One other key area of social policy where the 1964–1970 Labour Governments grappled with the difficulties of securing an appropriate balance was that of old-age pensions, as examined by Stephen Thornton in Chapter 17. In the context of the aforementioned economic problems which beset the 1964–1970 Labour Governments, which led to a series of deflationary packages entailing public expenditure curbs or cutbacks, coupled with the mid-1960s rediscovery of poverty (in spite of the blithe assumptions about the affluent society and *embourgeoisement*), the plight of many old-age pensioners moved up the policy agenda, with Richard Crossman, in particular, ensuring that pensions reform moved from the systemic to the institutional agenda. However, as so often in politics, recognising the existence of a problem is often much easier than devising a practicable solution, and so it proved with pensions reform, for the ensuing proposals proved inordinately administratively complex and struggled to achieve sufficient political agreement and impetus, quite apart from the economic constraints which were imposing themselves. What had originally been an ambitious plan for pensions reform – one which was ultimately intended generously to benefit the lower-paid, via a significant redistributive mechanism – steadily became a pale shadow of its former self, to the extent that by 1970 no legislation to enact pensions reform had reached the statute book.

Harold Wilson's leadership

Harold Wilson's leadership still remains something of an enigma for many economic and political historians, for whilst the dominant view is of a Labour leader and Prime Minister who lacked political vision and purpose, and thus shoulders much, if not most, of the blame for the 1964–1970 Labour Governments' tendency to drift without any sense of direction, there remains a perspective which is much more charitable, at least with regard to the early years of Wilson's leadership. In Chapter 4, for example, Noel Thompson argues that, contrary to the common and condemnatory view that Wilson lacked a clear set of principles, 'there was such a thing as a distinctively Wilsonian political economy that underpinned a particular vision of what Britain might become', and a strategy to achieve this vision. Moreover, 'its failings were intrinsic to any late twentieth-century social democratic political economy ... rather than a consequence of ... [a] lack of political resolve, principle or courage of the politician who gave it expression'.

Elsewhere, a highly complimentary defence of the early Wilson leadership is proffered by Peter Hennessy, who asserts that

> His brief spell as Opposition leader between Hugh Gaitskell's death and Alec Douglas-Home's loss of Office was verging on the brilliant. . . . He was literate, numerate, witty, and possessed of what we would now call a 'big idea' – that through planning, and by the harnessing of science and technology for national purposes, the remaking of Britain was possible. . . . In the early days of his premiership, he was a genuinely shining figure. The dazzle of his political lustre was extraordinary, from the first weeks of his party leadership following Gaitskell's death in January 1963 to the desperate weeks of July 1966, when the unsentimental reality of the money markets . . . forced him into . . . a virtual abandonment of the big idea of growth-through-planning. The tarnish which resulted never left him, or his reputation . . . it still has not.
>
> (Hennessy, 2001: 287–8)

An even more sympathetic (but certainly not sycophantic) account of Wilson's 1964–1970 premiership was provided by Ben Pimlott, whose voluminous biography represented a serious and scholarly attempt at rehabilitating Wilson's tarnished political reputation and emphasised his Governments' various successes, often achieved in spite of extremely difficult circumstances (Pimlott, 1993: 363–6 and *passim*). Moreover, against the common charge that Wilson was unprincipled and excessively pragmatic, Pimlott suggests that on a number of occasions Wilson suffered by virtue of 'being too principled for his own good', particularly in his steadfast – or stubborn – refusal to devalue (until the 'decision' was effectively forced upon him) and his dogged pursuit of industrial relations reform in 1969 in spite of mounting opposition from the trade unions, on the Labour back benches and within parts of the Cabinet table (Pimlott, 1993: 562–3).

The alternative perspective, that Harold Wilson was devoid of a clear or coherent political strategy, lacked firm principles and was thus unable to provide firm or visionary leadership, derives very much from the unflattering observations of some of his own ministerial colleagues, which have in turn subsequently confirmed the views of those commentators who have been critical of what they perceive to be Wilson's aimless premiership and lack of political principles.

Richard Crossman was amongst those ministerial colleagues who came to the conclusion that Harold Wilson

> doesn't feel himself representing the Labour movement, really caring about the trade unions or feeling great loyalty to the party. He cares about being PM, about politics, about power. He has become de-partied to a great extent, an occupant of Downing Street who adores running things well.
> (Crossman, 1977: 180, diary entry for 4 September 1968 see also Wilson papers, MS Wilson C. 935, Crossman to Wilson, 19 June 1969)

On an earlier occasion, Crossman sought to gauge Wilson's political goals on key issues, but to little avail:

> What are Harold's long-term economic objectives in this country? Does he really want to go into Europe, or doesn't he? I don't think he knows himself. . . . And what about the long-term future of the Labour Party? Does he see it as a real socialist party or does he, like the Gaitskellites, aim to turn it into an American Democratic Party or a German Social Democratic Party. . . . I see him more than most people. . . . But he certainly doesn't confide in me any profound thoughts about the future of the Labour Party, and I'm prepared to say . . . that I don't think he has them. . . . I'm also more doubtful than ever whether he's going to lead us anywhere, whether he has any real vision of a future for this country which we in the Labour Party can achieve. . . . His main aim is to stay in Office. That's the real thing, and for that purpose, he will use almost any trick or gimmick . . . his opportunism . . . which makes him a most disappointing leader for a radical left-wing movement.
> (Crossman, 1976: 159–60, diary entry for 11 December 1966)

Similarly critical in this regard was Denis Healey, who recalls that Wilson 'had no sense of direction, and rarely looked more than a few months ahead', so that too many decisions and policies derived from 'short-term opportunism' (1989: 331), whilst Tony Benn (even before he had begun his ideological journey to the left) was criticising Wilson for having proven to be 'a small man with no sense of history, and as somebody without leadership qualities' (1988: 187, diary entry for 17 June 1969).

Even before Harold Wilson became Prime Minister, Aneurin Bevan alleged that he [Wilson] was 'much more dangerous than Gaitskell because he isn't honest and he isn't a man of principle, but a sheer, absolute careerist, out for himself alone' (quoted in Campbell, 1987: 350). Intriguingly, one of his biographers recalls that when he first approached Wilson about writing such a book and admitted that he, the author, was certainly not a 'committed socialist', Wilson 'replied, with some satisfaction: "That's lucky, neither am I"', and whilst the biographer acknowledges that Wilson 'was joking, there was enough truth in the joke to make me feel that, on political grounds at least, I was not unsuitable as a biographer' (Ziegler, 1993: xi).

This apparent lack of vision and purpose, coupled with his ultra-pragmatism and reliance on short-term political tactics, also meant that Harold Wilson was distrusted by some of his ministerial colleagues (although, of course, all Prime Ministers are vulnerable to such sentiments on the part of aggrieved or frustrated colleagues, many of whom will doubtless be convinced that they could do a better job!). According to Crosland, for example, 'The trouble with Harold is one hasn't the faintest idea whether the bastard means what he says even at the moment he speaks it' (Crosland, 1982: 184), a view clearly shared by Tony Benn, who recalls that 'In the end, the tragedy of Wilson was that you couldn't believe a word he said' (*Guardian*, 3 October 1987).

Of course, such distrust and criticism served to increase Wilson's own suspicions about the motives and reliability of some of his ministerial colleagues, thereby fostering a febrile atmosphere of political paranoia, with Wilson suspecting various of his colleagues of plotting to replace him as Labour leader and Prime Minister. As Douglas Jay (a Minister in the Attlee *and* the Wilson Governments) recalls, 'The Wilson Government was an unhappy one, in which unease and suspicion festered, in contrast to the sense of purpose and achievement which buoyed us up even in the most arduous moments in 1945–51' (1980: 411). Tony Benn was even more explicit, alleging that 'Harold is very paranoid . . . he is afraid, and isn't quite up to the job' (1988: 63, diary entry for 30 April 1968).

Among academic commentators, meanwhile, there are sharply divergent opinions about Wilson's intellectual qualities and the extent to which these contributed to his style (or lack) of leadership. Hennessy, for example, in eulogising the pre-July 1966 Wilson leadership, refers to 'a polymath premier' who relished occasions on which he could 'display his intellectual and technocratic prowess' (2001: 287). In sharp contrast, Marquand (citing Crossman) views Wilson as 'not merely unintellectual, but positively anti-intellectual . . . ideas, and people who cared about ideas, made him ill at ease', and suggests that as Prime Minister, Wilson 'had . . . little stomach for those who believed that good government entailed thinking long'. Instead, even before he had become Prime Minister, pragmatism had become 'a kind of religion' for Wilson (Marquand, 1999: 164).

Needless to say, many Labour backbenchers also became disillusioned or frustrated during the 1964–1970 Labour Governments' period in office, either with Wilson's leadership per se or with the policies variously adopted – or abandoned. Moreover, as was noted in Chapter 2, the social background of many Labour MPs elected in 1964 and 1966 was such that they were rather less deferential and quiescent, and thus were often more inclined to make their views and policy preferences known. Meanwhile, with regard to policies such as industrial relations reform and incomes policies, trade union-sponsored Labour MPs also proved willing publicly to express their discontent in the division lobbies, as well as more privately at the weekly meetings of the PLP. Consequently, as Shaw illustrates in Chapter 3, the leadership of the 1964–1970 Labour Governments also had to grapple with the problem of party management, so that at least some semblance of unity and cohesion could be maintained in the context of growing unrest and unease on the Labour back benches.

Conclusion

It is evident, therefore, that the 1964–1970 Labour Governments enjoyed mixed fortunes with regard to their feats and failures. The early optimism and sense of purpose which was proudly proclaimed, particularly by Harold Wilson himself, soon dissipated as serious economic difficulties engulfed the Cabinet and rapidly undermined the assumptions of economic growth on which so many of Labour's policies and objectives depended. The centrepiece of Labour's economic strategy, the National Plan – on which various other policies depended – was soon cruelly undermined, with depressing and debilitating repercussions for the policy initiatives and objectives which were inextricably linked to it. Having entered office determined to exercise a new mode of control over the economy, one which did *not* entail a significant extension of formal public ownership and nationalisation, the 1964–1970 Labour Governments increasingly found that they were effectively subject to a range of economic forces over which they were able to exercise little, if any, control. Long-term economic planning, predicated on both the prior existence and the continued attainment of economic growth and industrial expansion, was swiftly superseded by short-termism, crisis management and a series of deflationary measures. This rapid transformation in turn did much to tarnish the reputation of the 1964–1970 Labour Governments and Harold Wilson alike, and fostered an enduring image of an administration and its leader bereft of strategy or vision, and repeatedly at the mercy of events largely beyond their control. There was no longer much semblance of long-term purpose, particularly after July 1966, beyond political survival.

However, to be fair, it is doubtful whether any government, of any political complexion, could have mastered the economic problems which overwhelmed the 1964–1970 Labour Governments. Certainly it is perhaps easy to be unduly critical with the benefit of hindsight, and condemn a government for decisions taken, or not taken, without having directly confronted the problems, or experienced first-hand the forces and pressures, that exerted themselves at the time, and which thus limited the Cabinets' room for manoeuvre and range of policy options.

Not surprisingly, though, the impact of economic circumstances and crises on various of the 1964–1970 Labour Governments' other policies – in terms of either abandoning or postponing particular proposals, or hastily adopting controversial policies which had not been originally envisaged – had a corrosive and demoralising effect on many Ministers and Labour MPs, and did much to undermine unity and cohesion in the Cabinet and the PLP alike, as well as straining relations between Labour and the trade unions. Moreover, increasing criticism and dissent, concerning the Governments' general direction (or lack of it) as well as over particular policies, fuelled Wilson's own insecurity and alleged paranoia about disloyalty and leadership plots amongst his colleagues. Many of them in turn became increasingly critical of Wilson's leadership – or failure to provide any.

It is only really in the social sphere that the 1964–1970 Labour Governments can be judged to have achieved notable success, for it is here that several liberal and 'civilising' reforms were implemented. To a significant degree, therefore, these Governments continued to be progressive in the social sphere, even whilst resorting to orthodoxy in the economic sphere, displaying ambiguity in foreign affairs and evincing considerable conservatism in the constitutional sphere, and hence it is these social reforms which have partly salvaged the reputation of the 1964–1970 Labour Governments.

References

Note: all books listed were published in London unless stated otherwise.

Abel-Smith, Brian and Townsend, Peter (1965) *The Poor and the Poorest*, G. Bell.

Abrams, Mark and Rose, Richard (1960) *Must Labour Lose?*, Harmondsworth: Penguin.

Abse, Leo (1973) *Private Member*, MacDonald.

Alderman, Geoffrey (1966) 'The Conscience Clause of the PLP', *Parliamentary Affairs* 18 (2): 224–32.

Alexander, Philip (2002) 'From Imperial Power to Regional Powers: Commonwealth Crises and the Second Application', in Oliver Daddow (ed.) *Harold Wilson and European Integration: Britain's Second Application to Join the EEC*, Frank Cass.

Althusser, Louis (1973) *Lenin and Philosophy, and Other Essays*, New Left Books.

Anderson, Donald (1968) 'Parliament and the Executive', in Brian Lapping and Giles Radice (eds) *More Power to the People: Young Fabian Essays on Democracy in Britain*, Longman.

Anderson, Perry (1964) 'A Critique of Wilsonism', *New Left Review* 27: 1–27.

Anderson, Perry (1966) 'Origins of the Present Crisis', in Perry Anderson and Robin Blackburn (eds) *Towards Socialism*, Ithaca, NY: Cornell University Press.

Araki, H. (2000) 'Ideas and Welfare: The Conservative Transformation of the British Pension Regime', *Journal of Social Policy* 29 (4): 599–621.

Arthur, Paul and Jeffery, Keith (1988) *Northern Ireland since 1968*, Oxford: Blackwell.

Artis, Michael (1963) 'Balogh's economic policies', *New Left Review* 22: 106–11.

Atkinson, J. (1977) 'The Developing Relationship between the State Pension Scheme and Occupational Pension Schemes', *Social and Economic Administration* 11 (3).

Attlee, Clement (1957) 'Party Discipline Is Paramount', *English and National Review* 148.

Back, Les, Keith, Michael, Khan, Azra, Shukra, Kalbir and Solomos, John (2002) 'New Labour's White Heart: Politics, Multiculturalism and the Return of Assimilation', *Political Quarterly* 73 (4): 445–54.

Badel, L. (1999) *Le Role des ministères des Finances et de l'économie dans la construction européenne, 1957–78* (actes du colloque tenu à Bercy, 26, 27, 28 mai).

Baldwin, P. (1990) *The Politics of Social Solidarity*, Cambridge: Cambridge University Press.

Balfour, Lord (Chairman) (1954) *Report of the Royal Commission on Scottish Affairs*, Cmnd 9212, HMSO.

Balogh, Thomas (1962) 'The Radical Fallacy', *New Statesman*, 28 December.

Balogh, Thomas (1963) *Planning for Progress: A Strategy for Labour*, Fabian Tract 346, Fabian Society.

Banton, Michael (1985) *Promoting Racial Harmony*, Cambridge: Cambridge University Press.

Barberis, Peter (1992) 'Britain's Reforming Ministries: Benchmarks of Historical Comparison and Assessment', *Public Policy and Administration* 7 (2): 46–60.

Barker, Anthony (1968) 'Participation in Politics', in Brian Lapping and Giles Radice (eds) *More Power to the People: Young Fabian Essays on Democracy in Britain*, Longman.

Bartlett, Christopher (1992) *'The Special Relationship': A Political History of Anglo-American Relations since 1945*, Longman.

Barton, Brian (1993) 'Relations between Westminster and Stormont during the Attlee Premiership', *Irish Political Studies* 7: 1–20.

Bealey, Frank (1970) 'Introduction' to Frank Bealey (ed.) *The Social and Political Thought of the British Labour Party*, Weidenfeld and Nicolson.

Benn, Tony (1987) *Out of the Wilderness: Diaries 1963–1967*, Hutchinson.

Benn, Tony (1988) *Office without Power: Diaries 1968–1972*, Hutchinson.

Berkeley, Humphry (1972) *Crossing the Floor*, Allen and Unwin.

Bernstein, Basil (1977) *Class, Codes and Control*, vol. 3, *Towards a Theory of Educational Transmissions*, Routledge and Kegan Paul.

Bevan, Aneurin (1961) *In Place of Fear*, Macgibbon and Kee.

Blackburn, Robin (2002) *Banking on Death*, Verso.

Blake, Robert (1978) *A History of Rhodesia*, New York: Alfred Knopf.

Bleich, Erik (2003) *Race Politics in Britain and France: Ideas and Policymaking since the 1960s*, Cambridge: Cambridge University Press.

Block, Brian and Hostettler, John (1997) *Hanging in the Balance: A History of the Abolition of Capital Punishment*, Winchester: Waterside.

Bourdieu, Pierre (1974) 'The School as a Conservative Force', in John Eggleston (ed.) *Contemporary Research in the Sociology of Education*, Methuen.

Bourdieu, Pierre and Passeron, Jean-Claude (1977) *Reproduction in Education, Society and Culture*, Sage.

Bowles, Samuel and Gintis, Herbert (1976) *Schooling in Capitalist America*, Routledge and Kegan Paul.

Braverman, Harry (1974) *Labour and Monopoly Capitalism*, New York: Monthly Review Press.

Bridgen, Paul (1999) 'Remedy for All Ills: Earnings-Relation and the Politics of Pensions 1950s/1960s', unpublished paper given at the conference 'Relative Decline and Relative Poverty: Signposts to the Sixties?' at the University of Bristol, 13 May 1999.

Bridgen, Paul (2000) 'The One Nation Idea and State Welfare', *Contemporary British History* 14 (3): 83–104.

Bridgen, Paul and Lowe, Rodney (1998) *Welfare Policy under the Conservatives*, Public Record Office.

Brivati, Brian (1996) *Hugh Gaitskell*, Richard Cohen Books.

Brown, George (1971) *In My Way*, Book Club Associates.

Butler, David (1955) *The British General Election of 1955*, Macmillan.

Butler, David and King, Anthony (1965) *The British General Election of 1964*, Macmillan.

Butler, David and King, Anthony (1966) *The British General Election of 1966*, Macmillan.

Butler, David and Rose, Richard (1960) *The British General Election of 1959*, Macmillan.

Butt, Ronald (1966) *The Power of Parliament*, Constable.

Cairncross, Alex (1997) *The Wilson Years: A Treasury Diary, 1963–1969*, The Historians' Press.

Callaghan, James (1973) *A House Divided: The Dilemma of Northern Ireland*, Collins.

Callaghan, James (1987) *Time and Chance*, Collins.

Campbell, John (1987) *Nye Bevan and the Mirage of British Socialism*, Weidenfeld and Nicolson.

Campbell, John (1993) *Edward Heath: A Biography*, Jonathan Cape.

Carter, Bob, Clive Harris and Shirley Joshi (1996) 'Immigration Policy and the Racialization of Migrant Labour: The Construction of National Identities in the USA and Britain', *Ethnic and Racial Studies* 19 (1): 135–57.

Castle, Barbara (1973) 'Mandarin Power', *Sunday Times*, 10 June 1973.

Castle, Barbara (1984) *The Castle Diaries 1964–70*, Weidenfeld and Nicolson.

Castle, Barbara (1990) *The Castle Diaries 1964–1976*, Papermac.

Catto, Lord (Chairman) (1952) *Report on Scottish Financial and Trade Statistics*, HMSO, Cmd. 8609.

Christoph, James B. (1962) *Capital Punishment and British Politics: The British Movement to Abolition of the Death Penalty, 1945–1957*, Allen and Unwin.

Clifford, Christopher (1997) 'The Rise and Fall of the DEA, 1964–69: British Government and Indicative Planning', *Contemporary British History* 11 (2): 94–116.

Coates, David (1975) *The Labour Party and the Struggle for Socialism*, Cambridge University Press.

Coates, Ken and Silburn, Richard (1970) *Poverty: The Forgotten Englishmen*, Harmondsworth: Penguin.

Cook, C. and Ramsden, J. (eds) (1975) *By-elections in British Politics*, Macmillan.

Coopey, Richard (1993) 'Industrial Policy and the White Heat of the Scientific Revolution', in Richard Coopey, Steven Fielding and Nick Tiratsoo (eds) *The Wilson Governments, 1964–1970*, Pinter.

Coopey, Richard, Fielding, Steven and Tiratsoo, Nick (eds) (1993) *The Wilson Governments, 1964–1970*, Pinter.

Corbett, Anne (1966) 'How Comprehensive?', *New Society*, 7 July.

Cowie, H. (1964) *Why Liberal?*, Harmondsworth: Penguin.

Craig, F. W. S. (ed.) (1975) *British General Election Manifestos 1900–1974*, Macmillan.

Crick, Bernard (1964) *The Reform of Parliament*, Weidenfeld and Nicolson.

Crick, Bernard (1965) 'The Prospects for Parliamentary Reform', *Political Quarterly* 36: 333–46.

Crosland, Anthony (1956) *The Future of Socialism*, Jonathan Cape.

Crosland, Anthony (1960a) *Can Labour Win?*, Fabian Tract, 324, Fabian Society.

Crosland, Anthony (1960b) 'The Future of the Left', *Encounter* 14.

Crosland, Anthony (1962) *The Conservative Enemy: A Programme of Radical Reform for the 1960s*, Jonathan Cape.

Crosland, Susan (1982) *Tony Crosland*, Jonathan Cape.

Crossman, Richard (1952) 'The Price of Conformity', *New Statesman*, 25 October.

Crossman, Richard (1955) 'Reflections on Party Loyalty', *New Statesman*, 2 April.

Crossman, Richard (1960a) *Labour in the Affluent Society*, Fabian Society.

Crossman, Richard (1960b) 'Labour's Constitutional Crisis', *New Statesman*, 6 August.

Crossman, Richard (1963) 'Introduction' to Walter Bagehot, *The English Constitution*, Fontana.

Crossman, Richard (1965) 'The Lessons of 1945', in Perry Anderson and Robin Blackburn (eds) *Towards Socialism*, Ithaca, NY: Cornell University Press.

Crossman, Richard (1972a) *The Politics of Pensions*, Eleanor Rathbone Memorial Lectures no. 19, Liverpool: Liverpool University Press.

Crossman, Richard (1972b) *Inside View*, Jonathan Cape.

Crossman, Richard (1975) *The Diaries of a Cabinet Minister*, vol. 1, *Minister of Housing 1964–66*, Hamish Hamilton/Jonathan Cape.

Crossman, Richard (1976) *The Diaries of a Cabinet Minister*, vol. 2, *Lord President of the Council and Leader of the House of Commons 1966–68*, Hamish Hamilton/Jonathan Cape.

Crossman, Richard (1977) *The Diaries of a Cabinet Minister*, vol. 3, *Secretary of State for Social Services 1968–70*, Hamish Hamilton/Jonathan Cape.

Cunningham, Michael (2001) *British Government Policy in Northern Ireland 1969–89*, Manchester: Manchester University Press.

Dale, Iain (2000) *Labour Party General Election Manifestos, 1990–1997*, Routledge.

Dalyell, Tam (1989) *Dick Crossman: A Portrait*, Weidenfeld and Nicolson.

Darby, Phillip (1973) *British Defence Policy East of Suez, 1947–1968*, Oxford University Press for the Royal Institute of International Affairs.

Deighton, Anne (2003) 'The Labour Party, Public Opinion and the Second Try', in Oliver Daddow (ed.) *Harold Wilson and European Integration: Britain's Second Application to Join the EEC*, Frank Cass.

Department of Economic Affairs (1964) *Joint Statement of Intent on Productivity, Prices and Incomes*, HMSO.

Department of Economic Affairs (1965) *The National Plan*, Cmnd 2764, HMSO.

Department of Economic Affairs (1967) *Prices and Incomes Policy after 30 June 1967*, HMSO.

Department of Health and Social Security (1969a) *National Superannuation and Social Insurance*, Cmnd 3883, HMSO.

Department of Health and Social Security (1969b) *National Superannuation: Terms for Partial Contracting Out of the National Superannuation Scheme*, Cmnd 4195, HMSO.

Department of Health and Social Security (1974) *Better Pensions*, Cmnd 5713, HMSO.

Department of Trade and Industry, North-West Regional Office (1989) *British Regional Policy from the Aftermath of the 'Great War' to the 'Thatcher Era', 1920–1989*.

Department for Work and Pensions (DWP) (2002) *Simplicity, Security and Choice: Working and Saving for Retirement*, Cmnd 5677, HMSO.

Dobson, Alan (1988) *The Politics of the Anglo-American Economic Special Relationship, 1940–1987*, Brighton: Harvester Wheatsheaf.

Dobson, Alan (1990) 'The Years of Transition', *Review of International Studies*, 16 (3): 239–58.

Donnelly, M. (1995) 'Labour Politics and the Affluent Society, 1951–64', unpublished PhD thesis, University of Surrey, Guildford.

Donoughue, Bernard and Jones, G. W. (1973) *Herbert Morrison. Portrait of a Politician*, Weidenfeld and Nicolson.

Dorey, Peter (1995) *The Conservative Party and the Trade Unions*, Routledge.

Dorey, Peter (2000) 'The Labour Party and the Problems of Democratising the House of Lords', *Representation* 37 (2): 117–23.

Dorey, Peter (2001) *Wage Politics in Britain: The Rise and Fall of Incomes Policies in 1945*, Brighton: Sussex Academic Press.

Dorey, Peter (2002) 'Industrial Relations as "Human Relations": The Conservatives and Trade Unionism, 1951–1964', in Stuart Ball and Ian Holliday (eds) *Mass Conservatism: The Conservatives and the People, 1867–1997*, Frank Cass.

Dorfman, Gerald (1973) *Wage Politics in Britain, 1945–1967*, Charles Knight.

Doxat, John (1984) *Shinwell Talking: A Conversational Biography to Celebrate his Hundredth Birthday*, Quiller Press.

Drewry, Gavin and Butcher, Tony (1991) *The Civil Service Today*, Oxford: Blackwell.

Drucker, H. M. (1979) *Doctrine and Ethos in the Labour Party*, Allen and Unwin.

Drucker, Henry and Brown, Gordon (1980) *The Politics of Nationalism and Devolution*, Longman.

Durkheim, Émile (1947) *The Division of Labour in Society*, New York: The Free Press.

Durkheim, Émile (1957) *Professional Ethics and Civic Morals*, Routledge and Kegan Paul.

Eckstein, Harry and Gurr, Ted (1975) *Patterns of Authority*, John Wiley.

Edgerton, D. (1996) 'The "white heat" revisited: the British government and technology in the 1960s', *Twentieth Century British History* 7 (2): 53–82.

Ellis, J. and Johnson, R. (1974) *Members from the Unions*, Fabian Research Series 316, Fabian Society.

Evans, Douglas (1975) *While Britain Slept: The Selling of the Common Market*, Victor Gollancz.

Expenditure Committee (1977) *The Civil Service*, Eleventh Report, HC 535, 1976–77.

Fabian Society (1964) *The Administrators: The Reform of the Civil Service*, Fabian Tract 355, Fabian Society.

Favell, Adrian (2001) *Philosophies of Integration: Immigration and the Idea of Citizenship in France and Britain*, 2nd edition, Basingstoke: Palgrave.

Fawcett, Helen (1995) 'The Privatisation of Welfare: The Impact of Parties on the Private/Public Mix in Pension Provision', *West European Politics* 18 (4): 150–69.

Fawcett, Helen (1996) 'The Beveridge Strait-jacket: Policy Formation and the Problem of Poverty in Old Age', *Contemporary British History* 10 (1): 20–42.

Fels, Allan (1972) *The British Prices and Incomes Board*, Cambridge: Cambridge University Press.

Fenwick, Keith (1976) *The Comprehensive School, 1944–70: The Politics of Secondary School Reorganization*, Methuen.

Flower, Ken (1987) *Serving Secretly: An Intelligence Chief on Record; Rhodesia into Zimbabwe, 1964 to 1981*, John Murray.

Foot, Michael (1959) *Parliament in Danger*, Pall Mall Publishers.

Foot, Michael (1973) *Aneurin Bevan*, vol. 2, *1945–60*, Davis-Poynter.

Foot, Michael (1984) *Another Heart and Other Pulses*, Collins.

Foot, Paul (1965) *Immigration and Race in British Politics*, Harmondsworth: Penguin.

Foot, Paul (1968) *The Politics of Harold Wilson*, Harmondsworth: Penguin.

Fry, Geoffrey (1981) *The Administrative 'Revolution' in Whitehall*, Croom Helm.

Fry, Geoffrey (1993) *Reforming the Civil Service: The Fulton Committee on the British Home Civil Service 1966–1968*, Edinburgh: Edinburgh University Press.

Fulton Report (1968) *The Civil Service*, Cmnd 3638, HMSO.

Garrett, John (1980) *Managing the Civil Service*, Heinemann.

Geddes, Andrew (2001) Review of Randall Hansen's *Citizenship and Immigration in Post-war Britain*, *American Political Science Review* 95 (3): 764–5.

Geddes, Andrew (2003) *The Politics of Migration and Immigration in Europe*, Sage.

Glennerster, Howard (1995) *British Social Policy since 1945*, Oxford: Blackwell.

Goldthorpe, John H., Bechhofer, Frank, Lockwood, David and Platt, Jennifer (1968) *The Affluent Worker: Political Attitudes and Behaviour*, Cambridge.

Goodman, Geoffrey (1979) *The Awkward Warrior: Frank Cousins; His Life and Times*, Davis-Poynter.

Griffiths, James (1969) *Pages from Memory*, J. M. Dent.

Haines, Joe (1977) *The Politics of Power*, Jonathan Cape.

Haines, Joe (1998) 'How Harold's Pet Project Became his Monument', *Independent* ('*Open Eye*' Supplement), 1 October.

Haines, Joe (2003) *Glimmers of Twilight*, Politico's.

Hannah, Leslie (1986) *Inventing Retirement: The Development of Occupational Pensions in Britain*, Cambridge: Cambridge University Press.

Hanning, Hugh (1966) 'Britain East of Suez – Facts and Figures', *Review of International Studies* 42 (2).

Hansen, Harry (1961) 'Socialism and Affluence', *New Left Review* 5: 10–16.

Hansen, Randall (1999a) 'The Politics of Citizenship in 1940s Britain: the British Nationality Act', *Twentieth Century British History* 10 (1): 69–95.

Hansen, Randall (1999b) 'The Kenyan Asians, British Politics, and the Commonwealth Immigrants Act, 1968', *Historical Journal* 42 (3): 809–34.

Hansen, Randall (2000) *Citizenship and Immigration in Post-war Britain. The Institutional Origins of a Multicultural Nation*, Oxford: Oxford University Press.

Hansen, Randall and King, Desmond (2000) 'Illiberalism and the New Politics of Asylum: Liberalism's Dark Side', *Political Quarterly* 71 (4): 396–403.

Hardie, Jeremy (1972) 'Regional Policy', in Wilfred Beckerman (ed.) *The Labour Government's Economic Record 1964–1970*, Duckworth.

Hargreaves, John (1996) *Decolonization in Africa*, 2nd edition, Longman.

Harvie, Christopher and Jones, Peter (2000) *The Road to Home Rule*, Edinburgh: Polygon.

Haseler, Stephen (1969) *The Gaitskellites. Revisionism in the British Labour Party*, Macmillan.

Healey, Denis (1980) 'Foreword' to John Garrett, *Managing the Civil Service*, Heinemann.

Healey, Denis (1989) *The Time of My Life*, Michael Joseph.

Heclo, Hugh (1974) *Modern Social Politics in Britain and Sweden*, New Haven, CT: Yale University Press.

Heidar, Knut (1994) 'Towards Party Irrelevance? The Decline of Both Conflict and Cohesion in the Norwegian Labour Party', in David Bell and Eric Shaw (eds) *Conflict and Cohesion in Contemporary Social Democracy*, Pinter.

Hennessy, Peter (1989) *Whitehall*, Secker and Warburg.

Hennessy, Peter (2001) *The Prime Minister: The Office and its Holders since 1945*, revised edition, Penguin.

Hennessy, Peter (2003) 'The Long March? Whitehall and Open Government since

1945', in Stephen Platten (ed.) *Open Government: What Do We Need to Know?*, Norwich: Canterbury Press.

Hill, Andrew and Whichelow, Anthony (1964) *What's Wrong with Parliament*, Penguin.

HMSO (1965) *Immigration from the Commonwealth*, HMSO.

Hollis, Patricia (1997) *Jennie Lee: A Life*, Oxford: Oxford University Press.

Houghton, Douglas (1962) 'Non-Manual Workers and the Labour Party', Labour Party Archives, RD.270/May.

Houghton, Douglas (1969) 'The Labour Back-Bencher', *Political Quarterly* 40 (4): 454–63.

Howard, Anthony (1963) 'Mr. Wilson's Grand Design', *New Statesman*, 4 April.

Howard, A. and West, R. (1965) *The Making of a Prime Minister*, Jonathan Cape.

Howard, Michael (1966) 'Britain's Strategic Problem East of Suez', *Review of International Studies* 42 (2).

Howell, David (1976) *British Social Democracy. A Study in Development and Decay*, Croom Helm.

Hughes, Emrys (1966) *Parliament and Mumbo-Jumbo*, London: George Allen and Unwin.

Hughes, Emrys (1969) *Sydney Silverman: Rebel in Parliament*, Charles Skilton.

Hunt, Norman *et al.* (1964) *Whitehall and Beyond*, BBC.

Hunter, Leslie (1959) *The Road to Brighton Pier*, Arthur Barker.

Ilersic, A. R. (1964) 'Paying for Regional Government', in Arthur Seldon (ed.) *Rebirth of Britain*, Pan in association with the Institute of Economic Affairs.

Illich, Ivan (1973) *Deschooling Society*, Harmondsworth: Penguin.

Inglehart, Ronald (1977) *The Silent Revolution: Changing Values and Political Styles among Western Publics*, Princeton, NJ: Princeton University Press.

Jackson, Robert (1968) *Rebels and Whips*, Macmillan.

Jarvis, Fred (1962) 'Non-Manual Workers and the Labour Party', Labour Party Archives, RD.270/May.

Jay, Douglas (1980) *Change and Fortune: A Political Record*, Hutchinson.

Jefferys, Kevin (1993) *The Labour Party since 1945*, Basingstoke: Macmillan.

Jefferys, Kevin (1997) *Retreat from New Jerusalem. British Politics 1951–64*, Basingstoke: Macmillan.

Jefferys, Kevin (1999) *Anthony Crosland. A New Biography*, Richard Cohen.

Jefferys, Kevin (2000) *Anthony Crosland*, Politico's.

Jenkins, Peter (1970) *The Battle of Downing Street*, Charles Knight.

Jenkins, Roy (1959) *The Labour Case*, Harmondsworth: Penguin.

Jenkins, Roy (1989) Review of Clive Ponting's *Breach of Promise*, *Observer*, 5 March.

Jenkins, Roy (1991) *A Life at the Centre*, Macmillan.

Johnston, Tom (1952) *Memories*, London: publisher unknown.

Jones, Barry (1983) 'The Development of the Devolution Debate', in David Foulkes, Barry Jones and R. Wilford (eds) *The Welsh Veto: The Wales Act 1978 and The Referendum*, Cardiff: University of Wales Press.

Jones, Barry and Keating, Michael (1985) *Labour and the British State*, Oxford: Clarendon Press.

Jones, Jack (1986) *Union Man*, Collins.

Jones, R. Merfyn and Jones, Ioan Rhys (2000) 'Labour and the Nation', in Duncan Tanner, Chris Williams and Deian Hopkin (eds) *The Labour Party in Wales 1900–2000*, Cardiff: University of Wales Press.

Jones, Russell (1987) *Wages and Employment Policy 1936–1985*, Allen and Unwin.

Jones, Tudor (1997) ' "Taking Genesis Out of the Bible": Hugh Gaitskell, Clause IV and the Socialist Myth', *Contemporary British History*, 11 (2): 1–23.

Jones, Tudor (2000) 'Labour's Constitution and Public Ownership: From Old Clause IV to New Clause IV', in Brian Brivati and Richard Heffernan (eds) *The Labour Party: A Centenary History*, Basingstoke: Macmillan.

Kaldor, Nicholas (1964) 'The Relation of Economic Growth and Cyclical Fluctuations', *Economic Journal*, 64: 53–71.

Kellner, Peter and Crowther-Hunt, Lord (1980) *The Civil Servants: An Inquiry into Britain's Ruling Class*, Macdonald.

Kincaid, J. (1975) *Poverty and Equality in Britain*, revised edition, Harmondsworth: Penguin.

King, Anthony (ed.) (1969) *The British Prime Minister: A Reader*, Macmillan.

King, John E. (2002) *A History of Post-Keynesian Economics since 1936*, Cheltenham: Edward Elgar.

Kingdon, J. (1995) *Agendas, Alternatives and Public Policies*, 2nd edition, New York: HarperCollins.

Kitzinger, Uwe (1968) *The Second Try: Labour and the EEC*, Oxford: Pergamon.

Kogan, Maurice (1971) *The Politics of Education. Edward Boyle and Anthony Crosland in Conversation with Maurice Kogan*, Harmondsworth: Penguin.

Labour Party (1939) *Annual Conference Report 1939*, Labour Party.

Labour Party (1952) *Annual Conference Report 1952*, Labour Party.

Labour Party (1955) *Annual Conference Report 1955*, Labour Party.

Labour Party (1957) *National Superannuation: Labour's Policy for Security in Old Age*, Labour Party.

Labour Party (1958) *Plan for Progress: Labour's Plan for Britain's Economic Expansion*, Labour Party.

Labour Party (1960) *Annual Report of the 59th Annual Conference*, Transport House.

Labour Party (1961) *Signposts for the Sixties*, Labour Party.

Labour Party (1962) *Annual Report of the 61st Annual Conference*, Transport House.

Labour Party (1963) *New Frontiers for Social Security*, Labour Party.

Labour Party (1964a) *Let's Go with Labour: The New Britain*, Labour Party.

Labour Party (1964b) Minutes of the Working Party on Regional Planning.

Labour Party (1964c) *Interim Report of the Working Party on Regional Planning*, first draft, February.

Labour Party (1964d) *Interim Report of the Working Party on Regional Planning*, second draft, February.

Labour Party (1964e) *Final Report of the Working Party on Regional Planning*, March.

Labour Party (1964f) *Labour Party Weekend Conference on Regional Planning*, July.

Labour Party (1965) *Report of the 64th Annual Conference*, Transport House.

Labour Party (1966a) *The Future of Regional Planning* (document presented to internal Labour Party Conference on Regional Planning, October).

Labour Party (1966b) *Regional Planning Machinery* (document presented to internal Labour Party Conference on Regional Planning, October).

Labour Party (1967a) *Report of the 66th Annual Conference*, Transport House.

Labour Party (1967b) Study Group on Regional Policy, minutes.

Labour Party (1967c) Development Area Policy Working Group B – minutes, Re.224/December.

Labour Party (1967d) *Future Regional Policy*, Re.112/March.

Labour Party (1968) *Report of the 67th Annual Conference*, Transport House.

Labour Party (1969) Study Group on Regional Planning Policy, minutes.

Labour Party (1970a) *Now Britain's Strong, Let's Make It Great to Live In*, Labour Party.

Labour Party (1970b) *Report of the Study Group on Regional Planning Policy*, Re.5871/February.

Labour Party in Wales (1970) *Evidence of the Labour Party in Wales to the Commission on the Constitution*, Cardiff: Labour Party in Wales.

Lapping, Brian (1970) *The Labour Government 1964–70*, Harmondsworth: Penguin.

Layton-Henry, Zig (1992) *The Politics of Immigration: Immigration, 'Race' and 'Race' Relations in Post-war Britain*, Oxford: Blackwell.

Leruez, Jacques (1975) *Economic Planning and Politics in Britain*, Robertson.

Leruez, Jacques (2002) 'Britain, France and Economic Planning in the 1960s: The Commissariat au Plan: Role Model or Counter Model?', in Philippe Chassaigne and Michael Dockrill (eds) *Anglo-French Relations, 1989–1998: From Fashoda to Jospin*, Palgrave.

Lester, Anthony and Bindman, Geoffrey (1972) *Race and Law*, Longman.

Lieber, Robert J. (1970) *British Politics and European Unity: Parties, Elites, and Pressure Groups*, Berkeley: University of California Press.

Lindley, P. (1982) 'The Framework of Regional Planning 1964–1980', in Brian Hogwood and Michael Keating (eds) *Regional Government in England*, Oxford: Clarendon Press.

Lipset, Seymour Martin (1969) *Political Man*, Heinemann.

Lipset, Seymour Martin and Rokkan, Stein (1967) 'Cleavage Structures, Party Systems and Voter Alignments: An Introduction', in Seymour Martin Lipset and Stein Rokkan (eds) *Party Systems and Voter Alignments*, Collier-Macmillan.

Lovell, John and Roberts, B. C. (1968) *A Short History of the TUC*, Macmillan.

MacArthur, Brian (1974) 'An Interim History of the Open University', in Jeremy Tunstall (cd.) *The Open University Opens*, Routledge and Kegan Paul.

McCrone, Gavin (1969) *Regional Policy in Britain*, George Allen and Unwin.

MacDonald, Mary and Redpath, Adam (1979) 'The Scottish Office 1954–79', *Scottish Government Yearbook 1980*, Edinburgh: Paul Harris Publishing.

MacDougall, Donald (1987) *Don and Mandarin: Memoirs of an Economist*, John Murray.

Mackintosh, John P. (1968) *The Devolution of Power*, Harmondsworth: Penguin.

MacLean, Iain (1970) 'The Rise and Fall of the Scottish National Party', *Political Studies*, 18: 357–72.

McLean, Iain (2001) *Rational Choice and British Politics*, Oxford: Oxford University Press.

Manners, Gerald, Warren, Kenneth, Kebler, David and Rodgers, Brian (1980) *Regional Development in Britain*, 2nd edition, Chichester: John Wiley.

Marquand, David (1961) 'Passion and politics', *Encounter*, 17.

Marquand, David (1991) *The Progressive Dilemma: From Lloyd George to Kinnock*, Heinemann.

Marquand, David (1999) *The Progressive Dilemma: From Lloyd George to Blair*, 2nd edition, Phoenix.

Marris, R. (1967) 'Have We an Economic Strategy?', *New Statesman*, 21 July.

Marsh, David and Chambers, Joanna (1981) *Abortion Politics*, Junction Books.

Marsh, David and Read, Melvyn (1988) *Private Members' Bills*, Cambridge: Cambridge University Press.

Marsh, Richard (1978) *Off the Rails*, Weidenfeld and Nicolson.

Mather, Janet (2000) 'Labour and the English Regions: Centralised Devolution?', *Contemporary British History* 14 (3): 10–38.

Meadows, R. (1978) 'Planning', in F. T. Blackaby (ed.) *British Economic Policy, 1960–74*, Cambridge: Cambridge University Press.

Mellors, Colin (1978) *The British MP*, Saxon House.

Messina, Anthony (1989) *Race and Party Competition in Britain*, Oxford: Oxford University Press.

Michels, Robert (1964) *Political Parties: A Sociological Study of the Oligarchical Tendencies of Modern Democracy*, New York: Free Press (originally published in 1915).

Middlemas, Keith (1990) *Power, Competition and the State*, vol. 2, *Threats to the Post-War Settlement: Britain, 1961–74*, Basingstoke: Macmillan.

Mikardo, Ian (1988) *Backbencher*, Weidenfeld and Nicolson.

Miliband, Ralph (1961) *Parliamentary Socialism: A Study in the Politics of Labour*, Merlin.

Miliband, Ralph (1972) *Parliamentary Socialism: A Study in the Politics of Labour*, 2nd edition, Merlin.

Miliband, Ralph (1973) *The State in Capitalist Society*, Quartet Books.

Miliband, Ralph (1977) *Marxism and Politics*, Oxford: Oxford University Press.

Minkin, Lewis (1978) *The Labour Party Conference*, Manchester: Manchester University Press.

Minkin, Lewis (1991) *The Contentious Alliance: Trade Unions and the Labour Party*, Edinburgh: Edinburgh University Press.

Mitchell, James (1996) *Stategies for Self-Government*, Edinburgh: Polygon.

Mitchell, James (2003) *Governing Scotland: The Invention of Administrative Devolution*, Basingstoke: Palgrave.

Morgan, Janet (1975) *The House of Lords and the Labour Government, 1964–1970*, Oxford: Oxford University Press.

Morgan, Janet (1976) '1966', in Richard Crossman, *The Diaries of a Cabinet Minister*, vol. 2, *Lord President of the Council and Leader of the House of Commons 1966–68*, Hamish Hamilton/Jonathan Cape.

Morgan, Janet (ed.) (1981) *The Backbench Diaries of Richard Crossman 1951–64*, Hamish Hamilton.

Morgan, Kenneth O. (1984) *Labour in Power 1945–1951*, Oxford: Oxford University Press.

Morgan, Kenneth O. (1987) *Labour People: Leaders and Lieutenants: Hardie to Kinnock*, Oxford: Oxford University Press.

Morgan, Kenneth O. (1990) *The People's Peace: British History 1945–89*, Oxford: Oxford University Press.

Morgan, Kenneth O. (1997) *Callaghan: A Life*, Oxford: Oxford University Press.

Morrison, (Lord) Herbert (1964) *Government and Parliament*, 3rd edition, Oxford University Press.

Myles, J. and Pierson, Paul (2001) 'The Comparative Political Economy of Pension Reform', in Paul Pierson (ed.) *The New Politics of the Welfare State*, Oxford: Oxford University Press.

NALGO (1969) *Public Service*, journal of NALGO, March 1969.

National Association of Pension Funds (1968) *The Future Relationship of State and Occupational Pensions*, National Association of Pension Funds.

National Board for Prices and Incomes (1968) *Third General Report*, Cmnd 3715, HMSO.

Norton, Philip (1975) *Dissension in the House of Commons 1945–74*, Macmillan.

Norton, Philip (1978) *Conservative Dissidents: Dissent within the Parliamentary Conservative Party, 1970–74*, Temple Smith.

Norton, Philip (1980) *Dissension in the House of Commons 1974–1979*, Oxford: Clarendon Press.

O'Neill, Lord (Terence) (1972) *The Autobiography of Terence O'Neill*, Hart-Davis.

Opie, Roger (1972) 'Economic Planning and Growth', in Wilfred Beckerman (ed.) *The Labour Government's Economic Record 1964–1970*, Duckworth.

Panebianco, Angelo (1988) *Political Parties: Organisation and Power*, Cambridge: Cambridge University Press.

Panitch, Leo (1976) *Social Democracy and Industrial Militancy*, Cambridge: Cambridge University Press.

Parr, Helen (2005) *Harold Wilson and British Policy towards the European Community, 1964–1967: Britain's World Role*, Routledge.

Paterson, Peter (1993) *Tired and Emotional: The Life of Lord George Brown*, Chatto and Windus.

Paton, Herbert (1968) *The Claim of Scotland*, London: George Allen and Unwin.

Paul, Kathleen (1997) *Whitewashing Britain: Race and Citizenship in the Post-war Era*, Ithaca, NY: Cornell University Press.

Pearce, Robert (ed.) (1991) *Patrick Gordon Walker Diaries*, Historians' Press.

PEP (1967) *A PEP Report on Racial Discrimination*, Political and Economic Planning.

Perkin, Harold (1989) *The Rise of Professional Society: England since 1880*, Routledge.

Perkins, Anne (2003) *Red Queen*, Macmillan.

Perry, Walter (1972) *The Early Development of the Open University: Report of the Vice-Chancellor January 1969–December 1970*, Bletchley: Open University.

Perry, Walter (1976) *Open University: A Personal Account by the First Vice-Chancellor*, Milton Keynes: Open University Press.

Philip, Alan Butt (1975) *The Welsh Question*, Cardiff: University of Wales Press.

Philips, Morgan (1960) *Labour in the Sixties*, Labour Party/NEC.

Pierson, Paul (1994) *Dismantling the Welfare State: Reagan, Thatcher, and the Politics Retrenchment*, Cambridge: Cambridge University Press.

Pierson, Paul (2000) 'Increasing Returns, Path Dependence, and the Study of Politics', *American Political Science Review* 94 (2): 251–67.

Pimlott, Ben (ed.) (1986) *The Political Diary of Hugh Dalton 1918–40 and 1945–60*, Cape/London School of Economics.

Pimlott, Ben (1993) *Harold Wilson*, HarperCollins.

Pine, Melissa (2003) 'Application on the Table: Britain's Policy towards the European Community, 1967–1970', DPhil thesis, University of Oxford.

Pine, Melissa (2004) 'British Personal Diplomacy and Public Policy: The Soames Affair', *Journal of European Integration History* 10 (2): 59–76.

Ponting, Clive (1989) *Breach of Promise: Labour in Power 1964–1970*, Hamish Hamilton.

Ponting, Clive (1990) *Breach of Promise: Labour in Power 1964–1970*, Penguin.

Postan, M. (1967) *An Economic History of Western Europe, 1946–64*, Methuen.

Pryke, R. (1966) 'The Predictable Crisis', *New Left Review* 39: 3–15.

Pym, Bridget (1974) *Pressure Groups and the Permissive Society*, Newton Abbot: David and Charles.

Race Relations Board (1967) *Report of the Race Relations Board for 1966–67*, HMSO.

Radice, Giles (2002) *Friends and Rivals. Crosland, Jenkins and Healey*, Time Warner Books UK.

Rees, G. Wyn (1999) 'British Strategic Thinking and Europe, 1964–1970', *Journal of European Integration History* 5 (1): 57–72.

Richards, Peter G. (1970) *Parliament and Conscience*, George, Allen and Unwin.

Rodgers, William (1966) 'Background Notes re Regional Planning Policy', submitted to the First Secretary, Michael Stewart, Department of Economic Affairs, 23 September.

Rodgers, William (1981) *The Politics of Change*, Secker and Warburg.

Rodgers, William (2000) *Fourth among Equals*, Politico's.

Roll, Eric (1985) *Crowded Hours: An Autobiography*, Faber and Faber.

Rose, E. J. B. (1969) *Colour and Citizenship*, Oxford University Press.

Rose, Paul (1981) *Backbencher's Dilemma*, Frederick Muller.

Rose, Richard and Davies, Philip (1994) *Inheritance in Public Policy: Change without Choice in Britain*, New Haven, CT: Yale University Press.

Royal Commission on Trade Unions and Employers' Associations, 1965–1968, *Report*, Cmnd 3623, HMSO.

Saggar, Shamit (1992) *Race and Politics in Britain*, Harvester Wheatsheaf.

Saggar, Shamit (1993) 'Re-examining the 1964–70 Labour Government's Race Relations Strategy', *Contemporary Record* 7 (2): 253–81.

Secord, Paul and Backman, Carl (1974) *Social Psychology*, 2nd edition, Tokyo: McGraw-Hill Kogakusha.

Shaw, Eric (1988) *Discipline and Discord in the Labour Party*, Manchester: Manchester University Press.

Shaw, Eric (1996) *The Labour Party since 1945: Old Labour, New Labour*, Oxford: Blackwell.

Shaw, Eric (2004) 'The Control Freaks? New Labour and the Party', in Steve Ludlam and Martin J. Smith (eds) *Governing as New Labour*, Palgrave.

Shinwell, Manny (1981) *Lead with the Left*, Cassell.

Shonfield, Andrew (1969) *Modern Capitalism: The Changing Balance of Public and Private Power*, Oxford: Oxford University Press.

Shore, Peter (1992) *Leading the Left*, Weidenfeld and Nicolson.

Short, Edward (1989) *Whip to Wilson*, Macdonald.

Shragge, Eric (1984) *Pensions Policy in Britain*, Routledge and Kegan Paul.

Shrimsley, Anthony (1965) *The First Hundred Days of Harold Wilson*, Weidenfeld and Nicolson.

Sillars, Jim (1986) *The Case for Optimism*, Edinburgh, Polygon.

Silverman, Sydney (1964) 'The End of the Noose', *Tribune*, 18 December.

Smith, Brian (1965) *Regionalism in England 2: Its Nature and Purpose 1905–1965*, Acton Society Trust.

Snell-Mendoza, M. (1996) 'A Review of Cabinet Papers, July–September 1965', *Contemporary British History* 10 (4): 139–49.

Solomos, John (2003) *Race and Racism in Britain*, 3rd edition, Basingstoke: Palgrave.

Spencer, Ian (1997) *British Immigration Policy since 1939: The Making of Multi-racial Britain*, Routledge.

Stacey, Frank (1971) *The British Ombudsman*, Oxford: Clarendon Press.

Steel, David (1968) *Out of Control: A Critical Examination of the Government of Scotland*, Edinburgh: Scottish Liberal Party.

Steele, David (1964) *More Power to the Regions*, Young Fabian pamphlet 3S 6D, Fabian Society.

Stewart, Michael (1980) *Life and Labour*, Sidgwick and Jackson.

Stone, Neal (1997) 'The Development of Labour Party Thinking on the Civil Service, 1945–1995: Ideological and Programmatic or Intuitive and Reactive?', unpublished MPhil thesis, University of Kent.

Studlar, Donald T. (1978) 'Policy Voting in Britain: The Coloured Immigration Issue in the 1964, 1966 and 1970 Elections', *American Political Science Review* 72.

Targetti, Ferdinando (1992) *Nicholas Kaldor: The Economics and Politics of Capitalism as a Dynamic System*, Oxford: Clarendon.

Taverne, Dick (1974) *The Future of the Left: Lincoln and After*, Cape.

Taylor, A. J. P. (1957) *The Troublemakers: Dissent over Foreign Policy, 1792–1939*, Hamish Hamilton.

Taylor, Robert (1982) 'The Trade Union "Problem" since 1960', in Ben Pimlott and Chris Cook (eds) *Trade Unions and British Politics*, Longman.

Taylor, Robert (1993) *The Trade Union Question in British Politics: Government and Unions since 1945*, Oxford: Blackwell.

Taylor, Teddy (1969) 'Inside Look at the Scottish Tories', *New Outlook*, November.

Theakston, Kevin (1992) *The Labour Party and Whitehall*, Routledge.

Theakston, Kevin (1995) *The Civil Service since 1945*, Oxford: Blackwell.

Theakston, Kevin (1996) 'The Heath Government, Whitehall and the Civil Service', in Stuart Ball and Anthony Seldon (eds) *The Heath Government 1970–74*, Longman.

Theakston, Kevin (1999) *Leadership in Whitehall*, Macmillan.

Theakston, Kevin (2003) 'Richard Crossman: The Diaries of a Cabinet Minister', *Public Policy and Administration* 18 (4): 20–40.

Thirlwall, Anthony (1987) *Nicholas Kaldor*, Brighton: Wheatsheaf.

Thistle Group (undated) *Devolution: A New Appraisal*, Edinburgh: Michael Ancram.

Thomas, George (1985) *Mr Speaker: The Memoirs of Viscount Tonypandy*, Century.

Thompson, Noel (2002) *Left in the Wilderness: The Political Economy of British Democratic Socialism since 1979*, Chesham: Acumen.

Thompson, Peter (1993) 'Labour's "Gannex Conscience"? Politics and Popular Attitudes in the "Permissive Society"', in Richard Coopey, Steven Fielding and Nick Tiratsoo (eds) *The Wilson Governments, 1964–1970*, Pinter.

Thorpe, Andrew (2001) *A History of the British Labour Party*, 2nd edition, Basingstoke: Macmillan.

Titmuss, Richard (1953) 'The Age of Pensions: Superannuation and Social Policy', *The Times*, 30 December.

Tomlinson, Jim (1997) 'Conservative modernization: Too Little Too Late', *Contemporary British History* 11 (3): 18–38.

Tomlinson, Jim (2003) 'The Decline of Empire and the Economic "Decline" of Britain', *Twentieth Century British History* 14 (3): 201–21.

Towers, Brian (1978) *British Incomes Policy*, Leeds and Nottingham: University of Leeds and University of Nottingham.

Trades Union Congress (1965) *Report of the 1965 Annual Conference*, TUC.

Trades Union Congress (1968) *Report of the 1968 Annual Conference*, TUC.

Trades Union Congress (1969) *Report of Special Conference*, TUC.

Vaizey, John (1962) *Education in a Class Society. The Queen and Her Horses Reign*, Fabian Society.

Walker, David (1987) 'The First Wilson Governments, 1964–1970', in Peter Hennessy and Anthony Seldon (eds) *Ruling Performance: British Governments from Attlee to Thatcher*, Oxford: Basil Blackwell.

Waltz, Kenneth (1968) *Foreign Policy and Democratic Politics: The American and British Experience*, Longman.

Warner, Nigel (1983) 'Parliament and the Law', in Bruce Galloway (ed.) *Prejudice and Pride: Discrimination against Gay People in Modern Britain*, Routledge and Kegan Paul.

Watkins, Alan (1966) 'Labour in Power', in Gerald Kaufman (ed.) *The Left*, Anthony Blond.

Webb, Sydney and Webb, Beatrice (1920a) *A Constitution for the Socialist Commonwealth of Great Britain*, Longman.

Webb, Sydney and Webb, Beatrice (1920b) *Industrial Democracy*, 2nd edition, Longman.

Williams, Marcia (1972) *Inside Number 10*, Weidenfeld and Nicolson.

Williams, Philip (1979) *Hugh Gaitskell. A Political Biography*, Oxford: Oxford University Press.

Williams, W. R. (1962) 'Non-Manual Workers and the Lab Party', Labour Party Archives, RD.270/May.

Willis, Paul (1978) *Learning to Labour*, Farnborough: Saxon House.

Wilson, Harold (1957) *Remedies for Inflation*, Labour Party.

Wilson, Harold (1961) 'A Four-Year Plan for Britain', *New Statesman*, 24 March.

Wilson, Harold (1962) 'Planning in a Vacuum', *New Statesman*, 26 October.

Wilson, Harold (1964a) *The New Britain: Labour's Plan Outlined by Harold Wilson*, Harmondsworth: Penguin.

Wilson, Harold (1964b) *Purpose in Politics: Selected Speeches by Harold Wilson*, Weidenfeld and Nicolson.

Wilson, Harold (1971) *The Labour Government 1964–70*, Weidenfeld and Nicolson.

Wilson, Harold (1986) *Memoirs: The Making of a Prime Minister 1916–1964*, Weidenfeld and Nicolson/Michael Joseph.

Wiseman, H. Victor (1970) 'The New Specialised Committees', in A. H. Hansen and Bernard Crick (eds) *The Commons in Transition*, Fontana.

Wolfenden Report (1957) *Report of the Committee on Homosexual Offences and Prostitution*, Cmnd 247, HMSO.

Wollheim, Richard (1961) *Socialism and Culture*, Fabian Tract 331, Fabian Society.

Woodward, Nicholas (1993) 'Labour's Economic Performance, 1964–70', in Richard Coopey, Steven Fielding and Nick Tiratsoo (eds) *The Wilson Governments, 1964–1970*, Pinter.

Wootton, Barbara (1954) *Social Foundations of Wages Policy*, Allen and Unwin.

Wright, Tony (1986) *Socialisms*, Oxford: Oxford University Press.

Young, John (1998) 'The Wilson Government and the Davies Peace Mission to North Vietnam, July 1975', *Review of International Studies* 24 (4): 545–62.

Ziegler, Philip (1993) *Wilson: The Authorised Life*, HarperCollins.

Index

Printed in the United Kingdom
by Lightning Source UK Ltd.
131492UK00001BB/133-138/P